Snakes in the Ganga

SNAKES IN THE GANGA

Breaking India 2.0

Rajiv Malhotra and Vijaya Viswanathan

An imprint of BluOne Ink

Published by BluOne Ink LLP
306, Tower-I, Assotech Business Cresterra,
Plot No. 22, Sector 135, Noida, U.P. India
Website: www.bluone.ink
Email: publisher@bluone.ink

Title: *Snakes in the Ganga: Breaking India 2.0*
Authors: Rajiv Malhotra and Vijaya Viswanathan

ISBN: 978-93-92209-09-3

First Impression: 2022

The moral right of the authors has been asserted.

Printed at Thomson Press (India) Ltd.

An imprint of BluOne Ink

Contents

Foreword

R. Vaidyanathan

India is reeling under pressure from persistent attacks on its ancient culture and civilization. These attacks are well coordinated, funded, and orchestrated from international locations and use Indians to exploit fault lines in India, which being a democracy and an open society, are quite visible. The caste system, for example, is painted dark; however, because of all the propaganda denouncing it, very little is being explained about the structure of Indian society.

One solid attempt to present how the ancient caste system was distorted into a flawed system and is now being exploited by an international nexus was made a dozen years ago. That was a pioneering work and a bestselling book, *Breaking India: Western Interventions in Dravidian and Dalit Fault Lines*. It created a thought revolution, because for the first time, there was a high level of clarity. The term 'Breaking India forces' along with an entire framework and vocabulary became part of this revolution. It explained, with evidence, the elaborate system working within and outside India to brainwash, manipulate, and evangelize the rural poor with the end goal of destroying the civilizational fabric. The social movement resulting in the aftermath of the work brought many hitherto unknown concepts into popular lexicon. It spurred a whole generation of social media icons in India, with their own spheres of influence in political and cultural discourse. This gave birth to innumerable legal, political, and social changes in the country at various levels.

But while there is growing recognition of what the earlier Breaking India forces are up to, there has been a qualitative change and expansion of threats from new Breaking India forces. As lead author of *Breaking India*, Rajiv Malhotra, along with his new co-author, Vijaya Viswanathan, analyze this situation in *Snakes in the Ganga*.

This book is even more important than *Breaking India* because today's 'Breaking India forces 2.0', as this book refers to them, are operating behind the scenes. They can only be understood upon careful and incisive investigation into their activities. Prestigious American universities like Harvard have been captured by them where they frame Social Justice theories designed to dismantle India. And Harvard has entered India and infiltrated its core institutions.

This book sheds light on the forces operating behind the social conflicts India has been facing recently while anticipating future attacks. Without this perspective on the global nexuses at work, Indian intellectuals are limited to reactive, rather than proactive, responses to the growing attacks on issues like Article 370, Citizenship (Amendment) Act, 2019, Babri Masjid, the farmers' revolt, and more recently, the Nupur Sharma saga, and the Agneepath scheme.

Snakes in the Ganga provides a balanced view and connects the dots between Marxism and Critical Race Theory (CRT), popularly known as Wokeism. It explains how Critical Race Theory/Wokeism has become the latest framework for interpreting India. Most Indians are unaware that this framework is being used to microscopically examine caste, Muslim grievances, Kashmir, gender and LGBTQ+ issues, communal violence, and even domains like public health, education, clean water, environment, and foreign policy. This analysis then provides the foundation for condemning India and passing judgment on social matters that haven't been understood adequately. This is the first book I am aware of that provides such a detailed analysis of this new force. It gives profound insights on the course of Critical Race Theory and other social theories developed by the far Left in the West. It describes the penetration and trajectory of this movement in India.

Many will be shocked to discover how Harvard is playing the lead role in building a troubling alliance between a few leading Black Americans and ambitious young Dalits, encouraging them to map India's caste system on to the Western concept of race. Theories known as Critical Caste Theory and Critical Dalit Theory are built on this framework and taught at Harvard as established fact in their curriculum. Despite the bogus comparison, no counter position is either presented or even entertained at Harvard.

Breaking India had already exposed the devious plan to map Black Americans to Dalits and White Americans to Brahmins, although the movement was only in its initial phases at the time. Today, it can no longer be considered a fringe movement. The American TV host, Oprah Winfrey actively promotes it and books that discuss it have become *New York Times* bestsellers. Harvard scholars are vigorously involved in mirroring the entire Black movement to a corresponding Dalit movement. There is a Dalit Heritage Month similar to the Black Heritage Month. There is a Dalit Lives Matter movement mirroring the Black Lives Matter movement. Like the Black Panther party, there is now the Dalit Panthers organization, and so on.

Considering the speed with which American systems are imported into India, Indians should be concerned about the divisive caste surveys being conducted in the US tech sector (especially in Silicon Valley). The information thus generated is not intended to be used for a reconciliation between people, but to help construct legal cases accusing upper caste Indian employees in American organizations of being akin to White supremacists. The US legal concept of 'protected classes' is being applied to people who could qualify as victim identities from India. Under the mask of philanthropy and development, they are being recruited and incentivized to produce information on India that could help Harvard build an archive and database for research that supports its pet theories and helps it generate atrocity literature. Such databases are also being used to train Artificial Intelligence algorithms to have an anti-India bias.

While America benefits from the enormous brain drain from India, Harvard academics have begun targeting Indian Science, Technology, Engineering, and Mathematics (STEM) institutions for their role in upholding meritocracy which Harvard scholars view as structures of Brahminical patriarchy. This is yet another way to break India by dismantling its institutions of excellence.

Because of Harvard's sheer power, this movement has taken India's divisive identity politics to a whole new level. *Snakes in the Ganga* draws parallels with the British 'civilizing' mission in India, which served as a divide and rule policy to control Indians. Sanskrit continues to be denigrated as an oppressive language. Hinduism is a prime target worthy of being dismantled while Islam has assumed a victim identity. Additionally, the Indian family system has now been declared an oppressive structure that is perpetuating patriarchy and Brahmin privilege. Even gurus have not been spared. There is an obvious and concerted effort to completely dismantle the foundations of Indian civilization.

Attacking India's legitimacy as a nation-state, its Constitution, and its ruling party, are Harvard's favorite themes for research projects and conferences. Its attitude to China, however, is the exact opposite. The book shows how cleverly China has used Harvard to further its own nationalistic agendas and also penetrate India.

A fascinating and original contribution of *Snakes in the Ganga* is the elaborate detail on Harvard's sprawling network of influence that permeates national borders, including those of India. This seminal work makes the unabashedly provocative statement that contrary to Indians' notion that India is guru to the world, in reality it is Harvard that is the guru. Even the Indian government's policies are influenced by it.

The information revealed provokes further inquiry into the role of the Indian billionaires and intellectuals that are sponsoring some of Harvard's research, education, and outreach. The book does not blame anyone; but we should dig deeper on our own to find out more. I found the billionaire involvement to be the most important revelation and urge them to take this in the right spirit as independent input for their own benefit.

Snakes in the Ganga is a path-breaking book. I urge every Indian with a genuine concern and love for the country to read this breathtakingly original book and organize a counter-movement in response to these Breaking India forces. Being pro-active is more important than re-active.

R. Vaidyanathan, Professor of Finance (Retd.)
Indian Institute of Management Bangalore
June 2022

Foreword

Peter Boghossian

In just under a decade, the United States has experienced a seismic shift in both cultural and moral values. Gone are the debates from older culture wars about evolution versus creationism, the existence of God, or American occupation of foreign lands. They have been replaced with questions revolving around identity markers like, 'Who is a woman?' and historical grievances like, 'Should the United States pay reparations to African American descendants of former slaves?' These questions are not raised in a genuine spirit of inquiry. Instead, they come with designated answers and anyone who voices a divergent opinion is viewed not merely as having incorrect perspectives but as being a bad person. And once declared a bad person, such a dissenting voice gets punished—through employment denial, ostracization, social media bullying, and the rest that is synonymous with professional and personal 'cancellation'.

Undergirding the 'correct' answers to these questions is a moral infrastructure which lends not just support but also the scholastic imprimatur of knowledge. Entire bodies of academic literature have been manufactured to lend legitimacy to morally fashionable conclusions, which by design eliminate any alternative views from serious consideration. Such trendy 'scholarship' includes Fat Studies, Feminist Geography, Queer Studies, and so on.

This is perilous to the functioning of modern civilization for many reasons, chief among them being we can no longer trust our academic institutions to produce non-ideological, independent, evidence-based sources of knowledge upon which we can rely to form public policies and enhance our lives. With each university that has experienced ideological capture, and each peer-reviewed journal that has bartered truth for Critical Social Justice ideology, we base our beliefs upon their conclusions and act in ways we think brings our flourishing but in fact, are not. We are making laws—and training a new generation of lawyers to make laws—that allow radical departures from historical norms, for instance, allowing 'gender affirmation' surgery for minors (sex changes, including removal of young girls' breasts and young boys' penises), often without parental consent.

However, there is something even more disturbing at play with this moral takeover: We are losing the ability and freedom to voice dissent. Our cognitive liberty—the ability to think according to our conscience—has rapidly eroded. We can no longer speak freely and are held hostage by the need to conform to the dictates of the dominant orthodoxy.

Bestselling books like Helen Pluckrose and James Lindsay's *Cynical Theories: How Activist Scholarship Made Everything About Race, Gender, and Identity – and Why This Harms Everybody* and Douglas Murray's *The Madness of Crowds: Gender, Race, and Identity,* have deftly explained the genesis of these phenomena and their ongoing consequences. *Snakes in the Ganga* builds upon these works and explains how this occurred not only in the West but also in India. The book is a clarion call to place truth at the center of our institutions and restore our ability to think freely and speak openly, honestly, and fearlessly.

Snakes in the Ganga is not limited from the confines of an American or European perspective, but examines these interlocking phenomena from a global perspective, starting by shining the spotlight on a conspicuous area of ignorance about India. While mainstream America has started to understand the problems around Critical Social Justice, Wokeism, and Critical Race Theory, this is not the case with India. This book highlights that Critical Race Theory and other related theories have entered India stealthily and—unbeknownst to most Indians— started pervading every strand of society and government. And with this ideological takeover, Critical Social Justice is destroying the legitimacy of venerable Indian institutions. For instance, the highly acclaimed Indian Institutes of Technology (that have the distinction of producing a large share of Silicon Valley entrepreneurs and corporate CEOs in the US tech sector) have been declared a structure of social oppression by a Harvard University professor of Indian origin (discussed in Chapter 4). The concept of meritocracy in Science, Technology, Engineering, and Mathematics (STEM) education is being declared abusive, and there is a demand to produce equal outcomes regardless of merit, rather than offering equal opportunities. In this context, *Snakes in the Ganga* shows the disastrous consequences of these invasive ideologies given India's delicate equilibrium of diverse identities.

The American export of Wokeism is also causing misunderstandings. In the absence of a clear understanding of American scholastic exports like Critical Race Theory, Indians tend to blame all Americans for certain aspects of US foreign policy. For instance, the US Commission on International Religious Freedom (a formal body that reports to the US Congress) in its annual report admonishes India for what it considers Islamophobia. The reality of inter-religious relations in India, however, is far more complex and has a long history that needs to be considered in any nuanced, balanced analysis. A number of Indians do not realize that such ideological biases are not representative of the entire United States and are merely the tip of the new moral orthodoxy's academic spear.

India is also significant in the spread of Wokeism globally, and this should be considered in developing any counter-movement. While many Americans are aware that India is an outsourcing supplier of Information Technology personnel, few know that the Indian Left too is a major provider of young scholars for training in the latest American Leftist ideologies like Critical Social Justice; and once trained are used as foot soldiers to spread tendentious scholarship and ambitious activism. *Snakes in the Ganga* points out that American Ivy League institutions like Harvard University recruit large numbers of these Indian Leftists who are funded, supported, and thus transformed into members of the Global far-Left army of knowledge workers.

While this activism is dangerous for any country to which it is exported, it creates perhaps the greatest threat to a country like India that comprises a significant diversity of identities and hence, the greatest scope for social disruption. Genuinely open-minded and liberal Indian intellectuals must, therefore, be brought closer to their American counterparts in addressing the global threat.

Snakes in the Ganga exposes the Indian funding of far-Left scholars-activists that push the tenets of the new moral orthodoxy. It also raises the puzzling question of why some capitalists are indirectly promoting neo-Marxism.

Once in a generation, a book comes along that has the possibility of changing the course of a civilization. *Snakes in the Ganga* is that book. It offers profound insights on the dangerous trajectory of Critical Social

Justice theories and untested moral orthodoxies born in the West when exported to other cultures. *Snakes in the Ganga* is our best hope of pushing back on illiberalism, recentering truth as our North Star, and changing the course of our civilization.

Peter Boghossian, Founding Faculty Fellow
University of Austin
June 2022

Introduction

Background

India, once again, is at the threshold of importing a large-scale sociological doctrine along with its varied practices, activism, trained manpower, and institutional apparatus. Like many other foreign imports of social sciences in the past, this movement is on a collision course with Indian society and politics. Yet, there has been very little attempt to study this latest force on India's own terms. On the contrary, the elites in government and industry are complicit in this infiltration. This statement should not be taken in any accusatory sense, and rather seen as a presentation of publicly available information as a red flag, calling for further discussion into the matter.

Before explaining further, we must first remind ourselves of the prior waves of socio-political disruptions caused by theories and doctrines that were imported into India. The discredited Aryan/Dravidian divide that haunts south India was an entirely European theory brought to India where it took several generations to become rooted. Only after that did we realize how deep its roots were established inside India's educational, social, media, and political fabric. It is now one of the most resilient paradigms accepted by the political spectrum in south India. Despite the evidence suggesting that the historical facts are more complex and nuanced, it has become domesticated, and the burden of proof is on those who disagree with it.[1]

The Indian sociological notions of *varna* and *jati* were very old, complex, and fluid. In different periods of history and across different regions, social structures differed considerably. But the foreign term *casta* that was brought to India by the Portuguese, led to the development of 'caste' as a European lens to view Indian society. This was later adopted as the official framework by the British Census of India to map their race theories onto Indian society from 1871 onwards. New laws were enacted by the British based on this imported rigid system replacing the flexible structures of the past. This served their divide and rule strategy.

Like the imported Aryan theory, the colonial premises of caste were at first resisted by Indians of all strata and even by many British officials. Gradually, however, the caste theories were accommodated by Indians, and eventually adopted as the normal frame of reference. After India's Independence in 1947, the caste system was further solidified into law, and has now become a resilient weapon spurring divisiveness.

Marxism, too, was imported, which gave birth to multiple communist parties in India, which were greatly influenced by the Soviet Union or China. Subsequently, India's Marxist intellectuals imported many new American theories like Orientalism, Postcolonialism, and Subalternism. The difference between Postcolonialism and Subalternism may be summarized as follows: Postcolonialism blamed foreign colonizers for biases and oppression and the natives of India were considered colonized victims. This changed in India when Subalternism began blaming India's Brahmins as the oppressors, while the oppressed victims were lower castes, Muslims, women, and others. This led to the rise of minority politics. While Orientalism and Postcolonialism unified Indians in countering the foreign colonizers, Subalternism became the divisive foundation of the Breaking India forces.

Each of these intellectual systems first established a foothold in academics. It spread to the writing of Indian history and educational curriculums, as well as the training of India's civil servants. Indian intellectuals have a fetish for importing foreign theories that are in vogue, and many careers and lineages are built this way.

What starts with Indian intellectuals does not stay limited to the intellectuals. Each of the above referenced imports is being supported by a network of Non-Governmental Organizations (NGOs), pipelines of foreign funding, and multinational political and legal support. The ecosystems are well-managed and efficient, and operate across national boundaries at the speed of light. Any event in one corner of the world spreads like wildfire throughout the ecosystem with consequences on the ground even in triggering off violence.

Let us turn to the core of this book. It may surprise the reader that something as seemingly idealistic and humanistic as Critical Race

Theory (CRT) is being exploited to break down a society built over several millennia. We are talking not just about the United States of America, where Critical Race Theory originated and has become all-pervasive, but also about India, a land on the other side of the world with a completely unique history and socio-political dynamic.

For the benefit of readers who might not be familiar with Critical Race Theory, Chapter 1 is devoted to examining its premises, history, major players, and tactics. It will become clear that this movement is weaponizing victimhood as a Breaking India force.

At the outset, we must make some important clarifications to avoid a knee-jerk reaction. Our focus is not on the application of Critical Race Theory to American society, but rather, on the way it has been incorrectly adapted for India and applied rashly to its vulnerable social ecosystem. Interestingly, unlike the way the adaptation of prior imports took place in academic institutions within India, in this instance, the Indianized versions are being formulated not inside India but at places like Harvard University. And this is being done largely by Indians based at Harvard. A large number of them are involved in this enterprise, performing roles from top professors to junior scholars, all the way down to students.

Finally, and the most unexpected of all findings in this book is that Indian billionaires are funding this movement, and lending their family names and contacts. Indian support of various kinds is involved throughout this pipeline: from the research done at Harvard, to the Harvard conferences and events where this material is discussed, to the training seminars where Indian political and business leaders are influenced, to the creation of India-based organizations that help source raw data and serve as the ideological distribution channels into Indian society.

This is indeed a very big story. First, the ground has to be prepared in the reader's mind to receive all this logically, and in a structured manner. There are many parts to the thesis and the picture must be understood in its entirety rather than piecemeal. The reader, otherwise, might take away some incorrect conclusions.

We will start systematically by presenting the multi-layered thesis, one layer at a time. The intellectual and socio-political weapons being imported to India have to be explained in their United States of

America context. Only then will the reader fully comprehend what is so dramatically new about them compared to the past ideologies that were imported.

What is essential to explain is the way African Americans and Dalits are being brought together for this purpose so that the latest shock waves of racism in American society can be transported to India. Caste censuses of Indian Americans are being carried out in American businesses and on campuses, with the prejudiced reports thus produced being used to poison public opinion on Indians. The same 'caste experts' that are responsible for these censuses have suddenly turned into elite consultants conducting caste sensitivity training inside the vast Silicon Valley corporations, much to the embarrassment of the large numbers of Indians that work there. And this is already causing the enactment of new laws and regulations on caste in American organizations.

Four Big Stories

This book is the result of an exhaustive investigation involving several domains both in the US and India. It has been organized into four distinct stories to help the reader understand its depth. Each story is self-contained and could be a book by itself. But each needs to be seen in the context of the others to appreciate the significant message in this book.

These stories are summarized below:

1. How Critical Race Theory has taken over the Leftist rhetoric in the West even though it often espouses ideals that are inimical to many core components of classical Liberalism.
2. Harvard University has brought together some leading Blacks and bright young Dalits, and they have adapted Critical Race Theory into Critical *Caste* Theory by mapping 'Caste = Race'. The old Afro-Dalit thesis exposed in the book *Breaking India: Western Interventions in Dravidian and Dalit Fault Lines*, claimed that Dalits are the Blacks of India, and Brahmins are the Whites. This hyphenation has catapulted into the latest sociological thesis that takes divisive identity politics to a new level. The door has flung wide open to bring all American race theories, legal frameworks, activist toolkits, and institutional

networks into India. So today, American anti-racism movements are the engines driving India's social revolution. While it is imperative to solve India's social injustices, this wholesale transfer is exploiting victimhood politics in India. One can draw parallels with the British 'civilizing' mission in India, which basically served as a divide and rule policy to control Indians. The implications for India must be understood clearly.

3. Harvard has become the academic nexus for this project. It is developing the atrocity literature to support the use of Critical Caste Theory to dismantle India.

4. Harvard is rapidly exporting this scholarship and activism to India. It has infiltrated Indian industry, government, media, philanthropy, and just about every segment of civil society. Parts 2 and 3 will give numerous concrete examples. Under the umbrella of philanthropy and development, a new generation of elite activists and institutions are being mentored.

Each of the four significant stories is of considerable importance by itself. When taken together, they uncover what is nothing short of a major intellectual and social revolution under way. The figure below shows how these stories flow into each other.

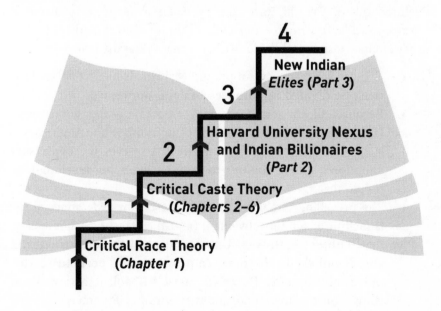

Story 1: The Americanization of Marxism

To understand this phenomenon, we must trace the evolution of Marxism in Europe and its arrival in America. This new Americanized version is fomenting and spreading from the US to the rest of the world, including, with devastating impact, India.

While most Americans have disdained Marxism throughout history, Marxist thought is, however, at the very core of American academic institutions, thinktanks, and powerful NGOs. It is not being called Marxism, as that has negative connotations; rather, it comes camouflaged within a powerful movement to dismantle systemic racism. At the heart of it, though, it is just old wine in a new bottle. In fact, America has become the global hub for developing and propagating this latest manifestation of Marxism.

We are sympathetic to many aspects of Marxism, especially its systematic analysis of the history of exploitation. But we wish to critique the extreme forms it is taking in dismantling traditional societies and the radical implications.

The new paradigm known as Critical Race Theory began with good intentions – to fight against the injustices suffered by Black Americans at the hands of White Americans. But in its merger with Marxism and Postmodernism, Critical Race Theory is on a dangerous trajectory towards a similar destructive impact that Communism and other Marxist experiments caused worldwide. It shares many Marxist principles:

- Critical Race Theory adopts the Marxist dialectic that **society must be divided into oppressors and oppressed**.
- Because all the discourse was created by the bourgeoisie (European ruling elites, now substituted with White Americans), it has been a hegemonic narrative that serves the oppressor. Therefore, **a new counter-hegemony must be developed** to topple that.
- The prevailing established order (thesis) must be attacked by launching a counter-movement (anti-thesis) with such intensity that both get destroyed. Unless and **until the old structures are demolished, all social reforms merely perpetuate the old establishment**. This clash must be violent and without compromise. Only then can a new social order emerge.

- All friendly negotiations and attempts to reform the system are flawed because they end up being within the old hegemonic narrative and its rules of engagement. Therefore, open dialog is a bad idea. In fact, **freedom to think and speak must be curtailed** to create the counter-hegemony, i.e., a new biased discourse to respond to the old bias. This intolerance is reminiscent of the Soviet dictator, Stalin. It is present in Critical Race Theory in the form of Cancel Culture that has spread across American campuses and society.
- The destruction of the established order can only be achieved by extreme intolerance, including the use of violence.

Chapter 1 will give ample evidence of each of these features of Critical Race Theory that find their origins in Marxism.

There is also an important point of difference between Marxism and CRT: Prominent leaders of Critical Race Theory have rejected rationality, objective evidence, and even science. An example is the rejection of the biological gender binary of male-female in Lesbian, Gay, Bisexual, Transgender, Queer+ (LGBTQ+) discourse. 'Lived-experience' is considered the final verdict and all rational and counter-debate gets shut down. Subjectivity rules while objectivity is considered patriarchal. Cancel Culture is applied when an opponent attempts to counter-argue. Unlike this, Marxism prides itself on its focus on rationality and the scientific method. While Marxist revolutionaries on the ground were radicals and intolerant towards opponents, the intellectuals did engage in rational debates.

Marxism, Postmodernism, and Liberalism are three important theoretical frameworks studied in the humanities and social sciences. The ideological camp that is broadly referred to as the Left uses these as building blocks with various permutations and combinations defining a range of 'Leftist' postures. All Leftists are not the same. Some are diehard Marxists, some rely more on Postmodernism, some are Liberals who use only diluted forms of these two, and so forth.

The situation gets even more complex if one goes deeper. One finds that even Marxism, Postmodernism, and Liberalism are not single ideas but that each has its own complex history with multiple sub-camps. This book does not intend to delve into the history and ideas of the Left in

Snakes in the Ganga

any detail because that would be beyond its scope. Rather, Chapter 1 will merely explain that Critical Race Theory has borrowed elements from all three – Marxism, Postmodernism, and Liberalism – while rejecting many of their key premises.

Ironically, most traditional Leftist thinkers that define themselves in terms of some combination of Marxism, Postmodernism, and Liberalism, have not come to terms with the fact that Critical Race Theory contradicts their fundamental premises. In other words, there is a serious clash within the Leftist camp. The Old Left is being challenged by the New Left that has emerged out of CRT.

The figure that follows shows the historical origins in Europe of what is commonly known as the Left. In the 1930s, a new form of Marxism, the Frankfurt School, started in Germany. During the Second World War (1939-45), its leaders migrated to the US to escape the Nazis. The German philosophers, Jürgen Habermas and Herbert Marcuse were among the young leaders from Europe and attracted a new generation of Americans into the Marxist movement. Columbia University in the US became an important base.

In parallel, Postmodernism had its origins earlier in twentieth-century France, where it underwent a series of developments through prominent thinkers. In the US, the literary theorist, Gayatri Chakravorty Spivak became one of the initial American contributors through her translations of important French thinkers into English. The other person that helped bring Postmodernism to the US was also of Indian origin, namely, Homi K. Bhabha, who is now at Harvard University. He is the subject of Chapter 10. This Americanization of both Marxism and Postmodernism was significant because it turned the US into the global base of the new Left.

Later, the Americans developed Critical Race Theory as a serious school of thought. Chapter 1 is devoted to this topic. The theory begins with the premise that there is systemic, unconscious, and pervasive, racism embedded in the core framework of Western society, including institutions (governmental, financial, and corporate), which results in the continued oppression of certain minorities. It draws a distinction between being 'not racist', which is considered insufficient to overthrow and eliminate the systemic racism, and being 'anti-racist', which calls upon people to actively challenge their own biases and mindsets, and to question institutional frameworks and practices, in order to create a more inclusive, and just, society.

Critical Race Theory gained mainstream visibility in the aftermath of the recent Black Lives Matter (BLM) movement when longstanding police brutality against Blacks came to light in a manner that was no longer ignorable. These events catalyzed CRT into an important discourse in the media, in schools, and at the workplace.

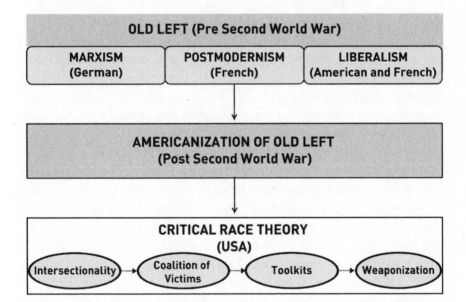

We believe that while these goals are laudable and the problems confronted are real, some of the methods of redress are ultimately problematic and more destructive than constructive.

A major premise of Critical Race Theory is that rights must be fought, not by individuals for individuals, but by groups for their members. This is an important shift from classical Liberalism where rights are as individual citizens and not as group identities. But in CRT, the social position of a *collective identity* determines the privilege or oppression of all its members. This is not about any individual but the way one's collective identity is categorized and operates in society.

As an example, former US president, Barack Obama, was a classical Liberal who did not want to create conflict by dismantling the old institutional structures. He wanted to get justice for Blacks within the framework of modern institutions, and not by dismantling them. Obama did not want to play identity politics that would pit Blacks against Whites. He sought unity as the way forward and was against creating rupture.

In his public speeches, Obama frequently advocated for societal integration through the pursuit of color-blindness; he specifically refused to concede that American society and institutions were irrevocably and irredeemably racist. Of course, as the first Black president of the United States, he was perhaps constrained by his unique position in history and the need to bridge the gap between White and Black citizens. However, he consistently articulated a thoughtful, constructive, and inspiring vision on creating a more just and united country. His vision needs to be appreciated while understanding and analyzing Critical Race Theory's contrasting position.

Obama's position on color-blindness represents classical Liberalism. The Liberal ideal has been that opportunities must not prefer one race over another, and injustices must be eliminated irrespective of race, i.e., a color-blind policy. Critical Race Theory complains that color-blindness allows a status quo in which the injustices continue. To dismantle racism, one must bring what amounts to reverse-discrimination.

Another key difference is that Liberals espouse equal opportunities whereas Critical Race Theory demands equal outcomes. According to the former principle, every individual must get equal opportunities, and outcomes are then determined based on merit. This is in line with the American ideal of meritocracy, also espoused by Obama. But Critical Race Theory states that the equal opportunity system is rigged because it produces unequal outcomes. This view ignores the fact that many factors including individual competence and pure luck, play a part in unequal outcomes. Critical Race Theory's goal is 'equity', which means equal outcomes. This is being demanded in all areas including college admissions, corporate and government jobs, and even math exam results.

Meritocracy, on an objective basis, is rejected because it fails to produce equal outcomes. The diversity of experiences from different identities is considered more valuable. Traditional ideas of hard work and merit, and traditional systems of rewards are called into question by Critical Race Theory.

The legal concept of 'protected classes' is being used to recruit newer kinds of victim groups. Federal laws of the United States of America define the following nine protected classes and grants them special protection from discrimination or harassment: sex (including sexual orientation and gender identity); race; age; disability; color; creed; national origin; religion; or genetic information. Individual states in the US can, and do, create other classes for protection under state law. The strategy of Critical Race Theory is to identify as many groups as possible that claim to have been oppressed historically, and to organize them into a coalition that fights the established order. This ensures a constant supply of disgruntled groups with grievances that will continue to break down society and its institutions.

The following diagram lists some of the important differences between Classical Liberalism and Critical Race Theory.

Classical Liberalism		Critical Race Theory
• Right of Individuals		• Rights of Group Identities
• Equality		• Equity
• Colorblindness		• Counter-hegemony, not Neutrality
• Reform Old Structures Incrementally		• Dismantle Old Structures
• Intellectual Freedom and Free Speech		• Cancel Culture
• Science and Rationality		• Dogma of Critical Race Theory
• Civilization has Advanced a Great Deal		• Civilization has been Oppressive

Critical Race Theory projects the Black American experience of racial discrimination as the universal lens applicable to racism and other prejudices in all the cultures of the world. We disagree. While in the US, the White/Black dichotomy is relevant to represent the oppressor/oppressed, the circumstances in other cultures can be more complex and multipolar.

For instance, how would the Critical Race Theory framework apply to Asian Americans? Are they the oppressor or the oppressed? How would the simplistic binary system of oppressor/oppressed deal with a situation where a community like the Hindus could be seen by some as oppressors (of Dalits), and by others as oppressed (historically by invaders and colonialists who were Muslims and Christians). This is rendered even more difficult in light of the fact that defending Islam has been subsumed into Critical Race Theory such that Muslims are now perceived as systemic victims, like Blacks.

Cornel West, one of Harvard's most influential Black scholars, openly supports the CRT argument that Hinduism's structures should be dismantled to protect the oppressed Dalits. But in the context of Hindus being oppressed by Muslims, Christians, and Western hegemony, one could argue that it is Hinduism that is protecting Indian minds from further colonization by the global nexuses. We thus have a complicated situation that cannot be reduced to a simplistic oppressor/oppressed situation.

Could one build a case that the *global oppressors* (Abrahamic religions and Western Leftist nexuses) are trying to use the *local oppressed* (Dalits within India) as a weapon to dismantle the structures of Hinduism, so that India becomes vulnerable to yet another takeover? This is a common strategy known as 'the enemy of my enemy is my friend', namely, a pragmatic way to use Dalits as a weapon against India's sovereignty. People familiar with Indian history will easily see this as yet another divide and rule game being played.

Story 2: The Indianization of Critical Race Theory

A major development out of the US is that caste has been mapped as race, which has become the basis for developing Critical Caste Theory. The Afro-Dalit movement that was in its nascent stages when discussed in the book, *Breaking India*, has now matured and solidified into a robust movement. Chapters 2, 3, 4, and 5 are devoted to discussing how this has come about so rapidly. Each chapter focuses on one aspect of this Indianized version of Critical Race Theory by addressing the most important protagonist in that aspect.

The following figure shows the four main protagonists discussed in these chapters, each of them examined in depth and given a rebuttal.

Caste → Cause of all Racism (*Isabel Wilkerson*)	⏩ Caste Enters US Pop Culture and Mainstream Discourse
Caste Surveys in American Workplaces (*Equality Labs*)	⏩ Caste Surveys Used to Prove Brahmin Racism in US Workplaces
Indian Tech Meritocracy Masks Brahmin Privilege (*Ajantha Subramanian*)	⏩ Silicon Valley Indians Bring Casteism to America
Critical Race Theory → Afro-Dalit Solidarity (*Suraj Yengde*)	⏩ Harvard Campaign to Dismantle Hinduism

This is not a fringe movement. The American TV host, Oprah Winfrey actively promoted Isabel Wilkerson's book, *Caste: The Origins of Our Discontent*, promoting this thesis. The book went on to become a *New York Times* bestseller. Harvard actively promotes Wilkerson's work to its student body. It is extremely well written for the mainstream and argues in an authoritative tone that caste is the underlying structure that has created racism worldwide. We take Wilkerson's thesis apart point by point in Chapter 2, citing her own statements and giving our responses.

Chapter 3 explains that caste surveys are being conducted in the US, led by the New York-based Equality Labs to build legal cases accusing American organizations of caste bias by their Brahmin employees. As a result of this legal threat to US organizations, various new laws and regulations are being rapidly enacted that officially classify casteism as a form of racism. Corporate America is fearful of being considered complicit, and Silicon Valley, especially, is conducting training workshops to educate senior management on caste oppression. Brahmins are being depicted as the equivalent of Whites, and Dalits as Blacks of India. This has turned into an attack against Indian Americans, branding them as casteists, the equivalent of White supremacists.

Critical Race Theory opposes meritocracy based on science and rationality, seeing these structures as a way to perpetuate White privilege. This argument has been turned into a movement starting from Harvard by Prof. Ajantha Subramanian through her influential book *The Caste of Merit: Engineering Education in India*, attacking the Indian Institutes of Technology (IITs). She argues that the IITs have institutionalized racism in the form of casteism that oppresses the minorities, especially the Dalits. This is examined in Chapter 4.

Harvard's Dalit poster boy, Suraj Yengde, is the most vocal, and high-profile, Afro-Dalit. He uses the oppressor/oppressed frameworks of CRT to interpret Indian society in every institution. Chapter 5 discusses his vicious attacks on Brahmins, Hinduism, and everything related to the Indian civilization. He has mirrored the entire Black movement to form a corresponding Dalit movement. There is Dalit Heritage Month similar to Black Heritage Month. There is a Dalit Lives Matter movement mirroring the Black Lives Matter movement. Like the Black Panther party, there is now the Dalit Panthers organization, and so forth. Yengde is senior fellow at the powerful Kennedy School of Government at Harvard.

While race is the primary category of oppression in Critical Race Theory, in its application to India, it is caste. A large archive filled with sensational and emotional atrocity literature has been systematically built by Yengde and others at Harvard.

Just as Black Americans have been officially declared a 'protected class' under American law, so also Dalits are being championed to become a protected class. The effect is that one can neither question nor challenge whatever a Dalit leader says in the US for fear of legal action or public shaming.

According to Critical Race Theory, the lived experiences of oppressed groups override any objective evidence or logic. The stories of this lived experience must become the basis for developing the counter-hegemony to fight the structures of oppression. Our concern is that by insulating this very lived experience from scrutiny, analysis, criticism, or refutation, one creates greater distance between communities. This exacerbates conflicts, rather than helping people unite at a higher level of consciousness. Also, this prevents Dalits from achieving excellence because they end up seeing themselves as perpetual victims that are dependent on reparations.

In the weaponization of Critical Race Theory for India, any group that can be convinced to oppose Indian civilization is a useful ally and is given the status of a victim. Besides the Dalits, the most important among them are the Indian Muslims and the LGBTQ+ communities. Once these victim identities are crystallized, they are weaponized to dismantle the structures, and provoked to attack in all directions. The following aspects of India's civilization are being formally designated as targets:

- Sanskrit: Sanskrit is being declared an oppressive language. Critical Race Theory argues that languages contain structures of 'White privilege' in the case of the West, and by extension, Sanskrit perpetuates Brahmin privilege as a tool for exploiting the lower castes and Dalits. The book, *The Battle For Sanskrit: Is Sanskrit Political or Sacred, Oppressive or Liberating, Dead or Alive?* explained this allegation and gave a systematic rebuttal.[2]
- Gurus: Because the Indian equivalent of Whites are Brahmins, all gurus are deemed guilty of asserting their hegemony over society. The institution of gurus is considered akin to White supremacy.
- Deities, festivals, pilgrimage centers, symbolism, rituals: All these structures from the past were constructed by Brahmin elites to establish hegemony. The charge is made that by design, these structures have in-built mechanisms for perpetuating exploitation. Therefore, it is important to prosecute all such structures looking for every instance of abuse. The dirt that is dug up is used to build an archive and database for research. The endgame is to dismantle it all.
- Vedic *shastras* and *Itihasa*: Vedic texts and related works are seen as hegemonic. Using the Marxist doctrine promoted by Antonio Gramsci, founder of the Communist Party of Italy, a counter-hegemony must be constructed and implanted into the discourse on Indian traditions.
- Family system: The traditional family structure is openly being attacked as a mechanism by which parents pass on the oppressiveness to the children, and Indian students are being advocated to revolt against their parents.

In other words, everything that allows India to succeed has to be deconstructed and dismantled under this theory. Chapters 2, 3, 4, and 5 give numerous examples of this kind of application of Critical Race

Theory to Indian society, with Harvard-based scholars leading this scholarship and activism.

While Dalits and Muslims are known to have been appropriated by Critical Race Theory and turned into pawns in this identity war against India, the LGBTQ+ community is a relatively new group being tutored using Western theories.

This is where the lived experience of Deepthi Rao, an Indian American software professional in Silicon Valley, is very insightful. Given the importance of her statement to our thesis on the divisiveness of CRT, and her audacity in expressing herself, we wish to quote in detail. She approached us as a Hindu lesbian with keen interest to connect and collaborate with the Hindu mainstream in dealing with the onslaught of Critical Race Theory. Here is her account:

> I was raised in India in a close-knit family. In my late teens I started feeling attraction to other women, but it was taboo to speak about being a lesbian. While working as a software engineer in the US, I decided to share my private feelings with close family. My parents resisted and tried to find 'solutions' to what they considered a behavioral problem that needed to be 'fixed'. My background in Hindu practices and Vedanta became important resources. I chanted the Vishnu Sahasranama and Hanuman Chalisa. I studied Vedic heritage and discovered the numerous references to people being non-heterosexual. But the modern-day Hindu practices were narrowminded and intolerant towards same sex relationships.
>
> Upon moving to California, I came out publicly as a member of the well-established LGBTQ+ community, especially with a sub-group of Asian origin members. This filled a void because we had comfort and safety as a family sharing common predicaments.
>
> As I got deeper into the American LGBTQ+ movement, I noticed that this new group of friends had antagonistic views about Hinduism and India. They were vocal about Hinduism being oppressive and casteist and in need of being dismantled. They attributed all the problems in India to 'Brahminical patriarchy' and called any positive policies and progress of India as fascist and nationalistic propaganda. Some even said that Silicon Valley tech

companies had a 'Brahmin problem' and that their success was
entirely due to caste privileges. Any alternative view I presented
was rudely dismissed. These individuals supported Muslim
culture, never once wanting to discuss Islam's anti-LGBTQ+
history and structural oppression. This is dishonest and bigoted.

I felt caught between two bad options: To have emotional
and political support for being a lesbian, I must serve as a loyal
member of the American LGBTQ+ community. But reject my
dharmic heritage. I do agree that societal norms that are toxic,
oppressive and divisive for the modern era must be removed.
But I find Vedanta very logical, and Gita provides great solutions.
Unfortunately, my LGBTQ+ friends pressured me to outright
reject my Hindu identity. I felt oppressed and kept my Hindu
identity secret out of shame and the fear of losing my support
system.

Eventually, I decided that my Vedic heritage was much more
important, even though I now face harassment as a Hindu![3]

Clearly, Rao has valuable experience and has reflected on the lessons
to be learned. She has offered the following analysis which we find
compelling. It shows how victimhood is being used to fight a culture
war against specific targeted cultures:

I have learned a great deal through all this personal experience.
The LGBTQ+ movement is a <u>false and forced unity</u> *because
different segments within it have incompatible views on sexuality.
As a lesbian, I am certain of my womanhood and do not want a
surgical sex change. But the Queer movement denies the very concept
of a woman, calling it a social construct that must be dismantled.*
This artificially unified movement assigns a single oppressor. In
the West it is White males, and this has been mapped to Brahmins
in India. I feel there are many kinds of oppressions and oppressors
in the different cultures. Our Hindu history of being colonized
by Muslims and then Europeans has left scars not understood
by other groups.

I disapprove of the movement's rigid internal hierarchy in
which all of us are expected to obey what the high priests have
dictated like some sort of religion. I disapprove of the Cancel

Culture that shouts down opponents rather than working together with well-meaning people of all backgrounds to explore paths towards a healthier society. I am especially troubled by the Marxist foundations that require conflict between identities. I do not like the demand to dismantle my civilization, especially when these leaders have no clue what to replace it with, or how to go about preventing anarchy.

Lastly, I can completely speak for how it feels when you are marginalized/ignored or shunned as a result of your identity. This experience wounds you emotionally and leaves you vulnerable. This is fertile ground to being hijacked by larger malicious forces. This is what happened in the case of Dalits. It started with being marginalized by the rest of the Hindu community, and they became the perfect target for religious conversion. Indians belonging to the LGBTQ+ community are being used by the Queer movement to provide them political strength in numbers, against our own civilization's survival.

What is needed is a movement within Hinduism that integrates, normalizes and protects the LGBTQ+ people using Hinduism's own traditional resources. This is not just a matter of passive 'tolerance' of diverse genders and sexualities, but an inclusive movement that creates sustainable changes within society for people of the LGBTQ+ community to co-exist with the regular heterosexual members as one unified community. It requires structures, institutions, leaders, and resources. Otherwise, we Hindus will not only lose a large number of our people to the Critical Race Theory movement, but also find them being used as a weapon against our heritage.[4]

Chapter 1 elaborates how the Critical Race Theory movement has become the umbrella for any and every kind of group with grievances against a culture that it chooses to attack.

We do not outright dismiss the theory, but when applied to India, Chapters 2 to 5 show that the evidence is shoddy, and the logic teeming with political rhetoric. The intimidation of critics with name-calling has thwarted free exchanges without which no proper diagnoses or solutions can emerge. To benefit from the many good things about Critical Race

Theory, there must be a nuanced approach and serious study at the university level just like the study and critique of any other philosophical system. The problem is that CRT's application to Indian society comes wrapped in a bundle of lies and exaggerations that nobody is allowed to question.

Chapter 6 gives a point-by-point rebuttal to the distortions concerning the history of caste in India. This is also intended as an important stand-alone monograph on the caste debate.

Story 3: Harvard University Churns Out Atrocity Literature

The important story in this book is that Harvard has become a global nexus for this kind of new Breaking India movement.

Part 2 analyzes three major centers at Harvard, those established by Anand Mahindra, Lakshmi Mittal, and Ajay Piramal, each in their respective family names. Each of them has donated several millions of dollars for the work being carried out. Though we discuss these three as specific examples, they are merely illustrative of the long list of wealthy Indians donating to Harvard for the study of India.

We discuss the nature of the work being carried out and its adverse impact on India. With examples, we show that Harvard is essentially setting the agenda that also includes anti-India biases. We contrast this with China's presence at Harvard: China has controlled the discourse and used it to pursue its well-crafted nationalistic agenda.

Attacking India's legitimacy as a nation-state, its Constitution, and its ruling party are among the themes of Harvard's research projects and conferences, often hidden beneath a veneer of social justice. For instance, India's enactment of laws that altered Article 370 of the Constitution, the Citizenship (Amendment) Act, 2019 (CAA), and the New Farms Acts 2020, became opportunities to rabble-rouse various 'victim' identities and encourage them to form coalitions against the government. Such agendas are under themes like Kashmir, LGBTQ+ rights, Muslim grievances, to name just a few. Naturally, the Indian military's actions against insurgencies are an easy target.

Many neutral or positive themes like public health, finance, entrepreneurship, youth training, technology transfer, and media training are being used as covers for highlighting the oppression of victim identities that fit into Critical Race Theory. Even Sanskrit studies

Snakes in the Ganga

uses the lens of human rights by claiming that its texts are driven by Brahmin supremacy and contain the oppression of Dalits, women, and others. We show how even the field of China studies in India is being used against Indian culture in this manner.

Harvard is a global hub that seeks to repackage Black/White history and laws in the US and apply them to Dalits/Brahmins in India. From this epicenter, the list of victim groups against India has been expanding. Each group is incentivized to dig up dirt on India and use an us/them and oppressed/oppressor rhetoric where possible. Borrowing a page from Gramsci's doctrine of building a counter-hegemony, Harvard has numerous projects we will discuss in Part 2 that build databases and archives for such research.

We see a clear bias of double standard in Harvard's treatment of Islam and Hinduism. The former is positioned as a victim deserving sympathy while the latter is positioned as an oppressor that needs to be controlled, or even dismantled. For instance, the website of the Harvard Graduate School of Education states: 'Islamophobia in the United States has become rampant' and it has established programs to monitor Islamophobia and fight it.[5] We certainly support the fight against all religious bigotry. But this should not be selective to protect only certain religions.

If Islamophobia is being monitored, and actively criticized by Harvard, the same approach must also be applied for Hinduphobia, for example. Unfortunately, the exact opposite is the case: Harvard has been found to perpetuate Hinduphobia in many instances.

One petition by Hindus stated: 'A Harvard Kennedy School academic has recently tweeted saying, "Hindus are sick people of India, it is their religious books who (sic) train the mind"'.[6] Another open letter to Harvard was sent by the Hindu Students Council complaining that Harvard had become a bastion for blatant Hinduphobia on its campus with the blessing of its faculty in some cases.[7]

With the political support of Harvard, the US Congress passed a bill making Islamophobia a crime worldwide and requiring the government to create a special organization prosecuting Islamophobia everywhere and to apply US sanctions against countries found guilty. The irony is that no such protection was offered to other religions. In parallel, Pakistan introduced a resolution in the United Nations General Assembly on

'International Day to Combat Islamophobia'. It stated that 'Hate speech, discrimination and violence are proliferating in several parts of world, causing great anguish in the Islamic world'. Though France desired any such resolution to be inclusive of all religions and not just for Islam, and India had similar views as well, there were many Muslim countries supporting the resolution. It was passed with a decision 'to proclaim 15 March the International Day to Combat Islamophobia'.[8]

Harvard seems to be especially obsessed with building databases and archives that can be of strategic value to Breaking India forces besides being a national security threat to India. Part 2 gives several such examples of sensitive data collection on minorities, insurgency-ridden regions, health and financial information of the vulnerable, and all kinds of social information that could be used to create dissent.

Part 2 also cites examples of Cancel Culture where opponents have been systematically excluded or blocked. People with opposing points of view can get branded as oppressors, and persistent voices subjected to public shaming. All this has serious implications when one realizes that Harvard is deep inside India's government organizations and industry, formulating policies, training civil servants and corporate leaders, and developing the standards for governance. It would not be an exaggeration to say that more than any other foreign institution, it is Harvard that is shaping India's young leaders in all sectors by using its research, education, training, networks of influence, funding, and brand name.

Story 4: Breaking India by the New Elites

All developments discussed earlier end up impacting India. This is the focus of Part 3. Critical Race Theory is having a global impact emanating from the US, and many countries have responded to it in different ways. France, Japan, Israel, and Singapore are examples of countries allied with the US that have reacted adversely to the way CRT threatens them. Russia and China have opposed it in strong ways as well, but that is to be expected.

Our concern is that India is likely to face more devastation than any other major country because its fragmented society is ideally suited for the disruptions that Critical Race Theory advocates. Also, India has an existing ecosystem of intellectual workers already participating in developing CRT in places like Harvard as well as helping it train an army of activists in India. Many Indians in high places welcome such interventions from the US, out of ignorance or personal opportunity.

Readers will be shocked to learn that Omidyar Network, owned by the US-based Iranian billionaire, Pierre Morad Omidyar, has established an elaborate network of investments across India that we believe pose a serious risk to India's sovereignty. This is evident in its ideological tilt towards CRT-driven projects. Its sophisticated public relations machinery has convinced Indians at highest levels that it is engaged in philanthropy and development. This is true, but the whole truth is far more complex and kept hidden. An entire chapter is devoted to Omidyar Network India.

Part 3 also discusses several other organizations in India that have controversial content. Ashoka University, based near New Delhi, is a major player, and is funded by influential Indians claiming to help India by introducing American style liberal arts. An entire chapter has been devoted to it. We also discuss Krea University as another India-based hub for such activities. There are activities funded by various others as well including the Abdul Latif Jameel Poverty Action Lab (J-PAL) (a Saudi funded initiative at Massachusetts Institute of Technology [MIT] that targets India on human rights).

The book, *Breaking India*, written over a decade back, discusses similar forces prevalent at that time. But the ground has shifted dramatically since then. There are now completely new players with different technologies and approaches to dismantle India's sovereignty.

The new threats, which we refer to as Breaking India forces 2.0, are based on Critical Race Theory which is radically different to the old Leftist ideologies. The new focus is not on poor, illiterate villagers in trying to convert them, but rather, on urban elites. The goal now is to establish a new generation of leaders across Indian society groomed by Harvard and others as part of its global network of influence. The Harvard name and its sophisticated approaches are powerful to get in the door.

The following table compares how the forces described in this book differ from the ones exposed earlier.

Breaking India 1.0	Breaking India 2.0
• Old Left Ideological Framework	• CRT Framework Extended to Indian Victim Groups
• Poor Villagers Target of Conversion or as Foot Soldiers	• Urban Elites Targets in Top Posts in Industry, Government, Civil Service, Entrepreneurship
• Stated Goal is to Deliver Basic Needs: Food, Clothing, Education, Water, etc.	• Stated Goal is to Deliver Development Through Technology, Leadership Training at Harvard, Prestigious Global Networking
• Targets are Isolated from the Global Nexuses; No Direct Contact with the West	• Harvard Trained Indian Intermediaries Run End-to-end Knowledge Channel at all Levels

Motives for Funding

Historically, many billionaires have made large contributions that have uplifted humanity in profound ways and we wish to recognize these honorable efforts. However, sometimes philanthropy has unintended outcomes. For funders of such projects, this book is a ready reckoner that critically examines the fruits of their philanthropy. The authors merely perform a due diligence on the state of the Indian nation, raising red flags on issues that may have gone unnoticed. We believe that the parties named in this book embarked on these projects with no malice, although the outcomes of such enterprises may include collateral damage that pose risks. We also hope that this book is received in the correct spirit to sharpen future philanthropic investments.

As with any due diligence done with objectivity, one has to ask why these billionaires are funding such activities in places like Harvard. We can conjecture several possible reasons but cannot conclude which ones might apply in any given instance.

Genuinely Aligned with the Ultra-Left

One of the ideological reasons could be that the billionaires, who accumulated this wealth suddenly in recent times, or their offspring who are spending it, are genuinely ideologically convinced of the entire thesis of Critical Caste Theory. In that case, they are ideologically ultra-Leftists.

Ignorant of the Big Picture

A second possible ideological reason could be that they haven't grasped this Critical Caste Theory of the ultra-Left but have sympathies with Dalits. They want to genuinely help the downtrodden but have not examined the details of what goes on in the social sciences using their money and family name. They are clueless about how dangerous some of these activities are. They have the naïve notion of helping humanity, but without knowing the full background. And without having done the due diligence on all the actors involved: the ultra-Leftist scholars' writings, their affiliation and ideologies, and their deep links with Breaking India forces.

In other words, in this category are those who are not intentionally breaking India. They are not ultra-Leftists like the first category, but think they are doing good, and have inadvertently ended up aligning with Breaking India forces.

Selfish

The third possibility is that the wealthy are seeking the limelight Harvard provides. They want a seat at the high table, sitting alongside the who's who of the elitist world. They want to be on par with the jet set global elites. So, it is basically to build a personal brand and get bragging rights. Besides glamor, they may benefit from getting their kin into Harvard as students or on various committees, boards, and affiliations that translate into tangible benefits. Joining the prestigious alumni is by itself considered a privileged membership.

Influencing the Left

The fourth reason may be that the donor is indirectly influencing the ultra-Left and in exchange, being spared by activists fighting capitalism and racism. To put it bluntly, this hypothesizes that some donors could be diverting the attention away from their own vulnerabilities.

The ultra-Left has seized the social sciences in prestigious academic centers and weaponized them to demand deep structural changes for the Dalits, Muslims, and others considered by Harvard to be 'protected groups'. Their campaigns want to change the boards of these companies and place Dalits and those that identify as LGBTQ+. They want a certain representation in senior management and end certain types of commercial activities on grounds of social justice. They have already started litigating giant companies in the US, such as Cisco Systems. There is also the Environmental, Social and Governance (ESG) movement that assigns ratings, which entails evaluating the 'social conduct' of companies and their top executives. So, funding the powerful Leftists at Harvard could be similar to hush money in exchange for protection. Indian billionaires are known for their detailed due diligence and negotiations when making commercial investments and we humbly recommend the same be done when investing in India studies.

Key Takeaways

Following are some important takeaway points presented in the book:

The New Marxism:

1. Black Americans and Dalits have been made to unite and the war against White Americans has expanded to target Brahmins. Caste is now considered the mother of all racism against Black Americans and other victim groups worldwide. Upper caste Indians are the Whites of India.
2. The ultimate goal of this new movement is to dismantle the present world order and the institutions that support it. But they have no clear path toward a new viable world system, nor the prerequisite experience in managing such a dangerous transformation.
3. Our concern is that after Critical Race Theory is used as the wrecking ball to dismantle society, the reconstruction of a new social order will be done by those who control the new technologies like Artificial Intelligence (AI). Our earlier book, *Artificial Intelligence and the Future of Power: 5 Battlegrounds*, explains how AI is controlled by

a new breed of elites. Its trajectory is leading towards an extreme concentration of power and wealth reminiscent of the East India Company.

Harvard University's Central Role:

1. Our research suggests that Harvard University is the epicenter for developing this discourse and weaponizing it into activism, as well as training thousands of fighters in this new warfare. Harvard has developed its own *sangha* (community) with a vast network of *shakhas* (branches).
2. Indian billionaires are supporting this Breaking India work at Harvard by actively funding it and giving it legitimacy, knowingly or unknowingly.
3. A plausible explanation is that such funding helps the ratings of the donors in the new system called ESG which determines their access to international investments and commercial contracts. Funding Harvard also gives them seats on prestigious boards and committees. It is one of the most profitable investments they could make, classified as philanthropy.
4. Contrary to Indians' self-congratulatory notion that India is *vishwa guru* (guru to the world), in reality it is Harvard that is the vishwa guru. And India is vishwa *shishya* (student), with many of its people serving as vishwa *coolie* (laborer), and vishwa *sepoy* (soldier) in this ecosystem.

Response From Other Countries:

1. Many Americans are fighting against Critical Race Theory and its pop culture form, Wokeism. But they are unaware that this problem also inflicts India, and in a far worse way.
2. Some countries have launched campaigns against the movement, including China, France, Japan, Israel, Singapore, and so on.
3. China is playing a double role: opposing this ideology at home but helping those who bring it to its enemies like the US and India.

Impact on the Vedic System:

1. Critical Race Theory is being applied to dismantle the Vedic narrative using the argument that all social problems confronting

India today including caste, gender, sexuality, human rights, social justice, are the result of Vedic structures. Therefore, the demand is that we should not allow the Vedic structures to survive because we will fail to solve the social crises we face. This calls upon social justice advocates to completely dismantle the foundations of Indian civilization.

2. We respond that rather than being the root cause of the problem, the Vedic system holds the key to many solutions needed by humanity to survive. Ironically, Harvard is busy digesting the treasures of the Vedic system – such as the history of Indian science and technology, the science of yoga, meditation, vegetarianism, metaphysics, and alignment with nature – and turning these digested versions into its own intellectual property and that of the West. We approached Indian billionaires for such projects, but they have not supported them. Chapter 7 discusses many examples of specific digestions by Harvard that we brought to their attention in the past quarter century but to no avail.

India's Self-destruction:

1. India's ruling elites and so-called 'intellectuals' are largely ignorant and staggered about all this.
   Hence, their energies are being misdirected, scattered, and often counter-productive.
2. The Indian government is also committing itself to this latest form of Marxist revolution, knowingly or unwittingly.
3. A large number of Indians are employed by the Global Left at all levels, from the highest to the lowest. They are a key part of this latest incarnation of the Marxist revolution. The Global Left operates across national boundaries.

'Woke' is the popular equivalent for the more academic term Critical Race Theory. Woke started in the Black American community as a means of spreading awareness and meant being woken up to the social realities. While we believe Wokeism has succeeded in waking people up in positive ways, its further success requires it to become open-minded, which means welcoming debates.

Some Provocations:

As free thinkers, we wish to brainstorm fresh ideas without the fear of retribution or intimidation. For instance, can we explore that hierarchy exists not only in all human societies but also in every species of animals? And just like the members of an animal species have individual differences, strengths and weakness in various attributes, so do humans. No amount of social engineering can erase differences or hierarchies. Therefore, we should explore ways to bring justice without constraining ourselves to equal outcomes.

For instance, if one person is more capable to become a surgeon while the other is superior as a gardener, could there be a way to give them equal dignity and worth despite these differences? If outcome were measured in terms of happiness, could they be given equal happiness within their respective occupations? Would it be a better idea to develop a global program to raise human consciousness using the techniques found in Indian systems like the *Vedas* and Buddhism?

Should the dismantling of old structures also challenge Western Universalism's emphasis on consumerism as the criteria for success, and is this a root cause of competitive greed and the frustration with unequal materialistic outcomes? Are inheritance laws causing a concentration of inter-generational wealth?

One of the major debates needed is to challenge the whole dialectic method that started with Hegel, continued with Karl Marx and all the way to its recent use in Critical Race Theory. This construct is foundational in Leftist thinking. A serious problem is that it calls for a revolution to overthrow the prevailing thesis. But what about exploring alternative approaches from other civilizations? For instance, if we look at the thesis and anti-thesis as a pair of opposites, the teaching in Vedanta is to *transcend and include both*. The Marxist dialectic method results in a fight between two opposing egos for their mutual destruction so that some new ego will emerge, hopefully a better one. But this dynamic keeps humanity limited to the ego level. There is no transcendence to a higher level in this system, whereas Vedanta and Buddhism offer practical and proven techniques to raise our consciousness.

The irony is that a large portion of the Left in the West are practitioners of many spiritual practices imported from India, such as meditation.

Their practices are premised on the principle of raising consciousness through systematic methods. As a result of the proliferation of Indian meditation systems in the West over the past half century, a large movement has emerged that calls itself the consciousness movement. All sorts of books, videos, seminars, etc. are becoming popular that teach a certain degree of Vedanta's and/or Buddhism's posture: that only by raising consciousness can one solve problems, and not by fighting at the ego level.

Snakes in the Ganga is a metaphor for some foreign institutions that are mapping ideas of Wokeism to India, thereby undermining India's ancient civilizational fabric. This book intends to inform Indians who might be supporting such work, often unintentionally, without an in depth understanding of the end game of these projects. It is the result of years of interaction the authors have had with foreign institutions that have oftentimes tried to muffle debate on opposing views. The book does not intend to vilify the sponsors of such institutions. It is purely an honest exercise to invite healthy academic debate on intellectual issues. It is a critique of scholars' works, not on their personalities or the owners/sponsors of the institutions where they work.

We hope this book opens the door for such conversations and we invite serious thinkers from all positions to argue with our views and debate us with mutual respect.

Part 1

DEBATING INDIAN CULTURE'S LEGITIMACY IN THE UNITED STATES OF AMERICA

1

Dismantling the United States of America

Overview

This chapter provides a background on the recent social sciences theories and political disruptions that are being imported into India from places like Harvard University. These theories have their foundation in Marxism and Postmodernism. The two systems originated mostly in Europe and then took root in the United States of America where they have been used to develop the latest social sciences movements. Most people in the mainstream, however, do not recognize the presence of Marxism and Postmodernism in the current popular social movements.

Explaining these two prior theoretical influences is complex as both have undergone multiple transformations over time. This is a vast topic, and we can only do justice to a few areas that bear specific significance to the situation presently being discussed. Our account is not intended to be complete and it merely highlights certain developments and qualities in these two systems.

After establishing this European background, we will fast forward to recent decades during which Critical Race Theory emerged as the most powerful impact in present times. Initially developed as Critical Legal Theory to address systemic racism in the US legal system, it was then generalized to cover racism in all social institutions. Alongside, some important theoretical offshoots of CRT such as Intersectionality and Queer Theory, will also be discussed. These are significant because they have helped CRT's influence to spread rapidly in every domain of American society.

Wokeism is the popularized, mainstream culture form of Critical Race Theory. Its explicit rejection of rationality and science, and suppression of free speech will be explained by quoting its prominent leaders. We will discuss how all these influences have entered American institutions like government, private industry, media, and of course, the academia, where it all began.

The chapter concludes with the original insights of Vivek Ramaswamy, a young tech entrepreneur in the life sciences, and chairman of Roivant Sciences, who addresses the question: Why is corporate America encouraging Wokeism? His provocative thesis about Wokeism's relationship with the corporate world is compelling and shocking.

The new discourse discussed in this chapter has been developing over the past two centuries as follows: Marxism and Postmodernism (as the foundations) ➜ Critical Race Theory and adjuncts (the latest products) ➜ Popular Wokeism (the packaging for mass consumption) ➜ Dismantling all institutions (mass movement).[1]

This chapter sets the stage to discuss the impact on India.

European Origins of the Old Left

Marxism

Marxism is one of the theories of society, economics, and politics that has made a big impact over the past two centuries. The social sciences based on it have recently evolved all the way to Critical Race Theory. But Marxism itself did not emerge in a vacuum; its key concepts can be traced back even earlier to the great German thinker/philosopher, Georg Wilhelm Friedrich Hegel.

Hegel is considered one of the pioneers of modern Western thought starting at the turn of the eighteenth- and early-nineteenth century. One of his important theories was the *philosophy of history*. Hegel claimed that *history is driven by a system of causation*; it is not the occurrence of random and unrelated events that took place in different parts of the world with no common trajectory, purpose, or direction. Rather, all history follows certain patterns, and he claimed to have discovered these patterns or laws in the same way that natural scientists discover the laws of nature.

In Hegel's model of history, an invisible force advances human events, which is why history has certain patterns and humanity that can be seen following a journey with predictable milestones. He called this force, Weltgeist, often translated as '*world spirit*'. Weltgeist is roughly analogous to what the Vedic tradition might think of as the idea of *Saguna Brahman*, or Bhagawan – as a force that drives history, or the idea of *rtam* or rhythm as the fundamental patterns comprising the fabric of reality. The Vaishnava idea is that a supreme person moves history forward in a certain direction. Of course, this is merely an analogy to communicate the idea and there are key differences between the two ideas.

Related to this notion is another Hegelian term, Volksgeist, that refers to the spirit of a given people, i.e., a nation's spirit or national character. Volksgeist resembles what Deendayal Upadhyaya, leader of the political party, the Bharatiya Jana Sangh (the precursor to the Bharatiya Janata Party [BJP]) called the *citti* of a nation, the essence or foundation that drives its grand narrative.

A third term, Zeitgeist, refers to the spirit of the age or the spirit of the times; an invisible agency that characterizes a given epoch in world history. In the Vedic framework, we live in a particular epoch called the *Kali Yuga* that characterizes the nature of life and society.

The world spirit moves through a certain sequence of evolutionary stages through which all nations must pass but some are ahead of others. An important claim of Hegel's was that the West is at the forefront and ahead of all other civilizations in these evolutionary stages. This implies what the West is today, other nations must strive to become in their future according to the natural law of the Weltgeist. And the way the other nations are today, the West was in the past. Hegel is often regarded as the father of the idea of the modern West.

This linear theory of history got applied by Hegel to justify the atrocities against the Native Americans because they were deemed uncivilized. He also justified the slavery of Blacks as he felt they hadn't evolved enough along this historical trajectory to be capable of living freely. The British colonization of India was legitimate, according to him, because the British were civilizing India for India's own benefit, the same way adults discipline children. In other words, he defined the standard linear trajectory that all civilizations must go through as their part of world history. This was his philosophy of history.

The other big idea of Hegel that became very influential is the 'dialectic'. By which he meant that the prevailing paradigm of a society that he called the thesis, triggers an opposing force, he called the anti-thesis. The anti-thesis is a reaction that opposes the thesis. Because they cannot be reconciled any other way, the thesis and anti-thesis must necessarily clash. This destruction eventually produces a synthesis, and a new paradigm emerges; this becomes the new thesis. And this is the way the world spirit evolves. At any epoch or stage in time, a nation has a thesis characterizing how its society is organized. An anti-thesis then emerges that opposes it. The clash between thesis and anti-thesis produces a synthesis where a new truth is found, one that is higher than the previous thesis and anti-thesis. World history moves this way. What is important to note here is the principle that conflict is desirable for progress.

Marx adopted Hegel's dialectic as the foundation of his system. But he introduced a critical shift: Instead of the spirit driving material changes as in Hegel's system, in Marxism it is the material conditions on the ground that cause the anti-thesis to arise and clash with the thesis. So, Marxism is the theory of historical causation purely by materialistic factors. It is an economic theory of causation and not a metaphysical one. One might say Marx secularized Hegel's dialectic by removing the idea of world spirit as the causal agency that drives history.

According to Marx, the West has reached a stage in its evolution where the capitalists (the bourgeoisie) own the means of industrial production, and the working classes (the proletariat) are employed by them as labor in the production of goods. The two classes have perpetual and irreconcilable conflicting interests. The 'thesis' is represented by the established social and political system, and this system is propagated through education, media, official policies, and so forth. But at some point, the labor class starts a revolt, which is the anti-thesis. Importantly, in Marxist thought, it is necessary to precipitate a clash between the two classes in order to produce a synthesis from the thesis and the anti-thesis. Only then can there be progression in history.

Therefore, Marxism necessarily tends to be destructive and violent, because only through the destruction of the thesis by the anti-thesis can there be progress towards a new synthesis. There is no win-win outcome possible in which both sides can accommodate each other peacefully and make adjustments.

Marxist Critical Theory

While Marx himself was focused on economic haves and have nots, oppressor and oppressed, the ruling elite and its victims, Marxism was later expanded to apply to broader forms of power that are not just economic.

One of the most influential Marxist thinkers that expanded the scope of Marxism was Antonio Francesco Gramsci, the founder of the Communist Party of Italy. He was imprisoned by the fascists and his prison diaries from the late 1920s and early '30s became the seminal work on which a new line of Marxist thinking emerged. His focus was on locating the problems with the *discourse* and solving those rather than going directly to a physical revolution. He wanted to demolish Western hegemony by constructing a counter-hegemony as the anti-thesis to the West. Only after this was accomplished, he believed, would the physical revolution become possible.

Gramsci began his analysis by noting that the exploited workers during his time were not revolting and overthrowing the bourgeoisie. This troubled him. His reasoning was, rather than revolting against the dominant group, the workers had *acquiesced and consented* to the beliefs and values of the ruling elites due to the influence of institutions like schools, churches, courts, and the media – thereby expanding upon Marx's renowned statement that religion is the 'opium of the masses'. This led Gramsci to develop the concept of cultural hegemony.[2] Under his influence, Marxism takes popular discourse and culture very seriously. It is culture, and the discourse it produces that has kept the proletariat under the control of the elites. That is where the mental/ emotional revolution must begin, and not at the physical level of violence.

His solution was to first re-educate the workers on how to think about their predicament. This required constructing a counter-hegemony to completely demolish the old structures of thinking — regarding issues like family, nation-state, capitalism, and religion. Only then could a physical revolution take place.[3] The revolution of the discourse is necessary to prepare the ground for the violent revolution later.

Meanwhile, in Germany another vibrant group known as the Frankfurt School emerged during the time of the Second World War, and its leaders developed what became known as 'Critical Theory'. From the mid-1920s onwards, its prominent leaders—Max Horkheimer, Theodore Adorno and Herbert Marcuse—were frustrated with classical Marxism. Marxists had earlier celebrated their success in the Russian Revolution in the early twentieth century, in which Lenin led a peasant uprising to overthrow Czar Nicholas II. But in Germany, predictions of a similar revolution did not materialize despite a severe economic depression and exploitation by the elites.

The German masses did not mobilize against the state as in the case of Russia, and instead joined the Nazi movement. Why was Germany's proletariat behaving different than Russia's, they asked? Gramsci's explanation would be that the counter-hegemonic discourse had not been prepared.

The Frankfurt School explained that at times, the elites can in fact prevent the communist revolution by using art, popular culture, and myth to defuse the anger of the people. The masses exist in a myth and their anger can get channeled away from their misery. The Nazis were able to channel this anger against the Jews and Roma people as the scapegoats, thus preventing a revolution similar to the Russian one. In other words, the hegemonic discourse was used to maintain control.

So, they explored fresh ideas challenging the prevailing social theories and came up with the notion of critical theories as a class of theories. Max Horkheimer, director of the Frankfurt School, described any theory as 'critical' if it was seeking 'to liberate human beings from the circumstances that enslave them'.[4] The Frankfurt School criticized traditional Marxism's reliance on economic forces and placed its focus on the role of popular culture in society. They wanted the following sequence of events: Counter-hegemonic discourse ➜ Change in popular culture ➜ Takeover of social institutions ➜ Physical revolution.

Critical Theory became concretized when Horkheimer wrote an influential 1937 manifesto titled, *Traditional and Critical Theory*. He claimed that 'man could not be objective and that there are no universal truths'. This idea that all truth is relative was inherited from the German lineage of Friedrich Nietzsche followed by Hegel. The implication is that all discourse is fabricated and presented as so-called truth by various social forces. In the absence of a final truth, this reinforces Gramsci's idea that there must be a clash of discourses to topple the dominant ideas implanted in the masses.

Critical Theory can be seen as a Hegelian renaissance for modern times. While Marx emphasized class warfare based on economic exploitation, Critical Theory expands its scope into the role of *cultural warfare*.

The French Marxist, Pierre Bourdieu, further developed the theory that *culture is a form of capital*. His contribution to Marxism was to formulate the relationship between culture and power. He stated that people in power use culture as an emotional tool to exploit the public and protect the status quo of their power. Culture contains deep, and invisible, safety nets, and emotional shock absorbers. People exist with their economic miseries without revolting because the cultural structures protect the power structure. In this way, culture has hidden structures that enable the elites to assert power over the masses.

Critical theorists feel that capitalism is subverting the materialistic revolution by diverting the masses away from such a revolution. Capitalists are promoting emotional 'good feelings' among the working class that deflects their attention away from real-world physical experiences. Culture has been co-opted by capitalism, and the advertising industry is one of its devices. Popular culture and advertising serve as a soothing balm that the ruling elites use to brainwash the masses and placate them. The goal is to channel their energies away from any social and political activism. Consumerism thus, is the enemy of social and political activism.

Herbert Marcuse, the young follower of Horkheimer, famously explained how capitalism had won over the oppressed masses psychologically:

> If the worker and his boss enjoy the same television program and visit the same resort places, if the typist is as attractively made up as the daughter of her employer, if the Negro owns a Cadillac, if they all read the same newspaper, then this assimilation indicates not the disappearance of classes, but the extent to which the needs and satisfactions that serve the preservation of the Establishment are shared by the underlying population.[5]

These Marxists blamed Hollywood as the main culprit because it glorified a false idea of success. Capitalism's control of the media industry allowed it to manufacture values and ideas of the good life. This is how the masses started believing that capitalism was the path forward without any need for a Marxist revolution. Marcuse said:

> The irresistible output of the entertainment and information industry carry with them prescribed attitudes and habits, certain intellectual and emotional reactions which bind the consumers to the producers and, through the latter to the whole social system. The products indoctrinate and manipulate; they promote a false consciousness which is immune against its falsehood...Thus emerges a pattern of one-dimensional thought and behavior.[6]

According to this new Marxist theory, popular media has created a new lens through which consumers participate in society. Their natural and free will has been hijacked. People are being exploited like commodities. Real culture has been replaced by the infotainment industry and all knowledge is therefore being shaped by capitalists.[7]

Another big breakthrough in Marxism came during the violence of the 1960s and early '70s Civil Rights era and the anti–Vietnam War Movement. Marcuse had become established in the US as an important face of the latest form of Marxism. He discovered that American society had a substratum of ideological minorities and outsiders that could be mobilized by stoking grievances among them.[8] He helped the minorities understand they were being exploited by the elites through the projection of values and cultures. This became the beginning of the 'minorityism' movement that has swept the world ever since.

It is important to note that Marxism had only two classes: bourgeoisie and proletariat. The bourgeoisie was one single class and there were no separate minority groups or identities each vying for victimhood status and power. The replacement of one single victim class with several is a major recent adaptation of Marxism.

The focus of Critical Theory and all its offshoots and variations was to attack Western institutions and norms in order to tear them down. It was to disrupt traditional thinking that schools imparted and what the masses believed.

Marxists also formulated literary theories to interpret texts and other cultural products with a view to identify the hidden structures of power. When a Marxist analyzes a story, he sees it as a reflection of power dynamics in society and focuses on how characters behave based on their position in the power hierarchy. According to Marxism, the socio-economic circumstances shape the writings of authors, the types of characters they develop, the examples cited, and the political ideas emphasized in the literary work. All literature, according to this theory, reflects prevailing society, and the literature itself becomes a social institution disseminating a particular ideology.

Later in this chapter, the reader will discover that many of these Marxist ideas have found their way into the core of Critical Race Theory.

Postmodernism

Postmodernism is an intellectual movement characterized by its scepticism of any objective reality; the influence of Nietzsche, Immanuel Kant, Hegel, and others is evident. It became a movement to interpret history, cultural works, and all grand narratives as being relative to the power structures hidden in them. The job of the scholar is to discover these hidden structures.

It started as an independent movement that rejected the European Enlightenment project as well as Modernity because they were seen as structures built by the power elite.[9]

Postmodernism is based on the following principles:

1. General scepticism about the existence of objective knowledge or universal truths.
2. Boundaries between categories are considered inherently blurry and are merely arbitrary human conventions.
3. Power structures and hierarchies exist in all societies, and this is how knowledge gets created.
4. All knowledge is constructed in language games that are inextricably linked with power. Language itself embeds the power of the elites who have developed it. Hence, the use of language is always biased and oppressive.

In other words, all claims to truth are culturally biased and are constructed by the social power of the elites. One consequence of such a theory is that a critic cannot offer counter arguments against any Postmodernist statement using scientific evidence and methodology, because the criticism would itself be rejected as a product of elitism.

Postmodernism takes its scepticism very far and believes that all intellectual systems, theories, and meta narratives are mere social constructs. Science too, as a system of rational thought, is such a meta narrative and does not represent any objective reality. We will later see how this idea results in the disregard for rationality found in Critical Race Theory today.

The Freudian revolution brought another innovation of great value: the idea of an unconscious level of mind that the individual is unaware of, which requires a specialist (psychoanalyst) to tease out. This turned Postmodernism's deconstruction of all human productions and activities into witch hunt for unconscious and invisible power structures.

In other words, power is hidden in all human productions such as literature. One has to look for it. The Left began using Postmodernism to deconstruct all histories and works of art looking for structures of abuse. When they teach history, what they really want is to expose a biased structure.

An accomplished art critic, according to them, must excavate the artist's bias that lies buried within the art. He will say that the work is skewed by a male bias or reflective of the unconscious bias of the privileged class, and so forth.

At first there was a serious clash between Postmodernism and Marxism because the former deconstructs all meta narratives including Marxism's core narrative of class struggle. In Postmodernism, the oppressors and the oppressed all get deconstructed, but Marxism, however, needs to construct an identity that is perceived as real and foundational for the downtrodden and mobilize them as a weapon for the revolution. Hence, the two camps traditionally opposed each other.

To bring Marxism and Postmodernism together, critical theorists developed what is called the second wave of Postmodernism. Unlike the first wave that dismantled every meta narrative, the second wave *dismantled only those identities and narratives that were considered oppressive.* The narratives that are the anti-thesis to elitist narratives are permitted and in fact promoted, because the oppressed must have special rights. This became the new way of championing the downtrodden, and how Postmodernism got repurposed in the moral vision of the Marxists.

This marriage of Marxism and Postmodernism opened the door to bring Marxism and its social sciences into Postmodernism. It could apply different standards and lenses to the thoughts of the oppressors and the oppressed. In effect, this new form has betrayed the fundamental principles of the founders of Postmodernism.

One of the major applications of Marxism combined with the second wave of Postmodernism was to the field of Postcolonial studies. This is the study of texts and other cultural products from the colonial era to discover the colonizers' oppressive view buried in every text.

Gayatri Spivak's 1988 essay, *Can the Subaltern Speak*? was a big moment in this field. She championed the 'subaltern' people as those that cannot represent themselves because they are not included in the discussions. Spivak borrowed the Postmodernist deconstructive methodology of the French philosopher/historian, Jacques Derrida. She concluded that a large number of people in India are subalterns because they are not allowed to participate in policy discussions and the discourse concerning them.

This opened the door for Subaltern studies in a big way. Indian Marxist historians quickly adopted the ideas of both Gramsci and the Frankfurt School to champion the subalterns. This led to the rise of many scholars claiming to be speaking up on their behalf. Most of these scholars belonged to elitist backgrounds while serving as the powerbrokers purportedly giving voice to the subalterns.

The new discourse in social sciences was that the downtrodden have no voice in developing their history because it was written by the elites, and therefore, the scholars must speak up for them. They must deconstruct and dismantle the old literary works to be replaced with new literature and new histories using the voice of the subalterns. In effect, the Subaltern scholars became the arbiters deciding what was oppression and what was to be heeded as the real voice of the subalterns. In effect, they became the new powerbrokers and elites in this revised societal structure.

The following diagram shows our main points thus far concerning Marxism, Postmodernism, and Postcolonialism.

All this has broadened the field of Critical Theory which is now at the heart of liberal arts education. It is a methodology and framework

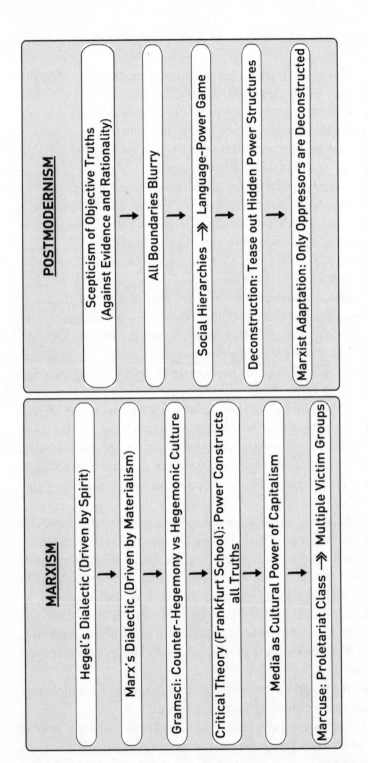

MARXISM

Hegel's Dialectic (Driven by Spirit)

Marx's Dialectic (Driven by Materialism)

Gramsci: Counter-Hegemony vs Hegemonic Culture

Critical Theory (Frankfurt School): Power Constructs all Truths

Media as Cultural Power of Capitalism

Marcuse: Proletariat Class ⟶ Multiple Victim Groups

POSTMODERNISM

Scepticism of Objective Truths (Against Evidence and Rationality)

All Boundaries Blurry

Social Hierarchies ⟶ Language-Power Game

Deconstruction: Tease out Hidden Power Structures

Marxist Adaptation: Only Oppressors are Deconstructed

POSTCOLONIAL STUDIES

Subalternism ⟶ History from Below

Deconstruct the Colonizer's Texts ⟶ Deconstruct Hindu Society to disrupt dominant paradigms by de-centering the grand narratives deemed to be oppressive. It identifies the master narratives as the overarching tropes, stories, concepts, images, and beliefs that comprise the dominant culture, institution, or worldview. This is equivalent to Marxism's thesis. The anti-thesis is developed in the form of counter-narratives to challenge such normative thinking with the intention of emancipating the oppressed.

Indians have quickly adapted these theories and positioned Brahmins as the oppressors. Indian scholars dig up Brahmins' hidden messages in traditional texts, to show that they oppress lower castes, women, minorities, and other victims. Every Sanskrit text, deity, guru movement, symbol, rite, festival, and other aspects of Indian traditions is being deconstructed using these tools to expose the in-built oppression.

It is important to point out that this deconstruction does not end with a critique, which would be a welcome form of introspection for any society, but rather, calls for the wholescale rejection of that which is being deconstructed, reminiscent of the Marxist call for revolution as a violent dismantling of the past structures.

Critical Race Theory

The foregoing developments originated mostly in Europe but had an echo effect in the US. The first big idea developed in the US specifically pertaining to its domestic society was Critical *Legal* Theory which later led to the more general Critical *Race* Theory.

Critical Legal Theory addressed the problem of systemic bias in the structure of the US law. Its proponents explained this as follows:

> The law supports the interests of those who create the law. ...
> a power dynamic which favors the historically privileged and
> disadvantages the historically underprivileged. ... The wealthy and
> the powerful use the law as an instrument for oppression in order
> to maintain their place in hierarchy.[10]

Its leaders acknowledged their theory to be greatly influenced by the Frankfurt School. Like the Marxist Critical Theory discussed earlier, it seeks to dismantle social structures, except that its target is a reformation of the legal system. It sees the law as cultural hegemony codified in statutes and defended by jurisprudence.

The first major discussion on Critical Legal Theory was held at the University of Wisconsin in Madison in 1977. Cornel West, an iconic Black American philosopher and activist, now a senior Harvard figure championing Dalit activism, was one of its early proponents.

Another influence on Critical Legal Theory came from Postmodernism which *shifted the focus from the individual to the group identity*. Now the fight for legal rights was on behalf of a group rather than an individual. Each group identity could demand that it be recognized collectively as a victim, not necessarily because of what was taking place then but because of what occurred in history. The focus was on criticizing the legal system as a hierarchical structure that helped Whites dominate Blacks, men dominate women, rich dominate the poor, and so forth.

The next step was to expand Critical Legal Theory into Critical Race Theory which holds that all aspects of American life (not just the law) should be seen through the prism of race. This applies not just to activities visible on the surface but also the invisible structures that control these activities. And racism cannot be understood without looking at history. Therefore, one must look beneath the surface to expose the hidden structures, and at the history of these structures.

Derrick Bell Jr., the first tenured African American professor at Harvard Law School, is considered the originator of the doctrine developed in the 1970s that later became known as Critical Race Theory. The movement initially distanced itself from Postmodernism for being too abstract and not practical enough. As explained earlier, Postmodernism was considered counterproductive by Marxists because it would also deconstruct the very notion of minority identities that the politics of Critical Race Theory depended on. Eventually, by the 1990s, Postmodernism got repurposed within a Marxist framework and is now an important foundation of the movement.

Critical Race Theory began with a revolutionary diagnosis of society and then mobilized a social movement based on it. It states that the structures of White privilege are the foundation of everything in literature, art, social norms, civil and criminal laws, the constitution, real estate practices in neighborhoods, financial conventions in banking, who gets loans, and so on. It includes the education system, the structures of media, the structures of government, the structures of corporations and who runs them. All of these institutional structures in modern society hide systemic racism.

The broad and sweeping impact of this theory is captured in the following summary:

> ... (CRT) makes race the prism through which its proponents analyze all aspects of American life — ... with a degree of persistence that has helped CRT impact all of American life. ... (It) underpins identity politics, an ongoing effort to reimagine the United States as a nation driven by groups, each with specific claims on victimization. In entertainment, as well as the education and workforce sectors of society, CRT is well-established, driving decision-making according to skin color—not individual value and talent. As Critical Theory ideas become more familiar to the viewing public in everyday life, CRT's intolerance becomes 'normalized,' along with the idea of systemic racism for Americans, weakening public and private bonds that create trust and allow for civic engagement.[11]

The basic claim is that the Whites formulated the idea of Black inferiority to justify their slave trade and colonization over the past five hundred years, and these ideas are embedded in the deep structures of society. Even the language we use reinforces these structures.

What is to be done once you understand this racist history of the past that persists in the structures of modern society? Being based on the dialectic of Hegel and Marx, Critical Race Theory demands its followers to construct an anti-thesis that will fight every kind of old structure. This can easily translate into activism on the ground, such as: opposing how universities admit students and the way American history is taught, undermining the founding fathers of the constitution, and so forth. Nothing is to be spared. Every aspect of society must be exposed and dismantled. Those who don't fight are actually part of the problem. They are protecting the elite. The only correct way forward is to support the anti-thesis, which is deconstructing, revolting, arguing against these structures, and dismantling them.

One must note that the famous book, *Hind Swaraj* or Indian Home Rule, written by Mohandas K. Gandhi over a century ago, made a similar argument: all Indians who function in the British colonial system in any capacity are upholding the British Empire and helping it function. This includes Indians serving not only in the army but also in the civil services, education, and so forth. Gandhi's *satyagraha* (civil disobedience) movement was designed as a sort of anti-thesis even though he did not use that framework. Satyagraha was used to topple the British thesis built into its colonial civil society and thereby bring down their Empire.

The proponents of Critical Race Theory broke ranks with old-school liberals that championed the 1960s and early '70s' movements of civil rights, racial integration, affirmative action, and other measures of equality. The approach of traditional liberals was to emphasize the material progress of the underprivileged. But proponents of CRT assert that civil rights laws are dependent on old structures that, in effect, perpetuate the oppression. The demand is to dismantle the structures rather than tolerate them.

An important principle championed by Rev. Martin Luther King Jr. and other civil rights leaders is 'color-blindness'. This espouses that all individuals should be treated equally regardless of color or identity and so create a level playing field. This is also being challenged. It is no longer acceptable to be neutral and unbiased towards identities; the established structures contain historically built-in biases that have to be actively countered. If someone claims to be merely neutral (by being color-blind), it is seen as a mask for hiding power. Later in this chapter, we will discuss how former US president, Barack Obama advocated color-blindness and how the CRT proponents have opposed him.

The husband-and-wife duo and legal scholars, Richard Delgado and Jean Stefancic, are considered to be among the pioneers of developing Critical Race Theory into its present form. They explain why the old liberal thinking must be rejected:

> Critical race theory questions the very foundations of the liberal order, including equality theory, legal reasoning, Enlightenment rationalism, and neutral principles of constitutional law.[12]
>
> Many liberals believe in color blindness and neutral principles of constitutional law. They believe in equality, especially equal treatment for all persons, regardless of their different histories or current situations.[13]

The Black Lives Matter movement had started in 2013 to protest against the prolonged and systematic American police brutality and unfair treatment of Black Americans. But the egregious murder of George Floyd by a White policeman in 2020 and many other similar incidents awoke large swathes of Americans to the reality faced by many Blacks in America. This also raised mainstream awareness and support for Critical Race Theory.

In effect, the BLM movement has catapulted Critical Race Theory with vigor greater than any previous Marxist-inspired movement in American history. Now a large segment of the Democratic Party's progressive Left sees the United States as a nation of victim groups and has discarded traditional Liberalism and progressive goals in exchange for identity politics.

Intersectionality

Intersectionality is an adjunct added on to Critical Race Theory. It is the view that when a person shares multiple identities, the *combination* of identities suffers a *unique* set of issues. The common example given is that Blacks have a certain set of issues and women have another set of issues, but *Black women* have issues that are not appropriately addressed by either group. Black women are not adequately understood simply as Blacks because Black organizations tend to cater largely to the men. Nor are Black women adequately understood simply as women, because most women's groups are dominated by White women. The kinds of prejudices a Black woman faces differ from those faced by Black men, and those faced by White women.

Black women therefore cannot be assumed to have been taken care of by the separate movements championing Blacks and women, respectively. Their experience of prejudice is not simply the sum of the two separate experiences. For example, when jobs were mobilized for Blacks, they went mainly to the men. Likewise, the mobilization of jobs for women went mainly to White women. Black women have benefited neither by the Black movement nor by the women's movement. This is why Intersectionality urged the creation of Black women as a separate and distinct category. Kimberlé Crenshaw, professor at Columbia Law School is credited for introducing the concept of Intersectionality.[14]

A major turning point in support of Intersectionality came when University of Maryland's Patricia Hill Collins' 1990 book, *Black Feminist*

Thought: Knowledge, Consciousness, and the Politics of Empowerment,
openly advocated identity politics over the idea of individual Liberalism.[15]
In *Intersectionality*, a book that Collins co-authored with Sirma Bilge,
they wrote:

> Shaped not by a single axis of social division, be it race or gender
> or class, but by many axes that work together and influence each
> other. Intersectionality as an analytic tool gives people better
> access to the complexity of the world and of themselves.[16]

According to the concept of Intersectionality, one cannot simply
understand the oppressor/oppressed dynamics based on a single type
of social division, such as race, gender, and class. There are multiple
social forces, identities, and ideologies that express and legitimize the
dynamics of power over the disadvantaged sections of society. The
primary category is race, which is combined with other identities to
create numerous victim identities.

We recall that in classical Marxism the notion of class subsumed all
kinds of oppressed people. It was important not to divide the oppressed
into small groups that could end up fighting each other and diluting
the collective impact. But due to Intersectionality, the list of separate
minority identities is exploding. For example, Feminism has fragmented
into numerous sub-identities. Now there are feminist ideological camps
that refer to themselves as: liberal feminist, neo-liberal feminist,
Marxist feminist, socialist feminist, radical cultural feminist, radical
lesbian feminist, radical libertarian feminist, psychoanalytical feminist,
womanist, Christian feminist, Jewish feminist, Islamic feminist, Indian
feminist, etc. These various groups oftentimes are attacking each other.

One can go on defining any number of Intersectional groups by
mixing and matching identities, leading to a proliferation of identities
considered to be marginal that need special treatment. This shift has
opened the floodgates of identity politics because more victim identities
emerge. Academic fields now include Critical Grievance Studies, Critical
Gender Studies, Critical Sexuality Studies, Critical Fat Studies, and
Critical Caste Studies.

Muslims have started what is known as Critical Islamophobia Studies
to position themselves as victims in the US and elsewhere.[17] This has
turbocharged the Islamic lobby in the Democratic Party with some new

audacious initiatives targeted against India. One of their successes has been to bring a bill to the US Congress that makes Islamophobia illegal worldwide and requires the US State Department to set up a special group to monitor Islamophobia in every country. If a country is found to have Islamophobia, it would be recommended for US sanctions.

This bill passed the US Congress with almost every Democrat supporting it. It was then introduced for discussion in the US Senate. We protested against this bill with an open letter. So far, the bill has not advanced in the US Senate, but it has not been withdrawn.[18] The instant success of such a bill in the US Congress illustrates the success of this movement to club together certain identities as victims and weaponize them to topple traditional Liberalism.

The various victim identities are being organized into a hierarchy of oppression. Those located at low positions in this hierarchy are being called 'protected classes' which gives them a special status under various laws, in terms of protection against discrimination.

The question being raised by critics is, who gets to define which identities are legitimate victims, and on what basis will the list of protected classes be determined? The present reality suggests that the loudest, most aggressive, and best organized activists tend to win in this societal game of victim rights. This is an entirely political matter in the hands of those that control the discourse on Critical Race Theory. We point out there are no special Intersectional categories of victimhood available for Kashmiri Pandits, Punjabi Hindus from Pakistan who became refugees, Tibetans living in exile in India, and so forth.

The political goal of the movement is to identify many marginalized identities using Intersectionality and then bundle them together to overthrow the so-called oppression of the privileged elite.

We appreciate that the brutalities faced by several identities have deep historical structures and need to be exposed and dismantled. However, there are several anomalies and contradictions that people should be able to discuss openly. For example:

- The Princeton Nobel Laureate economist, Angus Deaton, shows that White Americans suffered far more than others in the US over the past few decades in terms of mental health, addiction, suicide, employment loss, reduced lifespan, etc. Rather than clubbing all Whites as oppressors, might it be fair to include the marginalized Whites as victims of society's structures?

- It is unreasonably difficult for Asians and Jews to get admission into certain prestigious colleges like Harvard despite their merit, because they are being designated as a privileged group like Whites. American colleges and other institutions are taking the liberty to define Asians racially without the consent of various Asian communities. University of Maryland has defined its own racial categories for freshman enrolment. It combines Asian students with White students. The categories are: 'Students of Color minus Asian' and 'White or Asian Students'.[19]

- Asians are under-represented in American sports while Blacks are over-represented. This is because Blacks have superior physical abilities for sports such as basketball and American football. Should we call this 'Black privilege' and 'structural racism' by Blacks, and designate Asians as oppressed? Otherwise, if we celebrate that Blacks have stronger bodies suited for sports, why is it a problem if Asians by the same token are better at math? Merit is being seen as a form of privilege belonging to the elites in the case of Science, Technology, Engineering, and Mathemathics (STEM), and Indians are accused of enjoying White privilege in this regard. This forms the crux of Chapter 4.

The elephant in the room is that there was racism and social injustice for thousands of years prior to the rise of White people. And racism is caused not only by Whites. For example, Africans and all other cultures too have a history of group identities exploiting and oppressing each other. Africans practiced slavery among themselves, which had nothing to do with their encounters with Whites. There were African oppressors, and African oppressed.[20] There were Arab oppressors and oppressed among themselves, and there was slavery in Muslim kingdoms. There were Whites who were slaves of other Whites in Europe. The ancient Greeks had slaves. So did the ancient Romans, and so did the Chinese. Nor are all White people necessarily exploiters or privileged.

Also, Indian Americans present a dilemma for Critical Race Theory: Are they oppressed given that they suffered prolonged periods of colonization under a combination of European and Muslim conquerors?

Or are they enjoying privilege given their educational and financial success in the US? Clearly, the premise of Critical Race Theory is too simplistic because of the binary oppressor/oppressed it has inherited from Marxism.

The same could be asked of Christians. Historically, Christianity has a dreadful record of oppression of the natives of all continents. The Pope has apologized to many native peoples for the Church's past atrocities. Should the Christian structures (which amounts to the entire institutional apparatus of the Church) be dismantled as per the tenets of Critical Race Theory? Or are Christians to be treated as victims of laws in some countries that limit their ability to evangelize?

There is a rush to claim minority status within the Intersectional framework. Like the Muslims who want to make Islamophobia illegal, Christian leaders have come forth to establish their entitlement as part of the diversity movement. A good ambassador of this view is Pat Gelsinger, CEO of Intel. He asserts that publicly wearing one's Christian identity in the corporate environment should be welcome. When asked about diversity in the workplace, he supported it, but emphasized that this should include respecting someone like himself, an open Christian that described his work as ultimately in the service of 'honoring God'. This is how one can 'bring one's whole self to the workplace', asserting: 'I'm a Christian. If I can't express my Christian faith in the workplace, [it's] not a diverse workplace.'[21] Hindus as a group have not asserted themselves in a similar manner in American multinationals.

Queer Theory

Though Queer Theory started separately in the LGBTQ+ community, it has rapidly merged with Critical Race Theory because both deal with those deemed to be oppressed. Combining them into one super-theory makes it more powerful.

Dismantling all Categories

Queer Theory is widely misunderstood to mean something limited to sexuality. However, those who came up with Queer Theory gave it a much deeper meaning. To them, queer means that which falls outside of all categories. It is used mainly to challenge normative definitions of gender, masculinity, femininity, heterosexuality, homosexuality, etc.

But more broadly, *queer is a worldview that challenges all categories because categories are based on binaries, or pairs of opposites.* One is reminded that Vedanta has a similar deconstruction of categories and pairs of opposites, and so does the Buddhist thinker, Nagarjuna's work on Buddhism.

Queer Theory turns the criticism of binary categories into a social theory of power. It states that *stable definitions and categories are oppressive* because those who constructed them were the dominant ones. All human products, including language, are social constructions that embed bias and oppression in their very structure. Oppression is built into the history and usage of these categories even though it might hide beneath the surface. And recognizing this fact makes you a queer activist.

Queer Theory directly derives from Postmodernism and is therefore radically sceptical of any objective gender or sexual categories based on biology. Querists reject the categories of male and female as well as categories of being straight, gay, lesbian, etc. They believe that regardless of one's physical body being male or female, gender is fluid and one's psychological sexual orientation is socially constructed. What we consider normal and natural is deceptive; we have been brainwashed by the dominant culture to accept these categories as universals. We have internalized the categories of oppression and accepted them as natural. Therefore, all such categories ought to be dismantled.

Queer Theory states that because categories like male-female, masculine-feminine, and heterosexual-homosexual serve the oppressor, we too are participating in the oppression when we use them. This theory wants us to delete these binary categories and see all sexual boundaries as fluid and malleable. It believes that one can simultaneously be masculine and feminine, heterosexual and homosexual, and so forth. And in fact, there is an unlimited number of categories that blend what appear to be mutually exclusive. Let us take a deeper look.

The theory emerged in the mid-1980s, and its three main founding figures were Gayle Rubin, Judith Butler, and Eve Kosofsky Sedgwick. Rubin wrote *Thinking Sex: Notes for a Radical Theory of Sexual Politics* in 1984 in which she is outright sceptical of any biological foundation of sex or sexuality. She rejects *sexual essentialism* which she defines as 'the idea that sex is a natural force that exists prior to social life'. She maintains: 'Sexuality is impervious to political analysis as long as it is primarily conceived as a biological phenomenon or an aspect of individual psychology.'[22]

Judith Butler is the most influential among these theorists. She is influenced by French Feminism and considers gender to be *completely* socially constructed. She uses the term 'gender performativity', which means that people are taught to perform stereotype gender roles. In her major book titled *Bodies That Matter: On the Discursive Limits of Sex*, she defines gender performativity as the 'reiterative power of discourse to produce the phenomenon that it regulates and constraints'.[23] In other words, the way we behave and talk and expect each other to behave is a performance of these gender roles defined by society.

Butler, in her other book, *Gender Trouble: Feminism and the Subversion of Identity*, elaborates further that gender roles are taught and learned knowingly or unknowingly through socialization, as a set of actions, behavior, mannerisms, expectations and so forth. Eventually, people begin to perform such roles automatically. The scripts become installed internally and people are not even conscious they are performing them. It is like the roles performed on stage becoming the actor's self-image.

Her view is that people are not born knowing themselves to be male or female, straight or gay, and hence there are no such innate or natural factors; these are later constructed by society. By performing these roles, people are creating the illusion that the roles are real and inherently meaningful. This is their oppression, and it is society that is to be blamed.

As a result, everybody who uses such binary terms is an oppressor because they are reinforcing the structures built into these concepts. Butler says that the concept of gender identity is 'a regulatory fiction' that must be exposed and undermined. She believes that the problem is the reification of gender categories and relations, and unwittingly, people keep repeating and therefore strengthening this form of oppression.

Eve Kosofsky Sedgwick is the third pioneer of Queer Theory. She advocates breaking these categories by taking liberties to make them seem incoherent and ultimately chaotic. Sedgwick's book, *Epistemology of the Closet*, took French philosopher Michel Foucault's Postmodernism approaches and applied them to sexuality. For her, *sexual binaries are the foundation of all social binaries*. Like the other pioneers, she is against stable categories like gay, lesbian, bisexual, etc.

According to these three Querists, none of these categories is permanent in any individual, changing constantly from one context to another. Therefore, any use of such categories as being fixed is itself oppressive.

It is important to note that before Queer Theory, Liberal Feminism and LGBTQ+ activism considered sexual categories to be well-defined entities with clear boundaries; their movement was to alter the prejudices against people in these categories. But Queer Theory opposes the legitimacy of the categories and believes that bringing them equality normalizes them and increases their oppressiveness.

Another strategy of Querists is to make the categories irrelevant by making them appear baffling, chaotic, irrational, and illogical. When these theorists talk about 'querying a topic', they are referring to blurring the boundaries of all binary categories within that topic.

We are in sympathy with the ideas of the Querists presented above. However, things don't stop here. An important result of Queer Theory we note is that *one cannot argue against them because they reject outright, any opponents using scientific and rational categories.* Therefore, their discourse is more like the dogma of a Church, and it is blasphemy to challenge their thesis using evidence-based logic. We disagree and would like free speech. No discussion should be declared final and closed to further development.

Such theories reject science's claim to understand nature objectively, because all knowledge about nature is the result of human social construction. Querists have even dismantled the notion of childhood innocence, calling it a social construction by parents to perpetuate their own biases of White supremacy.[24]

Turning the theory around, could one say that victim identities, too, are socially constructed? If there is no such thing as childhood innocence, could we also say there is no such thing as a victim? It is a role performed since childhood that society has reinforced. We do not take a stand on the answer but would like such questions to be discussed openly.

Comparison with Vedanta

It is interesting to compare Queer Theory with Vedanta and Buddhism both of which consider linguistic categories as *relative* to our world of cognition. Categories are seen as constructed by the ego's cognitive system. The relative realm we live in is the *laukika*/empirical realm. The *paramarthika* or absolute reality transcends all categories. In this sense, what Queer Theory is claiming has long ago been thoroughly explained in Indian thought.

An important difference is that in the case of Vedanta, the conditioning is within each individual whereas in Queer Theory it is socially caused. Another difference is that Vedanta asks the individual to transcend the categories by transcending the ego, whereas Queer Theory mobilizes one social group ego to fight another group ego. Querists seek a clash between identity camps. Therefore, the outcome being desired by Querists is not beyond, but within, the ego.

The other difference is that as per Vedanta, upon transcending the ego's conceptual categories one experiences the state of nondual consciousness, whereas Queer Theory is not based on the existence of any higher state of consciousness. Queer Theory wants freedom from social oppression but does nothing to bring *freedom from one's individual ego*. In fact, Queer Theory, like the rest of Critical Race Theory, emboldens the ego of what is seen as the victim identity and channels its anger against others.

Queer Theory is aligned with Critical Race Theory in believing that language was shaped by the history of Western colonization, thereby making all linguistic categories oppressive. The assumption being made is that all languages were shaped by colonizers. This may well be true of the English language but there is no such projection of power over people built into Sanskrit categories. In fact, Sanskrit is liberating, and not oppressive. One cannot apply the same logic to all languages and their linguistic structures. Sanskrit-speaking people were not world conquerors and oppressors. This is a serious point. Critical Race Theory is being applied to implicate Sanskrit as a language of oppression used by Brahmins, and this is being claimed by categorizing Brahmins as the Whites of India and Dalits as the Blacks of India.

Interestingly, in support of Queer Theory, in the Vedic system, *Ishwar* (God) is represented often as half male and half female, and a blurring of boundaries between masculinity and femininity even in the understanding of divinity. Therefore, what the Querists are saying has already been respected in the Indian tradition.

But a key difference is that the Indian tradition did not reject the laukika and the practical use of these categories. It simply states that no categories are ultimate and absolute. Yet, we must keep them for worldly/pragmatic purposes while knowing at the same time that in the paramarthika realm these categories are transcended.

The diagram opposite shows how Marxism, Postmodernism, and Postcolonial Theory (mostly developed for societies outside the US) have been incorporated to build Critical Race Theory for American society. In other words, the realities of Black/White racism in the US have been merged with these prior theories to create the latest social theory being addressed by us.

The Church of Wokeism

Liberal Arts Becomes Dogmatic

The stated goal of liberal arts education is to equip students to process complex and diverse ideas, engage in abstract thinking, and consider opposing opinions with open minds. The teacher should provide students theoretical grounding from multiple perspectives and encourage them to engage each other and the faculty, and debate opponents with mutual respect. Such education should enable them to challenge beliefs, assumptions, and conventions.

In practice, however, liberal education has become the exact opposite. Students are no longer encouraged to think for themselves but are tutored in the teacher's specific ideology and social justice morality. Academic institutions are not sanctuaries for open inquiry and alternative viewpoints. The conservative thinker Allan Bloom was blunt in his influential book, *The Closing of the American Mind: How Higher Education Has Failed Democracy and Impoverished the Souls of Today's Students*, attacking American universities for spreading dogma as theory and for indoctrinating in the guise of scholarship.

Ironically, in the name of ridding society of its power structures, academicians have created their own enormous power structure. Since the old structures are seen as stumbling blocks, they are to be demolished. This includes not just dismantling structures like religions, nation-states, and traditional values, but also objectivity, rationality, and meritocracy.

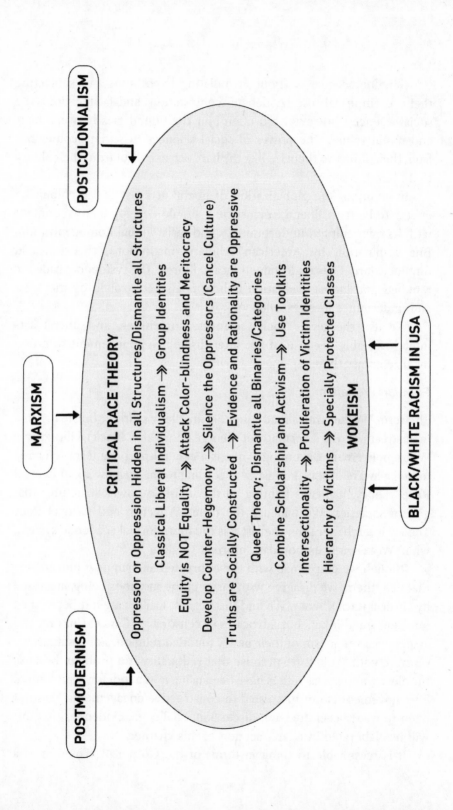

POSTCOLONIALISM

MARXISM

POSTMODERNISM

CRITICAL RACE THEORY

Oppressor or Oppression Hidden in all Structures/Dismantle all Structures

Classical Liberal Individualism → Group Identities

Equity is NOT Equality → Attack Color-blindness and Meritocracy

Develop Counter-Hegemony → Silence the Oppressors (Cancel Culture)

Truths are Socially Constructed → Evidence and Rationality are Oppressive

Queer Theory: Dismantle all Binaries/Categories

Combine Scholarship and Activism → Use Toolkits

Intersectionality → Proliferation of Victim Identities

Hierarchy of Victims → Specially Protected Classes

WOKEISM

BLACK/WHITE RACISM IN USA

Genuine science is about formulating hypotheses and subjecting them to empirical testing, debate, contestation, and falsification. The social sciences, however, too often blur the boundaries between facts and moral values. The power of social sciences in society comes not from their ability to theorize like the hard sciences, but from their ability to undermine societies.

In addition, the globalization of liberal arts has had a colonizing effect. To be truly liberal, each society should develop its own content with its own cultural underpinnings and resist global homogenization. But domination by American scholars, institutions, theories, and funding sources has undermined local cultures. The system of academic rankings and global evaluation indices is also controlled by the West and undermines local excellence.

We use the terms social sciences, humanities, and liberal arts interchangeably because of the inter-disciplinary movement to cross-fertilize across them.

Popular Wokeism

The term 'Woke' was already popular in Black culture, but it became mainstream in the aftermath of George Floyd's (a Black) killing by a White policeman. Becoming Woke is a general-purpose term referring to being aware of social injustice according to the framework of Critical Race Theory. It means fighting all the invisible power structures that govern societies. We will use the terms Wokeism and Critical Race Theory interchangeably; the latter is the more formal academic system, while Wokeism is its popular, informal version.

Though we empathize with the oppressed and support movements that help them, we disagree with many of the methods being suggested by Critical Race Theory. We find that activist leaders are not persecuted innocent freethinkers but advocates of censorship, Cancel Culture, and aggressive evangelism of their newly founded religion. For instance, we disagree with Wokeism's premise that rationality is a problem because the clever, upper-class elites have been using it as a tool for exploitation. The movement is not interested in constructive engagements. It is not open to free speech, debate, discussion, challenge, evidence, etc. This will be elaborated in a later section of this chapter.

It is reasonable to think in terms of the Gospel of Wokeism as a dogma belonging to a new kind of Church. The high priests of Wokeism are the autocrats deciding who is underprivileged and entitled to special treatment. This is a powerful new institution with its own ideas of blasphemy. Those who disagree are to be attacked viciously. Dissent is not allowed.

Woke is a form of groupism and tribalism, seeing society in terms of us/them, and waging an all-out war against its opponents.

The table below shows some of the similarities between this movement and the dogmatic structure of some Churches.

Church of Christianity	Church of Wokeism
• Adam and Eve's Original Sin	• White Ancestors' Construction of Oppressive Structures
• Sin Built into the Very Act of Reproduction	• Racism Built into all Structures Including Language, Knowledge, Institutions
• Everyone is a Born Sinner	• Every White Person (Mapped also to Brahmins) is a Born Oppressor
• Bible as Dogma	• Critical Race Theory as Dogma
• Evidence that Contradicts is the Work of the Devil	• Evidence that Contradicts is Caused by Racist Structures
• Church Appoints High Priests	• Self-appointed Authorities with Absolute Power
• No Free Speech. Dissenters are Heretics	• No Free Speech. Dissenters are Racists
• Infidels can only be Saved by Confession	• Oppressors by Birth can only be Saved by Confession of Guilt and Unconditional Submission

Vivek Ramaswamy, author of *Woke Inc.: How Liberal Activists Are Seizing Control of Corporate America*, has studied Wokeism. His comparison to an organized religion is interesting:

> Diversity has become a term of art, a symbol, one so powerful that the symbol is now more important than the thing it was supposed to represent. Wokeness sacrifices true diversity, diversity of thought, so that skin-deep symbols of diversity like race and gender can thrive. Just like Christ in the story, true diversity of

thought now represents a threat to the Church of Diversity.[25]

Wokeness states everyone who is born into the structures built by White supremacists becomes a born racist, just like the Church demands everyone to accept they are born sinners:

> Wokeness is the new orthodoxy, the new religion, one that disguises itself in secular clothing. Because its disciples worship the secular forces of identity rather than any supernatural one, it's much easier for the Church of Diversity to infiltrate the workplace.[26]

Joshua Mitchell, another critic, elaborates:

> America has not lost its religion. ... has relocated its religion to the realm of politics. ...Identity politics transforms politics. It turns politics into a religious venue of sacrificial offering. .... Without the sacrifice of the innocent Lamb of God, there would be no Christianity. Christ, the scapegoat, renders the impure *pure*— by taking upon Himself 'the sins of the world.' By the purging of the scapegoat, those for whom He is the sacrificial offering purify themselves. Identity politics is a political version of this cleansing for groups rather than for individuals. The scapegoat in the case of identity politics is the *white heterosexual male* who, if purged, supposedly will restore and confirm the cleanliness of all other groups of communities. He is the transgressor; all others— women, blacks, Hispanics, LGBTQs—have their sins *covered over* by the scapegoat, just as the scapegoated Christ covered over the sins of all the descendants of Adam.[27] [...]
>
> Those enthralled by identity politics seek redemption by purging the uncleanliness they claim is *external to themselves*. The white heterosexual male is the first unclean transgressor in their sights; but because the innocence of those enthralled by identity politics must be purchased through the sacrifice of a transgressor, once he has been purged, another transgressor *must be found*.[28]

Just as Adam and Eve committed the Original Sin that has inflicted everyone ever since, so also systemic racism is the Original Sin of the founding fathers and all others involved in nation-building. Individual merit is overshadowed by the structural Original Sin.

> It's a system of beliefs that stands as one indivisible unit and touches on all aspects of one's existence. You aren't allowed to consider the evidence and pick and choose which parts of wokeness you like. ... Like Christianity and Islam, wokeness purports to provide a system of beliefs that explains everything, and it doesn't allow its believers to pick and choose ... ... wokeness gives commands, not suggestions. ... You're not allowed to be a little woke, just like Christians can't follow their five favorite commandments. [...] It's the structure that they use to make sense of the universe. Where a nonwoke person sees ordinary interactions, ... a disciple of wokeness sees microaggressions. Just as a Christian sees God's hand in all of Creation, someone who's woke sees the guiding hand of identity-based power relations everywhere they look.[29]

Another similarity we find with organized Christianity is the use of victimhood. Wokeism inherited this from Marxism's Frankfurt School whose leaders defined a new class called 'the subaltern' as 'the oppressed'. This was a new kind of proletariat defined as those deprived of cultural power. This cultural hegemony has many names and forms: feminists call it patriarchy; sexual minorities call it heteronormativity, and racial minorities call it White supremacy.

The principal criterion for deserving entitlement as an oppressed community is *suffering*. The ideal way to have a public voice is to become, or to represent, a *victim*. This has been explained as follows:

> The politics of the victim ... are in some ways the residue of Christian thought and ritual in a Western world that offers little traditional religious education or formation. The premise of victim politics is like a mirror image of devotion to the Suffering Servant. Just as in Christianity, so in social-justice politics: The wounds of the primordial victim testify to the broken state of human nature and society at large. For Christians, the cross is a kind of throne, and the crown of thorns becomes a sign of authority. The paradox of Christianity is that the Lord reigns as King precisely because he offered himself as Victim.

Putting this Victim at the center of the social order, in
ritual or in preaching, begins the redemption of all humanity.
The faithful confess to the ways their sins contributed to the fate
of the victim. The ritual is meant to moralize and inspire those
who witness it and motivate them to more fully participate in
the effort of redemption. It can also provide its adherents with
a demonology that fills the world with invisible oppressors and
tormentors, making them oversensitive and fearful.[30]

The political vocabulary is about who is entitled to be a protected class
and what they are entitled to receive regardless of their merit.

Overall, the Marxist influence from Gramsci to Marcuse has brought
intolerance to dissention in the Woke movement. One is reminded of
the medieval Church's persecution of heretics. Someone who walks into
these environments looking for a stimulating intellectual engagement is
told to sit quietly and listen.[31] This is like the silence when the Gospel
is being read at a Church service. If you offer a rational response, you
are accused of heresy. Identity politics demands that oppressors being
sinners must atone or else they must be punished in perpetuity for the
sins of their ancestors. Ironically, this is a birth-based designation of
someone being considered an oppressor.

When certain oppressed people decide not to join the Critical Race
Theory revolution, they are accused of imbibing the beliefs of their
oppressors, and therefore in need of being sent to rigorous re-education
camps. This is analogous to the Church wanting an inquisition to exorcise
those accused of being under the influence of the Devil.

Troubling Attributes

Though we sympathize with the problems of systemic racism and the
movements emerging to eliminate them, it is important to analyze the
main tenets and debate with open minds. This section presents some
of the issues that have not been examined in constructive debates.

Rejection of Science, Rationality, and Meritocracy

This new movement considers science and rationality as products of
the White dominated culture. As mentioned earlier, one influence was

from Marxism's Frankfurt School whose philosophers stated that 'a true epistemology must end the fetish of knowledge as such, which as Nietzsche demonstrated, leads to abstract systematizing'.[32] They rejected objective and universal truths.

Truth is therefore said to be formed by political battles; one set of egos fighting another set of egos. The outcomes are decided by those with louder voices, more power and violence, and better organization.

Another approach to rejecting rationality and merit is the theory known as Research Justice. It states that science, reason, empiricism, objectivity, universality, etc. are all overrated compared to personal emotional experience and traditional narratives. The sociologist and author, Andrew Jolivétte defined Research Justice as a framework that gives 'equal power and legitimacy for different forms of knowledge, including the cultural, spiritual, and experiential...'.[33] This theory demands science and objective reasoning to be downgraded while emotions, subjective experience, and one's personal narratives take precedence.

On this, we agree with the Indian Marxist scholar, Meera Nanda, who does not accept that science and reason should be attacked as something strictly Western. She says such a posture is a disservice to India's traditions where science and reason have always enjoyed a strong place long before Western Enlightenment. Nanda says: 'If we grant the very foundations of objectivity to the West, are we not back to the old stereotypes of irrational emotional narratives?'[34] According to her, such theories prevent India from achieving progress using science and rationality because these have been conceded as a domain belonging to the West. She also feels it is demeaning for Indians to be assigned irrationality and superstition.

Even STEM education is being criticized by this wave of anti-rationality. The book, *Engineering and Social Justice: Synthesis Lectures on Engineers, Technology and Society* recommends: 'Getting beyond views of truth as objective and absolute is the most fundamental change that we need in engineering education'.[35] Another paper states: 'I argue for a movement *against* objects, truths, and knowledge towards a way of being in the world that is guided by first principles'.[36]

A problem with rejecting the objectivity of science and rationality is that such a society will lose to countries like China that are driven to dominate in science and technology. Also, the internal divisiveness within a society that such an irrational posture brings will result in people becoming subjugated to a foreign power like China.

Robin DiAngelo, one of the best-known proponents of Critical Race Theory, believes that scientific methodology, rigor, and hard work are all 'hallmarks of whiteness'. She holds that meritocracy is a White myth to justify White privilege. She feels policies must be evaluated not based on rationality but on whether they have caused the minorities to get ahead. Critical Race Theory dismisses hard work and merit as genuine factors in determining outcomes and considers winners as the result of structural racism.

We wish to point out a double standard on the importance given to the lived experience of a people as compared to objective, rational views based on evidence: For the past several decades, we have had numerous altercations with the American academia on its prejudiced representation of Hinduism. We offered facts, hard evidence, and logic to make our case on several topics. Each time we were dismissed on the technicality that we did not come with 'academic credentials' and that our claims were not approved by 'peer reviews'. On saying that we spoke from personal experience as insiders to the tradition, we were mocked at and denied the prerogative to speak as Hindus. Blacks, however, are encouraged to speak from personal experience and this testimony supersedes the academic findings.

The difference, we are told, is that Blacks are victims; as per Gramsci and Marcuse, this entitles them to the special rights of a protected class. Hindus, and most Indians by implication, are deemed-oppressors – entirely based on the allegations of Hinduphobic and Breaking India forces. This justifies the double standard.

Equity and Equality

A major policy issue at stake here is the difference between *equity* and *equality*. Equality means equal opportunities to all. Equity means achieving equal outcomes by reallocating the level of resources required to achieve this.

The previous form of Liberalism espoused that every individual deserves equal rights and freedom independent of their group identity. The new principle is based on identity politics: each group identity based on race, sex, sexuality, gender identity, nationality, and creed experiences life differently; and their inequality of power needs to be compensated by giving them *unequal rights*.

As a result, the notion of diversity in offices and campuses no longer refers to the diversity of ideas but to the diversity of identities. Because different groups produce knowledge differently, the theory is that the diversity required must reflect the views of different identities. But some identities have dominated and oppressed others and built structures of privilege; therefore, these oppressor identities need to be curtailed in order to create a more equitable playing field.

The posture of equity opposes the principle on which the United States of America was built, that meritocracy rewards people who work hard and play by the rules. The idea was that the middle class works to create the wealth it deserves.[37] This is now being thrown out of the window.

This rejection of merit also leads to problems in places like Harvard where admission policies officially discriminate against Asians. They have come up with arguments for imposing a ceiling on admitting Asians.

Another problem is that though it wants to fight hierarchical structures, Critical Race Theory is itself a reductionist system because it fails to consider the multiplicity and complexity of factors involved in the structures. All identities are classified very simply in a binary system as oppressors or oppressed. But a given individual holds multiple identities. One could simultaneously be a father, husband, employer, Indian, Hindu, philosophically oriented, scientifically minded, argumentative, politically incorrect, worshipper of Shiva and Goddess, meditator, animal lover, lover of music, cuisine and fashions, resident of a certain town, alumnus of a certain university, speaker of a particular language, and so forth. The same individual could be dominant or even oppressive in one context and yet oppressed in another.

Furthermore, Critical Race Theory explains every social ill in various contexts over thousands of years as the product of a single cause. This is ridiculous. Nor does it apply the remedy in a fair and equal manner. For instance, should monuments built by Muslim heroes in countries they conquered (like India) be dismantled just as old slave owners' statues are being dismantled in America? Should the English language be dismantled as a language of the oppressor? Clearly, it's not easy to universalize Critical Race Theory.

We cannot assume that all members of a given identity behave in the same homogeneous way as per some kind of normative code. There are individual members that deviate from their stereotyped behaviors. Human attributes are individual and not fixed for all members of a given identity. This is also the principle of diversity in nature. It works for the individuality of trees, plants, animals and indeed all life.

Cancel Culture and Suppression of Dissent

As noted earlier, Herbert Marcuse was one of the leaders of the Frankfurt School who relocated from Europe to the US and helped bring Marxism across the Atlantic. In 1968, he wrote that society should only allow the ideas from oppressed groups and conservative ideas should be repressed. He wrote that civil rights must be a zero-sum game: to give rights to the oppressed, they must be taken away from the oppressors:

> The exercise of civil rights by those who don't have them presupposes the withdrawal of civil rights from those who prevent their exercise, and that liberation of the Damned of the Earth presupposes suppression not only of their old but also of their new masters.... Withdrawal of tolerance from regressive movements before they can become active; *intolerance even toward thought, opinion, and word, and finally, intolerance in the opposite direction*, that is, toward the self-styled conservatives, to the political Right—*these anti-democratic notions respond to the actual development of the democratic society* which has destroyed the basis for universal tolerance.[38] (emphasis added)

This amounts to a system of revenge. The original purpose of such thinking was to demolish traditions of Western Universalism and replace them with the counter-hegemony of the oppressed, as proposed by Gramsci.

The Liberal idea that free speech is a cornerstone of society is being rejected. The ideology being implemented encourages students to shout down professors, guest speakers, and even other students across American campuses. This is considered a legitimate method to replace what is considered 'cultural hegemony' with a 'counter-hegemony'. The proponents of Critical Race Theory make their position clear:

Being committed to 'free speech' may seem like a neutral principle, but it is not. Thus, proclaiming that 'I am committed equally to allowing free speech for the KKK and 2LiveCrew' is a non-neutral value judgment, one that asserts that the freedom to say hateful things is more important than the freedom to be free from the victimization, stigma, and humiliation that free speech entails.[39]

This is the ideological basis for today's Cancel Culture in liberal arts universities. It empowers the leaders of this movement to decide who the oppressors and oppressed are, and on that basis decide whose speech must be blocked.

Robin DiAngelo's 2011 paper (later published as the book, *White Fragility* in 2020) popularized the term *white fragility* to refer to the defensiveness of Whites when race is discussed. Because they evade discussing race, she feels they are emotionally 'fragile' when the topic is broached, and their responses are evasive and counterproductive. The result of their non-engagement is that 'racial equilibrium' continues favoring White privilege. She defines white fragility as follows:

... a state in which even a minimum amount of racial stress becomes intolerable, triggering a range of defensive moves. ... (they) include the outward display of emotions such as anger, fear, and guilt, and behaviors such as argumentation, silence, and leaving the stress-inducing situation. These behaviors, in turn, function to reinstate white racial equilibrium.[40]

Her book became the number one *New York Times* bestseller in 2020. Corporate America and universities are clients of DiAngelo, spending millions on her services for diversity training.[41] She relies heavily on personal anecdotes and her own 'lived' experience as evidence to make her case. She makes bold claims about how Whites react when told they are racist. These reactions convince her that they are indeed racist. Only their total submission to her theory would satisfy her. She wants her large number of followers to denounce anyone who questions her views. In essence, Robin DiAngelo closes all doors for a productive conversation or dialogue if you disagree.

Seeing through her binary lens, she says that if you are not fighting to dismantle those she opposes, you are a racist:

> A critical approach to social justice refers to specific theoretical
> perspectives that recognize that society is *stratified* (i.e., divided
> and unequal) in significant and far-reaching ways along social
> group lines that include race, class, gender, sexuality, and ability.
> [...] Each of us does have a choice about whether we are going
> to work to interrupt and dismantle these systems [of injustice]
> or support their existence by ignoring them. There is no neutral
> ground; to choose not to act against injustice is to choose to
> allow it.[42]

Even science is subjective according to her:

> All knowledge is taught from a particular perspective; the power
> of dominant knowledge depends in large part on its presentation
> as neutral and universal. In order to understand the concept of
> knowledge as never purely objective, neutral, and outside of human
> interests, it is important to distinguish between discoverable laws
> of the natural world (such as the law of gravity), and knowledge,
> which is socially constructed. By *socially constructed*, we mean that
> all knowledge understood by humans is framed by the ideologies,
> language, beliefs, and customs of human societies. Even the field
> of science is subjective.[43]

Because oppression by the dominant group has become institutionalized,
she says, 'No individual member of the dominant group has to do
anything specific to oppress a member of the minoritized group'.[44]
Merely being a White (and by extension a Brahmin in the Indian context)
is enough to be considered a racist.

We agree with much of her diagnosis of structural biases but disagree
with her position that anyone raising issues and arguing with her is to
be condemned as racist. Any disagreement by a White person shows
what she calls 'internalized dominance'. In effect, her theory of race
becomes the dogma for a new religion, with her as its absolute prophet.
All dissenters are to be condemned as blasphemous:

> If and when an educational program does directly address racism
>   and the privileging of whites, the common white responses

include anger, withdrawal, emotional incapacitation, guilt, argumentation, and cognitive dissonance (all of which reinforce the pressure on facilitators to avoid directly addressing racism). So-called progressive whites may ... insulate themselves via claims that they are beyond the need for engaging with the content because they 'already had a class on this' or 'already know this.' These reactions are often seen in anti-racist education endeavors as forms of resistance to the challenge of internalized dominance. ... it may be useful to also conceptualize them as the result of the reduced psychosocial stamina that racial insulation inculcates.[45]

Another good example of scholar-activists advocating the suppression of free speech in classrooms is Barbara Applebaum, a PhD from the University of Toronto. She writes about a student trying to raise questions in class: 'Allowing him to express his disagreement and spending time trying to challenge his beliefs often comes at a cost to marginalized students whose experiences are, even if indirectly, dismissed by his claims'.[46]

This means it is now considered dangerous to allow students to express disagreements. If counter arguments are allowed, the teacher's prescribed theory may be undermined and place doubts in the minds of the oppressed they are trying to save. Applebaum argues that 'language constitutes our reality by providing the conceptual framework from which meaning is given'.[47] Any conceptual framework or argument expressed in language will itself be flawed and will perpetuate the hegemony built into that language. Since there is no other way to argue except through language, the practical result is that we must not challenge these theories.

Similarly, author Alison Bailey argues that anyone who disagrees with people like her can do 'epistemic violence': 'Treating privilege-preserving epistemic pushback as a form of critical engagement validates it and allows it to circulate more freely; this as I argue later, can do epistemic violence to oppressed groups'.[48]

Activism and the Toolbox

A new trend repositions teaching from being purely educational to becoming highly prescriptive and activist oriented. There is a blurring of boundaries between scholarship and activism. Teaching becomes inseparable from politics. Faculty can now openly declare they are activists and that their college course comprises teaching their own ideology. Dissent is banned. This is more like a Church classroom or a madrassa.

As a proponent of this politicized form of education, activist-scholar Sandra Grey writes:

> Part of being academic citizens involves challenging our students to do more and be more. ... There is a need for academics as part of their normal working lives to form alliances and connections, and even at times to become members of political advocacy organizations.[49]

In 2018, a group of activist-scholars compiled an anthology of essays, *Taking it to the Streets: The Role of Scholarship in Advocacy and Advocacy in Scholarship*.[50] This is a significant move: While many scholars have also been activists, these roles are now no longer separate but merged. Scholars are openly driving their scholarship to push their own ideologies. The big casualty is objectivity, which has traditionally been the hallmark of academic scholarship.

This activism-scholarship hyphenation has opened the floodgates to bring all kinds of ideology and politics into the classroom. A teacher's political issues, what he/she finds ethical and which products he/she likes, etc. all of this is considered legitimate to thrust upon students who are a captive audience with no choice to dissent.

To attract more people into activism, it has become necessary to replace some complex theories with simple 'how to' approaches. This is where scholar-activist and cultural historian, Mary Poovey has played an important role by developing what she calls a 'toolbox approach' to make the social movement less academic, and more activist, oriented. Complex ideas have evolved into simple, easily articulated, bite-sized terms that have become weaponized. This opened the doors for large numbers of activists to join in without having to understand the ideas and history of complex subjects like Marxism, Postmodernism, Critical Race Theory, Intersectionality, Queer Theory, and the like.

It is common now to encounter feminists, anti-racists, and LGBTQ+ activists who have no understanding of the above mentioned theories even though what they promote is based on them. Their toolbox uses vocabulary like oppressor/oppressed, dominant/marginalized, and rhetoric about society being culturally constructed through a clash of identities. They can spew a lot of jargon which they do not fully comprehend. Most followers who jumped on the bandwagon are unable to defend their positions intelligently if subjected to cross-examination. At the end of the day, the old structures of oppression are being replaced by new structures that are not truly liberating.

The Postmodernist view that social reality is constructed by dominant discourses has been turned into the demand that the speech of the oppressed must prevail over that of the oppressor. This has toppled the previous liberal view that in the 'marketplace of ideas' the bad ideas will automatically get defeated by the better ones. A big shift in Liberalism is that free thinking is being replaced by the dogma that only one particular ideology is acceptable, and this is the ideology of identity politics.

To allow individual outpourings of emotions, the leaders of this movement encourage students to express their individual experiences in a political framework. By the time they graduate, they are brainwashed with the new dogma replacing their own critical thinking faculty. We are therefore not removing structures to set people free; we are merely replacing one scaffolding with another.

The assumption being made is that reliable knowledge can be obtained without evidence, reasoning or cross-examination. It can be obtained simply by listening to the lived experiences of those who have been designated as marginalized groups, and this designation is fixed by the authorities of this Church and cannot be questioned. Because only lived experiences are valid, all traditional and authoritative texts must be discarded because they contain language that is oppressive.[51]

Attacking Individualism

Liberalism, until recently, had as its main characteristic the principle of *equal individual* rights for every citizen. France is an example of a democratic country where the clash with Wokeism has intensified. Let us discuss France as a way to open up a broader topic on the toppling of classical Liberalism.

The political ideology known as French Republicanism originated in the French Revolution (1789-99) and served as the core of the French grand narrative. This system is a form of social contract in which each citizen is engaged in a *direct* relationship with the state. France's approach to protecting minorities is that everyone is equal and should be treated as such. This is their principle of universal rights.

On the other hand, Critical Race Theory and Intersectionality champion the rights of *group identities*. According to CRT, society does not comprise individuals with individual rights. It consists of group identities and special importance must be given to those that claim to be oppressed by the rest of society. Woke thinkers claim that race, religion, gender, and sexuality give people different kinds of lived experiences and therefore public policies need to differentiate between groups. Wokeism considers France's Universalism ridden with elitism and an excuse to resist change.

These two worldviews diametrically oppose each other and so far, there is no win-win solution.

A member of a French government thinktank said: 'Wokeism puts people into tribes in order to control them. It says you belong in my tribe, and the leaders of my tribe will tell you how to behave. This is foreign to French mentality.'[52]

Another anti-Woke activist characterizes it as an all-out war against the founding principles of French Liberalism:

> We are in a country where the freedom to talk about anything and everything is taken for granted. When you have minorities who say such and such a subject is off-limits, people instinctively say that's censorship, and we can't accept it.[53]

President Emmanuel Macron has attacked Critical Race Theory because it undermines Individualism, which is at the very heart of the French Republic ideology. It states that everyone is an individual with equal rights from the state, and that groups are not intermediaries between the state and the individual citizens. Critical Race Theory and Intersectionality assert that the leaders of group movements are the ones who must negotiate on behalf of their respective members to get them rights.

Critical Race Theory has been adopted by Muslims in France to claim victim status for their collective identity. During a speech in 2020, President Macron expressed anguish at the lawlessness and gradual radicalization of his country's social fabric. He singled out Islam and criticized it for creating separatist identities among the French population:

> I'm asking every citizen, of all religions and none, to abide wholeheartedly by all the Republic's laws. And in this radical Islamism – since this is at the heart of the matter let's talk about it and name it – a proclaimed, publicized desire, a systematic way of organizing things to contravene the Republic's laws and create a parallel order, establish other values, develop another way of organizing society which is initially separatist, but whose ultimate goal is to take it over completely. And this is gradually resulting in the rejection of the freedom of expression, freedom of conscience and the right to blaspheme, and in us becoming insidiously radicalized.[54]

He blamed external influences and named names to get to the root of the problem:

> External influences and systematic organization by political powers and private organizations have pushed these most radical forms. ... we've let it happen, both at home and abroad. Wahhabism, Salafism, the Muslim Brotherhood – many of these manifestations were also, initially, peaceful for some. Their discourse has gradually deteriorated. They themselves have become radicalized. They've promoted messages of separation, a political project, radicalism in the denial of gender equality, ... and through external funding, through indoctrination from outside, they've reached the heart of our country.[55]

As in the case of France, Critical Race Theory's vision is to reimagine the US as an amalgamation of disparate groups of victims and not as a single nation of individuals. These group identities are what Marcuse wanted to arouse as the oppressed masses demanding entitlements.

The US census is also forcing identity politics by creating new identities. For instance, consider the category 'people of color'. Surveys show that many Hispanics do not wish to be classified as people of color and prefer to integrate into the American mainstream. Rather than being classified racially, they want to get ahead through hard work. A bitter lesson can be learned from the British censuses of India from 1871 onwards. This was a persistent campaign that distorted Indian society's self-images, leading to the rise of the divisive caste system.

All members of a marginalized group are assumed to have the same views and their voice is being represented by those designated as activists. Others are not invited, or are dismissed or filtered, or are told to get coaching and tutoring to make sure they fall in line. The bottom line is that only those who agree are considered authentic voices. Everything is turned into a zero-sum political game in which the way forward is by knocking down the oppressors in an all-out war.

Attacking Barack Obama's Color-blindness

Former US president, Barack Obama made a famous election speech, where he said 'there is no Black America or White America, Asian America, Latino America; there is the United States of America'.[56]

This is now up for criticism by the Wokeists. They feel Obama's vision cannot address the problem of racial inequality. What Wokeism demands are '*structural* solutions to racial problems' even when these turn into reverse racism.[57]

Obama's approach to the problem of race is being criticized as color-blindness. A color-blind society is one in which there are race-neutral governmental policies that reject discrimination in any form in order to promote the goal of racial equality.[58] Color-blindness was also the foundation of Rev. Martin Luther King Jr.'s and Robert Kennedy's Civil Rights Movement and the related anti-discrimination movements of the 1950s and '60s.

In other words, in Obama's approach, one does not fight prejudice against Blacks by legalizing prejudice against Whites, for instance. This concept formed the basis of US Supreme Court Chief Justice John Roberts Jr.'s opinion when he said: 'The way to stop discrimination on the basis of race is to stop discriminating on the basis of race'.[59] The color-blind approach essentially means that the government must create a level playing field in which individuals must put in effort and earn merit to improve their outcomes.

There is disbelief among many that Critical Race Theory demands reverse-discrimination. But this ideology of reverse-racism to solve past discriminations is loud and clear from the foremost ambassadors of the movement. For example, the number one *New York Times* bestselling author and National Book Award winner, Ibram X. Kendi, has famously said:

> *The only remedy to past discrimination is present discrimination.*
> *The only remedy to present discrimination is future discrimination.*[60]

This amounts to an 'eye for an eye' form of social justice!

Obama audaciously called out certain patterns in Black society that are detrimental to its progress. He wanted to hold Blacks accountable and be responsible for improving their lot. He pointed out that there is 'too much television' in their homes. They do not know when to put away their game box or to put kids to bed. He criticized his fellow African Americans for too much consumption of 'poisons', and the lack of 'emphasis on educational achievement'. 'I don't know who taught them that reading and writing and conjugating your verbs was something white.'[61]

He also stressed the importance of 'taking responsibility for our own lives by demanding more from our fathers and spending more time with our children' and called out the lack of 'two-parent households' in Black society. He chastized those refusing to acknowledge how these values were contributing to their predicament.[62] He was emphatic in making this point:

> The civil rights movement wasn't just a fight against the oppressor;
> it was also a fight against the oppressor in each of us.[63]

When questioned on his motives for picking on Blacks in particular, Obama refused to apologize:

> ... I am a black man who grew up without a father and I know the cost that I paid for that. ... I have the capacity to break that cycle, ... my daughters are better off. ... for me to have that conversation does not negate my conversation about the need for early childhood education, or the need for job training, or the need for greater investment in infrastructure, or jobs in low-income communities.[64]

He wanted to talk about both, the problems within the Black community *and* the need for affirmative action. This was to be based on 'class' and not 'race', so reparations/remedies would not be reserved exclusively for Blacks. Other deserving individuals, including Whites who were suffering, would have access to it, in keeping with his color-blind approach.

There are many criticisms of Obama's approach that seeks to solve racial problems by focusing on national unity rather than disunity. Color-blindness can seem like a bad deal to many Blacks because it is tough to accept criticism and change one's own habits. It is also hard to sympathize with others who also have problems, especially when one is told to see them as a group of oppressors.

The main fear is that color-blindness ignores the implicit racial discrimination caused by structural problems. In his book, *Racism Without Racists: Color-Blind Racism and the Persistence of Racial Inequality in America*, Eduardo Bonilla-Silva reflects on this view:

> Race does continue to shape social outcomes (e.g., in the labor
> market, wealth, education, interactions with police, and everyday
> encounters), and by ignoring this—or by being colorblind—we
> help perpetuate and reinforce the system of racial inequality.[65]

According to him, the policy of color-blindness is responsible for the lack of 'gains made by Obama in regard to race, a topic that is not targeted in his social policies and is almost never addressed publicly'.[66]

In another publication, Bonilla-Silva and his co-author David Dietrich explain 'how the election of Barack Obama is not an example of America becoming a "post-racial" country'. Rather, 'the Obama phenomenon as a cultural symbol and his political stance and persona on race are compatible with color-blind racism'. They complain that 'under the Obama administration, the tentacles of color-blind racism will reach even deeper into the crevices of the American polity'.[67]

They interpret Obama's broad appeal amongst both Whites and people of color as a political masterstroke because he tells all sides what they like to hear:

> Obama has become a symbol with especially different meanings
> for people of color and whites. For non-whites, Obama became a
> symbol of their possibilities in what they hoped would become a

more egalitarian America. For blacks, the possibility of having a black president became a symbol of their historical aspirations as a people, of 'a dream deferred, now realized'. For older generations of blacks desperate to see racial equality before they die, and for many post–Reagan generation blacks and minorities who have seen very little racial progress in their lifetimes, Obama became the new messiah of the civil rights movement. In contrast, the symbolic meaning of Obama to whites was compatible with their belief that America was indeed a color-blind nation. Obama quickly became for whites an Oprah- or Tiger Woods–like figure, a black person who has 'transcended' his blackness to become a national hero. Thus, for whites and other supporters around the globe, Obama also represented 'possibilities,' the American promise of the Horatio Alger myth that "no matter how humble the beginnings, or how tattered the overcoat, once washed up on America's shores anyone can attain anything".[68]

Blacks who advocate Critical Race Theory argue that Obama's success was attributable to the fact that he discarded or minimized his Black identity instead of embracing it. In essence, Obama accepted a position of inferiority and that if he hadn't done so, the political outcome could have been different:

> Obama's popularity also lies in his adoption of a post-racial (racially transcendent) persona and politics. He has distanced himself from most leaders of the civil rights movement, from his reverend [a blatant racist from the black community], from his church, and from anything or anyone who made him look 'too black' or 'too political.' Obama's campaign even retooled Michelle Obama to make her seem less black, less strong, and more white-lady-like for the white electorate. For his white supporters, Obama was the first 'black' leader they felt comfortable supporting because he did not talk about racism; because he kept reminding them he is half-white; because he was so 'articulate' or—in Senator Biden's words, later echoed by Karl Rove—Obama was 'the first mainstream African American who is articulate and bright and clean and a nice-looking guy'. Furthermore, unlike black leaders such as Jesse Jackson and Al Sharpton, he did not make them

feel guilty about the state of racial affairs in the country. Instead, Obama preached unity.[69]

In all fairness to Obama, he never said that color-blindness had already been achieved. It was something he wanted all Americans to work towards. He wanted them to make the difficult personal changes immediately and not wait for structural changes. The fact that many members of the Black community support color-blindness shows that he drove home his point.

One must appreciate that Obama's victory ushered in a new chapter in racial discourse that brought Blacks and Whites together to discuss matters of mutual interest. But this engagement is seen as a problem by proponents of Critical Race Theory. A major book from some of them had the following reaction to Obama's presidency:

> Emerging in the wake of Barack Obama's monumental election, a new center of gravity took hold in American racial discourse, one that was framed as a racially pragmatic alternative to the polarizing and counterproductive contestations over race. This discursive shift bore significant consequences in the struggle against colorblind ideology. On the eve of the election, racial justice advocates were already facing increasing pressure to abandon remnants of race-conscious discourse in the face of colorblind victories in both the legal and political arenas. *The emergence of postracialism only deepened the erosion of race justice discourse.* Underlying postracialism's buoyant introduction to the American scene was a conservative riptide that pulled racial justice constituencies into a discourse that legitimized a morbidly unequal status quo. That postracialism's condition of possibility was a political victory that few stakeholders of racial justice thought they would ever witness is one of the great ironies of civil rights history.[70]

Kimberlé Williams Crenshaw is troubled by the way Obama boosted the color-blind approach, saying that 'postracialism rode to the center of American political discourse on Barack Obama's coattails, carrying along with it a long-standing conservative project of associating colorblindness with racial enlightenment and racial justice advocacy with grievance politics'.[71] The problem, she says, is color-blindness because it is a conservative project and therefore, cannot produce a solution.

Marcelle Mentor, faculty at Columbia University, offered a succinct explanation of why color-blindness is problematic:

> ... when we say that we are racially colorblind, we render black and brown bodies invisible and we render their experiences, lives, and traumas moot and mute. We silence whole truths and whitewash a very real and painful history of people across the U.S.A.[72]

The Civil Rights Movement's approach had stressed incremental step-by-step progress. But Critical Race Theory wants to instantly dismantle the very foundations of the existing order; all attempts to remodel it are considered equivalent to supporting the survival of the old structures. They completely reject equality, legal reasoning and constitutional law, Enlightenment, and rationality.[73]

Educational Battleground

American university campuses have become ground zero for Critical Race Theory warfare. That is where the dogma and intolerance are the highest. There are routine incidents of speakers and even university presidents being shouted down with activists standing on desks screaming until the police intervenes. Those who defy the dictatorship of this movement are subject to ridicule, public shaming, being cancelled or even fired. Studies have shown that one-third of students and scholars on American campuses who oppose Critical Race Theory have been threatened by disciplinary action for their views, and seventy percent of academicians who oppose it have reported a hostile climate among peers.[74]

There is a trend to introduce Woke-related topics in American K–12 school subjects like social studies, history, and civics. This has generated a huge backlash from parents who complain that this material distracts educators and students away from subjects like STEM that build careers and a chance to live the American dream.

For example, California is planning to implement a curriculum with an entire section devoted to Intersectionality. Fairfax County Public Schools District in Virginia paid a social justice consultant twenty thousand dollars to speak before district employees. The school board in Montgomery County, Maryland, plans to spend nearly half a million dollars on a consultant to conduct an 'anti-racism audit'.

Ohio is training its school board on Critical Race Theory and also requiring training for all state employees and contractors who work in education. The new teacher training program is introducing methods of activism advocating personal narratives over objective knowledge and historical facts. This, despite years of research showing that minority students still lag behind their peers in core subjects. According to reports by educationists, almost half of all Americans cannot name the three branches of government.[75] Yet, the pedagogy promotes activism despite the inabilities of most students to be able to make mature decisions and act responsibly.

American history is being rewritten as a chronology of past injustices, and various kinds of entitlements that are expected as compensatory justice.

Dismantling the Old Without Knowing How to Build the New

The nation-state is a potential victim of this latest dialectic of multiple victim identities versus the established order. What used to be a positive civic sense of responsibility is turning into a call to disruption, including violent revolution at times.

We must remind ourselves of what Abraham Lincoln said: 'There is no grievance that is a fit object of redress by mob law'. Further, we must 'let the proud fabric of freedom rest' upon a 'reverence for the constitution and laws'.[76] We find it undesirable to topple these fundamental notions of upholding the due process under the constitution.

The endgame of Critical Race Theory is to dismantle existing structures because they have caused so much historical oppression and injustice, and the promise is that something new, but yet undefined, will take its place and bring justice. However, we must look at the track record of similar disruptions:

- The Russian Revolution that established Communism was also carrying out the project of dismantling old structures. That experiment failed, whereas Western Europe continued developing itself within the old structures and performed far better.
- Likewise, Iran went through a revolution to dismantle the

secular structures erected under Western influence. These were replaced with Islamic structures that led to the rise of terrorism and not a better society.

- The US intervened to dismantle the Islamic dictatorships hoping to replace them with democracy. That, too, failed.
- China's Maoist revolution destroyed its traditional fabric in the name of starting afresh, but the new China is hardly an appropriate example of social justice.

In every case of a radical dismantling of old structures, the outcome was a mess that brought even greater injustices then before. So, what is the evidence that the Critical Race Theory revolution to break down old structures will bring about better outcomes?

The Corporatization of Woke

There is a proliferation of Critical Race Theory training workshops and seminars across America's workplaces. The management is pressed to adopt official policies formulated by the proponents of CRT. These training sessions are modeled after the brainwashing sessions that Gramsci recommended for European workers in the 1920s – their goal was to create a discourse of 'counter-hegemony' that replaces what is seen as 'cultural hegemony'.

A well-known example of such indoctrination took place in 2020 at the National Museum for African American History and Culture, a Smithsonian institution. The museum's education criticized the notion that hard work and the pursuit of objective and rational thinking is the key to success. It explained that such attributes belong to the 'White dominant culture'.[77] Such training courses are spreading like wildfire.

Human Resources (HR) departments are pressured by expensive Woke consultants, and if they resist, they run the risk of being attacked as racists. The Society for Human Resources Management (SHRM), the lobbying arm of HR professionals, has also become a major force in convincing corporate HR professional to undergo such training and certification. It offers diversity training using Critical Race Theory under the guise of bringing social justice into the workplace. The SHRM is influential, with a membership that includes over 300,000 human resource professionals and business executives in 165 countries, and its policies and ideologies impact 115 million workers worldwide.[78]

An example of a top consultant of Critical Race Theory making loads of money is author Robin DiAngelo. She charges tens of thousands of dollars as speaking fees. She is forthright in stating: 'This book is unapologetically rooted in identity politics.'[79] Ironically, DiAngelo is vehemently against free enterprise and yet the corporates fear her so much that they hire her.

Another example is Critical Race Theory leader Ibram X. Kendi, whose book, *How to Be an Anti-Racist*, also condemns capitalism: 'Capitalism is essentially racist; racism is essentially capitalist. They were birthed together from the same unnatural causes, and they shall one day die together from unnatural causes'.[80] Yet the biggest corporates want to be seen as aligned with her.

Critical Race Theory has also infiltrated the workplace through graduates hired from liberal arts colleges who bring this influence.

Most importantly, it is also embedded in the algorithms that determine how the accounts and messages on social media are treated.

Vivek Ramaswamy offers a compelling thesis that corporate Wokeism is a way to hide something dark. He writes: 'There's a new invisible force at work in the highest ranks of corporate America', a force that is 'the defining scam of our time – one that robs you of not only your money but your voice and your identity'.[81]

Ramaswamy exposes the hoax in corporate America to 'pretend like you care about something other than profit and power, precisely to gain more of each'.[82] In other words, there are rich and hungry tycoons pretending to be doing good, but this is a way to spread their power over every facet of society. He says that industrialists are using philanthropic policies that look progressive merely as a ploy to deflect attention away from their own abuses of power:

> By adopting these new 'woke' values, America's business leaders stumbled upon a once-in-a-generation opportunity to leap from heresy to sainthood. Corporations were no longer the oppressors. Instead, corporate power – if wielded in the right way – could actually empower the new disempowered classes who suffered not at the hands of evil corporations but instead at the hands of

straight white men – the real culprits who had exploited their power not only since the birth of the corporation but throughout all of modern human history.[83]

He writes that the big corporations are patronizing Wokeism to hide their culture of greed. By hiring expensive diversity consultants, their capitalism is spared by directing anger against White men. It is a marriage of convenience between corporations and Wokeism:

> Corporations never truly loved wokeness, even as they embraced it and married it to capitalism. They always intended to use it. But wokeness never truly loved capitalism, either. There was nothing fundamentally woke about capitalism, no natural compatibility. When corporations started proclaiming that wokeness and capitalism were inseparable and offering money and status to anyone who could help spread that message, each side accepted the proposal not because there was very much truth to it but because it was profitable. [...]
>
> The main thing wokeness gets out of this marriage of convenience is that it gets to use every major company as a platform to blast its message to the universe. Money was not the only dowry that corporations offered. What they really promised wokeness was a megaphone to turbocharge its message and make it mainstream. By turning wokeness into the default ideology of business, they offered to make it the default everywhere. In exchange, corporations got to wear the protective cloak of wokeness's moral superiority. It was a cynical arrangement.[84]

To sum up Ramaswamy's charge of hypocrisy: *'A corporation offers woke people money and influence, and in return they lend it the protective cloak of wokeness's moral superiority to hide its wrongdoing'.*[85] This cloak of philanthropy gives a better return on investment than the traditional public relations.

This is how the super wealthy are hijacking the rules of ethical conduct, which has traditionally been outside the scope of running a business. The marketplace of ideas was meant primarily for individual actors on a level playing field, not for identity politics. But we now find corporate power thrusting its views on society, bypassing the rigors of public debate. The big companies are deciding who they will prefer for investments and business transactions based on their social values. The problem, according to Ramaswamy is that 'When companies use their commercial market power to make moral rules, they effectively prevent those with less money from having the same say in our democracy'.[86]

Ramaswamy argues that the limited-liability company was a powerful tool invented for free-enterprise. But a key element was that *in exchange for getting limited liability, the corporations confined themselves to commerce, and did not expand into the roles set aside for government.* This separation was important to protect society from the rise of monsters like the East India Company in the past and the Googles of today.

But now capitalism's institutions are being turned into tools for disseminating and implementing Wokeism. And corporations are using Woke activism as a vehicle to go beyond their commercial boundaries and exert power over society and governments.

If Woke capitalists want to expand their scope beyond commerce and also control social morality, the limited liability provisions in corporate law should be ended, so that they shoulder the social responsibility and liability for their actions. Presently, the corporate shield of limited liability is being misused by conducting social activism behind that shield. Governments conduct social policy and are accountable through democratic elections. Corporations are not accountable to the general public, only to their own shareholders, and this makes their social activism an unreasonable expansion of power. A fairer approach would be to reduce the scope of limited liability protection and *exclude their social activism from protection.*

Indian social theory addressed this problem of too much concentration of power across multiple domains. It required a separation among the different varnas (forms of social capital). This ensured that businesses (Vaishya varna) focus on profits by optimizing their use of resources, while intellectuals and spiritualists (Brahmin varna) were leaders on moral issues, and governments (Kshatriya varna) focus on delivering the social goods to the public.

The new idea of 'stakeholder capitalism' challenges these boundaries and allows private corporations to determine the social interests of humanity at large. Just as the Indian Constitution forbids the government to suppress free speech, so must big business be prevented from intervening in public discourse. This could be accomplished by expanding the list of 'protected categories' – race, sex, religion, and national origin – to also include political ideology.

The Environment, Social and Governance movement sweeping the business world rates companies according to their conduct on all three. The level of investment available to a firm can depend on its ESG rating. But a reasonable question is, who decides the criteria for rating a company's ESG score, and on what basis? Presently, ESG avoids 'sin industries' like alcohol, gambling, tobacco, and weapons. But what about the meat industry and the pharma industry's use of animals for testing?

The premise of ESG is laudable, but one needs to make sure there is diversity of views represented on what constitutes good social policy. Critical Race Theory emphasizes that Blacks and other Intersectional identities must have their views represented over and above any rational or logical arguments, so by the same token, why could we not bring in diverse value systems to formulate the standards of ESG?

2

The Americanization of Caste

Overview

A vibrant movement has developed in the United States of America with the help of the Indian Left to position caste as the universal architecture for racism throughout world history. One of the consequences of this theory is the fabrication of a new identity being projected as the epicenter of victimhood, commonly known as the Afro-Dalit identity.

The Afro-Dalit movement was introduced in the book *Breaking India* as follows:

> In the 1990s, an African American scholar at Princeton University casually told me that he had returned from ... India, where he was working with the 'Afro-Dalit Project'. ...I found that this US-operated and financed project frames inter-*jati/varna* interactions and the Dalit movement using American cultural and historical lenses. The Afro-Dalit project purports to paint Dalits as the 'Blacks' of India and non-Dalits as India's 'Whites'...But this is a false equation of caste as race. While modern caste structures and inter-relationships have included long periods of prejudice toward Dalits, the Dalit experience bears little resemblance to the African slave experience of America.[1]

The book made a huge impact since it was first published over a decade ago and galvanized many responses. The Afro-Dalit project has advanced considerably, both in the US, and as its mirror image in India, and morphed into a far more insidious form. Underpinning the emerging Afro-Dalit identity is the theory that *caste equals race*. We will discuss this theory and its impact on the American mainstream.

The chapter explains the following:

- Critical Race Theory, as previously covered, has been mapped to Indian society. In principle, there is nothing wrong with this, but as we shall explain, the mapping has been shoddy, full of biases, and has reached false and dangerous conclusions.
- The recent bestselling book, *Caste: The Origins of Our Discontents* by Isabel Wilkerson, is discussed to lay the groundwork.[2] The thesis therein has been widely accepted in America and makes a strong case that race is the consequence of the deeper-rooted phenomenon of caste. In fact, caste is considered the underlying infrastructure on top of which racism operates. The anti-racism movement, therefore, needs to reinvent itself as the anti-caste movement. In other words, the Afro-Dalit project discussed in *Breaking India* has now become far more aggressive, because what were previously separate, and independent, movements – Dalits dealing with caste in India, and Blacks dealing with racism in America – have now merged into a single global movement.

Critical Race Theory's Passage to India

A large part of this book is about how Critical Race Theory is being mapped on to Indian society and exported to India aggressively. The Indian Left has thoroughly imported all prior Western social thought derived from Marxism and Postmodernism (such as Postcolonial Studies, Subaltern Studies, etc.), and now the newest obsession is to Indianize Critical Race Theory.

Many of CRT's ideas are being introduced in India one at a time, sometimes informally and casually under the radar. But it seems there is also a formal movement under way, thanks to Harvard University and its network in India, to transfer the entire Critical Race Theory mechanism to India. This includes bringing to India:

- The theory
- Its adaptations for radicalizing certain groups
- Toolkits for activism
- Development and consolidation of victim identities
- Large number of activists already trained at Harvard at various levels

Harvard also provides support from the US by way of arranging funding from India's own wealthy individuals, as well as legal and political support.

This large-scale network is a *top-down* movement which is in contrast with previous Breaking India movements that were infiltrating at the *grassroots*. The purpose of this new Breaking India movement is to install an elite leadership in India's institutions across all segments of society including the government, industry, academics, and NGOs. This will be detailed in Part 2, which is why we call Harvard the vishwa guru that is creating its own sangha comprising a vast network of *shakhas* (branches) in India.

The following diagram shows the problems we see with the import of Critical Race Theory to India. Parts 2 and 3 are devoted to discussing these topics in detail.

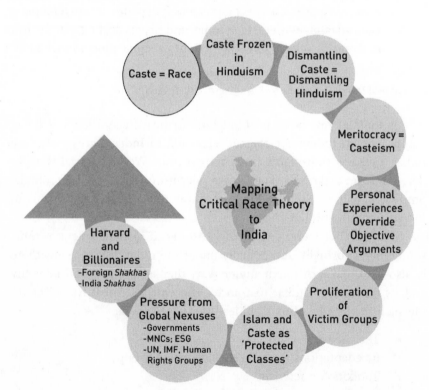

Going clockwise starting at the top, the main points of the diagram are as follows:

- The social structure of caste is said to be equal to the biological characteristics of race.
- Caste is treated as an indispensable part of Hinduism while caste systems in other cultures are ignored.
- The claim is that since it is an indispensable part of Hinduism, dismantling caste is possible only if Hinduism itself is dismantled.
- Meritocracy is claimed to be a product of caste structures and therefore a part of it.
- Since all objectivity is tainted with the bias of structural privilege, it is said that objective arguments must be replaced with personal experiences. Only the groups identified as victims are said to have valid personal experiences.
- Islam is assumed to be a victim group irrespective of numerous historical records to the contrary. Therefore, it is eligible for the status of 'protected class'.
- Global nexuses involving governments; multinational companies through their ESG programs; and international groups like the UN and human rights organizations are roped in to pressure India into accepting these frameworks.
- Harvard is playing a central role in creating and distributing this narrative through its vast and influential networks both in India and overseas.

We remind the reader that the end game of Critical Race Theory is to dismantle all structures that were historically built by those branded as oppressors. Working within those structures, modifying them or trying to correct their biases is explicitly and vociferously to be fought against as a ploy by the oppressors to preserve their status quo of domination.

When applied to India, the end game is to dismantle all structures of the Vedic/Hindu heritage, its texts, deities, symbols, rituals, festivals, customs, gurus, and institutions. Additionally, India's technology education, starting with the IITs, has become a target because, as we shall see in Chapter 4, scholars from Harvard have declared it a bastion of meritocracy, and meritocracy has been declared a structure of casteism set up by the Brahmins.

Once again, for removal of doubt, we are not denying the atrocities against various communities like the Dalits, and the imperative to address these. We are in total sympathy with *all* such communities. But we are against the wholesale dismantling of Vedic structures and prefer a more nuanced approach to adapt for modern times. One of the counter-arguments we will present in detail in Chapter 6 is that varna (loosely equated with caste) has not been uniformly abusive or fixed, but that (a) it has also been a positive force; and (b) it has been successfully modified from within many times in the past. Therefore, we reject the arguments calling for the wholesale dismantling of Hinduism.

The table below summarizes various positions from the Critical Race Theory camp and our response.

Position of Critical Race Theorists and Afro-Dalits	Our Position
✓ Dalits and Lower Castes Suffer Serious Biases Alongwith Many Other Groups	Agree
✓ Problems can be Deep and Systemic, not Superficial	Agree
✗ All Victims of Social Grievances Must be Unified Using Intersectionality	Disagree. Each Grievance has its Own Contexts, Causes, and Remedies. Cannot Club them all as One Anti-thesis
✗ Zero-sum Hegelian Dialectic Needed to Defeat Opponents; no Room to Collaborate	Disagree. The Ego Level that Created the Problem Cannot Solve it. Dialectic will only Create more Violence. Need to Raise the Level of Individual Consciousness
✗ Caste Problems Caused by Hinduism and Cannot be Solved within Hinduism	Disagree. Caste as Practiced Today is Neither Necessary nor Sufficient in Hinduism
✗ Free Speech of Opponents Must be Denied, and Dissidents Attacked as Racists	Disagree. Must Avoid Creating a New Religion with Dogma, High Priests, Blasphemy Laws
✗ Wokeism Must be Spread Across All Civil Society Using Intimidation	Disagree. Need Honest and Fair Approaches

Such social problems have existed in every civilization and in fact, continue to do so. Vedic tradition has often addressed its issues resulting in major social changes that will be explained, with evidence cited. Hence, the question is whether external interventions are required and would be the best solution.

On the other hand, external interventions by one civilization or nation in another's internal social issues have a deplorable track record. For example, when the Conquistadors conquered the North American natives, it was often justified on the basis that the natives committed crimes like human sacrifice, but this conquest resulted in their genocide. The same pattern is found in the way Africans were treated at the hands of Europeans. When the US invaded Mexico to grab the states of California, Texas, New Mexico, and Nevada, the real motive was pure and simple expansionism because oil had been discovered on those lands. But the reason cited in the US Congress to justify this invasion was that Mexicans abuse their women and children, and a lot of evidence was created and presented as part of what became known as atrocity literature.

The term 'yellow journalism' was coined to refer to *a style of newspaper reporting that emphasized sensationalism over facts and used to rabble-rouse American sentiments to invade other countries*. The term was coined in the mid-1890s to characterize sensational journalism in the newspaper war between Joseph Pulitzer's *New York World* and William Randolph Hearst's *The New York Journal*. During its heyday in the late nineteenth century, it was one of many factors that helped push the US into war in Cuba and the Philippines, leading to the acquisition of overseas territory.

Caste Considered the Architecture of Global Racism

During the colonial era, which lasted over three centuries, varna, a Sanskrit term that is non-translatable into English, was mistranslated as 'caste' by the British, both for ease of administration, and the subjugation of its colony. Worse still, the Indian Constitution later legitimized this new hierarchical structure of caste, which became a foundation of modern vote bank politics and Indian democracy. The long and convoluted history of caste is the subject of Chapter 6.

The caste idea has been further misinterpreted, this time with an American meaning in the framework of Black/White racial politics.

The recent entrant to the arena of misinterpreters is Isabel Wilkerson, a Pulitzer Prize-winning African American journalist and author. Wilkerson uses the term 'caste' to serve the purpose of describing racial tensions between Blacks and Whites in the United States. This newly defined idea that caste equals race has entered the American lexicon in the frontier of the social justice movement. Therefore, what we are dealing with is the double distortion that can be represented as follows: Varna ➔ Caste ➔ Race.

Wilkerson's core thesis is that India's social structure is 'the world's original caste system'[3] that lies deep beneath the surface of many societies and causes racism, both in the US and India. She translates caste as 'a graded ranking of human values producing an artificial hierarchy in society';[4] she links it to race, stating that race is the tool used by the underlying infrastructure called caste. In other words, caste is the foundation on top of which race serves as a tool. The following figure illustrates the grand sweep of her thesis.

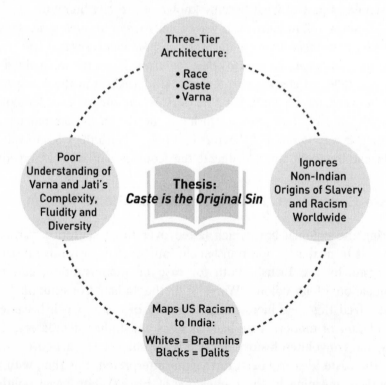

Three-Tier Architecture:
• Race
• Caste
• Varna

Poor Understanding of Varna and Jati's Complexity, Fluidity and Diversity

Thesis: Caste is the Original Sin

Ignores Non-Indian Origins of Slavery and Racism Worldwide

Maps US Racism to India:
Whites = Brahmins
Blacks = Dalits

This thesis has gained Wilkerson prominence as a public intellectual in the US and breathed new life into the discourse on racism. Oprah Winfrey boosted the sales of Wilkerson's book through her book club, while *The New York Times* called it 'an instant American classic'.[5] The popularity of her bestseller in mainstream media and in American thinktanks has given caste a new meaning, making it a household word. However, as we shall elaborate, this is just the beginning of the far-reaching implications for Indians everywhere!

This is, however, not the first instance of caste being equated with race. In 2001, during a UN conference on race in Durban, South Africa, the Indian government found itself at odds with a resolution being proposed that caste was a form of racism. Among the arguments used was the standard (but false) rhetoric that '*devdasis* face the threat of everyday rape by the representatives of Hindu gods right in the temple premise'. The government succeeded in getting this clause removed from the final resolution.[6]

But in those previous instances, caste was seen as one form of racism alongside many others in different parts of the world. All these forms had a peer relationship with one another; none was primary or the cause of the others. However, there is something fundamentally new and different in this latest claim of caste as racism: In the new theory, caste is the original sin of racism and has been *causing* racism globally. The adoption of the term caste is not merely as a metaphor or analogy, but as a theory of causation according to which caste is responsible for causing racism found everywhere. We will explain Wilkerson's thesis and the new movement being based on it.

Skin color is often regarded as a marker for caste. It is oftentimes assumed that low caste persons in India are dark-skinned and upper castes are light-skinned. This is used to support caste as being somehow linked to race. Wilkerson also refers to one of her Indian interviewees mentioning the 'Indian fixation on skin-color' and 'hatred of darker Indians'.[7] The fact, however, is that *caste (unlike race) is not determined by physical looks*. This is just one of many such false assumptions she makes to appeal to race-conscious Americans because being Black in America is based on physical looks.

In fact, most Hindu deities like Krishna, Kali, and Durga are dark-skinned, a fact always glorified in hymns. Wilkerson cannot, on the one hand, accuse Hinduism of being the cause of racism and yet, on the other, fail to recognize that most Hindu deities are dark-skinned, a fact totally contrary to her thesis. Also, the famous rock-cut Ajanta Caves in India depict paintings of individuals of dark and light complexions in which the former are often shown wearing lavish clothes and jewelry while the light-skinned attendants appear to be their servants. These cave paintings are dated to before the Islamic era (seventh century) and remained untouched by Islamic rulers because they were hidden from public view for centuries until discovered by the British. There are many such examples to prove that using skin color as an absolute marker of caste status is fraught with risk, and such an attempt by Wilkerson betrays her agenda to appeal to the emotions of Blacks in America.

One could easily argue in reverse: that the contemporary preference for light complexion in Indian society was the result of invaders from Arabia, Iran, and Turkey who brought with them the new aesthetics of light skin as a marker of beauty. To the extent Islamic, and then European, colonization shaped Indian aesthetics, and these two forms of colonization together lasted more than one thousand years, one must doubt the theory that it was India's 'original' caste system that downgraded the position of dark-skinned peoples.

Wilkerson gives examples of caste manifestations in America from the Jim Crow era, a horribly racist period in the country's history. Jim Crow was not a person, but an epithet based on a popular nineteenth century minstrel song that stereotyped African Americans. 'Jim Crow' became a popular term to personify the system of racial oppression and segregation officially sanctioned by the US government. 'Jim Crow laws' were in place from 1877 until the Civil Rights Movement in the 1950s and '60s. Wilkerson's claim that caste oppression was similar because that implies it was *officially sanctioned by governments,* is false. Except during the British rule in India, it was not the official state policy to enforce any such caste-based oppression. There is a difference between social practices and government laws, a distinction that Wilkerson misses.

Wilkerson correctly states that a problem cannot be fixed unless and until you look beyond the surface of plaster and wallpaper. This requires an x-ray vision into the social problem, and she presents her thesis as an x-ray of the American race issue. Just like old houses have a deep structure hiding the area where the real problem lies, she says, so also American society has the caste system as its invisible skeleton that is central to the operation of racism. Her thesis is that caste is the infrastructure of American society's divisiveness and internal conflicts. Using the analogy of a physical building, Wilkerson calls caste the engineering structure of studs and joists that support a physical building but cannot be seen by ordinary people; only an engineering expert can explain it to us. She is that expert in explaining caste to the American people. She writes:

> Caste is the infrastructure of our divisions. It is the architecture of human hierarchy, the subconscious code of instructions for maintaining, in our case, a 400-year-old social order. Looking at caste is like holding a country's x-ray up to the light. A caste system is an artificial construction, a fixed and embedded ranking of human value that sets the presumed supremacy of one group against the presumed inferiority of other groups on the basis of ancestry and often immutable trades, trades that would be neutral in the abstract but ascribe life and death meaning in a hierarchy favoring the dominant caste whose forebears designated it. A caste system uses rigid, often arbitrary boundaries to keep the ranked groupings apart, distinct from one another and in their assigned places.[8]

Another powerful analogy she uses is with the body's DNA: 'Just as DNA is the code of instruction for cell development, caste is the operating system for economic, political and social interactions in the United States from the time of its gestation'.[9]

According to her, the relationship between caste and race is simple and direct: *Caste is the grammar of racism.* She writes:

> Race does the heavy lifting for a caste system that demands a means of human division. If we have been trained to see humans in the language of race, then caste is the underlying grammar that we encode as children, as when learning our mother tongue. Caste, like grammar, becomes an invisible guide not only to how we speak, but to how we process information, the autonomic

calculations that figure into a sentence without our having to think about it. What lies beneath each label is centuries of history and assigning of assumptions and values.[10]

Interestingly, she considers race to be flexible and caste to be rigid. Hence, caste is the real problem: 'Caste is the bones, race the skin. Caste is fixed and rigid. Race is fluid and superficial, subject to periodic redefinition to meet the needs of the dominant class in what is now the United States'.[11] Caste, she says, is holding us prisoner for centuries: 'We are all born into a silent war game, centuries old, enlisted in teams not of our own choosing'.[12]

Even when in passing she briefly acknowledges that the Bible has racist ideas, she points out that Biblical racism was based on the pre-existing idea of caste that began before the Bible.

Wilkerson spent time in India with Dalits, followers of Dr. B.R. Ambedkar, a pioneering intellectual and politician, who chaired the committee framing the Indian Constitution. That is where she started developing her systematic list of parallels between the hierarchy of caste in India and the hierarchy of race in America. This work led to her recent bestseller.

She regards Ambedkar her hero, referring to him as the Indian equivalent of the American activist and Baptist minister, Rev. Martin Luther King Jr. She cites Ambedkar's interactions with one of the best known African American intellectuals, W.E.B. Du Bois. 'There is so much similarity between the position of the untouchables in India and of the position of the Negros in America', Ambedkar wrote to Du Bois. And Du Bois wrote back to Ambedkar expressing sympathy for the untouchables of India.[13]

All this is true but only part of the story. What is totally ignored in Wilkerson's book is King Jr.'s very explicit expressions of debt to Mohandas Gandhi. King Jr. was in awe of Gandhi, as is the political activist Rev. Jessie Jackson, and many of King Jr.'s predecessors and mentors. If she had mentioned this as part of the history of the African American movement, it would have compelled her to discuss Gandhi's support for varna, even while he fought modern caste biases. That discussion would require a far more nuanced understanding on her part. Such an analysis would take her down the rabbit hole of caste's complexities, making it problematic for her to pour out sweeping statements that appeal to the uninformed emotions of her readers.

The fact is that King Jr. was inspired by Gandhi to start his Civil Rights Movement in 1954. Additionally, the entire African American struggle of the twentieth century was classified by its early leaders as a Gandhian movement using Gandhi's ideas of satyagraha, or peaceful civil disobedience. Many prominent African Americans traveled to India to study and learn from Gandhi's movement. Wilkerson is selectively attacking Hindu dharma by characterizing caste in a certain manner while blatantly ignoring Hindu dharma's potential as a resource to address modern racism and other systems of bias.

The African American digestion of Indian ideas went through two phases. The first phase was during the twentieth century when Indian culture was seen as a resource to liberate Blacks with Gandhi considered the thought leader. The second phase started towards the end of the twentieth century during which Indian culture was seen as a scourge causing racism due to its caste system.

Wilkerson says that prior to the experience of caste-driven racism in America, there was no such identity as Black people, because their identities comprised their particular tribe in Africa. Similarly, there were no such people as Whites, because they saw themselves as Irish, Italians, Germans, French, and so on, and only became 'White' in America, thanks to the caste system. However, in theorizing the American history of racism, she ignores the role of the fifteenth-sixteenth century explorer Christopher Columbus treating the Native Americans as subhuman people by projecting his Christian prejudices. She writes: 'The American caste system began in the years after the arrival of the first Africans to Virginia Colony in the summer of 1619'.[14] In her analysis, the prior period during which Spanish Conquistadors, with the blessing of the Pope, committed the most unspeakable atrocities on the Native Americans, is not given the prominence it deserves.

She is rightfully concerned about endogamy which means restricting marriage within a birth-based community. She justifiably criticizes many Americans who joined the eugenics movement of the early twentieth century, including the inventor Alexander Graham Bell, industrialist Henry Ford, and the academic and president of Harvard University,

Charles William Eliot. But she incorrectly conflates eugenics with caste by quoting the American racist Madison Grant who was known for his eugenics proposals; she uses Grant as one of her subject-matter experts on caste. This makes caste seem like a eugenics project. Wilkerson says that the upper castes in India wanted to 'preserve the purity of their blood, and this persists till this day'.[15] She is unaware that many Indian communities of all strata choose endogamy to preserve their specific identity, customs, and traditions.

Wilkerson seems unaware of the historical fact that the upper castes were also Indians and not foreign conquerors. Indian history has no parallel to Africans being brought from another continent (and hence from a different race) and forced into servitude, except during Muslim rule as explained later in this chapter. Her book is full of anecdotes and quotations from people assumed to be legitimate authorities with no counter voice offered from the Hindu perspective. This, despite the fact that several Hindu intellectuals have written extensively on, and refuted, the kinds of statements she makes about caste.

Her book applies caste selectively to describe America and show the equivalences with race. She crisscrosses between random anecdotes from India and juxtaposes those with experiences of Blacks in America. For example, she refers to White America's racism using terms like 'dominant caste', 'ruling majority favored caste', or 'upper caste'. Asians and Latinos in the US are labeled 'middle castes', while African Americans are referred to as 'subordinate caste', 'lowest caste', 'bottom caste', and 'disfavored caste'.[16] This is a simplistic way of juxtaposing Indian and American histories.

Wilkerson says that both America and India were conquered by Aryans, in one case crossing the Atlantic Ocean while in the other, crossing the mountains from the north into India. They are the genesis of the global caste system which they took with them wherever they went. Democracy, she says, has not uprooted the caste system in either country. Despite such fundamental differences in histories and outcomes, both share the caste system as their deep structure. In other words, according to her the Aryan structures of social hierarchy got incorporated into societies everywhere.

She writes:

> Their respective hierarchies are profoundly different. And yet, as
> if operating from the same instruction manual translated to fit
> their distinctive cultures, both countries adopted similar methods
> of maintaining rigid lines of demarcation and protocols. Both
> countries kept their dominant castes separate, apart and above
> those deemed lower. Both exile their indigenous people – the
> Adivasis in India, the Native Americans in the United States – to
> remote lands and to the unseen margins of society. Both countries
> enacted a network of laws to chain the lowliest groups – Dalits
> in India and African Americans in the United States – to the
> bottom, using terror and force to keep them there.[17]

And elaborates further:

> The United States and India would become, respectively, the
> oldest and the largest democracies in human history, both built
> on caste systems undergirded by the reading of the sacred texts
> of their respective cultures. In both countries, the subordinate
> castes were consigned to the bottom, seen as deserving of their
> debasement, owing to the sins of the past.[18]

Nazism, associated with Hitler's Germany, too, gets blamed on the caste
system because Wilkerson assumes the Aryan invasion theory to be
true. But this theory has been rejected based on evidence from science,
linguistics, archaeology, and art history. The figure on the following
page shows the premises behind Wilkerson's thesis.

The deep structures of the Church as a cause of racial bias in European
cultures are simply ignored by her. In explaining the rise of Nazism, she
ignores the role of the Church and pre-Christian European structures
that had nothing to do with India or Vedic thought. She completely
ignores how the persecuted Jews found a new home in India; clearly,
that would not fit her thesis. Wilkerson diverts attention away from
other causes inherent in Western society for its home-grown slavery,
genocide, racism, eugenics, etc. In effect, she normalizes Western racism
as something foreign and Asian.

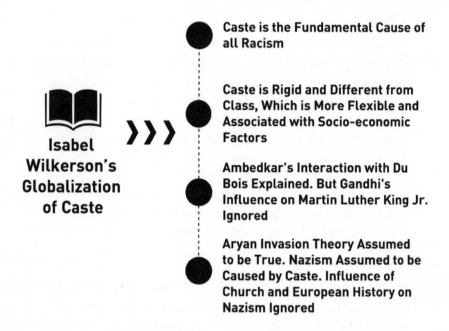

Isabel Wilkerson's Globalization of Caste

Caste is the Fundamental Cause of all Racism

Caste is Rigid and Different from Class, Which is More Flexible and Associated with Socio-economic Factors

Ambedkar's Interaction with Du Bois Explained. But Gandhi's Influence on Martin Luther King Jr. Ignored

Aryan Invasion Theory Assumed to be True. Nazism Assumed to be Caused by Caste. Influence of Church and European History on Nazism Ignored

Hindu Dharma Dismissed as a Frozen and Abusive System

What is being omitted in such definitive conclusions is the history of varna's fluidity, not only across time but also in the diversity across communities. Wilkerson makes it appear as though the Hindu social structure is something permanent, similar to the way Abrahamic religions are frozen in one book. She assumes that social norms have been applied uniformly throughout time and across all Hindu regions. This is simply not the case.

For instance, the history of Indian science and technology reveals that several of India's path-breaking accomplishments in metallurgy, textiles, agriculture, and other fields were pioneered by communities that are presently classified as lower castes. Socio-economic changes caused structural shifts that led to the disempowerment of certain professions. There was fluidity of professions and some that are now considered subordinate and low caste, were actually dominant players. The caste dynamic differed in nature during different periods of Indian history.

The pre-colonial, and pre-Islamic, prosperity of Indian masses of all strata is bypassed by Wilkerson. She also does not adequately consider the impact of one thousand years of colonization, resulting in a culture that has still not been fully decolonized. This experience is unique to Hindu civilization as compared to any other major civilization because neither Christian nor Islamic societies were ever colonized so intensely and for such a prolonged period. One must examine the effects of these different kinds of colonization rather than condemn ancient Vedic culture. This kind of nuancing, contextualizing, and historicizing caste dynamics is absent from Wilkerson's book.

Wilkerson fails to acknowledge solutions to social problems that have risen from within India itself. She totally ignores various religious orders that came about as a way of society correcting course. She also ignores the fact that some of the greatest sages of India, held at the highest altar of worship even today, like Valmiki to whom the *Ramayana* is attributed, were from the lowest strata.

A more balanced view would acknowledge that economies are never static and there is no fixed economic status of a community. Different professions move up and down in their relative financial standing. Market circumstances, politics and other factors change, and power structures are dynamic.

Different regions of India likewise have had different dynamics of caste. The situation in the north is not the same as the situation in the south. Hindus in the Caribbean do not have the same caste dynamics as in India; Hindus of all castes were brought to the Caribbean and enslaved under the cover of indentured labor. Wilkerson is silent on this. Hindus in the US and Canada have adapted socially to their new lands while remaining Hindu. The Hindu diaspora in countries like Hong Kong is also very different. Hinduism, therefore, is not a uniform, homogenous society.

Another blind spot of Wilkerson is that she seems unaware of the strict varna restrictions on Brahmins and Kshatriyas that do not apply to the lower castes. In matters concerning accumulation of wealth and enjoyment of materialistic pleasures, the lower castes are given greater latitude than Brahmins. In the varna system, there are four separate hierarchies corresponding to the four separate varnas, each having its own hierarchy of responsibilities and rights. For instance,

- Brahmins are at the top only as subject-matter experts in formal texts and in the authority to perform rituals. *They are forbidden from holding material wealth,* and most of the material prosperity was earned and enjoyed by the other castes. Thus, they were asked to be poor.
- Kshatriyas have political power, serving in military, courts, and as judges and kings. They are not meant to control economic capital.
- Vaishyas have the dominant position in business and commerce, the equivalent of modern capitalists. But they are not to enter politics.
- Shudras specialized in expertise that is embodied and hands-on. This includes areas like surgery, arts, farming, and so on. Shudras flourished in some past eras and there was even a Shudra dynasty of rulers.

Most Brahmins in the modern workplace are violating their scriptural injunctions that prohibit them from accumulating wealth or holding political power. As per their traditional rules, Brahmins are not supposed to be technology entrepreneurs and wealthy capitalists, nor are they allowed to enter politics. Similarly, industrialists (being Vaishyas) are not meant to enter politics, but many do. Those claiming to be Kshatriyas are not allowed to invest in capital markets. The varna system has fallen apart because the boundaries of each varna's rights and privileges have been violated. These transgressions of traditional safeguards have created some of the problems being criticized.

Clearly, there was no uniform and linear ranking of privileges. The four varnas were parallel and complementary to each other, with separate internal hierarchies. The varnas are better seen as occupational specializations that were initially based on individual qualities and merit. Later, this collapsed into an inherited form of social capital. All these transgressions are fair game for people to criticize, debate, and propose new formulations.

Contrary to the separate prescriptions assigned to each varna, White Americans are not restricted by any such codes. In the United States of America, there are no partitions of the different kinds of social capital into segregated buckets. Whites have enjoyed the top spot in a single homogeneous hierarchy. Therefore, conflating Brahmins with Whites is ridiculous and also self-serving, because it seeks to lay all the blame for any social evils within Western society at the door of the foreigner, thereby strengthening Western Universalism as a standard for the world to follow. The schism between American Blacks and Whites is being explained away by blaming Indians.

Wilkerson equates Brahmins and Whites by saying that they are considered the highest standard of normalcy, beauty, and so on. While this could be considered true of Whites in America because they are projected as possessing the qualities that all non-Whites should aspire to achieve, the same is untrue of Brahmins. She writes:

> A caste system centers the dominant caste as a sun around which all other castes revolve and defines it as the default setting standard of normalcy, of intellect, beauty, against which all others are measured, ranked in descending order by their psychological proximity to the dominant caste.[19]

There is no such thing as Brahmin qualities being the holy grail that all castes must aspire toward. Nor is there any indication in the Indian system of *Natyashastra*, a treatise on the performing arts which also details the concept of beauty, that Brahmins are the most beautiful and Shudras the least.

Wilkerson does not realize that the Indian people, even when poor, take pride in their specific community. It is an identity with cultural significances: festivals, traditions, foods, and specific village deities. This is the richness of Indian diversity. There is a nuanced distinction between the healthy variety of diversity and discriminatory difference; the latter should be fought but not the former. Indian culture is built on contrasts unlike the monoculture of the West. This is not meant to imply that one community is superior and the other inferior but rather the need to recognize, appreciate, and accept the differences, despite the discomfort or anxiety this could create on either side.

One can criticize the varna structure as being outmoded because technology today replaces, or at least disrupts, many of the earlier professions, and it is no longer possible to keep them isolated in separate communities. In fact, 'success' is presently considered the accumulation of all forms of capital (social, wealth, and intellectual), requiring multi-varna competence to succeed. For instance, a businessman (Vaishya) who also has scientific competence (Brahmin) is often found at the height of success – as seen in examples like Elon Musk, Bill Gates, Mark Zuckerberg, Larry Page, and so on.

Varna is one of the most complicated and misunderstood concepts once removed from its Sanskrit context and digested into some other framework. As for caste, there is no universally accepted definition, neither uniform actions on the ground, nor a common understanding among those Indians who are ostensibly inflicted by it. It is being incorrectly essentialized as a rigid pyramid of power and oppression, with no variances over time, location, or any other context, and with no flexibility or possibilities for changes from within the tradition.

Ignoring Other Caste Systems

A crucial point Wilkerson completely misses is that there was no slavery in India before the arrival of the Muslims. (The allegation of slavery in ancient scriptures is based on a mistranslation of the term *dasa* as slave, Shudra as slave, Kshatriya as feudal ruler, and so on.) That slavery was introduced in India during the Muslim rule was evidenced by a major exhibition in 2013 at the New York Public Library organized by African American scholars on how Africans were brought to India as slaves, how several of them later assimilated into Indian society, and how some became local leaders and rulers in their own right.[20]

Academic works also describe the widespread slavery of Hindus during Islamic rule.[21] Indians were routinely taken to slave bazaars in Central Asia and sold, the prices depending on the value of labor in the case of males, and age and looks in the case of females. Eventually, after several generations, some of the survivors managed to reach different parts of Europe where they became outcasts known as the Roma people of Europe (pejoratively called gypsies). Their horrifying story continued in Europe over several centuries of persecution. It culminated in the gas chambers of the Nazis – they were among the millions killed although they aren't included as victims of the 'Holocaust'. (The term 'Holocaust' is reserved only for the Jewish victims.) These are the Dalits of Europe, the result of centuries of Christian persecution.

Another inconvenient fact ignored by Wilkerson is that of a Muslim caste system prevalent in South Asia.[22] The Ashraf caste are the highest and claim to be descendants of Prophet Muhammad, or other Arab chiefs, or Turks, or Persians. The Ajlaf are people of Indian origin who got converted by Islamic invasions; the Arzal are the lowest castes among Muslims. The Urdu word, *quam*, refers to caste and is commonly mentioned in matrimonial advertisements in Pakistan. In theory, caste is ostensibly banned in Islam, and so the politically correct interpretation of quam is ethnicity or community with common heritage. There are communities that identify themselves as Dalit Muslims.[23] Chapter 6 discusses the writings of Ambedkar on the Muslim caste system, and Wilkerson ignores this even though she considers him her icon.

In discussing various systems of bias around the world and linking them to India's caste system, Wilkerson fails to problematize the caste systems within European societies, both pre-Christian, and Christian. European societies were historically stratified according to closed, endogamous social systems with groups such as the nobility, clergy, bourgeoisie, and peasants. A caste system exists in the British royal family that includes privileges by birth, and a certain kind of guaranteed professional hierarchy; there is also pressure to marry internally with other European royals although this is often transgressed in practice.

An especially dark chapter of history omitted by Wilkerson is the record of the Church in India being built on conquests starting from the arrival of the Portuguese in the late fifteenth, and early sixteenth, centuries. This support for the Church continued during the British era when the East India Company and the British government gave away large grants of prime land to the Church. This is the reason that innumerable graveyards, Young Men's Christian Associations, churches, and Christian missionary schools occupy the most prestigious locations in cities across India. Even though Christians comprise less than three percent of India's population, the Church and other Christian institutions own real estate of value far greater than the percentage of the people. Besides, they have a disproportionate ownership of educational institutions that bring in huge revenues and facilitate the enjoyment of political and social oppressive power over the Hindu masses.

In an overcrowded country where demand for education vastly exceeds the supply, some Christian educational institutions sell access to vulnerable families in exchange for their conversion to Christianity.

The carrot is that by converting, one's education fees get waived, that are otherwise extortionist for the average family. These schools with huge financial, cultural, and political capital were created during the colonial era using native land captured by the British. The main call to action by Critical Race Theory is to dismantle all structures erected by oppressors. The Church would have to be included in any such exercise in India.

There is a parallel argument for Muslim rulers' oppression of Hindus. This is about past invaders and has nothing to do with whether today's Indian Muslims are good or bad. Most of them are decent people. The parallel argument would be about the disproportionate amount of land in north India being used up for ostentatious Muslim monuments, massive graveyards, mosques, madrassas, and other developments created during the Islamic era sometimes by breaking down Hindu temples. Muslim rulers also imposed *jizya*, the tax on infidels which forced many Hindus to convert because they could not afford to pay it.

Wilkerson's book has a whole chapter devoted to symbolism in which she justifies the 2017 riots in Charlottesville, Virginia, to bring down the statues of the past White slave masters. She explains that this act was completely justified by Blacks who wanted to rid the symbols of their past oppression. This would have been a good opportunity for her to correlate with India in the way she does on other points throughout her book. But she is completely silent on this issue. She should have stated the fact that in India, Muslim monuments that symbolize past centuries of oppression were built by Muslim rulers to honor themselves.

The reason for her deafening silence is to hide a double standard. When Hindus demand back their sacred sites and the old Islamic colonial structures to be dismantled, they are accused of committing crimes simply for wanting what is legitimately theirs. When Blacks, on the other hand, take over monuments and dismantle the structures of the Whites that symbolize their oppression, it is not considered to be a crime, but rather, an appropriate response.

The reason for this asymmetrical approach is that in India, the present-day minorities (Muslims and Christians) have inherited the structural privileges enjoyed by their ancestors who ruled over the Hindu majority. Yet, nobody dare suggest they are the privileged community.

One should also point out that there is a Harvard University caste system, of which several of Wilkerson's colleagues are privileged members. Indeed, caste-like systems have existed in all cultures worldwide and continues to this day. Much information is available about the Spanish caste system, the varieties of caste systems in African countries, the American caste system, Pakistan's caste system, and even caste systems in China and Japan.[24]

None of this justifies the caste-based biases in India or elsewhere, but the proper diagnosis of a disease is the requisite first step to the development of a viable treatment plan.

Dismantling Hindu Dharma Is Considered Necessary

As is often the case with such writings, Wilkerson focuses on the *karma* (work, action, merit) system as the culprit that has perpetuated the caste abuses. Karma theory, she states, justifies punishing the low caste people:

> The Indian caste system is said to be stable and unquestioned by those within it, bound as it is by religion and in the Hindu belief in reincarnation, the belief that one lives out in this life the karma of the previous ones, in a past life, and that the more keenly one follows the rules for the caste they were born to, the higher their station will be in the next life. Some observers say that this is what distinguishes the Indian caste system from any other, that people in the lowest caste accept their lot, that it is fixed and unbending, that Dalits live out their karma decreed by the gods, and do their lowly work without complaint, knowing not to dream of anything more. In order to survive, some people in a subordinated caste may learn and believe that resistance is futile.[25]

She feels this is similar to how the plight of enslaved Africans was rationalized and, in both cases, there is disregard for the fundamental truth that all human beings want to be free. Equating karma theory with the cause of caste abuse, she sets the stage for arguments to dismantle Hinduism.

Wilkerson does allude to some established theories of caste, including those by prominent Western scholars, that caste is a form of *class* which can be remedied for bias without dismantling the entire system.[26] Such a position is open to the possibilities to remedy caste biases by creating better economic and social opportunities for the lower classes. There are several humanitarian projects where people of all castes unite to help the less fortunate, a trend that has accelerated.

But after briefly acknowledging these views, she is firm in claiming that caste is fundamentally different from class:

> It is the fixed nature of caste that distinguishes it from class, a term to which it is often compared. Class is an altogether separate measure of one's standing in a society, marked by level of education, income, and occupation, as well as the attendant characteristics, such as accent, taste, and manners, that flow from socioeconomic status. These can be acquired through hard work and ingenuity or lost through poor decisions or calamity. If you can act your way out of it, then it is class not caste.[27]

What clinches this deal in her mind is her dogmatic belief that caste is permanently fixed and beyond repair by way of any policies or social remedies. The implication of such a conclusion is that *Hindu dharma must be dismantled to rescue the lower castes.*

Wilkerson falls into the trap of reductionism. She wants to portray 'Caste ➜ Racism' as a single, overarching, universal cause of social abuses. A more coherent analysis would consider multiple causes for social biases. For example, could masculinity also be a cause for social bias, in which case it would have nothing to do with India-specific caste issues?

Wilkerson celebrates a Hindu man's gesture of casting away his *janeu* (sacred thread worn mostly by Brahmins) as an anti-caste gesture. She calls this a powerful renunciation of caste. The implication is that just as Critical Race Theory demands all to prove their anti-racist bona fides, Hindus must be pressured to renounce their symbols, traditions, practices, texts, festivals, and rituals in order to be Woke. But she has not asked her Black community to give up the Church and renounce Christianity to demonstrate that they are being anti-racist.

In response to her book, we raise the following ethical questions: Are such critics going too far in blaming the caste system and as a result, making all abuses inseparable from Hinduism, such that Hinduism must be dismantled? Would one take a similar position that because of sexual abuses in the Catholic Church one must dismantle Catholicism? Or that because of abuses in Islam, one must dismantle Islam? Or because of abuses of racism and casteism in Africa among the Africans, one must call for all Black culture to be dismantled?

On the one hand, Wilkerson is very concerned about dehumanizing any group because it is then easy to harm individuals within that group solely because of them belonging to it. But she needs to know that her work plays into the hands of those very forces that are dehumanizing Hindus. This is happening rapidly and turning Hindus into a defenseless people that do not deserve to be treated fairly because of allegations that they are predators and oppressors. She disapproves of people becoming slaves to group think and yet, group thinking against Hinduism is precisely what her work is causing. She is also against the use of oppression to assert control but does not address that the academic harassment of Hindus on campuses is actually a form of that very oppression.

Finally, the entire movement calling for Hindu dharma to be dismantled ignores the Hindu contributions to raise American consciousness through yoga, meditation, vegetarianism, ecology, and so on. One could argue that only at higher levels of consciousness can we solve these problems and not from the lower levels of consciousness prevalent today. Problems are best solved by transcending them and looking at them from a higher viewpoint. The Hindu idea of *tat-tvam-asi*, that everyone is originally divine and there is no eternal sinner, and the idea of *vasudhaiva kutumbakam*, that all living creatures are one family, are examples of built-in resources to help humankind. Wilkerson ignores the Bhakti Movement, a devotional movement that removed caste boundaries across India. This was an internal development that transcended social barriers.

Chapter 6 gives a more detailed response to her misrepresentations of Indian social structures and history.

3

Indian Americans Equated With White Racists

Overview

This chapter details how biased research driven by deep envy against the Indian American community has been causing mayhem in American workplaces where large numbers of employees are of Indian origin. It explains the following:

- A new ecosystem of American activism has emerged that has been collecting data on caste in America – spanning industries, universities, and government – and lobbying to change laws and policies that would result in caste becoming formally recognized as a form of racism under the laws of the US.

- Equality Labs, an organization run by Thenmozhi Soundararajan, is at the heart of a smear campaign against Indians. She uses her Dalit identity and plays the victim role to appeal to the guilt of White Americans. Her organization is not registered as a non-profit because that would subject it to disclosing its sources and uses of funds transparently to the public.

- Its flagship product is a single report on caste in the American workplace. The methodology used was full of glaring problems. At least two other reports on the same subject by well-established research organizations have disagreed with its findings.

- Equality Labs has scored significant legal and policy victories using US laws on racism to file charges of caste bias. Its actions will have devastating consequences for Indian Americans and Hindus everywhere, as well as the institutional structures of the US, India, and worldwide.

- There is a systematic incubation of Dalit leadership underway in Western universities and Leftist organizations that is then exported back to India. As we shall see in Part 2, Harvard University is the main hub where this is being done. This US-centric ecosystem has its tentacles deep into Indian institutions.
- Equality Labs has gathered a coalition of US-based organizations that share a common anti-India posture. It has used sensationalism and a well-coordinated campaign to become positioned as the authority on caste for American organizations. It demands employers to conduct caste censuses of Indian employees as a step towards dismantling casteism in their employees. Such censuses and training workshops for management have become a major source of income for Equality Labs.
- Equality Labs, it seems, assumes every Indian and Hindu is guilty of casteism unless proven otherwise. There is no other national origin or religion that has been singled out and treated likewise in the US.

As mentioned earlier, we are very concerned about any kind of bias, including those based on caste. Whenever there is a legitimate case, it should be addressed through legal means. But we oppose exaggerations, falsifications and reductionist theories of blame, excessive victimhood, divisive approaches, and so on.

Compiling US Databases of Indian American Caste Abuses

The US-based Equality Labs group is self-described as a Dalit 'power-building' organization. It suddenly became well-known after publishing a report alleging widespread caste discrimination in the United States within the South Asian diaspora.[1] Through effective messaging to impact progressive Western audiences, the organization has successfully convinced several governmental, educational, and corporate institutions to accept its views and policy recommendations regarding Indian Americans, especially Hindus. In 2016, it received its first grant and began collecting responses for its marquis survey on caste in the United States.[2]

The founder and chief firebrand of Equality Labs, Thenmozhi Soundararajan, was born in California to a cardiologist father, an immigrant from Tamil Nadu, India.[3] She studied at the University of California, Berkeley, and the University of Southern California, School of Cinematic Arts.[4] She has also been affiliated with the MIT Open Documentary Lab, a project that brings 'storytellers, technologists, and scholars together to explore new documentary forms'. Imitating Black History Month, she has launched Dalit History Month.

Soundararajan's methods include media activism, litigation, and diversity and inclusion-related training courses. Equality Labs' website states that its mission is to use

> community research, political base-building, culture-shifting art, and digital security to end the oppression of caste apartheid, Islamophobia, white supremacy, and religious intolerance. Through these methods, we provide practical tools for communities to make new interventions in longstanding systems of oppression and advocate for themselves.[5]

Its flagship accomplishment that gave Equality Labs considerable political clout was its 2018 report, *Caste in the United States*. This fifty-two-page report immediately generated substantial media coverage in the US, India, and even China. Some of its key claims included the following shocking statistics concerning Dalits living in the US:

- Sixty-seven percent reported unfair treatment in their workplaces
- Twenty percent encountered caste discrimination at a place of business
- Forty percent experienced a romantic rejection based on caste
- Twenty-five percent faced caste-related verbal or physical assault

The reader must note that these surveys and the report pertain to Dalits based in the US and not India. Several issues have been raised about the methodological sloppiness and built-in prejudices that undermine the reliability of the conclusions. For instance:

- The US census has never identified Dalits as a category, so it is impossible to estimate the number of Dalits in the US.
- No distinction was made between unfair treatment at work

due to racism from non-Indians and specific caste-based discrimination.

- The survey was distributed by Equality Labs' activists to people they selected and was not representative of the broader Indian American population. This could be the reason that almost thirty percent of respondents identified as non-heterosexual (further categorized into bisexual, homosexual, pansexual, and queer). These numbers appear statistically skewed.

- Equality Labs eliminated twenty percent of the responses for being 'extreme or illogical' entirely using its own subjective criteria that have never been disclosed transparently.

- It also admitted that there was no scientifically valid statistical sampling. For example, there was no external verification of reported caste affiliation (and no consistently applied methodology for self-identification as one 'caste' or another).[6]

The results of this report must be compared with two other caste-related surveys outside India conducted by well-established institutions. One was on caste in the Indian American community undertaken in 2021 by Carnegie Endowment, in partnership with Johns Hopkins University and University of Pennsylvania (UPenn). The report stated the following concerning the claims in the Equality Labs findings:

> This study [by Equality Labs] relied on a nonrepresentative snowball sampling method to recruit respondents. ... respondents who did not disclose a caste identity were dropped from the data set. ... the sample does not fully represent the South Asian American population and could skew it in favor of those who have strong views about caste. While the existence of caste discrimination in India is incontrovertible, its precise extent and intensity in the United States can be contested.[7]

The Carnegie Endowment report discovered that the majority of approximately 4.2 million people of Indian descent in the US do not 'personally identify with a caste group of any kind', and that only 1% of Hindus reported belonging to a Dalit or Scheduled Caste (SC) community. Less than five percent of Dalits reported having faced caste-based discrimination. A significant number of those claiming caste-based discrimination said that they faced such discrimination at the hands of non-Indians.[8] All this contradicts and undermines Equality Labs' findings.

The other, far more thorough survey on caste discrimination in UK, was carried out by the National Institute of Economic and Social Research. Their 121-page report stated that 'caste exists in Britain: this is not in dispute' but went on to acknowledge that uncovering the extent of caste discrimination in the UK would require an extensive survey entailing complexities, resources, and timelines beyond the scope of their study.[9] This would be particularly challenging given that the British population has not been segmented by caste and hence reliable data on who belongs to a given caste is simply unavailable.

Despite the obvious flaws, biases, and sweeping nature of its conclusions, the Equality Labs report received extensive mainstream media coverage in *The New York Times, The Washington Post, BBC, NPR, Bloomberg*, and other prominent publications.[10] These media outlets did not care to do any due diligence before supporting the report's findings as the gospel truth. Many public intellectuals, such as Harvard Divinity School's former professor from the Black community, Cornel West, also endorsed the report, without addressing any counter positions on the subject as a scholar must when reviewing peers' work. The media did not bother to invite Hinduism experts to their interviews and discussions.

An Indian American Democrat member of the US Congress, Pramila Jayapal, provided a major boost to Equality Labs. In 2019, she partnered with Equality Labs, South Asian Americans Leading Together, and API Chaya to organize a Congressional briefing on caste.[11] Jayapal along with Ro (Rohit) Khanna, a fellow Democrat member of the US Congress, went on to partner with Equality Labs in 2021 to introduce a resolution commemorating B.R. Ambedkar.[12] We want the world to honor Ambedkar, but this should not get muddled with agenda-driven mediocre reports.

Equality Labs is not registered as a non-profit organization obligated to publicly disclose finances or be subject to the same stringent limitations as imposed on political campaigners in the US. This seems like a clever ploy to keep its financials secret from the public.

But indirect sources confirm strong funding support from Leftist non-profits such as those related to Omidyar Network.[13] It operates as part of a broader coalition of South Asian activist organizations that help amplify its messages. The diagram below shows some of the organizations helping disseminate Equality Labs' propaganda.[14]

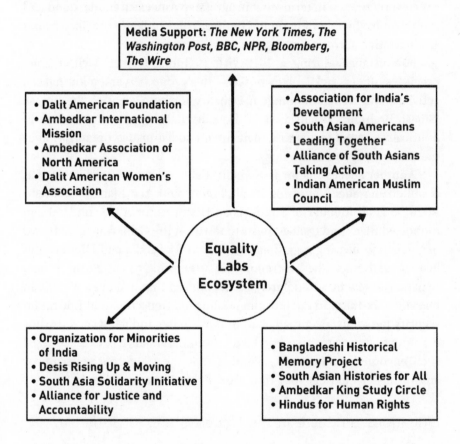

Some of these organizations were also associated with Rutgers University associate professor, Audrey Truschke, and her events such as the Dismantling Global Hindutva Conference held in 2021. For her work 'to fight impunity, state violence, anti-blackness, caste apartheid, and religious intolerance', Soundararajan was awarded the 'Atlantic Fellowship' by the renowned Rhodes Trust.[15]

Equality Labs has been particularly successful in garnering support from second generation Indian American social media influencers such as Alok Vaid-Menon and publications such as *Brown Girl Magazine*. An important reason for its success has been the sophisticated quality of its messages, tailored to specific audiences, especially non-Indians. Its views on caste, Hinduism, and the Indian American community are reductive, hateful, erroneous, and even ridiculous. Nevertheless, they are cleverly framed in terms that progressive Americans understand and can relate to, by mapping on to Hinduism and India the familiar tropes and narrative surrounding race in a Western context.

For instance, during a 2018 visit to India, former Twitter chief executive officer, Jack Dorsey posed with a group of women journalists, activists, and writers holding an Equality Labs poster with the phrase 'Smash Brahminical Patriarchy'.[16] Equality Labs' sponsors refer to it in politically correct terms as a mainstream social justice organization at the cutting edge of technology.

Another success factor is Equality Labs' aggressive leadership that is bulldozing ahead by using its alignment with the Black movement. In 2017, as co-founder of South Asian Histories for All, Soundararajan mobilized Black and Dalit activists to testify at the California State Board of Education hearing regarding the portrayal of India and Hinduism in history textbooks. She was reportedly attempting to cut ahead in line, bypassing a few hundred parents and children that had been waiting in line since six-thirty in the morning. California Department of Education security personnel eventually had to remove her and fellow activists for disruptive and aggressive conduct.[17] Soundararajan has characterized such encounters differently, claiming that the California government authorities ejected her four times for 'being Dalit American'.[18]

Litigations on Caste in the United States of America

There are three main areas in the US in which the research and lobbying activities of Equality Labs and its affiliates have started making shock waves: corporates, university and college campuses, and local governments. These will be illustrated with prominent examples as indicated in the diagram opposite.

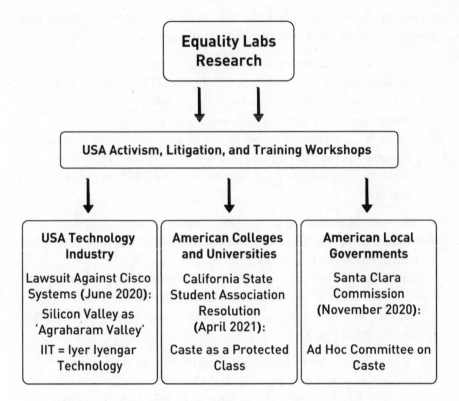

The US Technology Industry

The 2018 report by Equality Labs laid the groundwork for litigation targeting Indian and Hindu Americans, particularly in California. In June 2020, the California Department of Fair Employment and Housing filed a lawsuit against Cisco Systems for alleged caste discrimination on behalf of an anonymous 'Indian Dalit'. The agency claimed Cisco was over-represented by a 'South Asian Indian' workforce and neglected to protect the rights of Dalit employees that are 'the darkest complexion of castes' from facing discrimination and harassment from colleagues enforcing a 'strict Hindu religious and social hierarchy'. The complaint stated that Cisco had failed to prevent 'inequalities associated with caste status, ritual purity, and social exclusion' from its workplace.[19]

The supporting evidence for this was provided by Equality Labs. It further accused Cisco that its caste abusers came from the IITs, which according to Soundararajan, is 'notorious for casteist thinking and processes and policies'.[20] It complained that:

> Upper caste students and faculty that create that very hostile cultures in those academic institutions (like IITs), then go on to create casteist alumni networks in Silicon Valley tech companies. These companies often hire through a process called "internal referrals" ... it's basically caste networking, ... [which] often feed in same folks in same castes, so you have entire departments of multiple companies that are often made up of ONLY upper caste managers.[21]

Hence, Soundararajan wants to make companies 'caste competent'. She sees the Cisco case as having global consequences and feels that it will have an even bigger impact in India than in the US.

Cisco responded that it investigated the matter thoroughly and found no evidence of any caste-based discrimination. Though Cisco is defending itself, its vice president of human resources started to appease critics in a public post:

> While caste is most frequently used to refer to distinctions in Indian society, the concept is a useful one for understanding many different kinds of discrimination based on hereditary characteristics. Isabel Wilkerson, whose *Warmth of Other Suns* helped me understand the insidious nature of anti-Black racism in the US, has written a magnificent new book applying the concept to US racism, titled *Caste: The Origin of Our Discontents*.[22]

The Ambedkar International Centre (AIC) sought amicus curiae status in the case, and the Ambedkar King Study Circle and Hindus for Human Rights joined as well. John Rushing, an attorney representing AIC, told *The Wire*:

> Caste is also a form of race and colour discrimination, both of which are outlawed by California. ... All Dalits are South Asian, and in California, discriminating against someone based on race is illegal. ...If the complainant was not South Asian, and belonged to any other race, he would not have been subjected to caste discrimination.[23]

An article in *The Washington Post* accuses upper caste workers in the US of closing ranks and blocking the hiring of low caste workers. Equality Labs is cited as saying that Dalits have been subject to 'slurs and jokes, bullying, discriminatory hiring practices, bias in peer reviews, and sexual harassment' in tech companies including Google, Facebook, Microsoft, and IBM. Each of these companies has denied the charges of caste bias in their hiring or promotion policies.[24]

Two high-profile Indian American academicians from Harvard and New York University took the matter to *The New York Times*. They used the lawsuits against Cisco and BAPS (one of the largest Hindu organizations in the US) to lobby for the criminalization of caste under US law.[25] They said, 'Making caste a protected category is a critical step toward addressing the problem of caste in America'.[26] This means giving caste the same legal status as racism under the law.

Another article alleges: 'Students from Dalit and other marginalized castes routinely face comments about the color of one's skin, clothes one wears, and general ridicule even over surnames, often seen as classic markers of one's caste identity'. It cites a report by Equality Labs that low caste students face 'micro-aggressions' on American campuses. Equality Labs refers to Silicon Valley as 'Agraharam Valley' (Agraharam being an ancient farm grant given by royalty for Brahmins to practice their traditions). They have nicknamed the IITs as 'Iyer Iyengar Technology', Iyer and Iyengar being common Brahmin names.[27]

This level of media coverage is very unusual given the large numbers of employment discrimination cases filed every day across the US that do not receive similar, or any, attention. Equality Labs has become a catalyst for igniting conversations around caste in the tech world putting Indians and Hindus on the defensive. Such media activism also aims to lobby for caste-based quotas for H-1B work visas to US, replacing merit as the criteria.

We do not deny that there may well be individual instances of caste-based discrimination that take place in the American workplace. They can, and should be, redressed through the laws and corporate policies that are already broadly encompassing. The problem with Equality Labs' proposal is that caste would become the only protected category that singles out as the oppressor one specific religion (Hinduism), one country (India) and one racial group (Indian Americans). For example,

other protected categories like race, gender, sexual orientation, etc.,
are agnostic as to who may be the perpetrator and who may be the
victim (e.g., a woman can sexually harass a man). Here, Hindus and
Indians are being singled out as the only category of oppressor. This
demonizes one particular class of people unlike all the other categories.
For instance, there is no equivalent protected category of 'infidel' with
Islam designated as the oppressor.

Moreover, in an environment where it is inappropriate and
illegal to require people to disclose their racial, sexual, religious and
other affiliations, it would not be appropriate to require disclosure
of caste affiliations (especially when most Hindus in America do not
identify themselves with any caste) in order to monitor caste-based
discrimination. What if a Brahmin woman marries one from a lower
caste or a White person? In traditional Hinduism, birth caste has been
changed to that of their spouse; will corporate policies around caste-
based discrimination support this?

The media machinery of Equality Labs and its affiliated activists
have begun using the Cisco lawsuit to pressure other Silicon Valley
tech employers. Its messaging is that Cisco is guilty of hiring significant
numbers of employees from upper caste Indian Hindu backgrounds that
adhere to a regressive and rigid Hindu social hierarchy. Cisco should
have been aware that caste discrimination would exist among such a
workforce, and ought to have offered anti-caste training and included
caste in its corporate human resources policies.

Equality Labs has put out a call to collect information about instances
of caste-based discrimination in several US tech companies creating
an intimidating atmosphere to embarrass Indians. This also confuses
HR departments because they see two groups of Indians that look the
same and have similar sounding names. Corporate staff in diversity and
inclusion are also being forced to get involved; they are confused by
these heavily charged inaccurate and negative stereotypes. Activists are
demanding corporate management take a deep dive to understand caste
as an issue of racial prejudice.

Since American industry is uncomfortable dealing with this subject,
Equality Labs and its affiliates are offering 'caste competency trainings' to
become politically correct and safe from attacks. In other words, its team
of activists show up to coach large American corporates, and thereby

protect them from being accused of caste discrimination. Equality Labs has thus created a thriving business for itself.

In 2020, US companies promised thirty-five billion dollars toward racial equality efforts.[28] 'Several consultants in the diversity, equity and inclusion field say that summer 2020 was the busiest period of their careers to date'.[29] This was a combination of COVID-19, and protests over the killing of George Floyd. Companies often cut the risk of lawsuits by signaling their stance on diversity. They accomplish it by allocating a budget for Diversity, Equality, Inclusiveness (DEI) training:

> Dozens of companies and institutions have sought to deflect controversy over embarrassing missteps or revelations of homogeneous boards and workplaces by launching high-profile initiatives or enlisting a person of color for a prominent post.[30]

We have heard from Indians working in the US headquarters of Microsoft, Facebook, and others, that they are required to attend these 'caste sensitivity training' workshops. They find the content to be sensationalized, one-sided, and outright humiliating. But nobody speaks out from fear of being branded 'casteist', 'racist', etc.

The impact of such lawsuits and intimidating tactics is likely to be far-reaching for companies that employ large numbers of Indians. To track and prevent workplace discrimination, the United States Equal Employment Opportunity Commission requires firms with over one hundred employees to submit demographic data on employees' race/ethnicity, sex, job category, and salary.[31] Similar requirements exist at the state level. Once caste is classified as race and explicitly covered under such laws, *companies will be required to conduct a census and officially classify their Indian and Hindu employees by caste.*

The strange fact is that American corporate HR departments, civil rights enforcement agencies, and courts have gone on a frenzy of activities based on a single unverified report. This lack of due diligence should set off alarm bells even for those sympathetic to Equality Labs' agenda.

American Colleges and Universities

Similar to the tech industry, American college and university campuses also have large Indian populations. On some campuses, caste has recently been designated as a 'protected class', a formal term with legal consequences. Under US federal and state laws, a protected class is a group of people with a common characteristic that are legally protected from employment discrimination on the basis of that characteristic. Federal protected classes include race, skin color, religion or creed, national origin or ancestry, sex (including gender, pregnancy, sexual orientation, and gender identity), age, physical or mental disability, and so on.

Activists are lobbying to have caste added to this list. As a consequence, all kinds of US establishments will start compiling data on the castes of their employees, which in practice means profiling those of Indian origin, and report this data to prove that they do not discriminate based on caste. This will of course open the floodgates for 'caste experts' to offer consulting to the establishments.

We have written extensively about Hinduphobia being prevalent in US academia, particularly in South Asian Studies departments. This move, to profile upper caste Indians as oppressors that must feel guilty of their identity, would undermine all the work done over the past quarter century to fight Hinduphobia. Hindu students and faculty would hide their identity or feel apologetic for it, for fear of being targeted as racists.

Brandeis University in Massachusetts has now included caste in its anti-discrimination and harassment policy,[32] as has University of California, Davis.[33] Several other campuses are at various stages of adding caste to their official non-discrimination policies.[34] University authorities are responding to pressure tactics by some student and faculty activists. Presently, caste is under consideration for the California State University system that has twenty-three campuses across the state of California. In April 2021, the California State Student Association unanimously passed a resolution demanding the addition of caste as a protected class, directing the board of trustees to update their policies and provide resources to better their understanding of caste.[35] This was the first resolution of its kind in any statewide university system. It described caste as a 'structure of oppression that affects over 1 billion people across the world', and stated that the system comprises Brahmins, Kshatriyas, Vaishyas, and Shudras, and those outside the caste system entirely (i.e., Dalits).[36]

The resolution citing the Equality Labs report, and the Cisco case, stated:

> WHEREAS: All of these inequalities associated with caste status have become embedded in all of the major South Asian American institutions and ... American mainstream institutions that have significant South Asian immigrant populations, with some of the caste social locators being last names, whether a family eats meat, whether they own land in their country of origin, who they want to marry or be in romantic relationships with, and whether they are allowed to be out in their place of worship and community;[37]

The resolution also explicitly called for compliance with the mandates of Equality Labs:

> WHEREAS: The addition of caste within the anti-discrimination policy will make Cal Poly and the larger CSUs in compliance with the recommendations of Equality Labs, an international human rights organization;[38]

And concludes:

> THEREFORE BE IT RESOLVED: The addition of caste as a protected category should be paired with caste competency trainings during hiring at Cal Poly and the CSU at large.[39]

As with the Cisco case, such wording begs the question of who precisely would adjudicate whether a Hindu's vegetarian diet or marriage to a same caste person shows caste discrimination. Would Indian origin students and faculty be justified to complain against a university imposing the mandates of Equality Labs so blatantly, and using its 'training' to formulate its policies? Is it discriminatory on part of university administrators with little background on the complexities of caste to explicitly target Hindus?

American Local Governments

Caste has also made a sudden entry into politics at the county level of governments in the US. For instance, a proposal was submitted to Santa Clara County in the heart of Silicon Valley. This is where many of the tech giants that employ large numbers of Indian-origin workers are located.[40] Hence, it is a high-profile jurisdiction selected to maximize the sensationalism.

According to public records, Soundararajan met with the Santa Clara County Commission in November 2020 and convinced them to unanimously approve setting up an ad hoc committee:[41]

> Thenmozhi Soundararajan, Equality Labs, provided information relating to the historical background of caste systems, caste system hierarchy, and caste systems in the modern world. (and) ... relating to widespread caste discrimination in South Asia and the United States. Ms. Soundararajan recounted acts of caste discrimination in the workplace, education institutions, and everyday life.
>
> Chairperson Boren expressed appreciation to Ms. Soundararajan for bringing awareness to this issue. In response to an inquiry from Commissioner Chaykin, Ms. Soundararajan stated that the mission of Equality Labs is to establish caste as protected category, not the caste system to be a protected category, and expressed interest in a public forum to address the issues and provide a platform to the public to share their stories.[42]

A review began on whether to formally pursue caste as an issue, paving the way for policies to track and prevent caste discrimination. The local Indian community also got involved and participated in a public forum where invited 'experts' expressed their views to help inform the commission's decision.[43]

While ostensibly the ad hoc committee was an impartial volunteer body, its vice chairman, Justin Boren, associate professor of communication at Santa Clara University, tweeted a link on the public meeting in which he tagged the accounts of Equality Labs, Dalit Women Fight, Congressman Ro Khanna, Ash Kalra, and Rob (Robert Andres) Bonta (California attorney general). Khanna and Kalra are both well-known supporters of the Left-wing of the Democratic Party and Senator Bernie Sanders. Nobody representing an alternative perspective was included.

During the public hearing, Vice Chairman Boren and Chairman Bryan Franzen repeatedly interrupted representatives of Hindu organizations. They cut off a Dalit representing himself as a proud Hindu on the grounds that his criticism of Equality Labs was tantamount to 'attacking' it. On the other hand, the commission granted Equality Labs considerable latitude, and even allowed someone claiming to 'have caste privilege' with an insider perspective to lash out at upper caste people as being 'violently oppressive' towards lower castes.[44]

Among the 'experts' invited were several anonymous individuals, including one described as 'an expert on H-1B and caste'; another identified merely as a 'Pakistani Dalit professor'; and yet another who was a self-described 'Dalit Queer Non-Binary'. Ajantha Subramanian, professor of anthropology at Harvard was also an invited speaker. She justified the anonymity of these 'experts', saying that 'the number of Dalits testifying anonymously at this very forum attest to the fact that the stigma of caste and the fear of exposure has followed them to the US'. Subramanian advocated for systemic data collection on caste in the US because it could be used to compel academic and technology sectors to set up 'institutional mechanisms' addressing caste discrimination. Her work at Harvard is discussed in the next chapter, and her extreme bias comes out loud and clear.

Equality Labs and related organizations mobilized a considerable number of persons to testify in their favor, including multiple second-generation Indian Americans apologizing for being 'caste-privileged' and condemning the alleged rampant casteism, anti-Blackness, Islamophobia, and gaslighting within their families and communities. Several non-South Asians also testified in favor of Equality Labs.

The Ambedkar King Study Circle issued the following press release following the first session:

> Some of the sharpest commentary came from a speaker who argued that just as she, a white American woman, was in no position to define or refute non-white peoples' experiences of racism, members of dominant castes were in no position to deny that casteist discrimination exists. Her comment was clearly a response to the multiple dominant-caste speakers who repeatedly accused Dalit and Bahujan speakers of fabricating their stories.[45]

Members of the public waiting to testify exceeded the commission's expectations and the session lasted almost eight hours. A second meeting was held during which the commission deferred taking a final decision on whether to pursue caste in its work plan. Chairman Franzen admitted that the issue was far more complex than he had originally assumed. Nevertheless, documentation of the proceedings on the Santa Clara County website still relies on materials provided by Equality Labs and its allies. There are also numerous letters sent by members of the Hindu American community.

A particularly notable document listed on the commission's website is a resolution passed by the National Association for the Advancement of Colored People (NAACP), one of the oldest and most respected civil rights organizations in the United States. It starts with the mention of Rev. Martin Luther King Jr. identifying himself as an 'untouchable'.

The resolution's following allegations against Hindu groups are unsubstantiated and particularly harsh:

> WHEREAS any criticism of caste is lamented as attack on Hinduism by the Hindutva groups. In the Cisco caste discrimination lawsuit, a Hindutva group filed a motion in the California Supreme Court that allegation of caste discrimination is an intervention by the Department of Fair Employment and Housing in Hindu's religious liberty and rights. In California textbook issue the Hindu right-wing groups mobilized 1000s of people including the children to deny the practice of caste in the USA; and
>
> WHEREAS the practice of caste in the workplace is an extension of practice of caste by the South Asians in their day-to-day life; with privileged castes in the hiring-and-firing positions in big corporates, control the social and cultural organizations through money power and social networks and access to public offices; left the Dalits more vulnerable.[46]

Such an official resolution, passed by the powerful NAACP and used in legal proceedings across the US is potentially dangerous for Hindus in America. More specifically, Hinduism and 'Hindutva' are being explicitly targeted as the culprits behind this purported discrimination. This is tantamount to ascribing slavery and apartheid to Christianity and monitoring one's adherence to Christian tradition as a metric for determining how racist they are. No one would dare that with any other major religious tradition in the world, except for Hinduism.

Issues and Challenges

Equality Labs is playing the lead role in all the legal cases and proposals/ resolutions. It is using its strong presence among students and scholars to promote theories of a rigid caste system, the culprit of which is Hindu dharma. Its allegations claim caste as a Hindu doctrinal practice of a criminal kind. The low castes are said to be dark-skinned and upper castes as light-skinned as a way to play into the emotions of America's Black/White race politics.

Media coverage in all cases across the board has the same narrative and it is the same experts that are paraded from one interview to another. This amounts to branding the entire Indian American community as racists that deserve to be attacked by the ultra-Left Woke movement. Corporations and campuses are being pressured to become suspicious of Indians as a liability. This could impact their hiring and professional advancement, and make them insecure in their inter-personal dynamics in the workplace.

All these cases are premised on defining Hinduism as inherently bigoted and oppressive. But the American Constitution prohibits an organ of the state to delve into questions of religious doctrine, and the government does not have the right to define what a person's religion is. Besides, every citizen has the right to know his/her rights and responsibilities, and any notice about violations must clearly point out how the law is being violated. Such laws and their enforcement cannot be subjective, arbitrary, based on hearsay, and so on. The fact is that if one asks a random panel of Indians what the meaning of caste is, varying answers will come forth. Without a formal, widely accepted definition, how could caste become a cause for litigation? Even if there was consensus on a definition, it would be challenging for corporates or campuses to go about determining what a given individual's caste is.

There is the unsubstantiated presumption that a Hindu of Indian descent is necessarily identifying himself/herself by caste and exercising prejudice as per the theory of caste hierarchy. Would people with Indian sounding names therefore, be required to carry certificates of their caste? If this were done to Hindus, why would the same not apply to other ethnic or minority groups and people of other national origins? There is also the issue that many Hindus do not know anything about their caste, such as those whose ancestors came as indentured laborers to Guyana, Trinidad, Bahamas, etc. Second- and third-generation Hindu immigrants to the US, those born of mixed-race marriages, and those who are White Hindus or Black Hindus – most of them are clueless about their caste.

This opens up challenges of equal protection that is guaranteed under the American Constitution, because these activists want to create a class that will be suspect in the eyes of the law, and also because a special set of policies will be applicable only to them.

Of special concern to Indian Americans are the following issues: In a situation involving workplace discrimination, how might an American corporate human resources executive, judge, or jury harbor preconceived prejudice? Would businesses ask employees of Indian origin to list their caste? Would they adopt the Indian government's official caste classifications? Would they assume that a Marathi Brahmin enjoys hegemonic caste privilege over a Telugu Reddy in the same sense as Whites do over Blacks? Would a Gujarati Patel's vegetarian diet be considered evidence of casteism in a discrimination complaint? Would Hindus become subject to blatant hate speech because it becomes tougher for them to defend themselves? Will the bullying of Hindu students being documented in US schools get worse? Will it be justified for Jewish students to demand kosher kitchens in colleges, but considered casteist if Hindu students demand vegetarian food choices?

These must be addressed as American issues under US laws, (even if hypothetically, the Government of India was truly 'fascist') because Hindu Americans have the same right of religious freedom.

Globalizing the Dalit Empowerment Movement

In a 2014 interview, Thenmozhi Soundarajan explained that although she 'came out' as Dalit during her undergraduate studies, it was in the fifth grade she discovered that the Bhopal chemical disaster (a gas leak that occurred at the Bhopal plant of Union Carbide India Limited pesticide plant in 1984) had impacted a group called the Untouchables, which is when her parents told her about her ancestry. In another interview she claimed that Indian Americans in southern California would not allow her to use their main dishware and cutlery at parties hosted in their homes. She says her family had left India to escape caste, and when she publicly announced her Dalit identity, she got blacklisted by upper caste Indian professors and even received death threats.

Soundararajan is being groomed as a leader evidenced by the sheer number of awards she has received.

> Her work has been recognized by the Producers Guild of America Diversity Program, The Museum of Contemporary Art, The Robert Rauschenberg Foundation, Chicken & Egg Foundation, The Annenberg Innovation Center, Slamdance, MIT Center for New Media Studies, The Sorbonne, *The Source* Magazine, *Utne Reader*, The National Center for the Humanities, The National Science Foundation, The Indian Film Festival of Los Angeles and The Alfred P. Sloan Foundation.[47]

Equality Labs describes itself as an Ambedkarite power-building organization, representing both a specific Indian religious and political lens, as well as contemporary American social justice in its messaging and political organizing. Its grassroots agenda involves targeting various expressions of Hindu faith and identity. For example, in a blog titled, *Why Do We Say No To Holi? A Guide To Challenge Casteism*, it excoriated the festival of Holi due to its alleged connections with the 'violent overthrow of an Indigenous king', the murder of Holika (a Dalit), and its marginalization of caste oppression and indigenous peoples' traditions by 'settler colonial' Brahmins. Its call to action was:

> Desist from celebrating it yourself and resist cultural attempts to saffron-wash its violent history.... Share the Bahujan version of the story during dinner. Educate folks about the Brahmanical (sic) control of the history of India, and connect it to the rise of the BJP, Hindu Fascism, and upper caste networks of power. ... Similar to how progressive Americans do not celebrate Thanksgiving to honor Indigenous resistance, think about ways to build power, and support efforts of caste abolition. Share a meal, read Dalit and Bahujan history, and honor leaders who are not from upper caste and Brahmin families.[48]

It has rapidly adopted political mobilization strategies tested in multiple marginalized communities, including those without substantial financial resources. Equality Labs focuses on building a grassroots network of sustainable professional organizations and mobilizing people for direct action in the form of protests, participation in public forums, engaging the media, and crafting legislation.

Within five years, it has successfully reinterpreted the popular narratives of Indian and Hindu Americans being a successful American minority community. The new narrative it has established widely is that the reason for the community's success is the regressive and discriminatory practices they embody due to their religious affiliation. Thus, the new branding is: Wherever Indians go, they take caste with them.

Equality Labs has generated highly impactful atrocity literature tailored to mainstream donors as well as decision makers in government, academia, and corporations. It has the capacity to run multiple campaigns in parallel that set the public narrative using the media very effectively. The doors of elite media, academia, and top-level policy-makers have been thrown open to them. As a result of its orchestrated legal action against BAPS, the Hindu American population, despite its claims of being powerfully positioned in US industry and politics, has been put on the defensive and made to look suspicious in the eyes of the public. We support pursuing justice where crimes have been committed. If, for example, BAPS violated labor laws, it ought to be held accountable. But that should not implicate an entire community just like crimes committed by Muslims, Blacks or Christians in America do not result in such branding of those identities.

The concept of Hinduphobia is also being challenged because Hindus are being stigmatized as perpetrators of criminal hostilities against their oppressed Dalit fellow-Americans. As is clear from the legal cases discussed earlier, the presence of a large Hindu population of well-established individuals makes little difference in officials' and administrators' willingness to support Equality Labs.

Equality Labs' activism is loaded with false allegations. For instance, in 2020, a Dartmouth College student accused three Hindu professors of harassing her for being a Muslim. She also said that 'she believed that Hindus like seeing Muslims being tortured'.

Maha Hasan Alshawi further alleged that Prof. Prasad Jayanti was a member of an 'Anti-Muslim organisation named Rashtriya Swayamsevak

Sangh (RSS)'. She also claimed that he directed a graduate student to inquire about her religion. As to the report that Respondent Jayanti was a member of an anti-Muslim organization, there was insufficient information to support that allegation.[49]

Unfortunately, there is no comparable Indian grassroots organization in the US constantly carrying out similar activities on behalf of Indian Americans operating across corporates, governments, campuses, and media. It will need to be proactive and continuous, and not just reactive to problems. It will need to be professional according to the highest American standards, and frame issues in American idiom.

A Silver Lining

The work of Equality labs may have a silver lining, after all. Finally, it forces the Hindu to fight for himself or herself because the battle is becoming personal. The battle is entering each Hindu's workplace, home and family, and they can no longer run away from uncomfortable situations like they have been doing to date.

But even more encouraging is the recent shift in what Thenmozhi Soundararajan has said. She has started advocating the use of Buddhist meditation (i.e., Vipassana renamed as mindfulness).[50]

She is especially impressed by the work of Ruth King, a Black meditation teacher and author of several books including *Mindful of Race: Transforming Racism from the Inside Out*.[51] This can be a gamechanger, and something everyone involved in the issues should support.

On multiple occasions in this book, we have advocated raising the level of consciousness that comes through the various meditation systems developed in India. Only from a level higher than the ordinary ego, which is what Ruth King calls 'from the inside out', can humanity transcend the horrible boundaries of race and other identities. We hope Thenmozhi Soundararajan is genuinely pursuing the path of raising consciousness and we would welcome collaboration to achieve this for all stakeholders.

4

Attacking Meritocracy at the Indian Institutes of Technology

Overview

Ajantha Subramanian, professor of anthropology at Harvard, has written a widely publicized book, *The Caste of Merit: Engineering Education in India*, which claims that the Indian Institutes of Technology are factories that reproduce and perpetuate caste privilege. She is influential in academia and plays a prominent role in the Mittal Family Institute of South Asian Studies at Harvard where she chairs seminars such as *Building Nations, Breaking Communities: The Locality of Caste Violence in Colonial North India*.[1] She is also the Mehra Family Professor of South Asian Studies at Harvard.

This chapter delves into the following:

- A foundational idea of her thesis is the mapping of White American elitism to the upper castes of India. She makes this clear at the very outset of her book: 'To understand upper caste consolidation, I have turned to scholarship on the production of whiteness in the United States'.[2]
- Subramanian applies Critical Theory to develop her conceptual framework that Brahmins are the cultural capitalists and IITs their mechanism for the production of more upper caste engineers. This cultural capital is being mischaracterized as merit because it appears objective, autonomous, and a genuine type of competence. She debunks meritocracy as a veneer behind which Brahmin privilege perpetuates its supremacy.
- Her special targets are the IITs and their alumni. She accuses

them of a conspiracy against the lower castes which they bring to Silicon Valley and elsewhere.

- The key point is that even when an individual IITian is unbiased, she considers him guilty of benefiting from the institutional structure and thereby perpetuating, and reinforcing, its abusiveness. According to her, by their very structure, the IITs enshrine caste privileges even in situations where a Brahmin student is from an economically poor background, or where a low caste student belongs to a financially empowered and well-educated family. Chapter 1 explained the focus of Critical Race Theory on a clash of group identities and not on individualism.

- Subramanian applies the iconic Pierre Bourdieu who said that prestigious examinations and elite higher education guarantee the reproduction of old social hierarchies. By citing this, she assumes her case is made that the IIT exam and curriculum is reproducing caste hierarchies in India. But she offers no concrete proof of casteism in the exam or curriculum itself. All she does is cite numerous personal anecdotes with self-identified 'victims'.

- Subramanian advocates dismantling the IIT institutional structure and thereby liberating the underclasses that are exploited by this oppression. Her broader activism is to bring about social engineering, which feeds into political vote banks and legislation, as well as corporate policies for diversity.

- Her attitude is patronizing toward the lower castes, implying that they lack merit, and that meritocracy of any kind is a conspiracy against them. What she is essentially insinuating is that the lower castes cannot compete on merit even when provided equal opportunities.

- She ignores that the technology-heavy makeup of Indian immigrants in the US is not caused by caste privilege but a result of its immigration policy that prefers merit and those who can contribute to its society.

- To be consistent, Subramanian would also have to target other kinds of elitist hierarchies, such as Indian Muslims' social organizations, Jawaharlal Nehru's socialist structures, the alumni networks of Harvard's Business- Medical- and Kennedy School.

- As we will point out, her views on caste are full of reductionisms, over-simplifications, and selective use of evidence to support her positions.

• Our issue with her work is that it feeds communalism, divisiveness, and anti-nationalism in India. The divide and rule policy enforced by the British is being reinvented in the form of inter-caste identity wars managed by Harvard professors like her.

The Origin of Western Meritocracy

At the outset, we take exception to Subramanian's idea that modern meritocracy can somehow be blamed on the Indian caste system. The idea of meritocracy in the West can be traced to early Judeo-Christianity, the view that good things happen to the virtuous and bad things happen to bad people. We may think of this theological principle as *Biblical meritocracy*. It was enforced by an all-good, all-powerful God. Every stroke of good fortune is a reward, and every misfortune a punishment.

Centuries later came the Protestant Reformation. As argued by the German sociologist and political economist, Max Weber, this resulted in what he called the Protestant work ethic. In his notable book, *The Protestant Ethic and the Spirit of Capitalism*,[3] Weber advanced a sociological and economic theory that the values of the Protestant faith result in diligence, discipline, and frugality, which became the foundations for modern capitalism. This encouraged Protestants (especially the followers of the sixteenth-century theologian, John Calvin) to accumulate wealth, and many of them saw their materialistic success as a sign that they had earned eternal salvation from God.

In America, this evolved further into the idea that free, globalized markets reward people commensurate with their talents and initiative. Because such qualities for success were not necessarily moral ones, *technocratic meritocracy* was born.[4]

The secular counterpart was espoused by Adam Smith, the 'father of economics', in his 1776 book, *The Wealth of Nations*. Ever since, economists have promoted the concept that everyone pursuing their self-interest would produce the best outcomes for society. This ideology pushed free market competition as the most efficient way to allocate scarce resources. Everyone competes for limited goods and limited number of jobs, and these are allocated based on the ability (or merit) of the consumers and the workers.

This historical origin and development of meritocracy in the West may be shown as the following chronology: Biblical Meritocracy → Protestant Ethic → Modern Capitalism → Technocratic Meritocracy → Adam Smith.

Lately, there has been criticism that the US places excess emphasis on meritocracy. For example, Michael J. Sandel, professor of political philosophy at Harvard writes in his recent book, *The Tyranny of Merit: What's Become of the Common Good?*[5] that his own students are convinced that their success is entirely due to merit, even though two-thirds of them are from the top strata of income.[6]

Numerous authors have likewise highlighted problems with meritocracy and cited various reasons. But none before Ajantha Subramanian have singled out Hindu caste as the main culprit. The history of Western meritocracy summarized above shows the logical absurdity of Subramanian's attack on Hindus for 'merit' when the true target of her attack is the Western system itself.

History of Separating Artisans and Engineers in India

We will now summarize Subramanian's thesis that she formulates using her historical analysis of technical training in India.

It is widely accepted that traditionally, technical knowledge in India was the purview of artisans who tended to be from lower castes. This is documented in many works such as those of Dharampal and the History of Indian Science and Technology series published by Infinity Foundation.

The British changed all this because technical education and practice became integral to state power and economic development, and they repositioned it as having upper caste status. Subramanian traces the history of this change that culminated in Brahmins controlling the engineering profession. The rise of engineering was based on colonial practices that distinguished low caste from high caste, manual work from conceptual, and artisanship from professional white collars.

There's little to dispute in this part of her thesis. The East India Company Act of 1813 had stated the goal of promoting the knowledge of sciences among the Indians, and the Company's directors decided that the existing institutional structures of education for social elites would remain in place. The turning point came in 1823 when Ram Mohan Roy, the founder of the Brahmo Samaj – a movement that worked on social and religious reforms – wrote a game-changing letter to Lord Amherst, governor-general of Bengal. Roy criticized the proposal by the British to establish a Sanskrit college in Calcutta (now Kolkata) and urged the government that instead they should 'promote a more liberal and enlightened system of instruction'. By this he meant an English language system to transfer scientific thinking from Britain to India. In doing so, Roy became the originator, in fact the first, to actively promote the anglicizing of the Indian education system.

Initially, the British did not pay heed to Roy and Sanskrit-based education continued. But later, the directors of the East India Company adopted Roy's posture that there was a fundamental error in teaching Hindu knowledge because it was frivolous and not useful. This triggered a debate in the British Parliament between the two camps, those advocating Sanskrit and English education, respectively. In 1835, the debate culminated in the historian, Lord Thomas Macaulay's famous *Minute on Indian Education* that ultimately led to English replacing Sanskrit in India's system of education. Macaulay has been much maligned for creating this tectonic shift, but what is often forgotten is Ram Mohan Roy's role to instigate the process a decade before Macaulay adopted this idea.

The traditional system of learning was thus replaced by British training in law, medicine, and civil engineering. The College of Civil Engineering in Roorkee was founded in 1847 as the first engineering college in modern India. *The British continued their typical divisiveness by projecting that engineering is inherently hands-on, and therefore the upper castes were not meant for such work.*

They split the discipline to create a two-tier system in their vision of a hierarchical society. For the top tier, they created professional engineering programs theoretical in nature that promised social status and well-paying careers. This was sold as a prestigious white-collar profession and a pathway for Brahmins to enter elite society. It led to a cadre of Indian college-educated engineers, primarily comprising upper caste Brahmins. The second tier was created to equip artisans that tended to be from the lower castes, with modern industrial manufacturing practices.

Some British officials resisted this move, while others were in favor. Those who opposed it, such as Lord Curzon, British viceroy of India from 1899-1905, said that modern industry was a mimicry of Western culture, whereas the policies for India had to be loyal to the traditional customs. Many British officials wanted to champion artisans from lower castes as makers of industrial goods. The debate was resolved in favor of the two-tier approach as a good fit with the Indian caste system. By the early twentieth century, engineering had transformed into a gentleman's affair, conducted between British White people and elite Brahmins, with the lower castes performing hands-on work.

This is how artisanship and engineering became poles apart with engineering coveted as high-class and suited to the upper caste. Engineering became disassociated from manual work which was relegated to the lower castes.

Subramanian elaborates:

> The career of technical knowledge from the mid-19th to the mid-20th century is one of shifts from guild to state, shop floor to classroom, and lower to upper caste. These shifts were conditioned by processes at an imperial scale: the transfer of power from the East India Company to the British Crown in 1857, Inter-Imperial industrial competition over the latter half of the 19th century, efforts to minimize the cost of colonial rule, and nationalist critiques of under-development.[7]
>
> The shift ... also clinched the identity of the British-Indian engineer as a member of a colonial elite who was to embody the hierarchies of the colony. Initially, this meant racial exclusivity. But dual pressures – from England to do colonialism 'on the cheap' and from nationalists charging Britain with under-development – led to a lifting of racial glass ceiling, an entry of upper castes into the engineering service.[8]
>
> The development of technical education along two tracks was informed by and, in turn, reinforced caste differences. By the advent of independence, the status of technical knowledge have (sic) transformed; while engineering was now an upper-caste intellectual aspiration, intimately tied to nation-building,

artisanship had been demoted to a form of unskilled labor seen
as far less instrumental to economic development.[9]

The account that follows is a summary of Subramanian's explanation of
the history of how the IITs evolved. According to her, the two tracks
of industrial-schooling and college-engineering diverged and went their
separate ways. Lower castes, that had the history of technical skill and
knowledge, were displaced and placed below the glass ceiling of upper
caste engineering. Engineering thus evolved as a discipline of conceptual
knowledge in which the lower castes were left behind.

Brahmin intermediaries played a role in creating the notion that
Brahmins were innately more knowledgeable and destined to lead. Most
engineers in colonial India were from upper class backgrounds. A large
number abhorred manual labor, yet embraced engineering because it
was seen as a white-collar profession of conceptual knowledge with
proximity to the East India Company. It offered a fast track to the colonial
civil services and other privileges.

There was a brief struggle to topple the two-tier system in the
IITs when Germany offered help in establishing IIT Madras. The
Germans pointed out that at least half of their technicians were drawn
from small-scale industries and handicrafts and not from large-scale
projects.[10] Hence, IIT Madras emphasized practical training in manual
skills. But, according to Subramanian, the Germans found the Indians'
attitude frustrating because they were dismissive towards craftwork.
This was because during the colonial period, the Madras Presidency, an
administrative unit at the time, had introduced technical education in a
way that reinforced social hierarchies. Subramanian says that by 1921,
Brahmins comprised approximately seventy-four percent of engineering
college students in Madras even though only three percent of the area's
population were Brahmins.

She says that by the 1970s the German model of hands-on education
installed at IIT Madras started to decline, partly because of large-
scale migration of IITians to the US where engineering theory was in
greater demand. Over time, this led to IITians shifting away from core
engineering jobs toward academia, management, and the private sector.

The stratification into caste hierarchies was further reinforced when
the IITs decided to distinguish themselves in theoretical areas such as
computer science.

We agree with much of the historical account given by Subramanian as summarized above. We now turn to her logic claiming that the upper castes cunningly camouflage their caste privileges behind the veneer of merit.

Merit Considered a Form of Cultural Capital

To make her case, she imports the ideas of cultural capital propounded by the French Marxist and sociologist, Pierre Bourdieu, and applies them in the context of Indian STEM education. Bourdieu became well-known for enhancing Marxism with his theory of different forms of cultural capital. Besides Marxism's notion of economic capital, there is also cultural capital which Bourdieu defines as 'familiarity with the legitimate culture within a society'. This capital is about accumulating what is considered the 'high culture' and includes the skills, education, norms, and behaviors acquired by members of a social group that give them advantages over others. Being considered cultured, according to the norms of the ruling elite, becomes a form of capital one can use.

Bourdieu identifies three types of cultural capital:

A. Embodied capital: Special talents embedded physically in a person's body, such as singing, having a certain accent, knowing math, or playing a sport.

B. Objectified capital: Physically separate from the individual, such as intellectual property created by the person but with its own separate existence that can be bought and sold.

C. Institutionalized capital: The means of producing and reproducing cultural capital, such as prestigious universities, Hollywood, Research & Development (R&D) labs.

The value of cultural capital is society specific. What may be of high value in one society may be of little, or no, value elsewhere. Accumulating cultural capital can be a route to upward mobility. One can accumulate cultural assets like credentials, prestige, relationships, and networking connections. An individual's family history and social class are also an integral part of cultural capital.

While type 'A' cultural capital is not transferrable to another person, type 'B' is, just like other forms of capital. This is an important way power can be held and transferred and social hierarchies maintained. Type 'C' is far more prone to monopolization because its owner can produce and control the distribution of accumulated cultural capital.

Of special interest to our present discussion is that academic qualifications bestowed by recognized institutions are a form of cultural capital.

Subramanian's key point is her claim that:

1) The academic qualifications at the IITs are a form of cultural capital of which the upper castes are the capitalists; and
2) This form of capital is considered as merit because it *appears* to be objective, autonomous, and a genuine type of competence.

In essence, Subramanian uses the history of engineering education in India to claim that it became a form of cultural capital. And merit serves as the public marker to hide and substitute caste-based privileges. Upper castes across India embrace merit as a *collective caste trait* to distinguish themselves from lower castes. This is how, she insists, merit has become a way to commodify caste identity.

The leveraging of merit, she claims, is an upper caste conspiracy to perpetuate its capitalism. This is the reason IITians stick together and close ranks to prevent the emergence of an egalitarian society, because that would wipe out their cultural capital advantages. She has taken up the responsibility of dismantling this institutional structure and thereby liberating the underclasses that are exploited by this cultural capital.

Subramanian says that the Brahmin tech community likes to characterize its own success as a form of cultural capital based on a genetic predisposition to education and preordained capacity for entrepreneurial action. She points out that unlike the previous kinds of elites whose capital was in the form of land that was physically immovable, the new form of elitism based on meritocracy, caste privilege, and prestigious affiliation is highly mobile and internationally marketable. Merit is therefore the new currency. The IITs are analogous to central banks and print this money.

Cultural capital too can be contested the same way people war over economic capital. She claims that when the lower castes used vote bank politics to threaten the institutional structures, the upper castes started relying even more on merit to stay ahead:

Democracy – as ideology and a set of structures for making political claims – does provide leverage for subaltern politics that challenge the status quo. As a result, structures of inequality do not seamlessly reproduce themselves. Rather, upper caste claims to merit are emblematic of an ongoing war of maneuver in reaction against lower caste assertion.[11]

We understand her thesis but wish to raise the following issues. For instance, we make a similar argument, but in the reverse direction. We have previously argued that the construction of 'critical theories', and social sciences theories in general is itself an institutionalized system of privileges with hidden structures. This was argued nearly two decades ago during an important public debate – *The Peer-Review Cartel*.[12] We made the case that scholars like Subramanian are cultural capitalists in the liberal arts because their institutional status gives them special privileges they do not deserve. The following excerpt from that debate summarizes this point:

> The nature of the peer-review process is creating a knowledge production cartel that gives the Western academy neocolonialist control over the means of production of knowledge. Any critique from outside the elite cartel is sidelined (especially if it is seen as a serious enough threat) by invoking the 'peer-review' as a silver bullet. One of the most cherished myths of the Western-controlled liberal arts intellectual apparatus is that its peer-review is a fair system. The criticisms we make of their scholarship are considered illegitimate because their writings have been peer-reviewed. ... all our rejoinders get classified as 'attacks' on them, and not as fair criticism, because these do not emanate from within the peer-review cabal. ... those who are not licensed by their academic union should not be allowed to argue against their positions, and certainly not as equal partners. This attitude is, ... part of a larger problem in academic discourse, especially in anthropology, sociology and the study of religion, where it is assumed that (i) the non-academician can only be positioned as a native informant, and (ii) the native informant should not talk back. This allows mediocre scholars to close ranks and emphasize the schism between 'we the scholars' and 'you the ignorant consumers'.

Clearly, the peer-review process has acquired tremendous symbolic value. This blind spot in the academy prevents it from much-needed self-reflection.[13]

In fact, many academicians have expressed the view that without a well-placed patron in academia, it is difficult to publish and get ahead based purely on merit. The 'academic truth' in the humanities and liberal arts is often a façade of gibberish, false evidence, and politically and emotionally charged rhetoric. From Marxism onwards, Critical Theory has been very closely linked to political ideologies. Higher education teaches picking or mixing from the toolbox of approved theories and constructing a synthetic argument for whatever the agenda might be.

Proponents of liberal arts proudly claim that they no longer study literature, art or culture in and of themselves; rather, these are 'objects' to be processed via suitable 'theories'. This makes the legitimization and promotion of particular 'theories' very serious business because whoever controls the theories controls the discourse. This raises the following questions: Who has the power, and by what authority, to decide which among the theories on the market shall belong to the toolbox approved for scholarly usage? To what extent is popularity (by virtue of trendiness, money, and powerful backing) the dominant criterion? Does this suggest a vicious cycle, whereby usage of a theory by the peer group of intellectuals promotes that theory and helps it gain market share, a process of assigning value not commensurate with merit? The academic cartel, like any trade union, decides which theories are approved.

This highlights that Subramanian's own Harvard University is guilty of the following: By providing certifications and by its mere brand, it endows its students and faculty with one of the world's largest, and most prestigious, kinds of cultural capital. It, too, claims this to be *merit* and nothing more. For example, the coveted Harvard Business School program touts that the networking it provides via its elite alumni is one of the most valuable lifelong assets its graduates acquire. When students enter Harvard, they become part of the global networking club that looks after each other. Membership into the Harvard gentry is elitist, for sure.

One can list several other institutional mechanisms at Harvard as the means of producing cultural capital: the peer-reviewed prestigious journals controlled by the cartel; the use of Harvard University Press to publish books like Subramanian has done to gain an unfair advantage of credibility; and the highly political process of getting tenure. Part 2 is devoted to exposing Harvard's numerous institutions as the nexuses of cultural capital development against India.

Subramanian does mention Harvard's emphasis on meritocracy as a form of hidden bias. She suggests that there should be 'proportional representation' of students and that admissions should be a 'mirror of society'. But we feel that these changes would further expand Harvard's capital. It would, in fact, empower the Harvard elites by allowing them to select the marginalized people brought in and then to brainwash them with their pet theories.[14] Should there be a *Critical Harvard Theory* deconstructing all this?

American institutions have a history of attracting the best talent globally. And US immigration laws give highest priority to 'persons of extraordinary ability' in the arts, sciences, education, business, as well as to outstanding professors and researchers holding advanced degrees. Subramanian is eager to bring proportional representation into all these fields. But would she also demand proportional representation in the sports teams at Harvard and all other major league American sports? Would she prosecute all competitive fields like the Olympic Games, Oscars, Nobel Prizes and other awards to force them to replace merit with proportional representation to mirror society?

Another massive system of cultural capitalism ignored by Subramanian is that Muslims in South Asia climb the social ladder of Islam by accumulating cultural attributes valued in their society. This involves growing a beard, speaking Urdu with the correct intonation, promoting halal practices, adopting hyper-masculinity in one's body language and demeanor, and so forth. These are identifiers of what is called the Ashraf caste of Muslims, their highest caste. Such topics would be too politically incorrect for the otherwise provocative Subramanian. She ought to note Ambedkar's criticism of Muslim elitism as summarized in Chapter 6.

Entrance Exams Conceal Caste Privileges

The entrance exam to the IITs is considered one of the most standard, objective, and neutral measures of modern meritocracy by the youth of India. But Subramanian says the in-built social and cultural capital structures have not been adequately dismantled. She feels there are economic, social, and ideological factors that make the exam unfair to the lower castes. Therefore, they cannot succeed in engineering professions.

She fails to provide concrete examples or logic to prove that the exam privileges certain castes over others. All she does is cite numerous interviews with self-identified 'victims' from which she selects random anecdotes to support her theory. She repeatedly claims that she is speaking for the downtrodden, that she is their voice. But this is a common anthropological device and there is nothing scientific about such a methodology.

Subramanian's argument is shallow because she merely cites Bourdieu who said that prestigious examinations and elite higher education guarantee the reproduction of old social hierarchies. She then assumes that looking at India through Bourdieu's lens, she has made the case that the IIT exam and curriculum are reproducing caste hierarchies in India too. Her attitude is patronizing towards the lower castes, implying that they lack merit, and that meritocracy of any kind is a conspiracy against them. What she is essentially insinuating is that the lower castes cannot compete on merit even when provided equal opportunities.

A stronger case would be that the lower castes were not prepared through primary education because during the British era there was no universal education policy for the masses. This continued post-Independence under the leadership of Jawaharlal Nehru (independent India's first prime minister) and Indira Gandhi (India's longest serving prime minister). Therefore, by the time these youth try for engineering, they are already at a handicap. This is a secular issue caused by colonialism and the subsequent elitism that continued during the Nehruvian era.

Subramanian is also critical of the Union Public Service Commission exam that admits candidates into India's elite government services, alleging it comprises elitist structures. However, the exam also has a heavy dose of social sciences, and the social sciences taught in India are entirely imported from the West. It is she and others like her at institutions like Harvard, themselves products of the Western social sciences, that have created these elite structures in India.

The underlying reason for opposing entrance exams is her adoption of the Critical Race Theory tenet favoring equity over equality. As explained in Chapter 1, this means advocating equal outcomes and not equal opportunities. Such a view places less emphasis on equipping institutions to better prepare underprivileged students and help them perform on par with the best. The implicit assumption is that the underprivileged are incapable of learning, and hence the outcomes should be institutionalized to mirror the composition of society. An equitable admissions policy, according to her, would focus primarily on each student's history and identity and not consider aptitude for a given field.

Merit as Male Dominated Capitalism

One of Subramanian's major allegations is that the majority of IITians are male. She further asserts that male bonding on campuses was preconfigured by male relationships within the Hindu family. In other words, the Hindu male hierarchy in families brings about the masculine quality into the engineering profession. However, the fact to note is that in the US too, STEM education is male dominated and hence it is not something unique to Hindu societies.[15] Our position is that STEM should be encouraged for all genders and identities. The solution to a lack of performance by certain groups should not be based on the flawed diagnosis of blaming a convenient scapegoat. Subramanian also ignores the fact that India produces the world's highest number of females in STEM education.[16]

Institutional Kinship Among IITians and Brand Development Considered Casteist

Subramanian finds it unusual that IITians stand up for each other and is troubled by their brand becoming a form of cultural capital:

> The institutional kinship within the overwhelmingly upper-caste IIT diaspora has become an even more potent form of capital. Diasporic IITians have been at the forefronts of efforts to sustain and consolidate their effective ties and to make the IIT pedigree into a globally recognized brand. Much of this work of branding has been driven by IITians in Silicon Valley, for whom entrepreneurial success has further reinforced their sense of being self-made individuals.[17]

However, fostering cooperation among its members is the nature of every university's alumni association. She is unhappy about the success of the IITs in this regard:

> The IITians of Silicon Valley have been at the forefront of professional networking and image making to ensure that the Indian technical professional is immediately recognizable as a global commodity. Their networks of affiliation and accumulation work to reinforce the upper caste under pilings of Indian technical merit even while caste disappears from view.[18]

It is unclear what caste has to do with the fact that IITians like all other alumni, promote themselves, build their image, and help each other on a global level just like any other institution. Networking is a key benefit and aspiration for any student body; an intangible benefit. It is an inherent feature of any modern educational system and any criticism of this kind needs to lay at the feet of the Western education system itself and not selectively scapegoated upon Indians or Hindus.

Subramanian also takes a pot-shot at TIE, i.e., The Indus Entrepreneurs, a group created in 1992 mainly by IITians in Silicon Valley.[19] The Indus Entrepreneurs has spread worldwide with chapters in several countries. It is a non-profit organization for networking among tech entrepreneurs, venture capitalists, employees, and employers. Such organizations exist in business, medicine, the hospitality industry, the legal profession, and even in anthropology, which is her field. There is nothing amiss if Indians have taken the lead to create the world's premier professional association for technologists.

Subramanian is also troubled that many Indians own Silicon Valley companies and are angel investors favoring those with similar backgrounds. But this is a common trend across all professions: people giving preference to those from the same university, village or other affiliation based on one type of identity or another. In fact, proponents of diversity strongly encourage minority communities to organize such formal and informal networks to break the monopoly of White elite strangleholds over access and traditional networks. Belonging to associations like TIE and encouraging lower castes to build similar networks are not mutually exclusive.

What upsets her further is that Silicon Valley IITians have created the Pan-IIT Alumni Association which too has spread around the world. She acknowledges that this is similar to the Harvard Business School network but does not go to the same lengths criticizing either that or the Harvard Medical School network or the Harvard Kennedy School of Government network. Attacking them would be risky for her Ivy League career.

Among her targets are a wide range of individuals that have championed the IIT brand. These include Vinod Khosla, renowned venture capitalist and co-founder of Sun Microsystems, N.R. Narayana Murthy, founder of Infosys, and various others. She mentions that former and current US presidents, Bill Clinton and Joe Biden also praised the IITians, as did Bill Gates (of Microsoft), Jeff Bezos (of Amazon) and Nobel Prize winner, Prof. Amartya Sen. She is upset about the success of the IITs: 'Lost in this rhetorical echo chamber are the forms of inherited caste capital and state patronage that have gone into the making of the IITs'.[20]

The US-based Patel community is known to help each other get into the hotel business. Sikhs in New Jersey own most of the gas stations; they train, mentor, and finance each other get into the business. Similarly, Koreans own most of the laundromats. This is a fact of American society: When people migrate from a certain country, they stick together, and become professionally specialized in some area. Similarly, there is nothing unusual about IIT graduates standing up for each other, even if, for reasons beyond their control, they happen to be Tamil Brahmins of proven merit. Subramanian calls it 'institutional kinship' and considers it a Brahmin conspiracy to create a brand that makes IIT more attractive among employers the world over. The fact is that India's outsourcing industry wants to market its people, and it is a good business strategy to project a positive brand to its clients.

Subramanian mentions that IITians are treated very differently than students from India's Regional Engineering Colleges that cater to the lower strata of society. And it is an issue for her that the IITs are considered the benchmark of meritocracy. She mentions that many followers of Gandhi's ideology initially found the IITs to be elitist, but later maintained that even the ancient Buddhist university of Nalanda became renowned the world over because it was elitist and picked the highest caliber of talent regardless of social status.

Another point of concern for her is the success of the diaspora entrepreneurs because this has become a pride of Indians. She says that IITians in Silicon Valley have become 'self-styled neo-liberal capitalists'. But this is the very nature of the global capitalist society we live in; it is the nature and structure of free enterprise and has nothing to do with being Brahmins or IITians, or caste in the least.

She is disdainful of IITians criticizing the underdevelopment of the Indian public sector and the underachievement of engineers based in India. But why should she have the sole prerogative to develop a critique of Indian engineers; why can't others develop their own thesis on the problem? In fact, IITians are better qualified than an anthropologist to recommend policies on engineering education in India.

We, too, have criticized India's policies for failing to use its engineers but in a different way: Our criticism is that India is basically selling its engineers as raw labor and making a few billionaires even richer, while the technology produced belongs to a foreign client who then licenses it back to India.

Throughout her work, her contempt for the accomplishments of Indian American technocrats is clearly evident.

Attack on Silicon Valley

Subramanian's goal is to cause fissures in the sensitive US landscape of race tensions by wanting to pit one minority group against the other. She writes:

> ... people in the United States who are really committed to elevating the IIT brand and creating this myth of the technological Indian are also involved in politics in India. [They] push certain forms of entrepreneurialism in India, sometimes through the IITs, but often in other ways ... Some of them are consultants ... And they're really invested in certain forms of economic and legal transformation that allow for more unfettered foreign investment and more deregulation of public sector industries. It's both a project with a U.S. specific focus, but it also has a transnational dimension. What does it mean to be a model minority? It means that you are exceptional and ... can be held up as a model for

other less successful minorities. ... your success is pitted against
those other minorities in a way that completely obscures the forms
of caste and class capital that most of Asian Americans enjoy.[21]

She is a staunch supporter of Equality Labs that helped build the recent
case against Cisco alleging caste discrimination. She writes 'caste is a
travelling category' and that caste privilege in the form of social and
cultural capital is a 'transferable form of capital' that Indians have brought
to the US.[22]

She freely opines about caste being alive in American corporates,
and echoes Critical Race Theory to say that the policy of neutrality
towards all castes protects caste privilege:

It's not an accident that the vast majority of South Asian-
Americans are from privileged caste backgrounds. ... if one doesn't
subscribe to a caste identity, one is still a beneficiary of caste
privilege. So caste is here, it has been here, and it will stay here.
So one has to actually contend with it and not pretend that it
doesn't exist.[23]

Ironically, many people of upper caste backgrounds have immigrated
to the West in response to reservations policies in India that make it
much more difficult for them to gain access to educational institutions,
relative to other castes and backgrounds. She says the upper caste Indian
migrants' success is not self-made, but a success resulting from caste as
social capital transferred from India. She accuses Indian Americans of
preserving this upper caste capital but fails to acknowledge that most
Indian Americans do not identify themselves with any particular caste
and often marry out of caste. If a typical Indian American is asked their
caste, in many cases they will not have an answer.

Rather than be proud that IIT Madras has an entrepreneurship cell,
she criticizes this group for taking credit for forming 130 start-ups and
creating 250 internships. She is concerned that these collaborations
between the diaspora and the homeland is evidence of IITians and other
Indians having subscribed to the Silicon Valley model of meritocracy.
Every sign and instance of Indians' success is seen by her as a conspiracy
against the lower castes. Even India's former prime minister, Dr
Manmohan Singh, and Raghuram Rajan (former chief economist of the

IMF and former governor of the Reserve Bank of India) are quoted among those that praise the IITs, and hence they too, are part of this caste conspiracy.

'The Cisco case is a threat because it makes the diaspora Indians less secure,'[24] she says, and explains why it should become a tipping point:

> The Cisco case ... fits a broader pattern of dominant caste discrimination and oppressed caste marginalization. ... caste continues to operate in the U.S. despite its invisibility to most Americans. Alumni of Indian institutions, like the IITs, have brought their caste prejudices with them into the U.S. tech sector where they attempt to once again assert their dominance. By "outing" the Dalit engineer from IIT as a "reserved category" student, his dominant caste bosses expressed their casteist belief that he had gained admission to the IITs illegitimately, that he was intellectually inferior and unworthy of a job at Cisco, and that he needed to be put in his place. Moreover, they acted with a sense of impunity because caste is not legally recognized as a basis of either advantage or disadvantage in the U.S. It is this impunity to discriminate on the basis of caste that the Cisco case promises to end.[25]

She goes on to claim that,

> ...many of the same forms of descent-based discrimination that exist in India – from the practice of untouchability to discrimination in the workplace and in associational life — continue to find expression in the U.S.[26]
>
> The Cisco case holds out the hope that such policies may be applied more broadly within the academic and tech sectors. The addition of caste to U.S. non-discrimination policies will check the sense of impunity enjoyed by dominant castes and enable oppressed caste students and employees to more openly address ... discrimination. But to more comprehensively address caste discrimination, U.S. institutions should go beyond simply recognizing the caste backgrounds of their students or employees and monitoring on-site social interaction.[27]

Companies that hire offshore contractors and vendors often require those third parties to be subject to standard policies and protocols of their home country. Which means that any caste-related policies that are adopted in the US could be imposed on Indian contracting firms and vendors. This would have a momentous impact on Indians and more broadly, on the tech industry.

Subramanian wants the Cisco, and similar cases, to result in a deeper investigation into caste as a phenomenon on par with American racism. Just like race, caste bias is embedded in institutional structures that continue reproducing caste privilege:

> The protected category provides a legal basis to address experiences of discrimination. ... allow for more comprehensive data collection on caste as it's not a well understood category ... And this is not going to lead to a sense that South Asians are somehow backwards (sic) or non-modern. The U.S. is a race society. It's ... segmented along all kinds of lines. And caste is yet another of those forms ... And it's not one that is reducible to race or class. It has its own logic and sort of patterns that need to be attended to. ... caste is no more of an embarrassment than race is. These are both forms of descent-based structures of discrimination that are thoroughly modern. There's nothing archaic about either of these categories, when they're not just holdovers from a premodern or a pre-colonial or colonial past. (They) ... are reproduced through everyday forms of affiliation through marriage, schooling, and more.[28]

Subramanian positions her following statement in the context of criticizing the IITs, when in fact, most IITians would regard it as a matter of pride:

> IITians were able to bring the spirit of entrepreneurship to India and cultivated a new generation of capitalists who ... removed the nation's shackles of socialism. With ... diasporic entrepreneurship, brand IIT becomes brand India. This diasporic liberal theology raises the nation's deliverance, squarely in the hands of the US based IITians.[29]

She wants anthropologists and social scientists like herself to be the ones delivering fresh ideology to the downtrodden and is resentful that

IITians have achieved more success than her own cabal. What is also troubling to her is that IITians have resisted victimhood branding.

> Equating India's development status with brand value, it reduces the social, political, and even ethical complexity of development to market price. ... the capacity to attract investment and accumulate wealth becomes the preeminent index of social value and intellectual merit.[30]

It is true that structural socio-economic factors result in disparate levels of access to resources that help make one successful and be meritorious. Those issues absolutely need to be addressed. However, what is insidious about Subramanian's line of argument is that the very concept of 'merit' itself is being delegitimized. Any differentiation at all is blamed on conspiracy and structural elitism. The natural corollary that follows is that there can be no valid system of meritocracy. The target of such an attack is capitalism and free thinking; this is pure totalitarian Communism sneaking in through the guise of anti-racism and anti-casteism.

Breaking Ranks with Afro-Dalits

While Subramanian is clear about the mapping *upper caste = Whites*, she does not want to equate *lower caste = Blacks* to the same extent as do Isabel Wilkerson and Suraj Yengde (of Harvard Kennedy School, discussed in the next chapter).

She disagrees with Wilkerson's use of caste as the fixed, permanent architecture in which racism plays out universally. Her main issue with Wilkerson's thesis is that Subramanian regards caste as specific to India's history and not something that could be plucked out surgically and inserted elsewhere out of context. It is a by-product of a unique experience of foreign colonialism and capitalism combined with internal developments.

Another contrast to Wilkerson is that Subramanian does not want to disregard the social struggles of the past two centuries. She argues that both caste in India and race in America have undergone considerable change, and that there is much fluidity and mobility within each system. The social and political life of caste is far more complex, and she opposes simplistic comparisons of caste and race.[31]

But we cannot help speculating that there is a turf battle between them: *Subramanian wants to <u>own</u> the discourse on caste in the American academy*. Her criticism of Wilkerson suggests that she is willing to concede the criticism of race to Wilkerson, a Black scholar, in exchange for caste being uniquely Indian becoming *her* exclusive domain. She must make her argument different from the widely popular Wilkerson thesis, so as to carve out a space for herself where she would dominate as the academic expert.

The Politics of Jawaharlal Nehru v/s Narendra Modi

After India gained Independence in 1947, Jawaharlal Nehru dreamt of building a nation based on modern science and technology. Hence, he was very big on the idea of the IITs as well as large-scale steel plants and other infrastructure projects with foreign help. Subramanian takes Nehru to task that these new engineering colleges were kept insulated from caste politics, thereby enabling them to reproduce caste hierarchies. Nehru had even characterized science and technology as something Brahminical in the spirit of service. She feels that this further entrenched the idea of the scientist as an elitist, and the material and physical aspects became the domain of the less privileged, the lower castes. As per her, Nehru, in effect, mimicked Europe by making the IITs as part of the two-tier engineering system.

But she neglects the deeper root cause: Nehru and Indira Gandhi neglected mass education at the grassroots level, which has created the present stratification in higher education. Nehru's state socialism as the model for the planned economy was also elitist but has not been adequately examined by Subramanian.

Subramanian's posture on Narendra Modi is far more antagonistic than her calm reflections on Nehru. She outright dismisses all of Modi's accomplishments as authoritarian:

> The rise of Narendra Modi has ordered another shift in IITian projects of self-fashioning. In the United States this has been most clearly seen in the IITians endorsement of the BJP's neo liberal capitalism. ... Modi's style of authoritarian populism has

also garnered support in both the United States and India. ... this
is evident in an escalation of cultural nationalist politics on IIT
campuses. It is to this most recent expression of upper casteness
within India, and its implications for the ongoing dialectic of
upper caste claims to merit and lower caste claims to rise that
we turn to in the conclusion.[32]

She conveniently ignores the fact that Modi's electoral victories (both
in 2014 and 2019) were largely due to the massive support he received
from the lower castes. It is ironic that even after acknowledging the long
history that led to what she considers IIT elitism, she ends up blaming
the ruling BJP as the culprit.

She is troubled that a spokesman for the IITs praises Modi's policies
on technocrats and capitalists. She picks on him for saying that the
IITs have been a beacon of light in contrast with state socialism in
India. His statement that those IITians who migrated to the US did very
well as self-made entrepreneurs while those who stayed in India have
languished, reflects on the character of the US. Whether it is immigrants
from China, Japan, Germany, Russia, Poland, or anywhere else, the US
is a land where people compete on grounds of meritocracy and free
enterprise. This ethos has nothing to do with Hinduism or any kind of
caste privilege of Indian Brahmins.

Yet, she says that the election of 'Hindu nationalists' in India led
to a reinforcement of caste power that is reflected in the diaspora. The
reason cited is that Modi is caste-oriented (even though he does not
belong to the upper caste community) and is supporting upper caste
privileges. She writes:

> As with other majoritarian nationalisms, Hindu nationalism has
> long had a social base among the upper caste middle class. Most
> IITians are the perfect combination of both constituencies having
> emerged out of the upper caste middle class members to become
> capitalist class, spanning homeland and diaspora.[33]

Subramanian, however, gives no evidence as to which policies of
Modi's government are anti-lower caste. On the contrary, a lot of
infrastructure, job development, and several social programs have been
pro minorities and lower castes. A good scholar ought to have made

factual comparisons between the progress of lower castes during various political governments in India. But that seems beyond the scope of Subramanian's work. In fact, in the conclusion to her book, she makes a list of what she considers to be the great achievements of the previous Congress government in helping alleviate poverty and give rights to the downtrodden; but doesn't provide any statistical comparison to back her sweeping generalizations.[34]

She depicts the IITs as institutions preventing the redistribution of wealth from the rich to the poor, and preserving the separation of upper and lower caste work:

> In the successive fault lines between the mental and the manual, the gifted and the coached, the general and the reserved, the diaspora and homeland, and authoritarianism and lower caste rights politics, we see the dynamic and sustained forms of maneuver through which the possessive investment in upper caste-ness is expressed and secured.[35]

Concerns with Subramanian's Thesis

The diagram that follows next summarizes Subramanian's thesis, the activism resulting from it, and the impact on Breaking India forces.

Subramanian does not want caste to be treated like economic class because that would make caste biases solvable through economic development. Her agenda requires that caste is a permanent long-term structure, and she wants nothing short of dismantling everything built on top of that structure. We find this view short-sighted and dangerous in this age of competitive globalization. She fails to analyze the broader implications of STEM education in nation-building and uplifting of *all* communities.

Subramanian totally ignores the hard work required to gain admission into the IITs that leads to the success stories of thousands of students. In fact, *she argues that the very act of defending merit-based outcomes is itself a manifestation of caste privilege.* As we saw in Chapter 1, this close-mindedness is directly lifted from Critical Race Theory, shutting the door to any rational argument against her position.

```
┌─────────────────────────────────────────────────────┐
│              ANTI-MERITOCRACY THESIS                  │
│  • Caste = Cultural Capital                           │
│  • Upper Caste = Whiteness Equivalent in India = Capitalists │
│  • IIT Replicates Caste Hierarchy and Perpetuates Casteism │
│  • IIT Alumni Networks Continue Caste Oppression Worldwide │
│  • IIT Meritocracy a Sham Cover-up for Brahmin Privilege │
└─────────────────────────────────────────────────────┘
                        ↓
┌─────────────────────────────────────────────────────┐
│                     ACTIVISM                          │
│  • Caste Discrimination = Racial Discrimination       │
│  • Indian Immigrant Success is a Caste Conspiracy     │
│  • High-profile Lobbying Against IITs                 │
│  • Brainwashing Indian American Youth Against Parents │
│  • Supporting Kashmir Separatism                      │
│  • Helping US Government's Criticism of India's Human Rights │
└─────────────────────────────────────────────────────┘
                        ↓
┌─────────────────────────────────────────────────────┐
│                  BREAKING INDIA                       │
│  • US Ivy Leagues as Venues to Prosecute India        │
│  • Dismantling of IITs and STEM                       │
│  • Social Engineering of India                        │
│  • Communal Divisiveness and Anti-Nationalism         │
└─────────────────────────────────────────────────────┘
            ↙                        ↘
┌──────────────────┐        ┌──────────────────┐
│ POLITICAL VOTE   │        │   CORPORATE      │
│ BANKS AND        │        │   POLICIES       │
│ LEGISLATION      │        │                  │
└──────────────────┘        └──────────────────┘
```

She seems unfazed that US universities are known for Hinduphobic attitudes in South Asian Studies departments, which puts Hindu students at a psychological disadvantage compared to students of other faiths. To make matters worse, some academics like Ajantha Subramanian and Suraj Yengde are busy brainwashing young Indians in universities to look down upon their parents with disdain for being 'casteist'. She ignores the fact that it is common for Indian parents to invest their life savings for their children's college education which can run into the hundreds of thousands of dollars. She wants to brainwash the Indian American youth into revolting against what she sees as their family's caste privilege:

... South Asians of the younger generation that do make common cause with other social justice movements. ... there is a reluctance to think about privilege. There's an ignorance of caste in particular among U.S. born South Asians because they haven't been told about the structural conditions that allowed for their families to migrate and succeed. ... South Asians are aware of their own class privilege and grapple with how to think about that intersection of racial minority status and upper middle-class status. But the caste dimension of the story is often invisible. ... (do not) conflate non-whiteness with a lack of structural privilege. ... important for South Asian Americans, if they want to be productive allies in the fight for social justice.

... be willing to recognize the operations of caste in the United States and the parallels between racial and caste privilege. ... important to think about what it means to be a minority in the United States in comparison with ... a minority in South Asian countries. India right now has an authoritarian, some would say fascist government, and ... enjoys a huge amount of support among South Asians in the diaspora. So if you want to be allied with social justice movements, it's important to do that not just here but transnationally, about the scapegoating of minorities and oppressed castes in the subcontinent. And to not fall into the trap of supporting a majoritarian project in an ancestral homeland as an extension of your own racial, national, or religious identity here.[36]

She ignores the fact that the pattern of highly educated techies coming to the US and occupying prestigious positions has to do with the US immigration policies based on merit and not a result of Indian caste privilege. If the US were to give preference to farmers, carpenters or masons, surely many would end up migrating. If the floodgates were opened without restrictions, the diversity of people migrating would be huge.

Subramanian is a major political activist prosecuting the IITs as reproducers of caste privilege. Indians from privileged caste backgrounds have brought caste into the US, she argues, and the recent lawsuits in the US against caste discrimination are just the tip of the iceberg. She writes that,

...the vast majority of South Asians in the U.S. come from privileged caste backgrounds, and caste has been a form of capital that they've been able to leverage both in their taking advantage of opportunities for migration and also in achieving certain economic and professional successes in the U.S.[37]

Collaborating with other activists, she has been building a social, political, and legal case against IITians. She has positioned herself as the chief witch hunter determined to demonize the IITs at every forum she can get invited to. But absent from her thesis is any self-awareness that she is helping the Breaking India forces by creating communal violence and divisiveness.

The real question is whether the US Ivy Leagues are a suitable venue to prosecute Indian society, define India's policies, and apply heavy-handed geopolitical pressure. Does the US have the moral authority for making such interventions given its own track record of human rights violations, both domestically as well as internationally? Does the US have any record of success in other parts of the world to solve historical issues of a domestic nature?

One is reminded of US allegations of human rights violations in the Middle East that led to the deployment of the military. But it was later proved to be motivated by a desire to capture oil. Social scientists have a notorious history of becoming foot soldiers in America's dirty interventions, and the production of atrocity literature by them has been used to justify criminal acts of aggression and conquest in the past.

These fashionable ideas are being imported to India to shatter an already broken education system. The Mittal Institute at Harvard not only supports Subramanian's scholarship, it also conducts seminars to study the role and definition of merit in India. While China forges ahead in raising a generation of top STEM scholars, these Woke ideas are finding fertile ground in India helped by our very own billionaires and academicians like Ajantha Subramanian.

Postmodernism has aided the social sciences and humanities to slowly permeate the hard sciences of STEM, bringing in politics, sociology, and anthropology. This is happening worldwide. In Canada, for instance, award-winning scientist and chemistry professor of Indian origin, Patanjali Kambhampati, was refused two federal government grants because he said, 'We will hire the most qualified people based upon their skills and mutual interests.' The Natural Sciences and Engineering Research Council of Canada turned down his $450,000 grant application because 'the Equity, Diversity and Inclusion considerations in the application were deemed insufficient'. The application was rejected at the bureaucratic level without making it to the stage where other scientists could review his proposal.[38]

We have discussed that caste has become equated with American-style racism, databases are being compiled to highlight caste prejudice by Indians in the US, legal action is alleging caste abuses in American workplaces, and the IITs are being attacked as racist organizations. The next chapter examines a key US-based Dalit activist who has integrated all these building blocks and merged the Dalit movement with the Black American movement.

5

The Rise of the Afro-Dalits

Overview

Suraj Yengde has emerged as a central player in the field of expanding Critical Race Theory beyond its original scope of racism in the American context. He is senior fellow at the Harvard Kennedy School, research associate with Harvard's Department of African American Studies, fellow at the Hutchins Center for African & African American Research and is part of the founding team of the Initiative for Institutional Anti-racism and Accountability, also at Harvard.[1]

Yengde is prolific, sharp, audacious with a no-nonsense assertiveness, and has a natural wit and charm that makes him an attractive public intellectual. We take him seriously as a pioneer in the future of this discourse. We sympathize with his cause but point out serious flaws in his work.

He is on a mission to find a parallel between every atrocity on African Americans in the US to an equivalent issue in India. When the George Floyd incident on US police brutality broke out, Yengde immediately wrote:

> No one, it seemed, was interested to look at obvious parallels. I had to force this analogy into the discussions. One panellist in a TV debate said it was a US-centred conversation and, hence, bringing up caste issues of India would be a diversion.[2]

The American media has been celebrating him for championing the Afro-Dalit project and making it global:

> Yengde also discussed his personal connections to Black activism. His father, he said, was a member of the Dalit Panthers, an

organization inspired by the Black Panther Party that works to resist the caste system.[3]

'Caste is the mother of all problems' is Yengde's core mantra, and he vigorously chants it at every given opportunity.[4] And this holds true of him not only in India, but worldwide: 'Caste obviously transcends geography and takes on new forms feeding on native practices, like a parasite'.[5]

The framework of the Black movement in America has been appropriated to create Dalit History Month, Dalit Lives Matter, and Dalit Panthers. The *Al Jazeera* reports: 'In the Boston area, the "Dalit and Black Lives Matter" movement stands as a testament to the renewed, re-energised solidarity of the younger generation of Dalit and black activists'.[6] Even the title of the well-known book by Cornel West titled *Race Matters* has been borrowed by Yengde to write his book, *Caste Matters*.

We have previously criticized Indians like Piyush 'Bobby' Jindal who fake Whiteness to benefit from membership in the American Right-wing. Is Suraj Yengde the Black equivalent? He re-styled his hair in an Afro, traditional to African communities, and has manufactured a new kind of Dalit discourse that fits Critical Race Theory. In the process, Yengde has become the poster boy at Harvard's thinktanks being sponsored by Indian billionaires.

Yengde's most consistent passion has been his fixation on Brahmins as the villains entirely culpable for caste abuses; all other factors that may have contributed to the plight of Dalits and others are side lined. He insists that the ideological, religious, and social causes of caste and all its abuses are rooted in Hinduism. He says that the rigid caste hierarchy is built into the core DNA of Hinduism and this system has taken the lives of hundreds of millions of innocent people during its long life. In fact, it is so deeply entrenched in the structures of society at all levels and in everyone's personal lives that it is impossible to remedy merely by changing one's individual posture and actions towards injustice.

And since the injustice cannot be separated out of Hinduism, one must attack Brahmins, the keepers of the tradition, and dismantle Hinduism which gives them their power of oppression. The *structures must get dismantled in total* as a prerequisite for change. And it must be on a global scale. And in Yengde's view, until this is achieved, all progressive movements will be inadequate.

So, similar to Ajantha Subramanian's position, all attempts to reform the social system with initiatives like 'equal opportunity' will fail because the deep structures continue to reproduce unequal outcomes. And those that support reforms within the established institutions are only perpetuating the problem. They, too, are to be condemned as casteist no matter how good their intentions. In other words, Yengde makes no compromises with the world's present social order because he says it has caste embedded in its very fabric.

Yengde's thesis is based on Marxism's dialectic principle: That *every thesis must be opposed by its anti-thesis in an all-out war of mutual destruction.* Out of the rubble of the clash between thesis and anti-thesis will emerge a new kind of synthesis; this synthesis will become the next thesis. This new thesis will again result in an anti-thesis and a new conflict. This process will continue, as explained in Chapter 1. The diagram below explains the process.

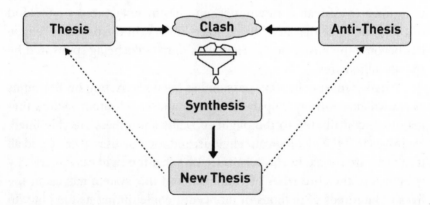

Hence, progress requires a series of such on-going clashes between the established structures and the counter forces that are designed to dismantle them. In other words, an all-out battle that results in the overthrow of the system is the only viable path forward.

When Yengde applies Marxism to deal with societal problems, his logic is emphatic: Hinduism is the institutional system responsible and hence, the main culprit; Brahmins are controlling it; and caste is the device being used to oppress humanity. Therefore, his life's purpose is to launch a revolution that will be the anti-thesis to defeat Brahmins, Hinduism, and caste in an all-out war.

There is much truth in his positions. Our issue with him is that he dismisses attempts by sceptics to raise serious questions. He denounces them as casteist, thereby thwarting what could otherwise be meaningful debates. According to him, the only noble thing for Brahmins is to simply accept his thesis in total, confess their sins against society, disown family members who disagree, and support his campaign to launch a global 'fourth world' movement. We find him dogmatic and blind in his ambition.

Drawing inspiration from Ambedkar, he has anointed himself his successor. He believes he is picking up from where the historical Ambedkar left.

The above summary is intended to present Yengde's positions, so that we can perform our due diligence and develop what we consider a fair assessment. We must repeat that we *do* take his cause seriously, even though we disagree with his arguments and recommended solutions.

Our analysis is based on reading his works and viewing the large number of his videos on talks given in the US, India and elsewhere. We summarize our overall response to his work:

- There are serious flaws in his factual claims and analysis. He is excessively reductionist in his diagnosis of a wide range of social evils; he repeatedly makes some serious factual errors, and fails to nuance issues that are either subjective, debatable, or have multiple layers of reality.
- He provides limited evidence in support of many of his claims.
- There are problems with his implicit zero-sum dialectic approach that is designed for maximizing social conflict. This is fundamentally in contradiction with the Buddhist path that he claims to follow.

Questioning Yengde's Core Historical Assumptions

Too many of Yengde's claims are based on premises that are outright false or exaggerated. Often, there are counterclaims that are substantial and deserve to be addressed. That he gets away with irresponsible statements more often than not, is troubling because it indicates that the academicians who sponsor and promote him are simply not interested in a proper peer review of his work. Let us examine a few examples.

Without citing any reliable evidence whatsoever, Yengde makes the sweeping statement that a race of foreigners known as Aryans had invaded India several millennia ago, bringing with them the problem of caste. Without supporting data and analysis, he wants us to be convinced of the 'alien invasion' which he says, 'is of course now proved'. He claims that genetic evidence has proven this Aryan invasion theory conclusively.

The facts are completely different:

- The Aryan invasion theory was a hypothesis concocted during the colonial era that served European interests and was in fact the type of racist and imperialist doctrine he should be repudiating rather than espousing.
- It was never subject to any academic due diligence whatsoever.
- In recent decades, the theory has been thoroughly refuted using evidence from multiple disciplines – archaeology, linguistics, geographical markers, genetics, and so on.
- Genetic evidence points to considerable internal unity across India.

He also argues against well-established scholarship that shows that the British, through their censuses, froze a fluid caste structure into a formal legal system. His main argument against this is that the British had ruled India for only ninety years, and hence their influence was limited. What he forgets is that before the British Crown ruled India for 90 years, the British East India Company had ruled it for 258 years. The British era, from the start of the British East India Company in 1600 till India's Independence in 1947, spanned a period of nearly 350 years.

Yengde offers a simplistic explanation for the way Indians were defeated by the British, and by various other invaders including the Portuguese, French, Muslims, Mongolians, etc. His theory is that the upper castes refused to let the lower castes get armed because they wanted to control them. In fact, he says, the Brahmins colluded with foreign invaders while the Shudras wanted to defend the country. The lower castes were loyal to India, but the upper castes betrayed the nation.

'Dalits were endangered and were thrown somewhere as slaves', while the upper castes aligned with the colonizers.[7]

The truth, however, is that the dynamics were far more complex. While there was indeed troubling complicity on part of many elites with Muslim and British invaders, there was also widespread resistance and battles for self-rule throughout the colonial period which is what ultimately led to India's Independence and national unity.

Another of his outlandish claims is that Hinduism didn't exist until the mid-nineteenth century. He considers Hinduism to be 'a political invocation to unite Brahmins when they thought their privileges were going away'.[8] This claim is a common one made by Hinduphobes, but there's an inherent contradiction: On the one hand, Hinduism gets blamed for creating the caste system in *ancient* times, and yet, on the other, it is claimed that Hinduism did not exist until *recent* times!

At the same time, we must appreciate that many of his points on history are true. He makes the valid point that Mangal Pandey is erroneously credited for starting the First War of India's Independence in 1857, when the real hero was a Dalit named Matadin Bhangi who had first inspired Mangal Pandey. He is also correct in stating that Gandhi explained caste in spiritual terms rather than eradicating it. Because of this, Yengde calls him 'the new modern political Manu'.[9]

Further, to his credit, Yengde also acknowledges Ambedkar's claim that *Vedas do not talk of varna by birth*, and that a later change made it birth based. This should have led him to introspect rather than place the blame squarely on Hinduism. After mentioning this critical point casually, he immediately returns to fixing the blame on 'the cunning brahmins and their progenies'.[10]

His overall position on the subject is inconsistent. At times he says that the caste system was brought by the Aryans when they invaded India. He then states it was not in the *Vedas* and was later created by Brahmins. And then again, he claims that 'It is no accident that Aryans found a spiritual homeland in India's Hindu laws and its callous caste system'[11] which seems to imply that the Hindu laws and callous caste system had existed *before* the Aryans.

So, he appears to be willing to twist the narrative depending on the circumstances and the audience, while consistently chanting the refrain about the toxicity of Hinduism and Brahmins.

Opportunistic Use of Ambedkar and Buddhism

Yengde considers himself the torchbearer of Ambedkar's movement. But he conveniently ignores Ambedkar's sensitivities and redefines the objectives of Ambedkar's movement to suit his agenda. Ambedkar was first and foremost an Indian nationalist and proudly declared himself as such. Therefore, even when young and vulnerable, he was able to ignore the materialistic temptations that the US and Europe offered him. He chose not to lean on foreign institutions or religions and after studying abroad, gave it all up to return to his motherland. We don't see similar sentiments coming out of Yengde.

We question how much value Yengde places on India's integrity and sovereignty. Making Harvard his base, he has positioned himself to work against Indian interests. And sitting atop that high pedestal, he is enjoying the limelight. His priorities (and loyalties) appear to lie outside India. It is not surprising that he has taken a completely different path from Ambedkar.

Ambedkar's lasting impact was that he adopted the identity of being a 'Dalit', a group *encompassing all depressed people irrespective of their caste*. Ambedkar staunchly *argued against Indians converting to Christianity or Islam*. His writings elaborating what was wrong with both Christianity and Islam are well known as will be discussed in the next chapter.

In a recent discussion between Yengde and a Theravada Buddhist monk, the host questions him on how Ambedkar embraced Buddhism. Yengde replies that Ambedkar 'couldn't find anything more convincing than the Buddha'.[12] This is not the whole truth. What Yengde wants to avoid mentioning is that Ambedkar went through a detailed and systematic evaluation of all the religious options available, and very emphatically *rejected both Christianity and Islam* before adopting Buddhism.

Yengde vaguely alludes to Ambedkar's discomfort with 'other religions' without being specific, saying, 'if Ambedkar had gone to any other religion than Buddha there would have been several wars'.[13] As if Ambedkar hadn't clarified his reasons for not doing so. This blind spot is very likely motivated by Yengde's agenda of bringing down Hinduism at any cost, even if the means go against the thrust of Ambedkar's thesis. Seen in this light, his ignoring Muslim atrocities on Hindus and Buddhists begins to make sense. He is eager to blame caste issues on Brahmins, even in Muslim and Christian societies.

Ambedkar's solution to caste abuses was that Dalits should convert to Buddhism. This point is central to Ambedkar's worldview and social activism. This means that as a new leader of Dalits, Yengde's relationship to Buddhism is of special importance and must be examined closely.

His discussion with the Buddhist monk provides some surprising insights.[14] Throughout the interview, the monk is very direct in his questioning; he puts Yengde on the spot several times to bring out the extent of his understanding of Buddhism. He is polite enough to not expose Yengde's shallowness, but this shallowness, nevertheless, stands out. For instance, the host questions the basis for his claim that the *Dalits were originally Buddhists*. Yengde's explanation goes as follows:

> When the Buddha came on to the consciousness of India, he became a biggest threat to the Vedic caste system because Buddha just crumbled the house of cards of caste system. Because Buddha offered that many tribes, which were eventually declared untouchables, become part of Dhamma and because they were part of dhamma, there was a repeated assassination of the people who were identifying themselves in the pathway of dhamma. Buddha himself was subjected to several attacks, physical, spiritual.[15]

This response sounds garbled and does not provide any convincing evidence to Yengde's claim that Dalits were originally Buddhists. And later, in the same interview he says, 'Ambedkar is born as a Hindu and born as a low caste untouchable Hindu', thus contradicting his earlier claim of Dalits being originally Buddhists.

To strengthen his position that 'Dalits are not Hindus'[16] Yengde assigns various attributes to them, whereas the fact is that Dalits are not a homogeneous group at all. The notion of a unified identity called Dalits is a recent invention to bring together all marginalized communities for the political cause of fighting injustice. But the move to homogenize their cultures for the purpose of attacking Hinduism is a violation of their pluralism. Especially since it is well established that they never had an internal unity of language, history, geographical proximity, spiritual traditions, culture, or professional status.

It is ironic that such a posture of homogenization comes from the liberal academy that champions diversity so fondly.

When Yengde hosted the Jharkhand chief minister, Hemant Soren at Harvard, he got his guest to say, 'Adivasis (indigenous people) were never Hindus. All our customs, traditions are completely different from Hindus'.[17] One of the differences cited to prove they are non-Hindus was that Adivasis are nature worshippers.[18] But Hindus too are nature worshippers! Surya *deva* (Sun god) is worshipped in numerous forms. Air, water, fire, and earth are manifestations of deities. There are sacred mountains and rivers. The peepal tree is sacred. Nature and Hinduism are inseparable.

Yengde says that Hindus assimilated Buddha by calling him the ninth *avatara*, the reincarnation of Lord Vishnu, and this was done to make Buddha secondary and subordinate to Hindus. What Yengde should know is that avatara is a Sanskrit term that refers to a manifestation of God/Supreme Being and calling Buddha an avatara can hardly be considered subordinate or demeaning. Also, many *sampradayas* (traditions) do not necessarily accept the positioning of Buddha within the official list of avataras. There is greater nuance to the Hindu response and receipt of Buddha and Buddhism than Yengde credits. This kind of shallow caricaturing is not serious scholarship.

He preaches about the victimhood of Buddhists at the hands of the Hindus. He refers to 'a genocide of Buddha, of Buddhists, and his Dhamma, repeated genocides'.[19] He refers to Acharya Adi Shankara, revered by Hindus as one of the greatest Vedic scholars and one of the foremost spiritual leaders, in the most derogatory manner. He tweets: 'This ugly head dumpster—Shankaracharya is responsible for crimes such as this'.[20] He accuses Shankaracharya of murder: 'Killing many monks who were killed during the onslaught of Adi Shankaracharya'. There was an 'onslaught and attacks to eliminate Buddha from this land'.[21] And of course, he offers no supporting evidence for his outlandish claims.

Claiming to be echoing Ambedkar, he says that Hindus desecrated Buddhist temples and viharas, and 'the monks were killed en masse by the invading kingdoms of the so-called invading Brahminic order'.[22] He fails to mention that Buddhist monuments were destroyed by marauding Muslim invaders and rulers. Shankaracharya just taught Vedic thought that inspires many. While he challenged Buddhist thought and doctrine, he did so through discussion and debate which was rigorous, open, and free – not through violence. That was the Indian tradition of intellectual debate for genuine truth. The Buddhist organizations in India were not eradicated by Hindus but by foreign invaders. Hindus and Buddhists generally enjoyed peaceful relations.

Yengde announces that it is *his responsibility* to continue Ambedkar's work of re-converting Indians to Buddhism. He does show the true spirit of Buddhism when he says that converting one's oppressor to the dharma is a good way to create a fellowship of the larger sangha. We would very much support Yengde if he were truly wanting to expand Buddhism's spirituality worldwide. That would be an amazing movement to be involved in.

But as we shall see now, his activism from his Harvard perch is hardly compatible with the Buddhist ethos: *The Marxist dialectic is incompatible with the Buddhist path*! And it was Ambedkar who said so, as we shall see in Chapter 6.

Buddha's signature teaching comprised two parts: the diagnosis, and the solution:

1. Buddha diagnosed the human condition in his famous *Four Noble Truths*. This is a nuanced, profound, and sophisticated insight and entirely different from Yengde's angry and divisive theory that is based on blaming Hindus for causing all the social problems. Yengde does not understand the nature of suffering and the means of removing that suffering from the perspective of the Four Noble Truths. Therefore, he is exploiting Buddhism very superficially merely to cloak himself with its cultural capital. His understanding is from the level of his ego, whereas Buddhism deconstructs the ego to achieve a higher state of consciousness.

2. Buddha's solution is commonly referred to as the *Eightfold Path*. This path focuses on uplifting one's own level of consciousness by transcending the level of ego, and then helping others to do the same. This is diametrically opposite to the Marxist dialectic that calls for a clash with other egos. Yengde is operating at the level of an ego driven to fight for power by bringing down an opponent. His path is a call to a revolution at variance with Buddhism.

Buddha takes us inwards to explain the problem as well as the solution. His premise is that better human beings will make a better and more responsible society. Yengde, on the other hand, externalizes both the problem and the solution. Ironically, the thesis he is building resonates with Buddhism while his anti-thesis is designed to clash with it.

As the conversation moves deeper into Buddhism, Yengde's claim to be a Buddhist falls apart. How Yengde explains his relationship with Vipassana (popularly called mindfulness), leaves a lot to be desired. Vipassana, after all, is the technique of meditation taught by Buddha that is now a worldwide movement and considered the fundamental practice for Buddhists.

But when the host asks if he has done Vipassana, he looks uncomfortable and mumbles: 'I did one ten-day course, three years before.'[23] His experience was not fruitful. He says: 'These teachers always tell keep practicing and keep practicing. I was lazy and I was not doing it.'[24]

Any practitioner of meditation would find it amazing how he trivializes the practice when he admits that upon meditating, 'my thought came that I am having too much saliva in my mouth'.[25] He says he found it 'difficult to detach' and be able to meditate. He concludes that he has been thinking for over a year to do some Vipassana. Clearly, he is no meditator, nor has he accorded it the respect required by the Buddhist tradition.

Being a non-meditating Buddhist is an oxymoron. It is a self-contradiction, for no true advancement toward liberation is possible as long as one is fighting from the ego level of consciousness. Viewed in Buddhist terms, Yengde is grasping an identity, projecting anger on his adversaries, and calling for a war between identities. This is against the path of Buddhism.

Also, he makes the false statement that 'the dhamma was an oral tradition. It was never written down'.[26] The fact is that originally it was oral, but then written in Pali, and thereafter translated into Sanskrit where it was formalized and developed extensively. He appears ignorant about the fact that Buddhism decided to write its texts in Sanskrit because Sanskrit offered a standard of rigor not available in any other language. This importance given to Sanskrit is well known to historians of Buddhism.

Furthermore, he says: 'It gives me goosebumps, Ambedkar calling Buddha, my master, the intimacy of that.'[27] But of course he has no idea that a core tenet of Buddhism is to avoid deifying any personality.

Eventually, Yengde concedes in the interview: '*I don't practice Buddhism. I go to temple maybe once a year. And I don't even know what to do once I go.*'[28] In other words, his claim to be a Buddhist is a ruse. His relationship with Buddhism appears to be driven by other motives. And it's easy to see how positioning himself as Ambedkar's successor would advance his career at Harvard.

He wants to fulfil Ambedkar's dream project of creating a political union of various Buddhist countries, in effect making a political bloc that would come to each other's defence. But his method for achieving this global Buddhist movement and unification is to promote the Dalit Panthers, which he says are like the Black Panthers in America. He claims that the Dalit Panthers are Buddhists and that Dalits have never instigated violence. Although he advocates developing more empathy towards other groups, this differs in practice from the Dalit Panther path of aggressiveness that he embodies.

Dalits as Perennial Victims

Yengde applies Critical Race Theory to caste and is developing what he calls Critical Dalit Theory that would supersede the former by going into the deeper cause of prejudices. One must understand Yengde's interpretation of Dalits as perennial victims in this context.

Critical Race Theory maintains that privileges enjoyed by White Americans are so deeply embedded in US institutional structures that these biases operate even unconsciously. This is how the oppression of the underclass carries on from one generation to the next. Yengde has taken this idea and applied it to caste. In his mapping, Brahmins are like White Americans and Dalits and other lower castes are akin to Black Americans. The following statements explain his thinking:

> The resources one [i.e., a Brahmin] is having is not earned on merit. It is by looting; it is by thuggery.[29]

Nobody is asking you to pay for the sins of your ancestors. ...
In many ways, you are reaping the benefits of what your ancestors
had done, by maintaining the status quo and by harassing the
majority of the population.[30]

In other words, Brahmin 'thugs' did not earn their privileges based on
merit but accumulated them by looting. The premise for this logic is
that today's Brahmins are merely reaping the benefits of these structures
in society established by their ancestors to pass on privileges. By 'the
majority of the population' he refers to the Dalits, and they are being
'harassed' by Brahmins who perpetuate their own privileges.

The following passages further elaborate his theory. Those Brahmins
that fail to admit these abusive structures from the past and continue
to perform patronizing acts to appear as though they are helping Dalits,
are perpetuating the abuse. They are also part of 'the casteist regime':

Unless we recognize those structures exist around you, you will
still be a part of a casteist regime because you have slowly in your
patronizing charitable ways very subtly contributed to espousing
casteism.[31]

Therefore, what we call tradition is itself an abusive structure, including
all its festivals and values:

Tradition does not exist. We have created this to bring out our
own values and impose on the rest of the majority things like
festivals and all become part of 'tradition'.[32]

He does not want people to think that affirmative action or quota
systems are a favor to the Dalits. According to him, the Dalits have
been productive in society for which they were robbed of their share
of fair compensation. Hence, educational subsidies are merely giving
back what was owed to them:

Dalits are actually paying for their own education. Because they
actually produce a certain economy which then gets into state
coffers and the state then gives them back. In this case, many
times the state doesn't give them back. ... I appeal people to look
at how much Dalits put into the state coffers each year and how
much do they get in return.[33]

The next chapter will explain the Dalits' contributions and economic conditions during different periods of history.

Another issue we have is with Yengde's position on *class*. While we empathize with the plight of the Dalits and lower castes, we find it problematic when he insists that caste is not similar to class. *Class is changeable* through education and economic reforms, but *caste is permanent*. He writes that the difference is due to the karma theory:

> Caste supersedes class. ... the labor is tied within the scriptural karmic theory, so they are "paying their penance" in this context. The classed people in India are the people who are fundamentally owners of capital brahmins and baniya groups.[34]

The capital is owned by Brahmins and *baniya* (businessman) groups, he says. The Dalits and lower caste people are denied capital because the karma theory is used to claim that their bad karma from past lives caused them to be born in an inferior status. Hence, their plight gets explained as a case of 'paying their penance'. This spiritual justification of birth-based bias makes it different than class, and hence impossible to eradicate. The scale of this abuse is horrendous, he says. He cites some statistics, including some numbers that appear serious exaggerations to sensationalize his point:

> In India, casteism touches 1.35 billion people. It affects 1 billion people. It affects 800 million people badly. It enslaves the human dignity of 500 million people. It is a measure of destruction, pillage, drudgery, servitude, bondage, unaccounted rape, massacre, arson, incarceration, police brutality and loss of moral virtuosity for 300 million Indian Untouchables.[35]

'India is probably the only country that has apartheid-era type of slaves,'[36] he claims. The statistics he cites, if taken at face value, make it seem that India is the world's worst human rights nightmare:

> From 2006 to 2016 about half a million atrocities were committed against Dalits. It's a genocide that we saw under our eyes and yet this is not a new incident. This has been happening since the independence era, prominently with immense amount of brutal

massacres, yet Dalits have not invoked civil wars. They have every reason to.[37]

All this violence against the Dalits falls at the doorstep of the 'Hindu religious order'. He maintains:

> The people made outcastes by the Hindu religious order, deemed despicable, polluted, unworthy of life beings whose mere sight in public would bring a cascade of violence upon the entire community.[38]

Many 'facts' used by him to argue his case are clearly out of line. He is incorrect in saying that upper caste people from India come to the US and enjoy reservations as minorities. His following statement that US reservations help upper caste Indians get into Ivy Leagues is incorrect:

> Many people who clamor against reservation in India get into line for reservation here [i.e., USA] to get into Ivy League schools and other university and other jobs and this is very ironical.[39]

Yengde has a flawed understanding of affirmative action in the US:

> Why are you applying for a diversity quota which is reservation? You want to get promotion, you cry hoarse that 'I am a person of color, I am an Indian, I don't get ahead because white people are dominating and all' and then you want to get the promotion. So, they get reservation promotion here. They get job on promotion reservation here, they get admissions on reservation here, yet they don't see the same thing applying to India.[40]

There is a distinction between affirmative action as practiced in the US today versus the reservations policies implemented in India. Traditionally, the US has resisted quotas; this is coming under pressure now from those demanding metrics to hold institutions accountable. But still one does not see in the US the widespread use of quotas or reservations in the same way it is aggressively pursued in India.

Yengde is right in complaining that India's modern education system has been woefully inadequate – '85% of population [of India] was not given access [to education], and to add, ... the rest 10% were given meagre education, not complete education'.[41] This made large segments of the population unable to perform useful work and earn a living. Here, one must refer to the writings by Dharampal who showed that till the mid-1800s, the Indian masses were receiving good education relevant to their occupations. These statistics are well documented in British surveys and discussed in the next chapter.

Subsequently, the British takeover of education produced a class of Anglicized Indians fit for low levels of administrative work in the British colonial system. Large Indian industries (like textiles and steel) got dismantled and taken over by Britain's Industrial Revolution. From being the world's largest export economy, India got reduced to a mere consumer of British goods. Yengde is silent on all this.

Beyond economic oppression, Yengde points out that Dalits also face humiliation. There is pressure on them to not speak up and confront the upper castes. He feels issues like Dalits wearing designer clothes, riding a horse, or even keeping a moustache are unacceptable in India. He adds that his standing tall at Harvard is considered dreadful by some.

Dalits are being blamed for identity and vote bank politics in India, Yengde says, while they are also pursued by upper castes: 'Don't you think brahmins, don't you think Thakurs, don't you think Marathas, don't you think baniyas are part of identity politics? They are. So let's apply the same lens to that caste politics.'[42] He is right. Identity and vote bank politics has become the norm in Indian democracy and the biggest cause for fragmenting and slipping towards breakup. No community has been able to rise above this; and blaming one another for being responsible is not constructive.

Since Yengde views through the lens of the Marxist dialectic, it is a zero-sum game for him. Brahmins must be condemned and brought down so that their structures get dismantled. Until that happens, Dalits cannot become free people.

> 44% of the CEOs in various companies and various board members are Brahmins. We need to question this, that how come a minority exerts so much influence and power.[43]
>
> Why is it singularly the Brahmins continue to be temple priests across the rich temples, sitting on so much amount of exploited wealth. It is the working class, the peasants' wealth that they are sitting upon.[44]

The first statistic is true in that Brahmins are over-represented in top corporate posts; one can debate whether this is entirely merit-based or whether their networks of privilege and influence play a role. But the second claim is false. Non-Brahmin priests run large numbers of temples across India. As far as the wealth of temples is concerned, most of it is in the hands of the government because the coffers of large Hindu temples are controlled by it. This has been a major issue from the Hindu side: Unlike churches, mosques and gurdwaras, Hindu temples continue to be run by the government ever since the British put in place discriminatory laws against Hindus that have never been repealed.

He is also wrong in his statement that when it comes to reservations 'your fellow Brahmins are taking your seats. It is not Dalits or Adivasis who are taking your seats'.[45] The quotas for Dalits and lower castes are indeed high and this is a matter worthy of debate.

What is especially troubling about the quote above is that it uses the same kind of anti-Semitic logic that hounded Jews out of many different territories when they were accused of being a well-to-do minority that was oppressing the poor natives of Germany. This kind of vilification of Brahmins is very dangerous.

Yengde's analysis of oppression concludes with a declaration that Brahmins are criminals. He says:

> If a community commits a crime repeatedly, what would you call that community? ...in African American struggle, they're straight up: white supremacist. ...Tell me, when we are going to call 'brahmin supremacists'? ... From my vantage point these are criminal castes. There is no other way I will identify them; they have committed a crime on my community, and they are criminals to me. If Thakurs have committed crime, they are criminal caste for me. They have to now work a lot to remove the stigma and stay in my mind.[46]

He wants to brand Brahmins the criminal caste. He has repeatedly insisted that Brahmins must be targeted and not the others, not even other upper castes. His formula for attacking Hinduism goes as follows:

- The Brahmin scriptures sanction caste. He claims that *Purusha Sukta*, a hymn from the *Rig Veda*, is 'the holy spirit of this superman, Brahma' and has organized the world according to birth.

- All forms of oppression are based on this hierarchical structure where Brahmins remain at the top. All patriarchy is Brahminical, and it subjugates not only women but also the poor.
- Brahmins will use all methods and creative ideas to retain their top position.[47]

He has been questioned why communities known as Other Backward Castes (OBCs) are not given their share of blame because a large number of acts of violence against Dalits are committed by OBCs. Why does he target only Brahmins? His response is radically anti-Brahmin:

> OBCs are responsible for violence but they are imposing violence under a structure. Without caste, OBCs are humans, brahmins are humans, Dalits are humans. With caste one becomes brahmin, one becomes OBC. OBCs are basically the servant castes of Brahminism where they like to serve because the structure grants them superficial superiority. If an OBC is committing a crime, it is because someone above him is authorizing to offer that violence, and for that he or she is compensated spiritually, politically and in various ways as we see in today's India.[48]

This means the Brahmins are responsible even for those crimes committed by others because the caste system they have ostensibly erected is causing all the crimes committed by third parties.

He makes contradictory statements depending on who he is addressing. For instance, he says, on the one hand, 'Dalit is not a subdued category. ... It is not problematizing the oppressor'.[49] But in fact, as the previous pages illustrate, he is not only problematizing the oppressor, but also engaging in the worst kind of reverse-discrimination against Brahmins. And to top it all, he is using many false allegations, highly exaggerated, and one-sided claims.

Yengde borrows the language and logic used by Black Americans to claim that reparations are needed for Dalits:

> Reparation is one way to tell the oppressor that you are also responsible. Now if you continue to inflict harm there would be more reparations on your side. Its (sic) not just material gain,

its (sic) acknowledgement to begin with first, that yes, we have benefitted out of the murders and rapes of the Dalits and continue to benefit even today.[50]

He wants that Indians must accept that most Dalits working on farms in the major states are landless and 'their landlessness gives a premium to the oppressor castes who are in the feudal setup to inflict violence'.[51] The way forward, he says, would be for the upper castes to 'Denounce your privileges. Give away whatever lands you have been possessing for thousands of years and redistribute'.[52]

Interestingly, one of the panelists in the above discussion pointed out that the Indian Constitution makes provisions for reparations for past atrocities (thanks to Ambedkar), while the US Constitution does not.[53] But he is blind to this kind of logic. Backed by Western institutions, Yengde believes Indian taxpayers must spend even more in developing a large army of sepoys. To end caste discrimination, he demands:

> Sending 10,000 Dalit and tribal students every semester to foreign universities from the dedicated fund meant for them would be a good idea. Empower the Dalits - materially, educationally as well as spiritually.[54]

He wants large-scale wealth distribution to Dalits:

> In India, about 70 percent of Dalit labourers are landless. If they are given land, he/she will take care of the land well and yield more. And I think for me that has to happen with nationalising land. Once that happens, we will create a society which is at least trying to slightly come off an equal. Affirmative action is just one policy, there will be more aggressive policies that we will need to democratise our institutions.[55]

Despite the intensity with which he champions the Dalit cause, he does not welcome the instances of their successes. During one of his panel discussions in the US, some panelists suggested that US business schools could teach Dalits the skills for upward mobility which will help them on their return to India. This made Yengde uncomfortable, especially when one panelist mentioned that there is a Dalit Chamber of Commerce in India providing Dalit entrepreneurs access to capital. Yengde immediately declared that the head of the Dalit group of entrepreneurs was 'a product of RSS' (Rashtriya Swayamsevak Sangh) Right-wing manipulation' and it was dangerous to let him represent Dalits.[56] He holds the RSS responsible for establishing this 'Brahminical supremacy',[57] and any initiatives by them to help Dalits must be condemned.

Clearly, Yengde prefers those Dalits he can parade as 'victims' and not those who have climbed the ladder within the system purely through merit and entrepreneurship. All progress that India has made on caste disparities is denied by his divisive rhetoric. Ram Nath Kovind, who completed his tenure as president of India in July 2022, is a Dalit. Furthermore, the current president, Smt. Draupadi Murmu, is herself a Santhal, one of the so-called scheduled tribes.[58] Yengde also ignores the dramatic progress on the ground that has been made in providing life amenities to Dalits, especially women, such as clean water, sanitation, free medical facilities, housing, etc.

Elsewhere, he has written:

> The Right wants to claim Ambedkar because Dalits are a potential challenge to the Brahmanical (sic) project. If the Right can't fight them, then they try to assimilate them. The Right has made its enemy it's (sic) best friend because they can't kill Dalit assertion.[59]

In other words, Hindus simply cannot do anything he will find acceptable. The complete, and final, dismantling of Hinduism seems to be a necessary condition for any solution, according to him.

He does not tolerate competing Dalit leaders, especially those wanting to improve the economic lives of Dalits in constructive ways. And if an upper caste scholar discusses Dalits, even while showing sympathy, he protects his turf. He advocates: 'Need greater scrutiny of Dalit studies done by non-Dalits'.[60]

Brahmin Patriarchy

Yengde says that the Aryan men came alone on horses without any women. As a result, 'The Aryan invasion was built on the separation of womenfolk, and women were not considered here as someone equal'.[61] Brahmins continued the Aryan traditions that caused all the problems. This is laughable and no one with even a basic knowledge of India would accept this. But being branded 'Harvard', Yengde gets away with such nonsense.

A core tenet for Yengde is that Brahminical patriarchy gets its legitimacy from Hindu codes that assign supremacist status to Brahmins.[62] It is 'the elephant in the room that continues to operate in every one of us. ... Brahminical equals patriarchy and patriarchy equals Brahminical. They are not different'.[63] He explains:

> If women and Dalits are not oppressed, caste society will not function. The oxygen of casteist society is the death of the Dalit and woman.[64] The origin of this can be traced back to the Vedas: 'In Rg Vedic times, women were the first slaves'.[65]

And what is Hinduism? He says it is merely an expression of Brahmin patriarchy:

> When we talk about Hinduism, we mask Brahminical patriarchy. If you have to talk at all about Hinduism, you have to talk about Brahminical patriarchy as a starting point. It is upon this that civilizations of various Hindu orders have been built.[66]

The very nature of Brahmins is to demand that a man be anti-women, he says. From a young age, boys are taught to be a strong alpha male character.[67] One that is not male is considered a curse to society.[68] Brahmin supremacy is imposed on society through five institutions: family, parents, marriage, reproduction, and the sexual control of women.[69]

He says that any attempt to expose the Brahminical privilege is resisted.[70] Women who are well-informed and confident are considered a threat:

> An independent autonomous and confident woman is an atom bomb to the Brahmanical (sic) Vedic system.[71]

Upper class Brahmin women were coerced into accepting Brahminical patriarchy. 'If she were to protest, she had to go and jump into the funeral pyre, the burning pyre of her husband'. Protesting would invite torture upon herself.[72]

The Brahmin guise of guarding a woman is not for protecting her, but to 'keep a watch on her every activity'. Women are put under surveillance and policed, he says, to prevent them from reproducing children that would not fit the caste structure. Even the systems of sati and widowhood were invented to control women. This is why a widow is required to shave her head, wear a certain type of sari, and live as an outcaste. 'Her life is a hell hole as long as she lives'.[73]

To keep women ignorant and vulnerable, they are not given access to *Vedas*, he says:

> Manusmriti gives an effective doctrine that women cannot have access to Vedas because they are born sinners and the chapter is closed. ... It becomes a very hetero-normative sexualized discourse that confines the independence of women's autonomy. [74]

Brahmin patriarchy even causes many women to get murdered, not only Dalit women, but all women:

> If a person was to marry second wife, most likely he murdered the first wife. And these murders went under the norm of suicide - she got burnt while cooking the food or she went to draw water from the well and slipped her feet. ... Not just Dalit, any women's murder committed by husbands were written down as an act of nature or she was just tired and committed suicide.[75]

Yengde insists that a woman's orgasm is a threat to male orgasmic powers. In fact, anyone who suppresses sexual desires and independence of the female body, is participating in Brahmin patriarchy, regardless of gender, caste, class, or religion. To make the woman feel helpless, he says Indian males created the requirement that the wife must want him as her husband for the next seven lives. That is required as per Yengde's understanding of the karma theory of rebirth.[76]

He argues that to maintain caste hierarchy, the role of women is strictly as reproducing units; they are the factories meant for reproducing caste purity. This, he claims, has been enforced through punishments and laws found in *Manusmriti*, *Ramayana*, and other 'so called spiritual texts'. Yengde says that *Manusmriti* became the law of the land. It put women at the same level as animals.[77]

> That's why Ambedkar resigned from his post as a law minister, saying if this new country cannot grant independence to women, I refuse to be a part of anything that is going to reproduce age old norms.[78]

Yengde also attacks the family system as a sinister structure to preserve caste abuse. 'Anyone operating beyond the framework of the monogamous family is considered a prostitute'.[79]

> When one is born into a certain Indian family that practices certain faith, they're actually coming into a family that is conditioning the behaviors. The pronouns are already granted, and the role of a woman is already destined. You can't break those regulations and norms and if you challenge, you are a woman who is bitter tongued. [80]

This abusive system is self-perpetuating because parents teach it and deny the youth their independent choices. The Indian diaspora parents in America enforce who their children hang out with, and the lifestyles they lead. He feels that 'parents effectively become the caste police' for their children.[81]

When parents help their children, they are using caste privilege and creating criminals, he says.[82] Yengde appeals to the Indian youth to reject their parents and get rid of casteism, patriarchy, homophobia, transphobia, xenophobia, and all other forms of inhumane values that are rooted in Indian culture. He says:

> Parents are the first casteist teachers. They are responsible for damaging their child's mind. When youngsters ask me how to get rid of caste, I tell them to disown their casteist parents.[83]

So, not only does he want to dismantle the societal system but also to break apart families and demolish familial structures. This kind of movement is not even a revolution; it is plain annihilation and tantamount to cultural genocide. He blames Brahmins for similar problems that exist in other religions as well. The impact of Brahmins has been so serious, he says, that these problems got adopted by all religions, including Islam and Christianity.[84]

Marriage, Yengde feels, is a way parents transact in the 'sexuality market'. Children are raised to prepare themselves for marriage. This 'hyper capitalist celebration of marriage' is so overarchingly present that people eagerly look forward to that specific day. This is why a woman in India gets tortured by her in-laws and even parents in some cases, if she does not bear a child. She must pray to God to grant a boy. Brahmin patriarchy causes all this anxiety in upper caste males and compels them to control lower caste men and all women.[85]

The *Manusmriti*, he claims, required families to control the purity of caste and in many instances, they had to marry and reproduce among themselves. Manu made women into mere property, like slaves to be transacted. Because a woman is considered equivalent to an animal, according to Yengde, it gives permission to invoke violence and 'that's why every week we have 21 Dalit women getting raped'.[86]

Given this dire predicament of women, all other projects should be set aside, and the central goal ought to be to rescue women from 'Brahminical violence'.[87] But only he and his movement are equipped to perform this act of liberation. Upper caste women scholars that engage in such issues is not the way forward; he accuses them of stealing feminist theories from the West to protect their own men. They rarely pay attention to the Brahmin patriarchy all around them, he says, because it has become normalized in everyday actions.[88]

Yengde also ignores or downplays Islam's role as an oppressor of women's issues. He gives Islam a free pass in its structural treatment of women, customs of marriage including polygamy and nikaah, halal, and the hyper-masculinity that Muslim men openly show off and brag about. Nor does he seem comfortable pointing out to his Black American collaborators that the history of African societies includes numerous structures of oppression of women and inter-ethnic violence.[89]

Yengde's tirade accuses Brahmins of creating myths to celebrate the murder of Dalit and Adivasi women. The festival of Holi is one such example. According to his interpretation, it enacts the story of Holika, a native woman who is depicted in Hindu texts as an *asura* or demon like the Dalits. These texts depict the upper caste as gods, he says, while those protesting against Hindu oppression are considered demons. This is the myth of Holi as a celebration of an asura's death.[90] All this is asserted by Yengde without evidence.

Another theory he has borrowed directly from missionary propaganda is the view that temple devadasis were sex slaves. According to him, Hindu priests were constantly seeking sexual favors, and therefore created a system of sexual slavery called devadasi. *Deva* means God and *dasi* means a female slave of God, he says. He claims that Brahmins are treated as gods, and Dalits are slaves forced to send their young girls, age five-six, into the temples to become slaves under the pretext of serving God. This, he says, was a forced custom. It was essentially a system of raping women constantly and using them as instruments for entertaining the Hindu gods, and in return, the gods showered blessings. This is why he claims that Hindus parade Dalit women naked or make them perform all kinds of acts that please men. But the upper caste men cannot tolerate an upper caste woman raping a Dalit man, according to him, because they are insecure about their own masculinity.[91]

The diagram below shows the main assumptions behind Yengde's uncompromising stand to dismantle Hinduism.

Suraj Yengde's Formula for Attacking Hinduism

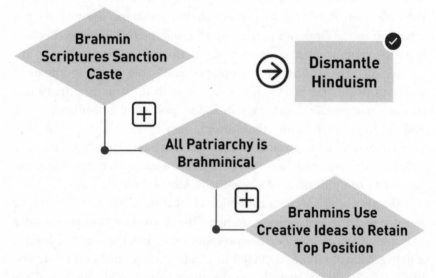

Caste Globalization and the Fourth World

Yengde points out that four million people of Indian origin reside in America, including almost two hundred thousand Indian students. Indians rank at the top in getting the H-1B visa for skilled labor force. In addition, large numbers of Indians are getting the Green Card or becoming naturalized as US citizens. He calls out many movers and shakers like Sundar Pichai, Satya Nadella, Kamala Harris, Bobby Jindal, and so on. What America does not know, he says, and he wants to educate them, is that they bring caste structures along with them.[92]

Yengde has a clear-cut and well-defined view on Indian immigrants in America, attributing their success to their caste elitism and proximity to White Americans:

> Why is it that so many persons of Indian origin thrive in America? ... many ... titans of big industries are brown people from South Asia. Why is it that so many Indian doctors or dentists take care of American ailments? And that the culture, literary, and media industries also have so many Indian people? What is that secret sauce that makes this possible? To understand this better we need a caste lens. The many Indians who sit at the top of the American dream are largely from the dominant castes of Indian society. Their upbringing, mannerisms, deftness, way of thinking and claiming pride, belief in culture, dominant oppressive status, easy access to lowest caste labor, and the confidence to 'walk in and win' are all traits shared by their 'cousins' on American soil. Indians coming to America is a homecoming of dominant castes. The many Indians who are invested in a politics of supremacy, hatred, and profit over human values find a natural home in the Republican Party.[93]

Ironically, many Indian Americans are actually Liberal and disproportionately support the Democratic Party and progressive causes. He says, the Indian diaspora is hiding its dirty dark secret of caste oppression behind exotic images of elephants and yoga, while sidelining caste as a topic for discussion. He explains:

> When people leave India and become de facto ambassadors, they promote India as a clichéd image of elephants on the street, yoga, meditation and other spiritual practices. ... you don't see caste being brought up and interrogated despite it being the fundamental aspect of everything that happens in India. Most of the time, caste is Orientalized and understood as India's own creative flavor of dividing labor. It does not come across as what it truly is – as caste apartheid.[94]

One of the culprits is Neo-liberalism because it enables the global elites to continue their exploitation. The deep structures of abuse have not been dealt with by the global multilateral institutions:

> ... World Bank and the IMF impose their exploitative policies, which is the reason that each country's elite continue to retain power unabashed and with massive aggression. ... caste, like social laws, continue to dominate the societies through the affixed institutions of culture inbred into the society. Thus, structure and cultures dominate societies which have been conveniently upheld as sacrosanct in the western human rights regime, discounting the oppression it produces.[95]

The problem according to him is that India lost a golden opportunity post-Independence to determine the proper direction for the nation. The elitists that replaced the British were Indians who had proximity to the British, and

> ...who went to institutions like Oxford and Cambridge, who had gone to America. They were the people traditionally in the positions of power, such as the Brahmin community or the Baniya community in India. Gandhi and Nehru are the classic examples of Brahmin Baniya representation. When the British left, those elite Indian communities took the reins from them. That is why we still see unrest.[96]

Though there is a lot of truth in what he says, Yengde refuses to credit Indian Americans in any way for their achievements in the highly competitive American landscape. He trivializes their achievements by calling it their 'inherited' caste privilege in India which is aligned with White privilege in US, Germany, and elsewhere:

> The inherited traits of being from a dominant caste give one what it takes to thrive. A dominant-caste immigrant, even if poor, is still advantaged with the cultural traits, societal building of confidence, and social and professional techniques needed in an ugly age of caste-capitalist competition. ... dominant-caste immigrant groups thrive and excel in America. American society has unwritten codes for that encourage harmony between groups who favor and

validate casteism. It is easy for the dominant "upper" castes not to upset the foundations of casteist society, which hinges on making the lowest group untouchable and unseeable. In every upper-middle-class, non-Americanized-accent-speaking household ... one could notice the immense faith that the dominant castes had in the validity of the American caste system. They held on to the values of hard work and merit-based advancement, denigrating the lowest castes as lazy and unworthy. Without a significant presence for more than a few decades, the dominant-caste immigrants ally themselves with their long-lost cousins of other societies—Aryan Germany, white America, or Brahmin India. It is no accident that Aryans found a spiritual homeland in India's Hindu laws and its callous caste system.[97]

In other words, he explains, 'Caste is as American as white supremacy'.[98] It is the same caste system that has adapted to various countries.

Yengde mentions that even in the 1800s certain scholars explained caste as a *global* social phenomenon, not just in Hindu society.[99] But no global movement was possible for all the outcastes in various countries to unite. In the following century, Ambedkar too began the process of connecting with outcastes in several countries, but the initiative did not produce a lasting outcome. He points out that recently there have been some cross-national meetings in which he is rising as a leader for collective actions.

The path forward for him is to convince philanthropists to make Harvard the center for uniting lower caste thinkers from around the world. He laments that he has not yet met at Harvard, the oppressed representing countries like Nigeria, Japan, Senegal, Mali, Mauritania, Kenya, Somalia, the US, South Africa, Eastern and Western Europe, Nepal, Pakistan, Sri Lanka, Israel, Afghanistan, and so on.

His next project, he says, is to champion the cause of communities worldwide that have been marginalized for thousands of years. The ruling classes use partial solutions like affirmative action to keep the present structures intact. This must change:

I am envisioning a fourth world, a think tank, a concept that goes beyond first, second and third world. This fourth world embraces the people who have never even participated in the project of third world because it reproduces a certain form of elitism. These marginalized folks would be invited to come and talk to each other and think of the ways that they want to live in the world, the way they want to see themselves. Currently, by virtue of non-accessibility and lack of access to resources, they cannot talk to each other.[100]

He wants to be the man at Harvard who brings together the downtrodden from the 'Fourth World':

> Due to abject poverty and lack of representation, many untouchables of the world are still unable to challenge mainstream narratives in their societies. Through my travels and research, I also discovered that the postcolonial scholarship and activism were another stratagem of the elites of native societies to hide the oppressions they practice and redirect public attention towards the external 'other' – the moribund colonial state.[101]
>
> There is what we can call a Fourth World of outcastes around the world who have been left out of the prominent discourses and debates concerning human rights and social and economic justice. Today, there is an urgent need to identify these underprivileged groups and establish international solidarity networks.[102]

His vision for a Fourth World thinktank is ambitious and deserves careful attention:

> An organisation dedicated to this task, seeking to challenge mainstream narratives, a Fourth World think-tank, could serve this purpose. It would provide the most vulnerable groups around the world with a platform to discuss and share their experiences of marginalisation and learn ways to fight discrimination and oppression. It would take solidarity work to the grassroots and help build knowledge and activism structures among underprivileged groups across the world. The oppressed castes need to come under one roof to develop a collective egalitarian vision for the future of the world. Coming together and working collectively is the only way in which we can break the bonds of oppression.[103]

At numerous venues worldwide, Yengde is making his case for funding such an organization, and repeatedly asks: 'Will universities fund research on caste in America and around the world?'[104]

Though Harvard is elitist, he finds it a useful base because he comes across intellectuals with similar backgrounds from other countries. 'Their love to (sic) humanity is a true testament of hope. They have truly worked with the community, and their scholarship is cutting edge. When I speak with these professors, we are actually not in that bubble'.[105] He wants to set an example for others in the underprivileged communities:

> I would like to tell people about what it is like to be at Harvard and boost their confidence to apply with the hope that the next generation that comes to Harvard will be socially conscious, practically informed, and particularly armed with not only scholarship but a desire to upend the structures that they have struggled with.[106]

Yengde is embedding himself in African American academia in the US and wants to use it to create a body of literature around the history of caste. This would become the standard reference library and be used to legitimize his worldview with the support of American academia. A report stated:

> Yengde said he hoped to revive a rich tradition of global literature, dating back to the 1820s, chronicling systems that oppressed Black and Dalit people. "I've been trying my best to create an archive for the future," ... he cited James McCune Smith, Frederick Douglass and Charles Sumner as American historical figures who spoke out against the caste system. Douglass, he said, recognized that slavery directly produced a racial caste system in the United States.[107]

Such a global scale archival project would address the need for Black Americans to read Dalit scholars like him. Until they do that, he says they will not understand caste and thus cannot fully understand American racism.

For instance, he points out that the Black Panthers were ignorant of the Dalits, and this is why his Black-Dalit hyphenated movement is necessary to educate the Black Americans. Another example of ignorance he points out is that Black Americans celebrate Kamala Harris as vice president, but they ought to know that she is half Brahmin. The way forward is to create a Dalit archive to educate future generations, and he wants to oversee this global project.[108]

He does not consider the negative impact of such movements that could harmfully dilute the requisite attention local issues in local communities require, and are best redressed by local solutions: by genericizing oppression and victimhood in this way, there will be such dilution and scapegoating that no one will seriously tackle the specific issues needed to be worked through to reach constructive aims. Instead, one will just lament that the world is unfair and call for a revolution that will never really take place. In the process, he gets to be a messiah figure and traditional institutions that uphold society will be weakened or destroyed. This is dangerous and destructive.

Yengde is also consolidating multiple outreach activities of the Breaking India forces. Sikhs with separatist leanings have been absent in caste related matters. But he is co-opting them as part of his grand alliance. For example, he is a frequent guest at Chetna, a Canadian organization run predominantly by Sikhs. Chetna describes itself as follows:

> It was established in 1999 with a primary objective of raising awareness about the caste-based issues globally. [It] ... promotes the benefits of creating casteless, respectful and inclusive communities through dialogues, discussions, presentations and seminars. The members of Chetna take inspiration from Baba Saheb Dr B R Ambedkar, the champion of human rights in India. [It] ... has a strong partnership with Dr Hari Sharma foundation, Institute for the Humanities at Simon Fraser University (SFU), and various departments of University of British Columbia (UBC). The partnership has planned and delivered Dr Ambedkar Memorial Lectures since 2016.[109]

Readers familiar with earlier movements like the Third World Project and the Subaltern Project, will wonder what is new and different in this Fourth World Project. It seems that now there is better coordination among the world's downtrodden and there is a new generation of leaders, hence the new term. But the essence of the grievances remains the same.

Catfight to Represent the Victims

Yengde is encountering internal battles for a market share among the champions of the downtrodden. Equality Labs' Thenmozhi Soundararajan is on a collision course challenging Suraj Yengde, Harvard's resident Dalit supremo, on his own turf. She outsmarted him by convincing Harvard to add caste as a 'protected category' following few other universities.

Yengde accused Equality Labs of appropriating his hard work, reports *Outlook India*: 'Dr Suraj Yengde, a senior fellow at the Harvard Kennedy School, and the most influential Dalit voice of Harvard University said that he wasn't informed about it'.[110] Yengde was clearly peeved: 'How can you exclude the one proud Ambedkarite on [the Harvard] campus who's been in the corridors for longer and has been actively lobbying for caste-sensitive policies?' He called this move by Harvard, a 'classic case of savarnas and sinister NGOs [seemingly referring to Equality Labs] appropriating the hard work of Ambedkarites in the US'.[111]

Soundararajan and Yengde are in a catfight among the oppressed. Each is competing to become the top Dalit champion in a cottage industry that offers huge grants and consulting fees for those that represent the victims.

The real issue raised by the decision made by Harvard is that if Dalit oppression was such a significant issue on campus, why was its outspoken champion, Suraj Yengde, sidelined by someone outside Harvard?

Aggression Redefined

There is a certain violence in Yengde's words, positions, and activities that seem representative of a new class of people given to justifying aggression and destruction in the name of human rights, social inclusion, and upliftment. Irrespective of how underhanded the tactics adopted, or how brazen the display of falsehoods, this attracts kindred spirits. And for many people in this group, the end justifies the means.

6

A Response: History of Indian Social Organization

Introduction

The foregoing chapters introduced the application of Critical Race Theory to caste and its transformation into a Breaking India force. This chapter consolidates the issues and our responses and offers a far more detailed and systematic analysis.

It also intends to serve as a stand-alone presentation on the history of Indian social organization. This is a topic of considerable importance, yet we haven't discovered any comprehensive treatment that responds to the broad range of claims made by the Critical Race Theory camp. This chapter aims to fill the gap by supplying evidence-based claims to balance the discourse on this complex topic. Our purpose is to invite all-round healthy debate.

One of the reasons for the misunderstandings on this subject is the persistent mistranslation of the two terms, varna and jati, as caste. The terminology and the idea of caste was imported by Europeans and in their minds, it referred to a hierarchy of races. As a result, this framework became projected to depict varna and jati as systems of exploitation. The varna system also became compared with systems like slavery or serfdom prevalent in the West. Varna and jati were thus held responsible for many of India's present social problems.

We will use the term caste in the context of present times and varna-jati for earlier periods before the European social engineering that ossified a fluid system into caste.

The serious implication of this error in framing Indian society is as follows: Because varna and jati are referenced extensively in key Hindu texts, scholars have made three cardinal errors:

1. The social organization of India has been assumed to be fixed for the past thousands of years and across the diverse range of Indian social groups.
2. All sorts of present-day social problems have been projected back on ancient origins. Vedic or Hindu foundations have been accused of the problems that Indian society faces today.
3. The massive disruptions that have occurred in India's long history, not once but repeatedly, have been ignored or glossed over without factoring in their impact.

The characterization of varna-jati as racism has become a powerful weapon in political movements to dismantle Hinduism. If racism is inseparable from Hinduism – as the claim goes – then as reasonable people, we must all join hands to get rid of Hinduism itself in order to free society of this scourge.

There is a lot at stake in this discussion. Hence, it is important to gain a proper understanding of the nature of Indian social dynamics since ancient times. This chapter explains how traditional Indian society evolved during several periods and under various influences, all the way up to the latest social engineering.

It is notable that earlier Western anthropologists and philosophers had opined favorably about India's varna-jati structures. Many of them wrote that the reason for India's survival in spite of numerous invasions, famines, revolutions and social upheavals, and conquests by invaders of alien religions, was largely due to these resilient social structures. It was explained that varna-jati also enabled Hindus to resist aggressive campaigns to convert them to Islam or Christianity.[1] For instance, the nineteenth century French missionary Abbé Dubois, who tried but failed to convert Indians to Christianity, acknowledged that the varna-jati system was responsible for protecting India from barbarism. He said it also provided a responsible government, prevented despotism, and preserved the indigenous arts and culture even under foreign rule.[2]

One of the important functions of varna and jati has been to integrate the various diverse social groups into one ecosystem in which communities cooperate, transact, negotiate, evolve, and adapt.[3] This stabilized villages for centuries and helped them function as independent and self-reliant units.[4] It enabled each ethnic, social, religious, or occupational group to function as a part of the social whole while retaining its distinctive character.[5] The rich members of a varna or jati helped the poor members and provided them necessary security. It also resulted in the absence of excessive competition, the root cause of exploitation of the weak in many societies.[6] A healthy society requires a division of labor to function efficiently, and varna was a division of labor based on the natural diversity of individuals. This is evident in India's diversity preserved to this day to a large extent: in languages, deities and ways of worship, food habits, culture, value systems, family and way of life.

Contrary to these descriptions, the ancient varna-jati system is presently portrayed as the caste system of exploiting the Shudras and those presumably outside the varna system. However, historical evidence, as we shall explain, does not present such a one-sided picture.

Today, the big debate on caste revolves around the following questions:

- Is caste a *necessary* condition for Hinduism – i.e., to be a Hindu can one avoid caste?
- Is caste a *sufficient* condition for Hinduism – i.e., does conforming to caste automatically make one a Hindu?
- Is there any version of the varna-jati system that would be compatible with modern- day democracy and capitalism, or are the two fundamentally irreconcilable? In other words, does the Hindu have to abandon caste in order to assimilate into the West, or can the varna-jati be modified to serve as India's own social system with *freedom at the individual level*?
- Was caste present in ancient Vedic society? When and why did caste enter Indian society? How has caste evolved over the centuries and what were the causal factors?
- Is the caste handicap fluid enough to be resolved by education and economic advancement, or is it fixed and birth-based, in which case it is more robust and difficult to overcome? And in the absence of birth-based caste, have Western societies managed to resolve the massive class and wealth disparities? Would the West be willing to abolish birth-based inheritance of wealth from

one generation to the next, as a way to resolve this?

- Is caste only abusive, or only positive, or does it have a combination of good and bad qualities?
- How grave is caste oppression today? What is being done about it and what is the progress report?
- Who are the Dalit activists working in the West? What is their position, who supports them, and what is their present global impact?

As we shall see, Indian society has been extremely diverse, fluid, and continually evolving. No single framework can be applied consistently over time, and it is misleading to assume a fixed and normative view.

Scholars who study modern caste and social structures typically use the voluminous texts known as the *Dharmashastras* as their main historical source in which jati structures became codified. These were written by multiple authors over a period of several centuries. Let us take a brief look at what the *Dharmashastras* have to say.

One of the most comprehensive studies of the *Dharmashastras* was done by P.V. Kane, a Sanskrit scholar, in his multivolume, *History of Dharmashastras,* published more than half a century ago. Some of the main insights from his research were:

- It is impossible to attribute the origin of what is today called caste to any single source. There are numerous flows and complex interactions that shaped and reshaped the social structures in India.
- There is a great difference between the popular caste practices of today and the conceptions about varna-jati in the ancient and medieval *Dharmashastras.*
- Many statements in the *Dharmashastras* are metaphorical, allegorical, and many of the verses are enigmatic.
- There are contradictions, not only between different texts but at times within the same text. This is exacerbated by the fact that Sanskrit terms often have multiple meanings. For instance, varna can also mean 'color', but it was not used to specify the skin color of people until recent times when scholars began racial interpretation.

- There are also many factual errors made by Western and modern Indian scholars in their understanding of the *Dharmashastras*.

There is little evidence to suggest that the bulk of the rules and injunctions in the *Dharmashastras* were ever enforced by Hindu rulers, though these texts were sometimes cited in debates between individuals. They were used as reference works when it suited one to support his position, but not considered enforceable or the final authority. They mostly concern ritualistic practices and are descriptive of cosmic consequences of breaches.

In light of all this, it is difficult to define Indian social groups into neat, absolute categories with clean boundaries. The matter becomes even more complex when one considers that the *Dharmashastras* are merely one of several spiritual texts of the Hindus. In fact, *the* Dharmashastras *are not required in practicing Hinduism.* Let us take a wide-angle view of Indian spirituality:

- In order to practice Hinduism, one must uphold the dharma. Indian traditions are not based on a 'one book' system like the Abrahamic religions. There are numerous texts from multiple exemplars.
- The high level of education in India meant there were always many voices and views, arguing and debating among themselves. The result was the development of the world's largest library of intellectual works. A knowledge system of this kind does not lend itself to uniform ideas and enforced implementation. There were numerous counter movements to the prevailing consensus, and new ideas and groups emerged to challenge the established authority. From its very inception, Hinduism has been a tradition of transmission and lineage. Many different branches emerged from the Vedic tradition with diverse viewpoints, traditions, and ideologies. This produces an open architecture that allows for reform and evolution such that a Hindu of every persuasion could find his or her spiritual home most conducive to his or her growth.
- There was no tradition of burning the sacred books of adversaries or condemning prior works as heresy or blasphemy. And hence, the proliferation of sacred texts and practices that are sometimes

apparently divergent or contradictory but still rooted in the same Vedic worldview.

- Among the various Hindu texts, the *Dharmashastras* are not used in the daily lives of Hindus. The texts used by practitioners are the *Vedas, Upanishads, Bhagavad Gita, Itihasas,* and *Puranas.* It is rare to find any practicing Hindu who reads the *Dharmashastras* every morning for guidance on how to live his day. On the other hand, many Hindus read the *Gita* on a daily basis, or the *Ramayana,* or chant Vedic mantras, or contemplate on the metaphysics in the *Upanishads.* Unlike most Hindu homes that keep the *Gita, Ramayana, Upanishads,* or *Srimad Bhagavatam,* almost none keep the *Dharmashastras.* If one were to survey the number of Hindus who have ever come across a copy of various Hindu texts, the *Dharmashastras* would rank below every other text commonly referenced.

- The point being made is that the much-maligned *Dharmashastras* were modulated through the guru lineage, so it never had the dogmatic impact similar to Abrahamic laws. It was the British in the late eighteenth century, who turned to the *Dharmashastras* to compile what they called *The Laws of the Gentoos* ('gentoo' being a slur referring to 'gentile' people in the Bible). Later, this was replaced by *The Laws of the Hindoos,* an exercise led by Sir William Jones, who called himself Pandit William Jones. Its purpose was to fix one 'standard law' for adjudicating legal cases in the Supreme Court set up by the British in Bengal where he was chief justice.

- Traditionally, there was no centralized Church-like structure with the authority to interpret and adjudicate on social theories. The adjudication of disputes was highly contextualized and based on specific circumstances and individuals concerned.

- The karma theory states there is a universal divine agency dispensing justice. This is different from God's injunction in the Abrahamic religions imploring humans to enforce God's commandments. Hindu rulers were unconcerned about individuals' spiritual compliance or transgressions, and their jurisdiction of law was limited only to worldly matters. The focus was on the self and not on harvesting souls in the service of religious zeal. Hence, there were no Hindu world conquerors using religion as their basis to colonize.

- Finally, what the *Dharmashastras* state does not match the anthropological evidence on what people practice. The latter describes the ground reality based on all kinds of empirical evidence including Indian and foreign records. This suggests that the texts were descriptive, rather than prescriptive, in the way society perceived them.

Because there is no normative institutionalized 'law' on these matters, many textual statements are opposed by other textual statements. For every practice followed by one, there are different practices followed by others. Questions about society often have answers that are *both* 'yes' and 'no'.

Hence, there was no single 'caste system' that could be applied uniformly to India through the ages or across its vast diversity of geography and communities. Because Indian society is frequently seen through the lens of a single 'caste' system, it presents contradictions. The term 'caste system' is misleading too because it suggests a framework that can be applied consistently and universally.

Like many other facets of Indian civilization, jatis were more like an open architecture of social organization in which communities of many kinds existed, adapted, digested others or become digested by others, and in many cases, disappeared.

As the West prefers simple frameworks, such a nuanced understanding of jati is considered too chaotic and complex, and this is the crux of the problem of scholarship on this subject. However, the following general statements can be made about the nature of Indian society through time:

- In terms of the dignity, prosperity, and vibrancy of social life of the masses, there were good periods and bad periods, good regions and bad regions, good examples and bad examples.
- Overall, compared to the *prevailing* practices in the Western world at any point in time, Indian society was highly advanced, mobile, flexible, and prosperous, and far from being backward or oppressive as commonly stereotyped.
- There were frequent challenges to the established social norms

including challenges to the foremost spiritual experts by ordinary, humble individuals. Many homegrown social reform movements brought about major changes. This evolution required no foreign or external intervention of any kind.

Seven Historical Phases

We have organized Indian social history into the following seven periods, proposed as a loose, informal chronology for the purpose of discussion.

1. Early Vedic
2. Late Vedic and *Itihasic*
3. *Dharmashastras* (overlapping with 2)
4. Muslim rule
5. European colonial rule
6. Post-Independence
7. Globalization

These periods are not defined by any precise characteristics or timeframes, nor are they mutually exclusive. They partially overlap and each contains some attributes of the others. The central characterizations that follow are purely illustrative and not meant to give a reductionist picture of a uniform system at any point.

Let us take a brief look at each of the seven periods in order to understand and appreciate the transformations that happened in the organization of Indian society through its history.

During the early *Rig Veda* period we come across artisans, farmers, priests and warriors; society was basically egalitarian. *We do not have evidence of a deep-seated, institutionalized, and hierarchical classification of people.* Women and Shudras were also composing Vedic hymns and other seminal works.[7]

Even during the later Vedic and *Itihasic* period, the idea of varna was in its nascent form and not rigidly dependent on birth. Artisans such as metalworkers, chariot-makers and carpenters were not necessarily birth-based occupational jatis. The *Mahabharata* states that one does not become a Brahmin by birth alone but also by conduct. It declares that a Brahmin could be born of a Kshatriya or a Vaishya mother.[8] There was also some ambiguity regarding the relative position of the varnas and these were related to each other in a fluid way.

The Greek traveler, Megasthenes, who came to India during the time of Emperor Chandragupta Maurya (reign c. 321-297 BCE), affirmed that slavery was unknown in India, that no Indian slave existed, and that all Indians were free.[9] Greek writers refer to the Shudras as Sodrai and describe them as an important community of northwest India at the time of the Macedonian king, Alexander (326 BCE).[10] This is contrary to the view presented by modern scholars that Shudras and Dalits have been slaves since Vedic times.

Jati was largely ignored in ancient texts and appears to be a later phenomenon. Initially, jati generally meant a kinship group whose people followed the same occupation and a shared lifestyle. This jati structure within the varna system seems to have evolved a few centuries before the Common Era.[11] Only later did these structures become more formalized.

The *Manusmriti* explains that jatis originated due to intermarriage between different varnas. This shows that different varnas *did* intermarry. Thus, sixty-one jatis are mentioned in the *Manusmriti* and more than one hundred are mentioned in the *Brahmavaivarta Purana*.[12] Kautilya, (more commonly known as the philosopher Chanakya) author of the celebrated *Arthashastra*, also refers to at least fifteen jatis which were the result of marriages between different varnas. During the post Maurya period (187 BCE-320 CE) there were intermarriages between different varnas, and jatis were giving birth to newer jatis.

The origin of jatis can also be based on the physical movement of communities. Such migrations allowed people to redefine themselves by combining their previous identity and their new profession. Their varna might change in this relocation. There are numerous examples of such migrant groups all over India. For instance, among the Brahmins such migrations led to numerous jatis like Vadamas, Andhra Dravidas, and Mulukanadu in the south. A group of Brahmins from Saurashtra in the west, became artisans in Madurai in the south and call themselves the 'Saurashtra jati', but this has not been accepted by Tamil Brahmins. The Kongu Gauda (Vellala) jati of Tamil Nadu are migrants from Bengal in the east.

The theory of *apad-dharma* (dharma in times of distress) in the *Dharmashastras* reveals a gap between theory and practice in the prescribed vocations of the varnas. One finds evidence that the textual prescriptions of different professions for the four varnas was often not followed in practice.

Thus, the *Manusmriti* mentions that in times of distress, people switched from their traditional occupations to that of other varnas and jatis. It was documented that people changed their professions to suit their needs. Buddhist texts also narrate that a jati was not rigidly tied to a particular profession. We find examples of a Kshatriya warrior working successively or concurrently as a potter, a basket-maker, a reed-worker, a garland-maker; and a Vaishya cook working as a tailor or potter, without any social pushback or loss of prestige.[13] Jatis proliferated further in Gupta- (fourth century CE-late sixth century CE) and post-Gupta times. It is also notable that Shudras had far more internal divisions among their jatis than did the other varnas.

As an example, some medieval inscriptions indicate that very few donors that set up various endowments described themselves in terms of their varna or jati. Instead, the inscriptions provide only their names and those of their parents. This is because varna and jati were not the most important aspects of one's identity in that period.[14]

Things changed dramatically with the Muslim invasions. The Muslim period is characterized by the decline of towns, trade, and agriculture. The progress of the Indian masses was stifled, and they became helpless, immobile, and poor. This environment of despair was not conducive to either economic enterprise, trade, or industrial growth. At times, agriculture too could barely sustain itself. The best hope for many people was to just survive. The jatis were less enterprising and resorted to ossifying their hereditary occupations and to endogamy.

The Mughal rulers exploited the masses ruthlessly and this created economic inequalities. During Shah Jahan's reign, from 1628-58, 37 percent of the entire assessed revenue collected was assigned to 68 princes and emirs, and a further 25 percent to the next 587 officers. This means as much as 62 percent of the total revenue of the empire was given to just 655 individuals. The distribution of income became even more inequitable during Akbar's reign (1556-1605), when the top twenty-five persons took over thirty percent of the total revenue.[15]

The ostentatious lifestyle and the monuments built during the Mughal period were based on aggression and pillage, not on new investment or education or development activities. They had taken over one of the world's wealthiest economies and lived the good life for a few centuries. Meanwhile, Europe had been in its 'dark ages' as a backward region of the world, but it suddenly accelerated ahead of everyone else.

The Mughals seized nearly all the surplus wealth by extortion, taxation, or direct confiscation. A stupendous amount of wealth was turned into unproductive luxuries. This resulted in frequent and catastrophic famines.[16] Such factors hampered economic dynamism. Artisans and traders lost mobility. Occupations became hereditary. The jati system became more rigid in matters of marriage and sharing food, and disintegrated into opportunism and social stratification. There is considerable evidence that in the Muslim period, jati groups became defensive for survival and there was a collapse in social mobility.

By the time the Portuguese came to India in the sixteenth century, they found the society (both Hindu and Muslim) to be organized into various occupational jatis. They called them *casta*, meaning tribe, clan, or race. There is no precise equivalent for the word 'caste' in any Indian language. Gradually, the term 'caste' became accepted as equivalent to jatis. During British rule, jatis got re-characterized as the formal 'caste system'.

Even during the colonial period, Indians had complex and multiple identities. Depending on the situation, one or another identity could take prominence. Therefore, when colonial censuses attempted to ascertain caste affiliations, the responses ranged from names designating endogamous groups or occupations, to titles, and surnames. There was no single category that people universally claimed affiliation to, which corresponded to the Western framework of 'caste'.

British census officials have documented their frustration that many Indians did not seem to know their caste, and in many instances, had to be coached for the census forms. The colonial classification system assumed that castes were well-defined standard entities whose members could be enumerated, and characteristics clearly specified. Large volumes of data were accumulated through such censuses, and this needed to be put into meaningful templates. Colonial officers deliberated among themselves and considered different approaches to resolve this paradox. This system of tagging helped them 'herd' these groups to submission during their colonial regime. They also deliberately tagged certain jatis 'criminal' and enforced genocide against them.

All modern sociological studies on caste use these arbitrary colonial conceptualizations. After India's Independence, the democratic system turned castes into vote banks which have been manipulated by politicians ever since to serve their vested interests.

In the present age of globalization, things are once again taking a different turn. Today, when food or any product gets delivered, who knows, or bothers to know, what the person's caste or sexual orientation is? The free exchange of goods and services is driven by market competition and meritocracy, and nobody cares about the old social classifications. Regardless of one's birth-based factors, one can work, get paid, advance in one's career, and move socially with freedom. Efficiency and optimization are the key success factors overriding everything else.

Capitalism is making caste obsolete, but it does not free society from structural biases. The new dynamics brings challenges as well as opportunities. The only caste system left in the rapidly urbanizing India is the one enforced by the government's formal identities given to people. This is India's curse: the birth-defect enshrined in its Constitution. This is fodder for the toxic identity politics.

The chronological sequence of the evolution of Hindu social structure can be represented as follows: Varna ➔ Jati ➔ Caste ➔ Political Vote Bank ➔ Global Caste Wars. The figure on the following page shows the evolutionary history of Indian social structures.

The metaverse goes even further by making many assets virtual and devaluing their physicality. The question is whether a whole new kind of 'Metaverse Caste System' will emerge on a global scale, and what its characteristics might be.

The table that follows organizes the trends into the seven periods that are illustrative of the way varna turned into jati, jati into caste, and now into vote banks.

History of Indian Social Structures

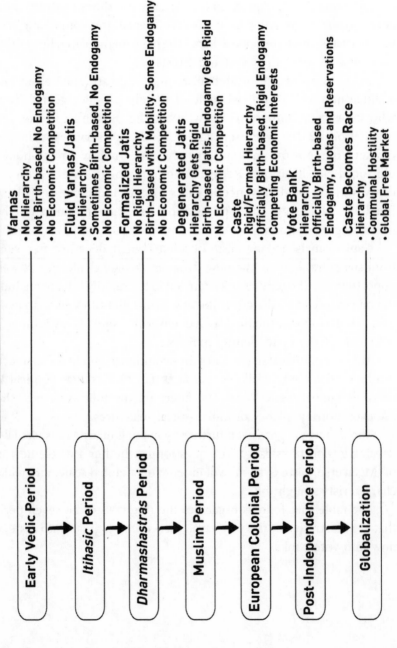

Early Vedic Period

Varnas
- No Hierarchy
- Not Birth-based. No Endogamy
- No Economic Competition

Itihasic Period

Fluid Varnas/Jatis
- No Hierarchy
- Sometimes Birth-based. No Endogamy
- No Economic Competition

Dharmashastras Period

Formalized Jatis
- No Rigid Hierarchy
- Birth-based with Mobility. Some Endogamy
- No Economic Competition

Muslim Period

Degenerated Jatis
- Hierarchy Gets Rigid
- Birth-based Jatis. Endogamy Gets Rigid
- No Economic Competition

European Colonial Period

Caste
- Rigid/Formal Hierarchy
- Officially Birth-based. Rigid Endogamy
- Competing Economic Interests

Post-Independence Period

Vote Bank
- Hierarchy
- Officially Birth-based
- Endogamy, Quotas and Reservations

Globalization

Caste Becomes Race
- Hierarchy
- Communal Hostility
- Global Free Market

PERIODS	1 Early Vedic	2 Late Vedic & Itihasic	3 Dharma-shastras	4 Muslim Period	5 European Colonial	6 Post-Independence	7 Globalization
Key character	Varna	Fluid Jati/Varna structures	Formalized jati	Jati degeneration and abuse	Caste	Vote bank	Critical Caste Theory
Hierarchy	No	No	Multiple hierarchies and privileges	Hierarchy becomes stronger	Rigid and formal hierarchy	Yes	Yes
Birth-based	No	Not always	Yes, but mobility possible	Yes	Officially birth-based	Officially birth-based	Equated with race
Competing economic interests	No	No	No	No	Yes	Quotas; competition	Global free market
Communal hostility	No	No	No	Sometimes	Yes	Yes	Yes
Endogamy	No	No	Yes, but flexible	Yes	Yes	Yes	Yes
Untouchability	No	No	Little	Yes	Yes	Yes. But illegal	Cancel Culture
Top-down power (as opposed to lateral peer groups)	No	No	No	Yes	Yes	Yes. Lobbying	Globalized
Political groupings	No	No	No	No	No	Yes. Communalism	Global social justice

The table summarizes our discussion and lists the various characteristics of varna, jati, and caste across the history of India. It can be seen that varna, jati, and caste are presently mistaken and equated with each other, resulting in confusion. We will further elaborate the key points in the table. (The absence of hierarchy in the early periods needs to be qualified. There was in fact a hierarchy in the specific context of performing rituals, though not in the broader social sense.)

What the Ancient Texts State

We shall now examine the major ancient texts as sources of evidence.

The Vedic Era

The earliest reference to the four varnas appears in two verses of *Purusha Sukta* of the *Rig Veda*. It mentions four social groups: Brahmin, Rajanya (instead of Kshatriya), Vaishya, and Shudra, but the term varna is not mentioned. The following two verses have created a huge controversy because they are commonly used to claim that the *Vedas* discriminate against the Shudras by equating them with the feet of the cosmic person.

> When (gods) divided Purusha, into how many parts did they cut him up? What was his mouth? What arms (had he)? What (two objects) are said (to have been) his thighs and feet?
>
> The Brahmana was his mouth; the rajah (king or kshatriya) was made his arms; the being called the vaishya was his thighs; the Shudra sprang from his feet.[17]

B.R. Ambedkar and many other scholars considered these verses to be a later interpolation. Along these lines, the renowned social scientist, R.S. Sharma, wrote:

> It is evident then that the shudras appear as a social class only towards the end of the period of Atharva Veda [chronologically the last of the Vedas], when the Purusha Sukta version of their origin may have been inserted into the 10th book of the Rg Veda.[18]

Regardless of their timing, these verses do not support a birth-based and hierarchical system. Rather, they present a metaphor for society as an organic whole in the same way as a unified person with several parts. The purpose is to bring out the psychological inter-relationships and dependencies among different aspects that comprise an integral unity. There is interdependency like in the case of various organs of the body. A healthy body would not have conflict among its organs or some sort of exploitative hierarchy of oppressor/oppressed. And the various organs in a body are integrally unified with a common structure, namely the DNA.

No person would want his feet compromised just because their physical location is 'low'. Being low physically does not correspond to having lesser importance. Moreover, the cosmic person is often depicted lying down horizontally, in which case there is no 'upper' or 'lower'.

The *Brihadaranyaka Upanishad* explicitly uses the human body as a metaphor to explain the different seasons, clearly not intending to classify some seasons as 'low and inferior' relative to others. It also describes the cosmos using different parts of a body to represent the constellations, clouds, sand, rivers, mountains, trees, and plants.[19] The body has been used in ancient texts as a metaphor for an organic unity of diverse elements.

Furthermore, there is nothing *prescriptive* in these verses. They merely indicate how the various organs of society specialize in their respective roles. Such symbolism was commonly used to explain diversity built into the unity. Unfortunately, Western scholars obsessed with depicting Hindu society as an oppressive hierarchy claim that because the Shudras were seen as analogous to the feet, they were treated as being inferior to the rest.

Prof. Arvind Sharma of McGill University has offered yet another interpretation of these verses: Each individual is being inspired to master diverse areas of competence and bring them together. This means the individual should be able to perform various duties across the spectrum: physical and mental tasks, management or governance of the community including offering military service when required, business activity, and other professional work. He writes: 'The idea is that all varnas are contained in every individual, instead of every individual being comprised within one of the varnas'.[20] We could extend this to society and say: Just as Purusha, the cosmic person, integrates multiple specializations, so also our society must harmonize and optimize all faculties.

The bottom line is that the *Rig Veda* emphasizes the equality of all human beings: 'No one is superior, none is inferior. All are brothers marching forward to prosperity'.[21]

The Upanishads

The entire metaphysics of the *Upanishads* emphasizes the ultimate unity of all humans, living entities, and indeed, all existence.

Furthermore, the *Upanishad* titled *Vajrasuchika* focuses entirely on refuting birth-based social identity. It is concise, comprising only nine short paragraphs, and S. Radhakrishnan included it in his book, *The Principal Upanishads*.[22] After giving direct point-by-point statements based on *Advaita Vedanta,* it calls upon everyone to meditate on the Supreme, removing all distinctions and egoism from the mind. The *Vajrasuchika* leaves no doubt that social discrimination is antithetical to the worldview of the *Upanishads.*

The Bhagavad Gita

The *Gita* is far more relevant and far more influential among Hindus than the *Dharmashastras.* Wherever there is disagreement between the *Dharmashastras* and the *Gita,* the latter gets predominance. Let us examine the *Gita's* stand on varna.

The *Gita* is clear that varna is not birth-based. The key quotation is where Krishna says: 'The four varnas were created by me on the basis of character and occupation.' (*Gita* 4.13) Krishna says explicitly that they were created on the basis of *guna* (natural aptitude, character) and karma. There is no reference whatsoever to birth as the basis for the fourfold division of varnas.

In the *Mahabharata* war, some individuals not born as Kshatriyas also participated in that role based on their *svabhava* (individual nature). Krishna enlightens Arjuna, the Pandava, to follow his *svadharma,* meaning that one has to follow one's own aptitude and qualities. This is a way to optimize the resource utilization in the best interests of society.

The *Gita* explains the Vedanta principle that there is divinity in every creature. Krishna says: 'He who sees Me in all things and sees all things in Me, never becomes departed from Me. Nor am I lost to him'. (*Gita* 6.30) And a subsequent verse: 'He who judges pleasure and pain in others by the same standard as he applies to himself, that yogi is the highest'. (*Gita* 6.32)

In the sixteenth chapter, Krishna lists the virtues he considers important. These include non-violence, truth, compassion towards all, absence of anger and hatred, doing charity and service selflessly, forgiveness, and modesty. (*Gita* 16.1-3) None of these virtues are based on birth.

Krishna's life itself is an expression of all the varnas. He was raised in a Vaishya home with cowherds. He ruled over Dwaraka as a Kshatriya. He accepted the role of Arjuna's charioteer as a Shudra and taught the *Gita* as a Brahmin.

The Mahabharata

The *Mahabharata* mentions that in Satya Yuga (the first and considered the most idyllic of all epochs) there was only one varna of human beings – that of the children of Vivaswata Manu.[23] The *Puranas* and other Hindu scriptures also show no evidence of separate social categories in that period.

The *Mahabharata* emphasizes that character overrides birth.

> High birth cannot be a certificate for a person of no character. But persons with good character can distinguish themselves irrespective of low birth. (*Mahabharata, Udyoga Parva*, Ch 34.41)
>
> A shudra who is ever engaged in self-control, truth and righteousness, I regard him a brahmin. One is a twice-born by conduct alone. (*Mahabharata, Vana Parva*, Ch 216.14-15)

In a dialogue between Krishna and Arjuna, when Arjuna specifically asks how varna is determined, Krishna replies: 'Birth is not the cause, my friend; it is virtues, which are the cause of welfare. Even a Chandala (untouchable) observing the vow is considered a Brahmana by the gods.'[24]

The famous story of Karna being prohibited from participating in an act for being the son of a charioteer shows that a sense of jati connected to varna did exist in that society. However, what is more interesting is that he is offered the throne of a kingdom thereby causing a change in his varna which was also possible in the flexible framework.

Dipankar Gupta, the sociologist writes:

> It was well after the Vedic period, after even the period of the Mauryan empire, that the notion of untouchability came into being. In *Satapatha Brahmana,* the chief is advised to eat from the same vessel as the commoner. In the Rg Veda there is no mention of untouchable either. It was only around second century AD that the stratum of untouchables and the notion of untouchability became evident for instance in *Apasthambha Dharmasutra.*[25]

Ambedkar speculates on the origin of bias against the Shudras. He says that some Brahmins felt insulted and harassed by the Shudra kings (in medieval times) and as revenge they stopped performing *upanayana* or the sacred thread ceremony ritual. That is when the Shudras became the fourth varna because their ritual privileges were denied.[26] Another theory he proposes is that untouchability started under Buddhist influence when Hindus gave up sacrifice of animals and beef-eating, and those Hindus who continued to eat beef were regarded as untouchables.[27]

Regardless of their stance on this thesis, most scholars do agree that birth-based varna came after the Vedic period and untouchability after Buddhism.

Arvind Sharma also cites that many *rishis* were born as non-Brahmins. He gives the examples of Valmiki (author of the *Ramayana*) and Vyasa (author of the *Mahabharata,* and editor/compiler of the *Vedas*) and even the great sage, Vasishta. They were all born in the lowest strata. Kalidasa, respected as the greatest Sanskrit poet came from a humble and obscure origin.[28]

The Dharmashastras

The *Dharmashastras* are often portrayed as supporting the caste system and abuses of all kinds. But these texts were never considered an absolute dogma like the Bible or the Quran. There was never any kind of blasphemy preventing people from rejecting any one or more *Dharmashastras* or specific verses from any text whatsoever. And as mentioned earlier, the *Dharmashastras* never had the same status as other texts like *Vedas* and *Upanishads.* Given all this, how could scholars essentialize the nature of Hinduism by referencing a few isolated verses from the *Dharmashastras* and positioning these as the inviolable 'Hindu law'. Even among the vast literature under the category of *Dharmashastras* there is no unanimity on the number and nature of jatis, and Ambedkar himself provides counter examples.[29]

Though *Manusmriti* is the text most easily used to prove the caste system in ancient India, it, too, qualifies its position: One should renounce any rule of conduct if it results in unhappiness or arouses peoples' indignation. (*Manu* 4:176) In other words, it is self-correcting and does not claim to be absolute and frozen permanently.

More broadly, in the first verse of Chapter 2, *Manusmriti* defines dharma as follows: 'Know that to be true dharma, which the wise and the good and those who are free from passion and hatred follow, and which appeals to the heart'. Gandhi often quoted this verse in his lectures. The implication is that if the wise and the good that are free from passion and hatred reject the caste system based on birth, according to the *Manusmriti*, the system can be discarded. There is no requirement to wait for a prophet of some kind, prove himself with miracles, and then alter the teachings.

An important point often overlooked is that the *Dharmashastras* impose the heaviest restrictions on Brahmins. They are held to the highest standard and severely confined in their activities. This is in complete contrast to the common claim that the texts favored Brahmins and discriminated against Shudras. Therefore, the life of a Brahmin, as per the *Dharmashastras*, was tougher and stricter. Brahmins were required to follow an austere code of conduct:

- A Brahmin was required to sustain himself by following a livelihood that caused little, or no, harm to creatures.
- He could accumulate only the minimum wealth needed for his subsistence and that too through certain activities specific to him.[30]
- Punishments were harsher for Brahmins. In instances of theft, the liability for a Shudra was 8 times the money stolen; for a Vaishya, 16 times; for a Kshatriya, 32 times; and for a Brahmin it ranged from 64 times to 128 times. The reason given was that a Brahmin was expected to practice his lifestyle at the highest standard.[31]
- Brahmins were forbidden from earning money by selling meat,

lac, or salt. And if a Brahmin sold milk for three days, he would become a Shudra.[32] Manu recommends that those Brahmins that take on the occupations of craftsmen must be treated as Shudras.[33]

- The *Dharmashastras* prohibited Brahmins and Kshatriyas from charging interest against lending.[34] The renowned Muslim scholar Al-Biruni who came to India in the first half of the eleventh century, writes in his work *Kitab-ul-Hind* (around 1030 CE), that usury or lending money at an interest was allowed only to a Shudra in the Indian society and forbidden to all other varnas.[35]
- The *Dharmashastras* also stated that a Brahmin should not take a weapon into his hands even if just to examine it.[36]
- Brahmins were told to avoid seeking praise just like one avoids poison.[37]
- A Brahmin was not allowed to expect gifts from a Shudra except under special restrictions.[38]

Modern scholars falsely accuse the *Dharmashastras*, especially *Manusmriti*, of sanctioning the practice of untouchability. We point out the opposite evidence.

- The texts state that persons following certain disapproved vocations (hunting, butchery, etc.) became untouchables. These texts classify one as untouchable solely based on pursuing certain occupations. Some occupations were considered impure in the path to spiritual liberation, and there was emphasis on not coming in touch with individuals performing these impure activities. These restrictions were due to a metaphysical sense of hygiene and not the result of hatred or any kind of ethnic prejudice.[39]
- Even one's intimate friend was not to be touched for several days while the latter was in mourning because the dead body holds the *samskaras* (karmic imprints) of the deceased person.[40]
- Untouchability also arose due to several different reasons unrelated to birth in a particular varna. Some persons became outcastes for committing grave crimes.[41]
- Untouchability started as a way to maintain ritual purity. For instance, many families have a specific ritual passed down for

centuries, in which family members are careful not to touch the one member designated in charge of the ritual till it is complete. Even the clothes worn for the ritual are washed separately and not touched by others. This could be seen as 'untouchability' even within a family due to ritualistic protocols on physical contact.

Contrary to popular belief, the *Dharmashastras* do not consider every kind of physical contact with a Shudra to be polluting. For example, the Vedic sage Atri and the deity Brihaspati, each state that there is no taint caused by any contact in temples, religious processions, marriages, sacrifices, or festivals.[42]

Another false statement commonly made is that the varnas were always endogamous. But *Baudhayana Dharmasutra* allows marriages between Brahmins and Shudras.[43]

Contrary to popular misconceptions, ancient Vedic texts testify that Shudras performed Vedic rituals:[44]

- *Rig Veda* mentions five individuals from all social categories that performed rituals to Agni.[45]
- The authors of some Vedic texts were also Shudras. For example, the author of *Aitareya Brahmana*, was a Shudra.[46]
- The *Chandogya Upanishad* mentions that King Janasruti was taught the knowledge of *prana* and *vayu* by a Shudra sage.[47]
- *Ramayana* mentions that the people of Ayodhya were well-versed in the *Vedas*.
- The *Arthashastra* considers almost all indigenous communities to be Aryas, including the Shudras and most lower-class communities.[48]
- In *Atri Samhita* the Shudra, Nishada, Chandala, and Mleccha are considered to have Brahminical origin.[49] The *Dharmashastras* also prescribe various samskaras for the Shudras, implying that they were an integral part of Hindu society.[50]

The foregoing analysis of core Hindu texts indicates that modern scholarship has been unreliable and reductionist and deserves to be contested.

Is Hinduism Fixated on Caste?

This section gives further historical arguments in response to the charges that caste has always been inseparable from Hinduism and is a scourge unique to it and no other belief.

Hinduism's Open Architecture

It is commonly alleged that a whole assortment of Hindu taboos, restrictions, and prejudices are sanctified by core Hindu texts and its authoritative institutions. But Hinduism is not canonical or defined by the *Dharmashastras*; the *Dharmashastras* too, as we noted, have a variety of views that are sometimes contrary to each other. Nor do the three eminent acharyas (Adi Shankara, Ramanuja and Madhva) or the multitude of popular saints and movements provide the only interpretations that all Hindus must accept.

Every text, exemplar, and social movement of Hinduism is to be respected for its contributions the same way we respect various leading scientists in history. But none of them is absolute or final.

Hinduism is an open architecture offering a vast library of texts providing guidance and this is why there are multiple choices. Every Hindu can, and does, cherry pick his personal choices of metaphysical interpretation, of guru for guidance (or no guru), of *ishta devata* (special deity), of rituals, of festivals, of pilgrim centers, and of lifestyle.

From this library of choices, diverse individuals and groups emerge as system integrators to build specific systematized solutions catering to different kinds of people. There are many such turnkey 'Hindu paths', each like a start-up and public offering that may or may not succeed in the spiritual marketplace.

Caste is Not Sufficient to Be a Hindu

If caste were a sufficient condition to be a Hindu, then everyone practicing caste would be a Hindu, including caste practitioners that are Christians, Muslims, or members of other non-Hindu faiths. But the fact is that caste, and even untouchability, are very common among Indians who are non-Hindus.

Even among those untouchables whose leaders claim to be non-Hindus, there is a gradation of hierarchy and pollution. For example, *bhangis* (scavengers) are considered more polluted than *mahars* (agricultural laborers). If caste practice automatically made them Hindus, they should not be calling themselves non-Hindus.

Some Lingayats claim to be non-Hindus because they do not accept the *Vedas* and varna, yet practice caste and ritual gradation. Basaveshwara was a prominent leader of the Bhakti movement in Karnataka and his followers are known as Veerashaivas or Lingayats. He was vehemently against social discrimination and yet failed to prevent the caste system among his followers.[51]

Buddhism and Varna

The Buddha is often presented as a social reformer against the varna system, and Buddhism is explained as a revolt of the Shudras against the hegemony of the higher varnas. However, Buddhist texts reveal a different reality. Buddha was a Kshatriya who denounced the varna system when it helped the Brahmins, but not when it helped the Kshatriyas. Buddha also was a believer in endogamy (marrying within one's varna) and commensality (eating only with people of one's varna) – at least where his own Kshatriya varna was concerned.[52]

The Buddhist criticism against the varna system came later and it was not anything new or radical. It was shared by many earlier and contemporary religious sects. A similar stress on deeds, rather than birth, was given in the enlightened and liberal sections of Vedic society. The *Chandogya Upanishad* (IV.4) says that good conduct makes a man the best Brahmin.[53]

Moreover, most of the intellectual stalwarts of Buddhism were themselves Brahmins. The intellectual power of the Buddhist sangha was maintained by the regular admission of learned Brahmins into the Buddhist fold. From the very beginning, Brahmin adherents functioned as the pillars supporting Buddhism.[54]

Those who became serious Buddhists in the early period left their households and became monks in monasteries.[55] When a follower of Buddha remained a householder, he did not give up the old varna identity or duty.[56] Even according to Ambedkar, Buddhism had no separate *dhamma diksha* for those who wanted to be initiated into the dhamma but did not wish to become monks in the sangha. This is why Ambedkar invented his own dhamma diksha ceremony for the laity.[57] Therefore, in the history of Buddhism, the lay community never quite acquired the status of a separate and distinct 'Buddhist' identity.[58]

Scholars like P.V. Kane and S. Radhakrishnan have opined that Buddha himself did not feel he was establishing a new religion.

Many Indians found no difference between the worship of Vishnu and Buddha, or between Shiva and Avalokitesvara, or between Parvati and Tara.[59]

Muslim Castes in India

Evidence that Indian Muslims have strong caste prejudices among them is compelling. Early Muslim historians of medieval India like Minhaj-i Siraj Juzjani and Ziauddin Barani (thirteenth-fourteenth century CE) denigrated the Indian converts to Islam. Barani advocated that the sultans should employ only those persons in government service that had aristocratic backgrounds by birth. He advised that children of low caste Hindu converts to Islam should not be admitted into madrassas because this education would qualify them for government jobs.[60] Sultan Ghiyasuddin Balban (r. 1266-87 CE) made noble birth a prerequisite for state service and rejected candidates for official positions if they were low caste converts to Islam.[61]

It is also notable that when Sir Syed Ahmed Khan founded the Aligarh Muslim University in 1875, it banned admission to low caste Muslims.[62]

An overwhelming majority (seventy-five percent) of the present Indian Muslim population is called Dalit Muslims. Caste and untouchability are a lived reality for Muslims in South Asia, and untouchability is the community's worst-kept secret. Many studies have claimed that concepts of 'purity and impurity'; 'clean and unclean castes' definitely exist among Muslim groups. A 2009 study found there was not one 'Dalit Muslim' leader in any of the prominent Muslim organizations, which were dominated essentially by upper caste Muslims.[63]

In another 2015 study of seven thousand Dalit Muslim households across fourteen districts in Uttar Pradesh, many testified that they are seated separately at Muslim feasts. Respondents also confirmed that they eat only after the upper caste Muslims. Many said they are served food on separate plates.[64] Around eight percent reported that their children are seated in separate rows in classes and also during school lunches.

Similarly, at least a third of them stated that they are not allowed to bury their dead in an upper caste Muslim burial ground. They are told to go elsewhere or provided a corner of the main ground.[65]

It is noteworthy that when Dalit Muslim respondents were requested to share their experiences in the homes of upper caste Muslims and Hindus, around thirteen percent of them reported receiving food/water in separate utensils in Muslim homes whereas this proportion was close to forty-six percent in the case of Hindu homes.[66]

A later section in this chapter gives the scathing criticism of Muslim caste abuses by B.R. Ambedkar.

Caste and Christianity

In 2003, Pope John Paul II criticized caste discrimination in the Catholic Church in India when addressing the bishops of Tamil Nadu. He said: 'It is the Church's obligation to work unceasingly to change hearts, helping all people to see every human being as a child of God, a brother or sister of Christ, and therefore a member of our own family.'[67] Despite his appeal, one can still see advertisements in newspapers in which Christians seek 'Catholic Brahmin' spouses.

The website Dalitchristians.com is devoted to an active movement demanding the Church to end its caste discrimination and cleanse itself of this hypocrisy. It gives extensive details on caste and untouchability among Indian Christians.

After many years of denial about caste in their community, the Church in India finally admitted to internal discrimination and began demanding special quotas for jobs and education for their own Christian Dalits and lower castes.

Even among Indian Christians in the US, there are separate churches for the Kerala castes and the Tamil castes.

Caste is Not Necessary to Be a Hindu

There are many Hindus that do not practice caste, and therefore it is not a *necessary condition* for being a Hindu. For instance, Hindus have settled down in Surinam, Mauritius, Bali, Fiji, and other places outside India for many generations. They are staunch Hindus, but do *not* practice caste. Many of them do not even know their caste since their ancestors left India as indentured laborers more than a century back, and they lost touch with their historical lineages. They intermarry Hindus of all kinds freely, and there are no taboos for inter-dining or sharing places of worship. (On the other hand, some diaspora jatis like Marwaris and Patels have maintained their distinct identities.)

The above facts prove: Caste is neither a necessary, nor a sufficient, condition for being a Hindu. One can be a Hindu without practicing caste; conversely, one can practice caste without being a Hindu.

Challenges to Birth-based Hierarchy in Actual Practice

Several well-known incidents show that even the highest strata of Hindus have been confronted and challenged when they exercised prejudice on grounds of birth. One example is of Adi Shankara: He asked a Chandala to move out of his way, who challenged him on whether the acharya's behavior was consistent with his philosophy. Shankaracharya then prostrated before him as one would before a guru, reiterated his nondual philosophy, and chanted a famous set of verses. The first verse states that a person who knows the Supreme, regardless of social status, is a guru for him.[68] Many important modern gurus have not been Brahmins by birth, such as Swami Vivekananda, Sri Prabhupad of ISKCON, and Swami Chinmayananda.

Because there was no central authority interpreting or enforcing any 'caste rules', such challenges and mobility were voluntary on part of common citizens. Given this free negotiation of a community's status, the ranking of many jatis was a matter of contention. Many jatis competed in claiming their superiority over others. Some did so by observing the rules of purity or by practicing the sacred thread ceremony and certain pujas. In many instances, those considered to be Shudras thought of themselves as Kshatriyas.

The anthropologist and sociologist, M.N. Srinivasan, well-known for his work on the caste system, called this the process of Sanskritization.[69] This was a means by which entire groups upgraded themselves in jati status since there was nobody to pass final judgment with any Church-like authority. Only the British made official caste laws and enforced them.

Shudras and *Vanavasis*

This section responds to several erroneous views that scholars have spread about Shudras being slaves and oppressed since the earliest Vedic times. Of course, one must fight against all abuse, but this is best achieved with an accurate view based on facts and evidence. A false diagnosis is always counter-productive and leads to incorrect solutions. This is especially true if identity politics is involved.

Shudras as Emperors, Kings, and Soldiers

What is clear is that the varna system was not fixed and unchangeable upon birth. Though in ancient India, occupation frequently coincided with the parents' varna, the testimony of the great epics, the Buddhist *Jataka* stories, and the lists of crafts in Hindu and Buddhist literature, also proves that a person born into a family of one varna or jati could shift to another if he was unable to follow his hereditary role or was attracted to another by inclination or talent.

As a matter of fact, we see Shudras occupying the position of kings and emperors in Vedic times.[70] Some Dalit scholars claim that Shudras were the non-Aryan aboriginal race of India who were conquered and enslaved by the invading Aryan race. However, Ambedkar strongly rejects this theory and asserts that Shudras, like all other Indians, were indigenous people. He further confirms that some of the most eminent and powerful kings of ancient India were Shudras.[71] The *Mahabharata* mentions a Shudra king conducting *yajnas*.[72] And Ambedkar identifies this king with Sudas who is mentioned in the *Rig Veda*.[73]

Ambedkar's view is corroborated by further historical evidence:

- The Nanda dynasty rulers of northern India in the fourth century BCE were Shudras as per Hindu, Jaina, and Buddhist sources. This means Mahapadma Nanda, the great emperor of northern India, was a Shudra.
- Likewise, the next great emperor of India, Chandragupta Maurya was also a Shudra. The Maurya empire was the biggest that India ever saw, and for the first time an all-Indian nationality was achieved under a centralized government. It is important to note that a Shudra was the head of such an empire.

- Later, during the Gupta period there were Shudra kings ruling in the regions of Saurashtra, Avanti, Arbuda, and Malwa.[74]
- Buddhist sources regard the powerful Pala dynasty, which ruled Bengal and other parts of eastern India for nearly four hundred years, from the mid-eighth to the eleventh century, to be of Shudra origin. The Buddhist text *Manjushri-mula-kalpa* states that Gopala, the founder of the Pala dynasty (750-1160 CE), was a Shudra.[75] The Pala dynasty monarchs were great patrons of Buddhism, and their copper plate inscriptions begin with an invocation to Buddha.[76]
- In medieval India, the Kakatiya dynasty monarchs (c. 1163-1323 CE) who ruled the Telugu-speaking Andhra region claimed themselves to be Shudras in their inscriptions. One peculiarity of medieval Andhra society was that many leading warrior families made no pretensions to be Kshatriyas and instead, proudly proclaimed their Shudra status by mentioning their descent from that of Lord Brahma's feet. Shudras possessed the greatest degree of actual political power in medieval Andhra.

Shudra kings always regarded themselves as an integral part of Hindu society. There is no evidence in ancient India indicating that they ever considered themselves otherwise.

An important Sanskrit inscription of the Andhra chief, Prolaya Nayaka mentions a Shudra's movement to liberate a large territory from the Muslims in 1329.

> Then arose chief Prolaya of the Musumuri family of Shudra caste. Unable to resist his might, the Yavanas abandoned their forts and fled to unknown places. He restored the agrahara lands to the Brahmins and revived the performance of Vedic sacrifices. He cleansed the Andhra Pradesha of the pollution caused by the movements of the Turushkas by means of the butter smoke arising out of the sacrificial fire pits.[77]

There was another instance when Hindu rule was established in 1320 by a Mahar (Ambedkar's community) after he reconverted from Islam to Hinduism. Arvind Sharma feels this indicates the Mahars saw themselves within the Hindu fold.[78]

It cannot be assumed that only a few fortunate Shudras became rulers while the masses led a marginalized existence. The Shudra varna as a whole played an important role in the socio-political life during Vedic, and subsequent, periods and enjoyed a considerable share in the governance of the state and in senior positions in the military.

- During the *Ashvamedha yajna*, the Shudras acted as armed guards protecting the horse sent out on an expedition of worldwide conquest.[79]

- During the period 800 BCE to 400 BCE, Shudras found a place in the exalted body of about a dozen 'high functionaries of the state' called *ratnins*.[80]

- The *Mahabharata* also recommends that there be a body of eight ministers to advise a king comprising four Brahmins, and three Shudras.[81] It also mentions that Shudras were invited to the great coronation of Yudhishthira as king of Hastinapur.[82]

- In the later medieval period, we find Shudras being commonly employed as soldiers in the mighty warrior Chhatrapati Shivaji's (r. 1674-80) army and other rulers of India. Many of them belonged to the so-called untouchable jatis like the Ramoshi, Mahars, and the Mangs.[83]

- This continued in British India and the soldiers perceived it as a continuation of their earlier Kshatriya tradition.[84] Even today, the Indian Army has a Mahar Regiment that has produced two army chiefs, won several battle honors, and received the nation's highest gallantry award, the Param Vir Chakra.[85] Many Dalit communities presently claim Kshatriya ancestry and often have Kshatriya names, which is verified by the Anthropological Survey of India.[86] There are many such examples of Dalits regarding themselves as Kshatriyas across India.[87]

- Mahar soldiers were particularly reputed for their loyalty in military service to the Marathas and other rulers. The Hindu Peshwas also had Mahars guard the women of the royal household.[88] Upon the killing of the Maratha prince Sambhaji by Mughal emperor Aurangzeb, one Sidhnak Mahar was honored by Sambhaji's son for raising an independent Mahar platoon to serve the Maratha state.[89]

Economic Power and Social Status

Contrary to the portrayal of Shudras as perpetually helpless and poor, records show that they formed the backbone of the Vedic economy. The *Vedas* mention many kinds of technological crafts and industries associated with them.[90] P.V. Kane mentions sixty-two different Shudra industries which included leather work, metallurgy, and textiles, all owned, managed, and controlled by them.[91] In other words, they were self-employed and not laborers.

The Shudra artisans and craftsmen were imparted training in big educational institutions and the *Vedas* clearly state that the king's duty is to build such institutions.[92] Many mantras of the *Rig Veda* state that the king should also protect and help the craftsmen and artisans.[93]

It was not unusual for Brahmins and Kshatriyas to work under Shudras.[94] Many Ayurvedic physicians and Sanskrit scholars in Kerala belonged to the Shudra Ezhava community.[95] For instance, Itty Achudan was a distinguished Ezhava herbalist of the second half of the seventeenth century, whose statement appears in the beginning of the renowned book *Hortus Malabaricus*. This botanical treatise on the medicinal properties of plants is considered one of the earliest sources of Europeans' knowledge of botany. It was published in twelve volumes from Amsterdam between 1678 and 1703.[96]

In ancient times, the Shudras and Vaishyas that worked together in the same economic fields were jointly called Sudraryau.[97] Numerous inscriptions show that these guilds also functioned like banks, receiving deposits from the public for interest and lending money to borrowers.[98]

The lawgiver Medhatithi's commentary on *Manusmriti* says that Shudras teach grammar and other sciences, a fact also mentioned in the *Brihaddharma Purana*.[99] The *Apastambha Dharmasutra* states that *vidya* or knowledge that exists traditionally among the women and Shudras is a supplement of the *Atharva Veda*.[100]

Ancient texts like *Yajnavalkya Smriti*, *Narada Smriti* and *Vishnu Smriti* prove that Shudra guilds of artisans and craftsmen were part of the state machinery and were held in high regard.[101] These guilds also formed part of the judicial tribunals of the country. The *Gautam Dharmashastra* mentions they had the right to make their own laws which were respected by the king.[102] Throughout recorded history, these guilds are shown to have worthy social positions.[103] In fact, the Shudra guilds enjoyed considerable economic prosperity in ancient India.[104]

The guild system functioned in the north till as late as the twelfth century, after which Muslim invasions made the guilds immobile and ossified, resulting in their degeneration and subdivision.[105]

Being part of the wealthy class of the times, they also made large donations. The evidence lies in numerous inscriptions that mention Shudras as philanthropists.[106] The Jain *Agamas* dated around the sixth to third century that comprise Mahavira's teachings, provide a picture of the economic prosperity of Shudras and the social respect for them.[107] Hiuen Tsang, the Chinese traveler who visited India in the latter half of the seventh century, mentions Shudras as a class of agriculturists.[108]

The figure on the next page shows the multifaceted role played by the Shudras in the traditional Indian society.

Untouchability Between Shudras

It is generally believed that untouchability was practiced only by the higher varna as a form of oppression against the Shudras and Dalits. However, untouchability was also present within the latter communities, and persisted even after they converted to Christianity or Islam. There is evidence that by the beginning of the Common Era, the outcastes themselves had developed a caste hierarchy and had their own untouchables. Thus, Manu mentions that the *antyavasayin*, one born of a mixed marriage between a chandala and a *nishada*, (also a low caste) was despised even by the chandalas.[109] In a similar manner, nearly every untouchable group felt that another group was lower than theirs.[110]

Even in present times, Scheduled Castes in every region have a hierarchy that restricts the acceptance and exchange of water and fruit from certain communities. For example, in south India, a Mala considers a Madiga an untouchable, and for both, a Thoti is an untouchable.[111] Similarly in north India, for a Meghwal, a Regar is an untouchable, and for both, a Bhangi is an untouchable.[112] Likewise, the Adi Dravida do not accept food and water from the Dhobi, Mala and Madiga communities.[113] Ironically, many Scheduled Castes (ninety-six percent) currently are endogamous.[114]

Multifaceted Status of Shudras

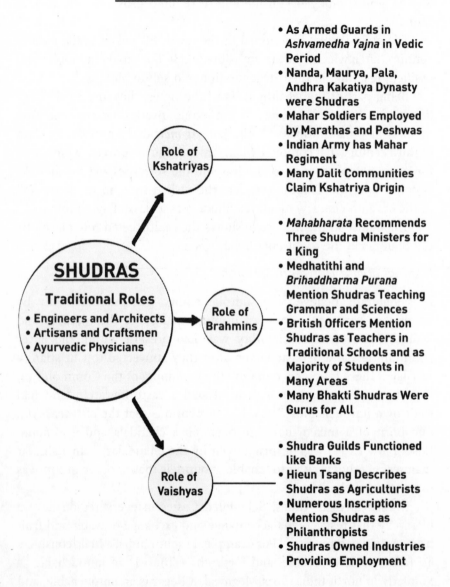

Role of Kshatriyas
- As Armed Guards in *Ashvamedha Yajna* in Vedic Period
- Nanda, Maurya, Pala, Andhra Kakatiya Dynasty were Shudras
- Mahar Soldiers Employed by Marathas and Peshwas
- Indian Army has Mahar Regiment
- Many Dalit Communities Claim Kshatriya Origin

Role of Brahmins
- *Mahabharata* Recommends Three Shudra Ministers for a King
- Medhatithi and *Brihaddharma Purana* Mention Shudras Teaching Grammar and Sciences
- British Officers Mention Shudras as Teachers in Traditional Schools and as Majority of Students in Many Areas
- Many Bhakti Shudras Were Gurus for All

SHUDRAS
Traditional Roles
- Engineers and Architects
- Artisans and Craftsmen
- Ayurvedic Physicians

Role of Vaishyas
- Shudra Guilds Functioned like Banks
- Hieun Tsang Describes Shudras as Agriculturists
- Numerous Inscriptions Mention Shudras as Philanthropists
- Shudras Owned Industries Providing Employment

Indigenous Education Before the British

Some scholars presently allege that Shudras were not given an opportunity to become educated. According to these theories, Shudras were steeped in illiteracy due to this discrimination. It is widely assumed that education in India, whether in the ancient period or until British rule, was the privilege of Brahmins and Kshatriyas. This view maintains that Shudras became emancipated only when the British introduced English education in India and provided them equal opportunities. However, the truth, is the exact opposite.

The scholar Dharampal, considered one of Gandhi's most earnest followers, spent considerable time in England studying their official records on India. His goal was to bring back an archive on the state of pre-colonial indigenous Indian education as per official British records. His books are a great reference source that refute many false claims made by eminent historians.

Dharampal writes:

> Madras Presidency and Bengal-Bihar data presents a kind of revelation. The data reveals the background of the teachers and the taught. It ... is in sharp contrast to the various scholarly pronouncements of the past 100 years or more, in which it had been assumed that education of any sort in India, till very recent decades, was mostly limited to the twice-born amongst the Hindoos, and amongst the Muslims to those from the ruling elite. The actual situation which is revealed was different, if not quite contrary, for at least amongst the Hindoos, in the districts of the Madras Presidency (and dramatically so in the Tamil speaking areas) as well as the two districts of Bihar. It was the groups termed Soodras, and the castes considered below them who predominated in the thousands of the then still-existing schools in practically each of these areas.[115]

In other words, Shudras and other lowest social strata communities had good access to traditional Indian education. Dharampal presents precise statistics using the British surveys on the indigenous education system of India. The table on the following page summarizes his findings of Madras Presidency in 1825.

Community Profile of Boys Undergoing Instruction in Schools and at Home in the District of Madras, ca.1825

	Brahmins	Vaisyas	Sudras	Other Castes	Hindus	Muslims	Total
Instructed in Schools	410	853	3,678	447	5,370	153	5,523
% of Total	7.42	15.12	66.59	8.09	97.23	2.77	
Instructed at Home	7,586	6,132	7,589	3,449	24,756	1,690	26,446
% of Total	28.68	23.19	28.70	13.04	93.61	6.39	
Total	7,996	6,967	11,267	3,896	30,126	1,843	31,969

Source: Dharampal, *The Beautiful Tree*

Clearly, the percentage of Shudras in schools (66.59) is higher than that of all the other varnas combined. Also, more Shudras were instructed in schools than at home which indicates easy access to formal schooling.

Similarly, Dharampal states that in the Malayalam-speaking Malabar, Shudras and other such castes accounted for some fifty-four percent of school-going students.[116] In the largely Kannada-speaking Bellary, the proportion of Brahmin and Vaishya students was thirty-three percent, while Shudras and the other lower strata accounted for sixty-three percent of school-going students.[117] The position in the Oriya-speaking Ganjam was similar: Brahmins and Vaishyas accounted for 35.6 percent of the students, and the lower strata around 63.5 percent.[118] The table on the following page shows the varna breakdown percentage of students in indigenous schools in the various regions of Madras Presidency.

This trend was not just confined to primary school education. According to Madras Presidency surveys, those practicing medicine and surgery belonged to a variety of castes. Amongst them, according to British medical officials, the barber jati were the best surgeons.[119] Astronomy was another subject in which the majority of students were Shudras.

The findings of Dharampal are supported by the fact that the British administrator Thomas Munro, in his survey of indigenous Indian education in Madras Presidency in 1822, explicitly stated that *there is no indication that a Shudra status prevented children from instruction in vernacular schools.*[120]

Community Profile of Boys Studying in the Indigenous Schools, ca.1825

Linguistic Region		Brahmins	Vaisyas	Sudras	Other Castes	Hindus	Muslims
Odiya	Students	808	243	1,001	886	2,938	27
	% of Total	27.25	8.20	33.76	29.88	99.09	0.91
Telugu	Students	13,893	7,676	10,076	4,755	36,521	1,639
	% of Total	36.41	20.12	26.40	12.46	95.70	4.30
Kannada	Students	1,233	1,004	3,296	1,332	6,865	329
	% of Total	17.14	13.96	45.82	18.52	95.43	4.57
Malayalam	Students	2,230	84	3,697	2,756	8,767	3,196
	% of Total	18.64	0.70	30.90	23.04	73.28	26.72
Tamil	Students	11,557	4,442	57,873	13,196	87,437	5,453
	% of Total	12.44	4.78	62.30	14.21	94.13	5.87
Presidency Total	Students	29,721	13,449	75,943	22,925	1,42,528	10,644
	% of Total	19.40	8.78	49.58	14.97	93.05	6.95

Source: Dharampal, *The Beautiful Tree*

Shudras not only dominated as students but also formed a large section of teachers. The Britisher, William Ward, in his early nineteenth century account of indigenous schools in Bengal, states that *teachers in schools were generally Shudras and occasionally Brahmins.*[121]

Dalit Hindu Pride

Some modern scholars claim that Shudras and Dalits are not Hindus. This serves the agenda to divide and fragment society. However, if we look at the various population census reports and comprehensive surveys carried out by the Indian government, it becomes clear that an overwhelming majority of Shudras and Dalits proudly classify themselves as Hindus.

A reliable reference is the study the Anthropological Survey of India carried out under its massive *People of India* project (1985-92). The intention was to present the anthropological profile of all the communities of India. The report reveals many interesting facts:

- 96.9 percent of the SC communities identified themselves as Hindus.[122]
- 79.8 percent of the SC communities share water resources and 67 percent share crematoria with other communities.
- 91 percent of them visit the same religious shrines as other communities.

- 91 percent of the SC communities participate in traditional Hindu festivals and festivities, and 17.6 percent have a special role to play in these festivals.[123]

Furthermore, Ambedkar specifically argued using the physical anthropological data, that there was no ethnic difference between Mahars and some of the Brahmin groups in Maharashtra and the Chamars and Brahmins in Uttar Pradesh.[124]

Many investigators have also reported that the genetic differences between the regions are greater than the variations between the castes of a given region.[125]

There is hard evidence on the religious lives of the three largest Dalit or SC communities in India – the Chamar, the Adi Dravida, and the Pasi. It clearly shows that they have considered themselves Hindus.

The Chamars are the largest Scheduled Caste or Dalit community in India and are spread out in almost all the northern states.[126] In Uttar Pradesh they are known as Raidasis because they recognize themselves as spiritual descendants of the Hindu Vaishnava saint, Raidas.[127] In Punjab and Himachal Pradesh their marriages are performed according to Vedic tradition,[128] and besides Raidas, they worship Hindu deities. In Haryana, too, the followers of Ravidas called Jatavs[129] as well as the followers of Sant Kabir called Julaha,[130] worship Lakshmi and Kali, amongst others. They employ Brahmins to perform their birth, marriage, and death rituals. Durga puja and Holi are their major festivals.[131]

The Adi Dravida is the second largest SC community in India.[132] They identify themselves as Hindus, visit Hindu shrines, and celebrate Hindu festivals.[133] In Karnataka, they worship Hindu deities like Durgamma, Renuka, Parashuram, Laxmi, Venkataramana, and so forth.[134] In Andhra Pradesh, they profess Hinduism and celebrate festivals like Diwali, Dussehra, Ganesh Chaturthi, Pongal and so on.[135]

The third-largest SC or Dalit community in India, the Pasi, believe in the legend that they arose from the sweat (*pasina* in Hindi, hence their name Pasi) of Sage Parashuram to protect cows from being killed.[136] They are spread in many northern states and worship Hanuman, Devi and other deities,[137] and perform pilgrimages to sacred Hindu centers like Kashi, Prayag, Haridwar, Vrindavan, and Naimisharanya. Typically, a Brahmin officiates at their major rituals.[138] The Pasis share wells, water resources, and religious shrines with other jatis and join them in traditional festivals. The figure below gives a glimpse into the regional profile of some Dalit communities of India.

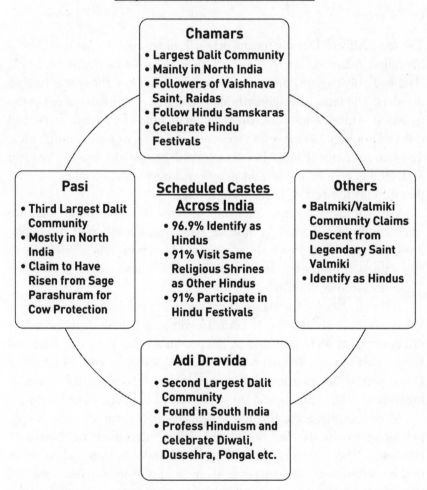

Regional Profiles of Shudras

Chamars
- Largest Dalit Community
- Mainly in North India
- Followers of Vaishnava Saint, Raidas
- Follow Hindu Samskaras
- Celebrate Hindu Festivals

Pasi
- Third Largest Dalit Community
- Mostly in North India
- Claim to Have Risen from Sage Parashuram for Cow Protection

Scheduled Castes Across India
- 96.9% Identify as Hindus
- 91% Visit Same Religious Shrines as Other Hindus
- 91% Participate in Hindu Festivals

Others
- Balmiki/Valmiki Community Claims Descent from Legendary Saint Valmiki
- Identify as Hindus

Adi Dravida
- Second Largest Dalit Community
- Found in South India
- Profess Hinduism and Celebrate Diwali, Dussehra, Pongal etc.

As per their own traditional accounts, until the medieval period, Pasis ruled in the area of Avadh in Uttar Pradesh. Some of their subcastes like Rajpasis claim descent from Rajputs.[139]

We must point out that there was no manual scavenging in pre-British times since there were no toilets in homes. Manual scavenging for Dalits was a British creation, modeled after scavenging practices in London those days. Communities like Bhangi, Mehtar and other castes became associated with scavenging during British rule. They are now unitedly called the Balmiki/Valmiki and claim descent from the legendary Hindu saint Valmiki. They also identify as Hindus.[140]

Vanavasis

The term Adivasi literally means original inhabitant. All Indians should be called Adivasis, but the British race theories of divide and rule classified only certain communities as indigenous and the rest as foreign invaders. The term 'aborigines' is also flawed as that invokes ideas of the natives of America and Australia who got subdued by foreign races, and this terminology has served to treat non-Adivasis as some foreign race. The Government of India has also argued against the use of the term 'indigenous people' for certain people at international forums because that implies the rest of Indians are foreign.[141]

We will use the term 'Vanavasi' to refer to communities that are traditionally forest-dwelling, making clear that the different geography does not correspond to a different race. However, when referring to governmental sources of data we will retain the official term 'Scheduled Tribe' to avoid confusion.

As in the case of the Dalits, there are many modern-day claims that Vanavasis were always non-Hindus. However, a British superintendent of census from 1931 said that in his provinces the Vanavasis followed Hindu customs, participated in Hindu processions, and worshipped Hindu deities. He mentioned that often it was impossible to distinguish them from other Hindus and they referred to themselves as Hindus.[142]

More recently, according to the *People of India* project, most people belonging to the various Scheduled Tribes identified themselves as Hindus.[143] They selected the category of Hindu as opposed to other options offered in the surveys, such as indigenous tribal religion, Christianity, Islam, etc. In the 1981 census, 87.05 percent of the total Scheduled Tribe population classified themselves as Hindus.[144]

The four largest Vanavasi communities in India are the Gond, the Bhil, the Santhal, and the Mina.[145]

Gond is numerically the largest Scheduled Tribe of India covering a vast geography across several states in central India.[146] They were once politically powerful and in the medieval period ruled over as many as four separate kingdoms.[147] According to their legends, their ancestors were adopted and nurtured by Lord Shiva and Mother Parvati. They worship Hindu deities and celebrate all major Hindu festivals like Holi, Diwali, Dussehra, Rakhi and Sankranti.[148]

The second largest Scheduled Tribe of India is the Bhil community, spread out in southern Rajasthan, western Madhya Pradesh, Gujarat, and northern Maharashtra. They speak Bhili which belongs to the family of Sanskrit. They are the largest Vanavasi community in Gujarat. Nearly all the Bhils identify themselves as Hindus and celebrate festivals like Holi, Diwali, Navaratri, Rakhi, etc. Historically, the Bhils played an important role in the coronation ceremony of many Rajput chiefs.[149]

Mina is the largest Scheduled Tribe of Rajasthan and the fourth largest in India.[150] They trace their descent from the *Min-avatara* or the fish incarnation of Vishnu, hence the name Mina.[151] Lord Shiva is their supreme deity, and they also worship Hanuman, Sita-Ram and Radha-Krishna.[152] In the 1961 and 1971 censuses, one hundred percent of Minas recorded themselves as Hindus.[153]

Like the Shudras, many Vanavasi communities have played a significant role in Hindu society as technologists and engineers. For example, the Agaria tribe (name derived from *aag* or fire) in Madhya Pradesh were traditionally ironsmiths and experts in smelting iron and making iron objects.[154]

People from the Munda community inhabit central and northeastern states.[155] The freedom fighter, Birsa Munda, who fought against British rule belonged to this community. He was influenced by a Brahmin whom he regarded as his guru. He learnt the Hindu epics and was inspired by their legendary heroes.[156] He became a vegetarian when he met a Vaishnava saint who taught him Bhakti.[157] Birsa Munda also raised his voice against Christian missionaries and the oppression of landlords and British administrators.[158] Many Vanavasi communities claim Kshatriya ancestry.[159]

It is noteworthy that despite the aggressive conversion drives by Christian missionaries over a long period, many Scheduled Tribes of northeast India overwhelmingly report themselves as Hindus. For example, among the Bodo-Kachari, which is the largest tribe of the Brahmaputra valley in Assam, ninety-five percent have reported themselves as Hindus in the 1971 census. They also visit the sacred shrines of the Vaishnav monasteries and temples.[160]

The Kachari Hojai Scheduled Tribe of Assam belongs to the Bodo linguistic group that observes major Hindu rituals like naming a child and the sacred thread ceremony. They belong to the Shakta tradition and claim to be Kshatriya. The 1971 census recorded one hundred percent of Hojais as followers of Hinduism. Another Bodo community is Kachari Barman and according to the 1961 and 1971 censuses, all of them classified themselves as Hindus.[161]

The Bhakti Movement

The Bhakti movement was the most prominent within the framework of Hinduism to fight against jati hierarchies and divisiveness. Across India it was led by several saint poets born in the so-called lower jatis and included female saints.

Bhakti (loosely translated as devotion) has always been a part of Hinduism. The *Upanishads, Bhagavad Gita, Mahabharata, Ramayana,* and the *Puranas* all comprise teachings of Bhakti. This old tradition was revived in a big way in Tamil Nadu in the sixth century CE by Shaiva and Vaishnava saints. In Karnataka in the twelfth century, it raised its voice against claims of jati exclusivity, to the extent of getting a Brahmin's daughter married to an untouchable's son.

The Bhakti movement democratized Hinduism into a grassroots movement. Its adherents emphasized that outward book knowledge is neither necessary nor sufficient for spiritual enlightenment. This effectively undermined the authority of anyone claiming exclusive access to the *Vedas*, because now the *Vedas* were not the only path available. However, it would be incorrect to say that Bhakti revolted against the *Vedas*; the fact is that its teachings are Vedic. In fact, many important Bhakti saints wrote commentaries on the *Vedic* texts and advocated studying them.[162]

The Bhakti movement was diverse and spread all over India. Kabir in north India, Shishunala Sharif in Karnataka, and Shirdi Sai Baba in Maharashtra were all born Muslim, but were Bhakti saints highly revered by Hindus. Maharashtra's Bhakti movement was similar, drawing from the lower caste working class as well as Brahmins.

Contrary to some modern claims that Shudras never considered themselves Hindus, there were many influential Bhakti saints from Shudra backgrounds. We will look at some prominent examples.

Ravidas and Kabir in the North

Swami Ramanandacharya was an imposing Vaishnava saint, a Brahmin by birth, who propagated the path of Rama bhakti in north India. He had twelve chief disciples, many of them Shudras like Sant Ravidas, Sant Kabir and Sant Sain.[163]

Ravidas traveled throughout north India to spread Bhakti and wrote profound hymns devoted to Vishnu. Ravidas' fame spread far and wide. Meerabai, the sixteenth-century celebrated woman, mentions meeting him in Kashi and acknowledges him to be her guru.[164] Sant Ravidas, in many of his devotional songs says that though he belongs to the Chamar jati of Shudras, the Brahmins of Varanasi prostrate before him with great respect.[165]

The fifteenth-century poet and saint, Kabir, was another influential disciple of Ramanandacharya. He was born in Varanasi to a family of weavers from the Shudra community.[166] He is among the most renowned of Bhakti poets and has a large following among the masses. His *doha*s, or two-line poems have a spirit of total surrender to Vishnu whom he calls Rama or Hari and are popularly recited by all sections of Indian society regardless of their varna or jati.

Hindu Saints of Maharashtra

Chokhamela, saint poet of Maharashtra's Varkari sect (late thirteenth and early fourteenth century) mentions in his works that he belonged to the Mahar jati, regarded as the lowest of the low.[167] He composed several devotional songs praising Vishnu and the *Vedas*. Other saints of his sect like Namdev, Tukaram, Gora Kumbhar, Savanta Mali also belonged to the lower jatis.[168]

The Vari pilgrimage is a living tradition of Maharashtra in which devotees march on foot chanting a mantra inspired by the names of two leading saints of the Varkari tradition – Jnaneshvar, a Brahmin, and Tukaram, a Shudra. This illustrates the unity of Brahmins and Shudras in this tradition. Tukaram was a firm believer in the Vedic tradition, and one of his songs says that one should not even look at a person who disbelieves the *Vedas* and *Puranas*.[169]

Hindu Shudra Saints from the South

The sixty-three Tamil Saiva saints called Nayanmars belonged to all varnas, including Shudras. Similarly, among the twelve Tamil Vaishnava Alvar saints, some were Shudras.

Among the large-scale social movements integrating Dalits into mainstream society, the Ezhavas in Kerala and the Nadars in Tamil Nadu were prominent. Both achieved their social transformations within the Hindu framework despite being under colonial rule.

In the case of Ezhavas, Narayana Guru was a powerful leader who upgraded their social status. When Ezhavas faced discrimination, he built and consecrated new Hindu temples where Dalits and non-Dalits prayed together.[170] He taught the philosophy of Adi Shankaracharya calling it a sublime contribution to the world.[171] He created Vedic schools to train Dalits as priests for performing Hindu rituals and teaching Hindu philosophy. As an educationist, Narayana Guru founded secular schools and colleges for all communities and several of his important disciples were Brahmins.[172]

He expanded beyond the Ezhavas, bringing other Dalits into the fold, in order to educate them to pursue professional careers. His was an all-encompassing program for comprehensive advancement of the Dalits that included the development of a financial credit system among them.

Narayana Guru trained his teachers to preach harmony with other castes and was supported by the upper castes. There were joint processions of all castes to call for Dalits' entry into major temples. Gandhi and he worked together to bring such reforms into the mainstream.

The Nadars did not have a charismatic leader like Narayana Guru yet managed to thrive under their own secular leaders. In their case, it was mainly through the medium of education and training in job skills. They helped each other through friendly credit arrangements and informal employment agencies, while also Sanskritizing themselves.[173]

The Nadars became economically powerful in industry. Modern scholars have highlighted that their community boasts some of India's richest industrialists.[174] Shiv Nadar, the founder of HCL Technologies, is a billionaire industrialist from this community. There are many lessons to be learned from their success. Their approach was diametrically opposite to that of Harvard University's Suraj Yengde. The goal was not to build rabble-rousing activist organizations for spreading awareness of their victimhood or protesting and making demands on the government and society.

Rather, they established constructive initiatives for their advancement. For example:

- They convinced parents to send their children to schools.
- They provided vocational training that qualified members to work outside their traditional professions.
- They helped their members relocate to places where jobs were available.
- They fought addiction in their community.
- Fellow Nadars looked after like extended family.

This was achieved without taking an adversarial stance against the rest of society. Success came about as a result of working with other communities rather than attacking them.

In modern Hinduism, there have been many other movements that have helped enrich the moral fabric and spiritual life of their followers. As explained by Swami Vivekananda, Sri Aurobindo and others, modern Hinduism has rejected the caste system. Likewise, for the groups led by Brahmakumaris, ISKCON, Sri Sathya Sai Baba, and Mata Amritanandamayi. They have shown that Hinduism can thrive without the caste system and needs no foreign intervention.

British Social Engineering

The British Admit That No Rigid Caste Existed

Prof. Simon Charsley, anthropologist at the University of Glasgow, explains how the British struggled to frame Indian society in terms of caste even as late as the censuses from 1871 to 1901. Considering that the East India Company came into existence in the year 1600, this is the situation even after 250 years of the British presence in India. Charsley's account begins as follows:

> When he [Sir Herbert Risley] became Commissioner for the
> 1901 Census of India, he was determined to carry out within its

framework a grand experiment in classifying and ranking castes in the sub-continent as a whole. ... Census-taking had often suffered ... from the difficulty even of identifying discrete castes and foundered in some census regions over the impossibility of finding any meaningful way of classifying them that did not release a hornets' nest of contention, as the Commissioner for the 1871 Madras Census put it. Commissioners in their reports often retreated from any greater ambition than providing a list of castes in English alphabetical order. It was clear ... uniformity of classification across the country could not be hoped for. Risley's scheme, therefore, was to send to every Census Commissioner, in each province, presidency, princely state, ... a standard scheme, inviting them to set up committees of 'native gentlemen' to consider its local applicability and to propose modifications as required.[175]

What this means is there was difficulty 'even of identifying discrete castes'. There was 'the impossibility of finding any meaningful way of classifying them'. Even after a few decades of attempts to study the castes, 'a uniformity of classification across the country could not be hoped for'. This tells us that after studying India so thoroughly for over two centuries, and engaging numerous Indian kings, scholars, and other significant persons, the British were clueless about caste. Every present scholar that makes tall claims of being an expert on 'the caste system' ought to study these British accounts with some humility.[176]

From the outset of the census project, the British reported resistance from the Indian communities being mapped as well as from the British officials carrying out the census. A persistent challenge was in identifying clear boundaries and definitions of 'the castes' in real life. This issue is well documented in official reports from the census authorities.

The problem was that of a deep civilizational clash. The British needed simple normative definitions of castes that would be mutually exclusive and clearly demarcated. The ground reality, however, was completely different. Indian society did not work the way the British wanted to see it. The British Privy Council also acknowledged that a better source of 'law for Hindoos' was custom and usage in real life as opposed to what was in texts like the *Dharmashastras*.[177]

Dharampal, after spending many years in British libraries concluded:

> For the British, caste was a great obstacle, an unmitigated evil not because they believed in castelessness or a non-hierarchical system but because it stood in their way of their breaking Indian society. ... caste did hinder the process of atomization of Indian society and made ... conquest and governance more difficult. The present fury and theoretical formulation against the organization of Indian society into castes, whatever the justification or otherwise of caste today, thus begins with British rule.[178]

Before Lord Risley decided to force a hierarchical framework, various European thinkers were speculating different kinds of conceptual schemes to capture Indian society in their imagination and make sense of its bewildering size, diversity, and depth. For instance, W.R. Cornish, who supervised census operations in Madras Presidency in 1871, wrote: 'Whether there was ever a period in which the Hindus were composed of four classes is exceedingly doubtful'. Similarly, C.F. Magrath, who authored a report on the 1871 Bihar census, wrote that 'now meaningless division into the four castes alleged to have been made by Manu should be put aside'.[179]

The Cambridge anthropologist Susan Bayly writes:

> Until well into the colonial period, much of the subcontinent was still populated by people for whom the formal distinctions of caste were of only limited importance, even in parts of the so-called Hindu heartland... The institutions and beliefs which are now often described as the elements of traditional caste were only just taking shape as recently as the early 18th Century.[180]

Different committees and commissioners established by the British came up with a wide variety of interpretations and often fell back on a simple list of castes without any hierarchy whatsoever. For example, in Baroda, the superintendent of census operations in charge said that Risley's terms were 'quite exotic' because in his province 'no such sharp distinctions are laid down here'. He took recourse to an alphabetical listing of castes without hierarchy.[181]

Despite Risley's determination, he failed to achieve a consensus among his officials across India on a uniform classification. All schemes of classification applicable in one province of India were rejected in others. Complaints were received from experienced and knowledgeable officers, both Indian as well as European. Charsley explains: 'One census commissioner after another struggled to discern some order amongst the differently-based groups.'[182]

It is interesting to note that the census commissioner for India complained from Bengal that 'the ignorant classes have very little idea of what caste means and are prone to return either their occupation, or their sub-caste, or their clan, or else some title by which they are known to their fellow-villagers'.[183]

But gradually, by the twentieth century, with repeated censuses and persistent inquiries from strangers landing up at their doorstep on how to identify their caste, *the Indian community leaders became schooled to give suitable answers that would be acceptable to the British.*

A vast literature emerged on how one's community should be classified. Many castes considered 'low' by the census-takers argued that they were high castes. Categories were hotly contested. A key basis for claiming castes to be mutually exclusive was that they practiced endogamy, but this too was not uniformly applicable. Key factors determining who would be eligible as a marriage partner included place of origin, occupation, language, and various combinations. Nor was endogamy universal as there were many exogamous groups also, i.e., those that married outside their community. Jati boundaries were often porous with many exceptions and contexts.[184]

Risley Imposes 'Caste = Racial Hierarchy'

Eventually, the template of Western race theory was adopted as the standard and Risley decided to forcibly fit India's diversity into it. That's how the imagined caste system emerged through trial and error over several censuses spanning half a century.

Sanjoy Chakravorty, professor of geography, urban and global studies at Temple University, Pennsylvania, summarizes the colonial agenda that is well accepted by scholars today:

> The colonisers invented or constructed Indian social identities
> using categories of convenience during a period that covered

roughly the 19th Century. This was done to serve the British Indian government's own interests - primarily to create a single society with a common law that could be easily governed. A very large, complex and regionally diverse system of faiths and social identities was simplified to a degree that probably has no parallel in world history, entirely new categories and hierarchies were created, incompatible or mismatched parts were stuffed together, new boundaries were created, and flexible boundaries hardened.[185]

The resulting categorical system became rigid during the next century and quarter, as the made-up categories came to be associated with real rights. Religion-based electorates in British India and caste-based reservations in independent India made amorphous categories concrete. There came to be real and material consequences of belonging to one category instead of another.[186]

Making 'Untouchability' Official

An important challenge for British experts was to decide whether there were four, or five, varnas. Besides the well-known four varna categories, Risley proposed a fifth which he defined as 'castes whose touch is so impure as to pollute even Ganges water'.[187]

But Risley's criteria, that untouchables were determined by Brahmins' unwillingness to take water from their hands, was not universally applicable. The criteria for physical segregation were much more complex. Few census managers wanted to take up Risley's suggestion for the fifth varna because applying his definition to concrete situations was very subjective, and a matter of opinion.

But gradually, this idea got traction. In Rajasthan, two British superintendents of census included the term 'untouchable' for the first time in print.[188] Others, however, pointed out that in the four-varna system these groups were included as part of the Shudras and there was no such category as untouchables. Evidence from the field differed from one province to another, from one census official to the next. Both, the four- and five-varna, versions were initially adopted in different locations.

Risley then decided to solve the problem by applying a racial theory. He started

> distinguishing 'tracts' according to their supposed racial composition and within which some greater uniformity might be expected. The North-West, today divided between India and Pakistan, he declared 'the Indo-Aryan Tract', consisting of the two Rajasthan census divisions, together with Punjab and Kashmir. Though the report for Punjab gave him no support and that for Kashmir rather little, he took his cue from the two Rajasthan reports and, on this slight basis, he set up for that tract a unified classification which included a 'Class VII: Castes untouchable'. No such term could be worked into any of his other tracts. From this unpropitious start, representing as it did more of a rebuff than a successful initiative, the career of a key term in modern India was launched.[189]

Under this experimental approach, British officials could experiment and project their own favorite theories with no objective checks and balances. One enterprising official began applying his own categories using the racial theory prevalent at that time. He defined Brahmins as 'Predominantly Aryan or their equals'; he had a category called 'Mixed castes'; another called 'Aboriginal tribes and wandering castes'; and finally, 'Impure Castes'.[190]

Indian Nationalists Accept the British Categories

This matter became a topic of debate among Indian nationalists who tended to be members of the English-speaking elite. Gandhi had experienced ill-treatment of Indians in South Africa and brought this sensitivity in the treatment of low castes in India. In 1903, the educationalist and Congress leader, Gopal Krishna Gokhale, moved a resolution on the elevation of the depressed classes.

The actual term 'Untouchable' had not yet emerged in the mainstream, and the idea was being expressed as 'Depressed Classes'. In the first volumes of the *Bombay Gazetteer* published in 1877, the term 'Depressed *castes*' was used, but subsequent volumes from 1879-80, the word '*classes*' began to be substituted and became the term used by the Reform movement. In 1906, the Depressed Classes Mission Society of

India was formed in Bombay, in 1909 in Madras, and in the north, the Arya Samaj had a similar approach. By the end of the decade, articles on the uplifting of the depressed *classes* were appearing in newspapers all over India.

This is when Sayaji Rao Gaekwad III, the maharaja of Baroda and progressive ruler of Gujarat, started making a big impact on the way communities were to be classified. He also encouraged leading activists, reformers, and writers to join the movement to uplift the depressed classes. Among these were the freedom fighter, Lala Lajpat Rai, Theosophist leader, Annie Besant, and renowned Buddhist thinker, Anagarika Dharmapala.

The maharaja preferred the term 'untouchableness' to the term 'depressed classes'. Given his stature, his choice of term tilted the discourse. He noted that the problem 'has varied at different times as the provinces, castes and communities of India have varied'.[191] Gradually, 'untouchability' replaced the maharaja's term 'untouchableness'. Under the presidency of the maharaja, the first All India Depressed Classes Conference of 1918 issued an 'All-India Anti-untouchability Manifesto'.

By the 1920s, the term was widely used in British writing, but Gandhi was hesitant. Sometimes he used 'so-called untouchables' or 'suppressed classes'. In 1931, he announced a change and decided the term 'Harijan' (man of God) was more desirable.

An important voice was Ambedkar, himself a Mahar from the Bombay Presidency, and a community to which the term 'untouchable' would certainly apply. But Mahars were once a large and widespread agricultural jati that were land owners but later got reduced to landless laborers due to political upheavals. By the time he returned to India in 1924 from his legal training in the US and Britain, Ambedkar was using the term 'Untouchable'. He asserted that the Untouchables were 'a separate element in the national life of India' and appointed himself as their spokesman.

Once untouchability became the identity of millions of people, there was a need to name its 'other'. At first, the term 'caste Hindu' was used, even by Ambedkar in 1930. But he later abandoned it and adopted 'Hindu' as the other, making the Untouchables non-Hindus as opposed to being out-caste Hindus. This was a major shift with huge implications.

Ambedkar argued that Untouchables were fundamentally different from Hindus, and capitalized it to emphasize a separate, and distinct, identity. As the chairman of the drafting committee for Independent India's Constitution and as first justice minister, he was responsible for firmly embedding the Untouchable identity.[192] The figure below shows how untouchability became a formal category during the British period.

How Untouchability Became a Category

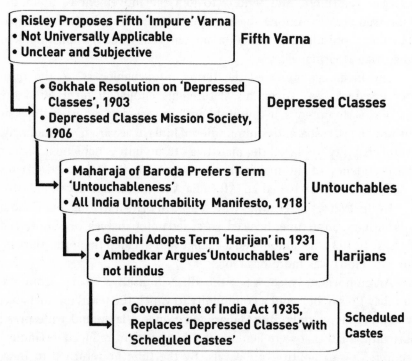

Scholars have identified many problems with Untouchability as a normative category, not just as a term but the category itself:

- It establishes an all-India homogeneous ethnicity when in fact each region's lowest strata of communities are distinct from one another in their histories, practices, relationships with the upper castes, and internal social-political organization. According to Charsley, the problem is that it 'masks local heterogeneity as well as setting up a uniformity more apparent than real between areas. It simplifies the problem of understanding Indian society, at the cost of obscuring the need to come to terms with one of its major and analytically important characteristics: diversity'.[193]

- Even within a given region, the term subsumes several communities that have carefully preserved their separate distinctiveness. For instance, each jati within this Untouchable grouping refers to itself having a distinct first ancestor, pointing to significantly different historical sources of identity.

- There have been tensions among the different Untouchable communities. Gandhi often chided them for prejudices against each other.

- Even the concept of impurity (the defining criteria) is too complex to be reduced into this homogeneous classification.

- It forces a dichotomy of victim/oppressor upon all its members when, in fact, each community's social narrative is distinct. It makes every such community feel like a disadvantaged people who ought to see themselves as victims and be hostile towards other jatis.

Charsley finds the category of Untouchability was an artificial imposition on India's social reality. He says:

> "Untouchability" thus suppressed diversity and variation, and set up a uniform and highly simplified structure in terms of which Indian society was to be understood. The positive practical importance of this conceptual development was great, but the negativity of the characterization needs to be firmly understood before considering the positive. It is this negativity which has become increasingly relevant to current developments as the twentieth century ends.[194]

> "Untouchability", however, not only imposes a hiatus upon the various social, cultural and economic links and continua but ... has the effect of hiding everything positive to be found below the division created. ... "Untouchable" refers to nothing those labelled do or are, merely to what others, negatively, do to them: they are excluded. ... They are not to be viewed as artisans, farmers or traders, nor in terms of their ritual contributions, but in terms of the undefined, unclear but certainly devaluing quality of Untouchability.[195]

Under the Government of India Act 1935, the term 'Depressed Classes' was replaced by 'Scheduled Castes'. It was difficult to reconcile that while the south had the phenomenon, in the north the situation was different. Many experts felt that in large parts of the country Untouchables did not form a distinct and separate group. The figure below shows how British social engineering gave birth to the modern caste system.

British Social Engineering and the Caste System

No Rigid Caste System Until Late Nineteenth Century
• British Admit no Rigid Caste System Exists
• British Struggle to Classify Indians into Hierarchy
• Resistance from Indians Against Census

Risley Imposes 'Caste = Racial Hierarchy' in the Early Twentieth Century
• Template of Western 'Race Theory' Adopted as Standard
• Risley Forcibly Fits Indian Diversity into Race Template
• Formal Caste System Emerges Through Multiple Censuses

Risley Makes Untouchability Official
• Risley Proposes a Fifth 'Untouchable' Varna
• Gradually Idea Gains Traction
• Risley Replaces Fuzzy Structures with Races

Indian Nationalists Accept British Classification
• All India Depressed Classes Conference 1918
• Gandhi Adopts the Term 'Harijan' in 1931
• Government of India Act 1935 Uses the Term 'Scheduled Castes'

This is how the Scheduled Castes were invented: starting with discussions on terms, then becoming structured formally by the British censuses, and subsequently being adopted by Indian nationalists and reformers. Finally, what was initially a theoretical structure, crystalized into substance at the ground level. This was incorrectly projected backwards to define the characteristic of ancient Vedic society.

Charsley states:

> Caste becomes a legally recognized group to which everyone either belongs unambiguously or does not. For castes with state-allocated benefits and privileges, certificates are to be obtained to prove membership and hence validate claims.[196]
>
> ... a transformation has been achieved of the far less tidy, less uniform and more ambiguous divisions of society in preceding centuries which we saw still represented clearly in the results of Risley's great experiment at the start of the century.[197]
>
> The current debate as to whether Untouchables replicate or reject the caste system which devalues them illustrates the danger here of creating an unreal problem by misreading the nature of the category.[198]
>
> ... the concept sets up a category defined as the bottom of a hierarchically ordered society but in practice traps and equates a variety of castes differently placed economically, socially, culturally and politically.[199]

B.R. Ambedkar and the Dalit Movement

No discussion on caste is complete without examining the thoughts of B.R. Ambedkar. He was a legendary intellectual that turned to politics during the Indian nationalist movement. Ambedkar received a doctorate from Columbia University under the renowned American philosopher, John Dewey. He fought for India's freedom and being from the Mahar jati, championed the cause of all lower castes, which included taking on his Hindu compatriots in the nationalistic struggle.

We examine Ambedkar's major positions on four topics relevant to this book. The following table lists the four major writings of Ambedkar we have studied. Each is discussed in a separate section.

Ambedkar's Major Works	Main Theme
Annihilation of Caste[200]	Severe criticism of caste abuses and Hinduism
Pakistan: The Partition of India[201]	Harsh attack on Islam
The Buddha and His Dhamma[202]	Explanation of his new interpretation of Buddhism
Buddha or Karl Marx?[203]	Argument on why Buddhism is superior to Communism

Ambedkar and Caste

Ambedkar had a complex relationship with Gandhi. The flashpoint was the issue of caste bias. Both agreed that there was deplorable mistreatment and inhuman bias against the lower castes and untouchables, but had fundamental disagreements on how to resolve the problem. Gandhi wanted to maintain caste as an intrinsic part of Hinduism and make amendments to get rid of the abuses. Ambedkar, however, wanted nothing short of total rejection of the caste system. Gandhi referred to Dalits as Harijans and worked hard to re-educate Hindus to accept them with dignity. Ambedkar felt this was a patronizing way to 'accommodate' the Dalits and did not go deep enough toward dismantling the abusive structures.

An important debate between Ambedkar and Gandhi includes Ambedkar's most direct, no-nonsense statement on caste. The background to this statement is interesting in itself. A Hindu reformist group had invited Ambedkar to deliver a speech on the caste system at their annual conference in 1936. Ambedkar sent them an advance copy of his draft for printing and distribution. The organizers were upset by several passages as they were critical of Hinduism and asked for them to be deleted. Ambedkar categorically refused. The organizers abruptly cancelled his talk.[204]

Ambedkar published his speech independently as an essay titled, *Annihilation of Caste*. It is likely (though unproven) that he made the published version even harsher against Hinduism to express his anger at the narrow-mindedness of the Hindu leaders he was confronting. This essay became a watershed event that started a vibrant debate among Indian nationalists.

Gandhi wrote a response to Ambedkar's essay and published it in his magazine, *Harijan*. Ambedkar followed up by writing a rejoinder to Gandhi, critiquing his *Harijan* article point by point.

For our analysis we have reorganized Ambedkar's essay into broad themes. There are several areas where *our positions coincide with his and contradict what the Global Left is claiming today*. For instance, he rejects the Western view that castes are separate races, writing: 'To hold that distinctions of castes are really distinctions of race, and to treat different castes as though they were so many different races, is a gross perversion of facts'.[205] He later reiterates this view in the same essay: 'The Caste system does not demarcate racial division. The Caste system is a social division of people of the same race'.[206] This is a major departure from present-day Dalit scholars who insist that Dalits are a separate race from other Hindus. This is a fundamental flaw in the Afro-Dalit movement that conflates Dalits with Blacks.

Ambedkar says that the untouchables in one region of India are different from those in another region. Therefore, they cannot be clubbed together as a single race. He writes: 'What racial affinity is there between the untouchable of Bengal and the untouchable of Madras?'[207] What he is saying is that while untouchables are a social division within the same race, they are not a homogeneous group.

An important statement comes after he has rejected Hinduism on grounds of caste. Despite this rejection, he feels that the *Upanishads* could be the basis for a new doctrine of Liberty, Equality, and Fraternity. He writes:

> You must give a new doctrinal basis to your Religion—a basis that will be in consonance with Liberty, Equality and Fraternity; in short, with Democracy. I am no authority on the subject. But I am told that for such religious principles as will be in consonance with Liberty, Equality and Fraternity, it may not be necessary for you to borrow from foreign sources, and that you could draw for such principles on the Upanishads.[208]

Though he uses the essay to announce that he is withdrawing from Hinduism, he wants to maintain harmony, rather than ill-will, towards Hindus. He writes: 'Even when I am gone out of your fold, I will watch your movement with active sympathy, and you will have my assistance for what it may be worth. Yours is a national cause'.[209]

However, his core message strongly opposes Hindu texts as well as practices. The overall assessment is captured in the following: 'Turn in any direction you like, and Caste is the monster that crosses your path. You cannot have political reform, you cannot have economic reform, unless you kill this monster'.[210]

Ambedkar's crisp and logical criticism of caste is impressive. He breaks down his argument into the following sharp statements. We summarize his views using mostly his own words along with some paraphrasing:[211]

- Divisiveness among laborers: Caste is not merely a division of labor. 'It is also a division of laborers. ... It is a hierarchy in which the divisions of laborers are graded one above the other'.
- Suboptimal economic use of individual talent: Caste prevents society from optimally using every individual's capacity because it assigns tasks to individuals in advance based on the social status of the parents. Changes in industries demand mobility to embrace new occupations whereas caste artificially freezes a worker. Nor is the division of labor based on free choice, personal sentiment, and preferences. It is based on 'the dogma of predestination'. Consequently, 'Caste does not result in economic efficiency'.
- Fragmentation among Hindus: Caste is not uniting the Hindus but keeping them fragmented. 'The Caste System prevents common activity; and by preventing common activity, it has prevented the Hindus from becoming a society with a unified life and a consciousness of its own being'. One result is that 'Caste prevents Hinduism from being a missionary religion'. Stated differently, there are separate caste-specific grand narratives rather than an overarching Hindu or Indian grand narrative. Ultimately, the loyalty is mainly to one's caste. 'This anti-social spirit, this spirit of protecting its own interests, is as much a marked feature of the different castes in their isolation from one another as it is of nations in their isolation. ... The Hindus, therefore, are not merely an assortment of castes, but are so many warring groups, each living for itself and for its selfish ideal'.

- <u>Indifference towards bigger causes</u>: 'Indifferentism is the result of the Caste System, which has made Sanghatan [community, congregation] and co-operation even for a good cause impossible'. As a result of this, 'Caste deprives Hindus of mutual help, trust, and fellow-feeling'. In fact, the opposite is the case. Rather than helping each other, 'The higher castes have conspired to keep the lower castes down'.
- <u>Blocking reform</u>: Those enjoying caste privileges want to maintain its structures and prevent reform. 'Caste in the hands of the orthodox has been a powerful weapon for persecuting the reformers and for killing all reform'.

Frankly, we find this diagnosis to be true, honest, and audacious. It is a provocation that Hindu reformists in 1935 ought to have heard, debated, and contemplated rather than uninviting Ambedkar. An excellent chance for genuine reform was lost. We cannot rewind time and determine whether India's future might have been different if the Hindu leaders had not become so defensive, and had, instead, collaborated with Ambedkar to explore various changes.

Ambedkar then moves on to discuss what ought to be done about these caste problems. He proposes: 'My ideal would be a society based on *Liberty, Equality and Fraternity*'.[212] This echoes the ideals of the French Revolution of 1789. It is ironic that his followers today have turned the movement into identity politics and Critical Race Theory whereas the French Revolution emphasized *individual* freedom and rights. The relationship has to be between each citizen individually and the state, *with no group identity serving as the intermediary* between citizens and the state. This point has been emphasized by France's president, Emmanuel Macron in his recent fight against Critical Race Theory, as explained in Chapter 1.

Ambedkar asks: What, then, prevents this from happening? Inter-dining to bring all castes together had already become prevalent but he finds this falling short. He wants inter-marriages which will bring about the necessary changes:

> Inter-dining has not succeeded in killing the spirit of Caste and the consciousness of Caste. I am convinced that the real remedy is inter-marriage. Fusion of blood can alone create the feeling of

being kith and kin, and unless this feeling of kinship, of being
kindred, becomes paramount, the separatist feeling—the feeling
of being aliens—created by Caste will not vanish.[213]

He now turns to Hinduism as the factor that is blocking the necessary
reforms. His verdict against Hinduism is devastating:

> Internal reform of the Caste System is virtually impossible. ...
> Caste has a divine basis. You must therefore destroy the sacredness
> and divinity with which Caste has become invested. In the last
> analysis, this means you must destroy the authority of the Shastras
> and the Vedas.[214]

In elaborating his attack on Hinduism, he explains his understanding of
what Hinduism is. Let us quote him first, followed by our response. We
will discuss whether he truly understands Hinduism broadly enough.

> What is this Hindu Religion? Is it a set of principles, or is it a code
> of rules? Now the Hindu Religion, as contained in the Vedas and
> the Smritis, is nothing but a mass of sacrificial, social, political,
> and sanitary rules and regulations, all mixed up. What is called
> Religion by the Hindus is nothing but a multitude of commands
> and prohibitions. Religion, in the sense of spiritual principles,
> truly universal, applicable to all races, to all countries, to all
> times, is not to be found in them; and if it is, it does not form
> the governing part of a Hindu's life. That for a Hindu, Dharma
> means commands and prohibitions.[215]

This is a reductionist view of Hinduism. Ambedkar sees it as nothing
more than a set of dogmatic rules, totally devoid of all spirituality. In this
pronouncement, he does not seem to consider the various dimensions,
such as:

- Profound philosophies contained in the *Upanishads.*
- Body-mind practices of yoga and meditation that have no
  restrictions based on caste whatsoever. There are numerous
  shastras on this subject.
- The entire Tantra system that is free from any form of birth-
  based privilege and is entirely in the control of each practitioner.
- The Bhakti movement that was an example of very successful

uprisings from within Hinduism to open doors for all segments of society. There have been many such mobilizations that transgressed the 'rules' which justifiably troubled Ambedkar.

Given this narrow understanding of Hinduism, he proceeds to declare the following:

> I have, therefore, no hesitation in saying that such a religion must be destroyed, and I say there is nothing irreligious in working for the destruction of such a religion. ... It is your bound duty to tear off the mask, to remove the misrepresentation that is caused by misnaming this Law as Religion. ... what they are told is Religion is not Religion, but that it is really Law, you will be in a position to urge its amendment or abolition.[216]

We wonder if Ambedkar would apply the same logic to the Greek classics. After all, Aristotle was a staunch defender of slavery. Both Plato and he also advocated infanticide. If Ambedkar applied the same criteria, the Greek classics would have to be banned along with almost all major European Enlightenment thinkers from Hegel onwards. Should we desist from learning from the Enlightenment thinkers? Furthermore, the American founding fathers too were guilty of theories and practices that are today condemned as violations of human rights and even criminalized.

We could take the conversation further back to the Bible in which there is no paucity of atrocities ranging from slavery to rape. Ambedkar's call to get rid of a vast tradition because it also contains objectionable material ought to require him to make a similar demand for dismantling Judeo-Christianity in total.

More recently, Einstein's diaries have shown that he made racial slurs against the Chinese. Would physicists want to reject all his theories based on that premise?

We agree that Hindu texts ought to be examined for modern times and selectively adopted. Where applicable there ought to be a fresh interpretation, even a rewrite to avoid misunderstandings. This approach is advocated by the *smritis* themselves. For instance, *Manusmriti* 4.176, advocates flexibility in its own implementation. It boldly states: One should give up any particular aspect of dharma if it is denounced by the public. The fact that many smritis were written over centuries and often presented opposing views, is testimony to the flexibility of dharma to adapt and not be a closed book like the Abrahamic books. Many mainstream Hindu organizations, the Arya Samaj being a prominent example, have modified and reinterpreted the *Manusmriti* to suit modern times.

Ambedkar makes his concrete suggestions to Hindus on how they ought to reform Hinduism. He lists the 'cardinal items' essential to this 'reform'. The first is a rather extreme form of the old Abrahamic tradition of burning books and outlawing their usage. This is contrary to Ambedkar's espoused liberal thinking and totally out of line with Buddhism that he embraced. He says:

> There should be one and only one standard book of Hindu Religion, acceptable to all Hindus and recognized by all Hindus. This of course means that all other books of Hindu religion such as Vedas, Shastras, and Puranas, which are treated as sacred and authoritative, must by law cease to be so, and the preaching of any doctrine, religious or social, contained in these books should be penalized.[217]

This is a bad suggestion. In fact, no Buddhist would appreciate a similar intervention by Ambedkar to ban all Buddhist books except one.

His second item for Hindu reform is to abolish priesthood, or else to remove the hereditary criteria for becoming a priest. The fact is that there is a range of temple traditions on the selection of priests, including those that *only select a lower caste priest by birth*. But then Ambedkar goes too far and wants the state to control priesthood the same way they certify civil servants. He says, 'It should be provided by law that no Hindu shall be entitled to be a priest unless he has passed an examination prescribed by the State.' In fact, he wants to make it a penal offense for anyone officiating as a priest without a government license. Every priest 'should be the servant of the State'. The state should limit the number of priests so that it is not a free-for-all system.

As noted earlier, Gandhi responded to this scathing article by Ambedkar, defending the caste system and wanting to reform it only to a limited extent. He wanted the basic structures to remain but without any prejudices towards the Harijans. This did not satisfy Ambedkar, who retorted:

I appreciate greatly the honor done me by the Mahatma in taking notice in his Harijan of the speech on Caste. ... My object in publishing the speech was to provoke the Hindus to think, and to take stock of their position.

He believed caste had ruined the Hindus and the varna system was 'like a leaky pot' that has an inherent tendency to degenerate into an abusive caste system. The principles of Liberty, Equality, and Fraternity were an absolute necessity. This required that 'the sense of religious sanctity behind Caste and Varna must be destroyed'. Therefore, the 'divine authority of the Shastras' must be discarded. No compromise was acceptable.

Ambedkar and Islamophobia

Islam was another major area of disagreement between Ambedkar and Gandhi. Gandhi appeased the Muslims, even supporting their global agenda outside India. Ambedkar, on the other hand, considered both Islam and Christianity dangerous options for Indians to adopt because he feared it would tear apart the fabric of Indian society.

Ambedkar's rejection of Hinduism is well-known, but it is falsely assumed that he was positive towards Islam, or at least neutral. This false assumption is made today to support the Global Left's strategic alliance with Islam. The Dalit movement is now aligned with Blacks in America and Muslims worldwide and has become grounded in new forms of Marxism we discussed as Critical Theories of various kinds.

Given the attempts worldwide to block criticisms of Islam, it is important to examine what would today be considered Ambedkar's Islamophobia. He writes that though Hindu society's social problems are widely discussed, he finds it utterly hypocritical that the same kind of open criticism is not given to Islam. To remedy this situation, he devotes much space in his tome of nearly five hundred pages, *Pakistan: The Partition of India*, to criticize Islam point by point.

His rigor, candidness, and audacity are remarkable, and it is surprising that despite his explicit and harsh condemnation of Islam, this work by him has received little attention.[218] We will quote him extensively because his views on the matter are being covered up.

He starts his scathing analysis by saying: 'One may well ask if there is any social evil which is found among the Hindus and is not found among the Muslims'. He then says, 'Take child-marriage', and using a table of statistics he makes the case that Islam suffers from this scourge worse than Hinduism.[219]

His next topic is the position of women. He says, 'The Muslim woman is the most helpless person in the world'. Here he cites a Muslim leader to elaborate: 'Islam has set its seal of inferiority upon her and given the sanction of religion to social customs which have deprived her of the full opportunity for self-expression and development of personality'. His lengthy analysis concludes with the verdict: 'No words can adequately express the great and many evils of polygamy and concubinage, and especially as a source of misery to a Muslim woman'.[220]

Then he takes up slavery in Islam and writes:

> Islam speaks of brotherhood. Everybody infers that Islam must be free from slavery and caste. Regarding slavery nothing needs to be said. It stands abolished now by law. But while it existed, much of its support was derived from Islam and Islamic countries. While the prescriptions by the Prophet regarding the just and humane treatment of slaves contained in the Koran are praiseworthy, there is nothing whatever in Islam that lends support to the abolition of this curse.[221]

Clearly, the prophet tolerated slavery and merely wanted that slaves not be ill-treated.

He then points out that Islam continues to have an appalling caste system. To explain this, he cites census data and other sources. Islam has designated most of its people as low castes and even untouchables:

> The Mahomedans themselves recognize two main social divisions, (1) Ashraf or Sharaf and (2) Ajlaf. Ashraf means 'noble' and includes all undoubted descendants of foreigners and converts from high caste Hindus. All other Mahomedans including the occupational groups and all converts of lower ranks, are known by the contemptuous terms, 'Ajlaf,' 'wretches' or 'mean people': they are also called Kamina or Itar, 'base' or Rasil, a corruption of Rizal, 'worthless.' In some places a third class, called Arzal or 'lowest of all,' is added. With them no other Mahomedan would

associate, and they are forbidden to enter the mosque to use the public burial ground.[222]

He then elaborates each of the Ashraf, Ajlaf, and Arzal castes by listing the names of the sub-castes within them. For instance, the Saids, Sheikhs, Pathans, and Moghuls are in the top caste. Most Muslims belong to the lower castes. Finally, he names the communities condemned as the untouchables in Islam.

He is especially troubled by the purdah system: 'Indeed, the Muslims have all the social evils of the Hindus and something more. That something more is the compulsory system of *purdah* for Muslim women'. He writes:

> As a consequence of the purdah system, a segregation of the Muslim women is brought about. The ladies are not expected to visit the outer rooms, verandahs, or gardens; their quarters are in the back-yard. ... young and old, are confined in the same room. No male servant can work in their presence. A woman is allowed to see only her sons, brothers, father, uncles, and husband, or any other near relation who may be admitted to a position of trust. She cannot go even to the mosque to pray and must wear burka (veil) whenever she has to go out. These burka women walking in the streets is one of the most hideous sights one can witness in India. Such seclusion cannot but have its deteriorating effects upon the physical constitution of Muslim women. They are usually victims to anaemia, tuberculosis, and pyorrhoea. Their bodies are deformed, with their backs bent, bones protruded, hands and feet crooked. Ribs, joints and nearly all their bones ache. Heart palpitation is very often present in them. The result of this pelvic deformity is untimely death at the time of delivery.
>
> Purdah deprives Muslim women of mental and moral nourishment. Being deprived of healthy social life, the process of moral degeneration must and does set in. Being completely secluded from the outer world, they engage their minds in petty family quarrels, ... they become narrow and restricted in their outlook. They lag behind their sisters from other communities, cannot take part in any outdoor activity and are weighed down by a slavish mentality and an inferiority complex. They have no

desire for knowledge, because they are taught not to be interested in anything outside the four walls of the house. Purdah women in particular become helpless, timid, and unfit for any fight in life.[223]

Ambedkar says the immorality of Muslim men is caused by purdah, because these men lack normal social contact with women. Isolation leads to unhealthy tendencies and sexual excesses according to him:

> The physical and intellectual effects of *purdah* are nothing as compared with its effects on morals. The origin of *purdah* lies of course in the deep-rooted suspicion of sexual appetites in both sexes and the purpose is to check them by segregating the sexes. ... *purdah* has adversely affected the morals of Muslim men. ... a Muslim has no contact with any woman outside those who belong to his own household. Even with them his contact extends only to occasional conversation. For a male there is no company of, and no commingling with, the females, except those who are children or aged. This isolation ... is sure to produce bad effects on the morals of men. It requires no psychoanalyst to say that a social system which cuts off all contact between the two sexes produces an unhealthy tendency towards sexual excesses and unnatural and other morbid habits and ways.[224]

The isolation also leads to segregation between Muslims and others, he claims. Furthermore, it causes Muslims to be unconcerned about the broader politics and social well-being of the nation: 'The evil consequences of purdah are not confined to the Muslim community only. It is responsible for the social segregation of Hindus from Muslims which is the bane of public life in India'.

Ambedkar next accuses Muslims of lacking political sensibilities beyond petty and selfish matters:

> The Muslims have no interest in politics as such. Their predominant interest is religion. This can be easily seen by the terms and conditions that a Muslim constituency makes for its support to a candidate ... does not care to examine the programme of the candidate. ... he should agree to replace the old lamps of the masjid by supplying new ones at his cost, to provide a new carpet for the masjid because the old one is torn, or to repair the masjid

because it has become dilapidated. ... a Muslim constituency is quite satisfied if the candidate agrees to give a sumptuous feast, and in other[s] if he agrees to buy votes for so much apiece. With the Muslims, election is a mere matter of money, and is very seldom a matter of [a] social programme ... . Muslim politics takes no note of purely secular categories of life, namely, the differences between rich and poor, capital and labour, landlord and tenant, priest and layman, reason and superstition. (it) is essentially clerical and recognizes only one difference, namely, that existing between Hindus and Muslims. None of the secular categories of life have any place in the politics of the Muslim community; and if they do find a place—and they must, because they are irrepressible—they are subordinated to one and the only governing principle of the Muslim political universe, namely, religion.[225]

What troubles him the most, he says, is the utter lack of any social movement to shake up the Muslims and improve their own lot:

But far more distressing is ... there is no organized movement of social reform among the Musalmans of India on a scale sufficient to bring about their eradication. The Hindus have their social evils. But there is this relieving feature about them—namely, that some of them are conscious of their existence, and a few ... are actively agitating for their removal. The Muslims ... do not realize that they are evils, and consequently do not agitate for their removal. ... they oppose any change in their existing practices. ... Muslims opposed the Child-Marriage Bill brought in the Central Assembly in 1930, whereby the age for marriage of a girl was raised to 14 and of a boy to 18, on the ground that it was opposed to the Muslim canon law.[226]

Digging deeper, Ambedkar explains the core of Muslim Canon Law according to which the world is divided into countries ruled by Muslims and those ruled by non-Muslims, i.e., infidels. There is no room for true democracy in such a system:

According to Muslim Canon Law, the world is divided into two camps, Dar-ul-lslam (abode of Islam), and Dar-ul-Harb (abode of war). A country is Dar-ul-Islam when it is ruled by Muslims. A country is Dar-ul-Harb when Muslims only reside in it but are not rulers of it. That being the Canon Law of the Muslims, India cannot be the common motherland of the Hindus and the Musalmans. It can be the land of the Musalmans—but it cannot be the land of the 'Hindus and the Musalmans living as equals.' Further, it can be the land of the Musalmans only when it is governed by the Muslims. The moment the land becomes subject to the authority of a non-Muslim power, it ceases to be the land of the Muslims. Instead of being Dar-ul-Islam, it becomes Dar-ul-Harb.[227]

When Muslim ruled countries cannot defeat non-Muslim countries, he says they resort to 'the extremist concept of Islamic Jihad'. He summarizes this as follows:

There is another injunction of Muslim Canon Law called Jihad (crusade) ... it becomes "incumbent on a Muslim ruler to extend the rule of Islam until the whole world shall have been brought under its sway. ... Technically, it is the duty of the Muslim ruler, who is capable of doing so, to transform Dar-ul-Harb into Dar-ul-Islam." And just as there are instances of the Muslims in India resorting to Hijrat, there are instances showing that they have not hesitated to proclaim Jihad.[228]

On the issue of a Muslim's loyalty to his country vis-a-vis his loyalty to Islam, Ambedkar exposes the potential duplicity:

... one that calls for notice is the tenet of Islam which says that in a country which is not under Muslim rule, wherever there is a conflict between Muslim law and the law of the land, the former must prevail over the latter, and a Muslim will be justified in obeying the Muslim law and defying the law of the land...The only allegiance a Musalman, whether civilian or soldier, whether living under a Muslim or under a non-Muslim administration, is commanded by the Koran to acknowledge is his allegiance to God, to His Prophet and to those in authority from among the Musalmans...[229]

Because Hindus are non-believers of Islam, they are designated as kafirs. This makes them unworthy of respect by Muslims. As a result, no government with Hindus at the top can be acceptable to Muslims, be it democratic or not:

> To the Muslims, a Hindu is a Kaffir. A Kaffir is not worthy of respect. He is low-born and without status. That is why a country that is ruled by a Kaffir is Dar-ul-Harb to a Musalman. ... no further evidence seems to be necessary to prove that the Muslims will not obey a Hindu government. The basic feelings of deference and sympathy, which predispose persons to obey the authority of government, do not simply exist. But if a proof is wanted, there is no dearth of it. It is so abundant that the problem is what to tender and what to omit...In the midst of the Khilafat agitation, when the Hindus were doing so much to help the Musalmans, the Muslims did not forget that as compared with them the Hindus were a low and an inferior race.[230]

Contrary to popular opinion in the mainstream, Ambedkar is convinced that Islam is highly divisive and tribalistic:

> Hinduism is said to divide people and in contrast, Islam is said to bind people together. This is only a half-truth. For Islam divides as inexorably as it binds. Islam is a close corporation and the distinction that it makes between Muslims and non-Muslims is a very real, very positive and very alienating distinction. The brotherhood of Islam is not the universal brotherhood of man. It is a brotherhood of Muslims for Muslims only. There is a fraternity, but its benefit is confined to those within that corporation. For those who are outside ... there is nothing but contempt and enmity.[231]

After many pages of this kind of analysis of the horrors of Islam, Ambedkar wonders, 'why are the Muslims opposed to social reform?' To answer this, he first goes through the reasons cited for Muslims worldwide being retrograde. He notes that Muslims have been globally declared 'an unprogressive people'. Islam has immobilized them 'in their native barbarism ... it is fixed in a crystallization, inert and impenetrable. It is unchangeable; and political, social or economic changes have no repercussion upon it'. He quotes the French orientalist, Joseph Renan on the Muslim hatred for science:

> What is ... essentially distinctive of the Musalman is his hatred of
> science, his persuasion that research is useless, frivolous, almost
> impious—the natural sciences, because they are attempts at
> rivalry with God. [232]

Ambedkar delves deeper into the situation specifically in India and
concludes that Muslims define themselves as Hindus' opponents. They
must constantly compete against Hindus: 'Their energies are directed to
maintaining a constant struggle against the Hindus for seats and posts, in
which there is no time, no thought and no room for questions relating
to social reform'. He says the Muslims do not want to collaborate with
Hindus for social justice even when there is common cause.[233]

For instance, he feels that poor Muslims do not align with poor
Hindus to fight the rich of all religions, because they do not want to fight
a rich Muslim landlord. Brotherhood among Muslims takes priority over
any, and all, kinds of social justice. This is evident in the way Muslims
agitate against states ruled by Hindus but not against states ruled by
Muslims even when it is the exact same issue. He writes:

> The dominating consideration with the Muslims is not democracy.
> ... (it) is how democracy with majority rule will affect the Muslims
> in their struggle against the Hindus. Will it strengthen them, or
> will it weaken them? If democracy weakens them, they will not
> have democracy. They will prefer the rotten state to continue in
> the Muslim States, rather than weaken the Muslim ruler in his
> hold upon his Hindu subjects. The political and social stagnation
> in the Muslim community can be explained by one and only one
> reason. The Muslims think that the Hindus and Muslims must
> perpetually struggle.[234]

Ambedkar does not even spare Gandhi, who he considers a hypocrite
for protecting Muslims and for overriding his espoused principles: 'He
[Gandhi] has never called the Muslims to account even when they have
been guilty of gross crimes against Hindus'.[235] Ambedkar goes on to
condemn Muslims' killings of Hindus in India and is troubled that Gandhi
fails to criticize such behavior:

> Mr. Gandhi has been very punctilious in the matter of condemning
> any and every act of violence and has forced the Congress, much

against its will to condemn it. But Mr Gandhi has never protested against such murders [of Hindus]. Not only have the Musalmans not condemned these outrages, but even Mr Gandhi has never called upon the leading Muslims to condemn them. He has kept silent over them.[236]

Ambedkar writes about the infamous riots by Muslims against Hindus:

The blood-curdling atrocities committed by the Moplas in Malabar against the Hindus were indescribable. All over Southern India, a wave of horrified feeling had spread among the Hindus of every shade of opinion, which was intensified when certain Khilafat leaders were so misguided as to pass resolutions of 'congratulations to the Moplas on the brave fight they were conducting for the sake of religion'.[237]

Despite all this horror, Gandhi praised them as the 'brave God-fearing Moplas who were fighting for what they consider as religion and in a manner which they consider as religious'.

Any objective reading of Ambedkar's extensive writings on Islam would find him to be Islamophobic by the criteria being applied worldwide today.

Ambedkar and Buddhism

Ambedkar wrote *The Buddha and His Dhamma,* a major tome that gives a lucid explanation of his interpretation of Buddhism. In the Introduction, he lays out what he rejects in the standard interpretations. The most relevant aspect he rejects is the very essence of Buddha's teachings: the Four Noble Truths, or the Four Arya Truths. Ambedkar writes:

The four Aryan Truths are a great stumbling block in the way of non-Buddhists accepting the gospel of Buddhism. For the four Aryan Truths deny hope to man. ... make the gospel of the Buddha a gospel of pessimism. Do they form part of the original gospel or are they a later accretion by the monks?[238]

His rejection of the concept of rebirth is ridden with contradictions. On the one hand, he says outright that there is no such thing as rebirth in

Buddhism, while on the other, he says that the Buddha was a Bodhisatta (Bodhisattva in Sanskrit), a concept based on rebirth that he explains as follows:

> Before enlightenment Gautama was only a Bodhisatta. It is after reaching enlightenment that he became a Buddha. Who and what is a Bodhisatta? A Bodhisatta is a person who is seeking to be a Buddha. How does a Bodhisatta become a Buddha? A Bodhisatta must be a Bodhisatta for ten lives in succession. ... In his tenth life he becomes Dharmamegha. The Bodhisatta attains the infinite divine eye of a Buddha.[239]

He describes specifically what the Bodhisatta achieved in each of the prior nine lives before becoming the Buddha in the tenth.

The reason for this contradiction is clear: Since Ambedkar wanted to distance himself from the concept of reincarnation in Hinduism, he wanted it absent from Buddhism, a religion he had adopted. The flaw is that Buddha himself says he recalls many previous lives. The entire tradition of the Dalai Lama and the Bodhisatta is based on rebirth.

Ambedkar's understanding of both Hinduism and Buddhism is erroneous:

- Hinduism has the notion of the ultimate Self (*atman*), and that Self is never born and never dies. Hence, that is not what reincarnates. The entity that reincarnates is something lesser, called the *jiva-atman*, which is the bodily form manifested by the Self, and is not the same as the Self.
- In Buddhism there is a stream of consciousness comprising momentary states with no permanent self or substratum. The experience of Self is an illusion. There is no 'entity' as such that reincarnates, but there is reincarnation as a process. Karma produces imprints on consciousness called *sanskara* or *vasana*. The energy of the sanskara is like a seed that produces an effect called *phala*. Upon the body's death, the sanskaras that remain unfulfilled set up the rebirth of a new body. But there is no Self that undergoes reincarnation.
- In one system (Hinduism) the ultimate Self exists but is not what takes birth or dies. In the other system (Buddhism) there is no

ultimate Self. Hence, neither system believes that any ultimate Self reincarnates.

Similarly, Ambedkar is also mistaken in his understanding of karma in Hinduism. He says that the Hindu idea of karma is based on the 'soul', but soul is an Abrahamic concept and hence it causes confusion. Though Buddhism does not have an entity that accrues karma, it says that the sanskaras or vasanas are karmic imprints that influence the process by which effects are produced. So, it doesn't discard karma.

Another serious conflict between Ambedkar and standard Buddhism is his attitude towards meditation. Buddha's Eightfold Path is his prescribed method for all Buddhists to follow. The seventh and eighth steps in this path are mindfulness and *dhyana* systems of meditation. The seminal Buddhist texts, *Satipaṭṭhāna Sutta* and *Visuddhimagga,* emphasize several systematic meditation techniques that Buddha practiced for his own awakening. Buddha's entire teaching is that these are universal paths available to everyone, and that he is teaching *only what he has experienced and nothing else.*

But Ambedkar bypasses, or under-emphasizes, meditation in his interpretation of Buddhism. For him, meditation is merely the pursuit of education and mental cultivation. To any serious Buddhist, meditation is entirely different from mental activity, and the entire basis of Buddhism is lost if meditation is trivialized.

Having done away with these core tenets of Buddhism, he invents a new version. At a press conference he called in October 1956, Ambedkar formally rejected Theravada and Mahayana Buddhism along with Hinduism. He launched his own Navayana Buddhism, just about six weeks before his death. The formal oath ceremony for his followers to join this new movement comprised twenty-two vows. Though one of them gives lip service to Buddha's Eightfold Path, there is no mention of meditation whatsoever.[240]

In essence, Ambedkar has secularized Buddhism and uprooted its spiritual dimension:

- He rejects the traditional idea of *nirvana* or enlightenment as something too otherworldly and escapist.
- He considers it irresponsible to spend too much time on meditation practice because it takes one away from social relationships.

- He does not believe nirvana to be a spiritual attainment but a social construct referring to a society founded on harmony and justice. Ambedkar's goal was to change Buddhism to a system of social justice. He wanted his version of Buddhism to nurture democracy with justice for untouchables and others.

It's important to note, however, that Ambedkar didn't consider spirituality to be worthless. He was merely attempting to remove untouchability that he felt was rooted in Hindu metaphysics. His problem arose because Buddhism shared much of the same metaphysics as Hinduism, making it impossible for him to adopt it without changes.

His followers have attempted to equate his movement with the kind of Buddhism that was brought to the West by the late Vietnamese monk, Thich Nhat Hanh. Westerners call this 'engaged Buddhism' because it uses meditation and other practices to raise human consciousness towards problems that confront society and the environment. It then applies Buddhist ethics and insights gained from practicing meditation to help alleviate suffering and injustices through social and political activity. Great emphasis is placed on non-violence, non-attachment with materialism, protection of animals and nature, and peace-making. But this is a difficult comparison because Ambedkar's version does not include meditation, which is where Thich Nhat Hanh's Buddhism begins. As a result, Ambedkar's Buddhism is strictly political.

Despite espousing what amounts to a secular form of Buddhism, Ambedkar claimed to oppose secularism; he wanted to operate within religion as his framework. He said: 'Those who deny the importance of religion fail to realize how great is the potency and sanction that lies behind a religious ideal as compared with that of a purely secular ideal.'[241] In an All India Radio broadcast in 1954, he said that secular mandates could be broken while religion has to be respected by everyone.[242] In other words, although his movement stripped Buddhism of key spiritual elements and turned it into a purely social justice movement, Ambedkar wanted to call it a religion to give it the sanctity that religion, and particularly Buddhism, had.

Regarding Christianity and Islam, he said:

What the consequences of conversion will be to the country as a whole is well worth bearing in mind. Conversion to Islam or

Christianity will de-nationalize the Depressed Classes. If they go to Islam, the number of Muslims will be doubled...and the danger of Muslim domination also becomes real. If they go to Christianity ...it will strengthen the hold of Britain on the country.[243]

He described his choice of Buddhism as the least harmful route for India since he considered Buddhism part and parcel of Indian culture. His motive was simple. Ambedkar was a staunch Indian nationalist and consistent in his priority to advocate a religion that would be good for Indian culture. His thinking is represented in the table below:

	Hinduism	Christianity	Islam	Buddhism
Good for India's unity	Yes	No	No	Yes
Good for overcoming caste abuse	No	N/A	No	Yes

Ambedkar and Communism

An important study done by Ambedkar was his comparison of Buddha and Karl Marx. This was later published as a small book, *Buddha or Karl Marx?*[244] He starts by saying that both systems oppose private ownership of property as that causes misery and suffering. The difference between them is in the methods to be used.

He then analyzes their methods and shows why Buddhism is superior to Marxism. The key difference is that Buddha wanted to first bring an inner transformation in a person's moral disposition and follow his path voluntarily, whereas Communism uses violence and imposes dictatorship. He writes:

... the means adopted by the Buddha were to convert a man by changing his moral disposition to follow the path voluntarily. The means adopted by the Communists are equally clear, short and swift. They are (1) Violence and (2) Dictatorship of the Proletariat. The Communists say that there are only two means of establishing communism. The first is violence. Nothing short of it will suffice to break up the existing system. The other is dictatorship of the proletariat. Nothing short of it will suffice to continue the new system. It is now clear what are the similarities and differences between Buddha and Karl Marx. The differences are about the means. The end is common to both.[245]

Ambedkar says that in trying to achieve their valuable goals, communists destroyed other valuable things. 'Could they not have taken property without taking the life of the owner?' he asks. In the long run therefore, he considered Buddha's voluntary approach superior to Communism's use of force.

The important difference, he says, is between external force being applied (in Communism) versus the individual being transformed from within (in Buddhism): 'One has to choose between Government by force and Government by moral disposition'.[246] He details a sermon by Buddha to show the difference between a rule by righteousness and a rule by force. Giving the example of the Russian Communist revolution, he says that the changes they achieved cannot be sustained except by force. When the force is withdrawn, there will be anarchy.

> This is probably the finest picture of what happens when moral force fails, and brutal force takes its place. What the Buddha wanted was that each man should be morally so trained that he may himself become a sentinel for the kingdom of righteousness.[247]

He says that only religion can sustain the change after force is withdrawn. He offers the Russians a lesson: 'The Russians do not seem to be paying any attention to Buddhism as an ultimate aid to sustain Communism when force is withdrawn'.[248]

Dictatorship is problematic for him because it requires ongoing force to sustain it. Buddha opposed this: 'As to Dictatorship the Buddha would have none of it. He was born a democrat and he died a democrat'.[249] The benefit of democracy is clear: 'In Parliamentary Government you have a duty and a right; the duty to obey the law and right to criticize it. In Dictatorship you have only duty to obey but no right to criticize it'.[250]

Dictatorship could be good only short-term just to bring about a safe democracy. 'Why should not Dictatorship liquidate itself after it has done its work, after it has removed all the obstacles and boulders in the way of democracy and has made the path of Democracy safe?'[251] He considered permanent dictatorship unjustified because it destroys spiritual values: 'Humanity does not only want economic values, it also wants spiritual values to be retained. Permanent Dictatorship has paid no attention to spiritual values and does not seem to intend to'.[252]

Ambedkar is proud that thousands of years before the Russians brought Communism, Buddha had already implemented it on a small scale in his sangha, and without resorting to force or dictatorship:

> The Russians are proud of their Communism. But they forget that the wonder of all wonders is that the Buddha established Communism so far as the Sangh was concerned without dictatorship. ... it was a communism on a very small scale, but it was ... without dictatorship, a miracle which Lenin failed to do. The Buddha's method was different. His method was to change the mind of man: to alter his disposition: so that whatever man does, he does it voluntarily without the use of force or compulsion. His main means ... was his Dhamma and the constant preaching of his Dhamma. The Buddhas (sic) way was not to force people to do what they did not like to do although it was good for them. His way was to alter the disposition of men so that they would do voluntarily what they would not otherwise to do.[253]

His ideal society would be one that achieves the aspirations of the French Revolution but with individuals acting voluntarily:

> Society has been aiming to lay a new foundation that was summarized by the French Revolution in three words: Fraternity, Liberty and Equality. The French Revolution was welcomed because of this slogan. It failed to produce equality. We welcome the Russian Revolution because it aims to produce equality. But in producing equality, society cannot afford to sacrifice fraternity or liberty. Equality will be of no value without fraternity or liberty. It seems that the three can coexist only if one follows the way of the Buddha.[254]

In a nutshell, the best way to achieve the goals of both Communism and the French Revolution is through the path of Buddha. Neither managed to achieve their stated goals, but Buddha had achieved them long ago.

The problem with his argument, as we discussed earlier, is that Ambedkar has already rejected the core tenets of Buddhism which include meditation. Buddhism requires one to first undergo a profound inner transformation and only *then* play an external role to help society. But Ambedkar does not accept the Four Noble Truths of Buddhism or its recommended meditation practices.

In essence, Ambedkar is sandwiched between Buddha and Marx, unable to follow either system fully. At one end, he has serious tensions with Buddhism as taught by Buddha. These disagreements are both with the foundational metaphysics of Buddhism (like reincarnation and karma) as well as with its meditation systems. At the other end, he wants to use Buddhism and its spiritual transformation to argue against Marxism.

So, he invokes Buddhism *as redefined by him* to make his argument against Marxism. The problem with this is that he offers Buddhism's solution without agreeing to its core tenets or practices.

This is a serious flaw: On what basis does he claim that such a method would work? Isn't it a fact that Ambedkar's primary teachers of Buddhism were books and not a living guru as required by the tradition? He was not a Buddhist in the conventional sense with a teacher initiating him into meditation and other practices. Has Ambedkar achieved spiritual transformation bypassing Buddha's prescribed path of meditation?

If Ambedkar's newly formulated Buddhism is to be taken seriously, and not seen as mere speculation, he would have to base it on actual experience. In *The Buddha and His Dhamma*, he correctly points out that everything Buddhism teaches is based on what has been empirically tested in practice. Buddha only taught what he knew first hand through personal inner experience. The same criteria must be applied to Ambedkar's new system. He can teach only what he has attained within himself. But Ambedkar never made any claims of having used his new methods to attain spiritual transformation.

In his system, the spiritual tools of Buddhism were rejected while the social justice goals were never demonstrated in practice, not even in a small pilot group. And yet, he rejects Buddha's method, substituting it with his own. It is unfortunate that he did not live longer, as that would have given him the opportunity to establish his ideas based on empirical results as did Buddha.

Despite all the achievements at the material level, humankind continues to be driven by the ego, and largely by the tribal ego of selfishness, greed, lust, attachments to bodily cravings, and so forth. In other words, precisely those mental afflictions that Buddha asked his followers to rid themselves of. The central thesis of Buddhism is that the problems we face cannot be solved at this level of mind. What is needed is a spiritual evolution beyond the ego.

Ironically, many of those doing lip service to Ambedkar have little commitment to practice Buddha's method and evolve their consciousness, and *then* become better positioned to help society. Instead, they bypass this serious inner work and crave political, social, or other kinds of power, all behind the lofty claim of being Buddhists. The figure below summarizes Ambedkar's philosophy as discussed.

Communism
- Communism Uses Violence and Imposes Dictatorship
- Buddha Implemented Communism in his Sangha Without Force
- Dictatorship Destroys Spiritual Values

Hinduism
- Opposes Hinduism on the Basis of Caste
- Says *Upanishads* could be Basis for Equality, Liberty, and Fraternity
- Declares no Internal Reform of Caste System Possible

Ambedkar's Philosophy

Buddhism
- Rejects the Four Noble Truths
- Rejects Rebirth in Buddhism
- Sidelines Meditation
- Launches Navayana Buddhism

Islam
- Most Dangerous Option for Indians
- Appalling Caste System and Untouchability
- No Room for Democracy
- Position of Women is Deplorable

The Pros and Cons of Jati/Caste[255]

In this final section, we give an overall assessment of the jati/caste system. The British economist, Angus Maddison, said that India was the richest country in the world until almost 1800, by which time the British were aggressively dismantling India's economic engine. Such a prolonged period of great prosperity does not fit with the assumption that caste, since ancient times, had made India economically regressive. Let us take a balanced view of the key advantages and disadvantages of this system.

Checks and Balances Against Totalitarianism

The jati structure was a system of decentralized self-governance in which numerous semi-autonomous social groupings provided services to their respective members. This is the reason for India's diversity of languages, customs, spiritual practices, popular arts, and culture – greater than any other country in the world.

As long as the jatis functioned based on their own local traditions, this structure was able to maintain a massive and diverse society without the need for centralized control. It avoided concentration of power in any varna or social capital. This was dismantled by the British because their interests were different and required top-down colonial control.

In the case of Brahmins, the *Dharmashastras* define a clear separation of ritual status from material power. Brahmins are to exercise ritual authority, and this was considered a responsibility they must carry. Their obligation to society is to pursue knowledge and preserve the Vedic tradition. It is not a 'privilege' as such because Brahmins are not allowed to seek either political authority or accumulate wealth. A Brahmin is not to solicit gifts or compensation and may only receive the material goods he needs for his livelihood. Accumulation beyond his maintenance leads to degradation as per the *Dharmashastras*.[256]

In the case of Kshatriyas, their duty (particularly of kings) is to maintain law and order, protect dharma and defend the public. They are not given any absolutist or dictatorial power. Their duty is to consult their ministers, listen to people, and address their grievances. The ministry comprised representatives of all sections of society including Shudras.

The *Dharmashastras* also provide for the removal of a king by his ministers with the support of the public in case he fails to uphold dharma or protect people and their property. Though in practice one cannot claim there was perfect governance, the point is that there was vibrant discussion, and political thought advanced from one time period to another.

During the British rule, many decentralized functions became consolidated under civil servants trained and appointed by the British. These British appointees served two primary purposes: In the upward direction, they collected taxes (at extortionist levels) that drained the Indian economy from being one of the world's wealthiest to one of the poorest. In the downward direction, the colonial civil system served the purpose of maintaining control through police, courts, and army – all of which reported to the British in an elaborate system of governance.

The British controlled the economy by enacting laws on who could engage in a particular economic activity. They controlled the education system; native education based on Sanskrit and other Indian languages got dismantled and replaced by English with the pedagogy and reading material determined by people sitting in London. They controlled religious life through a variety of laws such as the colonial control of Hindu temples and their daily administration (which has still not been dismantled). Civil servants controlled the physical environment, and this included massive deforestation projects to supply Britain's Industrial Revolution.

Division of Labor and Transmission of Expertise

We have seen how the initial social mobility and fluidity of varnas and jatis was lost. There was no public education as we have today, and from an early age children imbibed skills and knowledge from their parents. Gradually, nepotism set in and merit-based varna turned into a birth-based jati system. Occupations became associated with families and there was reduced mobility.

Epigraphic records show that many professional jatis were wealthy and well-organized, and strong professional associations known as *gana* emerged. Shudras could advance socially even to become kings; except they were not allowed to perform the rituals reserved for Brahmins.[257]

While Vaishyas and Shudras had professional associations or guilds, there was no such organization for Brahmins similar to a Church with its hierarchy of archbishops, bishops, and so on. This refutes the claim that Brahmins enforced the 'caste system'. In fact, they did not have any organizational mechanism to enforce anything. With all these instruments of power in the hands of non-Brahmins, it would be impossible for them to exert control.

The Brahmins' power came simply from the fact that they could refuse to perform a ritual and refuse to transmit their knowledge. It was a negative form of power rather than a positive act of asserting power over others.

Inter-dependency of Jatis: The Jajmani System

Jatis in Indian villages were always economically co-dependent and no single jati was self-sufficient without the rest of the village ecosystem. This is because none of them enjoyed absolute control over all the resources of the village. Most villagers tended to follow the traditional occupational specialization of their jatis. This specialization led to a healthy exchange of services. The relationship between the jatis was not contractual, individual, or temporary but based on long-term mutual trust.[258]

This is the *jajmani* system of traditional occupational obligations and is still prevalent in some measure in rural India. It was a system of inter-jati reciprocity.[259] Each jati plays a specific role in the overall village life. The role comprises economic, social, and moral functions and involves social support as well as economic exchanges.[260] The example below illustrates how the jajmani system functions:

> ... at the birth-feast of a child, Brahmin presides over the ceremony of 'Nama Samskaran' (giving a name), Sunar (goldsmith) provides the gold ornament for the new born, Dhobi (washerman) washes dirty clothes, Nai (barber) carries messages, Khati (carpenter) provides wooden stool (patta) on which the child is kept for ceremony, Lohar (blacksmith) provides *kara* (iron bangle), Kumhar (potter) provides *kulhar* (jugs) for keeping cooked vegetables and drinking water, Pasi provides *patal* (leaf-plates) for taking food, and Bhangi (scavenger) cleans the place after the feast. All people who help receive the gifts of food, money and

clothes depending partly on custom, partly on jajman's influence, and partly on the recipient's entreaty.[261]

The jajmani system comprises a network of roles and norms integrated organically and legitimized and supported by cultural values.[262] The system maintains the division of labor and economic inter-dependence of jatis.[263] The traditional method of payment in most regions is made during harvest; each landowning farmer distributes the newly produced food grains to various jatis. Additional payments may also be in the form of land for a house, areas for animals to graze, wood and cow dung fuel, loan for tools, and so forth. In addition, the landowning farmer gives clothes and gifts on ceremonial occasions and may also loan money in emergencies.[264]

For instance, the village officials or community servants (e.g., the watchmen) maintain jajmani relations with the whole village. Thus, a watchman's family gets a contribution at harvest from every landowner farmer's family in the village. The village servants may also have tax-free use of village land. Such families have rights to serve all those who live in a particular section of the village.[265]

Decentralized Lobbying

The jatis developed their own *panchayats* (jati-specific governance) to decide their internal affairs with no involvement of the king. This was an efficient and inexpensive way to settle many disputes internally. It also brought local stability because despite invasions and upheavals at the level of the king, the local life at the village level continued to function. It was a decentralized system of welfare and similar to democracy in some ways. This has been a reason for the long-term survival of Hinduism at the grassroots.

Gradually, the jatis became more self-sufficient and ossified. The panchayats enforced endogamy to maintain unity and strength of the jati. They could send someone into exile for a serious crime, considered a terrible disgrace.

In modern times, many jatis have merged to form bigger caste groups, each with its own political lobbies negotiating with mainstream society or central government. These caste groups are mainly political vote banks and much of their traditional function has dissipated.

Ecological Role

Jati groups had mutual understandings to define their professional boundaries. Only the fishermen jati went out to fish, only the farmer jati practiced agriculture, and only the chamar jati had the right to the dead animal's skin. Even among the fishermen, there were multiple jatis each specializing in a specific type of fishing. Over time, the jati panchayats evolved rules to prevent too much fishing, for instance, thereby avoiding destroying their stock of fish. There were jatis with the responsibility to preserve the sacred groves for the benefit of the entire village.

This way, the jati system reduced competition for natural resources and avoided over-exploitation. The internal specialization of a given jati ensured the efficient inter-generational flow of competence in specialized skills. The resources required by a given profession were better protected than would be the case with open competition in a free market system. The restrictions of professional territories among the jatis served as a form of limiting rivalries.

On the positive side, this was a harmonious steady-state equilibrium between societies and nature. On the negative, this slipped into stagnation and lack of innovation that comes with competition.

Economic Security

There developed a system of making annual payments in kind or cash, as soon as harvesting was done, for services rendered by village artisans, barbers, washermen, agricultural laborers and the like. The system of payment was not on quantity of output but the principle that landowners should take care of the local village workers and included expenditures for special situations and adversities. This evolved into a patron-client relationship in which landowners had power over the other working-class families. Naturally, as with any asymmetric situation, there were abuses and atrocities of all kinds. Harmony would break down into conflicts. Such tensions are not due to any 'evil Brahmin conspiracy' resulting from the *Vedas* or any such thing. This is simply class conflict among competing interests at the local level.

Though the economic system could optimize the use of local resources and demands, it was sub-optimal in the face of production and trade on a larger scale.

Jatis and Introvertedness: The Problem

A jati-based social ecosystem did have several advantages. Communities focused on managing their own affairs autonomously without the need to engage excessively with each other. There was a demarcation of the economic turf and boundaries. Each jati had its own leaders, customs, deities, rituals and festivals, 'laws' and adjudication of disputes. 'I mind my business and you mind yours' was the posture towards outsiders. This was a key to India's immense diversity because thousands of distinct cultures evolved in separate, and largely isolated, cocoons. It also allowed harmony because jatis were not prone to interfere in each other's lives.

At the same time, this disinterestedness in macro affairs beyond the boundaries of one's jati also developed into apathy towards outsiders. Ambedkar criticized this point as well: 'Indifferentism is the result of the Caste System, which has made Sanghatan and co-operation even for a good cause impossible'.[266] Since one's selfish interests were not impacted by whatever was going on elsewhere, there was little reason to keep track of external events.

Unfortunately, India's isolationism meant it could easily become outdated in understanding external threats. Though waves of invaders had entered and created havoc in other parts of India, the wealthy and powerful kingdoms of the time did little to send scholars to the invaders' lands to study them, i.e., to do what the tradition calls *purva-paksha*, or the objective understanding of opponents. Therefore, outsiders understood India and its people better rather than the other way around.

There were many counter examples of Indian rulers uniting to fight a foreign enemy. But this was mostly reactive when the enemy was already at the gates. They were not proactively coming together to pre-empt enemies and even conquer them. Indians lacked the expansionist mentality of the conqueror, being self-contented within their own local affairs. Therefore, Indians did not develop large-scale team building skills the way, for instance, the Romans did as part of their foreign campaigns and imperial rule.

Some would say that Indian traditions are not conducive to local kings and communities coming together for bigger causes, but we beg to differ. Krishna in the *Mahabharata* exemplifies the visionary who brings many disparate groups together to fight that cause of dharma. If the kind of jati fragmentation we describe above had been desirable, Krishna would not have strived to unite various leaders. Therefore, the excuse that Indians are supposed to be fragmented as a mark of lofty spiritualism is just that, an excuse. When personal selfish interests are at stake, Indian communities do come together, so why not act collectively in situations that are not driven by selfish factors. Otherwise, the proverbial Mother Teresa is needed to save Indians because their fellow-Indians wash their hands off social responsibility in times of need.

This inward focus is consistent with the teachings of Vedanta. Unfortunately, it has also led to lowering one's expectations in life rather than maximizing the joy of living. Indian traditions *do* want us to enjoy material comforts provided it is done in a dharmic way and not in violation of dharmic norms.

In conclusion, we feel that a lingering negative effect on the Indian mind has been the internalizing of jati fragmentation and introvertedness. This is yet another reason to update the social systems in keeping with the times and the latest technologies.

The Collapse of the Caste System

The original dynamics of the system were disrupted and undermined by many social and political upheavals. Over time, varna became jati, which then morphed into caste. The caste system is now mostly dead, but its ghost continues to haunt India.

The result of modern democracy and social mobility is a new kind of system which is primarily one of vote banks and lobbying for resource allocation. Public education and job mobility have reduced the interests of the younger generations to follow in the footsteps of their parents. Technologies and economic trends have rendered old models obsolete.

There is very little left of the traditional varna roles in practice. Brahmins, Kshatriyas, Vaishyas, Shudras and Dalits by birth are seldom limited to the roles assigned to them by tradition. Everyone, regardless of birth, freely moves into whichever profession they want to and for those they are able to compete for in the marketplace.

Many old professions have disappeared, and some of the most promising ones include those that did not exist in the past. Some previously 'dirty' professions like leather work are now multibillion dollar global industries run by ultra-wealthy industrialists. The old taboo and stigmas have lessened due to technology. For instance, when an elitist customer at a fancy bar in India orders a drink, he is unconcerned about the varna/jati/caste identity of the bartender.

Unfortunately, the old vocabulary of identities is still in use even though the referents are entirely different. This has caused confusion. People think that today's Brahmin is like the ancient one and therefore all his flaws are blamed on the *Vedas*.

We can conclude that the origins, sustenance, and dismantling of the caste system has been independent of Hinduism. It was always purely a social phenomenon that happened to be in a largely Hindu society. The *Dharmashastras*, including the *Manusmriti*, were descriptive of the social reality at the time and place, and not prescriptive. The *Manusmriti* (IV.176) clearly states that any rule ought to be rejected if it leads to unhappiness and indignation.

The collapse of the caste system does not pose a threat to Hinduism's survival. Hinduism is like a banyan tree with many different systems of roots, trunks and branches, with no single point of failure. Hence, those who do not practice Hinduism are fully capable of being Hindus.

Part 2

HARVARD VISHWA GURU AND INDIAN BILLIONAIRES

7

Thirty Years of Encounters with Harvard University

In Part 1, we discussed how Critical Race Theory originated in the US by applying European theories of Marxism and Postmodernism to American social oppression of Blacks and other victim identities. The goal of Critical Race Theory is nothing short of dismantling the underlying structures that support the present social order.

We also explained how Critical Race Theory is being applied to Indian society by mapping caste onto race. The work of four major leaders in the US was taken up in detail, one, a Black woman and the other three, Indians living in the US:

- Isabel Wilkerson is a Black author whose work has spread the idea that caste is the fundamental architecture of racism.
- Thenmozhi Soundararajan is responsible for founding the most important US organization championing the US campaign to survey caste biases by Indians based in the US, filing lawsuits using this evidence, lobbying for legal and policy changes to designate caste as the equivalent of racism, and conducting training workshops across American corporates on the caste system.
- Ajantha Subramanian, a Harvard professor, wrote a book that has shaken up Indians in Silicon Valley in which she attacks the IITs as a form of institutionalized caste oppression. We are not aware of anyone prior to this book having examined her argument in detail and given a comprehensive response.
- The fourth person we chose is Suraj Yengde, senior fellow at the prestigious Harvard Kennedy School of Government. He has

become the poster boy championing Hinduphobia very directly and in uncompromising ways.

We also devoted Chapter 6 to give a counter position on the history and nature of caste and its relationship to Hinduism.

In Part 2, we will dive deeper to uncover how this discourse on Indian society is being developed, Indian scholars being trained, activists being produced on a large scale, and in turn getting exported to India.

Harvard University is, by far, the most important hub for this work. It has numerous shakhas carrying out this work, which are spread in multiple schools and centers of the university. This is one part of the surprise we uncovered and will present.

The other, more shocking aspect is the key role being played by Indian billionaires in funding and championing this work at Harvard.

But we will first set the stage for this deep dive by explaining the thirty-year background of our dealings with Harvard in several capacities. We have funded multiple international conferences and visiting professorships at Harvard long before these billionaires stepped in. We have studied the scholarly outputs being produced at Harvard, written reviews, debated and argued with its faculty, and monitored its activities related to India and Hinduism. This chapter will provide helpful background information and set the stage.

Soon after Infinity Foundation was established in 1994 by one of the authors, Rajiv Malhotra began extensive engagements with American higher education institutions concerning the portrayals of India.[1] Given its significance in the study of India, Harvard University was accorded top priority in this engagement. Our hope was to collaborate constructively. No other organization was, at the time, funding and sponsoring academic work in the US specific to India's civilization. We were received with open arms and praised as pioneers. This chapter narrates an account of what turned out to be a rocky relationship that went through many phases.

A watershed event at Harvard University was around the year 2000. It was the retirement party of John Carman, one of Harvard's foremost professors on the study of Hinduism. His specialty was the works of the twelfth-century Hindu philosopher and theologian, Ramanujacharya, and his writings were considered as the final word on the subject by

Western academicians. Carman had trained several significant scholars, including Vasudha Narayanan, who later became president of the American Academy of Religion, a very distinguished post. A friendly and candid man, Carman's insights had a profound impact on us in the early years of Infinity Foundation.

Rajiv Malhotra was at the party, after which Carman was heading to Washington D.C., and they both agreed to travel together because Malhotra's home in Princeton was on the way. This gave them a chance to spend several hours in a relaxed atmosphere and the two discussed several issues. Carman was a good listener of our concerns about the academic biases and what Malhotra called the 'caste, cows, curry' stereotypes. He went on to suggest projects for Infinity Foundation to carry out its goals.

Carman said he was planning to return to India to live in the church in the south set up by his family for doing missionary work. This was not unexpected because many Harvard scholars of Hinduism maintain a dual posture: claiming to be objective and neutral in their academic work, but privately nurturing aggressive agendas that contradict this show of neutrality.

The more impactful point was his final one just as the train was approaching Princeton. Carman said something to the effect: One of the greatest assets of the Indian community in the US are their children who are outstanding and will be among the American elite.

He then said: '*They are being raised by us in the academy as far as their ideas about their heritage are concerned.* Their parents are too busy making careers and are not well informed to guide them on these things, and they look at us as the teachers and gurus.'

This statement had a chilling effect on Malhotra. He had been processing his experience of Harvard's academic biases for several years as a part of monitoring Infinity Foundation's sponsored projects there. Now things began to fall in place. He began observing how right Carman was. Indian students in American colleges are being 'raised' by the American higher education system. When the children step out of their parents' homes after high school, develop their own individualism and identities, this transformation takes place during their undergraduate years in American colleges. Thereafter, Malhotra became more vocal in raising issues of academic bias with Harvard's authorities.

One of the first areas of interest we brought to Harvard's attention was the digestion of Indian civilization into the West in which the institution played a key role. The concept of digestion of a civilization has been discussed in several of our earlier writings, and we will now provide concrete examples that are Harvard related. The second pattern we found in practice at Harvard was the denigration of Indian traditions. These two intellectual movements fed each other:

- The more Indian traditions were denigrated by Harvard, the more it encouraged scholars to appropriate from them without attribution. After all, a backward tradition/culture did not deserve to be respected as the source of great contributions. When we confronted Americans digesting the tradition by reformulating it as something original, a frequent defense was that they wanted to distance themselves from a tradition that burns its women, kills its lower castes, and Muslims.

- Conversely, once depleted of its treasures, the tradition appears like a hollow shell brimming with primitive practices, exotica, dangerous gurus, and deities. This was exactly how Christian conquerors had characterized the native peoples of the Americas; this narrative was used to justify capturing their lands and wealth. However, while there seems to be an attempt at reparations and apology towards other native cultures, the attitude of Western academia toward India remains one of blatant Hinduphobia.

In other words, the demonology of a tradition is a way to justify digesting, and denigrating or deleting, its original form. We will discuss both the processes that took place at Harvard. In our engagements with various departments, we aimed to initiate scholarship and discussions on these very topics.

In terms of the Critical Race Theory framework, the implication of digestion is that the traditions are seen as devoid of any usefulness. Its problems are emphasized and hence the case is easier to make that its structures should be deemed oppressive and dismantled. But if the positive contributions are acknowledged, they serve as a robust defence of traditional structures.

After all, how could one justify the global movement to dismantle

Hinduism (now underway thanks to Critical Race Theory) if that tradition is the mother of yoga, meditation systems, eco-feminism, and so many other facets incorporated into modern Liberalism? The only way to discard the underlying structures wholesale is by removing all the positive contributions from its history. This is what digestion accomplishes, as we see next.

Harvard University's Role in Digesting Indian Meditation Systems

The decade of 1970 to 1980 had been one of transformation for American society's large-scale discovery of Indian systems of yoga, meditation, and healing sciences. These had already arrived in America, but in this decade, there was expansive adoption by the public and serious scientific investigations conducted into the legitimacy of these ancient systems.

Having been a practitioner of Maharishi Mahesh Yogi's system of Transcendental Meditation™ (TM), Malhotra learned that a powerful Harvard medical researcher, Herb (Herbert) Benson had appropriated the technique without acknowledgment and claimed it as his own discovery. This led Malhotra to unearth the phenomenon of digestion of Indian spiritual and other traditions in America. He discovered that this digestion was staggering in its scale, and also that Harvard was a major epicenter for this activity.

Three Boston men were among those that played decisive roles as scientific investigators: Herb Benson, Daniel Goleman, and Jon Kabat-Zinn. While the first two were at Harvard, Kabat-Zinn was at the nearby University of Massachusetts with close ties to Harvard. Each of them had learned his knowledge from Indian gurus, and the trio collaborated.

- In Benson's case, he digested Maharishi Yogi's Transcendental Meditation technique and called it The Relaxation Response.
- Goleman's career took off when he used Indian models of psychology to write his blockbuster book, *Emotional Intelligence*.
- Kabat-Zinn learned Vipassana, considered one of the most ancient forms of meditation, from the Indian teacher, S.N. Goenka with full acknowledgment and gratitude and turned it

into his proprietary Mindfulness Meditation, positioning it as Mindfulness-Based Stress Reduction (MBSR).

The terminologies of the three men quickly entered American lexicon and their frameworks became seen as pioneering scientific breakthroughs attributed to them. In due course, each of these turned into a global movement taught to corporates and the public at large.

Malhotra is working on a multi-volume series on the history of how Indian knowledge got digested into the American scientific community and mainstream society. In this chapter, we shall provide a summary of the role played by Benson, Goleman, and Kabat-Zinn.

In the pattern that Malhotra refers to in his U-turn Theory,[2] the three went through the following stages in their relationship with Hindu and Buddhist sources and spiritual teachers:

- At first, they learned directly from Indian sources and were profoundly impressed. In the case of Goleman and Kabat-Zinn, this learning was publicly acknowledged. In Benson's case, however, he was cleverer in that he disguised the fact that he was researching meditators of TM and published his research findings in prestigious journals as being entirely original.
- All three went through an extensive period of learning Indian systems, both in theory and through laboratory measurements on meditators to study their medical effects. Many papers were published, and they received considerable funding both from the US government and academic institutions. There was great excitement in the American scientific community with this new frontier being discovered. India was the nucleus of importance and viewed as a source of great treasures.
- They initially positioned themselves before Western scientists as the translators and champions of Indian systems they had 'discovered' and wanted to bring to the attention of their peers. They presented Indian systems using Western psychological and medical terms to map them in meaningful, and credible, ways. To begin with, they continued referring to the systems as 'Indian' as this made them far more plausible.
- Gradually, the reference to Indian systems and teachers in their published works lessened, from being positioned as their main

'discovery' to becoming reduced to minor citations. What were earlier termed 'Vedic' or 'Hindu' traditions became referred to mostly as 'Buddhist', then 'Asian', and eventually as 'Eastern traditions'.

- Simultaneously, various other world religions (mostly Judaism, Christian mysticism, and Sufism) were introduced in their writings as having similar practices but not as widely known, or practiced, or explained in detail. In other words, the unique and valuable Intellectual Property assets of the Vedic systems were systematically diluted and turned into 'generic spiritual wisdom'.

- Eventually, by the 1980s, this knowledge was received as one pioneered by Americans who developed various trademarks, proprietary jargon, and established large institutions to build their own careers.

In the mid-1990s, when Malhotra began investigating, he approached Harvard numerous times to convince them to explore the Indian connections of such developments through research projects, conferences, talks, and courses. Infinity Foundation wanted to sponsor, fund, and play whatever role it could to facilitate bringing this history into the mainstream. But none of it materialized. One Harvard department after another gave a variety of reasons for their lack of interest. Some pretended they had no idea of any Indian influence. Some said that this belonged to the past and we ought to move on to the future, while there were those who felt that Indian traditions were so great that they did not need such petty acknowledgment.

The most disturbing logic put forth was that this spiritual-scientific knowledge was more secure and useful in Western institutions because Indian society was not trustworthy of being the custodian of such knowledge due to pervasive social abuses. Simply put, India was primitive and did not deserve to own these treasures, while the West, being the savior of humanity, would be more responsible in using this knowledge.

At least one Western author writing the history of that period was candid about the racist aspects:

We cannot ignore the possible effect of race in the situation ... Maharishi was a brown-skinned Indian man with a big beard and long, somewhat unkempt hair forward of the shoulders, who typically appeared in yoga robes with Hindu prayer beads. ... Reaction to TM was often mediated by stereotypes of 'Oriental monks' applied to the Maharishi, the iconic face of the movement. Jon Kabat-Zinn, the face of MBSR, is a clean-shaven white American doctor with short hair and rimless glasses, who delivers his teachings in business attire.[3]

There are dozens of such knowledge transmissions from India to the West described in the book series we have planned on digestion of Indian traditions. For this section on Harvard, we shall give brief snapshots of the three men introduced above.

Herb Benson

During the 1960s, when Maharishi's TM technique went viral in the new-age movement of the United States, he asked his young disciple Robert Keith Wallace, a medical student, to study the effects of TM with scientific rigor and publish the results. The very first paper on the findings was published by Wallace as sole author in the journal *Science* in 1970. He did his PhD on this research and published the results in the *American Journal of Physiology* in 1971.

Ever since, Wallace has had a close, and unbroken, relationship with Maharishi's movement. He became the founding president of Maharishi International University and established the first Maharishi Ayurveda Clinics in the US. By 1975, Maharishi's US organization had 370 centers and 30,000 people were signing on every month to learn Transcendental Meditation.

Meanwhile, Herb Benson was an established cardiologist at Harvard Medical School but with no prior research publication in the field of meditation. In fact, his early publications received funding from the Council for Tobacco Research, an initiative set up in 1953 by the tobacco industry to fund scientific studies addressing health concerns related to cigarette smoking.[4] This initiative was shut down in 1998 for legal reasons.

When Benson learned of the effects of Transcendental Meditation on the human physiology, he knew instantly that this was a huge opportunity. He had extensive personal meetings with Maharishi Yogi in the early days to gain a deep understanding of his teachings. Benson's wife too learned TM and was a practitioner.

Benson approached Wallace to collaborate on meditation research. For Wallace, this was an attractive offer given Benson's clout as a Harvard professor. Since Wallace had already published his maiden paper and completed his PhD, he accepted Benson's offer to continue his research at Harvard. Interestingly, Benson tried to discourage Wallace from publishing his PhD dissertation separately, suggesting they publish it jointly. But Maharishi asked Wallace to go ahead. Right from the start, Benson was determined to appropriate the research one way or another.

A joint paper by Wallace and Benson was published in 1971 in *Scientific American* (*SciAm*). The material was entirely Wallace's work and Benson's contribution was to use his influence to convince the magazine to publish the findings that were then considered controversial by the medical profession. In fact, a significant number of figures and data from Wallace's PhD dissertation are found in this co-authored paper. In 1971, at a scientific conference on meditation at MIT, Maharishi, Benson, and Wallace each spoke. So far, Wallace assumed that there would be an honest collaboration in which Maharishi brought knowledge and Benson brought the clout of Harvard.

But there was a turning point. Benson's superiors at Harvard got concerned that his links with Maharishi would bring notoriety to Harvard because the subject of meditation was in the news as part of the hippie culture, and therefore associated with drug people. Timothy Leary, author and psychologist, and others had been expelled from Harvard for taking drugs and the institution wanted to protect its reputation. The media often conflated drugs and meditation. Besides, anything to do with 'Eastern mysticism' lacked academic legitimacy.

Benson's dream was to win the Nobel Prize and he knew that these findings on TM had sweeping implications. And so, it became important for him to distance himself from Maharishi.

After validating the scientific effects of Transcendental Meditation, Benson broke off from the movement. He went on to publish his own paper without Wallace, presenting the entire material as his original, when in fact none of it was. He had merely regurgitated the same study using his own subjects to mimic the earlier research by Maharishi's people, but pretended it was original. As a result, Wallace moved away from Benson.

Benson launched his own trademarked technique in 1975 in a very popular book titled *The Relaxation Response*. The claim of originality was based on the single idea that he had replaced Maharishi's mantra with the word 'one'. He asserted that this made the technique generic and not specific to any religion or culture.

The similarities between Transcendental Meditation and The Relaxation Response are too glaring and obvious to be ignored. Benson states that all meditation systems comprise four common features that make them medically effective: a quiet environment; a mental device; a passive attitude; and decreased muscle tone/comfortable position. However, he never established through any scientific testing that these four features are either necessary or sufficient to produce the desired results. He simply duplicated this set of requirements because this was how Maharishi explained TM.

It is important to note that Benson describes The Relaxation Response as a 'non-cultic' technique and goes to great lengths to declare that this quality contrasts with TM and yoga. In the prestigious journal *Lancet*, he states: 'The relaxation response may be elicited by a non-cultic, simple psychological technique, or by yogic, religious, and secular techniques'.[5] This was a clever strategy using the fear of 'Eastern cults' in America at the time. Fearmongering of this kind helped him sell his claims as scientific and stripped of all cultish elements like the mantra.

Ploys such as these helped build his publishing career, both in serious academic medical journals and in popular books where he explained the Indian theories of mind-body relationship in medical terms.

Benson wrote more books on the same technique of meditation using his own jargon, with sales of forty million copies. He steadily moved his writings closer towards Christianity. In affiliation with Harvard Medical School, he launched the Mind-Body Medical Institute, a for-profit research and training initiative in behavioral medicine. By decoupling it from Indian spiritual traditions, his Mind-Body Institute was successful in introducing his trademarked technique to high schools. The institute launched training programs for healthcare practitioners in all aspects of what it called the 'Benson Method'. It franchised its model to hospitals and other healthcare facilities and started educational programs for the public.

The central focus of his medical research was to validate, and explain, the effects of ancient Indian systems repackaged as his *proprietary* Relaxation Response in scientific and technical language. For instance, the deep rest provided by the TM technique is renamed 'a hypometabolic state of parasympathetic activation'. Given his clout, funding sources, and sponsorship from Christian institutions, such as the John Templeton Foundation (brought in as a board member), he succeeded in rebranding Maharishi's distinctly Indian ideas as his own Benson Method. He became a significant bridge to bring the bounties of Indian mind sciences into Western frameworks and ownership.

Benson traveled to India with the intent of adding Tibetan Buddhism ideas on to his own meditation system to make it seem different than TM. In 1980, when Benson and Wallace met in India, Benson pretended he had done no wrong, to the contrary claiming he had contributed to Indian spirituality by popularizing Maharishi's ideas. Maharishi was asked several times about Benson's plagiarism; he was aware of it but wanted Wallace and others to ignore it and not pursue the matter officially.

Benson's thirty-page bio-data lists dozens of 'original' research publications, prestigious affiliations, and his various major accomplishments, but it carefully sanitizes the jargon to make all of his work appear as 'Western' science.

The academic world as well as mainstream American media gave Benson complete credit for the discovery of the science of meditation. Seldom mentioned was its debt to Maharishi's Transcendental Meditation. In fact, Benson was credited for having 'demystified meditation' by removing the mantra that seemed threatening to many Judeo-Christian Americans. He made a fortune and a great career at Harvard selling these techniques acknowledging neither the Indian origin of the practices nor the Sanskrit-based theories and epistemologies that interpreted and explained the higher states of consciousness.

Needless to say, Rajiv Malhotra tried hard to convince those at Harvard to discuss the relationship between the claims of their scholars with the Indian sources they had borrowed from. However, there was no interest on the part of Harvard to open this can of worms.

Daniel Goleman

Daniel Goleman is now an internationally acclaimed psychologist, bestselling author of several books like *Emotional Intelligence: Why It Can Matter More Than IQ,* and former chief editor of *Psychology Today.*

But his story begins when he was an undergraduate at Berkeley during the 1960s and became interested in Indian meditation systems. For his PhD research at Harvard and a pre-doctoral fellowship, he went to India to study meditation. There he became friends with Richard Alpert, who was fired from Harvard because of his experiments with the hallucinogenic drug, LSD. Alpert went to India and became a disciple of the guru, Neem Karoli Baba and changed his name to Ram Dass. Ram Dass, who died recently, was well-known for his association with Harvard and one who brought the Bhakti movement to America, becoming an icon of the new age/hippie era.

Goleman later returned to India under a post-doctoral grant. He, too, spent considerable time with Neem Karoli Baba and studied Indian spiritual traditions across a wide range, both in theory and practice.[6] One of his first research papers in 1971 as a doctoral student at Harvard was on Indian meditation in which he describes what the Indian texts say about the 'fifth state of consciousness'.[7]

Looking back, Goleman recalls when he brought these ideas to the US, yoga was 'very exotic' and meditation was 'practically unheard of '. He says he discovered the Indian concept of the 'transformation of being, that sounded very interesting to me from a psychological point of view. So, I grabbed that fellowship, ran off to India'.[8] He explains what he learned from India:

> ... a psychological system (was) at the heart of Buddhism ... absolutely unknown in Western psychology. ... I started to write about it, and the way it worked with the mind, the way it conceived of what you could do to transform the mind, ... meditation was very much at the heart of that. ... Western psychology did not understand that ... meditation did transform the mind, and now we know, the brain. No one had ever heard of the word, neuroplasticity in the 1970s, ... repeated experiences change the structure and function of the brain was implicit in Buddhist psychology and unknown in Western psychology. ...

you could transform the mind, to the point where, ... your inner emotional state was not at the whim of external conditions, but was an ongoing, ...equanimous state that was one of kindness. This was inconceivable. ... I would say psychologists in the 2010s don't think about it that much as whole.[9]

He describes working with Benson (well established in the Harvard faculty at the time) doing research on meditators practicing Maharishi's Transcendental Meditation. He explains the practice in detail as well as the clinical findings of its benefits considered a significant breakthrough in the scientific community. He writes that for the preceding three years he had tried several meditation techniques, and that,

> transcendental meditation (sic) as taught by Maharishi Mahesh Yogi is the one I've practiced longest, am most thoroughly familiar with theoretically, and about which I hypothesize here. Transcendental meditation (sic), or TM, like most yoga systems taught in the US, traces its roots back to the tradition of which Patanjali's Yoga Sutras is the classic statement.[10]

Goleman goes on to say: 'My hypotheses are generated from experience with TM but are framed in terms of meditation in general in the hope that they will be tested on a variety of different systems'.[11] He also acknowledges the pioneering research work in the scientific study of meditation being done by Keith Wallace (discussed above), a well-known long-time follower of Maharishi. He concludes: 'I must state that this paper is the bare beginning of the delineation of the process whereby meditation changes the meditator into the fifth-state being, nor does it do justice to describing what that state is like...'[12]

Goleman soon expanded his analysis to Buddhist meditation. In 1972, he wrote two influential research papers quoting both Vedic and Buddhist sources and comparing their teachings and meditation systems. He discussed the Bhakti and the Hare Krishna movements in a positive, scientific way. He cited Swami Vivekananda and his American disciple Christopher Isherwood and compared Bhakti with Raja Yoga, a technique that teaches controlling the mind. His survey of Indian systems includes Sri Aurobindo's Integral Yoga (a combination of several techniques), the renowned philosopher J. Krishnamurti's meditation,

Patanjali's *Yoga Sutra*, and the sage, Ramana Maharshi's teachings. Goleman achieved an impressive amount of theoretical knowledge of Vedic and Buddhist cosmologies and explained them as religious traditions without any apology or cover up. He then discussed Swami Muktananda, the founder of Siddha Yoga, who was already very popular in America, and drew comparisons between Kundalini Yoga, Tantra, and Tibetan Tantra. His work included an extensive glossary of Sanskrit terms he used copiously to explain Indian literature.[13]

These papers were among the most thorough early surveys of meditation in the West from a scientific perspective, referring to almost a dozen different Indian systems. Though Sufi and Christian mysticism were also mentioned, these were very brief and ninety percent of the study was on Hindu and Buddhist systems.[14] In his early publications, Goleman mainly cited Indian sources, such as Maharishi Mahesh Yogi and Sri Aurobindo, and scholars trained almost entirely on Indian sources, such as the American psychologist Charles Tart who had studied Indian yoga systems, and so forth. By 1975, Goleman was mapping his Indian knowledge on to the framework of Buddhist *Abhidharma* or texts, using substantial Sanskrit terminology.

Gaining confidence and legitimacy, Goleman started publishing in more prestigious psychotherapy scientific journals. This research became popular and led to what is now being called the field of mind sciences. Ironically, the field has almost totally scrubbed off references to Indian sources even though an entire generation of American thinkers and scientists was raised on them.

Gradually, he and his interviewees started omitting Vedic sources and began referring to the Buddhist ones. Goleman presented the *Abhidharma* system as the broadest, and most detailed, traditional psychology of states of consciousness.[15] By 1976, he was referring to this knowledge more in secular terms as 'Asian approach to mental health' and publishing it in prestigious mainstream scientific journals.[16]

His 1977 book, *The Varieties of the Meditative Experience*, was his first bestseller when it was republished under the title, *The Meditative Mind*. This book comprises what he has learned from Indian systems and maps it on to a Western framework, but without hiding the Indian sources at this stage. A Western biographer writes: 'As might be expected from a recently minted PhD on psychology, there is a persistent framing of the ancient source material in psychological terms'.[17] The book has a foreword by Ram Dass. The first edition was dedicated to Neem Karoli Baba and Lord Hanuman, among others. It was updated into a new edition by Penguin which became his first *New York Times* bestseller.

By the mid-1980s, Goleman had become one of the most popular writers on meditation with regular columns in *The New York Times*, educating Americans on his new system of mind sciences. In reality, this system was a restatement of what he had learned from Indian sources.

At times, he has continued to acknowledge his Indian sources, but largely confined himself to Buddhist sources. For instance, he regards the *Abhidharma* metaphysics as a scientific approach to psychology:

> ... I discovered ... an alternate psychological system. ... Abhidharma, which is the Sanskrit term for this model of mind. Then I started writing about it in psychology journals, albeit very obscure psychology journals, because they were the only ones that were interested. ... it was important to bring this news to Western psychology because ... it ...extend(ed) the horizon line of the potential of being human. ... if psychology's about anything, it's about the mind and what are it's (sic) upper limits; what are the worst places we can go, what are the best places we can go? And this described some best places that we hadn't heard of yet...[18]

Goleman remained close to the Dalai Lama and used him frequently to write introductions and endorsements for his books. His 1995 book, *Emotional Intelligence*, became an international bestseller and was translated into forty languages. It is an iconic book used by corporations for lessons in management and leadership.

Ironically, when he is invited by top multinationals in India, the fact that he is reselling Indian knowledge is seldom appreciated other than in casual references that he once travelled to India and could have picked up a few inspirations. Goleman now claims that he has superseded the Indian tradition with his own new and original scientific discoveries.

Goleman deserves credit for systematically testing the Indian systems using the scientific method and establishing their credibility. But this need not erase the source tradition in the process. When knowledge is appropriated from ancient Greece, for instance, it is duly acknowledged as such, and the same standard must apply in the case of

Indian knowledge. Such acknowledgment keeps the knowledge system alive in its native form so it can enrich us further.

Jon Kabat-Zinn

Though Jon Kabat-Zinn is not formally associated with Harvard, he is included here as he has worked closely with others at the institution and his influence there is clear.

In the late 1960s, when Kabat-Zinn was working on his PhD in molecular biology at MIT, he attended a lecture on Zen meditation. He started studying meditation with prominent Buddhist teachers, and at the Insight Meditation Center in Boston, where he later became a teacher. By 1979, he had thirteen years of training and practice, and during a two-week meditation retreat, he claims to have had a vision: His 'karmic assignment' in life would be to apply his learnings from Buddhism to help Americans deal with chronic health conditions and stress. To carry out that mission, he convinced the University of Massachusetts Medical School (now known as UMass Chan Medical School) to let him establish the Mindfulness-Based Stress Reduction Clinic.[19]

Kabat-Zinn packaged and marketed meditation in a way that led to his enormous success. The decision to name the technique mindfulness was well thought out, he says, as he didn't want to brand his product as overtly 'Buddhist' or foreign. In the 1970s, he realized that the average American regarded meditation as something associated with hippies, new agers, free spirited bums, and other counterculture dropouts. Very early he realized the value in overcoming this cultural barrier and prejudice among Americans. He decided to target the mainstream market by taking the medical route.

He formally trademarked the brand Mindfulness-Based Stress Reduction, popularly known as MBSR. He says the MBSR coinage sounds very corporate compared to terms like *samadhi*, *dhyana*, Vipassana or *pranayama*. And calling it stress management was more desirable than enlightenment. He renamed ancient Indian techniques with terms like 'body scanning' and 'guided meditation'. Kabat-Zinn says: 'I bent over backwards to structure it and find ways to speak about it that avoided as much as possible the risk of its being seen as Buddhist, New Age, Eastern mysticism or just plain flaky.'[20]

He has made millions by commercially franchising the ancient Vipassana system that Buddha himself taught. However, Kabat-Zinn markets the technique as his recent discovery. He learned to distance his work from Hindu and Buddhist traditions, and position it entirely as secular science with himself as the discoverer. When discussing with other scholars in the field, he admits to what he calls the 'Asian' origins of his methods, which he describes as a combination of three components: (1) Vipassana, a Theravada form of Buddhism; (2) Zen practices; and (3) Hatha Yoga, a kind of yoga that is more physical. Though these are clearly Indian systems with spiritual origins, those terms would undermine the clinical nature of his claims.

Another brilliant move was to establish the Center for Mindfulness in Medicine, Health Care and Society at the UMass Medical School. This paved the way for him to keep one foot in the medical research camp. It gave Kabat-Zinn enormous credibility compared to other Westerners positioning themselves like Indian gurus. He rapidly conducted one successful clinical trial after another to prove efficacy in treating a variety of conditions such as hypertension, heart disease, chronic pain, irritable bowel syndrome, and headaches.

Besides the US medical establishment, he started receiving funding from the US Army to develop special programs. The US military has used MBSR to improve the 'operational effectiveness' of combatants in the battlefield. He also received grants for research from some of the largest health insurance carriers. Maintaining a long-term close relationship with the Dalai Lama is yet another wise move because it enables him to claim authenticity among spiritual circles and protects him from criticism for his blatant appropriations. He is on the board of the Mind & Life Institute in Virginia, an organization that sponsors public dialogues between the Dalai Lama and leading Western scientists.

His biggest breakthrough was in 1993 when his work was prominently featured in the *PBS* television series, *Healing and the Mind with Bill Moyers*. This made him a household name as one of the foremost leaders of the American meditation movement.

Jon Kabat-Zinn's franchise has trained large numbers of medical and health professionals, corporate executives, and others. It has set up a few hundred franchisees to deliver clinical services in thirty countries and helped millions of patients. The benefit of Buddhist meditation is well established, except that it is not seen as Buddhist. He has now become too big to be criticized even by Buddhists. He fearlessly states that there is nothing particularly Buddhist about mindfulness, that 'Buddhists don't own mindfulness', and so forth.

In private conversations, Kabat-Zinn has been respectful of his debt to India, and admits he learnt these systems from Indian sources over a period of twenty years. But many teachers of his franchisees are embarrassed when we inform them that in his earlier books, he called his methods Vipassana because that helped him establish credibility for his teachings. Most teachers of mindfulness do not want to hear any of this. Any links with India, especially with Hinduism, are seen as negative associations that diminish the market value of MBSR. Some teachers display anger when it is explained to them that these are Indian techniques repackaged for Western markets.

Many Buddhist academicians and traditional teachers like the American Zen teacher, David Loy have criticized the way Kabat-Zinn has commodified Vipassana into a marketable service. And now, he is no longer the only player in the game. The American mindfulness industry has entered a new phase of cut-throat competition to certify mindfulness teachers although this greed is contrary to Buddhist values.

For instance, the International Mindfulness Teachers Association is a competing organization that too runs like a commercial venture. One of its services costs $22,500 to travel to what it claims are 'the seven chakras on our planet'. Another offering is a twelve thousand dollars per day consulting fee for training senior corporate managers in mindfulness. Organizations can become members for an annual fee of eight hundred dollars. There are fees for accreditation, license fees for using its logo, and so forth.[21] Another rival, Wisdom Labs, brags that it has sold mindfulness training to Ford Motor Company managers. It teaches sales strategies that help its franchisees go after business deals. 'Its (sic) all about branding and positioning', claims Wisdom Labs.[22]

But Jon Kabat-Zinn's brand, Mindfulness-Based Stress Reduction remains the undisputed industry leader. Over twenty-five thousand people have undergone its eight-week program with some one thousand certified practitioners/teachers. And it is taught in over six hundred clinics worldwide. It is a sort of pyramid scheme in which a student can advance to become a trainer of other aspirants.

Jon Kabat-Zinn has erected barriers for new entrants. His certification of teachers enjoys better reputation. And he has constantly identified new markets like corporations, schools, government, and the military.[23]

Digesting Indian Thought Into Western Philosophy and Psychology

Besides meditation, Western psychology too has been deeply influenced by India, but this is carefully concealed by academics. We will give a couple of examples to illustrate the importance of these digestions.

Alfred North Whitehead

Alfred North Whitehead was a renowned British mathematician of the late nineteenth and early twentieth century who subsequently made lasting contributions in the philosophy of science. His most celebrated student, the influential philosopher, Bertrand Russell, and Whitehead collaborated on several projects. In 1924, Whitehead moved to Harvard University where he developed his metaphysical system which he called the 'philosophy of organism', presently known as Process Philosophy.

Whitehead's exposure to Indian systems of philosophy was extensive and he has made positive observations, such as 'Buddhism is the most colossal example in the history of applied metaphysics'.[24] Some scholars have also remarked on the similarities between the central tenets of Buddhism and those of Whitehead's Process Philosophy. For instance, Charles Hartshorne, an eminent American theologian, said: 'Whitehead's mode of thought is, to a remarkable extent, reminiscent of ancient Buddhism... .'[25]

Western chauvinism unfortunately, has led most commentators, and even Western Buddhist scholars, to downplay the Buddhism contained in his ideas. They want to set forth that these were independent discoveries by him using scientific thinking that could not have existed in what is summarily dismissed as 'Indian mysticism'.

However, there is a very powerful smoking gun that points to his appropriation: The tenets of Whitehead's Process Philosophy are such that they *could not have been derived from mere analytical reasoning and scientific observations without the benefit of very advanced states of a meditative mind (required by Buddhism) which Whitehead did not claim to have achieved.* Certain premises of Whitehead's system are impossible to know in ordinary mental states, thus leading to the plausibility of plagiarism.

In a forthcoming book project, Rajiv Malhotra explains in detail that there are at least ten distinct points of convergence between fundamental Buddhism and Whitehead's central ideas of Process Philosophy.[26]

The German-Buddhist scholar Nyanaponika Thera explains why the key insight that Whitehead proposed can only be derived by an advanced state of meditation and not by intellectual reasoning alone. He asserts that Whitehead's claims 'cannot be observed, directly and separately, by a mind untrained in introspective meditation',[27] and continues:

> Just as the minute living beings in the microcosm of a drop of water become visible only through a microscope, so, too, the exceedingly short-lived processes in the world of mind become cognizable only with the help of a very subtle mental scrutiny, and that only obtains as a result of meditative training. None but the kind of introspective mindfulness or attention (*satti*) that has acquired, in meditative absorption, a high degree of inner equipoise, purity and firmness (*upekkha-sati-parisuddhi*), will possess the keenness, subtlety and quickness of cognitive response required for such delicate mental microscopy. Without that ... only the way of inference from comparisons between various fragmentary series of thought moments will be open as a means of research.[28]

An advanced meditative mind is a *prerequisite* for achieving insight into momentary occasions of experience, based on which Whitehead could have understood the relational structure of such phenomena. A merely inferential procedure can supplement the meditative insight and help one articulate it but cannot by itself penetrate the microscopic world of momentariness.

Buddhism recognizes three phases of understanding: (1) wisdom arising from study; (2) wisdom arising from contemplation; and (3) wisdom arising from meditative realization. Whitehead's discussions are entirely limited to the first two, and he never made any claims of having achieved the third phase. The purely inferential (inductive) method which Whitehead utilizes cannot even reveal what he calls the 'categorical scheme' or even the 'categories of existence'.

How then, could he possibly have developed these insights on his own? The resemblances of what Whitehead called 'actual entities' or 'actual occasions' with the Buddhist tenets are far too profound to be merely coincidental.

One must note that Buddhism was in vogue in Whitehead's milieu at Cambridge. Many leading intellectuals were strongly influenced by it. Whitehead and Russell were keen students of Buddhism, the prevailing intellectual fashion in Britain. At Harvard, too, the tradition of Buddhist studies was firmly established during Whitehead's tenure.[29] And Bertrand Russell shared his high regard for Buddhism.

What is surprising is Whitehead's determination to attribute the origins of his thought solely to Western sources. While the Western precedents he cites are at best weak analogues, the Buddhist tenets from which his system derives are clearcut and extremely detailed. His arguments are strongest and most lucid when they are framed using Buddhist models; they become vague and confusing when he turns speculative and tries to appear original in both terminology and framework. Anyone knowledgeable in Buddhism would find his attempts very unconvincing in their attribution to Western philosophers as his theoretical predecessors.

Whitehead made his theory Christianity-friendly by superimposing God upon the process. From the Buddhist point of view, this is both gratuitous and inconsistent.[30] His appropriation of Buddhism as a philosophy of science and then as a theology compatible with Christianity became very popular among Christian theologians. Several of them, including Pierre Teilhard de Chardin, Charles Hartshorne, John B. Cobb, Karl Rahner, started advancing a curious blend known as Process Theology.

This is now considered a mainstream Christian theology and pointing out its Indian origins is fiercely opposed, almost to the point of censorship. Because of the importance being granted to Process Theology in liberal Christian circles, with Whitehead positioned as its pioneering thinker, Harvard has had no interest in investigating our claims of this wholesale appropriation of Buddhism.

Swami Vivekananda and William James

It is well known that in 1893, Swami Vivekananda delivered a path-breaking speech in Chicago at the historic gathering at the Parliament of the World's Religions. Vivekananda's impact on eminent Americans of that era has not been adequately researched and published. He lectured and taught meditation to the New Thought movement in New England and started Vedanta societies in many parts of America that penetrated the intellectual elites of the time.

What is seldom given importance is the fact that he was invited to Harvard multiple times as special guest of the renowned philosopher and psychologist, William James, head of the philosophy department. In fact, at times Vivekananda stayed in James' house with the latter hosting Vivekananda's famous seminars at Harvard, which were attended by many prominent intellectuals.

William James is considered the father of modern psychology in the West. But what is not mentioned often enough is that he gained a great deal of knowledge about Samkhya, the branch of Indian philosophy that deals with the theory of mind, through his contact with Vivekananda. He also engaged important Buddhist scholars at Harvard and studied Madhyamaka Buddhism, the practice founded by Nagarjuna, as well as *Abhidharma*.

James became familiar with Vedanta and mentioned the *Upanishads* and other Indian texts in his popular book, *The Varieties of Religious Experience*. He acknowledged the profoundness and authoritativeness of Indian traditions, attempted to practice yoga, and felt that having a guru was important.

Rajiv Malhotra attempted to get Harvard's researchers in psychology, cognitive sciences, mind sciences, religious studies, and history interested in taking up projects on Vivekananda's influences on America. Unfortunately, Harvard has at best given lip service and preferred to ignore these significant topics.

Digesting Indian Spirituality Into Western Literature

During the 1990s, Malhotra also discovered that several eminent American writers associated with Harvard had, in fact, been deeply influenced by Indian spiritual traditions. Naturally, he brought these facts to the attention of those at Harvard hoping to get them interested in holding events to discuss this subject. We shall give a few prominent examples – the Transcendentalists based in the Boston area, and the

Nobel Prize-winning poet, T.S. Eliot.

Ralph Waldo Emerson

Ralph Waldo Emerson is well-known as the founder of the Transcendentalist movement as well as an important thinker for the Unitarians in the 1800s. Though in his early years he was a devout Christian, he underwent a transformation after his prolonged study of Hindu texts, especially the *Bhagavad Gita*, *Vedas*, and *Upanishads*. His transformation was impactful: the *Upanishadic* assertion that his own deep self is ultimately the divine led him to break with the Unitarian church and resign as a church minister.

Emerson had been accepted at Harvard Divinity School (HDS) in 1824 and then inducted into The Phi Beta Kappa Society, the highest academic honor. He became famous for his lectures and writings at Harvard. But after his transformation with Indian influence, when he was invited to deliver the graduation address at HDS in 1838, his lecture created a scandal. He publicly, and assertively, rejected miracles attributed to Jesus and the claim that Jesus was God. He was harsh in his criticism of Christianity terming it suffocating, obsessed with Jesus' historicity, and devoid of intellectual merit. His comments outraged the Harvard establishment and the general Protestant community. He was denounced as an atheist and a heretic. He was banned from speaking at Harvard for the next thirty years.

In 2003, Harvard celebrated Emerson's bicentenary as a great event with numerous talks on his life and an exhibition of his works.[31] However, they completely avoided discussing the embarrassing event of his lecture in 1838.

We wrote to the organizers that Emerson's writings on Hinduism should be featured, but never heard back. That is when Infinity Foundation sponsored Prof. Robert C. Gordon to write a book on the subject. *Emerson and the Light of India: An Intellectual History* was published in 2008 giving extensive details on these Indian influences.[32] Harvard had no interest in discussing it.

Walt Whitman

The second most famous Transcendentalist whose life and works became a part of American intellectual history was Walt Whitman, considered

America's national poet and one of the greatest of the nineteenth century. Once again, there are remarkable parallels between his views on liberation, on the nature of reality, and the teachings found in the *Vedas* and *Upanishads*.

Emerson once famously remarked that Whitman's *Leaves of Grass* was 'a mixture of the *Bhagavad Gita* and *The New York Herald*'. Whitman had himself said that he absorbed 'the ancient Hindoo poem' as well as some Western works in preparation to write his most famous work.[33]

In one of Whitman's India-inspired major poems, *The Sleepers*, he writes the quintessential Upanishadic statement that all entities are forms of Brahman:

> I am the actor, the actress, the voter, the politician,
> The emigrant and the exile, the criminal that stood in the box,
> He who has been famous, and he who shall be famous after to-day,
> The stammerer, the well-form'd person, the wasted or feeble person.
> ...
> I am she who adorn'd herself and folded her hair expectantly,
> My truant lover has come, and it is dark.

Compare this with what Krishna says in the *Bhagavad Gita* (9.16, 18-19):

> I am the ritual action, I am the sacrifice, I am the ancestral oblation, I am the medicinal herb, I am the sacred hymn, I am also the melted butter, I am the fire, and I am the offering.
> I am the goal, the upholder, the lord, the witness, the abode, the refuge, and the friend. I am the origin and the dissolution, the ground, the resting place, and the imperishable seed.
> ... I am immortality and also death; I am being as well as non-being, O Arjuna.

In his work, *Passage to India*, Whitman says his journey is not to 'lands and seas alone' but to 'primal thought ... Back, back to wisdom's birth, to innocent intuitions'.

He had a transformative insight into the Upanishadic idea of the unity of his deep selfhood with the ultimate reality. This led to an unconventional lifestyle by American norms – a life of wandering, isolation, and encounters with the political challenges of his time.

Henry David Thoreau

Thoreau was one of America's foremost naturalists, poets, and philosophers of the 1800s. He was one of the leaders of the Transcendentalist movement along with Emerson and Whitman. His writings on natural history and the environment have left a lasting impact.

Like the other two leaders of Transcendentalism, he was profoundly influenced by India's spiritual heritage. It was during his stay in Emerson's home for two years that Thoreau started reading Vedic books, and European translated accounts of the *Mahabharata* and *Manusmriti* among other *shastras*. He wrote about them with great inspiration in his journals. A friend later sent him a collection of twenty-one books on Hinduism that Thoreau treasured for the rest of his life. He fondly wrote that he had put 'these treasures' in a new case he made with his own hands. After reading them, he wrote to a friend: 'I am familiar with many of them and know how to prize them. I send you this information as I might of the birth of a child'.[34]

He translated a work from French into English, *The Transmigration of the Seven Brahmans* and read this as a philosophy of yoga which he clearly saw as an ascetic system of Hindu practice. In a letter to a friend, he wrote:

> The yogi, absorbed in contemplation, contributes in his degree to creation: he breathes a divine perfume, he hears wonderful things. Divine forms traverse him without tearing him, and, united to the nature which is proper to him, he goes, he acts as animating original matter. To some extent, and at rare intervals *even I am a yogi*.[35]

Another passage from his journal reads: 'One may discover the root of a Hindoo religion in his own private history, when, in the silent intervals of the day or night, he does sometimes inflict on himself like austerities with a stern satisfaction'.[36]

Overall, historians of that era feel Thoreau was more influenced by Buddhism than Hinduism. But his writings reveal the impact of both, and these made him interested in finding deep meanings in nature. As a mystic, he felt like a yogi.

Prof. Eugene Taylor, one of Harvard's foremost scholars of mind sciences who was also interested in writing about Indian influences, made an important observation:

> Henry David Thoreau's ideas on civil disobedience arose out of his reading of Hindu scriptures on meditation, yoga, and non-violence.[37]

This is a very significant statement because Thoreau's writings on civil disobedience later influenced Gandhi, whereas the common view is that it was an American idea that later went to Gandhi. What Taylor points out is that this was an old Indian idea digested into the West by Thoreau and re-exported back to India through Gandhi.

The book, *Thoreau's Ecstatic Witness*, discusses his spirituality and the deep links with Indian traditions becomes very clear.[38]

Ironically, Harvard has been in denial of Thoreau's Indian inspirations. Because he had been a Harvard student (1833-7), in 2017 the bicentennial of his birth was celebrated there. The *Harvard Gazette* exclaimed: 'Harvard profoundly influenced Thoreau and helped make him who he was... .'[39] The article, *The Harvard in Thoreau*, makes no mention whatsoever of what could be considered the Indian in Thoreau.

T.S. Eliot

T.S. Eliot, arguably the most significant American poet of the twentieth century, was intensely studying Sanskrit and Hindu texts like *Patanjali Sutras* while at Harvard. Several years of this study brought about a deep transformation in his thinking, and he is known to have said that 'their subtleties make most of the great European philosophers look like schoolboys'.[40]

He studied the *Upanishads*, *Bhagavad Gita*, *Vedas*, and several other texts, and scholars have remarked that they 'were the catalysts for some of his finest work, from *The Waste Land* through the plays to *Four Quartets*'. Hindu classics 'offered not simply points of confirmation of previously held ideas but valuable challenges to established points of view'.[41]

Even though Eliot's knowledge of Indian philosophy was profound and extensive, one rarely finds present-day English literature departments mentioning this influence, much less analyzing it to appreciate his poetry in a far deeper way. In college courses on the historical evolution of modern American thought and literature, only Greek and European influences are included, with some African and postmodernist Third World writers thrown in to make it multicultural. Iconic American thinkers like Eliot are not tainted with any sort of Indian underpinnings.

Eliot struggled with the fact that such spiritual influences from India were considered heretic by his American peers. He wrote that if he were to fully embrace the Indian insights, it would disconnect him from his familiar reference points of American culture, family, country, community, and even from the established American poetry tradition. Embracing Indian tradition would amount to a rejection of everything fundamentally Western. At the same time, the pull into Sanskrit texts was too powerful and irresistible.

He finally reconciled this inner conflict. He decided to return to his Christian faith to protect himself from being drawn too far into the Vedic worldview. However, he also wanted to continue studying Sanskrit texts without this threat. So, he got himself publicly baptized (for the second time), in the presence of the Harvard community. Having secured his Christian identity through this act, he continued with his Sanskrit scholarship, but now at arm's length and not with the previous immersion.[42]

When Malhotra met Prof. Cleo Kearns who had done her doctoral dissertation on T.S. Eliot's lifelong study of Hinduism, there was an instant resonance. Infinity Foundation funded her as a scholar on various projects and published her book, *T.S. Eliot and Indic Traditions* in India so those young Indians, in love with Eliot's writings, could understand that he had digested Sanskrit texts as part of his highly acclaimed poetry.

But all attempts to get Harvard interested in pursuing this research fell on deaf ears.

For the past thirty years, our attempts to get Harvard's religious studies, business school, social sciences, medical school, or psychology departments to showcase these as Indian contributions, have failed.

Atrocity Literature Developed by Harvard University

Infinity Foundation's second major discovery about Harvard's relationship with India was even more shocking. We found the institution to be a major center for producing atrocity literature on India. The term refers to literature Americans produce about another culture that depicts them as savages committing atrocities against their own people. This literature becomes an archive used for developing theories of human rights violations that are then used to accuse targeted societies. At some stage, such theories can be weaponized for political campaigns to invade, or somehow intervene, in those societies, as the savior bringing them social justice.

Atrocity Literature in the Name of Public Health

We were astounded to find the extent of such literature on India being compiled, curated and shared at Harvard in the name of public health. The Harvard School for Public Health (HSPH), later renamed Harvard T.H. Chan School of Public Health, had several forums on India. The complete list of these forums during the 1990s till just a few years ago, comprised the following:

- Child marriage
- Crimes against women
- Dowry
- Feticide
- Girl child
- Injectables/contraceptives
- Sati
- Tribals

Under each of the above topics, there were detailed websites on the home page www.hsph.harvard.edu. The websites have disappeared, but we have screen shots of large portions of the content. They contained articles, contact details of scholars being nurtured, resource material for research, legal cases in India, and so forth.

What is also interesting is that besides South Asia the only other region with a similar archive at Harvard was Africa. There was no such program on China.

When Harvard claims it wants to help India's public health, most assume it would be funding cures for dengue, malaria or other widespread tropical diseases. Or help champion India's medical tourism industry that brings in foreign patients for treatment. But there was nothing on these websites about curing serious diseases, or promoting traditional medicine systems, or improving India's facilities and equipment, or encouraging original drug discovery. The focus was only on social abuses and atrocity literature. We did not expect Harvard to be obsessed with digging up dirt to be used against India.

The blatant biases against India started to get cleaned up for public show at least to some extent from 2005 onward. That is when Harvard decided to solicit funds from Indian donors.

Weaponizing the Vanavasis

In the late 1990s, Infinity Foundation began discussions with Harvard scholars. This led to the funding of a series of Harvard Indology Round Tables by the foundation, with the German-American Indologist, Michael Witzel at the helm. Under this grant, scholars from various countries were brought to Harvard annually to work together on specific projects to do with ancient Indian history and archaeology. We met several eminent scholars, learned first-hand about their scholarship, understood the politics of academic research, and eventually were able to respond to them with our own scholarship. It was a significant learning exercise in *purva-paksha* (the systematic study of opposing viewpoints).

Something significant we discovered was Harvard's keen interest to study the Munda languages. This is a family of languages spoken in many parts of central India as well as Southeast Asia all the way to the aborigines of Australia. An early paper on this subject was presented at the Third Harvard Round Table on *Pre-History of Central and South Asia* sponsored by Infinity Foundation. The research was positioned as an aid in determining the possible Munda or Austroasiatic connection to the Indus Valley inscriptions and the substrate language in the early Vedic period.

We discovered that beneath this paper was a framework being researched and formulated at Harvard. Its implications were very serious. The thesis stated that the Aryan/Dravidian divide assumed by Western Indologists is incomplete, because neither the Aryans nor the Dravidians were the 'original inhabitants' of India. It was the Munda 'tribes' that preceded both. The aborigines in Australia are part of the same ancient family, the earliest Asians to occupy these lands.

According to this thesis, just as the Aryans conquered the Dravidians and pushed them down into south India, so also, *the Dravidians were the earlier conquerors from the West of India that invaded and overtook the Mundas of India.*

In other words, India's racial history has not two, but three layers. The first, and earliest, inhabitants were the Mundas who are now at the bottom. Then came the Dravidians to conquer and suppress them. And finally came the Aryans who suppressed both the Mundas and the Dravidians and are at the top.

By carefully cross-examining these scholars, it was clear to Malhotra that they wanted to encourage the fledgling Maoist movement in central India to incite separatism against India. The focus of these studies was to highlight the Munda languages as entirely different from Sanskrit as well as Tamil, making them the basis to show differences in culture and religion with the rest of India. The strategy was to highlight maximum dissimilarities from Hinduism and what they called the 'Sanskritized culture'. The Munda identity was blatantly framed as 'sub-nationalism'. They were being depicted as the Subaltern people to be championed as victims of oppression by *both* Aryans and Dravidians. India, in this scenario is an illegitimate nation created by foreign Aryans and Dravidians that oppresses the true natives.

Each of these three layers turned into their corresponding social groups today. The mapping on India's societal strata was being formulated as follows:

- Aryans ➜ Brahmins
- Dravidians ➜ Lower castes
- Mundas ➜ Tribals/Adivasis ➜ Dalits

This was not out of any genuine love for the Munda language or people, but rather to continue the fragmentation project started a century ago by the British and various missionaries. Once the foundation of a separate sub-nationalism is sown, a large amount of atrocity literature gets added to demonize certain people as oppressors. This turns into a deadly cocktail. The results are there for us to see.

Malhotra's attempts to alert Indians – government officials, gurus, academicians, politicians – failed because this seems like just another conspiracy theory. However, the result of this theory is presently evident in the Dalit movement to empower Vanavasis as 'tribals/Adivasis' by giving them an identity in conflict with the rest of India.

The Khalistanis and Kashmir Separatists

By the year 2000, a significant number of Indians living in the US began appreciating that Infinity Foundation had special first-hand expertise working with Harvard and the like on matters concerning India. This was when Pramathesh Rath, India's consul general in New York (2002-5) contacted Rajiv Malhotra, visited his home and invited him to the consulate, all for the purpose of picking his brain to understand the state of India studies in American universities, media, and schools. He was the first Indian in a position of authority to show interest.

One of the events Rath organized was a full-day seminar delivered by Rajiv Malhotra to a select list of influential invitees at the New York consulate. He expected them to be in sympathy with the range of issues Malhotra discussed. The response, however, was exactly the opposite. The attendees included many assumed to be friends of India, but when presented with uncomfortable details of the state of the discourse on India, they became defensive and closed ranks with the academic establishment. This was a wake-up call for Pramathesh Rath.

A few weeks later, Rath called Malhotra saying he was in his limousine on his way to Harvard where he was chief guest at a conference on India. He asked Malhotra for some pointers on what to say. Malhotra wanted to know who he would be sharing the stage with. Rath hadn't bothered to examine the list and just read out the names. That is when Malhotra informed him the list included well-known Kashmir separatists, Khalistanis, Pakistani scholars, and Indian extreme Leftists.

When Rath heard about their backgrounds, he understood he was being set up. This event was an ambush waiting for him at Harvard. He made the instant decision to return to New York and cancel his Harvard trip. It was shocking that India lacked (and still lacks) an effective research wing to monitor and track its opponents sitting in such a prominent place. This was just one of several similar encounters with Harvard-sponsored Breaking India forces.

Mapping Hindi on to Urdu

During our encounters with Harvard, we observed that their Hindi courses were not exactly teaching Hindi but Urdu, taught by Ali S.

Asani, a scholar of Indo-Muslim studies. Students taking these courses informed Infinity Foundation that Asani would mention on the very first day, that regardless of whether one had enrolled for Hindi or for Urdu, they would be learning the same things because the differences between the languages were unimportant.

Gradually, as the course proceeded, he would make Hindi seem as an inferior, and Urdu as the superior, language. Reading assignments, films screened, and cultural events would all feature Urdu as a language of beauty. He was looked up to as a father figure by the young and impressionable Indian students, one who would invite them to his residence for parties and gatherings. Asani is a well-known Muslim apologist who defends Islam's pluralism and human rights passionately at forums like the World Muslim Congress.[43]

He would carefully select Hindi reading assignments in which Hindu women bemoaned their culture, low caste and poor people spoke out in anger, and so forth. In other words, the Hindi content was generally negative unlike the positive Urdu content that discussed interesting and enjoyable issues.

At some point during the course, he would say that Hindi is too complex, and learning Urdu suffices. After the first level of the Hindi-Urdu course, each successive course in the series concentrated more on Urdu and with lesser focus on Hindi. By the time a student finished various 'Hindi' courses, the students would hate it and love Urdu.

We then spread our analysis of Harvard's Hindi-Urdu teaching among the community. Many parents were enraged. One Gujarati businessman sponsored a private teacher to teach a proper Hindi course, with permission from Harvard. Most Indian students migrated to that course and Asani felt abandoned. He pulled political strings with the help of people like Sugata Bose and had the competing Hindi course cancelled.

Asani has been determined to digest Hindi into Urdu and undermine Hindi as a separate language with its own beauty, literature, and ideas. This was something that took place around twenty years back and was one of the fights Infinity Foundation picked up with Harvard.

Indian Funding of Harvard University in the Early Years

Infinity Foundation Visiting Professorships

Infinity Foundation's initial approach to fix problems of academic bias was to fund institutions like Harvard in the hope they would change their approach. The foundation gave a grant to Harvard's Department of Sanskrit and Indian Studies the purpose of which was to bring a visiting professor to teach two topics we felt had been neglected:

1. India's contributions to Western civilization inadequately acknowledged.
2. Unfair treatment of Hinduism in the Western academy, i.e., Hinduphobia.

The first was Prof. Arvind Sharma, a renowned scholar of Hinduism at McGill University, Canada.[44] Our contact at Harvard was the well-known Indologist, Michael Witzel with whom we had numerous debates and disagreements, but also a respectful relationship of cooperation at the time. Witzel had confidentially shared with us that certain faculty members would most definitely oppose our plans.

Instead of identifying these topics the way true liberals should as the 'insider' perspective on Hinduism, there was a strong attack against the very idea of such a course before it could even start. According to some accounts, a team comprising three powerful faculty members tried to get the authorities to cancel the course. However, Witzel, as the host on behalf of Harvard of the visiting professorship, defended Sharma's courses. And so, they failed in getting the course canceled.

The following year, in 2002, Ashok Aklujkar, Sanskrit scholar and Indologist, and professor emeritus at the Department of Asian Studies at the University of British Columbia, became the second Infinity Foundation visiting professor at Harvard. He decided to play it safe and not engage in controversial topics. His wife, Vidyut Aklujkar, also a Sanskrit scholar, was given a lecturer's appointment at Harvard as well. Besides their teaching and research, they organized *Sangamani: A Conference for India Studies*, presenting a rare authentic portrayal of the Sanskrit tradition.[45] One of our goals was to put the spotlight on Prof. S.N. Sridhar, a linguist at the State University of New York, Stony Brook, so we could support his appointment as head of the Asia Center being planned there.

Infinity Foundation started alerting the community that South Asian Studies in America were replacing what was called Indology; this corresponded to a shift from Sanskrit-based studies of India to social sciences, hence the use of Left-wing lenses. In the case of China, however, it was not clubbed together with other neighbors into 'East Asia' and, instead, given its own prominence as China itself. The clubbing of India as one of eight South Asian countries was allowing Pakistan, Bangladesh, and others to each demand equal representation and voice in decision-making, at India's expense. Our campaign to call the programs Indic Studies or India Studies attracted pushback from the academicians.

Rejection by Dhirubhai Ambani

Sometime in the early 2000s, the late Rishi Kumar Mishra and his wife Renukaji visited the Infinity Foundation office in Princeton. Mishra was the late Dhirubhai Ambani's right-hand man and founder of the Observer Research Foundation set up by Ambani. They had heard of our opposition to places like Harvard and wanted specifically to get briefed on what to do about Harvard's request for Ambani to fund chairs there. After all, given Harvard's reputation, it was unusual for us to make a systematic argument against it. The couple spent a weekend at Infinity Foundation to hear out our concerns on Harvard.

Infinity Foundation brought in six scholars that were part of its team studying the state of South Asian Studies in the US. The presentations were eye-openers for Mishra, as he had never been made aware of the anti-India tilts at Harvard and the like. One talk compared how Harvard studies China with great respect, while India is seen through the human rights lens – caste, women's oppression, minority oppression, and so forth. Other presentations were about specific areas of biases such as the Aryan Invasion Theory. The result was that on his return, Mishra advised Dhirubhai Ambani to not give Harvard a single dollar until they made changes in their stance on India.

China, our team showed, gets treated as a serious civilization. One contributing factor is that China studies is done largely in Mandarin whereas India is studied in English. Also, China regulates visas for Western scholars such that it blacklists those it finds troubling, while India is open and welcomes everyone without supervision, and fails to do any analysis on the research undertaken. In fact, Indians take it as a compliment when Westerners study them, as though suffering from the inferiority complex of being ignored.

The intervention by Infinity Foundation was a temporary dampener on Harvard's crusade to dip into the pockets of rich Indians. And in the flurry of events that followed, where Harvard was campaigning to raise funds from Indian industry, Infinity Foundation was able to discourage potential donors. But all this put the foundation on Harvard's hit list. At around the same time, Infinity Foundation also ended its annual sponsorship of the Indology Round Table at Harvard.

The lure to become known at Harvard and dine with the who's who of the White American establishment is too powerful for Indians to resist. The real success for most wealthy Indians is when they are recognized and given a seat at the high table alongside White elites. Having studied Indian culture for centuries, this weakness is what the West knows and exploits well. It has used this knowledge to manage, control, and topple one raja after another in the seventeenth and eighteenth centuries. The British learned to take the wealthy Indian children to Cambridge, play polo with them, have White women available to flirt – so they could feel admitted to the club as honorary Whites in the presence of other Indians. After Independence, the Britishers got replaced by the Americans, hence the strategic importance of places like Harvard.

Anand Mahindra Jumps In

Infinity Foundation one day got a call from a prominent Indian that the Indian industrialist, Anand Mahindra was being roped in by Harvard, and he had given them office space at his Mumbai headquarters. Malhotra got an appointment for a personal one-on-one meeting with Mahindra and found him to be a very decent, gentle, and open-minded executive. He listened closely to the concerns expressed. He was unaware of these issues which clearly bothered him. But he also made clear that he owed a lot of personal moral debt to Harvard, as they had given him funding to support his studies. He said that for him, it was payback time, nothing more. Not to worry, he said, because he was giving only very small sums of money, such as twenty thousand dollars at a time, and that too for Indian students to visit as scholars.

Mahindra wanted to understand these objections concerning

Harvard so he could pass them on and make sure they changed their approach. A few days later, at Mahindra's suggestion, Malhotra had a brief phone chat with Harvard's Sugata Bose who was visiting India as their brand ambassador to raise funds. Malhotra had publicly criticized Sugata Bose for his writings that depict pre-Mughal India as uncivilized, exempt Islamic colonizers from criticisms, and promote the return to a unified South Asia under a quasi-Islamic civilization (positioned as 'secularism'). This, of course, his friend and co-author, Ayesha Jalal, had skilfully managed to incorporate into the core curriculum on South Asia at places such as Harvard. (Jalal, while not on the Harvard faculty, was on the committee of their South Asia program until Malhotra pointed out this strange anomaly, and then she suddenly stopped playing that role.) Bose was cordial and frank and agreed to continue to chat later with Malhotra – which never happened.

As we shall see in a later chapter, Anand Mahindra later donated ten million dollars to Harvard for the Humanities Center, which was then named after him. A straightforward and non-controversial man, Mahindra has never denied this.

Rajat Gupta

Around the year 2005, Infinity Foundation's Rajiv Malhotra and Krishnan Ramaswamy went to see Rajat Gupta (managing director of McKinsey at the time) to meet privately for several hours. The foundation explained that prior to Indian philanthropists giving funding to US universities, people like him should do 'due diligence' on what a given academic program has produced and how it compares with the philanthropist's image of India. We argued that no management consultant proposes an investment by his client in any venture without due diligence.

This struck a chord with Gupta. Malhotra and Ramaswamy pointed out that Infinity Foundation was the only organization that had attempted any such arm's length analysis of South Asian Studies in the US. It pointed that the Chinese government and their private donors prepared an annual report on the state of China Studies in the West, just like any industry analyst would do for an industry, and the report guides them where, and how, to invest. This gives the Chinese the basis for evaluating any given program and negotiating from a position of knowledge about the discipline.

Gupta was candid in confessing that he had not thought of it this way. He said that the persons involved in such India studies are good and decent folks. Malhotra responded that in evaluating a business investment, due diligence is not based on whether the management team were 'good guys' or decent folks at a personal level, but solely on objective criteria and evidence. He asked whether Gupta or anyone else to his knowledge had studied the writings of such India studies departments over the past fifty years, to be able to evaluate the situation from an Indian perspective. The answer to that remains the same today, no, they have not!

Lessons Learned

The result of the scrutiny of Harvard's position towards Indology and India, led the foundation to become increasingly public in its criticisms of the scholarship coming out of Harvard. A major turning point came in 2002 after Malhotra was invited to debate the top academic scholars of Hinduism at Harvard's annual American Academy of Religion Conference. This was a showdown between the camps of Wendy Doniger and Rajiv Malhotra. Harvard decided to throw its weight behind the Doniger camp. Jeffrey Kripal and Sarah Caldwell, both students of Doniger, got prestigious appointments at Harvard which they used to kick-start smear campaigns against Malhotra's critiques. A multipronged attack was launched with the full support of the Harvard cabal:

- The philosopher, Martha Nussbaum wrote a book titled, *The Clash Within*, in which she covered the Hindu thinkers in America she wanted to target, and Rajiv Malhotra was named as the primary person.[46]
- Jack Hawley, another peer of the same camp, started a project at Columbia University in which teams of students were sent to specific Hindu organizations to dig up dirt on them to be used to expose them. One of the five groups selected for targeting was Infinity Foundation. Among others was Swami Dayananda Saraswati's Arsha Vidya Gurukulam, where the FBI later showed up to make inquiries about their activities.
- Another prong of this attack was by Paul Courtright, exposed by

Rajiv Malhotra for his Hinduphobic writings on Lord Ganesha, who publicly stated in his campus tours across the US that he had reported to the FBI that certain 'Hindu extremists' were attacking him.

Since then, the Indian government and Indian billionaires have given major funding to Harvard for studies of South Asia – including both the ruling Bharatiya Janata Party and Congress-led governments. Yet there is not a single government or independent report on the state of this 'industry' that studies India, comprising several thousand full-time scholars from various disciplines – religious studies, history, anthropology, sociology, political science, human rights, and women's studies, among others. On the other hand, China Studies at the academy is secure in China's hands, with Western scholars positioned as outsiders craving to be allowed entry.

None of the reactions from 'Hindu activists' have made any effective impact because of their superficial nature and 'feel good' priority. Issuing petitions or writing angrily to their opponents is no good. They have failed to understand the deeper mechanisms at work. One doesn't fight a patient's ailment by holding placards and shouting slogans against the germs! The doctor must understand the mechanisms of the disease and figure out where and how to intervene. But a lazy, incompetent person (despite good intentions) would not go to medical school to learn all that, and *then* be ready to defeat the disease. He is in too much of a hurry, often lacks competence, and wants to make a big splash in public. And hence he stands outside the hospital shouting slogans against the germs. This may seem like a strange analogy, but if you closely examine Indian activists at work, many of them fit this picture.

8

China's Trojan Horse in America

Overview

India's precarious position in Western academia is perhaps best explained by contrasting it with China that also started from a position of disadvantage to skillfully maneuver itself into a position of strength. In this chapter, we take a short detour to look at China's positioning at Harvard. We will show how Chinese billionaires working in tandem with their government, use strategy and skill to drive Harvard's programs towards China's best interests. This is a significant study of contrasts that helps one understand the gravity of the situation India faces.

A major development of our times is the manner in which China has started showing off its technological prowess, for instance, its hypersonic missiles and target practices against mock-ups of US aircraft carriers. This has put China on a warpath to becoming the number one superpower. As China's status changes, it is apparent that it no longer needs to rely on the Western world. On the contrary, Western businesses need access to the Chinese market and have shown that they will compromise, if that's what it takes. The Chinese Communist Party (CCP) calls the shots on how Western business leaders behave. And there is a sense among Chinese intellectuals that it is now time for the rest of the world to adopt the worldview and culture of a dominant China. But this did not happen overnight. And Harvard was used by China as a part of its carefully crafted strategy to manage American opinion.

After studying the workings of American universities, the Chinese discovered how they are run like business organizations serving the interests of their funders and idealogues. Harvard, in particular, is able to offer more than the others in terms of its multinational network and influence at schools, companies, thinktanks, the public and governments around the world. This chapter details how Chinese funding has achieved the following specific targets involving each of these spheres of influence:

- At Harvard, the Chinese government's point of view is, at times, projected as the only relevant point of view on China. China's human rights abuses are seldom studied and have in fact been covered up. But Harvard regularly chides India on such issues. The US-China conferences have also served to build China's image.
- Harvard has continued to educate Chinese students and government officials on technology that would help China's development. This serves to strengthen China economically. But Harvard does not lecture China in the humanities and social sciences.
- China has funded Wokeism at Harvard and its distribution in America using the Harvard network. This has helped penetrate every facet of American life.
- Harvard and other American universities have close ties with the Chinese government and military and have been receiving funds from them. American universities providing military technology to China should be a concern for India.
- Representatives of American thinktanks and media are invited to China for participating in forums, thus increasing China's sphere of influence.

All this will be contrasted with Harvard's treatment of India in subsequent chapters.

China Enters Harvard University

China's entry into Harvard has been dramatic. It was in May of 1996 that a Hong Kong businesswoman Nina Kung,

> who wears her hair in pigtails, arrived unbidden in Harvard Yard. She had what Robert D. Blackwill, who runs the Russia and China programs for the Kennedy School [later the US ambassador to India], describes as 'an idea about Harvard helping interaction between American and Chinese elites'.[1]

The people Kung met at Harvard referred her to Joseph S. Nye Jr., dean of Harvard's Kennedy School of Government. She walked over to his office to present her plan. Her $3.3 billion in assets made her one of the richest women in the world at that time. She had high-level contacts in Beijing and had already cultivated close ties with then US president, Bill Clinton having become involved in his campaign fund-raising.

Kung's initial seven million dollars donation to Harvard was just the beginning of a long collaboration on terms set by China. Her program at Harvard's Kennedy School of Government won 'startlingly rapid approval from top brass of the People's Liberation Army', according to Robert D. Blackwill. He explained: 'We are not dealing with twenty-somethings here. These are senior Chinese military officers and civil servants. They are very serious people. They do nothing casually.'[2] Indeed, nothing done by China at Harvard has been casual ever since. Even President Xi Jinping's close relationship with it was skillfully developed when his daughter was there back in 2012.

During the past quarter century, China has pursued a long-term strategy at Harvard that requires foresight, consistency, attention to details of implementation, as well as endurance to withstand pain in the short-term. China entangled itself with the West in a very cunning and calculated way. Until very recently, every US administration was convinced that it was helping develop China into a major friend in the global system of free enterprise and multilateral institutions. The counterarguments, that it was feeding and building up its worst enemy, were never taken seriously.

But like everything else about China, its relationship with Western academics is complex and paradoxical. It has been building one of the world's strongest nationalist narratives for its citizens, while committing horrific human rights violations in Tibet, Xinjiang, and Hong Kong. This led it to outright reject the fashionable Left-wing social sciences the West wants to export to the entire world. One of China's amazing achievements has been its co-opting of Harvard despite it being the bastion of the intellectual Left. As a result of this co-opting, Harvard scholars have accepted that their social justice ideas are out of bounds while engaging with China.

To set the stage for subsequent chapters that discuss the various entanglements of Harvard with India's institutions – government, industry, media, and education – the reader must understand how China enjoys a completely different kind of relationship with Harvard. China's dealings with the institution demonstrate tremendous confidence and it has committed serious resources to realize its pernicious agenda of buying influence. This has been called 'sharp power' and goes beyond mere soft power. China's strategy is long-term, and its methods are coercive, opaque, and uncompromising.

Frankly, we were not surprised to find that China occupies a much stronger position than India at Harvard. But we discovered something far more worrisome: China's inroads into Harvard are also a gateway for it to penetrate India with influence and subversion.

Only in recent times has the US started waking up to the fact that its best institutions have been compromised by Chinese money. A 2019 Hoover Institution report raised serious concerns about Chinese infiltration of American thinktanks, media, and academic institutions.[3] The epicenter of this infiltration is the Harvard Kennedy School where China hires the finest American minds to implement its well-thought-out agenda on an unprecedented scale.

Harvard's dealings with the CCP are deep, extensive, and old. This is now being discussed as a risk to American national security, but as we shall see, it is also a risk to India. This chapter will expose that Harvard's coziness with China violates its image as the champion of democracy, human rights, and social justice it portrays to the world, and especially to India. Unfortunately, the Indian elites are clueless about this, and to the contrary, are complicit in making India vulnerable not only to the West but also to China.

China's influence at Harvard is illustrated by the story of Teng Biao, a Chinese dissident and activist who fled the country to come to Harvard through the Scholars at Risk program. Once at Harvard, Biao expected to have total freedom to criticize his country; after all, that was the very reason he had fled China. So, he organized a discussion at Harvard with fellow dissidents from Hong Kong with a shared history of being critical of the CCP. But to Biao's complete dismay, the associate dean of Harvard Law School *ordered Biao to cancel the event, claiming that it would 'embarrass' the university*. So much for protecting free speech and standing up for human rights.[4] A report in *The Harvard Crimson* admits:

... cancellation of Teng's event ... revealed that the University isn't immune from the CCP's reach. ... a reminder that Harvard's relationship with China doesn't exist in a vacuum. Even if higher education at times provides an alternative space for international dialogue and informal critique, the University cannot categorically evade the conflicting interests of state and academia, of politics and truth.[5]

There have been several reports about Harvard receiving large sums of Chinese money, indicating that corruption and greed at the institution has given the Chinese a seat at the high table from where it is calling the shots. This strategy to compromise Harvard's intellectuals has been accomplished meticulously over several decades.

Scholars are funded to help package China's political positions in ways that the West finds palatable; these narratives are then amplified using the credibility of the scholars and their access to media networks. In effect, Harvard has functioned as an important public relations arm of the CCP targeting the broad spectrum of American elites.

In later chapters we will detail how Harvard persistently, and extensively, attacks India on human rights and rebukes it for threatening democracy. On the other hand, its pro-China scholars control the very same issues in the case of China and silence all attempts to draw attention to these concerns. For example, in contrast to its discussions on India:

- We do not see Harvard rushing to organize conferences and seminars to highlight pro-democracy dissenters in China.
- Harvard does not delve much into the issue of Tibetan freedom, the democracy movement in Hong Kong, Taiwanese independence, China's monitoring of its citizens through a social credit system, China's crackdown on Mongolian culture and language or the human rights crisis of Uyghur Muslims.
- It does not discuss problems like the disappearance of well-known Chinese citizens who suddenly resurface only to publicly apologize.
- Harvard is silent on the Chinese government's muzzling and suppressing of Jack Ma (the billionaire founder of Alibaba Group) for becoming too successful and outspoken.
- There is no discussion on how a successful school tutoring

company in China was forced overnight to become a non-profit.

Harvard Praises China	• Harvard President Lawrence S. Bacow tells Xi Jinping it is 'Admirable that the Chinese Government Attaches Great Importance to Higher Education and Makes Huge Efforts in this Regard' • Confirmed Harvard will Continue Exchanges and Cooperation with Chinese Educational and Scientific Research Institutions*
Harvard Silent or Muted	• Tibet, Dalai Lama • Inner Mongolian Language/Culture • Pro-Democracy Movement in Hong Kong • Taiwanese Independence • Uyghur Muslims • Disappearance of Dissident Citizens
Harvard Helps China	• Training CCP Fellows that Run Uyghur Detention Camps • Social Credit System • Propaganda for CCP • Chinese Geopolitical Interests in India • Solving China's Environmental, Logistics, and Infrastructure Problems

* http://english.www.gov.cn/news/top_news/2019/03/20/content_281476571167688.htm

Harvard in particular, has a history of prioritizing self-interest above all: It supported South African apartheid by continuing its investments even when others pulled out, and despite protests on campus.[6] However, what makes its relationship with China so different is Harvard's active support of the Chinese regime. Even *The Harvard Crimson* criticizes Harvard for lacking basic human decency:

> Yet its attitude towards China — the silent abetting of a regime so outrageous in its actions, the willingness to use its influential brand to praise propagandistic institutions, the shoulder-rubbing with the chief executors of a humanitarian catastrophe — stands out as a particularly disgraceful stain on our history, a concerning disregard for basic human decency.[7]

American universities clearly understand the consequences of stepping on Chinese toes. For example, when University of California, San Diego, (UCSD) invited the Dalai Lama to its campus, it provoked the CCP. Many Chinese students on campus were organized to support the CCP's stance on Tibet and protest the Dalai Lama's visit:

> Many overseas Chinese students at UCSD view the Dalai Lama not as a messenger of world harmony, ... but as a separatist keen on splitting China and as a symbol of their country's feudal past. It's a view promoted by the Communist Party of China, which strictly controls within its borders what can and cannot be said about Tibet and the Dalai Lama, along with the 1989 Tiananmen Square massacre and relations with Taiwan ....[8]

An article titled, *Is China Punishing a U.S. University for Hosting the Dalai Lama?* explains the repercussions UCSD faced as China froze visas to its visiting scholars among other measures.[9] This was a way to send a clear message not to interfere with what China considers its internal affairs. Harvard has toed this line meticulously.

Harvard's Fairbank Center for Chinese Studies has held a series of conferences on Tibet over the past two decades that play along with Chinese interests but yielded no tangible benefit to Tibetans. Tibetan speakers were contained by the design of these forums in terms of format, framing of issues, and moderation. On the other hand, these forums presented the official Chinese government posture with no remorse or shame for all its human rights abuses. For instance, one of the speakers was Zhu Xiaoming, head of the Nationalities and Religion Bureau at the United Front Work Department in Beijing, which is responsible for internally managing China's Tibet policy. His position was:

> I think the negotiation should mainly discuss such questions as how the Dalai Lama and his followers should give up their stand for independence, stop carrying out separatist activities and contribute to the reunification of the motherland and national unity and progress, but not the question related to the legal and political status of Tibet. Tibet is an inalienable part of China. What questions does the US Congress want the Chinese Government

to negotiate with the Dalai Lama? The status of Tibet, a 'high-level autonomy', or other questions? All these questions are not negotiable.[10]

Zhu Xiaoming has gone as far as to claim that under Chinese rule, Tibet was a model of progress and human development that was never seen under Tibetan self-rule.[11] In other words, China's occupation of Tibet was for its own benefit. Since the Chinese generally outnumbered the Tibetan side, it was easy to divert, dismiss as false, or ignore all questions related to Tibet's autonomy from China or even as a separate state within China. There were no discussions on the many human rights abuses by the Han Chinese in Tibet, and the annihilation of Tibetan culture. Of course, Harvard has never tried to construct Subaltern identities within China or study the human rights abuses against its women and minorities the way that it has done in the case of India. Nor has it been necessary to blame the Chinese culture or civilization for these transgressions the way all wrongs in India are somehow traced back to its ancient culture.

The Harvard Kennedy School has the notoriety of training two CCP officials, Erken Tuniyaz and Yao Ning, that oversee the concentration camps for Uyghur Muslims. The Harvard Kennedy School graduates 'built or expanded nine detention centers since 2017', stated a report in the *Financial Times*:

> Two officials involved in overseeing China's detention camps for about 1m ethnic minority people in Xinjiang have studied on coveted fellowships at Harvard University ...
>
> Yao Ning, a local Communist party secretary who was honoured this year by Beijing for his work in Xinjiang, studied as an Asia fellow at Harvard University's Ash Center for Democratic Governance and Innovation between 2010 and 2011, according to the Australian Strategic Policy Institute.
>
> Erken Tuniyaz, chairman of the region, spent a few months at the Ash Centre as a new world fellow in 2012. Xinjiang's chair ranks as the region's top official after Chen Quanguo, party secretary ... Tuniyaz defended Xinjiang's internment camps as "counter-terrorism and deradicalisation measures". In an article published in 2012, the Ash Centre said the research of Tuniyaz and a colleague at Harvard "promises to inform their professional

careers and enrich the Center's portfolio of scholarship on innovation and democratic governance.[12]

Yao, 36, studied at Harvard as part of his PhD in public policy at China's Tsinghua University. ...he worked in Xinjiang's Kashgar prefecture, first in Yengisheher county ... predominantly Uyghur, and then in Maralbeshi (sic) county, said the Aspi (sic) report. In early 2019, Yao Ning was appointed party secretary of Maralbeshi (sic) County ... where ASPI researchers have identified nine detention facilities built or expanded since 2017," the report added.[13]

Harvard's Roy and Lila Ash Center for Democratic Governance and Innovation claims that in its training and fellowship programmes for Chinese participants, candidates are accepted only after being vetted by the US embassy in Beijing. Yet, those Chinese officials with serious records of violating human rights somehow slip past this vetting, even though the US government has openly accused Beijing of turning Xinjiang into an 'open-air prison'.[14]

The Ash Center flaunted its relationship with the two Chinese fellows in its program stating that they were among the 'new world fellows' it has selected. Harvard says it has brought

> a host of civil servants, policymakers and promising new leaders to further enhance their skills and broaden their capacity on relevant research ... Not only does the fellows program equip the next generation of Chinese with pertinent academic and government experience, the program also serves as a bridge between the US and China for future collaboration and knowledge sharing.[15]

In an interesting twist of fate and irony, Erken Tuniyaz, whom Harvard trained to 'bridge (the) US-China relationship', was later put on the US Department of Treasury Specially Designated Nationals (SDN) list.[16] The SDN is a blacklist maintained by the US under the Office of Foreign Assets Control:

> ... OFAC [Office of Foreign Assets Control] publishes a list of individuals and companies owned or controlled by, or acting for or on behalf of, targeted countries. It also lists individuals, groups, and entities, such as terrorists and narcotics traffickers designated

under programs that are not country-specific. Collectively, such individuals and companies are called "Specially Designated Nationals" or "SDNs." Their assets are blocked and U.S. persons are generally prohibited from dealing with them.[17]

Tuniyaz's assets are now frozen in the US, and every American institution including Harvard is banned from dealing with him.

Harvard did not as much as issue a statement to distance itself from such Harvard fellows for fear of upsetting the Chinese. This contrasts with the way Harvard scholars and numerous programs and events routinely focus on attacking India. The most favored topics on India at Harvard include criticizing the Citizenship (Amendment) Act, 2019 (CAA), removal of Article 370 on Kashmir, Hindu chauvinism, caste abuses, women's abuses, mistreatment of Muslims, and so forth. Harvard blacklisted Narendra Modi before he became India's prime minister, and continues to slam him personally as well as his party, the BJP, for every imaginable kind of human rights violation, even when he has been cleared by Indian courts.

Another hypocrisy is Harvard's claim to champion free speech, an argument it used to terminate Indian economics professor, Subramanian Swamy. Harvard's complaint against him was over his statement that India's Muslims had Hindu ancestors. This should have been debated at Harvard to nurture free thinking among its students. After all, Indian Muslims do not prefer calling their ancestors foreign invaders from the Middle East. Hence, who else could have been their ancestors if not the natives of India, i.e., Hindus?

We do not endorse Harvard's capitulation to China but are pointing out that India needs to learn how the game is played. A middle road needs to be found that balances protection of self-interest and academic freedom.

Chinese Funding

China funds American institutions through an intricate network of state-controlled entities and private businesses. For example, one of the donors at Ash Center is the China Southern Power Grid Company Ltd., wholly owned, operated, and funded by the Chinese government, and whose management is 'directly appointed by China's central government'.[18]

> Further donations also come from New World China Enterprises
> Project, a Chinese company whose board is composed almost
> entirely of CCP members. Its Chairman and Executive Director,
> Cheng Kar-Shun, for example, has served as a Standing Committee
> Member of the CCP's Political Consultative Conference. [19]

It is no wonder that Harvard was placed on the US Department of
Justice's radar for failing to disclose millions in foreign gifts from China.
And unfortunately, it is not the only American institution that has been
growing under Chinese influence.

According to the US Department of Education, the top three
American universities accepting Chinese funds since 2013 are Harvard
University, the University of Southern California, and the University
of Pennsylvania.[20] Stanford too is a big collaborator with China.[21] The
US government is concerned about the depth and breadth of China's
infiltration into key American institutions:

> A letter from DOE general counsel Rubinstein to Sen. Rob
> Portman (R-Ohio), the chairman of the committee that authored
> the report, said China's Communist Party 'invests strategically' in
> the U.S. education system and that 'the public lacks an accurate
> or complete picture of China's overall spending because nearly
> 70% of colleges and universities who accepted such donations
> from China failed to report them.' It said Chinese money comes
> with 'strings that can compromise academic freedom.'[22]

To probe China's penetration into US educational institutions, the
Department of Education has initiated an investigation into Harvard and
Yale for failing to report the foreign money received. These investigations
also revealed other shady dealings. For instance, Charles M. Lieber,
chair of Harvard's Department of Chemistry and Chemical Biology was
arrested for 'making "false, fictitious, and fraudulent statements" to the
US Department of Defense about his ties to a Chinese government
program to recruit foreign scientists and researchers'.[23] 'Lieber, who led
a group focused on nanoscience, had established a research lab in China's
central city of Wuhan, apparently without the university's knowledge'.[24]

The investigations are part of a bigger probe that have 'triggered the reporting of approximately $6.5 billion in previously undisclosed foreign money, much of it from China, Saudi Arabia, Qatar and the United Arab Emirates'.[25] Other universities under investigation are Georgetown University, Texas A&M University, Cornell University, Rutgers University, MIT and University of Maryland.[26] American authorities are also clamping down on Chinese students coming to American colleges.[27]

China Funds Wokeism in America

Foreign dictators often fund corporations through mechanisms that sound benign. Ramaswamy says that 'foreign dictators use the moral stature of woke corporations to whitewash their own oppression and also to damage the moral standing of the United States on the global stage'.[28] A good example is the way the CCP encourages Wokeism in other countries but bans it at home. Ramaswamy explains:

> The CCP flexes its muscle as a gatekeeper to the Chinese market to convince corporations to spread the CCP's own values abroad. It does this simply through the rise of woke capitalism – with companies like Disney, Marriott, Apple, or the NBA expressing their moral outrage about injustices like "systemic racism" and transphobia in the United States while staying completely silent about human rights abuses like concentration camps, forced sterilization of religious minorities, and beatings of innocent civilians in China.[29]
>
> Foreign authoritarian nations understand the weaknesses of America's new stakeholder model far better than America does and ruthlessly leverage their stakeholder status to selectively determine which causes the woke capitalists throw their weight behind. The NBA can put "Black Lives Matter" on all its courts because the CCP isn't threatened by that message. But the Communist Party would never allow the NBA or any of its employees to breathe a word in support of Hong Kong, Taiwan, or the Uighurs.[30]

We would add Tibet to the list of taboo topics that was at the center of activism against China until recently. But the Chinese seem to have succeeded in neutralizing those voices in the US. What this shows is how successfully the CCP has turned American and other multinationals into Trojan Horses to spread their long-term messaging. Ramaswamy sums up that 'woke capitalists in America get to make money with their dictator buddies abroad and act like they're saving the world back home'.[31]

According to a *Wall Street Journal* article, a new Chinese law has forced America's top universities including Harvard and Princeton to put warning labels on courses if they include any material that China considers sensitive. This is a large list that China continually expands. 'In response, Princeton students studying Chinese politics have started using secret codes instead of their real names on their assignments to protect their identities'.[32]

Ramaswamy says: 'The same companies that have improved consumer access and lowered the prices of technology are also the ones limiting options in the marketplace of ideas and raising the "cost" of ideological dissent.'[33] He calls this 'idea-fixing' and feels the anti-trust laws designed to fight price-fixing should be expanded to cover idea-fixing as well.

It is unfortunate that the US has been gamified by China on American campuses and removing China's deeply entrenched tentacles will be neither quick nor easy.

Harvard Kennedy School's China Program

Harvard Kennedy School has modified its multifaceted China program to better serve Chinese interests. Some of the past China related programs that have been cancelled were for training Chinese bureaucrats in governance, leadership, crisis management, and sustainability. These are listed under 'previous projects' on the HKS website.[34]

China's Carrots	China's Sticks
Strategic Funding	Block Access to China, Libraries, and Archives
Scholars Bought Out	Deny Visas to Scholars
Soft Lobbying	Close Joint Ventures that Give US Universities Access to China
Foreign Thinktanks, Institutions, Government, and Universities Bought Out	Use US Business Leaders that are Dependent on Chinese Markets to Put Pressure on Harvard

New projects are evidence of a strong, prudent, and focused China using Harvard to accomplish its strategic interests, and not the other way around. From the project descriptions, it is obvious that China is calling the shots and is very clear on seeking the following from Harvard:

- Make China the world's leading technology innovator
- Solve China's environmental problems as per its priorities
- Help China with logistics and infrastructure, such as streamlining China's social credit system
- Facilitate philanthropy funds for its education system infrastructure
- Be an extension of China's propaganda machine by showing that the Chinese people support their government, and that Communism has been a wonderful system to uplift China

It is important to note that China defines each of these goals and supplies the criteria for monitoring their success.

A good example of how China's propaganda machinery works in the US is HKS' partnership with the China Global Philanthropy Institute (CGPI) to launch the Global Leaders in Philanthropy Program. The CGPI is a Chinese NGO, except for two prominent foreign donors on its board, Microsoft's Bill Gates and Ray (Raymond Thomas) Dalio. Dalio is the billionaire founder of Bridgewater Associates, the world's largest hedge fund firm. In exchange for his support, the Chinese government gave Dalio approval to sell investment products to institutional, and high net worth investors in China.[35] During a *CNBC* interview, Dalio was asked how he reconciled human rights violations of the Uyghurs detained in Chinese concentration camps. He ducked the question saying he 'can't be an expert in those types of things'. He added that the US too has many social justice issues and that he did not want to get into politics. His job, he said, was 'to follow the rules':

> I look at the United States and I say, 'Well, what's going on in the United States and should I not invest in the United States because our own human rights issues and other things? and I'm not trying to make political comparisons, I (sic) basically just trying to follow the rules understand what's going on and invest properly.'[36]

The *CNBC* host called out Dalio on the flawed comparison, saying that while the US may not be perfect, the situation cannot be equated with China where people are made to disappear by the government. Dalio responded that while the US is a country of individuals and individualism, 'in China the government "is an extension of the family. ...As a top-down country what they are doing is they behave like a strict parent"'.[37]

Dalio's dismissal of the Uyghur human rights atrocities by explaining it as China acting like a 'strict parent' sits well with HKS. The HKS is perfectly comfortable with receiving funds for the 'Dalio Fellowships' that bring Chinese students to study in the China Program of HKS.[38] Anti-China candidates are filtered out of these fellowships.

Dalio himself has close ties to the CCP:

> Dalio is actually deeply knowledgeable about how things work in China. He has called Wang Qishan, the second most powerful man in the Chinese Communist Party, a "personal hero." In his 2017 book, *Principles*, Dalio confessed, "Every time I speak with Wang, I feel like I get closer to cracking the unifying code that unlocks the laws of the universe."[39]

The Chinese government has created a 'whitelist' to reward academics, scholars and businesspeople who speak positively about the US-China relationship and overlook Chinese human rights abuses. They are rewarded with contacts, multiple entry visas and other favors.[40] One radio station based in Washington D.C. has been paid millions of dollars by China to air its propaganda.[41] To be in China's good books, many American firms have formally apologized for their transgressions against Chinese interests.[42]

It is ironic that American businessmen go so far out to appease China and get on its 'whitelist' when the country has a long track record of stealing American Intellectual Property. In 2020, William Evanina, the then-director of the US National Counterintelligence and Security Center, stated that 'Chinese IP theft costs U.S. companies between $300 billion and $600 billion annually'.[43] The FBI report he cited stated that the Chinese Intellectual Property threat was the biggest law enforcement challenge for the FBI. Confirming this, a survey by *CNBC* found that one in five US corporations claimed that China had stolen their IP in the previous year.[44]

Harvard lectures India on the Western ways of philanthropy, but where China is concerned, it is the other way around. The HKS China Philanthropy Project pursues research on 'precedents and models of philanthropic giving' by using models which have, according to HKS, 'ideological, institutional, social and political similarities to China, but have remained understudied'.[45] This HKS program studies ex-Communist/Socialist countries like Russia and Eastern Europe to suggest solutions that fit the CCP's ethos and vision:

> ... we bring together scholars and practitioners from areas of the world that have clear ideological, institutional, social and political similarities to China, but have remained understudied. Russia and Eastern Europe are transitional political economies that share aspects of political and institutional foundations with China, and offer lessons for how philanthropic activities are shaped by - and interact with - the state. Philanthropic practices of Chinese in Southeast Asia offer instructive insights into geographies with cultural similarities to China. This project also includes a significant focus on China itself - what traditions does China draw upon and what precedents of state/society dynamics in limiting the growth of philanthropy persist to this day in China? This ... will result in a series of symposia, policy briefs, scholarly articles, and seed further fellowship collaboration internationally. [46]

Post 2013, the Harvard China conferences have been mainly on the

US-China relationship to show that China has come of age as a major superpower on the world stage.[47] A practical project of technological benefit is the Bay Area Development and Innovation Research Project being carried out for the Chinese Association of Development Strategy Studies. Its goal is to help the Chinese client build an ecosystem for innovation that they lack, by studying the factors that make true smart cities that spawn tech innovation:[48]

> The project will study the historical experience of the development of Shenzen Bay area; carry out comparative studies of different bay area development models including the Massachusetts Bay area; and strengthen the research base in the field of bay area development among China, the United States and relevant global bay areas. ...the Ash Center will be convening a number of Global Bay Area Forums to bring together scholars and practitioners from various Bay Area regions to discuss issues related to regional development and public sector innovation.[49]

Another project theme at HKS is China and Globalization, which too, veers away from politics and focuses instead on development and infrastructure in China.

The HKS Ash Center offers executive education to the Chinese under various programs:

> The China Leaders in Finance Program is a two-week program for senior executives from China's banking sector: 'Program skill sets relate to negotiation, corporate strategy, attracting 21st Century talent, and supporting innovation, among others'.[50]
>
> The Dalio Foundation funded Executive Leaders in Philanthropy Program aims to help leaders build effective public value organizations.
>
> The two-week Shanghai Executive Management Program aims to teach municipal agency officials 'strategy, leadership, management of service delivery, urban planning and development, crisis management, and social policy, as practiced in the United States and other countries'.[51]

All these activities carefully avoid dealing with issues like social justice, minorities, human rights, free speech and so on.

The funds from the Chinese government and businessmen with close links to the CCP that flow into US universities are receiving close attention. A Hoover Institution report mentions that China-United States Exchange Foundation (CUSEF) funds several US educational institutions, thinktanks, and non-profit organizations.[52] The HKS has a partnership with CUSEF whose mission has been to buy influence and spread Chinese Communist Party propaganda by targeting American universities through funding policy research, media coverage, and exchange programs.[53] Both, the CUSEF and HKS have also collaborated on several research projects.[54]

As part of the CUSEF partnership, the HKS sends student delegations to China on all-expenses paid trips:

> CUSEF was established in 2008 on the initiative of former Hong Kong chief executive and shipping magnate Tung Chee Hwa (C.H. Tung) who continues to be the chairman of the foundation. Tung is also the vice chairman of the Chinese People's Political Consultative Conference (CPPCC), China's highest-level "united front" organization and he attended the Communist Party's 19th Congress in October 2017. Moreover, *the number of mainland-based members of the foundation's official advisors and the foundation's easy connections with Chinese government organs belie the foundation's assertion that it is independent of the Chinese Communist Party and the PRC government. CUSEF undertakes a range of programs aimed at Americans that can accurately be described as "influence-seeking activities"; as such, it has registered in the United States under the Foreign Agent Registration Act (FARA).* Its lobbying activities include sponsoring all-expense-paid tours of China for delegations composed of what the foundation's website refers to as "thought leaders," including journalists and editors, think-tank specialists, and city and state officials.[55] (Emphasis added)
>
> In addition to meeting with Chinese Communist Party officials and state-run think tanks, schools, and influence groups, (HKS) delegation members reveal they've also <u>toured</u> Huawei facilities. CUSEF brochures contain pictures of the (HKS) delegation, showing students being lectured by professors at

state-run Peking University and by a former Major General of the People's Liberation Army.[56]

The HKS delegation was headed by a person of Indian origin, Sanjay Seth, who gave glowing reports about the China trip: 'CUSEF promotional brochures also feature testimonials from students, some of which praise China as a country that has made such incredible progress'.[57] Seth said:

> The delegation hopes to deepen their understanding of China's development through this visit and are willing to try their best to make positive efforts to deepen the friendship between the peoples of the U.S. and China and to enhance bilateral youth exchanges.[58]

According to a report by *The National Pulse*, the US Department of Justice's Foreign Agent Registration Act filings revealed 'a relationship spanning over a decade between establishment media outlets and the China–United States Exchange Foundation (CUSEF)'.[59] The article was titled *All Major Western Media Outlets Take "Private Dinners", "Sponsored Trips" From Chinese Communist Propaganda Front*.[60] It called out the involvement of *The New York Times, The Washington Post, CNN, Reuters, ABC News, The Economist, The Wall Street Journal, Agence France-Presse, TIME* magazine, *Los Angeles Times, The Hill, BBC,* and *The Atlantic* as well as most other well-known print media and TV outlets. A private Chinese lobby hosted dinners and meetings with CUSEF officials and arranged 'familiarization trips' to China for well-known media houses with an aim to spread propaganda about China.

> A 2011 FARA filing highlighted by Axios detailed CUSEF's agreement with American lobbying firm BLJ. It outlines how CUSEF set out to "effectively disseminate positive messages to the media, key influencers and opinion leaders, and the general public" regarding China.[61]

Not to be left out, the *Harvard Business Review* also joined the trip to China in 2015, indicating that the institution is compromised.

Unlike the Indian government and Indian billionaires, China and its business leaders are hard negotiators with their US partners. Their demands are sharp and well-defined, and many US institutions oblige in exchange for the vast sums of money they stand to gain. Below is another concrete example:

> A leading Washington, DC, university was approached by a Chinese university with a proposal for a $500,000 annual grant to establish a Center for Chinese studies in partnership with the Chinese university. The Chinese side had three main conditions ... : (1) that a series of Chinese officials and other visitors would be given public platforms for frequent speeches; (2) that faculty from the Chinese partner university could teach China courses on the US university campus; and (3) that new Chinese Studies courses would be added to the university curriculum.[62]

Clearly, China wants to educate the world with its own narrative and not let the Ivy Leagues write a critical narrative as is the case with India. To accomplish this, it has influenced senior persons at Harvard and been able to dictate the terms of the collaborations. In India's case, we shall show that Harvard has used the billionaires to penetrate the country through a network of programs that are spreading like wildfire both in the US and India.

Harvard's China-friendly Scholars

China's heavy-handed rule restricting basic freedoms of its citizens is no secret. However, it has ambitions of spreading its own values, language, and culture for the rest of the world to adopt. And Harvard scholars help to legitimize the China narrative. An interesting example is a survey conducted by Harvard's Roy and Lila Ash Center to demonstrate the resilience of China's Communist system; it concluded that CCP enjoyed the overwhelming support of its citizens.[63]

> The July 2020 report "Understanding CCP Resilience: Surveying Chinese Public Opinion Through Time" contends that the Chinese Communist Party (CCP) is "as strong as ever" and "under no imminent threat of popular upheaval."[64]

The poll was conducted by Horizon Research Consultancy Group, a Chinese company run by a former high-ranking CCP official. However, to prevent suspicion, Harvard withheld Horizon's name in its research report.[65] Foreign policy experts have doubted the authenticity of the report's findings.[66]

> The Harvard study, conducted by scholars affiliated with the school's Ash Center for Democratic Governance tracked public approval for the Chinese central government—as well as lower levels of government—between 2003 and 2016. ... public approval for all levels of government has increased during the 13-year period. The researchers published their findings in an academic journal in late 2019 and once again as a "policy brief" in July 2020.[67]
>
> In addition to concealing the researchers' ties with Horizon Research, the Harvard reports did not discuss the possibility that respondents might feel less comfortable giving honest answers to political questions. Cooper, the AEI scholar, said these ... studies should mention the possible impact of political pressure on the survey data. "I don't think there's anything wrong with attempting to do polling in China as long as you explain very clearly who was polled under what circumstances and note the fact that they may not have felt free to respond accurately," he said. "But if they didn't present that data, I think it's problematic."[68]

Edward Cunningham, one of the authors of the study, received $2.3 million from China Southern Power Grid Company, along with $3.9 million from the Tianfu Group, a China-based, billion-dollar management company.[69] The conflict of interest has been pointed out publicly, but Harvard remains steadfast in its opposition to change:

> Such financial ties call into question the Ash Center's (sic) to report objectively on the same government that gate-keeps many of the business deals the center's lead researchers appear to be involved with.[70]

Prof. Anthony Saich, director of the Harvard Roy and Lila Ash Center for Democratic Governance and Innovation, was another researcher in the study who worked with Horizon Research. Saich is a recipient of many awards from the Chinese government and is a trustee of the National Committee on United States-China Relations, a pro-China lobby group.[71] Such conflicts of interest abound. It is also a testament to China's successful grooming of pro-China scholars.

Like many China-funded researchers, Saich is extremely sympathetic to China and reluctant to call out its egregious human rights violations, let alone putting pressure. While India is looked upon very harshly by Harvard, China is constantly praised for its progress in human rights over the past three decades. It is never judged objectively on human rights and social justice but is instead applauded for the progress it has made. Research funded by China makes academicians take a gentler, and more accommodating, view. Saich is openly a China apologist, asking Americans to be patient for China to first become even stronger and then hope it will become more open:

> ... we misunderstand the Chinese from multiple levels. First, they are not really a threat to the US, which is the way its (sic) been often presented. ... As its economy becomes more sophisticated, as it develops more of an urban middle class, the pressure will increase for greater political freedom as well as the greater economic freedom that is already been a product to reforms in China. ... they will throw off the shackles. There's no doubt that China is a much freer much easier place to live in then it was 30 years ago.[72]

Anti-India and Pro-China Pivot

To illustrate that Harvard's pro-China position often corresponds to its anti-India posture, we take the case of the very powerful Harvard professor, Nicholas Burns.

Burns' very close ties to the CCP developed when he worked for a consulting firm that was part of the CCP's lobbying network in the US. He has been criticized as someone too close to the Chinese.

> Nick Burns – is a former adviser to a consulting firm employing Chinese Communist Party officials, a board member of a Harvard University program collaborating with China's military, and a contributor to Chinese state-run media outlets.[73]

Burns served as senior counselor at The Cohen Group founded by former US president, Bill Clinton's defense secretary, Bill Cohen. The Cohen Group is known to work closely with ex-CCP officials and is active in various Washington D.C.-based China lobbying groups. The group has also advised an entity sanctioned by former president, Donald Trump for human rights abuses against Uyghurs in Xinjiang.[74]

The Cohen Group's China Practice boasts that it facilitates 'constructive engagement and cooperation between leading multinational companies and Chinese enterprises around the world' and 'supports Chinese companies engaged in high-quality investments overseas'. To cement its relationship with China, The Cohen Group has two China-based offices in Beijing and Tianjin for over a decade. Burns has also appeared on Chinese state-run media outlets including China Global Television Network.[75]

Burns is on the board of HKS' Robert and Renée Belfer Center for Science and International Affairs, that has hosted cybersecurity drills with CCP government and military officials:

> The group roleplayed "fictitious cyber scenarios" and discussed sensitive technology matters relating to artificial intelligence, Huawei, arms control frameworks, ... Both sides worked through a fictitious cyber scenario to discuss what their respective governments and companies would do in the face of a third party cyber attack on critical infrastructure. The working group also discussed ... IP theft, supply chain security and ... and controlling the spread of malware over the dark web.[76]

Burns has assumed even greater significance because the current Biden administration has appointed him as US ambassador to China. In his new position, it will be interesting to see how Burns tackles the Uyghur human rights crisis in China. His track record over many years has been extremely sympathetic to China. 'We can't see them as the enemy because we need them,' Burns remarked in reference to China at a 2020 Aspen Institute event.[77]

But he has no qualms about calling out what he considers to be India's mistakes. In a 2020 article titled *On India, the U.S. Must Think Bigger*, he wrote: 'India would be well advised to temper those who practice an often-ugly Hindu nationalist agenda to the detriment of the country's large Muslim minority'.[78]

Clearly, Harvard Kennedy School with its various centers is well positioned to intervene in India's domestic affairs. This can, for example, be inferred from Nicholas Burns' invitation to Rahul Gandhi of the Congress Party in 2020 to its *Future of Diplomacy Project.* At the high-profile event, the naïve and vulnerable Gandhi poured out his grievances against Indian democracy to Burns' sympathetic ears. Pandering to Harvard, Gandhi sought validation when he expressed how India's Opposition parties were not being allowed to function democratically. He complained that the RSS and BJP were hijacking India's democracy.[79]

Gandhi asked Burns for US intervention. He wondered why the US was silent on such abuses of power prevalent in India: 'I don't hear anything from the US establishment. If you are saying "partnership of democracies", what is your view on what is going on here?' He called for American intervention to defend Indian democracy:

> I fundamentally believe that America is a profound idea, the idea of freedom, the way it is encapsulated in your constitution, it's a very powerful idea. *But you have to defend that idea.* And that is the real question.[80]

As the well-scripted conversation continued, Burns referred to the oppression of Black Americans in the US and then pushed Gandhi to comment on India's oppressive treatment of Muslims:

> I worry about the policies of the government and others to repress Muslims in India. ...we are both struggling with almost existential challenges inside the democracies, and until we overcome them we are going to be limited in our ability to be successful in our external policies. Do you agree? Do you disagree?[81]

Gandhi was diplomatic in saying that 'Hindu nationalism' Burns had earlier referred to should not be mixed up with Hinduism. But then he dished out what his hosts wanted to hear, saying that the Indian government's stand is

> against anybody who disagrees, so it is against Dalits, it is against tribals, it is against the Muslims, it is against the Sikhs, it is anybody who contests the idea that somebody has absolute power in India. This is going to create a real serious problem for our country.[82]

Gandhi has also urged the Harvard Business School to study the Narendra Modi government's economic failures. He later tweeted:

'Future HBS case studies on failure: 1. Covid19. 2. Demonetisation. 3. GST implementation'.[83]

This instance demonstrates the way Harvard takes sides in geopolitical issues and uses double standards in dealing with India and China. Harvard scholars have designed and deployed a huge machinery to dismantle this 'Hindu nationalist agenda' using Critical Race Theory. While the goal of CRT is to dismantle *all* structures that cause oppression, it is worth noting that Harvard has not launched a similar movement to dismantle the structures of the CCP although it has a well-established history of oppression.

Harvard and the Chinese Military

Harvard's close connections to China's military should also be of concern to India. An *NBC* News investigative report is informative in this regard; it shows how US universities retain ties with Chinese schools that support China's military buildup.[84] Another report claims that at least eighty-eight million dollars linked to the Chinese military has made its way to American colleges through a convoluted pipeline of partnerships. For example, one of the sponsors of the China Forum of 2020 was China Telecom, which the US Department of Defense has identified as a Chinese military collaborator. Another sponsor was the state-run media outlets China Central Television Network, *China Daily*, and *Xinhua News*.[85] Furthermore:

> Harvard University's annual China Forum – which advocates for a closer U.S.-China relationship despite the national security and the economic threat it poses – collaborates with a host of (CCP) linked entities including TikTok parent company ByteDance and Tencent alongside Chinese military proxies Huawei and China Telecom.[86]

In 2021, an independent report exposed that Harvard and other Ivy Leagues collaborated with both the Chinese military and CCP to develop technologies for Chinese defense and its nuclear program. The Harvard T.H. Chan School of Public Health, where the Piramal Center for Public Health is located, has partnerships with seven Chinese universities.

Harvard University's T.H. Chan School of Public Health runs a health partnership with seven Chinese universities focused on academic exchange and trains Chinese program participants to act as agents for reform in the Chinese health care system. At least six ... in Harvard's consortium have serious security risks, as they are tied to other research on behalf of the People's Liberation Army.

Three ... —Sichuan University, Xi'an Jiaotong University, and Tsinghua University—help develop technologies for Chinese defense, including the Chinese nuclear program. All three ... have links to Chinese cyber espionage efforts.

Ian Easton, a senior director in China policy at the Project 2049 Institute, said elite universities are inadvertently opening a new battlefront in the United States' competition with China: health care. ... could undermine patient privacy in both China and the United States. "You may not be interested in the CCP, but the CCP is interested in you. It wants to collect all your personal and private data. It wants to leverage your data against you, your values, and your way of life," Easton said. "The danger of that happening is very real. There is nothing benign or humanistic about the CCP's approach to medicine, and its exploitation of the global biotech industry ought to be repudiated."[87]

Piramal is providing Harvard (and hence indirectly the Chinese) a passage to India. The Piramal initiative is also supported by the Apollo Group of hospitals, Godrej, Tata Trusts, the Narotam Sekhsaria Foundation and other big players in India.[88] An open question is whether this indirect access allows the Chinese to turn public health into a Trojan Horse against Indians.

Harvard and COVID-19

Harvard's power to control the narrative and the HKS's close ties to the Chinese Communist Party became obvious in the handling of the COVID-19 pandemic. In late 2020, Dr Li-Meng Yan, a Chinese medical doctor and virologist published a study claiming that COVID-19 was created in a Chinese government research laboratory. Yan fled Hong Kong to the US once she became a whistleblower. Harvard's Shorenstein

Center on Media, Politics and Public Policy published a report to discredit Yan's work, calling it misinformation. The Harvard Kennedy School runs an initiative known as mediamanipulation.org that stated: 'The Yan Report is a misleading article masquerading as science, which falsely claims that the novel coronavirus was made in a Chinese lab'.[89] However, the references the Harvard report relied on come from institutions funded by the Chinese:

> Shorenstein Center's analysis points to a report by Johns Hopkins Center for Health Security to discredit Yan's work .... (it) cites numerous studies that have also received funding from the CCP. ... (the) Center also quotes a report by MIT that lists its first researcher as Dr. Robert Gallo. Gallo received an award from the Chinese state-run University of Chinese Academy of Sciences ... He is also the co-founder of the Global Vaccine Network, with several active branches in communist China. Given such strong ties to the CCP, it is unethical to cite these studies as proof invalidating Dr. Yan's analysis.[90]

Furthermore, Shorenstein Center was also exposed for having several CCP-linked fellows:

- Steven Dong was former director of the Global Journalism Institute at Tsinghua University, the educational institution attended by Chinese president, Xi Jinping. The dean has dubbed Marxist Journalism as the 'correct political orientation'. Dong is also a political communication professor at the CCP's Central Academy of Socialism and has lectured over twenty thousand senior Chinese officials.
- Zhengrong Hu served as chair of the CCP State Council's Discipline Evaluation Group of Journalism and Communication group. He was given a special governmental award by the State Council of China and a Cross-Century Excellent Personnel award.
- Li Xiguang was a former senior editor at CCP-backed propaganda outlet *Xinhua*. He is a professor at Tsinghua University and a member of the Chinese Foreign Ministry Advisory Committee on Public Diplomacy.[91]

The CCP-Harvard link (via Shorenstein Center) runs deep:

> ... Shorenstein Center has hosted at least 10 events alongside Harvard's Ash Center, which has taken millions from companies linked to and owned by the Chinese Communist Party and published studies popularized by Chinese state-run media outlets claiming the government enjoys record-high support. Among the events are "Combating Fake News: An Agenda for Research and Action," "Reporting from China: A Conversation with New York Times Correspondent David Barboza," and "Media Politics in China: Improvising Power under Authoritarianism".[92]

In 2021, Harvard invited Tedros Adhanom Ghebreyesus, director-general of the World Health Organization (WHO) as distinguished speaker at the Harvard T.H. Chan School of Public Health's commencement. Ghebreyesus was instrumental in protecting China from blame during COVID-19 under way at the time. He was the face of WHO which has been accused of lies, promoting conspiracy theories, and misinformation to mask China's role during the early days of the pandemic.[93] The Chan School hailed Ghebreyesus' 'great insight and the political leadership' and called him the right figure 'to restore trust in the WHO at a critical moment in its history'.[94] This resulted in a scandalous report:

> Harvard's decision to host Tedros calls into question the ongoing relationships between foreign nations and American universities, dozens of which <u>failed to disclose</u> donations from China last year. The Department of Education investigated Yale and Harvard ... for failing to disclose $375 million in funding from foreign nations, including Russia, Saudi Arabia, Iran, and China. In 2014, Harvard's School of Public Health <u>was renamed</u> for T.H. Chan, a Chinese businessman and Harvard graduate whose sons gave the school $350 million, the largest donation Harvard has ever received.[95]

Contrast this with India's handling of the COVID-19 crisis, for which Harvard has nothing but criticism and cynicism. For instance, K. Viswanath, director of Harvard Chan India Research Center, and Louise Ivers, professor of medicine at Harvard Medical School, talked about how India lacked leadership, about the dead bodies in the Ganga, and how deaths are being under-reported:

...the bodies are being washed up in the Ganges, the vast river. It's a very dramatic and tragic situation. And it's gotten so much worse since the winter.[96]

I'm talking about in terms of coordination and leadership at a national and state levels, where you're developing these guidelines, whether it's on a clinical level or in the public health level, developing policies, developing, implement, enforcement issues in a very unified way, and providing the appropriate information at the national level and at the state level. And now that kind of a leadership is really necessary. And it looks like it is just not there.[97]

The China-Brookings Institution Connection

The director of the Central Intelligence Agency (CIA) at the time, William Burns, warned Americans of the aggressive propaganda efforts by the Chinese. Ignoring this warning, many scholars from Brookings Institution, Carnegie Endowment for International Peace, Wilson Center, Asia Society, and other prominent US thinktanks, attended a summit hosted by the China Public Diplomacy Association, which is a CCP organization according to a *Washington Free Beacon* report.[98] Furthermore, the report stated:

John L. Thornton, the global co-chairman of the Asia Society and the namesake of the Brookings Institution's China Center, is ... keynote speaker at the event, as is Stephen Lakis, the president of the State Legislative Leaders Foundation. Daniel Victor of the Brookings Climate Change Initiative and Jerrold Green of the Pacific Council on International Policy are also listed as panellists (sic).[99]

According to another report,[100] Brookings is severely compromised by the Chinese. That and other American thinktanks have come under immense criticism for their links with the CCP:

John L. Thornton, the chairman emeritus of the Brookings board of trustees, has served since 2016 as chairman of the Silk Road Finance Corporation, a Communist Party-backed fund

that develops projects for the Belt and Road Initiative, which
the U.S. government considers a national security threat. He is
also affiliated with China's Confucius Institutes, which Beijing
allegedly uses to advance propaganda in American schools.
Scholars at Brookings's John L. Thornton China Center have
defended "Belt and Road" and Confucius Institutes without
disclosing that Thornton serves on organizations that support
the initiatives.[101]

This is considered serious because of the flow of top scholars between
Harvard and the US Federal government:

> A leading transparency watchdog group says think tanks like
> Brookings are vulnerable to foreign overtures because of their
> ability to influence public policy. At least 17 Brookings scholars
> have joined the Biden administration. Former Brookings China
> fellow Rush Doshi serves as director of the National Security
> Council's China portfolio.[102]

A 2017 Brookings Institution report titled *Benefits and Best Practices of
Safe City Innovation*, was written by an ex-Brown University professor
Dr Darrel West, in which West lauds the benefits of using (Huawei's)
technology in Nairobi and Lijiang (China) for policing. However, West's
relationship with Huawei, which sponsored this study at Brookings,
was not disclosed which raises serious questions about the Brookings
Institution. The *Washington Post* stated that Dr West had failed to
mention that

> the controversial Chinese telecommunications giant Huawei
> provided the technology for both cities, or that Huawei is one
> of the world's leading sellers of Safe City equipment, which the
> company describes as "cutting-edge" security to improve policing
> and oversight.[103]

The *Washington Post* also mentions that between July 2016 and June
2018, Huawei donated at least $300,000 to Brookings, via FutureWei
Technologies, Inc., a U.S.-based subsidiary of Huawei:

> Yet West's relationship with Huawei raises questions about the
> independence of his scholarship — and represents a worrying

example of China's influence on one of America's leading think tanks. [104]

If Brookings is compromised by the Chinese, one wonders about the motivation of the institution set up in India where children of many top Indian elites work in senior capacities. Are they an outpost of the CCP, clad in Western suits and spouting American accents? What is their real agenda? To what extent are Indians aware of the workings of Brookings? To what extent is national security being compromised through the relatives and children of Indian elites? These are real questions that India needs to address.

China's focus on breaking into American institutions and buying out the American elite appears to be achieving the desired results. China has three goals for working through the US university system. [105]

1. Influence the next generation of American leadership and how our rising crop of leaders perceive China.
2. Send Chinese students to American universities to acquire knowledge and skills and take that back to China.
3. Collect sensitive information from research labs especially at major research universities like Stanford and Harvard. [106]

The *Daily Wire* documentary reported[107] that university presidents are aware of the Chinese money flowing in, but they try to keep quiet about it:

> If you donate $1,000,000 or more, you are thinking about 'influence'; you are looking to influence the school to teach what you want to be taught; you are looking to offer research grants that give (sic) you insight into what the Americans are studying; give (sic) you access to America's most prestigious universities. Chinese gifts influence how professors teach about China, how they teach about that region – Taiwan, Japan, South Korea and others. This shapes how American students perceive China. ... Chinese infiltration is a result of American cooperation, a function of American greed. [108]

Regarding the Chinese infiltrations into India, there is a seventy-six-page report titled, *Mapping Chinese Footprints and Influence Operation in India*, published by Law and Society Alliance in India. [109]

9

The Importance of Investigating Harvard University

Overview

The nineteenth century French diplomat and philosopher, Alexis de Tocqueville, is believed to be the first to use the phrase 'empire of the mind' when he wrote:

> I consider the people of the United States as that portion of the English people which is commissioned to explore the wilds of the New World; whilst the rest of the nation, enjoying more leisure and less harassed by the drudgery of life, may devote its energies to thought, and enlarge in all directions the empire of the mind. The position of the Americans is therefore quite exceptional...[1]

The term was used in the context of the American empire after the Second World War (1939-45) when the late British prime minister, Winston Churchill, addressed a large gathering at Harvard University. He explained that the demise of the British Empire required the development of a different approach for the West to maintain its domination. He famously said: 'The empires of the future are the empires of the mind.'[2]

This chapter shows how Harvard professors behave like a cartel promoting a certain narrative about India while shutting out all dissenting voices. In effect, Harvard is stepping into the shoes of Oxford University of the British era, producing the same kind of effect that Oxford had on India. Harvard scholars studying Indian literature and translating it have the agenda of introducing Marxist interpretations to engineer Indians' perceptions of themselves and promote identity politics.

The Government of India has also been naïve in its approach towards

Harvard and doesn't appear to have done its due diligence. This has led to costly mistakes in policy making, in promoting Harvard, and in giving it the space to interfere in India's internal affairs. Building people and institutions within the country would have been cheaper and aligned with India's own interests.

Harvard University's Academic-Industrial Complex

Today, American colleges are not just empires of the mind but also run like businesses making money and managing their brand. Students are recruited to play in college sporting teams which earns them millions of dollars in ticket sales and TV rights. The alumni love to donate to their universities to support the teams. There are unspoken 'quotas' in admission for sports recruits who barely get any education. Colleges also make money selling sporting goods and branded college apparel. Apart from sports quotas, many colleges like Harvard give around thirty-five percent of seats to students with family ties to Harvard in the form of legacy admissions.[3] The regular students pay a hefty fee to become part of this brand. Most students graduate with huge debts. Student debt is at crisis levels in the US where total federal loans owed by 43 million students exceeds $1.5 trillion.[4]

In addition, American colleges serve as incubators and distributors of ideologies to a captive audience of students. This would be acceptable if there were a level playing field in which the diversity of ideas thrived openly. But, as we are illustrating in this book, the reality is very different: Faculties function like a trade union in which ideologically like-minded members support one another, and close ranks to keep critics and opponents out. The fashion for diversity focuses on biological diversity (race, gender, etc.) but is intolerant toward the diversity of ideas.

The following chapters of Part 2 will show the interactions between American universities, Indian billionaires, the Indian government, and various other stakeholders, and the risky consequences of such collaborations. Some of the collaborators might be unconscious of the outcomes being produced.

Harvard University's Ethics

Projection of Power
- Control Scholarship, Build Archives, Libraries, Maps
- Produce Atrocity Literature, Change Behavior/Culture
- Endorsements of People, Narratives, Build Sepoys
- Digestion/Appropriation/ Misinformation/Disinformation

China Ties

Toxic University Environment
- Professors Hire Like-minded
- Promote Woke, Marxist Ideas
- Cancel Culture and Disinvitation of Speakers
- Self-censorship by Students
- Administrators and Scholars Sold Out to Chinese

Undergraduate
- Admissions not Transparent
- Racial Discrimination Against Asians
- Profitable Tuition
- Grade Inflation
- Many Useless Fields – 'Grievance Studies'

Graduate School
- Profit Through Cheap International Labor for Research
- Causing Brain Drain in Other Countries
- Brand Harvard Built on Work of Foreign Students

We have focused on Harvard University to make the case because of the power it wields on the world stage. What starts at Harvard does not stay at Harvard. It spreads deep into intellectual and policy institutions everywhere. The term *vishwa guru* means the guru to the world. It is being applied to Harvard intentionally because it is fashionable among Indian elites to claim that India is the vishwa guru. Our thesis is that India is more like the *shishya* or student, with Harvard being the global guru. The figure above describes Harvard University's ethics.

We will discuss funding, some important scholars and their research output, and the ideological biases produced by Harvard. We will also lay threadbare the connections with Indian NGOs, institutions and media that widen, and strengthen, Harvard's clout. It will become known that these relationships can be dangerous for India's interests. With its deep pockets and influence, Harvard has penetrated the Indian government and civic society; it has been collecting sensitive data on Indians; it is receiving support from Indian billionaires; and is calling the shots on the future direction of Indian policies and the discourse on India. This will be amply clear from the mountain of evidence presented in subsequent chapters.

The figure that follows on the next page positions Harvard as the central player in the development and dissemination of the discourse on India. Its elements are briefly explained:

- The innermost circle shows the theories at work, with Marxism serving as the foundation. These were discussed in Part 1.
- Surrounding the theoretical frame is a box showing various Harvard schools and centers that both feed into these theories and draw from them.
- The outward arrows show the influence exerted by Harvard through these centers. There are numerous influences on India emanating from Harvard directly or via its network of collaborations and channels of distribution.
- The net result is the empowerment of what we call Breaking India Forces 2.0. This refers to our earlier book published over a decade ago, *Breaking India*, that first brought widespread attention to this phenomenon. Since then, the forces operating against India have evolved and entirely new forces have emerged that have taken the war to a new level.

Indians Build a Vishwa Guru Monster

In 2008, the Government of India awarded $4.5 million of Indian taxpayer money to Harvard to honor the economist Amartya Sen. The *Harvard Gazette* reported:

> The government of India has given Harvard University $4.5 million to support fellowships for graduate students from India. The gift recognizes the accomplishments of Harvard Professor of Economics and Philosophy and Thomas W. Lamont University Professor Amartya Sen and *his work for social and economic justice* across the globe. It also recognizes the work of Harvard's South Asia Initiative toward *establishing Harvard as a locus for the study of South Asia.*[5]

INDIAN BILLIONAIRES → HARVARD VISHWA GURU → BREAKING INDIA 2.0

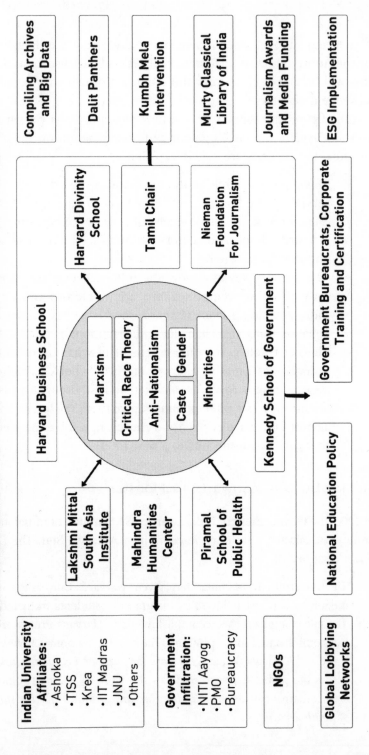

Indian University Affiliates:
- Ashoka
- TISS
- Krea
- IIT Madras
- JNU
- Others

Government Infiltration:
- NITI Aayog
- PMO
- Bureaucracy

Harvard Business School

Lakshmi Mittal South Asia Institute

Mahindra Humanities Center

Piramal School of Public Health

Marxism

Critical Race Theory

Anti-Nationalism

Caste | Gender

Minorities

Harvard Divinity School

Tamil Chair

Nieman Foundation For Journalism

Kennedy School of Government

National Education Policy

NGOs

Global Lobbying Networks

Compiling Archives and Big Data

Dalit Panthers

Kumbh Mela Intervention

Murty Classical Library of India

Journalism Awards and Media Funding

ESG Implementation

Government Bureaucrats, Corporate Training and Certification

Ronen Sen, India's then ambassador to the US, was instrumental in brokering this deal. He said: 'I am glad that Harvard has accepted this gift on the seventy-fifth birth anniversary of Professor Amartya Sen, who is a great son of India and one of the world's foremost contemporary thinkers.' He went on to praise 'the University's impressive scholarship on India' which the gift from India was intended to expand.[6]

This is the same Ronen Sen who in an official post had illegally granted Indian visas for Mormon missionaries, bypassing the bureaucracy of the Indian consulate which he headed. For this, he was praised by the US senator from Utah, Gordon Smith, which was exposed by leaked videos:

> In a leaked video in the year 2016, titled *Mormon Leaks* recorded on 8th February 2009, the then US Senator Gordon Smith "pressured" Ronen Sen to increase visas for Mormon Church members in India. ... Smith is a life-long member of the Mormon Church. ... [He] talks about how devout Mormons in the US Senate offer the Mormon Church access and influence [to India]. He further is on record saying how Sen and he came to a "pattern of dealing" to "get around Indian bureaucracy". Sen directly influenced 200 visas for Mormons. Smith then suggested how other Mormon Senators can be used in the same way. The leaked videos were shot from 2007 to 2012.[7]

For this 'service' to his motherland, Ronen Sen was awarded the Padma Bhushan in 2012 by the Indian government.

Prior to 2010, the largest gift ever to Harvard from a foreign donor was a whopping fifty million dollars given by Tata Companies, the Sir Dorabji Tata Trust, and the Tata Education and Development Trust. In exchange, Harvard agreed to name one of its buildings 'Tata Hall'.[8] This drew a lot of criticism, even from Western scholars. Given its special tax-exempt status, critics said that Tata was denying India income taxes and making their largest donation in 103 years to the most affluent university in the world:

> ... USD 50 million gift from Tata Trusts to the prestigious (HBS) in 2010 has come under scrutiny ... with questions being raised about public money from India being "apparently misdirected" to the

most privileged and wealthy in the world. Alan Beard, managing
director of Interlink Capital Strategies, ... in ... *The Daily
Caller* questioned 'how does one of America's most prestigious
institutions ... manage to have its silver spoon taken from the most
destitute? And how can such a revered institution of business
management be so blind to the ironies of accepting questionable
funds that go against every tenet of good governance?'[9]

'... Tata's gift may prove to be a public relations disaster
if the Indian government's investigation determines the funds
should have never been taken from poor Indians and sent to
rich Westerners,' Beard said. ... (He) cited media reports from
India ... that the ... gift is now under investigation by the Indian
government. ... India's Public Accounts Committee's (PAC)
sub-committee on Direct and Indirect Taxes has two principal
concerns – first, the ... donation in question came directly from
Tata Trusts, an Indian philanthropic organisation, rather than Tata
Group Chairman Emeritus Ratan Tata's personal funds, second,
this donation inappropriately took advantage of the tax-free status
of donations from charitable trusts.[10]

'... naming of Tata Hall at the Harvard Business School (HBS),
if true, are deeply disturbing and morally reprehensible,' Beard
wrote. The Indian government sub-committee ... has stated that
'construction of (Harvard's) Tata Hall did not amount either to
charity or international welfare in which India was interested,'
but ... was for the 'promotion of personal interest of one/some
of the trustees of various Tata Trusts'. Beard said ... the purpose
of a public charitable trust in India is to benefit the country's
poor and downtrodden.

'... public money has apparently been misdirected ... ,' he said.
Beard also questioned the 'conspicuous role' played by HBS Dean
Nitin Nohria in the 'now-questionable transaction', saying that
three months before the completion of Tata Hall in September
2013, Nohria was appointed a non-executive director to the board
of Tata Sons, the holding company of the Tata Group.[11]

In 2003, Harvard had established a modest initiative to study South
Asia, called the South Asia Initiative. This Tata gift, however, was the

turning point as it encouraged many other Indian billionaires to pivot into Harvard's magical spell.

In 2017, Lakshmi Mittal, the Indian billionaire who owns the world's largest steel company, further boosted the initiative with a donation of twenty-five million dollars. Harvard sealed the deal by naming the initiative after him and thus was born The Lakshmi Mittal and Family South Asia Institute. Soon after the cash infusion from Tata, Tarun Khanna advanced from being a Harvard Business School professor to head the South Asia Initiative, and now heads the Mittal Institute at Harvard. He is a commission member of the Atal Innovation Mission, which is advertised as 'a flagship initiative set up by the NITI Aayog to promote innovation and entrepreneurship across the country'.[12] He is also co-chair of the Committee on Developing Science and Technology Clusters at the office of the principal scientific adviser, Government of India. Thus, Khanna straddles both ends.

Harvard's penetration of India became much deeper when the government established the National Education Policy (NEP) in 2020. This was a windfall for US social sciences and humanities interventions. The new policy allows US universities to directly establish a trust in India for the purpose of fundraising from Indian donors of all sizes. Taking advantage of this policy, Harvard immediately established an office in Delhi. It now enjoys tax-free status in India, and Indian businessmen, NGOs and philanthropic organizations get tax-deductions for donating to Harvard in India.[13]

Indeed, the NEP has invited Western institutions without examining their track record on social engineering even in their home countries. Later chapters will show the disastrous consequences of Harvard's research on India's policies and civilizational narrative, and on the brainwashing of future generations.

Harvard as Good-Cop

When European settlers in North America were capturing lands belonging to the Native Americans, there were White persons (called 'good cops') that intervened to help the Native Americans. They sympathized with the natives' plight, fought on their behalf, and even represented them in negotiating with the White people in power. At first, these good cops won the hearts and trust of the natives. But eventually they betrayed the natives and aligned themselves with the bad cops. The natives ended up worse than if they had represented themselves and not trusted these middlemen. The good cops would absolve themselves of guilt by either saying they tried their best and failed; or they accused the natives for bad human rights as the excuse for switching sides.

In the long run it turned out to be a bad idea for the natives to let these White people serve as good cops and middlemen in dealing with the White establishment. There were numerous cases of this dynamics of good cops versus bad cops especially during the time of the seventh US president, Andrew Jackson in the late 1820s and '30s. The natives lost their lands and suffered cultural and physical genocides. The problem was that the natives had failed to develop their *own* leadership, getting lulled into becoming dependent on the good cops and their apparent generosity.

The same dynamic repeated itself in the case of Black Americans. After the period known as Reconstruction in US history (1865-77), Blacks also learned the same lesson: Relying on White leadership to champion their cause was a strategic mistake. That is when Blacks decided to develop their own leaders who were not under White tutelage, by independently experimenting with, and developing, their own solutions and policies.

This is the problem with Harvard establishing itself as the good cop to help India. It loves to jump into complex issues in India, take control over strategic databases, and frame the issues. The difference between the American Frontier described above and Harvard is that Harvard trains Indians to become the good cops under its tutelage. It nurtures future leaders that become the voices of India, and then instals and supports them throughout their careers. This eventually leads to a form of colonial control over one aspect of Indian society after another. It is similar to the way the British created a network of zamindars across India who received support from the British in exchange for helping them rule over the masses.

A lot of the content in the courses, seminars, and grants at Harvard can appear useful for India's development. However, the issue is about other influences that creep into young minds. As the examples given in the following chapters reveal, India has outsourced to Harvard the project of developing its future leaders' ideologies, affiliations and loyalties, and overall sense of identity.

But have the broad implications been thought through in this rush to bring Harvard into India? China has taken a totally different approach. It brings back US knowledge with a focus on strategic technologies related to STEM, and is specifically *not* interested in social, economic, political influences being imported from the US into China. In fact, while China rejects American Wokeism within its own borders, it uses Wokeism as an offensive to strike American society; China is promoting Critical Race Theory in the US by airing videos in English to target American children using the CCP funded China Global Television Network.[14]

It would be a mistake to see Harvard's India projects in isolation. These are part of a vast ecosystem this book uncovers. Hundreds of such projects and a few thousand, present and future scholars are involved in dismantling India's traditional grand narrative and replacing it with a new one that rejects many fundamentals of Indian sovereignty and especially its Vedic foundations.

One might say it is Harvard's grand narrative of India that is being developed and normalized as the mainstream one, all with the help of Indian money, Indian brains hired for the purpose, and Indians as intermediaries and distribution channels to bring this narrative to the masses in India and the world at large.

We will show that Harvard has developed a top-class intellectual garrison with powerful arsenal and stationed it in major cities like New Delhi and Mumbai. This infrastructure serves as a robust conduit for the flow of Indian scholars to Harvard. And Harvard gets to be the gatekeeper because of its brand value.

Consequently, through its ecosystem of India-based centers, Harvard is building a repository of India-specific knowledge in areas of public health, business, social sciences, Indology, history, humanities, and government, which can be strategically deployed to generate atrocity literature, engineer social and political changes, and further weaken India.

The government's New Education Policy 2020 has thrown the doors wide open: foreign universities are free to set up shop in India. The infiltration is public and with the full support of the Indian government.

Ironically, it is history repeating itself. Harvard is playing the same role Oxford played during the British rule of India. The latter was more transparent in training colonial leaders for ruling India. But Harvard's playbook is crafty and not so obvious, and the details of its activities need a lot of digging to compile and figure out. Indology was born in Europe and the message of the *shastras* was manipulated. This time, Harvard is the perpetrator. The following table highlights some of the key differences between Oxford's role for the British and Harvard's role for the Americans.

Oxford's Indology	Harvard's South Asian Studies
• Study of Sanskrit Texts and Ancient Thinkers	• Study of Contemporary Writings and Thinkers
• Large Translation Project of Classical Texts Using Max Mueller	• Large Translation Project of Classical Texts in all Languages Using Sheldon Pollock
• Replace Sanskrit Education with English. Introduce Colonial Thinking in India	• Introduce Leftist Social Sciences and Critical Race Theory Derivatives
• Replace Indian Business with British Industry. Work Through the Rajas	• Work Through Indian Industrialists and Government
• White at the Top with Indians in Lower Posts	• Train Indians to Think Like Americans and Place Them in Top Posts
• Divide Hindus and Muslims with Equal Enmity Towards Both	• Use Muslims and Christians as Weapons Against Hindus. Also Cultivate Dalits as 'Blacks of India'

If the tens of millions donated to Harvard were instead invested in India, it could build capacity and strengthen its own educational institutions. For every Harvard scholar being funded, one could fund twenty in India. Indians could educate diverse peoples and help build strong institutions to bring in many new participants for the future economy. Capacity building in high quality education is the need of the hour and where this work is done is important.

The ideological filter that Western scholars use to study India is the wrong one. The more mainstream the Harvard influence in India becomes, the more Indians will start viewing themselves through this lens. When people belonging to a civilization are unable to define themselves on their own terms, the civilization ceases to thrive. India should oversee India studies, just like China controls China studies. Only then can it prevent being misinterpreted and having its own people weaponized against its interests. We have already seen how the decades of research on Indian knowledge systems by the West has distilled into outcomes demanding the dismantling of Hinduism itself.

India's narrative being outsourced to Harvard is doubly negative for India, not only because Harvard is in the business of producing atrocity literature on India but also because the Harvard brand name gives its output high credibility. It is leveraging this brand to bring on board Indian thought leaders and politicians and is certifying Indian corporate leaders and bureaucrats. As a result, it is politically difficult to oppose any major report produced by Harvard on India's public health, human rights, minorities, caste, and women.

10

Databases, Taxonomies, and Archives

Overview

During British rule, there was a considerable transfer of knowledge from India to Britain that got digested as British knowledge. Evidence of this transfer is scattered but solid and requires extensive forensic work to collate the details. Fields like botany, mathematics, metallurgy, textiles, linguistics, and medicine are well-documented examples. In each specialized domain, the British would first set up an organization in India to work alongside Indian experts and learn from them. This involved replicating the Intellectual Property of Indians and then improving upon it. Gradually, and in stages, this reverse-engineering of Indian knowledge was transferred to Britain. Eventually, the Indian industry or discipline was shut down, often involving heavy-handed methods including accusations that Indian culture was primitive and abusive.

In recent times, the American digestion of Indian thought has happened along similar lines. The US-based Aveda is a good example of the systematic transfer of Ayurvedic techniques and formulations for skin care and beauty. This resulted in the development of the world's largest plant-based cosmetics brand. Its parent company, Estée Lauder Companies, made billions of dollars while relocating the farming of herbs from India to its own farms in the US and elsewhere.

Intentions can often times be good, and the work done by foreigners to study Indian knowledge can also benefit India. However, unless legal contracts exist from the outset on the fair sharing of Intellectual Property, there is every chance that the Western side will come out ahead, leaving the Indian side dependent solely as a consumer of foreign technology.

Far more serious today is the use of domestic knowledge as databases for training algorithms in Artificial Intelligence. The implications go much beyond mere economic value. It is important to understand the power of owning databases and knowledge about another country. The book, *Artificial Intelligence and the Future of Power*, explains the national security risks India faces because its databases are being siphoned off by foreign entities under various guises.[1]

Taxonomies: Indian and Western

Traditional Indian thought is rich with organizing principles one can think of as taxonomies: cosmology and metaphysics, linguistics, dance, music, botany, social structures, yoga, mathematics, medicine, and so forth. Pioneering Indian thinkers compiled and curated a large amount of information on a given subject and organized it using a Vedic substratum for understanding the world. This resulted in numerous taxonomies that serve as the grammars and meta-narratives of Indian civilization.

Vedic civilization may be viewed as an open architecture expressing itself in various domains through specific taxonomies. In modern terminology, one can say that Indian civilization comprises numerous domain-specific databases each with a well-defined architecture. All these architectures and knowledge systems follow the meta-architecture of the Vedas.

Two prominent examples are found in the works of Panini and Manu. The grammarian, Panini's *Ashtadhyayi*, describes how *bhasha* or language functions, based on his compilation of the characteristics of the languages during his time across India. By analyzing these languages, he discovered the patterns and principles in the syntax and semantics of the vast family of languages.

The rules of such a grammar can be descriptive or prescriptive. Descriptive rules merely state how something functions, how it *happens to be*, regardless of why it is so. Gravitation is what it is, and no physicist can say why it is so, or whether it *ought* to be a certain way. The job of physics and all modern science is purely descriptive. On the other hand, prescriptive rules specify how the behavior *ought to be*, such as laws established by a king or a constitution that citizens must obey. Prescriptive rules are human constructions, one might say, so they may be artificial and arbitrary.

An empirical scientist observes patterns of natural phenomena (such as gravity or light, for instance), and models them as a system of 'rules' being followed by nature. These rules become known as 'the laws of physics' and describe how nature functions. The reason they are called 'laws' is because Western thought emerged from religions where God is seen as the lawgiver who made these prescriptive laws that nature follows. Judeo-Christianity regards nature's behavior as God's prescription; humans discover these behavior patterns and hence, they are descriptive from the human point of view. Nature functions independently of the scientist, and science merely uncovers its patterns and puts them in the form of rules being followed by nature.

In the same manner, Panini's grammar captures *how* the various bhashas function. The important point is that Panini did not invent bhashas or establish the grammar they *ought* to follow. Rather, they pre-existed him just as the natural phenomena pre-exist the scientist who is discovering the laws.

However, once discovered by Panini, his rules of grammar began serving a prescriptive function as well: Learned people adopted these rules and started complying with them, in fact, even formalizing other languages using his grammar. In other words, *Panini's grammar has been used to re-engineer certain languages* that were previously not following these rules. Examples of this are found in the early centuries in India. More recently, after Europe's discovery of Panini's grammar, there was frenzied activity to upgrade European grammars. The point being made is that *taxonomies do exert very powerful influences* in the trajectory of an entire domain of knowledge, in this case, natural languages. They serve to channel the discourse in a certain direction.

The other significant example of an important taxonomy is the *Manusmriti*, a compilation and commentary on social conduct in India. Manu makes it clear that these are the customs being followed by people; he does not say these are a normative set of rules to be imposed universally. In fact, he makes it very clear that the customs in the north are different from those in the south, different from one local community to another, different from one period of history to another, different from one strata of society or one social context to another. Manu advocates adapting and rewriting such texts (called *smritis*) for each epoch and each context. The *Manusmriti* is a prominent example of an entire family of such texts about social organization known as the *Dharmashastras*.

It is a matter of debate whether the *Dharmashastras* became prescriptive, and if they did, to what extent, in what periods of time, and where. When prescriptive, such a set of rules would be enforced as law by courts and kings. Otherwise, such rules would be purely descriptive of the customs of a society at its own discretion, and not by force of some higher authority. Part 1 of this book discussed these *smritis* in detail.

Both these examples – curating and analyzing bhasha into a grammar and studying the social patterns and explaining them as *Dharmashastras*, respectively – are examples of building empirical databases of phenomena that already exist and providing a theoretical framework to understand them.

One could easily add other domains to this list of taxonomies. The *Natya Shastra,* for example, is the theory of performing arts and aesthetics. The important point is that India did not lack its own indigenous database developers and their profound taxonomies to understand India.

The West too has developed its own taxonomies. All the natural sciences – physics, chemistry, biology, etc. – are the great accomplishments of the West in developing systematic rules to model the behavior of nature.

Our criticisms pertain to other domains of Western taxonomies: the humanities and social sciences concerned about the systematic development of rules of social behavior. By calling them 'sciences', Western theorists of human behavior in a broad spectrum of topics, tabulated empirical data and developed theories, in many ways similar to the way physicists do their work. These domains included economics, politics, culture, sociology, history, and psychology.

However, while in principle these social sciences/humanities might be seen as sciences in the same sense as the natural sciences, in practice there are serious issues with this equivalence.

- First, human behavior cannot be modeled like inanimate objects because humans exert free will and choice, and can and do change over time, making it difficult to predict their behavior. This difference is well known and accepted.
- Second, in natural sciences, the state of mind, perceptions, belief systems, prejudices, biases, and agenda of the experimenter are less important in the result because the measurement itself is objective even when the interpretation is not. This is not true of the social sciences.
- The third difference that makes the social sciences lack objectivity is not clearly understood and is of great importance to this book: The West colonized the world in recent centuries through its hard power advantages, and in doing so imposed its thinking and hence, its taxonomies upon others.

The book, *Being Different: An Indian Challenge to Western Universalism,* uses the term Western Universalism to refer to the syndrome of turning the West's limited experience into an absolute, and universal, set of rules, both descriptive and prescriptive. Western Universalism was founded on the values and beliefs that emerged from the historical events in Europe. It assumes that those experiences are universal, and therefore, Western philosophy, ethics, social sciences, and history are suitable templates into which all other civilizations can be mapped.

Because Western civilization is considered the gold standard, non-Western civilizations are relevant only as origins of the former (as in 'our past') or as theatres in which the West operates ('our civilizing mission') or as threats to Western interests ('our frontiers'). The unique interests and identities of other cultures are of little consequence.

As a matter of fact, much of the development of the social sciences took place during Europe's colonization of the world, and its purpose was to serve as a tool for colonization. Anthropologists, sociologists, historians, political scientists, and other social scientists worked alongside colonizers, and in many cases were employed by them. Their work was to build a variety of taxonomies to understand the non-European peoples with the explicit purpose of defeating them, governing them, manipulating them, and in many cases, leading to their eventual destruction.

Therefore, Western Universalism in general assumes the supremacy of the West, and its social theories are tainted with the toxicity of denigrating others. This is not to suggest that all Western social thought is flawed or sinister and should be rejected wholesale. Rather, this implies that one should not accept it at face value without serious due diligence and scrutiny of each of its claims. Many aspects of Western social sciences are applicable in those countries but cause violence when imposed globally.

A serious problem with Western social sciences is that they have become *prescriptive*: first during the colonial era, and more recently, as part of what is termed globalization. Globalization has, in many ways, become the Westernization of the globe. The recent pushbacks from Islamic countries and from China should be seen in the context of Western Universalism having become too powerful. What started out as a heavy-handed imposition of Western thought has now become normalized and is accepted unconsciously as 'scientific'.

Given the power of Western institutions that put these theories together and deploy them globally, there is a lack of humility on the part of the social theorists, including, and especially people of color hired from non-Western countries and brought into the service of Western institutions.

In this chapter we will show the following processes at work in several examples:

> Databases, Archives, and Taxonomies ➜ Standard Western Frameworks ➜ Universalisms adopted globally and controlled by the elite

Colonization: The Clash of Taxonomies

In an encounter between two civilizations, there is inevitably a clash between their taxonomies. The side that dominates with hard power can also decide the fate of the taxonomy of the weaker or defeated side, and hence control the fate of its soft power as well.

In many cases, books have been burnt to eradicate all the knowledge of the defeated side, so future generations can be brainwashed and raised using the taxonomy of the victors. The Europeans did this in the

Americas and Africa, and China is doing this today in Tibet, Xinjiang, and Hong Kong. The Muslim conquerors and rulers of India also engaged in large-scale destruction of books, but they were more interested in quick wealth extortion.

The Western strategy is more sophisticated. They appropriate those parts of the colonized knowledge they find useful. This gets reformulated on their terms and turned into a knowledge system as something new they own. If they were to acknowledge that their intellectual systems include key elements borrowed from the colonized peoples, it would psychologically empower the defeated side, making it harder to rule over them. The asymmetry of power between the colonizers and the colonized allows the wholesale fabrication of the history of scientific ideas and cultures. This is the clash of taxonomies.

An encounter of civilizations typically results in an outcome we have previously described as *digestion*. This occurs when an aggressive, predatory culture dismembers a weaker one into parts from which it picks the pieces it wants to own. These appropriated elements get mapped onto the language and social structures of the predator's own history and paradigms, leaving little trace of the source tradition. The civilization that was thus mined gets depleted of its cultural and social capital.

Eventually, the depleted civilization enters the proverbial museum as just another dead culture, ceasing to pose a threat to the dominant one. What is left after digestion is waste material which is to be removed and destroyed. The dominant side superimposes its concepts, aesthetics, language, paradigms, historical template, and philosophy, positioning them as the universal worldview. At the same time, the images, symbols, histories, and languages of the weaker culture get distorted.

Simply stated, digestion is a way to map one civilization into another civilization's framework. The digested side loses control of its taxonomies and as a result its members become mental slaves. When a taxonomy/framework gets hijacked by the West and turned into something that fits its own agenda, we have criticized it as an act of digestion, a form of violence. The colonized people lose their way in their own physical and experiential space because their experiences become reframed in the meta-structure of Western Universalism.

Being very efficient at digesting others, the West maps alien civilizations into its own reference points as a way of capturing and controlling them as its property. In the end, Western experts and non-Westerners trained under their tutelage, become the subject-matter experts on that civilization. They now acquire the *adhikar* or authority to comment on it, formulate recommendations for policies, and eventually serve in the enforcement of those policies.

A major problem being exposed in this book is that the West, led by the United States, is in control of the construction of key databases and archives that fit into its social sciences taxonomies concerning India. This has invaded every conceivable domain of knowledge. This is what the various projects we critique are about, such as the mapping of the Kumbh Mela, mapping the public health of India, reinterpreting caste to make it appear as racism in America, building databases on genders in India by funnelling through the lens of gender conflict in the West.

The history of colonization needs to be better understood to appreciate how this book issues a warning on the possibility of India's re-colonization. British colonizers were pioneers in curating certain kinds of information about Indian society. This was carried out on India's education systems, agricultural systems, social stratification, systems of governance, linguistics, and so forth. The knowledge became vital and central to their project of empire building.

The strategy of the British was to build all kinds of maps – a 'map' being a kind of database. The political scientist, Benedict Anderson, documented the role of such map-building in creating European empires. His book, *Imagined Communities: Reflections on the Origins and Spread of Nationalism*, has become a classic since the 1980s and is widely taught in postcolonial studies, Indology, and South Asian Studies.[2] It explains how communities get shaped by the maps built about them. British colonialists were obsessed with mapping (in a broad sense of organizing databases) geography, population, religious practices, social and political structures, all for the purpose of developing a template for better negotiation and control. The same kind of mapping had earlier been done in North America by the European settlers, which helped their systematic aggression against the natives.

Such map-building continues today: Some of the best socio-religious databases on India at the district and village level are the ones recently developed by the Church and the Central Intelligence Agency.

There is an eerie resemblance between the colonial map-building project described by Anderson and the present research on India being done by America's Ivy Leagues like Harvard. This is very significant for the thesis of this book, and we will devote some space to summarize what Anderson wrote in his influential work.

Anderson provided extensive details of the colonial obsession for capturing all kinds of data concerning India and turning it into theories, frameworks, policies, and so on. One objective was to plagiarize whatever they found useful and claim it as their own Intellectual Property. This helped expand European knowledge in medicine, agriculture, botany, textiles, linguistics, metallurgy, and so forth.

The other, more sinister, goal was to understand how to predict and manage the Indian mind. This was used to help or undermine Indian society, depending on a given situation. Adding Indian knowledge into Western Universalism was for constructive purposes while undermining Indian society was for destructive purposes.

Anderson explains that the European project to record their colonial assets, both the territory and the inhabitants, was implemented through three institutions – *census*, *map*, and *museum*. These benefited from the use of the new technologies of mechanical reproduction. Anderson says,

> together, they profoundly shaped the way in which the colonial state imagined its dominion—the nature of the human beings it ruled, the geography of its domain, and the legitimacy of its ancestry.[3]

Censuses were very large-scale undertakings that eventually transformed society by the type of classification used to codify everyone's place in the hierarchy. The census-makers brought a passion for accuracy, and the sheer scale and rigor gave it immense credibility. Previous enumerations by native rulers had been only for the purpose of collecting taxes and did not introduce new kinds of social categories. Successive censuses from the late nineteenth century onward show important changes in the way categories are redefined: groups are continuously clustered, disaggregated, recombined, intermixed, and reordered. As the colonial period proceeded, the census categories became more visibly racial, whereas religious identity gradually disappeared as a primary census classification. Chapter 6 discussed the role of the British census in distorting social reality at the ground level.

Map-building took a big leap with the invention of the chronometer in the 1730s that made it possible to calculate longitudes precisely. The entire world could be represented on a flat geometrical grid. Into this empty template, the empirical data of the colonizer's choice could be inserted. Previously, what existed was an imagined map using cosmology. For instance, a Buddhist map might show the three worlds with heavens and hells and the earthly realm in between. A purely secular map might have diagrams showing military campaigns and shipping. But British maps represented the geography using context-free numbers with latitudes and longitudes.

The intersection between map and census created a whole new kind of power. Demographic data from the census was added to the maps and this turned them from purely topological to political tools. Discourse became reformulated in cartographic frames of reference. Traditional reference points were in terms of the sacred sites, rivers, seas, mountains, communities, religions, and languages. The new kind of map was detached from all these and became the new abstraction of one's physical reality.

> A map was a model for, rather than a model of, what it purported to represent.... It had become a real instrument to concretize projections on the earth's surface.... The discourse of mapping was the paradigm which both administrative and military operations worked within and served.[4]

The new approach to representing one's geography became an even bigger phenomenon with the help of the technologies of printing. The rulers carefully populated the new maps with content to show human hierarchies, histories, and relationships as it suited them. Maps serving as political-biographical narratives had a psychological impact. The result was an entirely new way for the natives to conceptualize their world.

The third institution – museums, are natural to Europe because European history is a story of discontinuities in which each epoch is marked by violence to destroy past cultures. What gets stored in museums thus belongs to the dead past and the present society can enjoy it as something belonging to 'those people'. This notion of being alienated from one's own past was exported to the peoples that

Europeans conquered. It was an act of violence because non-Westerners typically did not have the same sense of their past being something alienated from their present lives.

For instance, rituals for worshipping the living deity cannot be performed in the same way once its temple is turned into a museum or 'archaeology site' managed by the archaeological institution. The deity's statue placed in a museum is only a statue, not the *living person* it once was. Museums and archaeology thus worked hand in hand to define the 'dead past' and the living tradition. The colonizers decided which aspects of the natives' past could thus be 'killed' by classifying it as their antiquity as opposed to their living present.

At the same time, the colonizers sponsored huge projects of archaeological restorations to impress the locals of their generosity and good intentions, while sneaking in their biases under the veneer of scientific development. Reconstructed monuments often juxtaposed the symbols of the progressive West with the natives' primitiveness. The documentation of a colony's antiquity became a patronizing way to project the colonizer's superiority. Colonized civilizations could thus be museumized and repositioned as regalia for a secular colonial state.

To the three major institutions of census, maps, and museums, we can add the large-scale *translation* projects as another enterprise that comprise a form of intellectual and emotional conquest.

Anderson explains how these projects re-engineered the natives' ideas of their external spaces:

> Interlinked with one another, the census, map and museum illuminate the late colonial state's style of thinking about its domain. The "warp" of this thinking was a totalizing classificatory grid, which could be applied with endless flexibility to anything under the state's real or contemplated control: peoples, regions, religions, languages, products, monuments, and so forth.[5]

Another taxonomy developed by the West has been the caste framework for India's social organization. As discussed in Part 1, this has had a devastating effect. Though started by the British, it has continued after Independence and has now become even more rigid as a political identity. It is being morphed once again using Critical Race Theory into what is being called Critical Caste Theory.[6]

The book, *Sanskrit Non-Translatables: The Importance of Sanskritizing English* explained how the translation of certain Sanskrit terms into English has distorted their meaning and, in the process, imposed an alien worldview.[7]

Elitist frameworks, especially those controlled from foreign nexuses, have immense power. Those that cite them using the established references do not have the burden of proof because the validity of such frameworks is accepted as the gospel truth. Anyone daring to differ faces an uphill battle, as is clear to those who post controversial positions on social media and face biased algorithms running the platform. Such a knowledge system becomes like an echo chamber because new data is captured that fits the framework.

The British era saw dramatic re-imagining by the application of the contemporary technologies of navigation, astronomy, surveying, photography, and print. Similarly, today the new knowledge-maps of India being built at places like Harvard, are applying the latest technologies of Artificial Intelligence, Machine Learning, Big Data, Virtual and Augmented Realities, and so on. The use of information to colonize can now be carried out much more powerfully and intricately.

For instance, as we shall detail in a later chapter, the modern academic archive that Mittal Institute is developing at Harvard is the digital equivalent of a map, census, museum, social organization and much more, especially as the metaverse develops and our experience becomes more digital.

The following chapters will show that the various centers and projects at Harvard, ironically funded by Indian billionaires, are at the cutting edge of developing databases on Indian society, women, minorities, conflicts, public health problems, economic problems, development problems, grassroots entrepreneurship, educational policies, and so on. These databases will become extremely powerful to train AI algorithms. And it will lead to the next generation of colonialism.

This approach will shape how policy will be developed and debated, how governments and corporates will be rated and evaluated, and how individuals will be organized into a sort of digital caste system, shaping their careers and lifestyles. This influence will permeate all aspects of civil society, and the future will be built on the premises, conclusions, and biases built into the theories developed largely by the Americans.

Curating assets and assigning them a place in the metaverse through 'labelling' is therefore a strategic act of capturing and colonizing people, places, and things. The British called it the 'civilizing mission' where Oxford University played a strategic role. The book, *Oxford and Empire* documents the role it played in empire building at the intellectual level using this strategy.[8] The Indian elites then lapped it up as a great British gift to India. Today's Indians, likewise, are in awe of the kind of Americanization Harvard brings in their thinking about their own society.

During British times, the knowledge base about India was used to train British leaders to manage India. These young British men were then sent to India, where in turn, they trained junior Indians in the civil service, bringing their thinking in alignment with the colonizers. These native 'bicultural intelligentsias', i.e., those natives who get trained in the colonizer's language, idiom and ideology, play a significant role in the process of colonization and become part of the new elite.

Our study leads us to believe that American elite universities like Harvard have essentially stepped into the shoes of the British. Just like the British in the past, Americans have today successfully co-opted the most promising Indians to serve the American cause. The big difference is that the British employed Indians only in junior positions to do this work, whereas the Americans have successfully co-opted Indians to join their enterprises at the highest levels.

This kind of American map-building and database building is extremely dangerous. These databases are a real-time snapshot of what is happening at the hyper-local level in the lives of villagers, in micro-financing, in the Intersectionality with social issues, and other areas mentioned above. India is being captured into the overall meta-narrative and framework under Harvard's control.

This book unravels how it is all happening. Hence, it is of vital importance.

Kumbh Mela

A prominent example discussed earlier is Harvard's major surveillance project to capture data through videos, images, social demographics, blood samples, and movement of people during events like the Kumbh Mela. This is a massive database creation exercise dealing with information of almost one hundred million people from every corner of India, representing every community, across all strata. Harvard refers to its work as 'mapping' the Kumbh Mela.[9] A database creation of this scale is unparalleled anywhere in the world and has been carried out under the garb of academic research to help further India's public health.

These kinds of exercises violate the privacy of ordinary Indians and contradict India's proposed data protection laws. The information gathered is used to map the vulnerabilities and fault lines in Indian society, train algorithms, feed Hinduphobic movements that exploit the conflicts between ethnic, linguistic, and religious groups, and in general, interfere with India's sovereignty.

When The Lakshmi Mittal and Family South Asia Institute at Harvard created the Harvard Kumbh Mela Project, Indians felt proud. After all, it brought global importance to their heritage. However, a closer look revealed that the project diluted the mela as exotic tourism; it distorted and secularized its purpose; it used the information for appropriation and digestion; it extracted information for atrocity literature that can be developed to condemn India's 'human rights violations'; and it opened legal doors for infiltration by Christian evangelists and Islamic groups. And as explained earlier, these investigations were carried out using a Eurocentric worldview without proper consideration of the relevant Indian frameworks.

Prof. Diana Eck made a telling remark in the official video by Harvard's Kumbh Mela project team. She inadvertently gave away the hidden agenda, saying that she 'missed seeing' feminist NGOs at the mela.[10] This is exactly how Ford Foundation started its interventions in India several decades back: by training, funding and empowering several feminist NGOs in India, and then using them to dish out atrocity literature about Indian society, along with the large-scale training of a whole generation of Indian youth in Western social theories. The goal was to make Western feminism fashionable among the bright, young women of India by constantly encouraging them to study women's oppression in India. We certainly want gender issues to be studied and remedied but feel that the wholesale import of Western feminism models without careful consideration of its pros and cons is undesirable.

We believe that Harvard scholars were more interested in using the mela as an open-ended expedition exploring uncomfortable issues mentioned below, rather than treating it as a sacred Hindu event:

- Is the mela dominated by males? Do the *sadhvis* enjoy equal rights as the *sadhus*?
- Are women being exploited at the event?
- Are there rapes and harassment? Are there tantric sex orgies?
- Are Dalits being oppressed?
- Do the Hindu groups have equitable representation of LGBTQ+?
- Are people from the south and northeast being discriminated against?

The project researchers were essentially 'mapping' the mela into these oft-repeated tropes used in thousands of anthropological and social sciences projects that target India. The façade was to position this as diversity studies and hunt for caste and gender inequalities in the mela's facilities. The grand strategy included developing academic dissertations, investigative journalism, and television documentaries on issues like dowry, sati, idolatry, some naked sadhus allegedly eating human flesh, and so on. In the process, the mela was stripped of its original sacred purpose and turned into a pageant serving the sole purpose of furthering such agenda-driven research.

For thousands of years, India's diversity has co-existed in mutual harmony and respect, but this project would empower Harvard to interfere and disrupt it in the name of modernization, emboldening certain Indian NGOs in the process. Political groups representing various fragments would jump on the bandwagon to politicize the mela. Once unleashed, this trend would have a life of its own and fuel conflicts among various groups.

We have feared that the mela could turn into a big unexplored frontier of the exotic, 'uncivilized and dangerous' others. It is far too open, and offers huge opportunities for Western frontiersmen seeking adventure, fame, and fortune.

For the researchers, this is just another anthropological hunting ground for exotica and erotica. One immediate impact was a demand for large-scale distribution of condoms at the Kumbh Mela. The *Times of India* set the ball rolling on this sensation[11] and foreign media quickly picked up the hot story.[12]

None of the materials produced by Harvard's team has discussed the metaphysical meaning of the *yajna* (cosmic process of creation and equilibrium) being carried out at the Kumbh. When they discussed what they called the 'myth' behind the mela, it was presented as some exotic, primitive, fantastical story along the lines of *The Lord of the Rings*. They lack the spiritual expertise and interest to appreciate the metaphysics of *rtam* (cosmic order) and yajna, and how they manifest in the world. Such a profound insight is missing because there is no *shraddha* (spiritual posture) in the top leadership of the project.

A blog by the Harvard Kumbh Mela team reported: 'One of the major outcomes of this group's research was observing the concern many people at the Kumbh had about the pollution produced throughout the course of this festival'.[13] More research is bound to follow on how the mela causes pollution. Just as Diwali, Ganesh Utsav, and other Hindu festivals are targeted as environmental hazards, so will the Kumbh Mela be added to the list of primitive nuisance practices. We have expressed concern that students from Harvard and other places are already studying 'environmental issues' as a doorway to expose Hinduism's problems like immersing ashes, cremating dead bodies, and performing other age-old established rituals.

One enterprising American scholar bragged that he participated in the tradition of kite flying on the banks of the river Ganga because this allowed him to hide a video camera on his kite, turning it into a drone for filming. Imagine the treasure trove of scandalous and sensational video footage he collected for their archive!

Christian missionaries have made attempts to infiltrate the mela for proselytizing. Any restrictions against this are likely to be challenged by missionaries with the help of Western and Indian institutions. Arguments already abound that nobody owns the mela, the river Ganga, or any other public place where it is held, and therefore everyone has an equal right to participate in whatever manner they choose. Missionaries are experienced in entering as good guests using *sama* (friendship) and *dana* (charity). They will undoubtedly bring lots of freebies to impress the villagers who comprise a major percentage of the attendees. Harvard's Pluralism Project is easily able to disarm naïve Hindu leaders by praising 'Hindu tolerance' that stirs pride among them.

As an example of how such data lends itself to sophisticated analyses, we cite a 2016 paper published by a team led by Tarun Khanna.[14] The paper stated that it got cell phone data (including both phone calls and text messages) at the Kumbh Mela from a telephone carrier. The data was used for a detailed study of *homophily*, a term that refers to the way individuals behave in a group that includes some persons who resemble them and others who are considered different. The similar/different criteria could be caste-, religion-, language-, gender-, class of society-based, and so on. Such a study models the behavior of Indians from these groups towards those perceived as different.

The paper states: 'These communication metadata, at minimum, keep track of who contacts whom, when, and for how long'. The dataset they used contained records of 146 million text messages and 245 million phone calls for a total of 390 million communication events. A total of 207 cell phone towers at the mela were used to collect this data and was combined with the latitude and longitude of each tower to build a spatial map of the mela grounds.

The paper further states that the Kumbh Mela provided a unique opportunity to study such individual-level behavior in large settings of crowds. The team studied attendees from twenty-three states and developed separate results on each state and social group. As per their estimation, sixty-one million people attended the mela during the three-month period covered by their analysis.

The report gives its findings on the likelihood of various groups having the 'herding' tendency to do 'collective decision-making'. It looked at variables like 'linguistic origin, ethnic agglomeration, and preexisting social bonds and boundaries', while measuring 'associative homophily'. The researchers pointed out that such studies can predict a given group's vulnerabilities to situations like 'human stampedes'. Measures of homophily can also give the tendency for 'segregation' of certain people.

States represented at the mela with large populations had lower levels of homophily than states with fewer people. This is explained by the report as a measure of how comfortable or uncomfortable a variety of Indians feel towards those from a different kind of background.

None of this research is a violation of the law, and it is fair for Harvard to carry out such activities because it has been assisted by Indian authorities at every step. Harvard was easily able to secure a buy-in from many Indian elites by offering them prestigious association with Harvard's brand. Harvard's beautifully packaged book on its project titled, *Kumbh Mela: Mapping the Ephemeral Megacity*, was launched with great fanfare:

- In New York the launch was held with the sponsorship of Asia Society.[15]
- The New Delhi launch was held at the luxurious Oberoi hotel strategically timed after India's Independence Day. To secure his support, the limelight was on Akhilesh Yadav, the then chief minister of Uttar Pradesh.[16] He was grateful that Harvard's association boosted his personal status in the presence of the international media.[17]
- The following day, the Mittal Institute hosted the second launch in a series of five launches held at the iconic Chhatrapati Shivaji Maharaj Vastu Sangrahalaya in Mumbai in partnership with Asia Society India Centre and the Harvard Club of Mumbai.[18]

Harvard's prestigious Mittal Institute refers to this project as interdisciplinary, combining many departments, each with its own separate purpose. These included urban planning, logistics, public health, religious studies, business school, anthropology, design school, etc. Each of them had a highly secularized lens and were only looking for interesting specimens to study.

By leveraging its Kumbh Mela database, Harvard has spread its tentacles into healthcare. The initiative, known as the JanaSwasthya Project, is a collaboration with several partners including Harvard's own T.H. Chan School of Public Health. Its goal is the mass screening of the health of pilgrims, sadhus, and security forces at the mela. The report explains:

> The project builds upon the team's research at the 2013 Kumbh Mela in Allahabad, where they initially piloted their disease surveillance tool on iPads. ... The cornerstone of the 2015 JanaSwasthya Project is a unique interactive visual analytic tool ("dashboard") that provides critical disease surveillance data to health officials in real time. On the first day alone, the dashboard had tracked over 2,000 visits recorded on government issued tablet devices at over 30 fixed and mobile health clinics serving

pilgrims at the Mela. *This real-time disease surveillance program is unprecedented in its scale. Using all of this rich data, planners can see the data of patients organized by age, location, gender, disease, and disease frequency in all real time.*[19]

Harvard believes that such data has huge potential for bypassing traditional public health systems and helping refugees and minority communities that are facing challenges in Indian society.[20] It announced that the next phase will move from modeling to prescribing solutions, and then making socio-political interventions.

The funding by Indian billionaires causes other elite Indians and some naïve traditional Hindus to buy into Harvard's template to understand the mela. Such bicultural Indians get appropriated to spread Harvard's worldview.

The goal of any such database and archive construction is to get online search engines to supply the Harvard view as the standard one pertaining to India. Toolkits and dashboards developed by Harvard and its collaborators will thus become the standard user-friendly ways for the public to access their own heritage.

Many years ago, Infinity Foundation published a report on Harvard's surveillance of the Kumbh Mela. It warned that this was not the benign project it appeared to be because it was compiling socio-demographic, DNA, and psychological data of nearly one hundred million people from every corner of India. This is also feeding Harvard's machine learning systems to identify social and political divisiveness that could eventually be exploited in the name of human rights.

Our report, printed in both English and Hindi was widely distributed in many Indian state capitals, as well as in academic, media, and other institutions of civic society. Hundreds of thousands of copies were handed out to senior leaders at various Kumbh Melas, generating an emotional response.

In 2017, when Yogi Adityanath first became the chief minister of India's largest state, Uttar Pradesh, Rajiv Malhotra met him in person to present the report and request an investigation into such foreign projects. But no action was taken by India's Central or state governments. In fact, several months later there was a surprising press release that Yogi Adityanath had invited several foreign research agencies (including

Harvard) specifically to gather data at the Kumbh Mela. Ironically, the door was flung wide open to foreign institutions to carry out surveillance, completely unsupervised.

However, it seems that our persistent writing and speaking on this subject to expose Harvard, finally made an impact. Harvard's Tarun Khanna has made a quiet statement that the Mittal Institute has no further plans to investigate the Kumbh Mela. However, it remains to be seen whether Harvard has merely outsourced this project to its network of partners because its own direct entanglement has been exposed.

The Partition Project

Another significant example of building a strategic database archive with Harvard's own interpretation is the Partition Project.[21] It is funded by the Mittal Institute and headed by Prof. Jennifer Leaning, director of the Center for Public Health and Human Rights at Harvard. She has been working on this project for over a decade and plans to build the most comprehensive archive of materials from the Partition period from India, Pakistan, and Bangladesh. It will include voices from the public and media, as well as government sources. The project is a long-term one involving several faculty members. The ambition goes beyond the Partition era, and Jennifer Leaning wants to eventually cover the entire span of British India.

Leaning, an expert in human rights and international law, will be interpreting, classifying, and gatekeeping the access to the archive.

Tarun Khanna said the Partition Project captures what Mittal's South Asia Institute is all about: taking overall control of a subject of immense significance by bringing together scholars from different parts of the world, including those in South Asia as well as researchers and students at Harvard.

As an example of the work being done, a Harvard student interviewed the late Milkha Singh (popularly called the Flying Sikh), one of the finest athletes India has ever produced. The student, Akshay Veer, is a Partition ambassador at the Mittal Institute, and one of fifty-five students working on *Looking Back, Informing the Future – The 1947 Partition British India: Implications of Mass Dislocations Across Geographies*. This portion of the Partition Project has students collecting and documenting oral stories from survivors of Partition.[22] Mittal Institute states it wants to focus on oral histories of the 'underrepresented voices', namely, women and religious minorities.[23]

They claim to have collected more than 2300 narratives of survivors over a three-year period. The Harvard Graduate School of Design is involved in developing a 'deeper understanding of the displacement that occurred during the Partition in 1947'.[24] Numerous visiting fellowships from India and Pakistan are being given by the Mittal Institute to document the 'religious dislocations' that occurred.[25] The institute hosts a series of seminars on topics like *Gender and Partition*, and so on.[26]

An archive of this kind is designed to serve as the definitive historical record on a certain period. This means the most comprehensive archive on British India will rest with Harvard. All future scholars wanting to research this subject will need to approach Harvard and request access to it. The scattered material from India will be curated and archived by Harvard with funds received from the Mittal family.

This is similar to the way the archives on colonial era Indology are being controlled by universities at Heidelberg, Oxford, and Harvard. This is history repeating itself! India's rare manuscripts on Vedic knowledge systems are still in the hands of Western libraries and archives, with Indian scholars having to pay hefty fees to access them. A significant amount of Indian archival material is outside India, and the government should be focusing on bringing that back rather than putting more of it in the hands of places like Harvard.

Whoever ends up owning the archive of British India, will own the primary sources for writing the history of that period, and indirectly, a significant portion of India's grand narrative. This research can very well be done in India with Indian scholars. That would bring an insider's lens, thus developing an Indian indigenous model for social sciences. There is a need to research, rebuild, and update Indian models of society that are aligned with Indian civilizational values.

Medical Databases

Harvard's ambitions are not restricted to the capture of India's sensitive health database. It also intends to *develop the entire software and data collection mechanism and operate it in India*. This is *The India Digital*

Health Network and is led by Prof. Satchit Balsari, assistant professor in emergency medicine at Harvard Medical School and Beth Israel Deaconess Medical Center, and Global Health and Population at the Harvard T.H. Chan School of Public Health. The project is described as a research and policy collaboration and the goal is:

> The development of an application programming interface (API)-enabled health exchange ecosystem ... seeks to generate policy insights to shape ... India's digital health information architecture. ... proposal ... has been adopted and implemented by the NITI Aayog in its approach paper for the National Health Stack, and ... Ministry of Health and Family Welfare, Government of India (GoI), in its National Digital Health Blueprint. Key contributions include: a) the inclusion of the term "machine-readable" while mandating the portability of personal health data, setting the stage for health data interoperability in India; b) the concept of the personal health record, as opposed to a hospital-based electronic medical record, being the organizing core of India's digital health ecosystem; and c) inclusion of Regulatory Sandboxes in the National Digital Health Mission (NDHM) which are controlled testing environments within which existing regulations may be temporarily relaxed to allow experimentation for novel technologies.[27]

Harvard's project involves the development and installation of what it calls a 'toolkit' that 'identifies necessary documentation, personnel, and resources at the primary care level'. It goes on to brag about the strategic importance of this toolkit:

> We are developing a provider-driven, patient-centric design process for digitizing health data whereby doctors and administrators can quickly deploy easy-to-use customized solutions that can securely port data to and from other systems.[28]

Their partner in this project is Tata Trusts that will operate this toolkit and compile the databases, which will be shared with Harvard. 'Computer scientists, medical informaticians, healthcare providers, data scientists, and policymakers from India and Harvard provide technical and policy assistance'.[29] Harvard and Tata have also roped in other prestigious Indian research institutes.

Subsequently, Mittal Institute took this database collection venture even further on behalf of Harvard. Various seminars have been held and collaborations fostered between Harvard and Indian parties in which Mittal plays a key role. For instance, the following joint seminar with Radcliffe Institute for Advanced Study is described in its annual report:

> The Exchanging Health Information seminar sponsored by the Radcliffe Institute for Advanced Studies brought together experts in medicine, computer science, big data, public policy and law to identify a research and policy agenda that addresses implementation barriers to health information exchange.[30]

The report states that 'health information storage in India is extremely diverse' but scattered, disorganized and not fully electronic. It explains the opportunity for Harvard with Mittal's help:

> While this patchy ecosystem of largely absent health information data in India posits a formidable challenge to building out an effective exchange, the ubiquity of recent mobile networks and broadband provides a greenfield for bold, innovative solutions unencumbered by expensive legacy systems.[31]

There are also many well-intended initiatives like Project Prakash.[32] This is an independent non-profit organization based in Boston near Harvard that provides excellent assistance to treat visual impairment among India's poor. Who could fault such a noble movement? It provides people with the most sophisticated treatment available for curable loss of sight.

However, it is also building an ambitious digital database; a centralized repository that will 'provide crucial context to formulate policies regarding the types of medical and rehabilitation resources that are most needed to improve the health of children'. It is also developing 'regional Digital Health Innovation Hubs to provide a prototyping environment for scientists and industry partners to develop mobile and cloud-based solutions', as well as *testing labs to collect data for new technologies*. The project is funded by Tata Trusts while the Mittal Institute showcases and facilitates its work. [33]

The question is: Who will own, control, and use such databases and technologies? Will India once again become a consumer nation dependent on American generosity? Could this be an *unconscious/ innocent transfer of Intellectual Property and databases?*

Regular exchanges are also organized to build a network of Indian Ayurvedic researchers and transfer their knowledge on genetics to their Harvard counterparts. The New Delhi office of Harvard's Mittal Institute has facilitated exchanges on topics like 'mitochondrial disorders, infertility, sex determination, forensic genetics and the Genetic basis of Ayurveda prakritis'.[34]

Another sensitive project unconsciously throwing Intellectual Property related to India's rich biodiversity into Harvard's waiting arms is the collaboration with the Ladakh Nuns Association. This ecological and cultural documentation project is nicely dubbed 'Ladakh Nuns Association Digital Sustainability Project'.[35] The stated goal is:

> To create a record of plants and their medicinal uses, while recording and digitally archiving the experiences of nuns working at the intersection of conservation and healthcare. She (Lewis, scholar) performed her research through virtual interviews and obtaining photos taken by the nuns in a three-week collaboration.
> ... (Lewis will) develop the foundation for a digital archive that can document Ladakh's endangered medicinal plants and their uses, providing an evolving record of the education, healthcare, and conservation leadership of Tibetan Buddhist nuns.[36]

Notice the clever use of 'conservation', 'endangered' and 'healthcare'. Who would not support such issues! All this in the name of honoring the Buddhist nuns of Ladakh.

Yet another grant is to research legumes in Indian agriculture as part of building databases on 'Indian agrarian heritage, the history of botanical collection from India, and the governance of biodiversity'.[37]

Besides the above examples, Mittal Institute also sponsors a significant amount of work to promote the American approach to public health policies and reforms. The COVID-19 pandemic has given it a new kind of opportunity to penetrate deeper and spread its influence on the governance of public health in India. Naturally, public health also serves as a great window to bring in social justice and critical theories and establish leaders deep inside India with American values and support.[38]

Art and Aesthetics

Mittal Institute's Program for Conservation of Culture has developed an interesting database of art and museum artefacts. Harvard's faculty and students visit museums like Mumbai's Chhatrapati Shivaji Maharaj Vastu Sangrahalaya to study conservation and restoration practices in India. The institute launched a virtual workshop on Conservation Science, Training, and Research with the goal of building 'a virtual platform to bring together museums and cultural and academic institutions to collaborate and share best practices that constitute a viable ecosystem for museums and the scientific study of the cultural heritage of the region'.[39]

This is a fancy way of saying that Harvard will control the cloud system holding all the digital assets of the museum that will have immense value in the metaverse as well as big data to train future algorithms.

> The Mittal Institute's Executive Director, Meena Hewett, also visited the Indian National Trust for Art and Cultural Heritage's (INTACH) conservation laboratory in Lucknow, India to study the state of conservation science in India ... – from manuscripts to animal skins – building an understanding of the current conservation services available to art collectors.[40]

A similar project is the Project Mapping Color in History. This is a digital platform to 'compile and organize newly generated information on pigments and place these colors within a historical context'. It draws on scientific analysis of the unique pigments in Asian paintings through collaborations with Asiatic Society, Udaipur Museum, and Chhatrapati Shivaji Maharaj Vastu Sangrahalaya.[41]

Another grant was given to understand how the East India Company developed a painting style 'as a tool to construct and perpetuate an Indian identity' and used it to construct 'an anglicized Indian identity within the artworks' and how it 'presented an Indian identity through a colonial lens'. We presume that this research will be useful to reengineer Indians' identity once again, but this time making it more Americanized rather than anglicized.[42]

Other Databases

Some research projects compile the lists of players in India that could be weaponized against India at a future point. One such project lists feminist organizations on sexual violence in India.[43]

Another faculty grant was for developing an atlas on medium sized Indian cities. This is a database for making projections regarding 'where new population growth, industrial development, and potential infrastructure investment will be directed'. Another aspect is 'an in-depth look at the political, social and spatial aspects' of several such cities.[44] Numerous urban planners in India have been won over to these projects.[45]

Funding was given to the 'Seeds For Change Program', which has the goal of developing and maintaining a digital dashboard tool for corporations, investors, and NGOs that want to monitor human rights abuses and political risks. 'The tool aggregates news, social media data, and political economic indices to give the user an understanding of the disruptions and reputational risks in their complex supply chains and investments'.[46]

Loss of Intellectual Property and National Security

The most disturbing issue is the manner in which personal data belonging to Indians and everything they represent is being siphoned off and fitted into Western frameworks with the resultant new theories being exported back to India under the garb of development. This data belongs to Indians as their Intellectual Property. And it is being appropriated clandestinely, without transparency, regarding its intended usages.

Although initially there may appear to be some positive benefits, history has shown that civilizing missions are carried out with the goal of strengthening the colonizer's control over the colonized. The colonized people's history and culture gets reduced to incoherence, and the colonizer controls the meta-level framework that can make sense of it.

With key social, political, economic, environmental and all other information in the hands of foreign entities like Harvard, the government's ability to develop social welfare schemes is compromised. Armed with sensitive data on India's most vulnerable fault lines, Harvard can resort to blatant arm-twisting to change the laws and facilitate external aggressors, be they missionaries, economic forces, or political adversaries. It can engineer identity politics and social unrest to destabilize the country. It can foster mediocrity to hurt people's competitive prospects. It can dole out various benefits to win more people over. It can rewrite history to turn aggressors into saints, and victims into oppressors.

Since its brand attracts funding and has successfully influenced law-making to channelize tax exemptions for such funding, it can get positioned to circumvent the democratically elected governments and assume de facto influence over civic society.

It is possible that India is inadvertently failing to protect the assets belonging to its citizens. And it is outsourcing policymaking to people at places like Harvard University.

11

Anand Mahindra and Postmodernism

Overview

Over the next few chapters, we will do a literature survey of a wide swathe of projects being carried out at the various centers of Harvard University and funded by Indian billionaires. The source materials we use are mainly the writings or talks of the scholars themselves, as well as reports from the institutions where they work and the publicly available media.

Many of the topics are laudable and worthy of study. It is also not our contention that Harvard University and these centers do not have any *adhikara* or right to undertake this scholarship. Our critique merely raises red flags where these studies have serious implications for India's future and sovereignty.

There are certain core functions related to public policy, understanding of sensitive socio-economic issues, defining priorities and objectives for the nation's development, and research and development that are foundational to shaping society. These need to be home-grown. In other words, this is work which India needs to be doing itself, for India, and for Indians. This is a core competency that cannot be outsourced, especially to foreign institutions, for several reasons.

First, not owning the intellectual capital and the capacity to take it further will make India dependent on foreign parties, and therefore under their control. One has to look no further than Russia to see how even a major world power can be ostracized from the world stage overnight to such an extent that it can be denied access to basic financial infrastructure and world trade systems that were heretofore considered universal.

Second, the data being extracted and appropriated by these external parties rightfully belongs to India's citizens. This data can be used to glean important insights to understand how society functions and the same processes can be used to monitor the effect of unsolicited interventions, including rabble-rousing and social engineering, among other things. Many countries impose data privacy laws that assert sovereignty over the data generated from their citizens. But Indian data is being appropriated by subterfuge under the garb of helping society and in the process, avoiding scrutiny.

Third, in order for sensitive socio-economic, cultural reform projects to be successful, they need to resonate with the cultural context and norms of the people. We have seen how international criminal tribunals designed according to Western systems have failed to address the needs of Rwandans in the face of genocide and South Africans facing apartheid. In both cases, externally imposed systems were rejected, however well-intentioned they may have been, in favor of less formal mechanisms geared towards reconciliation rather than retributive justice. This ability to solve one's own problems is crucial to developing a healthy, functional, and resilient society that can be responsive to the needs of its citizens.

Fourth, there is inherent bias against Hinduism and India, which are seen as primitive, barbaric, and regressive. This is a recycling of old tropes from colonial days that weaponized atrocity literature to evangelize Christianity and Western ways. This has now been combined even more insidiously with a Marxist lens that seeks to foment revolution and violent confrontation, requiring total dismantling of the native systems in order to generate an 'anti-thesis', which precludes constructive, practical problem solving in favor of scapegoating and sowing dissent and divisiveness.

In other words, these projects are not always innocuous and well-intentioned. There is a consistent underlying structural agenda that is fervently pursuing the dismantling of traditions, practices, cultures, languages, and religions native to India only to replace them with ideas of Western Universalism or Abrahamic faith.

Throughout these chapters, we will be describing the alternative approach that China has taken to these matters. We are not advocating the adoption of the Chinese approach in toto. We do support freedom of speech and freedom of scholarship, but our contention is that these ideals become meaningless when there isn't a balance in views and topics, respectful and objective analysis, and appreciation for nuance. Those funding the initiatives should exercise due diligence and should assert their views on how their money is spent.

This chapter deals specifically with the Mahindra Humanities Center at Harvard and shows how it has been used (without necessarily the knowledge of its industrialist donor) to dilute India's position as one of the oldest living traditions in the world and therefore worthy of being studied in its own right. It points out how Harvard appoints as center-head a person known for his unfriendly view of this civilization even when his scholarship has been called into question by his peers. The central issue is the use of Postmodernism as the lens through which India is being studied. Chapter 1 discussed the issues with this lens from a native Indian point of view.

In 2010, Anand Mahindra, the billionaire owner of Mahindra & Mahindra, donated ten million dollars to Harvard, which thanked him by naming its humanities center the Mahindra Humanities Center. Mahindra was quoted saying:

> I am proud to be part of the intellectual legacy of India's contribution to global thinking across the arts, culture, science and philosophy. I am convinced ... for incorporating social and humanistic concerns into the core value proposition of business and have sought to do so with tremendous support from my peers and colleagues at work and outside.[1]

Mahindra's admirable goal is to encourage the cross-cultural and inter-disciplinary exchange of ideas in an international setting. In reciprocity, Harvard has appointed him to the Committee on University Resources, the advisory committee of the Harvard University Asia Center, the Harvard Business School Board of Dean's Advisors, and the Asia-Pacific Advisory Board. He co-founded the HBS Association of India and received the HBS alumni achievement award in 2008.

The *Harvard Crimson* reported: 'This was the largest gift directed solely toward the humanities in Harvard's history'.[2] Prof. Tarun Khanna facilitated this gift, and justified the money flow from a poor country to a rich country as a way to break cultural stereotypes:

In addition to being used well by the Harvard University Press, the
Business School, and the Humanities Center, these donations may
trigger a wave of consciousness in India and South Asia in general
that will encourage fortunate people to support good institutions
... International philanthropy like this—with money flowing from
a relatively undeveloped country to a more developed one—will
help break down cultural stereotypes ...[3]

Mahindra supported the appointment of Homi K. Bhabha as the head
of the center, saying that the Mahindra name, coupled with that of
the director, would make the center 'a symbol of India's heritage and
its contemporary contribution to the arts and the humanities'.[4] On his
part, Bhabha rejoiced that 'there is no other humanities center in the
US whose very name signals the global nature of its enterprise'.[5]

Bhabha was already among the most influential postcolonial
and postmodernist scholars in the academic world, and among the
most iconic ones celebrated by the Indian Left. Given his stature in
the humanities, and especially in critical theories, his impact on the
Mahindra Humanities Center has been powerful. Therefore, it is
important to explain Bhabha's status and intellectual contributions. This
background will also help in understanding the role of Postmodernism
in shaping Harvard's approach towards India. Postmodernism not only
serves as the launching pad for deconstructing India, but also supports
various fashionable social science theories like Critical Race Theory.

When Bhabha was first brought to Harvard, his appointment
was seen as a watershed event. The *New York Times* wrote that 'the
acquisition of Homi K. Bhabha from the University of Chicago this
fall is regarded as a major coup, as if Sammy Sosa had defected to the
Boston Red Sox'.[6] The Indian government has conferred Bhabha with
the coveted Padma Bhushan. He has served on numerous prestigious
committees, such as the humanities jury for the Infosys Prize.[7]

Homi K. Bhabha, the Pied Piper of Harvard

Bhabha, as the newly appointed head, praised Mahindra for his gift:

There are going to be such philanthropic gifts made to institutions
that stand worldwide for universal use of the arts and the

humanities. Man does not live by bread alone, nations do not make their names and their reputations only on their annual growth rates. To make a truly global presence, *you have to be seen, to stand for culture and human values*, and that I think is the distinction in particular of Anand's gift ... The humanities centre at Harvard, which I direct, is not so much a centre, as it is at the crossroads of the university.[8]

He went on to emphasize that the central importance of the humanities was to teach how to interpret facts. All the information in science, technology, business, arts, literature, and religion is useless unless it is interpreted correctly, he said. We agree with his generic statement below:

If you don't have the humanistic disciplines, which encourage our attention to ethics, morality, human life and its progress, concept of equality, fair play and justice, empathy, rights of minorities, ... sciences, technology ... financial sector will not have a strong framework of values. ... humanities create a framework that allows ... sectors of knowledge to come together. ... another central contribution that humanities make. ... There is this flood of information, facts. The way in which information becomes knowledge, is through the act of interpretation. Why am I watching these facts? Why is all this information being thrown at me? Why do I distinguish what is valuable and important from what is not? All of this needs interpretation. ... humanities ... literature, art history, philosophy, theology, or study of scriptures are about interpretation. And evaluating the information. And that's something people often don't want to talk about to the press. The press will say what is interpretation, what are the outcomes, what profits do you make. What is the market value of interpretation? Zero. But without interpretation, you will not ... understand how to intervene in the market, how to make judgments. ... in an age where information is thrown at you from all sides, it is interpretation that turns information into knowledge.[9]

However, the central issue is: *Whose* interpretation is to be used? *Which* civilization's lens? There is no such thing as 'the universal' interpretive lens in the humanities. Even within Indian thought, there are multiple systems of interpretation, and likewise in Western thought. However, there are significant commonalities among a given civilization's lenses that comprise a coherent worldview. The Western worldview is significantly different than the Indian one.

Bhabha is a well-known postmodernist scholar that has championed this genre of Western thought his entire career and used it to deconstruct and debunk the legitimacy of India as a nation, Vedic thought as a system, and other things Indian. The most fundamental point that emerges from our following analysis is that Bhabha emphasizes the *Americanization of humanities in India.*

Over a decade ago, Harvard's Prof. Michael Witzel had informed us that the Leftist crowd was determined to change the Indology department to South Asian Studies. He offered to help Infinity Foundation influence the new charter for South Asian Studies if we could fund it on a large scale and he would secure a few key appointments before his retirement. We were convinced of his sincerity and of the proposal, but we failed to raise the required level of funds.

As the years went by, Witzel's warnings came true. Harvard's new South Asia programs became increasingly distanced from what used to be Indology for the past several decades. By 2010, the following was announced:

> The Department of Sanskrit and Indian Studies has laid out plans to adopt a more interdisciplinary focus as the renamed Department of South Asian Studies. ... the department will draw from other departments like anthropology, history, religion, folklore and mythology, music, and archeology to expand its current faculty from eight to 15 professors, according to Sanskrit Professor Michael E. J. Witzel.[10]

Bhabha's Postmodernism

It is fair to point out that Bhabha has his share of critics among his own peer group in White liberal academic circles. They criticize his deliberate use of opacity, obscurantism, and ambiguity. Ensuring that very few can understand him is a terrific ploy because nobody can challenge what is tough to figure out.

> Interestingly, in 1998, the journal *Philosophy and Literature* awarded Bhabha the second prize in its Bad Writing Competition.[11] This is a way to spotlight a nonsensical academic publication. The award 'celebrates bad writing from the most stylistically lamentable passages found in scholarly books and articles'. Bhabha was awarded the prize for the following sentence in his widely acclaimed book, *The Location of Culture*:
>
> > 'If, for a while, the ruse of desire is calculable for the uses of discipline soon the repetition of guilt, justification, pseudo-scientific theories, superstition, spurious authorities, and classifications can be seen as the desperate effort to "normalize" formally the disturbance of a discourse of splitting that violates the rational, enlightened claims of its enunciatory modality'.[12]

When Bhabha was appointed to the Harvard faculty, Marjorie Perloff, professor emeritus of English at Stanford University, expressed 'dismay', telling *The New York Times* in an interview that 'He doesn't have anything to say'.[13] Mark Crispin Miller, a professor of media studies at New York University, also criticized his work: 'One could finally argue that there is no meaning there, beyond the neologisms and Latinate buzzwords. Most of the time I don't know what he's talking about.'[14]

Another Western critic has described Bhabha's most celebrated book as 'dense, pretentious prose, which is commonplace now among the humanists who feel inferior to scientists'.[15] Others point out that he hides the trivial nature of his ideas behind arcane poststructuralist jargon. He garners undeserved attention even though there is no thesis, no argument, no evidence. He goes through the motions of scholarship by making generic statements that overwhelm the reader's cognitive faculties. Using convoluted sentence structures and a few lofty quotes, he is the snake-oil salesman selling you what appears to be a thesis.

Robert Young, a prominent liberal academician and well known for his book, *White Mythologies: Writing History and the West*, criticizes Bhabha for shifting from one conceptual scheme to another. He says that none of Bhabha's ideas are established by empirical evidence or solid reason, and is disturbed by the haphazard, discontinuous jumping from one idea to another without justification.

> On each occasion Bhabha seems to imply through this timeless characterization that the concept in question constitutes the condition of colonial discourse itself and would hold good for all historical periods and contexts – so it comes as something of a surprise when it is subsequently replaced by the next one... Inevitably, of course, different conceptualizations produce different emphases – but the absence of any articulation of the relation between them remains troubling.[16]

Young goes on to say that Bhabha's 'theoretical anarchism' and lack of 'consistent metalanguage' makes his style incomprehensible. Someone once quipped: 'Does Homi Bhabha understand what Homi Bhabha writes?' As the saying goes, if you cannot dazzle them with brilliance, then baffle them with bullshit!

This reminds us of a dialogue between the postmodernist Michel Foucault and philosopher John Searle in which Foucault justifies the use of obscure language that nobody will understand. It is believed Foucault told Searle that he wrote in an arcane and impenetrable style because '25 percent of one's writing needs to be incomprehensible nonsense to be taken seriously by French philosophers'.[17]

Postmodernism is full of such scholarship. In fact, its scholars do not agree among themselves even on how to define Postmodernism. This is not surprising because one of its tenets that its scholars agree on is that *all ideas of absolute truth and objective reality must be rejected*. This has established Postmodernism as a field where anything goes depending on only one factor: whether one's theories and assertions get accepted by the peer group's leaders that have the power to determine the fate of every claim. There is no need for any semblance of evidence or rational proof.

A well-known scandal emerged in this light when Alan Sokal, a New York University physicist and mathematician, deliberately wrote a nonsensical article filled with gibberish. It claimed that quantum gravity was postmodernist in nature, and he loaded his paper with the kind of tropes postmodernists love. He used fashionable terms like 'transgression of boundaries', 'deconstruction', 'dominant ideologies and power relations', 'self-referential', 'counter-hegemonic', 'marginalized communities', etc. In other words, physics had finally concluded that reality is entirely a social construct. Sokal sent the article to one of the two most prestigious journals of Postmodernism, Duke University Press's *Social Text*. It was accepted. He then revealed that it was all a hoax and wrote about it in the other popular journal of Postmodernism, *Lingua Franca*. He said his goal was to demonstrate that even the most esteemed Postmodernism editors cannot identify something that is utter nonsense and a parody!

In a 2005 interview with *The Hindu* in India, Bhabha was upset at his critics, saying that a philosopher like him should not be required to use the 'common language of the common person'. He argued that scientists are given a pass for their use of technical language that is not immediately comprehensible to casual readers.[18]

This is an arrogant statement claiming that he can speak and write in illogical juxtapositions because he has declared himself to be a 'philosopher'. However, what is more troubling is his comparing himself with scientists who use technical terminology. He ought to know that technical terms used in science adhere to tight definitions, are precise, and accepted by the scientific community after extensive debate; nonsense cannot hide behind an aura of ambiguity that is so typical of Postmodernism.

Also, scientific claims are continually subjected to independent empirical testing and logical scrutiny at an intellectual standard that is well above the competence level found in Postmodernism. Once a given scientific term is comprehended by the reader, the text becomes perfectly clear and unambiguous, whereas in the case of Bhabha's postmodernist hubris, even his fellow-postmodernists are unable to explain or understand what he is trying to say.

What might be his motive in this method? We believe Bhabha is pursuing a cunning and deliberate strategy to throw up a lot of rubbish using Harvard's clout, causing cognitive dissonance in the reader's mind. And once the reader's rationality is broken down this way, gobbledygook is accepted as profundity and the reader can then be channeled towards the desired ideological position. The Pied Piper can lead the way.

The more challenged the readers have been in decoding his work, the greater Bhabha's reputation has become as an 'original' thinker. In fact, many scholars have said that his meaninglessness is what makes him awesome. But the use of obscurity and incomprehensibility is a camouflage and not some stroke of genius.

On the other hand, many Liberal thinkers have been clear in their writings. For instance, the French West-Indian, Frantz Fanon was an eminent postcolonial scholar whose style was free from the burden of nonsense and hence, his work was accessible to readers.

The imprint of European thinkers on Bhabha, especially the imprint of Jacques Lacan, Michel Foucault, Sigmund Freud, and Jacques Derrida, becomes clearer the more one tries to decode him.

What exactly are Bhabha's fundamental tenets on which all his fame rests? We have spent a couple of decades decoding him and below is a brief summary to the best of our abilities. We will explain in the most positive manner, four main ideas he focuses on, and even make them coherent and unified to give him the benefit of doubt:

- Hybridity or Hybridization: This is a convoluted way by which Bhabha refers to the process of adopting elements of multiple cultures, commonly known as multiculturalism.
- Ambivalence: Restated simply, this means that colonialism creates a split in the identity of the colonized. On the one hand, he has the identity given to him by the colonizer, but simultaneously, he retains a part of his own original identity.
- The Third Space: This is the mental area in between two conflicting identities because of ambivalence. It 'challenges our sense of the historical identity of culture as a homogenizing, unifying force, authenticated by the original past, kept alive in the national tradition of the People'. This is where the hierarchical claims of originality and purity about one's original culture get broken down and new statements about one's culture get developed. Bhabha believes there is nothing well-defined about culture because all the elements of a culture can be isolated, broken up, and deconstructed. Each of these can then be translated to suit one's purpose. Even its history can be rewritten in accordance with present needs.[19]
- Mimicry: This is the climax of his entire theory. It refers to the colonized people imitating the culture of the colonizers. The result

is a form of resistance. 'The effect of mimicry is camouflage... it is not a question of harmonizing with the background, but against a mottled background'.[20] Because hybridization is never a complete replication of the colonizer, it retains remnants of the original colonized culture that turns into a form of resistance.

What Bhabha calls hybridity overlooks the fact that when one culture colonizes another, the asymmetry of power results in what we have called the digestion of one civilization by another. He also wants us to simply accept, without any convincing logic, that the colonized culture imitating the colonizer represents *in all cases* a form of resistance that undermines colonialism. He says this resistance limits the range of exchanges between the oppressor and the oppressed.

But Bhabha ignores the fact that there are numerous kinds of cross-cultural transactions. For instance, the U-Turn Theory proposed by Rajiv Malhotra is a detailed description of the journey by which the colonizer experiences the civilization of the colonized. Along the way, he appropriates the alien culture as his own. The theory elaborately explains the diverse forces at work in each of the five stages of the process, and the different kinds of outcomes that might result. It also explains the overall impact such U-Turns have on the two civilizations engaged in this encounter.

What makes Postmodernism dangerous is that it removes the burden to prove any thesis with evidence. It relativizes the truth and turns it into identity politics. All truth-claims are dismissed as powerplays by the elitists. While we certainly see this to be true of some scholarship, postmodernists go too far. They deconstruct all knowledge, including natural sciences, mathematics, etc. as the result of power at the hands of the elites. This makes Postmodernism an enabler of Wokeism because political correctness overrides the need for empirical evidence and logical interpretation.

Devdutt Pattanaik is a prominent example of this genre and controversial for relativizing the Vedic *shastras*. For instance, he rejects all past interpretations of the *Bhagavad Gita* and claims his own 'My Gita' to be the valid interpretation. It's true that the tradition thrives on challenges and fresh ideas. But there are well-defined principles of interpretation within the tradition.

Postmodernist deconstruction of Indian texts leads to their trivialization, mistranslation, and breakdown into random parts that can be arbitrarily used and abused out of context. What Bhabha praises as hybridity is what leads to the digestion of non-Western civilizations into the stomach of the West.

It is not surprising that Bhabha supports people like the famous Carnatic vocalist, T.M. Krishna, whose signature work is to promote the digestion of Indian classical music into what Bhabha would call 'hybrid' forms. This was highlighted during a lecture at the Mahindra Humanities Center.[21]

Our take on Postmodernism is that it borrows many ideas from Vedanta and Buddhism, and this has been discussed in numerous academic writings. However, these borrowings are distorted as is often the case when knowledge gets digested from one civilization to another. Both Postmodernism and Indian knowledge systems deconstruct the ordinary reality experienced by our senses. Indian systems do this with the purpose of revealing a higher reality in a higher state of consciousness variously known as *moksha*, *nirvana*, and so on. Postmodernism, on the other hand, does not subscribe to any such higher state of consciousness.

So, what does a postmodernist deconstruction of the ordinary reality lead to, and what does it accomplish? This is the serious question postmodernists do not discuss. Both Vedanta and Postmodernism want to get rid of the mundane cognition we have, but Postmodernism lacks any kind of metaphysics of what lies beyond this ordinary consciousness. The reason is that Postmodernism was born as a political device to defy European injustice by fighting all grand narratives as they are deemed to be the result of power and domination. And hence, the entire movement has been stuck at the political level and has never advanced spiritually.

Indian Franchise

Bhabha is a clever middleman straddling two cultures. He has mastered the art of convincing Indians that he brings to them the trendiest American literary theories, while simultaneously selling himself to the Americans as their authentic voice of India.

He serves as a major American intellectual export to the Third World. His great mastery of the English language allows him to mesmerize

Indians with flowery and playful words. The Indian *chowkidars* or gatekeepers, guarding the fortress of Critical Theory consider him a legend. The senior members of the franchise are the high priests licensed to evangelize his works for the junior English Honors masses. The franchise operators in India build him up for their own credibility as cross-cultural brokers.

This manufactured popularity in India gets played back in the US to impress the White liberals. They feel he is representing the Empire talking back. This absolves the White guilt by making it seem as though the American academy is addressing its racism.

The worst harm one can inflict on the Indian youth is to take them further into confusion and moronization. Postmodernism is a horrible weapon to destroy a people's sense of self-esteem.

America is too practical a society to have time for such nonsense. Therefore, Bhabha did not serve any purpose in any practical sense in America and nor did the American government and corporate mainstream recognize him as a serious thinker. For many decades, his importance was mainly within the academic ghetto of Third World studies. Then, one lucky day, his legitimacy was broadened outside the academic cocoon. This is when Anand Mahindra launched Homi K. Bhabha beyond the small academic cliché to become an important commentator on India, influencing policymakers and the wider public.

Hinduphobia

Bhabha has been very critical of Hinduism and nationalism in India. He says: 'There is no question that certain cultural, religious, moral ideas like Hindutva are being presented to people as a platform for the construction of a national community.'[22]

He feels that while the BJP projects a very cosmopolitan image abroad, in India it is parochial, and involved in 'disempowering certain traditions, cultures and communities within the nation'. This dichotomy between the ideological stance at home and abroad troubles him consistently.

Bhabha draws a parallel with Donald Trump's slogan, 'Make America Great Again' (MAGA). He claims that a similar populist nationalism is alive in India, and 'the dangerous thing is that those who do not agree with it are not invited to be a part of a fair and free democratic process. They are stereotyped and scape-goated'. In order to resist such oppression, Bhabha wants Indians to have solidarity with foreign nexuses. He supported Indian writers that returned their Sahitya Akademi awards (for literary scholarship) to the government as a legitimate mode of protesting against the purported suppression of rights and freedom.[23]

When the Jawaharlal Nehru University (JNU) in New Delhi acted against student union president, Kanhaiya Kumar in a sedition case, Bhabha wrote to the vice chancellor criticizing this as the 'criminalization of dissent'. Ironically, he called for 'engaging with the diversity of opinions', something that his Ivy League fortress has repeatedly denied to those who disagree with its cabal.[24]

Bhabha has routinely promoted the idea that India has slipped into 'Hindu nationalism' and 'majority authoritarianism', and that the minorities have been denied their constitutional rights. The following statement by him in an interview is an example of this posture:

> There is a trend in India today to enhance political didacticism rather than democratic dialogue. The appeal to one element of the composite and syncretic culture of India — Hindutva, for instance — on the grounds of patriotism or populism is to distort the fine balance between cultures, beliefs and communities that represents the wonder that was India and could become the wonder of India once again. Our Constitution is a fine instrument of equality with checks and balances to protect minorities as a part of the larger national interest. Once the state devises majoritarian instruments of intimidation and exclusion and aims itself indiscriminately against the "enemy within" — Dalits, Christians, Muslims, the LGBT community, NGOs, etc. — then democratic participation is overshadowed by authoritarian paranoia.[25]

He falsely assumes that Hindu civilization legitimizes what he calls 'a mythical return to a state of racial purity; a closed-in cultural homogeneity; a sexuality that is deeply regulated; a walled insecurity of territorial sovereignty'.[26] Bhabha's ideal of a nation is based on Subaltern fragmentation where all values are tentative. He constantly accuses the Hindutva crowd of wanting to return to some ancient homogenous India.[27]

The problem with him and other postmodernists is their false notion that Hinduism wants homogenization. As the two books, *Being Different* and *Indra's Net* point out at great length, the case is the exact opposite. Hindu dharma is an open architecture and champions the diversity of views, methods for worship, deities, lineages, metaphysical frameworks, and so forth. Hinduism promotes diversity through mutual respect for difference.

As an example of the ideological tilt promoted by the Mahindra Center, let us examine an event it sponsored to launch an interesting book titled, *Indian Sex Life*, by Durba Mitra of the Radcliffe Institute at Harvard.[28] The book focuses on the use of caste as the lens to study sexuality in India with a special emphasis on prostitution. This is an interesting work based on the author's original insights and her review of colonial era literature. However, it suffers from bias, because of her sole reliance on secondary sources by Westerners and Indians trained by Westerners that stereotype Hindu caste. She cites the caste ideas of William Jones, Levi Strauss, David Emile Durkheim, and others, and does not reference sources from within the Hindu tradition itself. For instance, the *Dharmashastras* and *Itihasa* have numerous references to prostitutes that are mostly non-judgmental, and one could use these instead of Western works to interpret their lives.

Another methodological problem is that even though Mitra acknowledges that similar phenomena are described in Urdu and Persian writings, she ignores probing them. Only 'Hindu caste' is studied, and only upper caste Hindu men are problematized. As expected of such a scholar, her explanations are lavishly sprinkled with terms like 'elitist', 'nationalistic', 'misogynistic', 'patriarchal', 'majoritarian', etc.

Mitra contrasts two writings from a century ago: by a Muslim woman and a Hindu male. The Muslim's narrative describes a dream in which Indian women in the future dominate in public, innovate technologies and manage statecraft while men are secluded in the home. She contrasts this with the second narrative written by an upper caste Hindu male, and describes 'the decline and fall of high caste Hindu society as the result of unbridled woman's sexuality in a didactic scientific text'. The Hindu man is portrayed as the stereotype of patriarchy wanting to get rid of assertive women. She wants to spread memes making the Muslim look good while the Hindu is described as the 'upper caste Hindu elite' with his 'majoritarian patriarchal control' through 'Hindu monogamy'. That kind of identity politics has made her popular at Harvard.

Mitra projects her views to Twitter, saying there is 'a really, really good misogyny army on Twitter of Hindu rightwing men' that comprise 'a strategy that's part of Hindu nationalism from the beginning'.

The comments by panelists do not offer any diversity of perspectives. They support the book as an important contribution to Critical Social Theory, intellectual history, and the sociology of knowledge.

Another example is the Mahindra Humanities Center's support for Prasenjit Duara under the Environment Forum at the Mahindra Center.[29] Duara is a well-known scholar of China and an advisory board member of the Institute of Chinese Studies.[30] A recent report by The Law Society Foundation called this institute

> a Lutyens think-tank dedicated to Chinese studies which has tried to project itself as a 'neutral' research organisation, though in reality, is aggressively trying to build pro-China sentiments in India. Reportedly, through questionable studies and analysis, it tries to portray Communist China in good light and has never raised concerns over Beijing's expansionist agenda or human rights abuses – not even its incursions into the Indian territory! The organisation has been founded by a prominent pro-China voice in the Indian academia. Besides, a couple of prominent former diplomats are associated with the organisation. The think-tank also 'recommends' Indian students for post-doctoral studies in China through a tie-up with the Harvard-Yenching Institute.[31]

Duara has great things to say about China's environmentalism, and in his book, *The Crisis of Global Modernity*, he says: 'Among all developing countries, the Chinese government's efforts in environmental education are probably the greatest'.

In his discussion at the Mahindra Humanities Center, Duara discussed spirituality as a basis for ecology. He gives a lot of credit to Christianity while compromising the contributions of Hinduism in ecology. He also commends Alfred North Whitehead for using spirituality for ecology, not pointing out that this is a Buddhist idea that was digested by Whitehead. He also refers to Henry Thoreau being inspired by nature, again not recognizing that Thoreau himself was deeply influenced by

Vedic thought. While praising all the other major religions for their contributions to environmentalism, Hinduism is mentioned the least and he is quick to say that it is compromised because of Hindutva.[32]

In a *New York Times* interview, he praises China's environmentalism; but when asked to comment on India, he says that it has a hierarchical society, and though earlier there were movements that helped the environment, now it has a strong man like the Russians and Chinese.[33]

In conclusion, our analysis of the Mahindra Humanities Center at Harvard focuses on the use of the Postmodernism lens as exemplified by its head, Homi K. Bhabha, and on a sample of scholarship produced by some individual scholars. As far as Anand Mahindra is concerned, though all this scholarship enjoys affiliation with his name, we appreciate that his own views are not necessarily being reflected.

12

Lakshmi Mittal and Social Justice

Overview

As seen in the previous chapter, Harvard University's attitude towards India has often been hostile. The studies it conducts undermine India. This chapter shows how Harvard uses The Lakshmi Mittal and Family South Asia Institute to be critical of India's civilizational legitimacy. And as may be expected, it is headed by a person with a mixed-up posture on India.

The institute has an inordinately high interest in India's minorities, whether they are defined in terms of religion or social order, or gender, or any other criterion and consistently positions itself as the savior of these groups against their own government and fellow citizens.

India has a very long international land border and has suffered a multitude of tensions while protecting it, whether in the form of illegal occupation, or insurgencies, or both. The Mittal Institute is present at every venue, advocating for these groups, whether it is the Bhil region in the west, or the Naga and Manipuri land in the northeast. It is also defending the radical Muslim narrative on Kashmir. There is also a goal to rewrite India's history with a certain stated bias, especially with respect to specific periods or events (such as Partition); and to own the sources from which this story is derived. The Harvard brand name is enough to position this as the only authoritative narrative of the times.

Its scholars are constantly searching for an opportunity to take pot-shots at India's democratically elected prime minister, Narendra Modi. Here too, one sees an effort to support the Opposition parties. These postures are of course unscholarly in their lack of objectivity and interventionist in their motive.

To see that all its plans come to fruition, Harvard also maintains good relations with the Indian government, occasionally entertaining government officials and people in important positions.

In fact, with all this background work and funding by Indians, Harvard figures it has the wherewithal to set up an 'embassy' in India for more direct interference.

Harvard University Sets up its 'Embassy in India'

When Lakshmi Mittal, the steel tycoon, made his landmark donation in 2017, it breathed new life into a languishing South Asia Institute at Harvard. The Mittal Institute at Harvard is now well funded for research and training of scholars at a rapid pace. It is also the anchor investor that has encouraged other Indian billionaires to invest in Harvard. It proudly boasts:

> The Lakshmi Mittal South Asia Institute serves as a nexus for Harvard's engagement with Afghanistan, Bangladesh, Bhutan, India, Maldives, Myanmar, Nepal, Pakistan, and Sri Lanka, as well as diaspora populations from these countries. ... currently engages more than 250 faculty from a variety of disciplines across Harvard and peer institutions; provides annual funding for more than 50 students to participate in research, internships, and immersive language study; supports postdoctoral fellowships; hosts visiting artists at Harvard; sponsors lectures, conferences, and leadership training in the region and on campus; and works with government, academic, and civil society organizations in-region, especially through its local offices in India and Pakistan.
>
> 'We are so grateful for the Mittal family's support and what it will enable us to learn and share — across the sciences, social sciences, and the humanities — and the many people and institutions it will allow us to engage,' said (Tarun) Khanna. 'The world stands to benefit for generations from the work that these resources will generate.'[1]

Clearly, Mittal, like other billionaires, had good intentions for such a donation. A newspaper report stated:

> 'South Asia has played a dynamic and influential role in the
> development of our world since the very first civilisations,' said
> sixty-seven-year-old Mittal, chairman and CEO of ArcelorMittal,
> the world's largest steel company. 'Ensuring that we fully
> understand its history and unique dynamics is a critical enabler
> in helping to shape a successful future,' he added.[2]

But it isn't clear how the institute is furthering this laudable vision. We
will examine some of the specific socio-economic positions this institute
has taken over the past few years for a glimpse of how it embarrasses
India. We will pick some examples from its work on caste, meritocracy,
and political interventions in India's internal affairs.

In the year 2018, Harvard announced that this institute was its
'embassy' in India, and hailed this as a new era of Harvard's direct
engagement with the South Asian region:

> 'Harvard would not be what it is if it was not capable of attracting
> the best brains from all over the world,' said Mark Elliott, vice
> provost for international affairs and the Mark Schwartz professor
> of Chinese and Inner Asian History ... 'We intend to create a
> small embassy at the institute, which will help the students and
> researchers to study at Harvard.'[3]

What is being entirely ignored is that India has its own rich heritage in
the fields covered by the Western liberal arts. But unlike China, which
has been exporting its liberal arts via the hundreds of Confucius Institutes
and incorporating these ideas into all levels of education domestically,
in India's case there is no similar initiative. Instead, its billionaires
are helping to import Western liberal arts that denigrate India's own
traditions.

Political Interventions

As did Oxford University in the 1800s, Harvard projects itself as the
genuinely neutral player between the Global North and South to save
humanity. Once its reputation and clout were established, the Mittal
Institute began flexing its muscles more confidently to intervene in
India's internal affairs.

A good example to illustrate this is the work of Salil Shetty, senior fellow, Carr Center for Human Rights Policy at Harvard Kennedy School, who is regularly championed by the Mittal Institute. He is described as 'a long-term activist on issues of poverty and justice and has served as Amnesty International's Secretary-General'. The institute describes that he researches 'accountability and equity in governance in India across sectors. He seeks to understand strategies for more inclusive and accountable governance in India'.[4]

Shetty is an important activist turned scholar who is routinely promoted by the Mittal Institute. One of his talks was on *Kashmir: Decoding the Crisis*, on the revocation of Article 370 that gave special status to the state of Jammu & Kashmir. He said:

> Since the so-called war on terror was launched, we have seen huge backslide on human rights, specifically but ... on justice and democracy itself. The rise of elected populist authoritarianism using 'othering' techniques against Muslims, refugees, indigenous people, blacks, women, etc., powered by social media and the internet has created a new reality. ... Shutting down media and the internet, combined with curfews and bans on meetings, is the standard methodology used by governments ... to curb freedom of expression and assembly. This is only going to make Kashmiris angrier, particularly since thousands of leaders and activists have also been unlawfully arrested and restrictions on freedom of movement means that they cannot even communicate face-to-face within their neighborhood. ... by throwing a matchstick into a tinder box, it seems like the current regime in India has decided to sacrifice the people of Kashmir in order to achieve its Hindu national hegemonic goals in mainland India.[5]

His agenda is not consistent with the Mittal Institute's claim to be a neutral and unbiased player. But he clearly wants the 'progressive world' to intervene in India. He says, one should not expect that 'ordinary people who have a progressive world view will remain silent. That is where the hope lies'.[6]

As another example, in 2020-1 when farmers in Delhi protested against farm bills passed by the Indian Parliament, students at Harvard demanded the Mittal Institute to denounce Prime Minister Modi's actions concerning the bills on the basis of human rights violations. Harvard's campus magazine, *The Crimson*, reported:

> The Undergraduate Council passed legislation Sunday endorsing a petition calling on Harvard administrators and the University's Lakshmi Mittal and Family South Asia Institute to 'denounce the detention and repression' of protesters in India under Prime Minister Narendra D. Modi's administration... the government has cracked down on the protests with internet censorship and arrests. The petition decries actions taken against protesters by the Indian government under Modi, alleging 'grievous, unconscionable, and unconstitutional' human rights violations.[7]

Another political talk denouncing the Modi government was hosted by the Mittal Institute featuring a group of professors. The event was titled, *Voting for Strongmen: Nationalist and Populist Leadership in Brazil and India*. It compared Prime Minister Modi and President Bolsonaro of Brazil, as examples of 'a resurgence of strongman politics' that are 'bypassing democratic norms and embracing populist ideals'. The panelists discussed the nationalist and populist leaderships and implications for the global political system at large.[8]

Various joint seminars on politics in South Asia were coordinated by the Mittal Institute that included participation by Harvard, MIT, Watson Institute at Brown University, and the Weatherhead Center for International Affairs.[9] One of these was on 'armed politics' in South Asia.[10]

A pet theme for Mittal scholars has been the study of India's borderlands, with particular focus on promoting and championing insurgencies and separatist movements. For example, a sociology professor was invited to lecture on *Exploring the Roots of Insurgent Citizenship in India's Bhil Heartland*. The research focused on Subaltern groups that 'must resort to the universalizing vocabulary of citizenship to stake claims for redistribution and recognition. But on what basis do they do this – especially under severe coercion?' The lecture was advertised as an investigation on the 'movement patterns in the Bhil heartland of western India, where Adivasi communities have organized and mobilized against the tyranny of the local state'.[11] This is a sensitive region severely affected by insurgencies, exactly the kind of place Harvard loves to play in.

Also, under the guise of teaching 'critical thinking and problem solving' to high school students in the sensitive region of Manipur in the northeast of India, teachers sent from Harvard proudly declared their motive was to dig up dirt. From the very first day, they 'brainstormed a list of social problems in Manipur. They had so many ideas, from crimes against women to frequent strikes in the state'.[12]

Another inter-disciplinary project set up by the Mittal Institute is studying the controversial legal and constitutional issues of citizenship in India. It will cover the period starting from Partition onwards including the various counter movements. The intention is to develop a framework in which the recent laws on citizenship can be discussed and problems unearthed.[13]

Mittal scholars are also studying various issues related to the political and societal functioning in India with the goal of intervention at some later date. For example, a research paper by a Mittal fellow on India's Forest Rights Act 2006 highlighted how landless members of lower castes in the state of Uttar Pradesh were harassed by higher caste men.[14]

The institute is also helping Harvard's push to dominate as the largest database owner on social problems in India. For example, the Raghunathan Family Fellowship at the Mittal Institute was awarded for research on 'urban and residential segregation' and 'whether or not urbanization is a solution to breaking caste and religious barriers'.[15] The Raghunathan Family Seminar presented 'how residential caste-segregation is independent of city size'. It proudly reported that for the first time ever it used a large database of minute details from 147 of the largest cities in India. The work was showcased during talks both in the US and India:

> ...one of the central conundrums in Indian urbanism – the persistence of caste segregation across the country, and across cities of varying sizes. This finding punctures a hole in one of the central normative promises of India's urbanization: the gradual withering of traditional caste-based segregation. The talk will provide further fine-grained evidence on the ghettoization of the most spatially marginalized groups in urban India: Muslims and Dalits.[16]

Similarly, a seminar titled, *Na Hindu, Na Musalman: The Dilemma of A Bengali Artisan Caste*,[17] was conducted on the social predicament of a 'low-caste' community of West Bengal, the 'Patuas', who converted from Hinduism to Islam in the thirteenth century. The seminar's claim was that they have weathered the rough waters of double marginalization by Indian society, being both low caste and Muslim. Another example is the grant given to a PhD candidate in philosophy to study *The Dalit Middle Class: How caste, class, and market-centric discourses interact to shape it.*[18]

Tarun Khanna said in an interview that the Indian Public Sector Undertakings should 'be engaged in CSR (Corporate Social Responsibility) more productively'.[19] This is not a simple statement considering the way CSR and ESG are sometimes used for furthering specific socio-political agendas especially when combined with identity politics. Other Mittal researchers in the broad category of US-India ties have chosen issues including Indian diaspora politics, corruption, and governance in India.[20]

The following samples of supported projects illustrate Mittal Institute's interests in making social justice and political interventions. These include individual research projects as well as panel discussions. Some of the scholars supported are well-known names with strong political ideologies. The following titles of projects are a sample of the vast work done by Mittal Institute:

- Voices of the Rohingya
- Dreams of Independence: Vernacular Nationalism Among the Mizos of Northeast India
- Religious Nationalism, Ethnic Conflict and State Terror in Modern India: Cases From Kashmir, Punjab, Gujarat, and Nagaland
- Naxalite-Maoist Conflicts in Eastern India
- Relationship Between Neoliberalism and the Rise of Religious Fundamentalist Movements
- Deliberative Inequality: A Text-As-Data Study of Tamil Nadu's Village Assemblies
- Democracy in Distress in South Asia

- Role of Social Media as Propaganda in Sri Lanka's Post-War Religious Violence
- Decoding the Supreme Court Verdict that Decriminalized Homosexuality in India
- Crisis and Credibility: The Politics of Ideas in India and Developing Democracies
- Constructing a Majority: A Micro-Level Study of Voting Patterns in Indian Elections
- States-in-Waiting: Nationalism, Internationalism, Decolonization
- US-India Relations, Diaspora Politics, Anticorruption, and Global Governance

Caste Impact in America

An all-time favorite theme of Western intervention has been the wide range of social issues. And under that umbrella, there is nothing more explosive and high leverage than caste. The following examples are merely illustrative of the content being promoted at the Mittal Institute.

A special series on *Caste in America* was led by a television investigative reporter, with Mittal Institute's Tarun Khanna, Harvard Kennedy School's Suraj Yengde, and others. This was just one of numerous activities to get Harvard involved in the thesis that caste abuse is like American Black/White racism and has entered the US through the Indian diaspora.

The anchor confirmed at the very opening that the purpose of the series was to explore 'the discrimination Indian immigrants face in the United States as a result of this ancient hierarchical system of human classification', including the relationship of caste to race. Yengde emphasized that Americans must understand caste because it characterizes the large Indian diaspora in the US.[21]

The Mittal Institute has co-sponsored events with Equality Labs. Earlier chapters discussed Equality Labs – the main thinktank championing the Black-Dalit mobilization against the so-called 'Whites of India', namely, the upper castes. One such event was on *Caste in Town Hall* and its stated goal was to build momentum against 'America's casteist workplaces and the larger movement to add caste as a protected category across the United States in the battle to end caste in the US'. The event was moderated by Thenmozhi Soundararajan, executive director of Equality Labs. The speakers included Ajantha Subramanian (of Harvard), the subject of an entire chapter earlier, as well as representatives from Ambedkar Association of North America, and Ambedkar International Center.[22]

Women's Empowerment

The issues of women and gender make up yet another powerful domain being used to question traditions, in general and those of India, in particular. The Mittal Institute has carried out numerous activities to champion the human rights of women, such as the Harvard Gender Violence Project:

> ... the Harvard Gender Violence Project ... elevate(s) the status
> of South Asian women by engaging societies to reject violence
> and foster respect for all people. The Harvard Gender Violence
> Project (HGVP) is a collaboration between SAI, HLS, HBS,
> and the FXB Center for Health and Human Rights, and regional
> experts working in the area of gender violence prevention and
> intervention programs.[23]

While these are noble objectives, the problem is with the way Harvard gets between the Indian people and the Indian government as the intermediary representing the oppressed/victims of India, in this instance, women. The Mittal Institute also collaborates with Harvard's Francois-Xavier Bagnoud Center for Health and Human Rights on such issues. One such project involved producing policy frameworks on how to create successful educational outcomes for daughters of illiterate parents.[24] One of the key champions of Indian women's causes is Harvard Kennedy School's Prof. Jacqueline Bhabha, a well-known legal expert who is also the wife of Homi K. Bhabha.[25]

A look at the various conferences and workshops organized around women's issues reveals a pattern. For instance, the conference on gender justice, criminal law, and curriculum reforms was 'to explore current issues related to law enforcement, advocacy and curriculum reform'. And it led to a follow-up workshop on 'preventive approaches to gender violence'.[26] This was followed by another workshop titled *Gender, Civil Society, and the State in Contemporary South Asia:*

Preventive Approaches to Gender Based Violence.[27] The goal was to formulate legislative and policy changes that would be relevant to sexual assault and gender violence in India.[28]

The following sample of topics shows the broad range of gender issues being studied:

- Jacqueline Bhabha led a discussion with Indian feminists on 'the challenges young women still face when it comes to access to education and health while negotiating with the societal expectations'.[29]

- The Karachi-based artist, Numair Abbasi's paper investigated 'the construction and performance of binary genders, sexualities, and their panoptic behavior in South Asia as rippled consequences of colonization, and whether the practice, acceptance, and visibility of the spectrum of genders and sexualities pre-date colonization'.[30]

- Research is being done on 'adolescent risk for early marriage, family violence and sexual assault'.[31]

- Another professor's book investigates Indian reforms on gender equality.[32]

- An investigation was carried out on how gender and globalization intersect and impact the well-being of workers in the garment industry.[33]

- A seminar explained the intersection of poverty and women in India, focusing on discrimination due to Indian culture.[34]

- A webinar tackled gender-based violence and examined the lack of police training and accountability of elected officials. It proposed better policies to recognize domestic violence.[35] A related webinar took up the topic of women in Indian politics.[36]

Numerous activities are organized to encourage Indian women to voice their traumas. A panel discussion was held on a three-volume collection of essays on *Gender Challenges* that refuted standard economic analysis and assumptions.[37] A film on violence against women in India was screened followed by a question-and-answer session.[38] And a woman invited from India discussed issues she faced as a female artist in India. She compared a middle-class woman and lower-class woman both of whom were working and raising a family. She concluded that both are deprived of basic freedoms.[39]

The Mittal Institute also serves as an audit and review agency of sorts, keeping its eyes on what goes on in India with the goal of building a support base, initially state by state, and eventually on a pan-India level. One of its teams visited India to investigate women's social and educational empowerment. The report submitted by this team became the basis for further workshops at the institute. One such workshop brought together sixty-five leaders from fifty NGOs and the field visits that followed helped build a network of Harvard-friendly activists at the grassroots level.[40]

Another seminar brought together government representatives, researchers, NGOs, and academicians to find ways for 'reorienting gender stereotypes and traditional gender roles' to address gender-based discrimination and violence. The goal was to alter 'patriarchal and repressive mindsets' because Mittal Institute believed that India lacked a 'comprehensive nationwide program'. Harvard brought in the Population Foundation of India (PFI) as a vehicle to disseminate Harvard's messages.[41]

Harvard has also been conducting annual conferences on how to teach about India in American schools. The focus is on teaching about 'gender violence in India'.[42] There have been numerous campaigns to remove textbook and curriculum biases and stereotypes in US schools. This is a political issue and there are ongoing lawsuits.

We feel that the Mittal Institute ought to use its clout to invite all sides on such events for a more even-handed dialogue on the treatment of India. Of course, it is important to solve women's issues worldwide, but changes in India will not happen through US school classroom discussions.

The question is, should India's education system depend on Harvard to give it the legislative and policy frameworks for making its women safe? Does the dependency on places like Harvard create a long-term addiction to Harvard, i.e., should the government be waiting to be told what to do by a foreign institution because of its superior brand value? Even more fundamentally, before pontificating to India on policy changes, has Harvard solved women's problems in American society, or even on its own campus? The *Harvard Crimson* admitted that Harvard has a lot of work to do on this front[43] and even as recent as 2022, its own students accused it of ignoring sexual harassment by a Harvard professor.[44]

Digging Deeper

An example of a program set up at Mittal Institute for bringing social justice to India is a special gift from Dr Mukesh Prasad of New York. It specifically funds students under the Mittal Initiative's Prasad Fellowship. Students are funded to take on projects in India on issues 'ranging from the role of media in Indian democracy to environmental governance'.[45] It has also sent students to help advance healthcare rights in India.[46] Students proposed how the media ought to function to improve Indian democracy.[47]

One can't help but wonder how Harvard is more qualified than Indian institutions to give advice on bringing healthcare rights to Indians, improving democracy, and promoting environmentalism.

Major Themes

Social Entrepreneurship

One of Mittal Institute's programs is to mentor and win over young Indian entrepreneurs. The content being taught is standard, easily accessible in India itself. Harvard brings its brand value to recruit high potential youth and then mould them in its way of thinking. In return, it builds an alumni network of youth being mentored as the future leaders of India that remain loyal.

To illustrate this, their collaboration with Tata included an eighteen-month long research project, *Livelihood Creation in India Through Social Entrepreneurship and Skill Development*. It focused on three key areas: rural livelihood creation; educational, social and economic empowerment of women; and science and technology-based interventions for poverty alleviation. It claims to have impacted over one hundred social enterprises across fifteen Indian states.[48] In phase two, eight social projects were funded, including one on *Low-cost Toilets in India*.[49] A seminar was organized in New Delhi on *Fostering Entrepreneurship in Developing Countries* and involved several government ministers.[50] A massive online open course was taught by Tarun Khanna, with modules on healthcare, urbanization, and food security.[51] None of the content seems particularly advanced compared to what any major country's own education system should be able to provide internally.

An even more direct Harvard influence was a course providing 'a framework and multiple lenses through which to think about the salient economic and social problems of the five billion people of the developing world'.[52] This job of nurturing future leaders of poor countries on 'how to think' is precisely what nation building comprises. Has India outsourced its nation-building to Harvard?

The problem at times is not with what is taught, but what is *excluded*. For instance, Tarun Khanna co-directed a project with a Chinese colleague to study meritocracy in India and China. This was a perfect opportunity to discuss that the Chinese are going in a direction opposite to that recommended by his Harvard colleague, Ajantha Subramanian, whose work *attacks Indian meritocracy using Critical Race Theory*. The Mittal project failed to highlight this crucial difference: *While China pursues merit relentlessly, not bowing to international criticisms about its internal human rights, Indians on the world stage are being asked to apologize for meritocracy rather than being proud of it.*[53]

Economics and Development

Many of the topics taken up by the Mittal Institute are indeed important for India and it is entirely possible that the work done is of a high standard. But as a matter of principle, it is problematic for the Indian government to be outsourcing the fundamental policy functions to a foreign institute that is not accountable to the Indian people, and one that has an established track record not entirely consistent with India's best interests. The examples given here need to be seen in this context.

The institute conducted a workshop in which it assumed the role of an intermediary between people working in the informal economy and the Indian government.[54] A concrete example of such a role was its advocacy for the garment manufacturers of Bangladesh.

As part of its role to bring diversity into India's economy, the Mittal Institute organized a seminar on *Financial Inclusion* in India conducted by a former executive director of the Reserve Bank of India.[55]

The Mittal Institute is extensively studying urban development in India. A conference it conducted was to propose ways to achieve sustainability.[56] The topic of urban planning opens the door to social issues: A student project at Harvard was to research 'contemporary issues of spatial cleansing, social justice, and transformation in Delhi'.[57]

The environmental considerations in the growth of Mumbai, was the focus of Eduardo Peláez's thesis, *Learning from Slumscapes: Wet Grounds, Flooding, and Community-Based Initiatives in Mumbai.*[58] The purpose here was to understand the socio-political dynamics of migration from rural to urban areas, their poverty, lack of infrastructure, 'rubbish mountains' and other challenges. These projects go deep into the kinds of slums featured and exoticized in films like the Oscar-winning, *Slumdog Millionaire.* The idea is to build expertise and networks of contacts.[59]

Another study examined India's transportation needs from a policy standpoint. The goal was to model the transportation needs with a complexity of factors. This is the type of work one expects on a regular basis from a country's Planning Commission and ministries for urban planning.[60] Harvard is also building good relations with the Indian government, inviting senior officials for talks and discussions on subjects ranging from highway development to sanitation to housing projects.[61]

A frequent theme deals with migrant workers' experiences, aspirations, and worldviews in New Delhi, drawing on fieldwork among metal workers in the Okhla Industrial Area in Delhi.[62]

Harvard seems deeply concerned about the water crisis in Delhi and organized monthly round table discussions of experts to understand 'the importance of socio-political context in water problems'. The key crisis they identified was 'the social vulnerability of the populations impacted by infrastructure failure'.[63] Once again, it's the Harvard good cops preparing to rescue India's 'downtrodden' from half a world away.

Healthcare

The Building Bharat-Boston Biosciences Program is an important Indian government program that Mittal Institute helps operationalize in the Boston area, in Massachusetts. In fact, Harvard played a leading role in formulating this program and negotiating with the Indian government. A year-long fellowship went to a scholar from Punjab who highlighted his work *on injustice in Northeast states of India using anthropological and political approaches.*[64] Another scholar being featured is developing *policies on marginalized groups based on her work at Rohingya refugee camps.*[65] There are grants given to study governance in India and the relations between state and society.[66] There is also a project to uncover *social issues during the Kerala floods* and the *internal migration in Maharashtra.*[67]

A seminar on *Health and Human Rights in Burma* used healthcare as the vehicle to discuss human rights in Myanmar.[68]

Separately, the Tata Institute for Genetics and Society, San Diego funded by Tatas, collaborates with Harvard through the Mittal Institute. Its research includes 'developing alternative control methods for vector-borne diseases, developing better crops with higher productivity, and finding technological means to alleviate the global issue of antibiotic resistance'.[69] Mittal and Tata collaborate with other institutions based in India 'to train and help influence policymaking at the national and global level'.[70] Tata Trusts is also funding a Harvard project 'to build a digital platform to train frontline health providers to deliver psycho-social interventions of sustainable quality. A pilot test of the program has been done in collaboration with Madhya Pradesh Ministry of Health'.[71]

The Mittal Institute coordinates numerous events with medical institutions in India. These cover exchanges between researchers as well as projects to influence government policies in India. Its mental health projects in India include the study of alcohol, child abuse, violence, poverty and inequality, and social marginalization. Its meetings formulate policies and are used for training Indians in this space. A special focus is on the treatment gap for low-income people and the problem of being outcasts. Gender and human rights are frequently built into the discussions.

Arts and Culture

Mittal Institute has an interesting Visiting Artist Program to bring Indian artists and use them as a vehicle to study, and influence, Indian culture.[72] Some of the specific grants and programs are benign and purely about art for art's sake. Others deal with specific communal identities or use art to promote ideology because art has always been an effective medium for social and political messaging.

Mallika Sarabhai, renowned dancer, controversial activist, and daughter of Indian space scientist Vikram Sarabhai, is an example of the artists promoted. The theme of gender and sexuality naturally gets highlighted.

The film *Mandir, Masjid, Mandal, and Marx: Democracy in India*, by the Left-wing Harvard historian, Sugata Bose, also a senior politician in All India Trinamool Congress, a political party active, and in power, in West Bengal, showed Indian democracy through his ideological lens. The screening and discussion were promoted by Mittal Institute as providing 'a rare glimpse into the role of religion, caste and communism in India's democratic politics'.[73]

Among the miscellaneous assortment of activities, one finds Muslim qawwali performances being promoted. The symposium on art in Nepal discussed 'how to challenge the yoke of insularity' and bring in modernity and globality.[74] Another project on translating Bengali texts focuses on interpreting religious and racial elements.[75] Abhijit Banerjee is a Harvard Nobel Prize winner for economics, and yet Mittal Institute decided to screen his film on social messaging and not on economics.[76]

Art is also presented in more directly divisive ways. One Nepali visiting fellow dished out the social message that would fetch a pat on the back from his hosts at Harvard. He positioned his work as focusing on the 'layers of caste, class, gender, and regional inequalities throughout Nepal' and the 'deeply brahminical patriarchal thinking'.[77]

The vocalist, T.M. Krishna was invited to deliver a lecture on his 'philosophy on the possibilities for art to break through social habits and boundaries'. He discussed India's marginalized communities such as transgender performers from Karnataka being affected by environmental crises. Artistic entertainment can become a great channel to spread social memes, and Krishna is well known for this skill. Naturally, this fits Mittal Institute's vision for its role.[78] Such contexts provide the ideal setting for well-known ideologues like Homi K. Bhabha to discuss sophisticated issues that include 'the textures of vulnerability at play in the cross-community encounters' and 'tenuous micropolitics of polarized communities'.[79]

Other Diverse Projects

Some activities seem to be purely for the purpose of 'networking' where important people from India and the US are brought together including government officials, business leaders, and intellectuals. As the gatekeeper, Harvard boosts its status and hence, power brokering capital. The participants benefit from affiliation with the Harvard name and by joining these prestigious clubs.

Other activities are presented as First World technical assistance being given to the Third World. However, we failed to find any serious examples of advanced technologies being transferred. A study of urban wastewater or recycling agriculture water are hardly areas where India needs to send people to Harvard to learn. Rather, it could be the other way around. But the Indian participants sell out and become Harvard loyalists for life because of the panache and shine in the way Harvard treats them. Harvard routinely brings in other Indian brand names like Tata to add weight to its role, and Tata-like corporates too get a prestige boost in the bargain.

In some projects, we see a clear case of Indian innovations being showcased at Harvard under the guise of adding value to the Indian ventures, when in fact, the knowledge transfer is from India to the US.[80]

Under the Nepal Studies Program, the Mittal Institute coordinated with two Nepali government agencies and a university to study earthquake preparedness in the aftermath of the 2015 earthquake. Reading the report, one is left wondering what possible value the Harvard delegation could have added besides bringing back photographs of disorganized, poor, and helpless people.[81]

Another common theme is research into some sector of India's industry giving detailed analyses of the kind of work routinely being done in Delhi ministries and various related thinktanks. In what way does it help India to invest in Harvard for such straightforward research when all the data and stakeholders are located in India?[82]

In 2020, the head of Paytm, (the digital payment system), Vijay Shekhar Sharma also joined the elite group of Indian billionaires and donated an undisclosed sum of money to support the activities and research performed by The Lakshmi Mittal and Family South Asia Institute.[83]

Kushagra Bajaj, the scion of the Bajaj family, (manufacturers of motorcycles and three-wheelers) donated an undisclosed amount to the Mittal Institute to fund leading Indian scholars to visit Harvard and 'avail of the university's vast resources'.[84]

In addition to wealthy Indian donors with programs in Mittal Institute named after their families, there is another tier of influential Indians wanting a seat at the Harvard high table. They are included in the list of business leaders that are on the advisory council of the Mittal Institute. Depending on the level of funding committed, some of them get seats at higher levels of Harvard's hierarchy. A sample list of such families is provided in the endnote.[85]

In Contrast with Pakistan's Pride

We find an interesting contrast in the way Pakistani donors have positioned the work being done at Harvard. There are at least two Pakistani funded fellowships at Harvard that Mittal Institute implements. Under these fellowships, the institute offers two opportunities for scholars and practitioners to come to Harvard specifically for research on Pakistan. The Aman Fellowship supports doctoral and advanced professional degree holders working on research related to Pakistan's development. The Syed Babar Ali Fellowship supports doctoral and advanced professional degree holders working on issues relevant to Pakistan.[86]

The leading figure studying Pakistan in the Mittal Institute, Dr Mariam Chughtai, challenges Western stereotypes and assessments of the narratives on Pakistan. Mittal's website states that as the Mittal Institute's Syed Babar Ali fellow, she is writing a book that explores the tension between the politics and culture of Pakistan 'to rewrite the narrative that has been erroneously assigned to the nation'. In other words, her thrust is to criticize the American popular images of Pakistan and she wants to use her Harvard fellowship to write such a book. Specifically, it states:

> Her research stands to challenge the staunch Western notion that instances of violence in Pakistan can be generalized across an entire population as a violent nature. ... Through her book and field experience, Chughtai intends to demonstrate that the perceived narrative about Pakistan is not necessarily the correct narrative.[87]

Unlike the mindset of many Indian donors as well as the scholars funded by them, Chughtai openly confronts the established views on Pakistan one sees in America. She states the purpose of her dissertation:

> ... Pakistan cannot be understood in a linear analysis of simple trends and generalizations. There are many contradictions and dialects that need to be understood through a nuanced, historical analysis of Pakistan.'[88]

This was a project assigned by Syed Babar Ali, the inaugural donor from Pakistan to the Mittal Institute and funder of the institute's Syed Babar Ali Fellowship. It shows pride and audacity on the part of the donor. Sending a fellow to Pakistan is part of a bigger strategy. Their mission was to establish a first-of-its-kind School of Education at the Lahore University of Management Sciences, School of Education. This Lahore institution would be patriotic to Pakistan's interests. 'The main ethos of the school is to operate at the nexus of research policy and practice to enable our students to consume leading research and bring it into practice'. They have already trained 350 youth entrepreneurs in Pakistan on their ideology.

The effort to overturn narratives on Pakistan was also pursued by Imran Channa, visual artist and a Pakistani research affiliate at Mittal. The website states:

> He explores how fabricated narratives can override our collective memory to shape individual and social consciousness and alter human responses.[89]

In other words, Pakistanis spend a tinier sum compared to Indians, but they select scholars and topics that will have a direct positive impact on the Pakistani narrative. This is similar to the way China's projects at Harvard are patriotic rather than against their country's interests the way the Indian projects tend to be.

Nothing in our analysis suggests any problems involving the Mittal family whose name and money is being used to produce such scholarship. We merely highlight some red flags where one-sided scholarship or interventions of a sensitive nature are being carried out by a powerful foreign nexus, using Indian resources. It is up to the philanthropists to investigate further and determine whether a course correction is required.

13

The Piramals: Harvard University's Gateway to India

Overview

We have already exposed the close relationship Harvard has with China and how it protects China's interests to the detriment of other countries, including the US and India. This chapter shows how the Harvard T.H. Chan School of Public Health has a Chinese power broker with Chinese Communist Party connections at its roots who funds its activities through front companies posing as philanthropic organizations, and how an Indian billionaire has become mixed up in this.

This Chinese involvement is particularly concerning with respect to India given the research output it has produced. Most people would be surprised to discover how the topic of public health in the US can be diverted to one of caste in India. But the Chan School has perfected this art and has gone further to frame the issue of health in Harvard's favorite categories of race and Intersectionality, with Harvard appointing itself as the savior of the underclasses. While claiming to be advocating for the marginalized Roma people of Europe for instance, Harvard has not yet succeeded in developing an accurate account of their history or the causes for their marginalization. It is instead allowing Suraj Yengde to develop an 'alternate' history for them.

Indian billionaire Ajay Piramal has become a part of this operation to facilitate the Chan School's penetration in India. The Harvard Chan India Research Center in Mumbai that came out of the Piramal grant has attracted collaborators from the Indian elite, the government, the UN, UNICEF and others, and additional funding from Indian industrialists. And in the usual way that Harvard frames these attacks on India, the center is headed by people who are not necessarily committed to India's interests. Besides, its stated goals clearly reveal the risk of using Piramal's connections to infiltrate India's elite, build indoctrinated leadership at every level to take the movement forward, collect sensitive data (including genetic data) with the end goal of driving social change. Chinese connections can be traced to their Artificial Intelligence ambitions.

As in the case of other Indian billionaires discussed, in the case of the Piramals we do not find any violation or breach on their part. The purpose of any audit exercise is to look for areas that owners/managers of the enterprise ought to be made aware of, so they can exercise their judgment in taking any further steps towards greater clarity. Nor are we suggesting that the Piramal initiative at Harvard lacks positive aspects; it certainly plays a constructive role in public health.

China's Infiltration of Harvard T.H. Chan School of Public Health

While China systematically constructs its own narratives, its foreign strategy is to infiltrate and disrupts others. According to Michael Pillsbury: 'Chinese companies have begun to make substantial donations to think tanks and universities to fund U.S. policy studies of China that support Beijing's views.'[1] Pillsbury, who served in US presidential administrations from Richard Nixon (1969-74) to Barack Obama (2009-17), was a former analyst at the thinktank RAND Corporation, served in senior positions in the defense department and on the staff of four US Senate committees. He is convinced that China is buying its way into prestigious American universities.

The most prominent example we expose is China's deep infiltration into the heart of America through the Harvard T.H. Chan School of Public Health. The School of Public Health is a century old and was taken over by Chinese influence in 2014 with an initial donation of $350 million, the largest donation in Harvard's history.[2] This is when the school was named after T.H. Chan, the donor. The donation was praised for being 'unrestrictive', thereby giving the school complete freedom on spending it.

The euphoria was so magical that nobody bothered to do any due diligence into the source of funds, even though it was the first instance when an entire school at Harvard was being named after a donor. Press releases and media coverage focused on American billionaire, Gerald Chan as an individual donor, and ignored his brother Ronnie C. Chan. Both had co-founded Morningside Foundation, a US charity with no employees, as their vehicle to capture Harvard's prestigious and strategic School of Public Health and name it after their father.

There was closer scrutiny a few years later that resulted in a scandal: Two of the funding sources of Morningside Foundation were unknown entities raising suspicions of them being shell companies. The third funding source using Morningside as a conduit was the main source of the Harvard gift, and the Panama Papers (leaking information) revealed that it was an entity hiding behind Monaco's secrecy laws.[3]

Meanwhile, the public relations campaigns had branded Ronnie Chan a 'philanthropist', concealing the fact that he is not merely a real estate billionaire. He is a global powerbroker with close ties to the CCP. He has served as a senior adviser to a Chinese government thinktank that reports directly to the highest administrative authority in China.[4]

When he was exposed as 'a pawn of the CCP' by a Hong Kong pro-democracy newsman who got arrested, the Twitter page disclosing this information was deleted.[5] Ronnie Chan has defended Beijing's hostile takeover of Hong Kong and facilitated support to elect pro-China leaders there. When he was co-chair of Asia Society's Hong Kong Chapter, the screening of a film critical of China's human rights violations got canceled under Chinese pressure.[6]

After a Hong Kong-based investment company bought a majority stake in *Forbes*, a piece critical of Ronnie Chan was deleted from its website, and the contributor was terminated.[7] He is widely believed to be playing an important role in helping the Chinese government suppress free speech at home and abroad. His influence ranges from blacklisting and expelling foreign journalists, to pressuring the National Basketball Association to disavow tweets supporting pro-democracy demonstrators.

Ronnie Chan is presently being scandalized as a controversial billionaire donating huge amounts of money to influence Americans in strategic ways.[8] It is being pointed out that he is the governor of the 'China-United States Exchange Foundation' (CUSEF; introduced in Chapter 8) which is officially registered in the US as a foreign agent.

The organization has pumped large sums of money into multiple Washington D.C.-based thinktanks. One of them is the influential Peterson Institute for International Economics where he also sits on the board. The US-China Economic and Security Review Commission, a bipartisan congressional committee, concluded that the CUSEF is part of China's shadowy network that seeks to 'co-opt and neutralize sources of potential opposition to the policies and authority of its ruling Chinese Communist Party'.[9]

Harvard's student activists assert that Chan's infiltration into US colleges supports China's global propaganda campaign.[10] A backlash against Ronnie Chan's CUSEF has also started. For instance, the University of Texas at Austin rejected its funding because of concerns that it was spreading Chinese propaganda.[11] But the Chans are not easily deterred by reprisal. In March 2022, MIT announced that it received a one hundred million dollars gift from Chan's Morningside Foundation.[12]

Harvard's own *The Crimson* newspaper wrote: 'That a figure so linked to the polity behind these efforts could be honored by the University and even have a school named after his late father, is simply unconscionable'. The article calls him 'a cheerleader for a government responsible for significant humanitarian crises. Harvard is incredibly influential in shaping American perceptions of China'.[13]

Orville H. Schell III, who heads the Center on US-China Relations at the Asia Society in New York, says that every person who is a China specialist in the US is somehow associated with Harvard. The *Crimson* reports that Harvard's decision to 'cozy up to oligarchs (even having student delegations visit thinktanks that are legally registered as foreign agents) can have a tangible impact on future policy'.[14]

Ronnie Chan has already entered India serving as a governing board member of the Indian School of Business.[15] Chan is also a charismatic globetrotter supporting Christian missionaries. He has been criticized by mainstream American Christians for spreading controversial views on theology. He claims that when he was sixteen, the Lord visited him, and he compares this to the experience of John the Apostle. That was when the Lord told Chan what he should do with his life.[16]

Caste as Lens in Public Health

The Atlanta-based Centers for Disease Control and Prevention defines public health as follows:

> ... the science of protecting and improving the health of people and their communities. This work is achieved by promoting healthy lifestyles, researching disease and injury prevention, and detecting, preventing and responding to infectious diseases. Overall, public health is concerned with protecting the health of entire populations. These populations can be as small as a local neighborhood, or as big as an entire country or region of the world.[17]

An emerging trend in this field is the focus on delivering health services to marginalized communities, because one should not restrict the scope of health too narrowly. The health of a people also depends on factors like neighborhoods, policies, and the unconscious biases in those that implement these policies. On the face of it, this is a welcome trend.

Unfortunately, at times there are subjects and speakers that do not have adequate understanding of the context and resort to political correctness. In situations like this, Critical Race Theory and concepts like Intersectionality are brought forward without adequate scrutiny and opposing views being allowed. For instance, the Afro-Dalit alliance has become a vehicle to express ideas of race, identity, and oppression, and it has devised a path to globalize caste politics: A discussion on racism in America is started, it smoothly switches into a discussion on Dalits, and Hinduphobic agendas are pushed.

This approach was used when the Harvard T.H. Chan School of Public Health ran a six-month event titled, *Public Health Storytellers – Powerful Narratives for a Healthier World*. This was part of its Office of Diversity and Inclusion. One of the guests was Isabel Wilkerson to talk about her book, *Caste*.[18] The book was discussed in Chapter 2 where we showed that the complex subject is not adequately nuanced and contextualized in her work. Don Lemon, the *CNN* anchor, and Prof. David Williams were discussants at the event, which was supported by the Nieman Foundation. This is how a public health topic concerning Black Americans was switched to one of caste, without any other experts representing the complex aspects of the issue.

Another example is the work on caste politics being done at the Harvard Center for Population and Development Studies, part of the Chan School of Public Health.[19] Critical Race Theory has entered every discipline including public health and morphed into Critical Caste Theory. The pattern is for Indian Leftists to imitate the American Left at every step. It is not surprising that the issue of reparations for Blacks is now being echoed in a call for reparations for Dalits in India. Harvard has now become the nexus for taking this to the mainstream. In December 2021, a seminar *Making the Case for Reparations* was organized by the FXB Center for Health and Human Rights, again, part of Chan School of Public Health.

The director of human rights at FXB is none other than Jacqueline Bhabha, wife of Homi K. Bhabha.[20] Jacqueline Bhabha said: 'From France to California, from Belgium to India, the call for reparations can be heard.' This clubs India along with other places where the fight for reparations can be expected to accelerate.[21]

We are not against reparations. In fact, we believe it is important for societies everywhere to not only dismantle the legacy structures of abusive power but also compensate the victims for the past. What we are against is the blind application of Western Universalism to other countries. Each nation has its own historical complexities, and it is dangerous to impose any one theory collectively and assume a single cause of all problems everywhere. We are especially against the interference of institutions like Harvard that have the clout to influence American politics to act against another country.

The FXB Center has been holding regular events to highlight the racism and oppression that the Roma people have faced for a thousand years in Europe.[22] Sadly, a decade of Harvard's claims to be championing their cause has failed to yield even a single event where their history was elaborated with evidence. And while there is a lot of effort to win them over by showing sympathy for the racism endured by them, it is never acknowledged that they are Hindu Indians by origin. It is also considered politically incorrect to discuss their enslavement by Muslims. What Harvard likes to say is that they 'migrated' to Europe.

Infinity Foundation has carried out projects in support of the Roma people going back twenty-five years. Our approach has been grounded in their history. To evaluate the way Harvard Chan School has been politicizing the identity of the Romani to fit their agenda, we give a brief history of the Romani from the time they left India.

It is agreed that the Roma people originated in north India, mostly from Punjab and Rajasthan, and left India about one thousand years ago. They also refer to themselves as Romani people. Prior to being exported by the Muslims as slaves, many of their communities were traders of goods that required transportation across long distances, typically with long caravans of oxen, etc. Some of their communities were of traveling musicians and entertainers.

Scholars mostly agree that their exit from India was caused by repeated Muslim invasions and plunders of India. One of the best known and acclaimed scholars on the subject is Prof. Ian Hancock of the University of Texas, a proud champion of Romani history.[23] He refutes the theory being put forth by some ideologues that the Romani are descendants of low-caste Indians. He cites extensive evidence to prove that they descended from Indian warriors who lost when the Turk, Mahmud of Ghazni invaded India in the eleventh century. He cites the presence of words derived from Sanskrit among the Romani people across Europe today, specifically words of military origin in India. He also refers to Rajasthani oral legends according to which groups of Rajputs left India through the Himalayas during the Muslim invasions.

Ghazni used Romani slave warriors to destroy large parts of Sindh and Punjab in India. Some slaves became free and started long migrations out of India. In the 1300s, the Muslim ruler Alauddin Khilji legalized the enslavement of the Hindus who defaulted on the payment of *jizya*, a tax imposed on infidels. Many were sold in slave markets. There has been considerable scholarship on the thriving slave trade throughout the Indian Ocean in that era, and this trade was controlled by Muslims. Slaves were taken wherever the Muslims went, all the way to Central Europe and beyond. An exhibition in the New York Public Library in 2013 featured the history of Africans brought to India during Muslim rule.[24]

Prof. Christoph Witzenrath, a research fellow at the University of Aberdeen, has also investigated and written about this history. It states:

> From early on in the history of Islam, South Asian slaves were plentiful in Central Asia and Persia. The conquest of Sind in

712–13 yielded 60,000, and the Ghaznavids of eleventh-century Afghanistan drove home hundreds of thousands from India. The servile population of West Turkistan included many South Asians from at least 1326, and Indian slaves were routinely exchanged for inner Asian horses. In the late fourteenth century, the Samarkand-based Timur the Lame killed 100,000 Indians captured before reaching Delhi, but still brought thousands back to West Turkistan. As many as 200,000 Indian rebels were supposedly taken in 1619–20, for sale in Iran., [...]

By the sixteenth century the southern neighbours of the Eurasian heartland became 'gunpowder empires', stabilizing Islamic power. Their armies or those of their projecting allies, the Turkmens, Tatars and Maghreb corsair states extracted infidel captives on a grand scale from India to South-east Asia. ... The Mughals expanded further into southern India than any previous Muslim power, inundating Central Asia with Hindu captives. Nevertheless, these advances obscured structural flaws: newly conquered Christians and Hindus often refused to convert.[25]

When the Dutch East India Company arrived in India, it started trading in the enslaved Hindus, which was expanded to other regions outside India and became a major activity of the Dutch.

The present Romani in Europe had started their journey from different parts of India, at different times, and belonged to diverse caste backgrounds. They were captured and enslaved, often used as captive entertainers and engaged in other forms of low-level work. In Europe, many such groups coalesced because they faced a common plight of being persecuted. It was, therefore, a survival technique to stick together for safety in a hostile region where they were often legally hunted down as animals.

Suraj Yengde, Harvard's poster boy fighting racism in India, attends several Harvard events on the Roma. He uses his Harvard brand and clout to 'educate' the Roma about caste horrors of Hinduism and India while wanting to recruit them into his Ambedkar Dalit movement. He falsifies their history as people that were Dalits in India, who therefore, ought to join his crusade against Hinduism.

Chan-Piramal Collaboration on India

While all the foregoing activities have been taking place in Harvard's Boston area campus, the Piramal family has worked in parallel to bring Harvard into India and give a home base for these ideas. What has not received serious attention among Indian thinkers is that the Harvard T.H. Chan School of Public Health has been using the Piramals to enter deep into India. There is nothing wrong with the Piramals using their money and name to pursue whatever interests them. We merely draw attention to the controversy in the US regarding Chan's alleged or suspected links with the Chinese Communist Party.

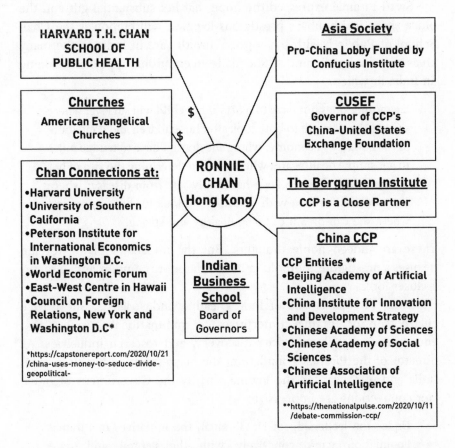

In 2014, the Chan School of Public Health received a generous gift from Ajay Piramal and his wife Swati, which allowed it to open a research and training center in Mumbai, right in the heart of India's foremost financial district. The space includes a classroom with a capacity of about fifty; an informal lounge/dining space that can host up to thirty-five; office and cubicle space for visiting faculty, staff, and students; and conference room space.

In exchange, Harvard has given Swati Piramal a seat on the Harvard Board of Overseers. Her LinkedIn profile describes it as 'one of the most prestigious and oldest Board's (sic) in the world – the Harvard Board of Overseers'. In addition, she was admitted as a member of the dean's advisors at the Chan School of Public Health and at Harvard Business School.

Swati Piramal expressed the hope that her substantial gift and the office space in Mumbai's prestigious location will empower the Chan School of Public Health to 'improve health care in India in the many areas where it lags behind'.[26] She made an emotional appeal envisioning an India in which

> ...a mother does not have to worry if her child will survive; where she has the strength to both look after her children and contribute to the country's economy; where she doesn't have to trudge miles to get simple health care; where she can determine the size of her family; where she can keep her family safe from disease; where she can look forward with a positive outlook for her future; and where she can dream of being healthy and strong.[27]

These are indeed noble thoughts. But the impact of giving foreign nexuses a prestigious foothold in India is far more complex and deserves a closer look.

Swati Piramal is one of India's leading industrialists. She is vice chairperson of Piramal Enterprises, a multinational business that encompasses healthcare, drug discovery, and research industries. As director of the Piramal Foundation, she helps promote health in rural India and was awarded the Padma Shri by the Government of India. Her connections are impressive:

> Under the leadership of Dr. Piramal, the initiatives of Piramal Foundation work cohesively with the central and state governments, as well as through collaborations with NITI Aayog,

The Rockefeller Foundation and The Bill and (sic) Melinda Gates Foundation, amongst several others.[28]

Piramal says: 'HSPH [Harvard School of Public Health] has vast global experience that can bring both technology and skills to find innovative solutions for India's healthcare needs. With the help of HSPH, we will be able to make an impact for millions of people—not only in India, but around the world.'[29]

At the head of this Harvard Chan India Research Center is Kasisomayajula 'Vish' Viswanath, professor of health communication at the Chan School of Public Health. He called the Piramal gift 'transformative'. The Mumbai base would be strategic for expanding deeper into India, he felt.

> Having this new space in Mumbai will provide HSPH with a platform to facilitate and stimulate the School's activities in Mumbai and throughout India. ... having a physical presence there will support our work in many areas, including research, training, and translation and communication around public health issues.[30]

The center's ongoing work in India includes projects in a wide range of public health issues that everyone would consider desirable. After all, the need is so desperate and far greater than the capacity of the Indian government to deal with presently. Humanitarian help is to be welcomed from whatever source, in this situation. Viswanath's strategies, however, go beyond providing immediate relief to India's masses. He expects the new center to spur numerous activities by the Chan School—such as providing training for public health leaders, running workshops on various public health subjects, and providing a home base for students doing research or internships in India.[31]

Viswanath leads another center within the Chan School. He is co-director at Lee Kum Sheung Center for Health and Happiness at the Chan School of Public Health. That center was established by yet another Chinese billionaire family that has old roots in mainland China. Its focus is on research to develop models for mental states such as happiness. It is well positioned to capture health and genetic related sensitive data in India that would be useful for training algorithms on mental behavior. This could teach future Artificial Intelligence systems how to push the buttons of the Indian peoples for generating specific feelings and moods.

The Harvard T.H. Chan School of Public Health India Research Center is part of a bigger Harvard presence in India. It works alongside the Harvard Global Research Support Centre India which is described as 'a social-impact organization, established in 2015 that works primarily in the domain of Education'.[32] There is an elaborate network being planted in India, some with the Harvard name directly, and others through collaborations under the umbrella of various institutions.

The India Research Center states it is designed to facilitate the development of new strategic relationships and build upon existing ones with organizations across India. It provides logistical support for its strategic goals of research, teaching, and knowledge translation and communication already underway by the school's faculty and students and their collaborators in India. Equally important, it offers opportunities to expand those activities and create new projects in the future.[33]

Alongside Viswanath, is his assistant director Ananya Awasthi who got her degree at Harvard's Chan Institute. She describes her area of focus as 'the intersection of government, non-governmental organizations and academic institutions to support the development of Public Health programming'. She has also worked at the Abdul Latif Jameel Poverty Action Lab (J-PAL), whose Breaking India activities will be discussed in Part 3. The center's advisory council is filled with people trained at places like Harvard's Chan Institute, J-PAL, and McKinsey, as well as those with strategic connections to India's NGO ecosystem and various government departments.

The Harvard Chan India Research Center lists powerful organizations among its collaborators and development partners: Tata Trusts, Ministry of Health & Family Welfare, NITI Aayog, Bill & Melinda Gates Foundation, Tata Institute of Social Sciences, Indian Institute of Population Studies, Narotam Sekhsaria Foundation (Ambuja Cements), UNICEF, UN-India Business Forum, and so on. Besides the Piramals, other Mumbai elite industrialists too have stepped in as donors.

To appreciate its vast ambition and scope of interests, one must start with its diagnosis of India's present condition. The Harvard Chan India Research Center explains:

There are disparities in health and health care systems between poorer and richer states and underfunded health care systems that in many cases are inefficiently run and underregulated. ... Public and private health systems are placing huge demands on the country's capacity to train exceptional health leaders and professionals. ... The Harvard T.H. Chan School of Public Health is collaborating with partners across India to address those challenges.[34]

It lists an ambitious strategy to be achieved in India through research, training, and knowledge translation. It has plans for the following activities:[35]

- Providing Harvard access to <u>local connections</u> at the highest levels in India.
- Convening conferences and workshops to <u>shape policies</u>.
- Establishing networks of activism (which Harvard refers to as 'education') in fields including <u>human rights</u>.
- <u>Training</u> public health <u>leaders</u>, researchers, and managers in state and Central governments as well as the private sector. Educating the future generations of public health leaders.
- Developing <u>research collaborations</u> across the field of health by organizing connections, providing technical platforms, facilitating logistics, cultivating wealthy Indians as potential donors, and facilitating Harvard field visits in India.
- Developing <u>databases</u> of population and primary health projects in India.
- Translating Harvard's research results for <u>implementing</u> in India. Building capacity for public health practitioners, researchers, and leaders on latest techniques developed by Harvard Chan School.
- Using the Harvard EdX <u>education platform.</u> Harvard Chan School has already awarded nearly two thousand training certificates to individuals from India.

The center's website announces its ambitions, and states that it has received funding from the Bill & Melinda Gates Foundation:

The goal is to make Harvard Chan School India Research Center a one-stop venue to collect and disseminate the latest knowledge

on major public health matters in India. This includes building
a comprehensive database with a dashboard to obtain the latest
facts on public health subjects from the public, nonprofits, and the
media, and installing Harvard systems as major stakeholders. The
proposed data portal, called Sanchar has already been launched
in its early stages and can be accessed at: https://projectsanchar.
org/.[36]

In its quest to accumulate as much data as possible, the India Center,
along with Harvard's John A. Paulson School of Engineering and Applied
Sciences, is collaborating with Indian organizations to hook them up
with Harvard tie-ups. For example, the Wadhwani Institute for Artificial
Intelligence and Harvard Chan Center organized a workshop on health-
related Artificial Intelligence.[37]

Piramal is also using its Harvard base to expand its footprint into
other American universities. In 2019, Piramal Foundation for Education
Leadership (PFEL) signed a Memorandum of Understanding with
Emory University in Atlanta to build the capacity of educators, including
headmasters, teachers and government officials, to implement a 'Social
Emotional Ethical Learning Curriculum' in government schools across
India. Piramal will pilot the curriculum across five thousand government
schools that will impact five lakh children across Gujarat, Jharkhand,
Jammu & Kashmir, Maharashtra, and Rajasthan, over a period of
two years. This work is commendable, but the question is whether
a curriculum for 'emotional and ethical learning' in Indian schools
should be developed in the US that has a vastly different culture and a
contrasting set of emotional and ethical issues than India.

Concerns

It is clear from the foregoing summary that the Chinese-controlled Chan
Institute of Public Health at Harvard now has a foothold in India with
the help of India's rich and famous.

The *Crimson* wrote that the Piramal donation solved many
problems, but still it looked 'wherever possible' for more donations.[38]
The Chan-Piramal India Center received funding from many other
Indian heavyweights including Rati and Nadir Godrej, Anupa and Rajiv

Sahney, Padmini Somani of the Narotam Sekhsaria Foundation, Mintoo Bhandari, Tata Trusts and Suneeta Reddy of Apollo Hospitals that have supported and donated large sums of monies to the Harvard T.H. Chan School of Public Health in India.[39]

India needs on-going due diligence of any foreign initiative that sucks out knowledge and databases and brings social and political influence and dependency. India is exporting knowledge without proper understanding, and this is getting digested by the West and China. It is importing a Western style of public health at the cost of uprooting its own native systems like Ayurveda.

At one end of this pipeline of information flow is China, in the middle is the Harvard T.H. Chan School of Public Health, and at the other end is the Piramal presence in India. There does not seem to have been interest in India to investigate Ronnie Chan's CCP connections and the implications of letting their Harvard base get inside India. This despite the fact that in recent times, some Harvard scholars have been getting arrested for their associations with China, and US authorities and media have been exposing serious national security issues concerning China's presence. This should be a matter of further inquiry.

The diagram on the following page summarizes the key relationships we have discussed.

The US has already begun addressing these problems and taking care of its own interests. But why would it bother protecting India's national interests, which should be for India's own luminaries to look into?

The support of Indian billionaires helps Harvard penetrate the Indian public health space and put pressure on its public health policies in the name of minorities, social justice, and the like. This opens the door for a social justice agenda to be introduced which helps the Breaking India forces. India seems complacent to the negative aspects of letting Harvard become the vishwa guru, one that imparts wisdom to the world in so many strategic domains.

What is not being said is even more troubling than the negative topics being given space. For instance, the COVID-19 pandemic exposed the Western bias against India's public health successes. India's tremendous achievement in managing the pandemic at a very low cost per population was a news blackout in the West. There ought to have been discussions at Harvard on various alternative healing systems, but this is seen as a

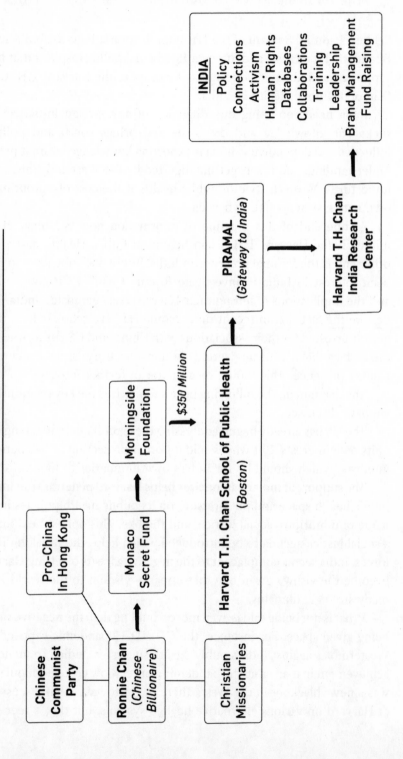

Harvard T.H. Chan School of Public Health

- Chinese Communist Party
- Pro-China In Hong Kong
- Ronnie Chan *(Chinese Billionaire)*
- Christian Missionaries
- Monaco Secret Fund
- Morningside Foundation

$350 Million

- Harvard T.H. Chan School of Public Health *(Boston)*
- PIRAMAL *(Gateway to India)*
- Harvard T.H. Chan India Research Center

INDIA
- Policy
- Connections
- Activism
- Human Rights
- Databases
- Collaborations
- Training
- Leadership
- Brand Management
- Fund Raising

threat to the Western and Chinese systems of medicine. Nor did India get the credit it deserved for managing the world's largest vaccination program, and its level of help in donating vaccinations to poor countries.

Furthermore, India's pharma industry has been locked out of drug discovery and has been contained in the role of providing generic substitutes. It is not for us to advise Piramal, but we point out that they could use Harvard's clout to lobby with the US Food and Drug Administration and WHO to admit India into the select club of countries whose original drug discoveries become accepted globally. One could aim even higher and place Ayurveda on the world map, at least on par with Chinese medicine.

A look under the surface reveals the following picture:

- China controls its own narrative and uses Harvard to disseminate it widely, whereas India has outsourced its narrative to Harvard and is sending its leaders there to get trained. China also uses Harvard to support woke and Critical Race Theory in the US, thereby disrupting America.

- China is using the T.H. Chan Center to nurture cultural and intellectual imports into India.

- At the same time, Harvard is heavily involved in researching and digesting Indian healing systems such as yoga, meditation, and Ayurveda. Infinity Foundation has been documenting these cases, and a brief summary of this digestion was provided in Chapter 7.

Our concern is that the Breaking India forces could get normalized under the guise of helping the country. We hope India's industrialists will investigate the digestion of Indian knowledge in healthcare the same way the Chinese industrialists and government have turned Chinese medicine into a massive export industry.

14

Harvard University's Control of the Media Ecosystem in India

Overview

Harvard's scholars have played varied roles in the study of India: digesting the valuable aspects within Indian traditions; diluting India's position by lumping it together with other Asian countries that don't share its civilizational heritage and worldview; systematically building narratives that can only be seen as atrocity literature; interpreting India's history and traditions in ways that aren't in consonance with India's own accounts and experiences; building databases of information under Harvard's control that can be used to further its agenda; and skilfully engineering India's elites according to its values.

As part of the agenda for the distribution of its content, Harvard aims to control India's media ecosystem. In other words, it is not enough to have its own views out there. There must, in addition, be suitable mechanisms in place to undermine, ridicule, remove, control, or simply swamp the stories that are outside its control and not in line with its narratives. Moreover, control over the Indian media has a dual purpose. Sponsored media outlets serve as Harvard's mouthpiece; and Indian government action against biased/divisive narratives can be milked to create stories about 'authoritarianism'. But Harvard goes much further.

It has the clout to see that the narratives it chooses enter the school curriculum to influence young minds. When you consider China's infiltration of this academic powerhouse, you can see just how dangerous this might turn out to be. In the US, this power is subjecting Indians to increasing discrimination in schools where a caste identity is being forced on them. In India, its own vulnerable citizens are playing into

Harvard's hands simply because the larger power games are unknown or unfathomable to them.

Harvard and various related institutions have made significant progress in collecting public data on various aspects of India and this data is already being propagated as material for future textbooks. These archives are also of tremendous economic value and the sheer detail makes this a national security concern.

Harvard has built a staggering machinery to disseminate and control its narrative using the infrastructure set up with the help of India's own billionaires. One such Harvard distribution channel is The Nieman Foundation of Journalism with its wide network of other non-profits that control the world of journalism.

The Nieman Foundation was founded in 1938 and offers fellowships to journalists across the globe for a year of study, seminars, and special events at Harvard. As far as India is concerned, Nieman is particularly active in its grants to Indian journalists after 2019, coinciding with the landslide win of Prime Minister Narendra Modi. Nieman also runs the following projects:[1]

- Nieman Watchdog Project: a website that encourages journalists to monitor and hold accountable all those who exert power in public life.[2]
- Nieman Reports: a channel for its fellows to publish their work.
- NiemanLab: the research arm for effective journalism and best practices in the digital age.
- Nieman Storyboard: a website for narrative-style of journalism.

The Nieman-Pulitzer Center Alliance

One of Nieman Foundation's initiatives is its strategic alliance with the Pulitzer Center on Crisis Reporting ('Pulitzer Center') to jointly work on crisis reporting. The Washington D.C.-based Pulitzer Center makes grants to journalists to write stories it considers underreported around the globe.[3] It is not to be confused with Pulitzer Prizes, although both are related to the same family but as separate legal entities. Of course, many Nieman fellows are recipients of the Pulitzer Prize as well.

This initiative strengthens Harvard's control over what gets reported the world over that Harvard considers 'underrepresented international stories':

> The partnership [between Nieman and Pulitzer Center] will also bring Pulitzer Center journalists to Harvard University for presentations and discussions on underreported international stories and provide an annual workshop for Nieman Fellows that will explore the Center's innovative strategies for using multimedia platforms effectively; placing news stories in the media for maximum impact; and employing social media, educational networks and other techniques to engage the public in important global issues.[4]

The close ties between the two organizations have strengthened even after the formal agreement expired. For example, a report titled *International Reporting Must Distinguish Hindu Nationalism from Hinduism* was published as a Nieman report with support from the Pulitzer Center.[5]

Besides funding journalists to write on specific topics, the Pulitzer Center also helps place their stories in various media outlets and wants to ensure that these stories reach young minds. It also plays a major role in education by developing curriculum for institutions worldwide[6] and guidelines for educators conducting classroom discussions. The center claims the following achievements:

> It assists all kinds of journalists: freelancers, which are increasingly relied upon and exploited as many full-service overseas bureaus vanish; and famous organizations, such as The New York Times, The New Yorker and PBS NewsHour, that need extra resources to do their most ambitious journalism.[7]
>
> The end result has been an impressive, 10-year-legacy in which the Washington-based nonprofit has supported 715 separate projects, a total of 6,168 stories in various outlets and dealt with 571 publication partners.[8]
>
> The outreach is impressive. It's got 31 members of a Campus Consortium, which range liberal arts institutions such as University of Chicago and The College of William & Mary to graduate journalism schools, including Northwestern's Medill and

American University, to more specialized partnership, ... Johns Hopkins Bloomberg School of Public Health and climate change at the Yale School of Forestry & Environmental Studies.[9]

... it works with elementary and secondary schools St. Louis, Chicago, Washington, Philadelphia, and New York, ... in the San Francisco Bay Area and Boston, along with a NewsArts initiative (exploring the intersection of news and arts) in Winston-Salem, North Carolina. ... more are detailed on the education page of its site.[10]

The Pulitzer Center often commissions stories it wants promoted to specific journalists. One such story was on the Namami Gange Project after the historic electoral victory of Narendra Modi in 2014. This story was commissioned to be published by *The New Yorker*. The agenda was to use the Ganga clean-up project as a doorway to turn environmental issues into a discussion on politics and religion. George Black, the reporter on the story, gives an insight into how such an agenda works:

> The New Yorker came to me about a year ago and suggested that I might be interested in doing a piece on the Ganges and I said yes. And *we discussed really what kind of a piece it should be*. We wanted a lot of colour because it's an extremely colorful story - you've got great locations, you got strong characters and ... a good way of getting to this mystery, the people; still I don't think can really resolve, you know, 'who is Narendra Modi the Prime Minister'; ... *he had a long reputation as the Hindu radical*, had been implicated in some nasty events ... in ... Gujarat, and ... came to power promising that he was going to solve India's economic problems. He was gonna clean up corruption in the government, he was going to compete with China as an economic power, he was very pro technology, he loves social media so you have these two images and I remember at the time of the election, two years ago, the Economist magazine had a cover that portrayed him (Modi) in a *very menacing light*. ... the editorial ... essentially said that 'this man should never be elected he's too dangerous, he has been denied a US visa for 10 years and then he went on to win the election six weeks after that story ...' And there he (Modi) is on the cover again, he's dressed all in white,

he's got this smile and it's like India's saviour. So, I thought the Ganges clean-up [story] was a really good way of getting at that. Is he one, is he the other, or is he both? And I think I pretty much concluded in the end that he is both.[11]

Clearly, this was commissioned with a well-defined bias but it gets portrayed to students as independent and objective.

The Pulitzer Center itself is funded by many of the usual Leftist charities including the Omidyar Network, Facebook's Meta Journalism Project, the Rockefeller Foundation, the Gates Foundation, and The Stanley Foundation:

> Primary core support for the Pulitzer Center has come from Emily Rauh Pulitzer, The Emily Rauh Pulitzer Foundation, The David and Katherine Moore Family Foundation, Barbara and Richard Moore, The New York Community Trust - Deborah W. and Timothy P. Moore Fund, Elkhanah Pulitzer, Joseph Pulitzer V, Michael Pulitzer Sr., Deirdre and Peter Quesada, William Bush, craigslist Charitable Fund, The John D. and Catherine T. MacArthur Foundation, Trellis Charitable Fund, Arnold Ventures, Omidyar Network, Humanity United, Henry L. Kimelman Foundation, Poklon Foundation, The Fore River Foundation, The Hollywood Foreign Press Association (HFPA), and The Kendeda Fund.[12]

To understand the political interventions of the Pulitzer Center, a good example is the high-profile project in which it developed the classroom curriculum for *The New York Times' 1619 Project*.[13] The project has raised controversy in the US. Whether one agrees or disagrees with this revised account of history is beside the point. We are highlighting the power of the Pulitzer Center to manufacture the grand narrative of any nation and planting it in the education system. In the above example, the center created the school curriculum and published reading guides, lesson plans, and extension activities for the 1619 Project.

The curriculum has been placed in over 3,500 classrooms in all 50 states. Five school districts, including Chicago and Washington D.C., have made it mandatory. The center donated 5,600 copies of the magazine length version of the 1619 Project to the Buffalo Public schools where it is a part of the required curriculum; this is enough to distribute free copies to all eleventh and twelfth grade students.

Despite the controversial claims attacking America's founding fathers, only one side of the debate was presented. However, in America's case, there is a well-organized sophisticated machinery fighting the Pulitzer Center's work with a counterpoint. India's curriculums being outsourced have no such counter voices, which makes Pulitzer's clout far more dangerous.

Indian Organizations Supported by the Nieman Institute and the Pulitzer Center

The Pulitzer Center gives grants to journalists to work on projects in India and then helps them publish their works in Indian media houses that are mainly Leftist with an emphasis on the topics of Kashmir, environment, Vanavasi/Schedule Tribes, and social and religious tensions in India.

The media houses it partners with in India are well funded with state-of-the-art websites in multiple languages. They focus on niche demographic markets and targeted media.

Sabrang is one such organization. It is run by Teesta Setalvad and her husband Javed Anand, both well known for openly criticizing the government and having encounters with the Indian law enforcement authorities for over a decade. In 2010, Setalvad architected what the National Council of Educational Research and Training (NCERT) called a 'venomous' curriculum for primary school children in Gujarat and Maharashtra.[14] Thousands of children were taught this program.

In 2018, she was caught up in an embezzlement scandal and 'charged with using the NGO's funds for her personal benefit'.[15] In 2021, one of her trusts was found to be in violation of the law because it used illegal channels to receive a Ford Foundation grant to 'address communalism, caste-based discrimination in India, including media strategies'.[16]

Case Study: People's Archive of Rural India and the Chinese Communist Party

Among the media houses associated with the Pulitzer Center, one stands out and we shall discuss it as a case study. This is the benign-sounding digital media platform, People's Archive of Rural India (PARI). It demonstrates the level of vulnerability in India's national security.

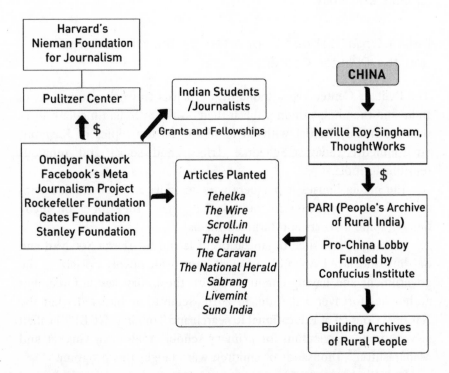

As the above diagram shows, the People's Archive for Rural India is well-funded and focuses on collecting information in the form of photos, videos, and articles about India's diverse peoples, their culture and society. This is a database archive of India's rural societies on an unprecedented scale. 'It's a project that will never be complete and should never be complete,'[17] says its spokesman. 'Write for us, shoot for us, record for us – your material is welcome so long as it meets the standards of this site and falls within our mandate: the everyday lives of everyday people',[18] states the PARI website. It continues:

PARI is both a living journal and an archive. It will generate and host reporting on the countryside that is current and contemporary, while also creating a database of already published stories, reports, videos and audios from as many sources as we can. All of PARI's own content comes under the Creative Commons and the site is free to access. And anyone can contribute to PARI. [19]

A call for donations states:

PARI is also building a Resources section, where we aim to put up (in full text and not just via links), all official (and unofficial but credible) reports related to rural India. For instance, every report of the National Commission for Enterprises in the Unorganised Sector, reports of the Planning Commission (now NITI Aayog) and ministries, the United Nations and much more. Researchers will not have to surf multiple sites to access important documents and studies from different sources.[20]

The scale of the project is staggering. The archives will provide details of the social, behavioral, and cultural knowledge base of ordinary Indian citizens, which as we have explained often enough is valuable for training Artificial Intelligence algorithms. This is not only a valuable economic asset, but also a national security risk:

Across 60 months or so, PARI will generate text reports, audio stories, videos, documentary films, photographs, music and 'talking albums' on the everyday lives of everyday people – from every part of the country. A database that will be truly representative of the Indian people, particularly of 833 million rural citizens. Of their labour, crafts, stories, songs, poems, art and more. The network of Fellows we build will also reflect the social composition of the country. Half of the nearly 100 Fellows will be women. And Dalit journalists, Adivasi journalists and those from the minorities, will also be represented in a fair manner. Many stories will be told directly by everyday people themselves. Among other legacies, this will give generations of students, all our children, living textbooks on the world around them. And give the nation itself a repository the like of which it has never seen.[21]

This is the brainchild of businessman and activist Neville Roy Singham, the founder-chairman of ThoughtWorks.[22] After selling ThoughtWorks, Singham moved into activism full time. Recently, *the Enforcement Directorate's investigation alleged that Singham has deep associations with the CCP and its propaganda wing.* Interestingly, Singham also seems to be interested in pouring money into other media companies.

> The Enforcement Directorate's investigation into a money laundering case against media portal NewsClick and its promoters has turned the spotlight on their financial dealings with Neville Roy Singham, a businessman of Sri Lankan-Cuban descent whom the investigators have identified as the key source of Rs 38 crore that PPK Newsclick Studio Pvt. Ltd. received between 2018 and 2021 from abroad. Sources in the agency who have been mapping the flow of funds to the media outlet alleged that *Singham was associated with the propaganda arm of the Communist Party of China CPC.*[23]
>
> In February 2021, the Enforcement Directorate had raided premises and the residences of several officials and journalists associated with NewsClick, a news media portal is (sic) most famously known for peddling fake stories. The officials had also raided NewsClick founder and Editor-in-Chief Prabir Purkayastha in connection with a money laundering case pertaining to foreign funding.[24]

Singham is also on the radar of American watchdog groups that claim he has strong ties with China and is undermining US national interests. Some consider him a part of the Chinese propaganda machinery in the US and at the center of a complex web of activity that denies the genocide of the Uyghurs in China:

> A monthslong (sic) investigation by *New Lines* can reveal that over the past five years almost $65 million has filtered through various entities connected with people who have defended the Chinese government and downplayed or denied documented human rights violations committed by Beijing against the Uyghur and Turkic Muslim minorities. This funding has moved through a complex series of mostly tax-deductible investment funds and

charities, all linked by virtue of their governance structures to one man: the 67-year-old American tech magnate Neville Roy Singham.[25]

The People's Archive of Rural India showcases its database archive of 'occupational, linguistic and cultural diversity' of India as a humanitarian project to help marginalized people. But this poses two big problems. One is that it builds sensitive archives related to India that is outside the control of the Government of India. The second is Singham's connections to the Chinese.

PARI as a Breaking India Force in Education

Besides PARI publishing stories claiming to be authentic, it also positions this database as a teaching tool: 'It's going to be a teaching tool for teachers to use. What is there is already being used by teachers in the classroom'.[26] The PARI education site boldly claims: 'At PARI, we're writing the textbooks of the future based on our numerous stories, photos and videos. Both students and teachers can contribute and develop course content'.[27]

And adds:

> Teaching and research materials, including textbooks, will increasingly move online in the next few years – that process is already on in some parts of the world. PARI aims to help create informative and lively resources for students, teachers, schools, colleges and universities. Done right, it could mean 'textbooks' or teaching material that can be added to, amended, updated or widened. As broadband access grows, it should also mean lower costs for many students, as PARI is a free-access-to-public site. [28]

Like Teesta Setalvad's ideology-based education curriculum that entered the schools of Gujarat and Maharashtra, and the 1619 Project of the Pulitzer Center taught in American schools, PARI's entry into the Indian education system is also designed to indoctrinate. It has partnerships with over sixty schools and colleges all over India: Flame, Mt. Carmel College, IIT Jammu, JNU, Lady Shri Ram College, etc. The long list of Indian institutions is available on the link in the endnote.[29]

This is a two-pronged approach: to spread its activism, and to recruit students to populate its archives. There is a call to activism in every message sent to school and college students as the following sample suggests:

> To the young student it's a fun and exciting story about unusual occupations, to the teenager discovering rebellion, it's an example of truth spoken to power, and to the young adult, it's an opportunity to contribute to a living archive and resource.[30]
>
> Young people are engaging in issues and processes of our times: they are on the ground at the farmers' protest, in the Jaunsar mountains recording the impact of climate change, speaking with daily wage earners such as railway hawkers, construction workers and fishermen, whose livelihoods vanished in the lockdown.[31]
>
> As educators, we are in danger of grooming a generation of Indians ... far removed from problems in their immediate surroundings, oblivious to social and ethical questions and detached from the growing inequalities around us. If we are to change this, we need to give them the tools and information to question stereotypes and think critically beyond their textbooks.[32]

The themes that PARI chooses are clearly designed to use children as its soldiers fighting its social justice wars:

> Rights and democracy: Do all citizens enjoy the same rights and privileges as per our Constitution? Social and economic inequalities and historical injustices have denied many citizens of their fundamental rights such as education and health. A set of stories which dive into how this plays out in the everyday lives of the underprivileged.[33]

Some projects indoctrinate young people and can be seen as a step towards rewriting the history of India. And the Pulitzer Center is facilitating this by providing grants to journalists who contribute to PARI's archives. The association with the Pulitzer Center also gives legitimacy to PARI.

Data is the new weapon and PARI is capturing private data of unassuming Indian citizens in the name of journalism and humanitarianism. It is using India's diversity to undermine India's integrity:

> PARI's content is broadly grouped into 'categories': 'Things we do' about labour and 'Things we make' about artisans, artists, crafts. There are categories about agriculture, sports, women, Dalits, Adivasis. And this list, though exhaustive, isn't final; other categories, the founders say, can and will come when they have the material.[34]
>
> But PARI already has broken new ground. There is a unique category called Faces, to which 40 photographers have contributed ... Faces — a celebration of the facial and occupational diversity of India — will include photograph of one male, one female and one child from every single district of India, along with metadata (name, occupation, village, district and details of the photographer/ camera). It was a terrific learning for the contributors to understand that you can have 100 faces and over 200 occupations, since many rural Indians do more than one thing to survive.[35]
>
> ... all the content ... — and the website itself — has been put together voluntarily. ThoughtWorks India, a global software company, has created, pro bono, an incredible, responsive platform ... Neville Roy Singham, ThoughtWorks founder-chairman remarked, 'This is an insane project, and a wonderful one.'[36]

As already described, the archive is both a national security risk and has economic value because of its unmatched details on peoples' lives, behavior patterns and psychological profiles, religion, age, demographics and social status, occupation, cultural preferences, songs, dances, craft, languages, dialects, even pictures and videos of faces. Such an archive of vulnerable people in sensitive rural areas could be misused to incite social unrest. This database is being crowd-sourced from innocent students in India's schools and colleges. It is unfortunate that nobody until now has delved into this issue.

Missionary projects like the Joshua Project could use this database to further attack indigenous cultures and traditions of India. It will serve as a database for Western, Chinese, and other foreign writers to manipulate the narrative by gaining access to people who do not have the foggiest idea of what is going on.

Case Study: Assault on Hindus in America

In 2018, the Pulitzer Center funded a journalist by the name of Philip Martin of the *WGBH* public radio station in Boston that is also a member station of *National Public Radio* (*NPR*) and *Public Radio International* (*PRI*). It has a focus on education and broadcasts news programming from both NPR and PRI.[37] The Pulitzer Center brought in Harvard fellow Suraj Yengde and commissioned the station to do an agenda-driven series called *Caste Discrimination in the USA*. The series was announced as follows:

> 'Caste Discrimination in the USA' is an original WGBH/PRI's *The World* multi-part, multi-platform journalistic investigation into casteism in the United States and Canada. [38]

Yengde was the lead actor in the episode titled, *Harvard Pedigree, Caste Follows 'Like a Shadow'*. It was promoted as his personal story as a Dalit at Harvard. Harvard and the Pulitzer Center used their channels to spread the message of this series in the form of radio series, videos, and articles.

The project's goal is to show that caste follows Indians everywhere they go in the world, like a virus being spread everywhere. Indians in North America have brought their bigotry with caste-based discrimination into the American workplace. This narrative was systematically constructed through a thirty-day blitz of stories in multiple media channels with the following list of episodes:[39]

- *Suraj's Shadow: Wherever he Goes, his Caste Follows—Even in America*
- *No Escape from Caste on these Shores, 'Untouchables' from India Say*, by Tinku Ray
- *Love and Marriage: Rebels Against an Indian Tradition that Endures in the U.S.*, by Kavita Pillay
- *Caste Bias Isn't Illegal in the United States. But this University is Trying to Fight it*, by Philip Martin
- *The U.S. isn't Safe from the Trauma of Caste Bias*, by multiple authors
- *Even with a Harvard Pedigree, Caste Follows 'Like a Shadow'*, by Philip Martin

- *WGBH News' Philip Martin Travels to India to Explore Caste*, Philip Martin with Suraj Yengde in India
- *Discrimination In America – Parts 1 and 2*, by Philip Martin
- *Caste Discrimination Exists on College Campuses. Some Schools are Trying to Change That*, by Philip Martin. With Jaspreet Mahal, DEI at Brandeis University – instrumental in making caste a protected category at Brandeis University, Thenmozhi Soundararajan, Equality Labs
- Philip Martin hosts panel discussion on *Caste in America*

The objective of this hit-job on Hinduism was to make caste a widely recognized category that has legal implications. The Pulitzer Center bragged its success:

> Even in the diaspora, away from the harsh realities that define everyday life for 'untouchables' in India, Nepal, and elsewhere, the inherent bigotry of caste has followed. This according to various studies and Dalit scholars and buttressed by a recent national U.S. survey carried out by ... Equality Labs. Examples have included students who, allegedly after divulging their surnames, were in some instances denied housing. Many first and second-generation South Asians in the U.S. seem to agree that marriage among Indians is indisputably influenced by caste. Many job-hires and job placements, in high tech for example, are also reportedly influenced by caste prejudice, ... (and) often represent the difference between those toiling in the kitchens of Indian restaurants in Boston, New York, or Houston, or at the helm of companies in Silicon Valley or Kendall Square, Cambridge. Dalits, in the most under-reported way, say they frequently encounter caste-based discrimination, for which there are no specific protections or references in U.S. constitutional law. But based on preliminary interviews, many middle-class Indians living in the U.S. do not believe that caste is an issue here.
>
> By contrast caste is recognized as a major concern in the U.K., though efforts to impose legal prohibitions have hit a wall. This project take(s) a closer look at on-going grassroots and parliamentary efforts to establish legal protections there and in Canada and the lessons for the United States.[40]

The media blitz proved effective, and the Pulitzer Center and Harvard achieved their goals: In 2022, California State universities and Harvard University made rulings to recognize caste as a form of racism and hence the caste-oppressed groups as a protected category under US law. Not surprisingly, the Catholic Church bestowed the 2020 Gabriel Award to this series:

> 'Caste in America,' an examination led by Phillip (sic) Martin of casteism in the United States and Canada for WGBH, was *awarded a 2020 Gabriel Award by the Catholic Press Association of the United States and Canada.* The radio series, part of the project 'Caste Discrimination in the USA: A Public Radio and Online,' received the first-place award in the 'Human Dignity – Radio – General Excellence' category. The team behind the radio series, videos, and articles in the complete project includes Tinku Ray and Kavita Pillay. The Gabriel Awards recognize 'works that support themes of dignity, compassion, community and justice.'[41]

Philip Martin also won the 2020 Public Media Journalists Associations Award for the Best Collaborative Effort:

> 'Caste in America' is a Pulitzer Center-supported project that delves into casteism, prejudice, and discrimination on the grounds of caste, along with its continued practice in the present day in the United States and Canada.

The above is a clear example of how Harvard promotes a scholar (i.e., Harvard's own Suraj Yengde) through its collaborators like the Pulitzer Center, which leads to new laws on caste in America. This affects Indian Americans. Such is the power in the hands of Harvard and its allies.

Pulitzer Center Funding on India

Following are some of the articles funded by the Pulitzer Center for just one sample year (2021 to February 2022).[42] Many of the media placements are also indicated. Some topics are repeated in multiple grants and stories.

PULITZER CENTER FUNDING ON INDIA – PART A (Sample Year – 2021 to February 2022)

POVERTY

- *The Hindu:* Hungry Nation
- Hunger: A Hidden Condition Exacerbated Further by COVID-19 Lockdown
- *The National Herald:* Opinion: What Do the Poorest Eat? Salt, Water and Pepper

TRIBALS IN INDIA

- PARI - We Will Be Kicked Out and No One Will Care
- India's Adivasi Identity in Crisis
- Sabrang: Adivasi Identity At Stake
- *The Wire:* Illegal Detention, Forced Marriage: What Happens After Alleged Naxals 'Surrender' in Bastar?
- *Tehelka:* Rise of Sati Pati Cult in Jharkhand
- *Al Jazeera:* Living in the Shadow of Rebellion: India's Gond Tribe
- The Gond Tribe of Central India
- PARI: We Have Been Pleading for a Bridge in Sautada
- PARI: In Marathwada: Forlorn Farmers, Fatal Fears
- PARI: In Beed: 'It Got Easier To Threaten and Harass Me' (Rape)
- Sabrang: Pathalgadi: Assertion of Adivasi Rights Over Land

COVID MISMANAGEMENT

- The Possibility of a Third Wave Is Frightening
- *LA Times:* A Lost Generation: India's COVID Crisis Reverses Decades of Progress for Children
- Societal Fallouts of COVID-19
- PARI: In Osmanabad: Dodging and Ducking the Virus
- PARI: We Didn't Know Our Situation Could Get Worse
- PARI: 'He Became Irritable ... He Would Snap at Us'
- *South China Morning Post:* China-India Border Dispute: How One Doctor Coped With Conflict and COVID-19 on the Front Lines of a Face-off Between Two World Powers
- Coda: How Healthcare Workers in India Fought a Surveillance Regime and Won

HINDUPHOBIA/RELIGION

- *The Caravan:* Ritual Killings: How Crimes of Superstition Thrive in the New India
- International Reporting Must Distinguish Hindu Nationalism from Hinduism
- Islamophobia and Coronavirus in India
- *The Caravan:* The Republic of Tantric Crimes
- Finding an Old Religion in a New India
- Religion, Populism, and the Media

PULITZER CENTER FUNDING ON INDIA – PART B (Sample Year – 2021 to February 2022)

ENVIRONMENT

- Event: India: Environment Undone
- Liberation: Reforestation compensatoire» en Inde: l'arbre qui gâche la forêt
- *Tehelka*: Unending Despair in India's Magical Land
- The Rise of Citizen Protest in India's Goa
- *Hakai Magazine*: In Goa, The Water Runs Black
- Sabrang: Under the Shadow of Coal Mining
- *The Caravan*: Rocks of Ages: Jharkhand's Millennia-old Megalithic Sites are Under Threat
- *Suno India*: Making Environment Political: The Save Mollem Movement
- Article 14: The Lack Of Evidence To Confirm Obvious Environmental Damage Is Derailing Local Battles For Justice
- Behind the News: India's 'Compensatory' Forests

GENDER

- PARI: Beed's Child Brides: Cutting Cane, Crushing Hopes
- PARI: In Beed: 'It Got Easier To Threaten and Harass Me'

KASHMIR

- In Kashmir: Mourning has Become Contentious
- *Scroll.in*: How Kashmir's Half-Widows Are Denied Their Basic Property Rights
- Years Out of School in Kashmir
- Solace in Spaces: About Kashmir
- Faith and Pandemic in Indian-administered Kashmir
- Sacred Peace Building in Kashmir
- *Haaretz*: Mourning Over Empty Graves
- *The Wire*: Secret Burials in Faraway Places: Slain Kashmiri Militants' Kin Are Denied Right to Grieve
- *Deutsche Welle*: World in Progress: Missing Out on Education in the Kashmir Region
- Islamophobia and Coronavirus in India

POLITICS IN INDIA

- Religion, Populism, and the Media
- Indian Government's Tech Imposition on Healthcare Workers
- *Livemint.com*: Why Childcare Workers Are Suddenly up in Arms

This is just a sample from one year, so one can imagine their long-term impact.

It is apparent that some of the topics used are a façade. The real motive seems to be to add supporting evidence of social injustice by showing the ill-treatment of the 'victim' communities. Categorizing a media project as 'environment' or 'tribal' or 'COVID' is just a nice way to show that Harvard is serving India's best interests.

The hard reality is that all this evidence being generated is being used in accordance with Critical Race Theory's goal to dismantle the underlying structures of nation, Hindu faith, and civil society – in other words, what holds India together.

The Nieman-Pulitzer Media Network in India

Media Houses Supported

The young journalists funded by the Pulitzer Center also get support to publish their work done by funding the following media outlets:

1. *The Wire*
2. *The Caravan*
3. *The National Herald*
4. *Tehelka*
5. Sabrang
6. PARI
7. *Livemint.com*
8. Suno India (co-founded by ex-Hindu reporter, and supported by the Independent and Public-Spirited Media Foundation [IPSMF])
9. *The Hindu*
10. *Scroll.in*

In addition, selective foreign publications like *Al Jazeera* are also being funded to write on India.

Nieman Reports

The Nieman Foundation runs the *Nieman Report,* a website and quarterly print publication

... covering thought leadership in journalism' as its website states. Its editorial mission mirrors that of the Foundation itself: "to promote and elevate the standards of journalism." Nieman Reports is home to the Nieman Watchdog Project, which chronicles how journalists can hold those in power to account, founded by longtime Washington Post reporter and 1950 Nieman Fellow Murrey Marder.[43]

Deep pockets and high-class relationships allow Nieman to cast its net wide and control the narrative in India. Just one year's output is enough to give the reader a glimpse of the Nieman Foundation's agenda. The list of projects funded through its partner, the Pulitzer Center, in one sample year (2021-February 2022) is given below:

- In India, the Last Few Bastions of the Free Press Stand Guard Against Rising Authoritarianism
- Arundhati Roy: 'We Live in an Age of Mini-Massacres'
- In India, Journalists 'Are Fighting For Whether Truth is Meaningful or Not'
- The Modi Government, *The Caravan* magazine, and the State of the Free Press in India

Nieman Grantees, Awards and Fellowships

The Editors Guild of India lists fifty-one organizations from overseas that offer fellowships and grants to recruit Indian journalists on specific topics. The Nieman Foundation is listed as the top source of funding:

> Nieman Fellowships at Harvard University offer fellows a chance to study at Harvard for an academic year; Knight Visiting Nieman Fellowships, which last 12 weeks or fewer, are also available for project-based work that will advance journalism in some new way.[44]

Let us look at some of the awards and fellowships given out by the Nieman Foundation recently. In 2021, it gave *The Caravan* magazine the Louis M. Lyons Award for Conscience and Integrity in Journalism. This prestigious award was given for 'investigations into Hindu supremacist terrorism, political murder, caste and gender injustice, and ethnic violence against India's Muslim minority'.[45]

The *Caravan,* according to Nieman, received the recognition for 'its unique and uncompromising coverage of the erosion of human rights, social justice, and democracy in India'.[46] It goes on to state:

> ... the selection of this publication comes under extraordinary and alarming circumstances. The Caravan's recent coverage of nationwide farmers' protests has drawn the ire of Prime Minister Narendra Modi's government, which has attempted to shut down the magazine's social media accounts and brought sedition charges against multiple Caravan employees. Under such intimidation, The Caravan embodies an urgent commitment to conscience and integrity. ... (it's) recent work is another chapter in a legacy of indispensable reporting in the world's most populous democracy. India's first publication devoted to narrative journalism, The Caravan, has persistently spoken truth to power while documenting the rise of political Hinduism in the country over the past decade. Risking violence and imprisonment, its reporters have written an essential series of investigations into Hindu supremacist terrorism, political murder, caste and gender injustice, and ethnic violence against India's Muslim minority. The Caravan has repeatedly demonstrated that it represents a beacon of moral clarity in Indian public life.[47]

One of the recipients of the Nieman Foundation fellowship for the class of 2022 was Pranav Dixit whose official role is to cover technology for India.[48] However, he has used 'technology' as a way to cover social justice issues as illustrated by the titles of his articles:

- *I Thought my Job was to Report on Technology in India. Instead, I got a Front-Row Seat to the Decline of my Democracy*
- *No Email. No WhatsApp. No Internet. This is Now Normal Life in Kashmir*
- *Kashmiris are Disappearing from WhatsApp*
- *Twitter Unblocked Accounts that Criticized India's Government. Now, its Employees are Being Threatened with Jail Time Unless it Blocks Them Again*
- *While Two Nuclear Powers were on the Brink of War, a Full-Blown Online Misinformation Battle was Underway*

- *Meet the Women who have to Sneak onto Facebook*
- *Here's How a Secret Meeting of Twitter Execs and Indian Activists Caused a Caste Scandal*
- *Older Indians Drive Millennials Crazy on WhatsApp. This is why they're Obsessed*
- *How India's Political Parties Hijacked Twitter's Trending Column for Partisan Bickering*
- *American Tech Companies are so Afraid of Offending Indians that they're Censoring all their Products*

In 2020, Vidya Krishnan of *The Caravan* was given the Nieman Foundation Fellowship.[49] A scathing article by her on the Modi government was featured in the Nieman Foundation reports in 2021, titled *In India, the Last Few Bastions of the Free Press Stand Guard Against Rising Authoritarianism.* Krishnan criticizes the Modi government by saying 'Discrediting and harassing journalists is central to how the Modi government operates, with severe paranoia and vindictive cruelty'.[50] She elaborates:

> Over the last seven years, newsrooms have found themselves in the trenches, holding the Modi government to account... On July 16, Siddiqui was killed by Taliban terrorists in Kandahar, Afghanistan. He was covering the clash between Afghan special forces and Taliban fighters for Reuters. At 38, he had already won a Pulitzer Prize for Feature Photography, in 2018, for documenting Myanmar's Rohingya refugee crisis. His colleagues described him as 'a man who cared deeply about the stories he covered.' Condolences poured in from around the world, with Afghan President Ashraf Ghani, the U.S. State Department, and United Nations secretary general António Guterres expressing grief at the tragic news. *Modi chose not to acknowledge Siddiqui's death.* ... the prime minister's followers called Siddiqui — an Indian Muslim murdered by the Taliban — a 'jihadi'.[51]

As other examples, in 2017, Raheel Khursheed head of Twitter India and Southeast Asia was given the Knight Visiting Nieman Fellowship.[52] And in 2021, the Pulitzer Center grantee Kalpana Jain and American historian John Fea were invited to speak on the relationship between religion and populism:[53]

'It was V. Savarkar, a former anti-colonial revolutionary, who translated this idea of Hindu unity, and he made it a more potent symbol: that of the Indian state,' she explained. 'He saw religious boundaries as national ones, and he considered Islamic and Christian traditions as illegitimate, foreign influences'.[54]

The Pulitzer Center praised Fea's work that was an effort to compare Christian nationalism in America with what the West perceives as Hindu nationalism:

Fea, discussing the story of one participant in the January 6, 2021, storming of the U.S. Capitol, observed a similar surge in Christian nationalism and how it can provide an outlet for those who feel that they do not have a voice in society.[55]

Jain talked about Hindu nationalism in contemporary India with a focus on a Vishva Hindu Parishad women's organization called Durga Vahini.

'Members of Durga Vahini are ordinary women from across India who seek greater agency in their everyday lives through the organization,' Jain explained. 'They have grown up under very strong patriarchal control,' she said. 'They have never been able to go out in the public and be seen as having a voice.'[56]

Jain criticizes Durga Vahini's approach to educating women and girls: 'In that training of Hindu culture, there is misrepresentation of history, there is misrepresentation of facts, and there is also this otherness created about the outsider: the Muslim.'[57]

Since 2018, there has been a steep increase in the number of Indian journalists funded by the Pulitzer Center. More remarkable is its interest in Kashmir, where a number of young journalists have been sent to write about the Indian government's activities.

Reinterpreting Indian Classics

Though Harvard University Press is totally independent of Neiman Foundation, it can bring similar effects as a publisher. It is one of the most powerful publishing houses in the academic world and what it puts out carries a lot of weight. Therefore, one expects it to manage this clout responsibly. But in many instances, it shows utter disregard for the ancient traditions of India. We do not suggest that all its publications are flawed but wish to point out that its brand is at times misused.

A good example is its largest ever project, the Murty Classical Library of India. Funded by the Indian billionaire N.R. Narayana Murthy, co-founder of Infosys, its purpose is to translate and interpret hundreds of classical Indian texts across a vast array of Indian languages.

While it is a noble gesture to showcase India's extensive literary tradition, the translations are under the editorship of Sheldon Pollock of Columbia University, a Sanskrit scholar known for his prejudices against the Vedic heritage. The book, *The Battle for Sanskrit*, gives a detailed critique of how this project distorts Indian classical traditions by interpreting them through the Western social sciences lens and taking liberties with the translations.[58] It shows that Pollock's positions on Sanskrit are fundamentally flawed. According to him, Sanskrit's primary reason for success was due to its use for political exploitation and oppression. He does not acknowledge its spirituality. He considers it a dead language, having been killed by Hindu kings in the past.

What Harvard University Press is essentially doing is taking Western conceptual categories and infusing them into Indian minds while claiming to be bringing the knowledge in these Sanskrit works to the masses. This makes Indians 'feel good' about their heritage.

15

Harvard Kennedy School: Geopolitics

Overview

The Harvard Kennedy School of Government is arguably the world's most prestigious and powerful academic center on political science, governance, and policymaking. It is training present and future world leaders and asserting its own political ideologies in the broadest sense. Its website announces:

> Harvard Kennedy School's mission is to improve public policy and leadership so people can live in societies that are more safe, free, just, and sustainably prosperous.[1]

This sounds like a great service to humanity provided there is no bias in their interpretation of safety, freedom, justice, sustainability, and prosperity. We shall examine these premises in this chapter as they pertain to India.

With an endowment of $1.7 billion[2] that is separate from Harvard's overall endowment of over $50 billion, HKS is one of the largest institutions within Harvard. It includes under its umbrella several other powerful centers, such as The Roy and Lila Ash Center for Democratic Governance and Innovation, The Belfer Center for Science and International Affairs, The Carr Center for Human Rights Policy, The Center for International Development, The Center for Public Leadership, The Institute of Politics, The Shorenstein Center on Media, Politics & Public Policy, The Malcolm Wiener Center for Social Policy, The Mossavar-Rahmani Center for Business and Government, The Taubman Center for State and Local Government, and The

Women and Public Policy Program.[3]

In addition, it also has collaborative programs with Harvard Business School, Harvard Law School, Mittal Institute, Mahindra Humanities Center, T.H. Chan School of Public Health, and various others at Harvard.

Its structures of power and networks of influence make the Harvard Kennedy School a seat of geopolitical clout like none other. Why the school matters to India can be seen in its ability to negotiate issues, set policies on the world stage and expose India to grave security threats. In addition, we will show that China became well-positioned to use the Kennedy School's resources to its advantage.

Harvard Sepoys Testifying Against India

We start by looking at five scholars nurtured by HKS: Raqib Hameed Naik, Rashad Hussain, Anurima Bhargava, Preeta Bansal, and Ashutosh Varshney. All five are of Indian descent and heavily trained by HKS and supported by it to shape world opinion. Each of them has given expert testimonies against India at US government hearings on various issues. One of the ways HKS wields power is by using such individuals to shape the foreign policies of the US and other countries.

The first individual nurtured by HKS we will discuss is Raqib Hameed Naik. He is an activist and independent journalist writing for *Al Jazeera* and *The Wire*. He was an expert witness at the US Congressional briefing on Kashmir in Washington D.C., where he said:

> With each passing day the humanitarian crises in the valley are intensifying and the grave human rights violations continuing; and let's not forget the brutal atrocities committed by the Indian state (in Kashmir) over the last more than 3 decades.[4]

Naik was one of the panelists at the Harvard India Conference of 2020 jointly hosted by the Harvard Kennedy School and Harvard Business School. The discussion was on the challenges of being Muslim in contemporary India.[5] He is sympathetic towards the Rohingya Muslim migration into India, and wrote an article titled, *India's far-right turns hostile toward Rohingya refugees*.[6] He is a prominent ally of the Indian American Muslim Council in its persistent anti-India lobbying in the

US and is well known as a Kashmir separatist fighting against India's sovereignty.[7]

At a typical one-sided panel at the Harvard India conference, Arfa Khanum Sherwani, senior editor of *The Wire*, compared Nazi Germany with India.[8] Aman Wadud, a human rights lawyer, was on the panel speaking against India's Citizenship (Amendment) Act, 2019 law. Another panelist was Hussain Haidry, writer and lyricist, who expressed strong disapproval over the court verdict on the Ram Mandir and called for 'progressive people' to unleash chaos and unrest in Ayodhya and stop the Bhoomi Pujan ceremony.[9]

As is normal in Harvard's panels on India, they failed to include any voice with an alternative viewpoint or anyone with evidence to the contrary. For example, Harvard never brings in experts to speak on Kashmir's spiritual and literary history, or the plight of the Kashmiri Pandits, or the legal position of the Indian side in this dispute, or Pakistan's violation of the UN Resolution on Kashmir, or on China's occupation of Kashmir territory.

This bias also shows that Indian billionaires who proudly sponsor such events fail to ensure that a fair and balanced view is presented.

Another tough activist educated by Harvard Kennedy School is Rashad Hussain whose parents had migrated from Bihar. He earned a master's degree in public administration at the Harvard Kennedy School and was the recipient of the Paul and Daisy Soros Fellowship named after billionaire George Soros's older brother.[10] In 2010, President Obama appointed him special envoy to the Organization of Islamic Conference. Many Americans opposed his nomination because of his pro-jihadist stance. A report in the American media stated:

> The turmoil caused by Hussain's appointment centers around comments he purportedly made in defense of Sami Al-Arian, a convicted terrorist and former leader of the Palestinian Islamic Jihad. Now, questions are rightfully being raised as to how a terrorist sympathizer has risen to such a position within the president's administration.[11]

Many years later, when Joe Biden became president, Hussain got yet another boost in his career. He was appointed US ambassador at large for International Religious Freedom. This is a powerful position reporting directly to the highest levels of the government as the official eyes and ears of the United States.

Unlike during Obama's tenure when the American Right-wing opposed him, Hussain has lately managed to close ranks with them in this new position. In his previous position, the American Right-wing saw him tilted towards Islam, but he has now found common cause by targeting India on the controversial issue of religious conversions. This is why the *Christian Post* and *Christianity Today* praised Biden's nomination of Hussain. Open Doors' CEO, David Curry, who has aggressive plans to convert Indians to Christianity asked for a swift confirmation of Hussain:

> David Curry, CEO of Open Doors USA, told Christianity Today that he was 'heartened' by the Biden administration filling the critical IRF roles. 'Rashad Hussain is a well-qualified nomination with a deep understanding of the factors at play in China, India, and elsewhere,' he said. 'We look forward to building together the diverse coalition of leadership necessary to counter the rising tide of religious persecution worldwide.'[12]

The diverse coalition of leadership brings certain Muslims and Christians together to counter India's attempts to stop the massive wave of Christian conversions. This is done under the guise of 'religious freedom', a code word to support foreign funded missionaries. Not surprisingly, during the 'Karnataka Hijab' controversy, while the Indian courts were deciding if individual institutions had a right to mandate uniforms, Hussain promptly interfered, tweeting the following from his *official* Twitter handle:

> Religious freedom includes the ability to choose one's religious attire. The Indian state of Karnataka should not determine permissibility of religious clothing. Hijab bans in schools violate religious freedom and stigmatize and marginalize women and girls.[13]

Interestingly, the US did not interfere when Denmark, France, Austria, and other Western countries banned the burqa. Despite the tensions among the Abrahamic religions, they close ranks to collaborate against non-Abrahamic faiths, of which Hinduism is the largest, and a different standard of 'religious freedom' applies.

This illustrates how HKS prepares its young scholar-activists and plants them in strategic positions to spread a specific agenda globally. Hussain's example shows Harvard's network of power that reaches beyond its Ivy League walls. Whatever ideologies are formulated at Harvard are meant to 'educate' the rest of the world. The Kennedy School is an important launching pad for interference in every country once it gets targeted.

We will later discuss Harvard's role in training the Indian civil service. They are also constantly using their connections to plant their own people into international organizations like the World Economic Forum, the US Commission on International Religious Freedom (USCIRF), and other institutions that help maintain the status of Harvard as the vishwa guru.

Anurima Bhargava is another familiar face involved in the proceedings against India at the USCIRF. She has close ties to Harvard where she spent substantial time. In 2021, the *Harvard Gazette* proudly noted her importance as a Harvard product. She has been deployed to mobilize 'brown and Black students' to serve the downtrodden voiceless people:

> Bhargava has kept close ties to the University. ... she addressed students and alumni on campus as the keynote speaker for the annual Public Interested Conference, coordinated by the Phillips Brooks House Center for Public Service & Engaged Scholarship. She has also served as co-chair for the National Advisory Board for Public Service at Harvard College, was a senior fellow at the Carr Center for Human Rights at the Harvard Kennedy School, and was a fellow at the Institute of Politics. Through her service to Harvard she hopes she can show students 'that service takes on many forms, including telling their story or giving solidarity and voice to the silences,' to help them 'build or find a lifelong community grounded in purpose,' to engage across difference, and to give brown and Black students especially 'a space to share their stories and to find community'. [14]

A decade after Bhargava graduated from Harvard, she was selected as a senior fellow at the Carr Center for Human Rights and fellow at the Institute of Politics, both at HKS.

Towards the end of her HKS Carr Center fellowship, Nancy Pelosi,

US speaker of the House, appointed Bhargava to the USCIRF where she now serves as vice chair. Bhargava appears to be projected as the 'Hindu voice' in the powerful USCIRF. But as an example of where she stands with regards to the CAA bill in India, Bhargava said that 'India's controversial citizenship laws are "troubling"'.[15] The *India Abroad* reported that 'the USCIRF slammed the CAA as "a dangerous turn in the wrong direction," and called on the Trump administration to impose sanctions on Home Minister Amit Shah — the catalyst behind this legislation'.[16]

In 2021, Bhargava continued her crusade against India at the USCIRF:

> Because of these systematic and ongoing egregious violations in India, the ... (USCIRF) has recommended that India be designated as a Country of Particular Concern (CPC). USCIRF commissioner Anurima Bhargava notes that such national and state policies 'create an ecosystem which is taking a turn from the historical protection of pluralism' typically seen in India, and many are worried about the government's efforts to silence those who speak about this issue.[17]

The condemnation of India to the list of Country of Particular Concern is quite typical of the Harvard educated anti-Hindu voices masquerading as Hindus. A generation before Bhargava, another woman became the first Hindu to serve in the USCIRF, and she, too, compromised the positions of Hindus in her official capacity. She was also a product that Harvard was proud of. Preeta Bansal graduated from Harvard in 1986 and became a visiting fellow at Harvard's Kennedy School of Government. Immediately after her HKS fellowship, Nancy Pelosi, speaker of the US House of Representatives, appointed her the chair of USCIRF in 2004. Indian newspaper headlines flaunted the achievements of the little girl from Roorkee, a city in the Indian state of Uttarakhand:

> Preeta Bansal, a former solicitor general of New York state, has been appointed a member of the ... (USCIRF). This is the first time an Indian American will occupy such an eminent position ... which advises the president, the secretary of state and Congress on religious freedom in other countries and how best to promote it.[18]

In 2004, under Bansal's watch, USCIRF placed India on the list of Country of Particular Concern.[19] For her work, Bansal has been richly rewarded. She received the National Organization of Women's 'Woman of Power and Influence Award' in 2006; was named one of the '50 Most Influential Minority Lawyers in America' by the *National Law Journal* in 2008; and was given the 'Pioneer Award' from the National South Asian Bar Association,[20] the Henry Crown Fellow at the Aspen Institute, and the Asian Pacific American Institute for Congressional Studies Stewardship Award.[21]

Our fifth and final example is Ashutosh Varshney who was a fellow at the Ash Center of Harvard Kennedy School. He, too, has testified against the Indian government's position before the USCIRF,[22] saying that the CAA 'creates an enabling atmosphere of violence against Muslims and marginalization of Muslims in politics'.[23] The damage from his scholarship, however, runs deeper, especially after Harvard placed him in strategic academic posts elsewhere.

In October 2021, as a leading columnist of *The Indian Express*, he published an article titled *Jim Crow Hindutva*.[24] He superimposes the Jim Crow laws that were at the height of American racism on to India. He says India is regressing to 'Jim Crow Hindutva', because the government removed Article 370 of the Indian Constitution that had kept Jammu & Kashmir isolated from the rest of India. What he does not inform his American readers is that J&K has been a territorial dispute in which every Indian government regardless of being Left-wing or Right-wing ideology has fought to protect India's sovereignty. One is left wondering how a political stand to resolve a territorial issue gets turned into a Jim Crow topic.

To make his case, Varshney incorrectly compares the practice of lynching during the Jim Crow era with isolated incidents of violence in India associated with issues like cattle theft and slaughter of calves. This is a projection of facts taken from one context on to an entirely unrelated context half a world away. As a political scientist, he has sounded the alarm that 'the liberalism of India's polity is in precipitous decline'. But his analysis lacks objectivity and conveniently overlooks significant facts that contradict his thesis. For instance, he fails to acknowledge that the move on Article 370 restores broader rights to Dalits and women, which were earlier denied in the Jammu & Kashmir region.

In his capacity as professor of social sciences at Brown University, he repackages Isabel Wilkerson's idea of 'caste = race' and exports it to India. His contribution is that he includes Indian Muslims on the 'caste' side of the equation. Muslims of India are akin to the Blacks of America according to him, and Hindutva is essentially the American equivalent of White supremacy.[25] This is a way to claim that Muslims ought to be designated as a 'protected class' that cannot be criticized.

When asked about how the US should respond against India, Varshney laid out a strategy to the US, including the options on the table, the pros and cons of such intervention, and the likely resistance. He discussed whether the US should place sanctions on India or use diplomacy; and the array of possible interventions available to the US to keep India in check, keeping in mind the possible counter responses from India. Essentially, he was advising the US on how best to prosecute India and keep it under check.

Varshney repeatedly asserts that there can never be anything like a Hindu *rashtra* or nation, saying, 'those who argue that (the) Indian nation is 5000 years old, democratic theory doesn't accept that claim, its simply an ideological claim'.[26] India has been a civilization and not a nation for five thousand years, he says. India as a political construct was thus born during Independence.

But why should the Western definition of nation and political construct be the criteria for evaluating India's legitimacy? Varshney's lens is so colonized that he cannot think outside of Western political theories. In fact, one could invert his logic and say that India was traditionally better off as a civilization rather than a 'nation' as defined by the 'political construct' in the Westphalia sense. And if he wanted to counter such a proposition, he would have to provide historical evidence that the ancient Bharat rashtra was dysfunctional. Otherwise, nothing is proven by simply pointing out that the idea of rashtra does not fit into the Western concept of nation state.

A better way to analyze would be to question whether the construct of rashtra, which is united by a common civilization was indeed successful in serving its citizens. Did it provide a good standard of living for its subjects, did it provide good education, and did it make progress? One would have to compare the ancient rashtra not with today's best examples, but with other ancient civilizations and countries at the time.

Such an approach would topple Varshney's thesis.

From all historical accounts written by the early Greeks, the Chinese, all the way more recently to the Europeans, Bharat rashtra was considered an advanced and successful society.

Upon Independence, India became a nation state as per Western norms with a Constitution based on Western style democracy. This was required because the world order dominated by the West had set the ground rules to determine when a given colony should be considered fit for self-rule, and this criterion was the Western notion of a nation state. This requirement of becoming a modern nation was forced upon all colonies as the precondition for their independence. By no means does it invalidate the idea of rashtra.

The rashtra notion has been evaluated using the constructs established by the Treaty of Westphalia in 1648. Today, the widely established concepts of state sovereignty, mediation between nations, and diplomacy all find their origins in this treaty. India, as a modern nation state in the Westphalian sense, is a child of colonialism, and this alien imposition should be evaluated as a possible cause for many of the problems that India faces today. One must appreciate the contradictions between Bharat rashtra as a civilization on the one hand, and modern India on the other, trying to become a Western-style nation. It is not obvious that the problem lies with the civilization and not the modern construct.

Clearly, though, Varshney, as a self-proclaimed post-colonialist, is using a colonized lens, thus failing to view the idea of rashtra on its own merits.

Varshney also criticizes historians for pointing out the well-established fact that Muslims invaded India twelve hundred years ago, imposing their religion and their Persian language as the official language in Indian courts; and that some of the most sacred Hindu sites were demolished and replaced with Islamic monuments. In the passage below, he condemns Prime Minister Modi for referring to that Islamic rule as a form of colonialism, because he feels it is

> a standard Hindu nationalist argument: that India's colonization
> began with the arrival of Muslim rulers in Sind in the eighth
> century, not with the Bengal conquest by the British East Indian

Company in 1757. The latter is the standard claim in history books, which also argue that while the first Muslims of India might have arrived from the Middle East, they settled down in the country, Indianized themselves, and broke links with the Middle East, except for visiting, once in a lifetime, the holiest shrine of Mecca, as Islam requires. This standard historical claim is not acceptable to Hindu nationalists. To them, Islam is a religion that forcefully conquered India, defeating and humiliating the Hindus, the original peoples of India.[27]

There are several flaws in his reasoning. Just because the view that Islamic conquest resulted in colonization is not 'standard', does not make it false. Whose 'standard' is this? While it is true that foreign Muslim rulers did Indianize themselves, this was solely for the purpose of enjoying the grand lifestyle India offered that was not available in their country of origin. The White European conquerors of America also left their homes, settled in the new land, and Americanized themselves by adopting many practices not found in Europe. Similarly, the European colonizers also settled in India. Therefore, just because foreign conquerors settle in the country after conquest and adopt it as their home, it does not mean they weren't colonizers. Each of these examples was an act of intercontinental conquest, plunder, and imposition of the aggressor's culture, religion, and language upon the defeated natives.

Muslim invaders brought their own scribes to document their plunder, taking Hindu slaves, and implementing large-scale slaughters of the defeated. These historical records of heroism written in Persian are found in museums and archives not only in India but also Europe and US. The large-scale sale of Hindus into the slave markets of Central Asia is well-established in the archives of the former Soviet Union and was explicitly the subject of a PhD dissertation by Scott Levy at the University of Michigan.[28]

That Indians did not earlier discuss these aspects of their past should be seen in the same light as women, Blacks and LGBTQ+ are. In all these cases, the victims are only *now* waking up to discuss their past victimhood. These are instances of re-examining the past and dealing with it in a responsible manner without turning them into acts of retribution.

We agree with Varshney that problems of past Muslim atrocities should not be blamed on present-day Muslims. Nobody is responsible for the conduct of their ancestors, and people should be judged solely on the basis of their own actions. But he is an apologist for Islamic horrors of the past:

> Muslim princely power has been used by Hindu nationalists to transform the conduct of some Muslim rulers, especially Babur and Aurangzeb, and before them, the invasion of Ghazni and Ghouri, into a larger anti-Muslim political narrative. [...] No serious historian finds an unbroken chain of Hindu-repression and India-hatred running across centuries of Muslim rule. More fundamentally, how are Muslim masses implicated in the princely conduct? Why punish them?[29]

We agree that past accounts must not be allowed to turn into present-day acrimony, but at the same time, history books must explain the atrocities against Hindus in the same manner that Black Americans and Native Americans demand the proper documentation of past atrocities against them.

The denial of the history of Islamic oppression is not only false but also causes jingoistic Muslim leaders to claim superiority of their religion as the justification for invading India and claiming it as their gift to liberate the Hindus from the scourge of caste and other atrocities. In other words, to salvage the reputation of the Islamic invaders, a common portrayal by today's historians and political leaders has been to argue that the inferior culture of the Hindu infidels needed foreign invasion to rescue the natives from their plight. This was also the argument used by the British to justify colonialism as a civilizing mission and the so-called White Man's burden. Muslim chauvinism has been fed by claiming that civilizing the infidels of India was the Muslim's burden for which they had to travel thousands of miles, all the way from the Middle East.

The truth is quite different. For one thing, there was a thriving slave trade under Muslim rule, both with Indians being exported to slave markets in Central Asia, as well as with African slaves being imported into India. It should not be considered politically incorrect to teach such facts in history courses, along with the flaws in Hindu society in the past and present.

In other words, truth shouldn't turn into negotiable claims with politicians taking control of the discourse, because if that happens, irresponsible manipulations are inevitable. Varshney could introspect and play a useful role given his prominent position.

Varshney is also critical of Indians advocating 'nationalism' and condemning 'antinationalism'. In a report resulting from a three-year project supported by Azim Premji University, Varshney jumps on this use of the word 'nationalism'. He is speaking to his US government handlers and his sponsors when he says: 'The U.S. State Department's religious-freedom reports have also criticized India's recent governments for not providing adequate support—including physical safety—to minorities, especially Muslims.' He warns that India's democracy is threatened by Hindu nationalism.

But this should be seen as a semantic issue in the use of English language nuance. Indians often use English terms in a different sense than Western academics. Until a few generations ago, the terms patriotism and nationalism were used interchangeably in the West as well. But nationalism was besmirched due to its usage by the Nazis and other fascists (who we might remind the reader were products of Western civilization). As a result, the term 'patriotism' is now being applied in the positive sense referring to love for one's land and culture without forcing it on anyone, whereas 'nationalism' has become a bad word referring to authoritarianism and intolerance towards diversity.

Indians (except those trained by the West) have not understood this shift in nuance, nor should they be expected to. In any case, the difference between nationalism and patriotism is subjective and not absolute. Varshney fails to explain this peculiarity of the Indian usage of English terms. One must look at the substance of a given situation and not whether the English vocabulary is being used accurately. The key point should be that Indians accused of promoting nationalism explain that their idea of India is one of inherent diversity based on Vedic metaphysics.

Misinformation Warfare

The Shorenstein Center on Media, Politics and Public Policy at HKS describes its charter as:

Dedicated to increasing understanding of how people access, create, and process information, particularly as it relates to news and societal issues, and describing potential solutions to the problems facing our information ecosystem.[30]

This is yet another powerful nexus at Harvard controlling the construction and flow of information. If you search for anything on India at Harvard Kennedy School, you are likely to find a lot of material on how terrible everything in India is, in terms of human rights, social justice, and attitudes towards sexual violence. The Shorenstein Center, for example, has a paper on rape culture in India and the role of the press:

After public protests and editorials from the press, the Indian government established a committee to examine the country's laws and attitudes toward women, producing an extensive report – yet the resulting media coverage was cursory, and the government has yet to enact suggested reforms. Jolly [the author] provides recommendations for how the Indian media and the government can work to improve conditions for women, addressing problems that are rooted in patriarchal structures. The paper also highlights the importance of sexual violence reporting in shaping public opinion and policy.[31]

As part of her recommendations, the author suggests that Indian newsrooms should appoint 'specially-focused gender reporters to ensure rape is not covered as a one-off event but is reported within the social context that it occurs'. This will ensure that more coverage is given to 'rape in rural areas, rape within the home and rape in conflict areas'.[32] It is definitely a good idea to call for more female journalists and increase focus on women's issues. But the problem is that by installing itself as the moral police charged with 'protecting the information ecosystem and supporting healthy democracy', the Shorenstein Center has at times abused its power and proved to be a generator of misinformation.

It is also troubling that the Shorenstein Center is said to have deep connections with the Chinese Communist Party. According to a report by the *National Pulse*,[33] the center has had many fellows from the CCP and is instrumental in pushing narratives that are aligned with the party.

Masquerading as an anti-disinformation platform, Shorenstein actually aids the Chinese Communist Party by knocking down narratives the CCP prefers not to be public.[34]

The center counts Chinese Communist Party advisers such as Steven Dong – who served as the Director of the Global Journalism Institute at the alma mater of Xi Jinping, Tsinghua University, and former presenter for state-run news outlet China Central Television (CCTV) – as fellows.[35]

Another fellow – Li Xiguang – is a Tsinghua University Professor, a member of the Chinese Foreign Ministry Advisory Committee on Public Diplomacy, and a former Senior Editor at the state-run media outlet Xinhua.[36]

The report continues:

Another fellow, Zhengrong Hu, was the Director of the National Center for Radio and Television Studies at the state-run Communication University of China. ... Zhengrong has also served as Chair on the Chinese Communist Party State Council's Discipline Evaluation Group of Journalism and Communication group, Chair of the Education Supervision Committee at the Ministry of Education, Chair of the China Association of Communication, and member of the Expert Committee of Courses Development and Disciplines Establishment at the Ministry of Education.[37]

And furthermore,

the Shorenstein Center has hosted at least 10 events alongside Harvard's Ash Center, which has taken millions from companies linked to and owned by the Chinese Communist Party and published studies popularized by Chinese state-run media outlets claiming the government enjoys record-high support.[38]

With so much Chinese influence, the Shorenstein Center can hardly claim to be the arbitrator on mis- and dis-information of any kind, let alone serve as an honest broker for information on India.

Since the explosion of the role of social media in affecting elections, Harvard has launched several initiatives in its self-appointed role of monitoring misinformation. For example, Campus Reform, a conservative watchdog site has reported that Harvard blacklisted many respectable conservative and libertarian news agencies as 'fake' news outlets while giving a free pass to liberal news outlets as credible:[39]

> Harvard's guidelines on fake news also recommend that students download browser plug-ins that theoretically detect websites that "may not be a reliable source," flagging well-known outlets like *The Drudge Report, Breitbart, The Daily Signal*, and even calling *LifeSite News* "clickbait." Harvard claims, however, that its guide merely "offers a brief introduction to the spread of misinformation of all kinds and tools for identifying it and reading the news with a more informed eye."[40]

The HKS *Misinformation Review* was launched in 2019 at the HKS' Shorenstein Center.[41] Its website gives a glorifying description of itself as

> The only peer-reviewed journal dedicated to publishing multidisciplinary research on mis- and disinformation. It operates on a 'fast peer review' process that ensures the academic rigor of the articles, but on a much faster timeline than traditional academic publishing, because the research being published is 'timely and of great importance to practitioners currently working to combat disinformation and its effects.'[42]

We shall discuss a few instances to illustrate the bias. The landslide victory of the BJP in India in the 2019 general elections shocked and disappointed those in the West who had been aligned with the prior regime. Harvard decided to study the technologies that amplified the election results it considered undesirable. One of the papers posted at its 'misinformation review' website studied the information on various platforms:

> We study a large collection of politically-oriented WhatsApp groups in India, focusing on the period leading up to the 2019 Indian national elections. By labelling samples of random and popular images, we find that around 10% of shared images are known misinformation and most fall into three types of images. Machine learning methods can be used to predict whether a viral image is misinformation...[43]

The project categorized misinformation into different classes with the goal of modeling 'the motives behind posting' misinformation, and eventually training algorithms to identify it based on factors including 'who spreads it'. It also wants to figure out how misinformation gets used for causing unrest and violence. Such a project has bias built into it. For instance, it hired three journalists to manually annotate 2,500 images and identify what they considered 'fake' and 'biased', which in itself is prone to bias. They also arbitrarily chose fact checking websites in India, yet another source of bias. Of special interest to them was misinformation that involved superstitions, historic and religious myths, nationalism and political memes – what appears to be a good way to target Hindu 'chauvinism'.

Another Kennedy School paper claimed that the propaganda and misinformation in the Global South (read India) needs different methods of monitoring than methods used in the Global North, because in the Global South 'a deep understanding of the political economy of propaganda and misinformation is urgently needed'.[44]

As an example, the paper claims that Facebook is by BJP-linked people and hence a different approach is necessary: 'In India, Hindu nationalist propaganda on Facebook and Facebook-owned WhatsApp has led to harassment, hate speech, lynchings, and pogroms against Muslims and lower castes'.[45] Because Harvard was unable to plant its own people as gatekeepers, it was assumed that the BJP must have planted them: 'It is difficult to expect institutional accountability when BJP-linked people run the Facebook India office'.[46]

Another paper discusses setting up real time tip lines to curb the spread of misinformation on WhatsApp during elections in India. Obviously, Harvard has the clout to develop and fund such tip lines that would be presented as neutral and objective sources.[47]

Harvard's misinformation research website promotes a study by Equality Labs, titled, *Critical Disinformation Studies: History, Power, and Politics*.[48] This accuses Hindus of Islamophobia and caste hierarchies as the causes for disinformation in India and resulting in the 'Rohingya genocide' in Myanmar. The report claims to be 'grounded in history, culture, and politics, and centers questions of power and inequality'. It sets the stage to gain a favorable reception at Harvard, stating:

In the United States, identity, particularly race, plays a key role in the messages and strategies of disinformation producers and who disinformation and misinformation resonates with. ... Disinformation is a primary media strategy that has been used in the U.S. to reproduce and reinforce white supremacy and hierarchies of power at the expense of populations that lack social, cultural, political, or economic power.[49]

It then goes on to apply this logic to India where thousands of Rohingyas have made their way: 'Anti-Muslim conspiracy theories on Facebook India against Rohingya communities have included calls to violence, like those leading to the Rohingya genocide in Myanmar'. It makes allegations of Islamophobia as misinformation that 'leverages existing religious and caste hierarchies as well as the unequal distribution of power and access on digital platforms'.[50] However, these statements were never subject to debate and were accepted at face value.

The anxiety about social media awareness in India troubles Harvard. An article recommends that Facebook and WhatsApp should change their approach to filtering misinformation and replace it with Harvard's own system. It claims to have a superior approach to detect misinformation from its fact-checking efforts.[51] It is ironic that the self-appointed police of electoral misinformation is in itself a source of one-sided rhetoric.

Harvard's goal is to instal ruling parties in various countries that align with its political doctrines. By investing in the elimination of a certain kind of misinformation, Harvard uses its deep pockets and wide network to run smear campaigns that crush those that oppose its ideology and promote those aligned with it.

An interesting example is the way Harvard attacked a small Black online organization, American Descendants of Slavery (ADOS) whose views threatened Harvard's political alignment. In a heavy-handed approach, Harvard discredited it in a widely disseminated paper in mainstream media alleging:

We find that the ADOS network strategically uses breaking news events to discourage Black voters from voting for the Democratic party, a phenomenon we call disinformation creep. Conversely, the ADOS network has remained largely silent about the impact of the novel coronavirus on Black communities, undermining its claims that it works in the interests of Black Americans.[52]

The CEO of ADOS lashed back, substantiating her claim that Harvard had used sloppy research to discredit her organization. She called it

a clear attempt to use the Ivy League institution's esteemed name to legitimize an ongoing smear campaign directed at the ... (ADOS) movement. The report ascribes a familiar set of demonstrably false motivations to our political advocacy, with the authors frequently substituting subjective claims, innuendo, and outright lies for the sort of empirically-backed assertions one would expect to find in a publication from such a prestigious university. ...

We reject in the strongest terms possible the allegation that ... ADOS ... has ever used breaking news to manipulate the Black community into voting Republican or, for that matter, abstaining entirely from the act of voting in the 2020 presidential election. And one will search the Harvard report in vain trying to locate a single piece of evidence that substantiates that claim.[53]

She also attacked Harvard scholar Mutale Nkonde for not disclosing conflicts of interest and voiced concern over the severe impact on her organization when an institution like Harvard spreads misinformation:

This article threw cold water on our momentum, an act which I can't help but wonder if this was intentional. Why would a wealthy white institution choose to put a small, Black group in its crosshairs? Why was MoveOn involved, given their blatant conflict of interest?[54]

The leading author of the "Disinformation Creep" article was Mutale Nkonde. NKonde (sic) is the founding CEO of AI For the People. There were numerous co-authors, including several affiliated with Media Matters and MoveOn.Org, both progressive political organizations. While conducting the research for this article, I noticed that there was no mention of Mutale NKonde (sic) as CEO on the official AI For the People's website; only the board and team are mentioned. She has become a star in the world of artificial intelligence and social justice, often speaking at predominantly white institutions. Her relationships span from the fashion industry to the White House and the UN.[55]

Perhaps fearing a lawsuit, Harvard retracted the paper by their scholar, Nkonde, acknowledging her sloppy research, and issued the following statement:[56]

> The external review found that Nkonde et al.'s study failed to meet professional standards of validity and reliability. ... "the conclusions drawn by the authors are supported primarily by their interpretation of a few selected tweets by ADOS leadership," and that "the quantitative analysis is insufficiently connected to the conclusions" of the paper.[57]
>
> After concerns were brought to our attention by (ADOS) ... challenging the validity of the findings reported by Nkonde et al., the journal commissioned an internal review, conducted by a Harvard researcher not directly affiliated with the journal. The internal review found flaws in the methodology, as well as discrepancies between the data and the findings reported by the authors, resulting in unsubstantiated conclusions drawn from their analyses. We then commissioned an external independent review to verify the findings of the initial investigation.[58]

Of course, Nkonde did not suffer any loss of funding for false and shoddy scholarship. In fact, her movement got promoted:

> Ironically, prior to the release of NKonde's now-unsubstantiated "Disinformation Creep" article, the MacArthur Foundation awarded AI For the People $220,000 between 2020 and 2021: two grants, including $200,000 for Journalism & Media and Technology and $20,000 in the area of Public Interest. The funding was to "create new knowledge about the impact of technology's design and governance on Black communities and to break down barriers for more African Americans to participate in public debate on important tech-related policy issues that affect them."[59]

Meddling with Indian Democracy

The Harvard Kennedy School clearly takes sides in India's political landscape with an intention to influence it. Narendra Modi's election win in 2014 was unacceptable to HKS and ever since, it has organized a staggering number of research studies, conferences, and seminars focusing on India. It shows a single-minded emphasis to change democratic outcomes in India, raising suspicions on its agenda and funding sources that make such investigations possible. These efforts by HKS to interfere in democracies reminds one of the way the US carried out regime changes wherever the government did not follow its mandates. The Kennedy School is a key institution in this global projection of power under the guise of academic work, with the additional assistance of its prestigious brand name.

In 2015, a one-year performance report of the new Modi government was issued by Ronak Desai of the Kennedy School's Belfer Center. He gave the administration a 'D' for what Harvard considered egregious acts: tightening restrictions on the funding of international NGOs and for the investigation of Greenpeace.[60] There was no discussion on the reasons for such clampdowns, which were necessitated due to the violation of Indian laws on foreign funding and the crimes by Breaking India forces.

The report is especially hypocritical because Harvard's multi-year study on China gave the CCP great marks and claimed it enjoyed overwhelming support of its citizens. Nor did the alarm bells go off in the Harvard Kennedy School when China cracked down on NGOs in 2017 on the basis that they posed a national security risk. China placed the NGOs under a different ministry to ensure proper oversight:

> When it comes to managing the affairs of foreign ... (NGOs) seeking to work in China, the Ministry of Public Security (MPS) is very much in charge. This is a significant departure from a previous 10 years of practice, when the Ministry of Civil Affairs was tasked with monitoring and reporting on the doings of foreign NGOs.[61]

In 2017, an article posted at the Harvard Kennedy School website claimed that India's Congress Party had a rare opportunity to exploit the state of the economy to win.[62] However, such plans did not materialize. Modi's 2019 landslide victory troubled HKS and it started producing more atrocity literature to feed the Breaking India thesis. Its scholarship is meticulously packaged with actionable programs to counter what it sees as dangerous. As a democratically elected leader, Modi got demonized as one of the world's most dangerous poisons of 2019. Stephen Walt, a Belfer Center professor of international affairs at HKS, wrote:

> It's not hard to think of worthy candidates in the category of 'most significant foreign-policy event of 2019.' Pick your poison: the Hong Kong protests, the whistle blower revelations that led to the House of Representatives voting to impeach U.S. President Donald Trump, the Amazon and Australian fires, British Prime Minister Boris Johnson's electoral triumph, or *Indian Prime Minister Narendra Modi's march toward a new and narrower conception of Indian nationalism.*[63]

Thus, Harvard has a complete program to train human resources in topics to research and fuel activism on the ground in India. Since 2019, the Kennedy School, it would seem, has gone to great lengths to destroy the Hindu renaissance in India. For example, it has scores of scholars studying social media messaging on WhatsApp and Facebook platforms to look for influences on elections. It has proposed Artificial Intelligence-based tools for its role as the media police and put immense pressure on Facebook to comply with its requests.

What happens when internal movements and strong voter turnout in foreign countries yield results counter to Harvard's plans? We will show instances in which, like a spoilsport, Harvard changes the rules of the game when its efforts to control the outcome have failed. It claims that such countries must be dying democracies, the death being caused by the very same elected leaders that democracy has produced.

To deal with adverse election outcomes, Harvard produces new political theories. Its scholars begin claiming that elections are merely one of the multiple conditions for democracy. They want to redefine what constitutes a 'real' democracy. For example, a book by Harvard's political scientists Steven Levitsky and Daniel Ziblatt, *How Democracies Die,* states:

"Democracies do not die the way they used to die," said Steven Levitsky, a professor of government at Harvard University ... "Democracies used to die at the hands of men with guns. During the Cold War, three out of every four democratic breakdowns took the form of a classic military coup. ... Today democracies die in a much more subtle way. They die at the hands not of generals, but of elected leaders, presidents, prime ministers who use the very institutions of democracy to subvert it. ..."

In those polities, what emerges is "competitive authoritarianism," ... where "the playing field is pretty heavily skewed against the opposition. ... Hungary is a clear case. Venezuela, maybe Poland, maybe India, hopefully not the United States."[64]

Once Harvard had the ball rolling on this new way to address unfriendly outcomes, with India flagged, Indian intellectual sepoys quickly focused on applying the doctrine to India. Ashutosh Varshney amplified the ideas put forth by Levitsky and Ziblatt in an influential article in *The Indian Express*.

India's democracy is backsliding, not because of the generals and soldiers, but because elected politicians are subverting democracy. Very soon, two of the most widely read annual democracy reports — by America's Freedom House and Sweden's V-Dem Institute — will be published. They had argued last year that India was on the verge of losing its democratic status. Let us see whether this year's reports call India undemocratic, or only "partly free". ...

For democratic theory, elections are necessary, but not sufficient. Elections alone cannot be equated with democracy. Democracy is measured by a composite index. The overall judgement depends partly on elections, and partly on what the elected governments do between elections.[65]

Varshney quotes Freedom House's report of the prior year:

Almost since the turn of the century, the United States and its allies have courted India as a potential strategic partner and democratic counterweight to China in the Indo-Pacific region. ... Indian government's alarming departures from democratic norms under Prime Minister Narendra Modi's Bharatiya Janata Party ...

could blur the values-based distinction between Beijing and New Delhi. While India ... held successful elections last spring, the BJP has distanced itself from the country's founding commitment to pluralism and individual rights, without which democracy cannot long survive.[66]

Freedom House is funded by the US government, and it faces criticism from US thinktanks for its pro-Left biases:

> Freedom House reports on all five countries [the United States, Great Britain, Israel, Denmark, and Poland] reveal a consistent pattern of partisan bias against mainstream conservative parties. ... On issue after issue, Freedom House monotonously repeats the talking points of the progressive Left.[67]

It is noteworthy that Vivek Paul, former CEO of the IT company, Wipro, serves on the board of Freedom House.[68] The incestuous relationship between self-righteous Harvard scholars, whistleblower institutions within HKS, and the media, help promote the narrative that Harvard has scripted.

Harvard's record over the past several decades shows that it attacks governments that oppose its hegemony, be they Left- or Right-wing. This is why nearly every major policy decision of the BJP government has been criticized by Harvard. When India implemented demonetization, the Kennedy School's Amartya Sen wrote: 'PM Narendra Modi's Notes Ban Neither Intelligent Nor Humane'.[69] In 2019, more than 220 Harvard affiliates signed a petition condemning India's Citizenship (Amendment) Act, 2019 and alleged suppression of student protests at Indian universities. Harvard's campus newspaper reported: 'The letter was sponsored by groups including the Harvard US-India Initiative, the Harvard Islamic Society, and the Harvard College Pakistani Students Association'.[70]

Students of the Kennedy School are often the ones being tutored to organize protests against the Indian government, for instance in January 2020 condemning the CAA. Harvard's Dalit leader, Suraj Yengde, was chief mentor:

> Suraj Yengde, a protestor and a fellow at Harvard Kennedy School, said demonstrators in the Square stood especially in

solidarity with women who have been leading the protests in India, including a group of hundreds who have been occupying a street in the Shaheen Bagh neighborhood of Delhi for weeks. ... "The purpose of this is two-fold," said Ruha Shadab, a student at the Kennedy School and one of the protest's organizers. "One is to express our discontentment with the act itself. And the other is in solidarity with all the student-led movements, which are now just civilian movements, across India."[71]

In the following month, HKS students protested the invitation of Indian consul general to the Harvard India Conference because of his pro-India statements on Kashmir. They chanted slogans and held placards reading, *'Kashmir wants Freedom'*, and *'From Kashmir to Palestine, occupation is a crime!'*[72] This despite the fact that it is the Hindu Kashmiris that were genocided and driven out of their homeland.

During the 2019 general elections in India, Varshney said that a majority victory for the BJP would be something influenced by Hindutva, which he equates with White supremacy and White nationalism:

Should the BJP gain an absolute majority in parliament, "it will head towards a Hindu nationalist version of the nation," ... The [BJP] party's platform this time has been influenced more heavily by Hindu nationalism, or Hindutva. [He] describes the concept as "a political doctrine, which makes the claim that the Hindus are the primary owners of the nation." He terms it a sort of Hindu supremacism in which the non-Hindu minority of India accedes to the control or ownership of the state by the Hindu majority. "White nationalists in the United States would make a roughly analogous argument," he added.[73]

The student-run *Political Review* at Harvard is also replete with anti-Modi articles. One article reads *Protecting Cows and Persecuting People*.[74] Another article titled *IPL During COVID: The Nexus Between Cricket and Politics in India,* talks about the sycophancy adulation of Modi by Indian cricket players:

The (cricket) team's flagrant embrace of militarism was an endorsement of the Modi government's efforts to whip up ultra-nationalistic sentiments in the country following escalating tensions with neighboring Pakistan, which ultimately contributed to Modi getting re-elected with a landslide majority. ...

Sachin Tendulkar, ... perhaps the only Indian athlete who can rival Kohli's stardom, rushed to congratulate Modi after his sweeping victory in 2019. Another celebrated cricketer, Ravindra Jadeja, hailed the victory, proclaiming "a victory of Believers over non-believers." Virtually all prominent cricketers have persistently engaged in this kind of sycophantic adulation of Modi, conveniently disregarding the worsening plight of religious and ethnic minorities in the country under his rule. Gautam Gambhir, who played a crucial role in India's victorious run in the 2011 World Cup, even won an election for the BJP from East Delhi and is currently a member of the Lok Sabha. ...

Nationalism and cricket are intimately linked in India, and the game has proved to be a prodigious tool in providing the political elites leverage over the public mind.[75]

Every center at Harvard seems to have an agenda to undermine India's legitimacy when it chooses its own path. The Indologist, Michael Witzel remarked: 'Organizations associated with India's BJP political party and the Sangh Parivar have attempted to fundamentally and inaccurately revise textbooks to propagate a Hindu nationalist view in Californian and Indian schoolbooks.'[76]

Michael Walton, a senior lecturer in public policy at the Kennedy School in a 2020 paper, said that India lacks what he calls 'inclusive capitalism':

> While a path to an inclusive capitalism can (still) be imagined, the political economy pressures, and authoritarian temptations, are unlikely to support this in the medium to long term. Under these conditions, India could face Latin American scenario of rising, entrenched inequality, slow long-term growth and, even, macroeconomic instability.[77]

Walton is also a visiting fellow at the Centre for Policy Research, New Delhi and was VKRV Rao chair professor, Institute of Social and Economic Change, Bengaluru. He is being boosted as some sort of authority on India's business and economy. His clear bias is evident in statements like:

> Modi 1.0, despite the pro-business narrative and some potentially important policy shifts, was a half-baked enterprise in terms of reforming capitalism, if anything, leaving state-business relations in an intermediate position with less credibility in transactions – except for the biggest and most influential business houses. This became more vividly apparent in the initial period of Modi 2.0. The production and, especially private investment, slowdown was probably going to occur in any case, but was not helped by the uncertainties of the transition and the "chill" around business interactions with the state – this interacting with the financial overhang.
>
> The short-run measures in Modi 2.0, while striking, smack more of desperation than a concerted policy design, and are associated with a mix of deficit expansion and absence of a credible policy mix for tackling the financial sector.[78]

Women and Public Policy Program

A center dedicated to Harvard Kennedy School's way of advancing gender equity, the Women and Public Policy Program proclaims:

> No other organization in the world builds on behavioral insights to create evidence-based organizational designs that can promote women's empowerment, overcome gender bias, and provide equal opportunities for women and men, like the Women and Public Policy Program at Harvard Kennedy School. [79]

An important aspect of its mission is to change the attitudes of Indian women to match those of Western women through 'studies' being conducted in India on Indian women. These studies also offer a mechanism to spew Hinduphobia in the name of scholarship.

An illustrative example is a Harvard research paper on Indian women and entrepreneurship, titled *Do Traditional Institutions Constrain Female Entrepreneurship? A Field Experiment on Business Training in India.*[80] The authors investigate whether poor Indian women have constraints in pursuing entrepreneurship and whether 'traditional' structures have a role in obstructing these women. The study was carried out in Ahmedabad in partnership with a local bank. It studied Muslims, Hindu Scheduled Castes or Dalits, and Hindu upper caste women. It is ironic that two of the three authors were upper caste Hindu women who seemed to have miraculously escaped the oppressive Hindu caste system which they describe in the paper. According to them, upper castes,

> maintain purity by avoiding sexual relations, marriage and, in extreme cases, contact with lower castes. Premised on men being a source of pollution, restrictions are placed on women to limit contact with men other than their husbands. ... a married woman remain (sic) veiled, not remarry if widowed, not interact with older men, and have restricted mobility outside of her house. These norms – particularly the latter two – significantly restrict female labor force participation.[81]

Although they find that Muslim women have more restrictions than upper caste Hindu women, the authors suggest a noble cause behind the Muslim restriction: 'Because Muslim women are entitled to a share in family real estate, controlling their relationships with males outside the family can be crucial to the maintenance of family property and prestige'.[82]

The report acknowledges that Hindu upper caste women responded favorably to the entrepreneurial training provided because it allowed them to 'challenge social norms that were distorting their business practices'. Since the Muslim women did not respond at the same levels, the authors felt compelled to come up with an explanation that would not be considered Islamophobic. One possibility they put forth was that the women at the local bank might not represent the broader population, a hypothesis for which they felt the required data was unavailable.

The other possibility offered was the fault of Hindus in Ahmedabad for discriminating against the Muslims. The paper puts forth the thesis that 'Muslims in Ahmedabad, which has a history of religious tension, face considerable discrimination in the marketplace, which business training could not undo'. No evidence was offered in support, as a mere accusation of Hinduism sufficed. The paper also dismissed the notion that Islam's restrictions on interest-bearing loans may have been a possible reason that the entrepreneurship training did not result in increased demand for credit among Muslims.[83]

To bolster their thesis that restrictive cultural practices keep women from engaging in entrepreneurship, another fellow from Harvard's Center for Population and Development Studies arrives at the same conclusion but from another angle.[84] Aashish Gupta says that patriarchy in gender norms discourages women from using cooking gas despite government subsidies in India. If at all the women use cooking gas, he claims it is because the patriarchal culture wants to keep them secluded, tied to the house, and restricted from going out to fetch firewood.

> North Indian society confers low status to women, promotes women's seclusion, and constrains women's engagement in economic activities outside of the home. These beliefs encourage women to preserve gas, promote women's work that facilitates the use of solid fuels, and hinder communication between the cook and the decision-maker regarding LPG (Liquefied Natural Gas) refills. When rural north Indian households use gas, it is frequently to facilitate the adherence to norms of seclusion that prevent women from leaving the home to collect solid fuels.[85]

Another HKS team of Indians undertook a study titled *Why Are Indian Children So Short?*[86] Stating that India's children are the most stunted in the world, they found that there is height disadvantage because Indian mothers are biased in feeding their sons more than their daughters. Seema Jayachandran and Rohini Pande squarely blame stunting in Indian children on the Hindu cultural preference for sons. With the authority that only Harvard can provide, the scholars conclude:

> First, the Indian firstborn height advantage only exists for sons. Second, an Indian son with an older sibling is taller than his African counterpart if and only if he is the eldest son. Third, the India-Africa height deficit is largest for daughters with no older brothers, which reflects that fact that their families are those most likely to exceed their desired fertility in order to have a son. [87]

Another research conducted by the team was to find whether exposure to more female politicians changed negative stereotypes about women's roles in politics. Their conclusion, not surprisingly, showed that Hinduism results in misogynistic social attitudes: 'Interestingly, while voters change their willingness to vote for women and alter their implicit biases reasonably fast, their explicit attitudes (and therefore social norms) are much slower to change'.[88]

The Carr Center for Human Rights Policy

The Carr Center for Human Rights Policy is yet another center within HKS. Sushma Raman, its executive director, had prior stints with the Ford Foundation and George Soros' Open Society Foundations. She managed a portfolio of grants on 'social justice philanthropy and strengthening civil society' and helped to launch new foundations focused on 'gender justice and human rights/social justice'.[89] She comes well qualified to serve Harvard's purpose as the vishwa guru bringing social justice to the world.

Interestingly, when at Ford Foundation in India, Raman was accused of violating Indian Foreign Contribution (Regulation) Act, 2010 (FCRA) laws in the Teesta Setalvad/Javed Anand case:

> "... Raman, program officer of Ford Foundation, received the first proposal from Sabrang for receipt of grant in 2004. Investigations revealed that Raman was aware that Sabrang was not eligible to receive funds since it was not in accordance with the provisions of FCR Act. She had communicated with Javed at that time of processing of the proposal for the grant. To circumvent the compliance requirements Raman connived with Anand who was trying to project the grant as consultancy charges", the charge sheet mentions.[90]

Such defiance of Indian laws can build the individual into a hero in American academic circles.

Another example is Carr Center's senior fellow Salil Shetty who was secretary general at Amnesty International, an organization that has had several issues with India's Enforcement Directorate for FCRA violations in India.[91] In 2021, Shetty was rewarded and made vice president of the global program at Open Society.

Shetty has complained about the Indian government's 'unethical, narcissistic, authoritarian and incompetent leaders' during COVID-19 against NGOs and Muslims:

> There is now a large campaign in sections of the Indian media and public that link the spread of COVID-19 in India to Islam, thereby advancing the core agenda of the Hindu fundamentalist regime in power. Even the slightest criticism of the government or call for government accountability is seen as anti-national! ... many of the largest and most influential countries in the world have unethical, narcissistic, authoritarian and incompetent leaders who have been elected through a process of othering minorities, refugees, and peddling lies about past national glory.[92]

In a talk at Harvard, he said that the world is struggling with the quality of leadership when it comes to human rights. He then worries about those leaders whose human rights records are taking humanity backwards, and Modi is named alongside Trump and China's Xi Jingping.[93] In another paper, he says that comparing India to China in economic and military terms is 'a bit delusional'. Though its potential cannot be denied, 'its weakening democracy at home could prove to be a big challenge'. He claims that the reports from India show that the biggest challenges to India's soft power are 'religious intolerance and the increased number of hate crimes' that erode its traditional democratic and secular values. He writes:

> India, under the current regime has become increasingly aggressive towards any form of dissent and the foundational checks and balances of any healthy democracy i.e. independent media, judiciary, civil society etc. The country's handling of domestic disputes – including but not limited to caste-based violence, lynching over beef allegations, rights of adivasis and taking away Kashmir's special status have all taken its toll on India's soft power.[94]

Shetty cites the various indices that measure democracy to argue that under Modi, India is no longer a good democracy. Freedom House dropped India's ranking as a liberal democracy from seventy to eighty-five. The NGO, Reporters Without Borders dropped India from 133rd to 140th place in press freedom. He says these reports 'raise an important concern that many share: whether or not India remains a democracy in spirit. There is little doubt that all of this has damaged India's soft power image globally'.[95]

India, according to Shetty 'behaves with a sort of cognitive dissonance'. India's 'human rights violations and violence' not only lessen its standing on the world stage, he says, it could 'even result in the imposition of sanctions'.[96] Though previous political parties were also hard on detractors, according to him the current regime of Modi has

> taken it to another level entirely. It is often described as the imposition of an undeclared emergency and all indications are that it will only get worse. Even as the domestic democracy deficit is growing, the current regime has alienated pretty much all its neighbours, some by choice, others by bungling. The collapse of constitutional morality, in particular, has reduced India's standing in the eyes of its neighbours.[97]

On India's relationship with Pakistan, he comes out hard:

> For India's current Hindu nationalist regime, attacking Pakistan as a Muslim state and a historical enemy, is a core part of its identity. With the unprovoked stripping of Kashmir's special status and rights of the people of Kashmir, India has consciously chosen to further alienate Pakistan and China.[98]

The HKS also does consulting work for clients like Amnesty International India. One such subject was *Media Manipulation in the Indian Context: An Analysis of Kashmir-Related Discourse on Twitter*.[99] The study states it selected the media coverage of Kashmir to study the problem.

> The Modi government's decision to strip Jammu & Kashmir of its statehood through the abrogation of Article 370 brought the region to the forefront of the news starting mid-2019. Severe restrictions placed on internet and mobile services, movement of people and freedom of the press left questions about the quality of information available to the public.
>
> Twitter was chosen as the platform for investigation; Two specific types of manipulation—driving division and polarization and spreading progovernment propaganda—were selected as

focus areas. Driving division and polarization in society was observed through the use of derogatory terms against liberals and government critics. Spreading pro-government propaganda was studied through the portrayal of the situation in Kashmir in late-2019 as "normal" (despite the enforcement of several restrictions, as described above).[100]

The paper analyzes the top one percent of influencers in politics and media who are alleged to be engaged in 'a variety of manipulative tactics' on social media. It is especially interested in investigating Prime Minister Modi's 'die-hard' supporters who 'defend him furiously while bashing the opposition'. The report finds that many of these accounts have spread false information (as per Harvard's criteria of truth). The prime minister's social media cleverly selects the accounts to follow to maximize his 'brand-building efforts'. It concludes:

> Research suggests that there could be a tiered structure of being followed, with Modi being at the top. Different tiers could gamify the experience for users such that they are incentivized to increase online support for the BJP to rise up the tiers.[101]

Narendra Modi's social media also uses 'strategic silence' on the Kashmir issue, the paper claims, which has produced a lack of accountability:

> Silence creates confusion and leaves holes in the information ecosystem. It protects Modi and Shah by keeping them away from controversial conversations that could affect their brand. Instead, it puts other users in the front-line of the conversation. Distraction through other topics diverts the conversation away from important political matters and results in a serious lack of accountability. Without a clear message from leading authorities in the country, the status of Kashmir is unknown to the public and, as a topic, can appear less important than it is in reality.[102]

The *Harvard Law Review* also joined the attack on CAA and Article 370 issues. In a report titled *From Domicile to Dominion: India's Settler Colonial Agenda in Kashmir*, it states:

> The abrogation of Article 35A and the laws that have followed it are quintessential settler colonial violence, but so too are the legal

regimes that came before the abrogation. Fuelled by a growing settler narrative around Kashmir, India has long utilized the law to not just colonially oppress Kashmiris but erase them altogether.[103]

A discussion titled *Reimagining Social Movements and Civil Resistance during the Global Pandemic,* was announced as follows:

Carr Center faculty and fellows outline how social movements and civil resistance can take shape in a time of social distancing, and how these efforts are more important than ever in holding governments accountable.[104]

Inayat Sabhikhi, a graduate student at the Carr Center, wrote an article in the student magazine titled, In Solidarity: Harvard Students Join Indian Demonstrations Against New Citizenship Bill, *about the solidarity of Harvard students against the CAA.*[105]

The Center for International Development

Our analysis reveals that the Center for International Development is another part of HKS that is constantly trying to impose Western cultural norms and practices on Indians. Multiple parallel tracks collaborate to look for vulnerabilities, identify and train sepoys that can be usefully deployed, and eventually wear down the Indian structures and systems. Carrots and sticks are combined. For instance, one set of Harvard studies do a deep dive into an Indian phenomenon being targeted. Another set of projects try out various tools developed by Harvard or other Western academics to change Indian behavior. A third research track develops atrocity literature that shows India as a human rights nightmare where victims are waiting to be rescued by the West.

The HKS research also tries to investigate what made Indian civilization so resilient for centuries. In this regard, there is an ongoing HKS study, *Why is Mobility in India so Low? Social Insurance, Inequality, and Growth.* It blames caste-based networks that provide a support system to members of the community for the lack of mobility of rural people in India.[106] Contrast this with the pioneering work done by Prof. R. Vaidyanathan of Indian Institute of Management Bangalore, showing how caste groups have provided social security, cost-effectively, compared to government programs, and fostered economic development in several communities. Harvard has never invited Vaidyanathan to any of its events on this topic although his lifetime of original research is precisely on this subject. He does not fit their echo chamber.

Like the Carr Center, the Center for International Development also studies the low participation rates of women in the workforce. One such study looks at constraints that prevent higher participation and suggests policy changes to remedy this.[107] Another study titled, *Male Social Status and Women's Work* presents what it considers 'novel data' on attitudes of male spouses and community towards female participation in the workforce.[108] Yet another study uses female leaders to change behavior and outlook of villagers about gender roles.[109] And one project examines the gender gap in mobile phone usage.[110]

Harvard incentivizes scholars to take up such 'save the savages' projects by giving awards to research that strengthens such narratives. For instance, the Center for International Development offers a Malcolm Wiener Award on Inequality Research.[111] One awardee produced a report saying that India should commit to move up the ranks on women's access to employment.[112] Another award went to a project to change gender norms of masculinity in Uttar Pradesh's youth: 'A vicious cycle operates between the internal (mental models of men) and interpersonal (societal/cultural masculinity norms) levels that reinforce each other, perpetuating regressive behaviors and violence – hence Harvard's reason to change attitudes of men'.[113]

Publications

The Harvard Kennedy School publishes articles like *Cow Vigilantes and the Rise of Hindu Nationalism*[114] and *How Weddings Condemn India's Poorest to Bonded Labor*.[115] The goal is to use various do-good sounding topics that lead to conclusions about issues like 'upper caste money lenders', low levels of education, poverty, and 'caste-based discrimination', 'bonded laborers who toil in brick kilns, rice mills, construction sites, mines, steel factories or fish farms', and so forth.[116]

Brainwashing India's Elites

The Government of India spends taxpayer money to train many of its bureaucrats at Harvard. We have shown that center after center, scholar after scholar, seminar after seminar is focused on undermining India's national interest with a goal to indoctrinate the young, recruit the vulnerable, and push an agenda on the unsuspecting. All this is done while blatantly ignoring the inconvenient side of the topics.

This started in 2006, when *Times News* published an article about the virtues of having Harvard's Kennedy School of Government train Indian civil servants. The article boasted that Harvard will not only train, but will also select, the candidates for this training. It said that 'this may be the best way to tackle red tape. Harvard University's highly acclaimed Kennedy School of Government will now train Indian civil servants in issues related to good governance'. There are three-month and one-year programs. And Harvard's faculty too visits India to give lectures under the program.[117]

It is disconcerting that India is unable to train and coach its bureaucrats. Given the power of the bureaucracy and the delicate sensitive nature of many policies, this is a dangerous path. Even if India thinks that HKS offers superior expertise, a better model would be the one followed by Croatia. Croatia's partnership with the HKS is to develop a *customized* program to solve *specific* policy issues facing Croatia. The agreement says that the training will address 'essential areas of need identified by the government' after holding 'consultations with the Office of the Prime Minister of Croatia'. It says that Croatia's frontline policymakers and practitioners will explain their needs to the HKS faculty.[118]

A tiny country like Croatia has the sense and courage to deal with Harvard on its own nationalistic terms, whereas India has outsourced the training of its elites on a carte blanche basis. Why is it better to let Harvard teach Indians about managing the Rohingyas, dealing with Sufis in Kashmir, sensitivity towards Indian Muslims, and so forth? Why is Harvard being empowered to determine how Indians feel about Article 370, or CAA, or the Ram mandir, or social justice, or the rights of LGBTQ+, and so forth?

The Indian government is so much in awe of Harvard and suffers from such an acute colonized inferiority complex that it has hoisted Harvard as the vishwa guru and turned India into its *shishya* (student). This is outright insulting for a country like India that prides itself as a major world power.

This program has now expanded. It might surprise many that the Indian government actually funds civil servants to get trained under a scheme known as Domestic Funding of Foreign Training for civil servants. There is a list of thirty-eight short-term programs and sixteen long-term programs in different universities in foreign countries where Indian civil servants are encouraged to apply for training. Besides Harvard, Berkeley, University of Chicago, and Cambridge feature prominently on these lists.[119] The government also funds degree programs overseas for Indians. Among the top universities, there are five Chinese universities, which means that Indian bureaucrats can get trained in China at the taxpayer's expense. Depending on the course and its duration, the Indian government pays up to fifty-five thousand dollars per candidate.[120]

India seems to have a fetish about university rankings as it uses these to decide a university's eligibility for training its bureaucrats. These ratings are subjective and highly suspect. A University of California at Berkeley study charged that these international rankings appear to be influenced by hiring certain consulting firms.[121]

For the US, it has been an important foreign policy strategy to educate the elite leaders of targeted countries in the Western narrative. This has now reached a new level because Harvard has lured Indian billionaires to give grants and lend their names for credibility. For example, the Indian billionaire couple Bharat Desai and Neerja Sethi are behind the Desai-Sethi Foundation, or the DS Foundation. Every year, it funds Indians to come as post-graduate fellows in public policy/public administration/international development to Harvard Kennedy School. The DS Foundation Public Service Fellowship is for active officers in the Indian Administrative Service and Indian Foreign Service.[122] In other words, Harvard's indoctrination of Indian bureaucrats is being funded by India's very own billionaires and its taxpayers.

The Harvard Kennedy School created this Public Service Fellowship program and the Indian administrative and foreign services actively encourage their officers to participate. The choice of candidates to receive such fellowships is purely under Harvard's control. Neither the

Indian government nor the DS Foundation has a say in the matter.[123]

To illustrate the way Harvard has infiltrated India's intellectual elites with its worldview, we take up the example of Mukul Saxena who was picked by Harvard with a fellowship to study public administration. The choice was strategic because he had served in the Indian Army for two decades. Saxena was a good fit being a sympathizer of Rohingya refugees and believing that actions of the Indian Army are not the internal matters of a sovereign state. His work includes the following:

- *Apathy and Inaction: The Plight of the Rohingya Muslim* (in progress).
- *Mapping the Jihad in Kashmir*: He claims that the Sufi tradition maintains tolerance in Kashmir, and therefore 'it is of paramount importance that all military operations and activities are carried out with immense sensitivity towards these religious and cultural beliefs'.
- *Lawfully Wedded to Democracy? India and the Armed Forces (Special Powers) Act*: He criticizes the Act, saying that 'such enactments do not have a place in democracy'.
- *French Headscarf Law and the Right to Manifest Religious Belief*: He criticizes the French law against public display of certain Muslim symbols because he considers it as impacting women's rights and creating conditions of gender discrimination.
- He has also been writing papers for the Indian Army advising it to soften its approach in dealing with Muslim violence.[124]

After Harvard, Saxena became a faculty member at the Kautilya School of Public Policy in Hyderabad. The name of this institute is misleading because it has nothing to do with Kautilya's (more commonly known as Chanakya, the ancient philosopher and strategist) approach to public policy. The school is politically aligned with important figures from the Congress Party, including individuals who served as spokespersons and campaign managers for Rahul Gandhi. The dean, Syed Akbaruddin, is a retired Indian Foreign Service officer, and former permanent representative of India to the UN.[125]

Harvard's ideological presence is clear from the fact that Kautilya's board includes two former Harvard Kennedy School professors, Steve Jarding and Moshik Temkin. Jarding was a former lecturer at the

Harvard Kennedy School and political campaign consultant of Rahul Gandhi. He helped Gandhi's 2019 campaign against Modi. Previously, Jarding was campaign manager for the Samajwadi Party in 2017, which was a failure.[126]

Temkin is associate professor of history and public policy at Kautilya. He compares the state of the Uyghurs in China to that of the Muslims in India.[127] He praised Senator Bernie Sanders for denouncing Modi's Citizenship (Amendment) Act, 2019:

> He (Bernie Sanders) took a principled stand against the authoritarianism and fascism sweeping much of the world today; when India's nationalistic Prime Minister Narendra Modi began his campaign to legally discriminate against India's hundreds of millions of Muslim citizens, Sanders was the only major American political leader to denounce him.[128]

Temkin sees the urgency to train Indians in American geopolitical ideology. Bringing Indian intellectuals for training at Harvard to turn into sepoys is slow and expensive. Kautilya solves that problem by functioning as Harvard's academic base in India:

> The days in which the lucky few who can afford it go to elite institutions abroad should come to an end; India now has its own top-notch public policy school. Kautilya School of Public Policy aims to educate and train the people that India needs, in order to claim its place as a global leader befitting its size, richness, and potential.[129]

Kautilya offers a master's degree in public policy with the goal of producing future leaders with the 'right outlook'. There are also some superficial aesthetic trappings of Harvard already being adopted. This was attested by UK's deputy high commissioner to Andhra Pradesh and Telangana, Andrew Fleming, who appreciated the 'excellent facilities with @Kennedy_School inspired decor'.[130]

Many in the US believe that the Harvard Kennedy School is more about politicking and networking than actual skill development, which makes such training of Indian bureaucrats at HKS a colossal waste of taxpayer money. Some independent reviews in the US have 'rated their HKS education as being the least effective in the skill areas of leadership, ethics, organizing/mobilizing, and managing people'. Some even doubt whether good policymaking can be taught sitting in an ivory tower classroom. Former New York congressman, Daniel B. Maffei, an HKS alum, remarked that 'politics can be an afterthought' in these programs because it is an elite education that is mainly about making connections.[131]

The Double Standards of Harvard University

Many universities in the US, Canada and Australia, and even corporates have begun acknowledging and honoring the Native lands upon which their plush buildings exist. At events like the Oscars, the announcement of native land takes the solemn form of a prayer. At Harvard, the native land acknowledgment is a formal statement:

> Harvard University is located on the traditional and ancestral land of the Massachusett, the original inhabitants of what is now known as Boston and Cambridge. We pay respect to the people of the Massachusett Tribe, past and present, and honor the land itself which remains sacred to the Massachusett People.[132]

These Native Land Acknowledgments as they are known, have found their spot adjacent to preferred pronouns on emails, and on building signs. At the beginning of major events, politically correct White folks usually go off on a self-righteous rant confessing to be a 'settler' on 'robbed land' and being 'complicit' in its occupation.

While this may sound authentic, it begs the question: When universities claim they are on stolen land, why are they not doing the right thing by returning it? That's what one does with stolen property. It has never occurred to Harvard to use its fifty-three billion dollars endowment to make reparations to the Native Americans.

Elizabeth Solomon, assistant director for academic affairs and fellowship programs in the Department of Social and Behavioral Sciences, was asked to open the 2018 convocation of the Harvard T.H. Chan School of Public Health. She began with an official acknowledgment of native land and peoples. As a member of the Massachusett Native Tribe at Ponkapoag, Solomon provided the context for why the acknowledgment of native space is practiced:

> When indigenous communities in the United States gather
> together, they traditionally acknowledge and honor the *ancestral
> holders of the land* they are meeting on.[133]

This is moving and very important to understand. The 'ancestral
owners of the land' must be acknowledged and honored by the present
occupants of the land.

This type of public acknowledgment should be a role model for
Harvard to practice in India and teach as part of its ethics. Should the
ceremonies at the Piramal Center which hosts the Harvard Chan School
in Mumbai begin with a ritual to honor the original Indians that owned
that land before it became Portuguese property? Similarly, Harvard's
New Delhi offices sit on the lands of the glorious Indraprastha, which
must be honored at the start of all their events.

Harvard's social justice ethics must pressure the Catholic Church to
start all its meetings in India by acknowledging and honoring the native
lands stolen by the British and bequeathed to the Church. Harvard
must advocate that all Muslim prayers in Indian mosques must begin by
acknowledging the original inhabitants of the lands. All these examples
in India were *more recent lootings* than the White landgrabs from the
Native Americans.

Such rhetorical speculations are merely thought experiments to
expose the double standard of Harvard University.

16

Harvard Business School

Overview

This is a short chapter explaining how the Harvard Business School acts somewhat like a brand ambassador for Harvard through the export of its library of case studies to management institutions across the world. It also shows how China has questioned the relevance of these largely American stories and has instead taken measures to build its own brand. India should perhaps also question its own leanings on Harvard given that it has been such a miserable failure at understanding and depicting Indian civilization and its assets.

Social Justice Through Business Lens

Most people imagine that Harvard Business School focuses solely on teaching about running a business, managing investment decisions, and the like. Few expect it to be immersed in identity politics with the agendas of the social sciences. Unfortunately, the facts are otherwise: HBS funds several sociological studies in India in the name of entrepreneurship and business, and such 'business themes' are a doorway to enter, and produce, one-sided portrayals of caste. We will illustrate how Harvard scholars blatantly ignore valid evidence and cherry-pick the data to suit their preconceived narratives. All this in broad daylight with funding from Indian billionaires.

As an example, a paper authored by Lakshmi Iyer and Tarun Khanna (both of HBS) and Ashutosh Varshney (Harvard Kennedy School), concluded that while certain lower caste members have made strides in political representation in India, that is not the case in entrepreneurship.

They claim that this happens due to the lack of networks to find workers and contacts with suppliers and customers. Because this problem persists even in states with 'progressive policies', they recommend further studies that would go to deeper levels of society. The goal would be to uncover the 'deeper mechanisms' at work.[1]

The topic is an important one, but one that should be pursued based on India's own principles. The Harvard theories developed from such research push for their policies within India and bring international pressure from global nexuses of power where Harvard rules.

For example, this research completely ignores the decades of scholarship by Prof. R. Vaidyanathan (Indian Institute of Management Bangalore) on the relationship between caste and entrepreneurship. Vaidyanathan's 2019 book titled, *Caste as Social Capital*, was a comprehensive study, systematically showing how caste networks helped many communities in their business success. This book was widely publicized and discussed in India and elsewhere. *Yet it was totally ignored by Harvard scholars*. One would expect that responsible scholars working at Harvard would live up to their reputation purporting to be rigorous and balanced.

Vaidyanathan's study divulges a different story of entrepreneurial success by Muslim and Dalit groups that have established their chambers of commerce. His conclusions are worth contrasting with those from Harvard:

> The main argument of the book is that the jati or community or caste plays a major role in entrepreneurship and also facilitates the upward mobility of the whole caste rather than the individual.
>
> The book looks at the role of caste in promoting education, entrepreneurship and business, and creating professional networks amongst the individuals. Thousands of caste-based economic clusters are spread across India, providing millions of jobs and creating wealth. Traditional business communities like Marwaris, Sindhis, Patels, Bohras, Kutchis have been extremely successful in forming global business networks. ... the book throws light on how castes have promoted entrepreneurship in different areas such as services, trade, construction real estate, transportation, tourism, ... Notable examples include clusters

formed by Gounders in Tirupur in Tamil Nadu, Patels in Surat in Gujrat, Nadars in Sivakasi in Tamilnadu, and Jadejas/Patels in Jamnagar Gujrat. Such clusters are promoted and run by ordinary persons, their members have high appetite for risk-taking, and ... their business is based on relationships rather than on formal contracts. Importantly, such economic clusters are usually self-financed. They maintain a fine balance between cooperation and competition.

... castes in India are increasingly taking to business and entrepreneurship. Tirupur ... has now become a world-leader in the knitted-garment industry. ... the kite-making industry in Ahmedabad, worth around Rs 800 Crores, is dominated by Muslim entrepreneurs. In leather business too, Muslims are present in significant numbers. Dalits are also taking to business. Some Dalit entrepreneurs have built large business empires. A Dalit chamber of Indian commerce and industry has been set-up.

In India, caste is closely linked with reservation and politics. The clamour for more reservations in government jobs and educational institutions is growing. Even forward castes want reservations. But how far do reservations help? Not much, some castes have done much better because of their 'Vaishyavisation' or entrepreneur skills rather than from reservations. In Tamil Nadu, some castes want to be delisted from being scheduled caste communities because they face social discrimination on that account.[2]

Vaidyanathan has argued persistently and convincingly that caste is a form of social capital that can be utilized by policymakers to play a positive role in helping the lower strata uplift themselves. Caste is a complex social institution with both positive and negative implications as far as business success goes. A book review states that this 'enriches the discussion about the role of caste in Indian society'.[3] His work is far deeper than the superficial treatment by Tarun Khanna's Harvard team, and it is no surprise that they have cancelled him.

In the absence of subject matter experts like Vaidyanathan, Harvard's numerous conferences and events are free to promote what must be Harvard's own parochialism and ideological bias. For instance, Isabel

Wilkerson was the featured speaker at a HBS event, *Managing Diversity: A Conversation with Isabel Wilkerson, Author of Caste*.[4] And a few months later she was invited to Harvard's School of Public Health.

And the Indian billionaires who fund Harvard have failed to hold Harvard accountable for such acts of 'Cancel Culture' boycotting scholars like Vaidyanathan with diverse research results.

Another one-sided analysis was an HBS paper by Abhijit Banerjee et al stating that 'certain groups hold power within society that is disproportionate to their size'. Obvious examples are Whites in South Africa in the Apartheid years and 'high castes in India through most of its history'.[5] This paper conveniently ignores counter examples such as Indian Christians, who despite being only two percent of the population, own and control a disproportionately large amount of real estate and corporate jobs because the British gave them land and educational privileges. The paper further states: 'The population share of Brahmans (sic) in a constituency is positively correlated with access to primary, middle and secondary schools, to post offices...'[6]

What is being ignored is that Indian Christians are overrepresented in controlling educational institutions, while at the middle level are the Hindus, and at the bottom are the Muslims. And when someone points out that Indian Christians are often the gatekeepers of education, the frequent response is that this shows they are a *progressive* community. Yet, the Brahmins' focus on education is branded as casteist rather than progressive. One would think that an erudite scholar and future Nobel laureate from Harvard would be consistent in interpreting the facts, and not selective in cherry-picking data to make his case.

At one of the lectures on *Managing Diversity* at HBS, Prof. Mihir Desai spoke on *The Tulsa Massacre and the Call for Reparations* and discussed reparations for Blacks in America. He used this opening to switch over to the Dalits in India. He said that the African American call for reparations should be used to trigger a call for Dalit reparations: 'I'm really proud of this part of the case, which is to look for parallels and to think about this in a global perspective.'[7]

In 2017, HBS explored long-running patterns in international business in developing countries. The section on India claimed that the root cause for the preference of light skin by Indians is the caste system and the Aryan invasion:

In the 1970s a handful of Western firms began to invest in product innovation designed to deliver products especially for emerging markets. Unilever's large Indian affiliate, Hindustan Lever, which had created its own research facilities in the 1950s, was among the pioneers. It began selling its own distinctly Indian shampoo and toothpaste brands, as well as brands from Unilever's global portfolio. More interesting, was the creation of 'Fair & Lovely' skin-lightening cream in 1978. This was cream designed to appeal to a traditional regard for fairer skin in India. *The origins of such preferences lay deep in Indian history, which some traced back to the origins of the caste system two and a half thousand years ago, when fair-skinned foreigners established a class system with the indigenous darker-skinned local population at the bottom.* ... British rule introduced a new set of rulers with lighter skins. Hindustan Lever now applied its scientific and branding capabilities to translate such cultural preferences into a highly successful brand, which became the best-selling skin care brand in India. 'Fair & Lovely' was based on a patented formulation containing an active ingredient which controlled the dispersion of melanin in the skin. The brand's advertising promised greater fairness within six weeks of using the product, and ... emphasized the improved marriage prospects of fair-skinned women. Considerable use was made of endorsement by celebrities from the huge Indian cinema industry known as Bollywood, whose leading actors and actresses were overwhelmingly fair skinned.[8]

We have already shown in Chapter 2 that preference for light skin is not due to Vedic culture but due to more recent developments resulting from Muslim and European invasions.

In a HBS report on how the religious identity of state legislators influences the socio-economic outcomes, the benefit of doubt is given to the hypothesis that it is Muslims who want to reduce Hindu-Muslim conflicts:

We find that increasing the political representation of Muslims improves health and education outcomes in the district from which the legislator is elected. We find no evidence of religious favouritism. ... Why are Muslim leaders more effective than other (primarily Hindu) leaders at delivering improvements in child health and education? One plausible explanation is that Muslims ... prioritise reducing Hindu-Muslim conflict, and equal provision of public goods is a means to this end.[9]

In 2018, Tatas spent $8.4 million to start a program to train its employees at HBS:

> Harvard University has announced a six-year, $8.4 million research partnership with a group of Tata companies that includes Tata Sons, Tata Communications, Tata Steel, and Jaguar Land Rover. Under an agreement coordinated by Harvard's Office of Technology Development, the partnership will support cutting-edge research and provide professional development programs to visiting business leaders through the Tata Fellowship Program at Harvard Business School. For each project funded under the arrangement, a veteran Tata employee will have the opportunity to spend up to a year in residency in the HBS Executive Education Program.[10]

Jumping on this bandwagon of the Indian billionaires are many Indians who are below the top-tier billionaire level. They too are donating serious sums. For example, Siddharth 'Sid' Yog of the Xander Group donated eleven million dollars to HBS, making it the single largest *personal* donation by an Indian. Yog said that this was the guru *dakshina* or offering to his professor at Harvard who he calls his guru. He said he was continuing the guru-shishya *parampara*, or the age-old Indian teacher-disciple tradition. To convince his professor to accept the offering, he narrated the story of Ekalavya from *Mahabharata*, who cut off his thumb and offered it as dakshina to his guru, Dronacharya.

Yog's intentions were clearly good, but the parallels can be questioned: His Harvard professor is the wealthy owner of a real estate development firm, not a Dronacharya. Nor did Yog realize that Harvard's mission is to dismantle the guru-shishya lineages of India, seeing them as a scourge to social justice, and replace them with Harvard's own lineages. Of course, the Indian press rejoiced that this young Indian entrepreneur now 'rubs shoulders with' international tycoons.[11]

Harvard and Cancel Culture

While Harvard has been all too quick to rebuke India for arresting students for sedition at Indian universities like JNU, it endorses Cancel Culture on its home turf when the narrative is not to its liking, even in business school alumni gatherings. Harvard wants total control of its alumni even after they graduate. A recent event hosted by the Harvard Business School Club of New York on the pervasive Cancel Culture in Western societies was itself, ironically, cancelled. This was reported:

> 'Have you ever wondered about the ideas behind the cultural and political wars that are wrecking the country and reached a crescendo last summer in the "Cancel Culture" movement and the violent outbursts in many cities around the country? Do we even understand the fighting words brandished by the social justice activists in this movement?... Join us for a presentation and discussion of the book with author James Lindsay, followed by a Q&A session,' the event description, now removed from the Business School Club's website, stated.[12]

Exporting American Principles

The Harvard Business School ranks number one among the world's most influential schools based on teaching power, which is a measure of how much their coursework is used by others.[13] The HBS' proprietary method is the use of case studies that its scholars generate and are a huge revenue generator for HBS. These case studies have become the core pillar of MBA education worldwide. In 2020, Harvard sold over fifteen million individual copies of case studies to business schools worldwide.[14]

China, however, is developing its own repository of case studies that the world must now buy from them. It claims that the HBS cases have a very narrow American centric worldview. Since China has become the focal point in the corporate ecosystem, one needs to understand China, and hence it has developed these case studies to educate the rest of the world.

Yubo Chen, associate dean of Tsinghua University's School of Economics and Management in Beijing, says the different demands of his students explains why his school is one of a growing number in Asia writing their own — often shorter, more practical — teaching cases. 'Our students are not satisfied with Harvard cases,' he says. 'The environment is changing so fast, and we need cases on China. It's very difficult to talk, say, about Amazon. They want to know about ecommerce in China.'[15]

Harvard is also positioning itself as the middleman channeling funds from Indian Corporate Social Responsibility programs into the causes it likes. It holds high-class events for tutoring Indian businessmen with the help of the World Bank and the Indian government.[16] The goal is to bring Indian business leaders into its intellectual wavelength. One such program stated:

> The main objective of the program was to strengthen the capacity of a cadre of senior managers of corporations. Through the case study approach, best practices and strategies in CSR development were highlighted. The workshop was modelled after the highly successful Strategic CSR executive education program developed at the Harvard Business School.[17]

Harvard has also been pushing a movement started by the WEF and other business elites to value companies based on the 'good' they do in the areas of ESG. The criteria for 'social good' is determined by the global elites and imposed universally.[18]

China's Business Leadership

It is noteworthy that China has its own institutions pushing its own business principles. For instance, the China Europe International Business School (CEIBS) is a joint venture between the European Union (EU) and the Chinese government. The CEIBS was co-founded by the Chinese government and the EU and has campuses in Shanghai, Beijing, Shenzhen, Accra in Ghana, and Zurich in Switzerland.[19] It is rapidly moving up the business school rankings and is only behind

Harvard Business School, Wharton, Stanford's Graduate School of Business, and INSEAD of France.[20]

The CEIBS distinguishes itself as a business school that is a conduit to study China on its own terms. It specializes in teaching the world about business in China and is controlled by the Chinese government.

An Indian, Shameen Prashantham is associate dean and director of the full-time MBA program at CEIBS.[21] The Chinese government is using this to educate the corporate sector worldwide to understand China on its own terms:

> What hasn't changed is the program's laser focus on the China experience. 'We have certain electives and this huge case center which produces the largest number of Chinese cases in the world,' he says. 'Digital China is one of many unique electives here. We are trying to increase the portfolio of Chinese-based modules (immersions). I will take students later this month on a module that explores the globalization of Chinese companies. A German colleague is doing a Shanghai-based elective on European companies in China and how they cope with local competition and the rise of digital companies in China.'[22]

Prashantham said: 'A lot of our international alumni are based in China, and we have an opportunity to deepen those bonds.'[23]

Tarun Khanna has been a visiting thought leader at CEIBS, and is also an adviser at NITI Aayog. This gives him the power to be a bridge between the Chinese Communist Party and the Indian government.

One is left wondering why the Indian billionaires never bothered to build something in India to project to the world the key traditional methods of business successes: communities serving as tight networks of trust and oral contracts? One wonders why they have not wanted studies conducted on traditional business family structures, and practices of funding family and community infrastructure (like financing guilds, funding ecosystems around temples, donating dharamshalas and schools for the old and the young)?

Part 3

IS INDIA FOR SALE?

17

The Ivy League Passage to India

Part 1 presented Critical Race Theory and its popular form, Wokeism. We showed how it is being adapted in the Indian context by equating race with caste. We also evidenced how Critical Race Theory is finding expression in policymaking in American academics, corporates, and governments, and the devastating impact it is having on ordinary Indian Americans. Caste is rapidly becoming a 'protected category' in the US, making it a weapon of litigation against Indians accused of being casteist. This is already turning into an effective device for Hinduphobic forces, legitimizing their agenda to dismantle the structures of Indian society.

The implications are serious both for the US and for India. In the United States, many present laws against racism are being applied to caste, and some local governments already have a mandate in place to classify caste as a form of racism. This project is now speeding ahead. Universities and schools are attacking Indian social organizations and social structures without giving adequate space to counter arguments or evidence. Corporates that hire large numbers of Indians want to make peace with the troublemakers by funding their cause, by appointing them as 'experts' who can inform their decisions, by changing the constitution of their boards, by discriminating against Hindus in the hiring process, and by introducing caste 'education'. Or else, they risk being dragged to court for caste prejudice as in the case of Cisco Systems.

Hinduphobic forces are entering corporate America via the Diversity, Equity, and Inclusion (DEI) route; and extremely well-funded 'consultants' like Equality Labs are milking the situation through 'caste sensitivity training programs'. As a result, perfectly innocent Indians are forced into confessing their 'inherent caste bias' and apologizing publicly for inheriting caste privilege. There is no room for refutation in the workplace because any attempt to protest is treated as proof of guilt. The only path open to Indians is one of passive acceptance of their systemic caste bias and Brahminical patriarchy that is ostensibly institutionalized in Indian society worldwide, just as race is in America.

What makes this movement particularly significant is that it unites different groups that have grievances and conflates their issues in order to force equal outcomes. In the process, and because it suits the agenda, it problematizes the very idea of merit. India's own quota system is designed to give a boost to the underprivileged, but without undermining the principle of meritocracy. As a result, India has been able to develop academic centers of excellence such as the IITs, which have created world class leaders. The new discourse, however, seeks to dismantle this pillar of Indian success that will have far-reaching consequences for India's future.

The Afro-Dalit movement described in *Breaking India* more than a decade ago, was at the experimental stage of this attack on India. The plan was to claim a common racial origin for both Blacks and Dalits so the same academic and activist machinery used for Black emancipation could be deployed for Dalit separatism. Not only has this machinery become far more sophisticated but it has also succeeded in mobilizing Black Americans against India on a far larger scale by connecting them to Dalits through the Critical Caste Theory, and through the funnel of Intersectionality.

Additionally, in the earlier Breaking India phenomenon (which we refer to as Breaking India 1.0), it was the rural poor being targeted by Marxist ideas on the one hand, and the evangelizing Christian machinery, on the other. But now, in what we describe as Breaking India 2.0, it is India's urban elite at the highest levels of social, political, economic, and government institutions that are being targeted and weaponized to dismantle Indian society.

It is imperative to understand the core difference between Breaking India 1.0 and Breaking India 2.0 because the latter version is fundamentally more dangerous. The narratives being pushed are more complex; the funding is much more substantial, coming from some of the wealthiest both in India and abroad; and the role of technology is insidious. This is now a top-down movement to dismantle Indian society.

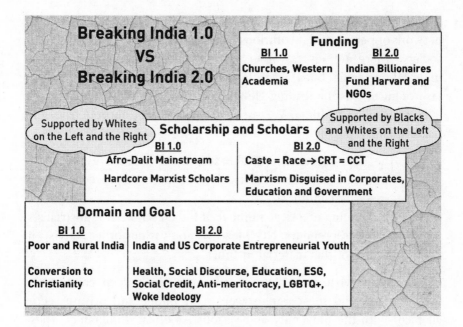

Breaking India 2.0 is not just a mere extension of Breaking India 1.0. Many new kinds of players have joined the game, both from within and outside India. Some of them are corporate leaders from all over the world. The technology sector, in particular, has been handsomely rewarded by the stock market, and many have cashed out and deployed their enormous war chests for social engineering in the name of philanthropy.

This new brand of philanthropy is worth dwelling upon, and it generates even more wealth and power for the philanthropists. But because it is presented as a benign, do-good activity, large portions of the public (and possibly some portions of the Government of India!) are buying into the game. The technology hides the agenda from public view.

A multitude of foot soldiers is being produced in India. In Breaking India 1.0, missionaries and Marxists resorted to subterfuge and inculturation to indoctrinate the hapless public. They initially set up funding pipelines from overseas and developed some atrocity literature. But it did not utilize the latest AI-based technologies, and it had not infiltrated the core of Indian industry and its elites. Therefore, the scale and scope of Breaking India 1.0 was insignificant compared to the current onslaught.

In Part 2 we gave details of how Harvard University and its vast network of people and institutions have infiltrated every facet of Indian society. There are several other foreign universities in this game of undermining India, but Harvard is the mothership we have termed the vishwa guru. It is the leading global nexus where Critical Race Theory is being applied to India. We showed two kinds of outputs from this massive effort:

- The development of CRT-based theories that are specific to India and can serve as atrocity literature to prosecute India, especially Hinduism.
- The training of a large number of Indian scholars, industrialists, tech entrepreneurs, NGO leaders, and various other activists in the use of this material in India.

Concurrently, what we also exposed was China's deep connections with Harvard and the complex web of its public and private sector alliances with the university and various American thinktanks. These relationships, along with the flow of funds to Harvard indicate that the elite institution has been compromised by the Chinese. This has serious implications for India, especially because it's an unequal exchange, with raw data flowing from India to Harvard, and social theories, ideologies, and trained intellectuals flowing back from Harvard to India.

Basking in the glory of American academic institutions, several prominent Indian billionaires have established centers named after themselves at Harvard. This has helped Harvard and its American and Chinese collaborators build bridges of access to India in various sectors, including government policy, public health, digital infrastructure, higher education, media, and culture.

In other words, foreign academic institutions, of which Harvard is primary, are gaining access to Indian data, Indian government organizations, the best Indian minds, and even fund raising from the Indian public. These foreign institutions create and own archives of Indian history, culture, and public health; build libraries of translated works of Indian literature; collect data on large-scale events like the Kumbh Mela that can pose potential threats to India's national security; and be used to train bright young Indians to become activists.

We must clarify that none of this is unlawful. Whether it is unethical and contrary to the national interests of India is also subjective and depends on one's worldview. There are large segments within India, US and elsewhere that want the disruptions being brought about, seeing these as the way forward for the Social Justice movement. At the same time, others are concerned about the vacuum created by the dismantling of old structures. Our purpose in this book is to highlight the examples that point toward this disruption, neutrally and dispassionately. It is for the reader to decide how to interpret the implications based on their own value system.

Indian and Western business leaders are participating in the adoption of the latest Harvard-spun corporate social credit rubric based on Western narratives (i.e., the ESG system of rating companies). Besides, some of them are also facilitating extensive data collection in India. They have access to numerous Indian fronts to access big data on population, public health and other sensitive information. They are running large-scale pilot projects as proof-of-concept for digital transformation, which allows them to experiment with strategies of social engineering. These public- and private-NGO alliances do appear to be uplifting the common person in India in the short term. But their sprawling apparatus also allows them to steal peoples' agency and manipulate their consent. In the process, India's wealth is in danger of being sucked out, with the potential for unprecedented concentration of wealth and power ending up in the hands of a few that have their own personal interests.

The Breaking India activity is a powerful machinery that has penetrated Indian society at its very core. Many of India's universities (both public and private), media houses, corporate houses, tech start-ups, and various other institutions have been compromised. One is left wondering if the Government of India too is looking to Harvard as the vishwa guru to solve all its problems. For instance, the Indian government trains its bureaucrats at Harvard and other elitist foreign institutions. There is inadequate concern about the way many top Indian minds are connected to the Western elite. Breaking India 1.0 may have been contained in scope, demographics, players, and resources. Breaking India 2.0, however, is a broader sell-out of our future generations, our customs, our history, our heritage, and our way of life.

The table that follows summarizes the key differences between Breaking India 1.0 and Breaking India 2.0.

	Feature	Breaking India 1.0	Breaking India 2.0
1	Funding	Marxists NGOs, Missionaries/Churches	Billionaires: Indians and foreign
2	Narrative	Afro-Dalit, Postmodernism Supported by • Left: White Liberal Americans • Right: White evangelical Americans	• Critical Race Theory ➔ Critical Caste Theory • Hindutva = White supremacy • Dalits + Black Americans ➔ Afro-Dalit Movement • Anti-meritocracy in academics and employment • LBGTQ+/Gender as victim categories • Corporate ESG, Social Credit Supported by: • Left: White and Black Liberal Americans • Right: White and Black evangelical Americans
3	Focus areas	• Religion, poverty	• Religion • Public health: big data on public health, children's health, nutrition • Cultural/Heritage: Kumbh Mela, religion and economics, archives on lived experience of victims • Digital infrastructure: digital ID, currency, Internet access, digital projects for public works • Education: NCERT – elementary through secondary • Education: public and private universities, research, training students and scholars • Corporates: frameworks for assessment, metrics using ESG • Administration: government policymaking

4	Target Demographic	Rural India, Poor, Dalits, Tribals: • Religious conversion • Atrocity literature • Cultural appropriation	• Urban middle class Hindu youth become Woke • Young entrepreneurs in corporates: incentivized by venture capital • Corporates pushing ESG: punishing businesses for non-compliance; Diversity, Equity, Inclusion • Media pushing Woke narrative: promoting gender fluidity and Woke activism • Universities: using academic talent to shape Woke-friendly government policy, grooming sepoys • Government: installing infrastructure for social credit system, shaping policy on philanthropy, skill development and public infrastructure. Big data at risk, foreign control of culture/history archives • Bureaucrats: trained by West resulting in deep colonization • In US: caste as a protected category like race in universities, US government and corporations
5	Infrastructure	• Bibles in native languages • Funding pipelines for missionaries • Media/TV channels acquisition • Instituting tithing • Local seminary training	• Infrastructure for archives: real-time updated archives • Infrastructure for big data: collection and monitoring systems • Digital infrastructure • Infrastructure for public health monitoring and data collection • Infrastructure alliances with global organizations like WEF, UN, WHO & NGOs • Infrastructure for scholarship: university conferences on Woke topics, preparation of students/scholars
6	Vulnerability	• India's discourse	• National security risks • Youth: social engineering • Indian way of life, religion, heritage, culture

In this, Part 3, we discuss how the entire movement discussed earlier is entering India. A vast network of organizations has emerged in recent years. Because nobody prior to this book has conducted a systematic study of this phenomenon and developed a framework to understand it, there is a lack of insight on the part of Indians regarding this development. Our main objective is to stimulate healthy debates across the spectrum of political ideologies so that more information can come about and be discussed openly.

We will look at Indian institutions that are on the frontlines working with Harvard University, MIT, Yale University and affiliate organizations. These forces, positioned as domestic within India, are building a new kind of sepoy army. Breaking India 2.0 is run by India's elites just like Indian kings and zamindars worked for the British in exchange for the status of local elites. Some of the business entrepreneurs, government officials, academicians, media persons, activists, etc., and the educated class of the youth are being weaponized to dismantle the civilizational heritage.

We will first discuss the Andhra Pradesh-based Krea University and its links with MIT's J-PAL (a Saudi funded project) and Yale, before diving into a more detailed analysis of Ashoka University. This will clearly show the direction that Indian academia has taken. Krea and Ashoka proudly project themselves as 'the Harvard of India', bringing American liberal arts to the country. But in the process, like Harvard, they are inadvertently dismantling many traditions of India.

The boards of both Ashoka and Krea sport a constellation of world class luminaries from India and overseas with deep connections to Ivy League universities. They are setting up infrastructure within and outside India, and the seamless pipelines they are building can be used to transport ideas for brainwashing young Indian students and siphon off big data. Our purpose is to present facts and not adjudicate. It is for the reader to draw inferences and probe deeper. The government hires some foreign professors as advisers and facilitates their collaborations in Indian industry, thinktanks and research organizations. The media is also being funded by a coalition that reduces the direct exposure of the participants.

As an example, Omidyar Foundation, run by a Silicon Valley billionaire, has become a big player in India with private and public alliances. Likewise, the Bill & Melinda Gates Foundation and other NGOs like Amnesty International that already enjoy support from Harvard are also partnering with the Indian government. They work with Ashoka and other universities to ensure that government policies are favorable to their ideologies. Indians are getting trained in various theories that support Western hegemony, while the West is gaining access to Indian big data and creating archives on India.

18

The Nexus of Saudis, Americans, and Indian Billionaires

Overview

Massachusetts Institute of Technology has traditionally been a source for technology, but is now rapidly building partnerships in India for meddling in economics and 'poverty elimination'. Noam Chomsky of MIT, arguably one of the most influential American intellectuals alive, summed up his institution's Hinduphobic attitude:

> The pathology of Islamophobia is growing throughout the West. It's taking its most lethal form in India where the Modi government is systematically dismantling Indian secular democracy and turning the country into a Hindu ethnocracy, with almost 250 million Muslims becoming a persecuted minority. The assault is taking other forms as well, including a general attack on independent thought and the educational system primarily directed against Muslim victims, but by now expanding beyond. That's apart from India's terrible crimes in Kashmir. Those crimes have a long history. They've been sharply escalated by Modi's right-wing Hindu nationalist regime. Kashmir is now brutally occupied territory under harsh military control, similar in some ways to occupied Palestine.[1]

Subsequently, Chomsky lashed out at the US government for supporting what he called a 'neo-fascist' India:

> ... United States is quite supportive of the Indian government. India has a neo-fascist government. The Modi government is

working hard to destroy Indian democracy, turn India into a racist, Hindu kleptocracy, attack Muslims, conquer Kashmir, crush Kashmir — not a word about that. The United States supports all that. It's very supportive. It's a close ally, a close ally of Israel — our kind of guy, in other words.[2]

Hypocrisy on Human Rights

Like its neighbor Harvard, MIT too is coming under the influence of foreign entities, causing concerns to the US government. It has deep connections with the Saudi royal family which generously funds many research initiatives and provides scholarships to Saudi students at the institution.

During his 2018 visit, Saudi Crown Prince Mohammed bin Salman made a twenty-three million dollars gift to MIT. A few months later, Jamal Khashoggi, a Saudi journalist working for *The Washington Post* was brutally killed and dismembered at the Saudi consulate in Istanbul. A member of the crown prince's entourage at MIT (who was photographed with the prince during the visit) was directly linked[3] to, and identified, as one of the perpetrators of Khashoggi's brutal murder.[4] As a result of the scandal, MIT faced tremendous criticism over the blood money it had received from the crown prince, who according to sources in the US government, had personally ordered Khashoggi's killing. Critics in the US started questioning Saudi funding and leverage at US institutions. Although many protested, an MIT report found no 'compelling case' to cut ties with the Saudis.[5]

This is the nature of the double standards of American universities: While decrying that India has become a fascist country, they roll out the red carpet for the de facto crown prince of Saudi Arabia who has a deplorable record on human rights including bombing of civilians in Yemen, and squashing of all domestic dissent. The situation on freedom of speech has indeed worsened according to a Saudi student who wished to remain anonymous in his remark to *The New York Times*.[6]

Massachusetts Institute of Technology also had close ties with Jeffrey Epstein, who ran a pedophile ring providing young girls for sexual pleasure to the rich and famous. Fully aware of Epstein's background,

MIT hosted him at least 9 times, and accepted $850,000 in donations from him.[7]

Yet, MIT's Hinduphobic machinery never loses a chance to attack the Indian establishment even on much milder grounds.

Saudi Funding of American Institutions

In a pattern similar to the Chinese, the Saudis fund at least sixty-two US institutions[8] either through Saudi state-owned companies like Aramco, the personal philanthropy trusts of the crown prince, or influential Saudi businessmen like Mohammed Abdul Latif Jameel who funds the Poverty Action Lab at MIT discussed in detail below. The *New York Times* reported:

> It shows that Saudi money flows to all sorts of American schools: M.I.T.'s elite peers, including Harvard, Yale, Northwestern, Stanford and the California Institute of Technology; flagship public universities like Michigan and the University of California, Berkeley; institutions in oil-producing regions, like Texas A&M; and state schools like Eastern Washington University and Ball State University.[9]

Between 2012 and 2018, the Saudi government donated $650 million[10] to American universities. The *New York Times* describes how the Americans host the crown prince as a celebrity and explains the successful rebranding of the Saudi image through such affiliations. In effect, this is building Saudi soft power:

> The benefits to Saudi Arabia from these relationships are clear. The kingdom gets access to the brain trust of America's top academic institutions as it endeavours to modernize its economy, an effort Prince Mohammed has named Vision 2030. ... entree (sic) to schools like M.I.T. serves to soften the kingdom's image. *Saudi Arabia is an absolute monarchy, hostile to women's and L.G.B.T.Q. rights and without protections for a free press or open expression, but its associations beyond its borders can make it seem almost like an honorary Western nation. Another way to view the Saudi relationship with American universities is as a form of branding;*

its recent moves to sponsor prominent sporting events serve the same purpose. "It's a way of spreading soft power," says Jordan, the former ambassador, "in the same way the U.S. has done for years around the world."

... Prince Mohammed spent a full day along the two-mile corridor that is arguably America's most hallowed academic ground. After the morning at M.I.T., he made the short trip in his motorcade to Harvard, where he participated in what was called a faculty round table, followed by a reception with local college presidents. No one asked him about Yemen or about much of anything else.[11]

Mohammed Abdul Latif Jameel Poverty Action Lab at MIT

Unlike Indian billionaires who seem to sponsor work at Harvard that undermines their own country, Saudi Arabian tycoons fund more strategically and patriotically. A good example is the Saudi funding of the Abdul Latif Jameel Poverty Action Lab (J-PAL) at MIT. Mohammed Abdul Latif Jameel, a MIT alumnus named it after his father, Abdul Latif Jameel. As the name Poverty Action Lab suggests, it claims to be a do-good philanthropic foundation that highlights the plight of women and minorities, and exposes the lack of democracy in several countries, especially India.

The irony is that J-PAL does not research social issues or lack of democracy within Saudi Arabia. With the Saudis as anchor investors, J-PAL is also a recipient of donations from various sources. Some of these funds are used on projects that target India's internal affairs. By funding J-PAL, the Saudis befriend American Left-wing intellectual circles and position themselves as champions of the downtrodden the world over. This is a clever way, almost like buying out the Left-wing watchdogs so they do not shine the spotlight on social issues plaguing Saudi Arabia.

Poverty Action Lab has received at least seventy-three million dollars[12] from Saudi's most influential businessman, Mohammed Abdul Latif Jameel[13] who MIT claims 'is a dedicated supporter of research initiatives at MIT to improve lives around the world'.[14] Jameel started the J-PAL endowment in 2005, followed by another substantial contribution

in 2009 to greatly expand its work. Critics have pointed out that both
Jameel and the crown prince are part of the closely knit Saudi oligarchy
that runs the country. An article in *The New York Times* points out that
'it is the giant oil company that funds the war in Yemen, the roundup
of dissidents and all else that occurs in the kingdom', and makes the
point that 'they are all part of the regime, part of the government'.[15]

Omidyar Network (the focus of Chapter 22) and the Bill & Melinda
Gates Foundation, among others, also fund J-PAL.[16] It is formally set
up as a research center in MIT's economics department. The Nobel
Laureate husband-wife economist duo, Abhijit Banerjee and Esther
Duflo, are among its founding members which gives it considerable
clout. The executive director of J-PAL is Iqbal Singh Dhaliwal, husband
of Gita Gopinath, who was chief economist at the International Monetary
Fund and then promoted to first deputy managing director. These are
well-connected elites hobnobbing in the highest circles of world power.
Dhaliwal and Duflo are co-scientific directors of J-PAL's South Asia
office from which they have entered India.

India's Krea University is their launchpad, by virtue of its aspirations
to be the MIT of India (minus the fields of engineering). Using the field
of economics to bring human rights is an interesting approach.

Indian Affiliates

The plot gets thicker as there are many more parties involved. Poverty
Action Lab's South Asia office is hosted by the Institute for Financial
Management and Research (IFMR), Krea University's parent. The IFMR
is headed by Shobhini Mukerji, who is also on the board of directors at
CARE India, an NGO funded by United States Agency for International
Development (USAID) and the Bill & Melinda Gates Foundation.
According to a report, CARE India funds Christian missionaries in
Kerala.[17]

Poverty Action Lab jointly hosts the Intersectional Sustainable
Development Goals (xSDG) conference.[18] It is run by members of
the Washington D.C.-based Dalberg Advisors and their Indian NGO,
Belongg Research Collective.[19] Using the lens of Intersectionality
discussed in Chapter 1, Belongg seeks out Indian data on discrimination
based on identity. It is still in its infancy but with a broad scope and

deep pockets. Belongg aims to be the expert on all diversity issues in India. It is building a database of 'experts' that corporates can hire to conduct training on discrimination, similar to what Equality Labs in the US has been doing for the multinationals. It advertises that it offers 'experts you can invite to understand religion-based discrimination in terms of access to development'.[20]

Its outreach includes seeking research papers on select topics, conducting a litfest, and building libraries with content on identity politics including video interviews with minorities to amplify grievances. While many of its causes seem worthy, Belongg's lens of Intersectionality theory gives many initiatives an unbalanced narrative. For example:

- It has a series of 'myth buster' videos to bust the stereotypes of Muslims and Islam. However, it does not have a similar effort to expose the Hinduphobia that exists in schools and at the workplace.
- It seems to push the American Left's methods of 'sexual grooming' of children in Indian schools under the garb of inclusive education. Its outreach and training programs on LBGTQ+ issues in Indian schools appear to be interested in grooming people to feel like victims.[21] Indian government officials also participate in 'inclusive' education seminars of Belongg.[22]
- Belongg's litfest seeks to amplify voices of Hinduphobic authors like Perumal Murugan with no counterpoint represented.

Belongg solicits research papers offering hefty grants to produce scholarship that sees Indian life through the lens of Intersectionality and discrimination. For example, a paper was funded to assess how the use of domestic LPG cylinders could be increased by 'overcoming the existing caste, class and gender-based exclusion'.[23] Its research stated that the government's LPG scheme is 'not gender-transformative in its approach'.[24] Another research study finds that landlords in Delhi are biased against Dalits and Muslims.[25] Belongg's involvement in the xSDG conference, jointly hosted with J-PAL, has a specific goal: 'Belongg believes that intersectional thinking linked to gender, caste, disability, religion and so on, needs to be much more deeply integrated in the overall SDG approach'.[26]

The xSDG website references a report titled *India Exclusion Report* (IXR). This was put out in January 2021 and prior years by an organization of prominent human rights activists called Centre for Equity Studies (CES), led by author and social activist, Harsh Mander.[27] The report received funding and support from the Tata Trust. From the US, Ashutosh Varshney, head of Watson Institute, Brown University, also supported it. The Centre for Equity Studies is funded annually (to the tune of rupees two to three crores) by the Azim Premji Foundation, apart from other foreign funding sources.[28] Mander is a frequent speaker at Azim Premji University. According to the watchdog group, Legal Rights Observatory, CES also receives crores from French and Danish Christian missionary organizations.[29] Other donors that contributed to CES during the Citizenship (Amendment) Act, 2019 protests in India include Action for Hope, a leading Pan-Arab cultural organization, US-based Indian Muslims Relief & Charity, and UK-based Minority Rights.[30]

Harsh Mander also comes with the backing of Breaking India heavyweights like George Soros, who has nominated him for the Nobel Peace Prize 2022. The Soros funded Peace Research Institute Oslo that nominates for the prize made the following announcement:

> Under Narendra Modi's Hindu nationalist administration, the situation for Muslims in India has become increasingly difficult, and the country has seen numerous incidents of religiously motivated violence. Responding to this violence, author, activist and director of the Center for Equity Studies in New Delhi, Harsh Mander, launched Karwan-e-Mohabbat, a campaign supporting and showing solidarity with the victims of hate crimes.[31]

In fact, Mander is one of Soros' proteges, having been groomed by him for a very long time. He is currently chairman of the Human Rights Initiative's advisory board which belongs to George Soros' Open Society Foundations. To better understand the significance of this connection, let's take a brief look at who Soros is.

George Soros is a Hungarian-American committed to fighting nationalists and conservative governments which he deems to be authoritarian. His organizations in India under his flagship Open Society Foundations, started out by offering scholarships and fellowships for pursuing studies and research, but rapidly built a vast network of journalists and media outlets across India that are fiercely anti-India.[32] At the World Economic Forum at Davos 2020, Soros said:

> Nationalism, far from being reversed, made further headway. The biggest and most frightening setback came in India, where a democratically elected Narendra Modi is creating a Hindu nationalist state, imposing punitive measures on Kashmir – a semi-autonomous Muslim region, and threatening to deprive millions of Muslims of their citizenship.[33]

In his speech he pledged one billion dollars to fund a new university network to tackle the spread of nationalism, especially in India.

During the farmers' riots in Delhi, *The New York Times* carried a full-page advertisement paid for by the Justice for Migrant Women and signed by seventy-six organizations claiming to be concerned farmers, activists, and citizens of the world. The headline read: *'We – Farmers, Activists, and Citizens of the World – Stand in Solidarity with Farmers in India Protesting to Protect their Livelihood'*. Among the farmers, activists, and citizens listed as supporters, was the Council of American Islamic Relations (CAIR) that has been backing Kashmir separatists by putting up billboards all over the US. It attacks the Indian government's decision on the abrogation of Article 370 and blames the Indian Army for atrocities against Muslims. Soros' Open Society Foundations is a major funding source for CAIR.

Another person roped in by Soros' Open Society Foundations is Amardeep Singh, co-founder of the US-based NGO, Sikh Coalition. He was appointed by President Obama to his advisory commission on Asian Americans and Pacific Islanders (AAPI). Since 2014, he has been working with Open Society Foundations as its senior program officer. The Sikh Coalition website supported the rioters, stating: 'The crackdown included tear gas, water cannons, baton charges, internet and resource shutdowns, censorship of journalists, the arrest and detention of activists, and concerted efforts from government leaders and state-aligned media to portray the protestors as terrorists'.[34] It added that

> ...the Sikh Coalition undertook several advocacy approaches to raise awareness and spur action on this issue, including direct outreach to elected and appointed policymakers, supporting

sangats' initiatives to raise awareness, and engaging with press to encourage coverage of this historic movement. ... We mobilized more than 6,700 community members and allies across the country to send nearly 20,000 messages to their elected officials in Congress asking them to support the farmers' right to peacefully protest and denounce the Indian government's anti-democratic behavior. We provided draft resolution language to sangats so that they could engage local lawmakers on the issue. We sent multiple letters to members of Congress and the Biden Administration...[35]

Research Output

The main areas in the purview of the Centre for Equity Studies are communal violence, citizenship, gender, labor and migration, social justice, and homelessness. While the objective seems well-intentioned, its India Exclusion Report showcases human rights issues of only Muslims and other minorities. The violence against Hindus is glaring in its absence and their intentional portrayal as perpetrators of violence is an obvious attempt to fit the evidence with the narratives espoused by international social sciences institutions. The 308-page India Exclusion Report, which is a collection of papers, suggests policy changes for the government towards Muslim and other minorities. The CES has put on one of the most organized and well-funded fights against the Citizenship (Amendment) Act, 2019.

The xSDG conference showcasing Mander's India Exclusion Report is moderated by MIT J-PAL's officials. The only reasonable conclusion is that J-PAL's goal is to change government policy, and to train local Indian scholars for this purpose. Scholars from Ashoka University, Azim Premji University, and Krea University are well represented. It is clear from a close analysis of their activities that J-PAL, Belongg, CES, Krea University, and Azim Premji University are well on their way to creating an elaborate ecosystem in India that develops research and trains activists with a specific ideological slant.

Poverty Action Lab seems obsessed with caste and has hired Western 'experts' on the subject. For example:

- Marianne Bertrand, an executive committee and board member of J-PAL, is professor of economics at the University of Chicago whose research combines racial bias in the US with affirmative action for disadvantaged castes, and corruption in India.[36]
- Another faculty at J-PAL is Jeanne Lafortune, economist at Pontifical Catholic University, Chile, whose focus includes 'the relationship between marriage market conditions and human capital accumulation, the role of caste in the Indian marriage market...'[37]
- Priyal Patil is a scholar with research interest in caste, racial/gender discrimination, health, and education.[38] Ankit Agarwal is yet another scholar whose research interests are stated as economics of gender, caste, religion, and education.[39]
- J-PAL is heavily involved in building its own infrastructure in India for data collection, social mapping, in-depth interviews, and conducting village level meetings.[40]

Poverty Action Lab is very imaginative in using any topic as an opportunity to study some divisive issue. For instance, cricket was used to study prejudice among different social groups and design strategies for inter-group dynamics in India.[41] Another study looked at how caste status is correlated with the grades given to students.[42] Another found that flood tolerant seeds had a clear advantage over traditional seeds used by Indian farmers, in effect undermining traditional farming techniques and increasing the dependence on foreign seeds.[43] There was also a study of caste and religious norms that negatively affect economic development.[44]

Poverty Action Lab's gender studies are most interesting. Teaming up with Harvard Kennedy School, it has studied the gender gap in micro-entrepreneurship and found correlations with caste that restrict female mobility.[45] There is nothing wrong with such studies, but one is left wondering why the Saudi funded J-PAL does not conduct such research in Saudi Arabia which deprives women of fundamental rights. Why aren't the Saudis compelled to spend their millions in their own country where freedom and human rights are of serious concern?

Other than social issues, J-PAL is also keenly studying voting and electoral outcomes in India. One study looked at the effect of the criminal backgrounds of candidates on the outcomes in elections.[46] Another study found that more transparent disclosure on candidates' policies and performance help the less corrupt candidates.[47] Strangely enough, one finds that the dictatorial Kingdom of Saudi Arabia is so concerned about the Indian democratic process and the political rights of Indians that it is sinking millions of dollars into a system that will rectify the situation. Even stranger is the fact that MIT, Dalberg Advisors, IFMR, Krea University, CES, Belongg.net and others don't question why the Saudis don't do this to rectify the situation in their home country.

Jameel-Poverty Action Lab's India Outposts: Institute for Financial Management and Research and Krea University

The IFMR was founded in the 1970s, funded by ICICI Bank, the Kothari Group, and other businesses. Today, it runs a host of organizations including:

- Krea University
- IFMR LEAD
- J-PAL South Asia
- Centre for Digital Financial Inclusion
- Initiative for What Works to Advance Women and Girls in the Economy
- Inclusion Economics India Centre
- Moturi Satyanarayana Centre for Advanced Study in the Humanities and Social Sciences

The IFMR has had deep ties with both Harvard and Yale and has more recently brought in MIT's J-PAL under Krea University. As far as we are able to uncover, it is now practically synonymous with Krea, serving as an umbrella organization which supports research for foreign agencies through Krea.

Many corporate heavyweights have joined in funding Krea, including Anand Mahindra, Kiran Mazumdar Shaw of Biocon, Aditya Mittal of ArcelorMittal, Dheeraj Hinduja of Ashok Leyland, Sajjan Jindal of JSW Steel, and Anu Aga of Thermax. The governing council includes high profile academics like former Reserve Bank of India governor, Raghuram Rajan, mathematics professor at Princeton, Manjul Bhargava, and John W. Etchemendy, ex-provost at Stanford, who also serves on the board of Infosys. Ramkumar Ramamoorthy, former chairman and managing director of Cognizant has joined as pro-vice-chancellor. Krea is also funded by the Bill & Melinda Gates Foundation to research on women's issues. Some of these IFMR organizations receive funding from the US-based Dalberg Advisors.

Quietly, India has become a fertile ground for importing Critical Race Theory. Krea has a star-studded panel of Leftist scholars and immense support from American academia. In the name of bringing liberal arts from the West, it is rapidly developing academically and in terms of its administrative control into a major nexus for Woke activism.

Krea is an outpost for J-PAL's work in India, as MIT begins building its network in India. What is interesting is that MIT's stellar reputation is primarily as a technology research center, but there is a glaring absence of MIT-backed engineering centers in India to bring scholarship in technology. That should be the natural choice for patriotic Indians to utilize a university of MIT's repute. Instead, all investments from MIT through J-PAL are in social sciences with caste as the lens.

Abhijit Banerjee and Esther Duflo (along with Michael Kremer) won the 2019 Nobel Prize for Economics by conducting randomized controlled trials in the field of experimental economics similar to how pharma companies use randomized clinical trials to test the efficacy of a drug.[48] Krea University (through IFMR) helped Banerjee and Duflo conduct these experiments for J-PAL. Duflo was added to Krea's governing council in 2021 and thanked it for help in her research that led to the Nobel:

> It is fair to say that we would not have received a Nobel prize
> had it not been for all the research we could do in India, thanks
> in large part to the support we received from Krea University's
> sponsoring body since 2008.[49]

Krea's partnership with J-PAL gives the Saudis tremendous power to meddle in Indian affairs under the garb of issues like poverty eradication. As an example of meddling, the American rock superstar, Rihanna, out of nowhere, extended her support to the protesting farmers of India on Twitter which catapulted the farmer's protest into a global issue.[50] She used her 106 million Twitter followers to add weight to the protest. (Rihanna was earlier in a romantic relationship with Hassan Mohammed

Abdul Latif Jameel,[51] son of J-PAL's founder, Mohammed Abdul Latif Jameel.)

Universities like Krea lack competence in Indian knowledge systems and assemble Western academics to earn credibility as institutions of eminence. These connections do not come for free: Krea has to pay for it by supplying big data on India. It facilitates the training of Indian scholars to become *shishyas* (followers) of Western Left-wing academicians and their political interventions in India.

Krea has become a gateway for MIT, Yale, the Saudis, the French, and foreign NGOs like the Bill & Melinda Gates Foundation. Krea has partnerships with foreign entities to produce scholarship on economics, gender, environment, and poverty. These projects bring Western values, regardless of whether they have succeeded or failed in their home countries, and with little respect for the Indian context. It is a large-scale social engineering movement to change the mindset of the masses.

The charts on page 512 and 513 show J-PAL's extensive network in India and its research output.

Krea's scholars and their research output reflect the ideologies of its leadership. Its economics professors like Sumit Mishra have tied up with scholars from Harvard and Cornell to produce papers in economics that show how caste-based segregation prevails in India.[52] But they fail to include the perspective that caste-based networks also contribute to the success of several communities, as IIM Bangalore's Prof. R. Vaidyanathan has established in detail.[53]

Another example is Sayantan Datta who has an MSc in cognitive sciences but teaches writing and oral communication at Krea. Datta received a 'Diversity Reporting' grant in 2021 from the National Association of Science Writers, an American organization, which claims it 'will explore an impressive range of issues affecting Indigenous peoples, neurodiverse individuals and the transgender/nonbinary community'.[54] He has imported the entire system of Intersectionality we discussed in Chapter 1 and applied it to India's caste, gender, and sexuality identities as the oppressed 'protected class'. Even the study of science in India is seen through this lens.[55]

When the IIT chief commented that there is no discrimination at his institute and that 'we will not allow it and if there is we will deal with it severely',[56] Datta tweeted:

This is really irritating. There is more than ENOUGH documentation that all IITs, and IIT Madras too, is a hotbed of casteist discrimination. In fact, IITs survive on casteism; IITs *produce* (sic) caste to continue the myth of merit.[57]

Datta's views on Ayurveda go as follows: 'Any analysis of Ayurveda without understanding how it is inexorably linked to caste and casteism is, for the most part, bullshit. Promoting Ayurveda = promoting caste'.[58]

Krea and Data Mining

Harvard Kennedy School's Evidence for Policy Design recruited IFMR in 2013 to study and gather data on Indian labor economics. The program was transferred to Economic Growth Center under Inclusion Economics at Yale.[59] The main focus of research is to mine data on Indian economics and environment in order to build a big data repository at Yale. In some instances, accessing the data on Indian economics and society requires special permissions from Yale. With so much valuable data being mined by IFMR/Krea for Yale, it is ironic that IFMR/Krea is recognized as an 'Institution of National Importance' by the Indian government's Ministry of Finance.

Yale hires many scholars for data collection and analysis focusing on gender as it relates to labor economics, economic empowerment, political economy, and environmental economics. The idea is to collect data to back policy interventions. Another goal is to promote the narrative to the general public and policymakers to effect change that fits Yale's ideology on inclusivity.[60] The Yale website has over a dozen fellowship positions at any given time to conduct such data driven research in India. Krea is helping Yale collect massive amounts of data on the Indian economy, environment, and social networks.

We are not claiming that any laws are being violated. Based on the arguments presented in our earlier book, *Artificial Intelligence and the Future of Power*, we are merely pointing out numerous instances in which sensitive data is being gathered and exported without the necessary level of government scrutiny.

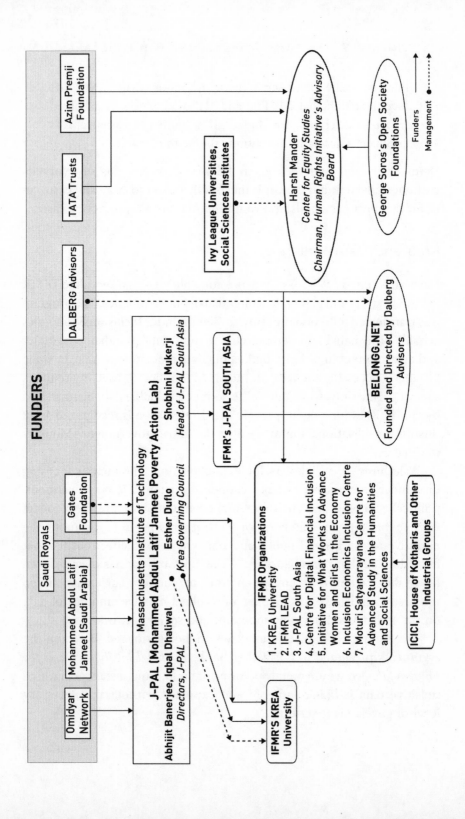

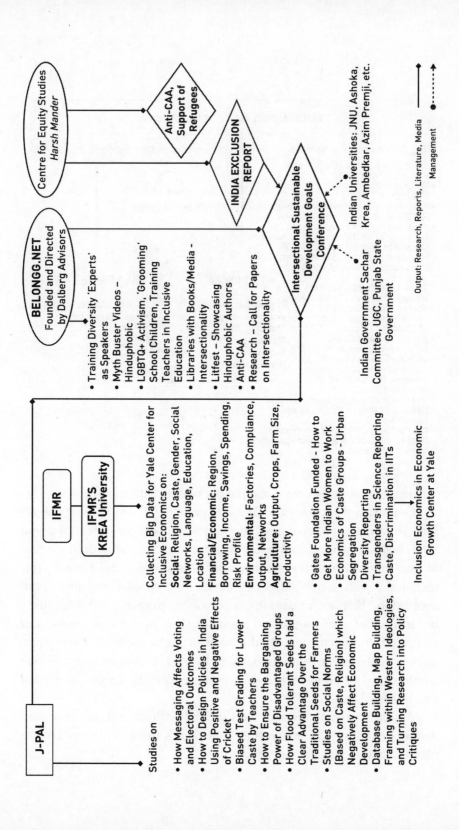

Centre for Equity Studies
Harsh Mander

BELONGG.NET
Founded and Directed by Dalberg Advisors

IFMR

J-PAL

IFMR'S KREA University

Anti-CAA, Support of Refugees

INDIA EXCLUSION REPORT

Intersectional Sustainable Development Goals Conference

Indian Universities: JNU, Ashoka, Krea, Ambedkar, Azim Premji, etc.

Indian Government Sachar Committee, UGC, Punjab State Government

Output: Research, Reports, Literature, Media

Management

- Training Diversity 'Experts' as Speakers
- Myth Buster Videos – Hinduphobic
- LGBTQ+ Activism, 'Grooming' School Children, Training Teachers in Inclusive Education
- Libraries with Books/Media – Intersectionality
- Litfest – Showcasing Hinduphobic Authors
- Anti-CAA
- Research – Call for Papers on Intersectionality

Collecting Big Data for Yale Center for Inclusive Economics on:
Social: Religion, Caste, Gender, Social Networks, Language, Education, Location
Financial/Economic: Region, Borrowing, Income, Savings, Spending, Risk Profile
Environmental: Factories, Compliance, Output, Networks
Agriculture: Output, Crops, Farm Size, Productivity

- Gates Foundation Funded - How to Get More Indian Women to Work
- Economics of Caste Groups - Urban Segregation
- Diversity Reporting
- Transgenders in Science Reporting
- Caste, Discrimination in IITs

Inclusion Economics in Economic Growth Center at Yale

Studies on

- How Messaging Affects Voting and Electoral Outcomes
- How to Design Policies in India Using Positive and Negative Effects of Cricket
- Biased Test Grading for Lower Caste by Teachers
- How to Ensure the Bargaining Power of Disadvantaged Groups
- How Flood Tolerant Seeds had a Clear Advantage Over the Traditional Seeds for Farmers
- Studies on Social Norms (Based on Caste, Religion) which Negatively Affect Economic Development
- Database Building, Map Building, Framing within Western Ideologies, and Turning Research into Policy Critiques

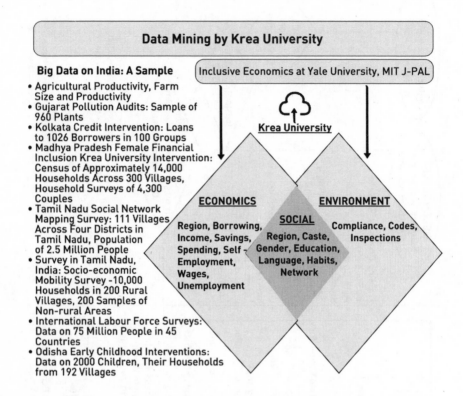

The diagram above shows a sample list of data gathering projects.

One example is Krea and Yale's Economic Growth Center's large-scale survey of socio-economic mobility with a sample of ten thousand households in two hundred rural villages, as well as two hundred samples of non-rural areas in the southern Indian state of Tamil Nadu.[61] This includes a village-by-village census on householder earnings, land ownership, housing conditions, age, caste, primary and secondary occupation of each household member, size of the household, and education and occupation of the head of the household. There were questionnaires at the household and individual levels with a specific one administered to all ever-married women collecting details on marital and fertility history.[62]

Another example is the Odisha Early Childhood Interventions dataset on 2000 children and their households from 192 villages in the eastern state of Odisha. Yale claims:

It contains demographic and economic data on the household as well as detailed and advanced measurements on child skills. It also contains network and community-level information. The size and the scope of this dataset allows research on poor communities well beyond the original research. It also forms the basis of a cohort with the potential of following the children and their families into the future with numerous research objectives, including a follow-up of the effects of the interventions that motivated it in the first place.[63]

The Tamil Nadu Social Network Mapping Survey is a large database of 2.5 million people of Tamil Nadu which maps financial and social networks. Social networks outside individual villages are also mapped meticulously in this dataset owned by Yale. The site boasts that,

> complete network data exist on both financial and social connections for almost all households in every village. ... there are data on both within-village contacts and outside-village contacts, which is very rare. Finally, the dataset includes detailed measures from all households on self-assessed well-being, income and wealth, public good provision and community participation, which is unique in the context of network mapping datasets.[64]

The environmental data collection includes surveys on air pollution, regulatory compliance, and factory inspections. Krea receives funding from the Government of India, Harvard University Climate Change Solutions Fund, Harvard University Sustainability Science Program, MacArthur Foundation and USAID for its environmental data mining projects.[65]

The Yale Inclusion Economics Center has also collected data about Indian agriculture to study agricultural productivity and farm size, as well as the role of insurance in agricultural inputs and crop yields. Electricity infrastructure data has been used to study costs and benefits of expanding India's energy infrastructure. This includes sensitive information on infrastructure that could potentially be used for cyber-attacks. In the guise of women's empowerment, the Yale Inclusion Economics Center gives women in rural Madhya Pradesh training; and it reports that Indian women prefer to be homemakers, which they see as a cultural defect they want to remedy.[66]

While Krea's activities seem above board, the recent Indian policies on data protection would suggest a closer scrutiny. We have shown one of the key bridges from a Western university to an Indian one bringing social justice agendas, and all this funded by foreign and Indian business people.

19

Ashoka University: Harvard University's Junior Partner

Overview

Ashoka University is the most significant venue for what many patriotic Indians characterize as Breaking India forces. It is where key databases on Indians are collected and analyzed, Breaking India theories are conceptualized and intervention strategies are developed, tested, and perfected. This is where many students are trained in ideological narratives and strategies, and then mobilized. New victim groups are identified and nurtured. Heavily backed by Westerners with vested interests as well as by Indians, it behaves in ways that its loyalty to the nation may be questioned. We point out a complex network of global connections – of people, infrastructure and institutions in India, which are concerning. We do not wish to adjudicate any kind of violation, and the purpose here is to present raw data that would need to be analyzed further before making judgments.

While other liberal arts universities springing up across India are playing a similar role, Ashoka is by far the most prominent. But this is not how it was envisaged by its founders. They were a group of well-intentioned, successful IIT/IIM and US-educated entrepreneurs with the desire to build a university along the same lines as top Western universities focusing on liberal arts education. Most of them had tech backgrounds devoid of an adequate understanding of Western liberal arts and how that differs from Indian traditions. It would appear that they were driven by the glamor of showing off their recently acquired wealth by hobnobbing with the global elites. Once a few big names got the ball rolling, many more wealthy Indians jumped on the bandwagon.

They did not delve into the track record of places like Harvard in the study of India. One would think they would have undertaken the kind of analysis we presented in Parts 1 and 2 before making their strategic plans. As successful business people, they know the importance of doing due diligence before making strategic investments.

In 2014, Sanjeev Bikhchandani, founder of Naukri.com and one of the early founders and funders of Ashoka University said:

> But for me the penny really dropped when St. Stephens college declared in 2007 that [they would have] 50% reservation with a 35% gap in the cut off [marks] between the general category and reserved category. And that got all St. Stephen's alumni up in arms saying that 'look with 35% gap, it's not about the reservations, it's about the gap.' But with the width of 35% gap, you know, you're going to kill the academic character of the place. But nobody listened. And so, a few alumni got together and said let's start a new college.[1]

Bikhchandani praised the merit and hard work the IITs and IIMs represent. He has not realized that Harvard's own professors are pursuing anti-India postures, including their attack on IITs as being casteist institutions hiding behind merit.

One possible explanation for the meltdown of Ashoka's founding principles could be the funders' ignorance of the ideologies incubated, nurtured, and promoted in liberal arts universities. They felt honored that Westerners and Indians trained by them were glad to take control of defining Ashoka's values, structures, and alliances.

For the Sonipat campus alone, these businessmen invested over Rs. 1,000 crores ($125 million). For the second campus, the fund-raising campaign for which started in 2021, the target was even higher – Rs. 1,500 crores. The IIT/IIM network was mobilized with Ashoka boasting 160-plus co-founders including businessmen, Non-Resident Indians, and high net-worth individuals from the UK, US, and Singapore.[2] The Bill & Melinda Gates Foundation and the Omidyar group also made grants to support certain projects in Ashoka.

The diagram that follows shows the major centers within Ashoka we will discuss individually, and how these are organized as a pipeline creating a new generation of Breaking India forces.

Ashoka University's Role in Breaking India

Description	Stage
Mining India's Big Data: Trivedi Centre for Political Data	Trivedi Centre for Political Data
Providing Access to Foreign Entities: China, France, NGOs: Ashoka Centre for China Studies	Ashoka Centre for China Studies
Working for Foreign Interests: Centre for Social Impact and Philanthropy	Centre for Social Impact and Philanthropy
Training and Grooming a 'Professional Class' of Marxists: Centre for Studies in Gender and Sexuality	Centre for Studies in Gender and Sexuality
Compromising India's Civilization: Centre for Social and Behaviour Change	Centre for Social and Behaviour Change

Breaking India Ecosystem: Built Brick by Brick

Financial investor, Ashish Dhawan, along with other founders appointed an academic council comprising Leftist scholars Pratap Bhanu Mehta (who served as vice chancellor till 2021), Ramachandra Guha, Andre Beteille, Kaushik Basu, and others, thus playing into the hands of the Western academic elites of the kind we have criticized in Part 2. This is why the premise of Ashoka has been flawed right from the start.

Dhawan and his team did not seem to have investigated the architecture of Western social sciences that we summarized at the introductory level in Chapter 1. They were not rooted in Indian classical studies. Their decision to learn from the Harvards and Yales of America treated those universities as the vishwa gurus with Ashoka as the leading shishya.

Ashoka University has grown into a Breaking India incubator that may be called the JNU of the rich. It is for privileged Indian kids of parents who can afford rupees thirty lakhs for a bachelor's degree that coaches them on how to denigrate and dismantle the heritage that their forefathers tirelessly built up over millennia.

We certainly support critical thinking among the youth, including criticisms of civilizations, religions, governments and all kinds of institutions. But this must always be balanced with multiple viewpoints present. We do not find this to be the case at Ashoka. Our intention is not to criticize any investor in their personal capacity, but to focus on the intellectual output of scholars. We present a survey on the works of Ashoka affiliated individuals from the vice-chancellor down to the regular faculty and students. These individuals have been very public about their agendas.

For example, back in 2016, when JNU was racked by anti-India slogans at a pro-Afzal Guru (the Kashmiri separatist involved in the terrorist attack on the Indian Parliament in 2001, later put to death) protest, which led to the sedition case against several persons, Ashoka's then vice chancellor, Pratap Bhanu Mehta wrote that 'we are living under a government that is both rabidly malign and politically incompetent'. He continued:

> It is using nationalism to crush constitutional patriotism, legal tyranny to crush dissent, political power to settle petty scores, and administrative power to destroy institutions. The instigation of this crackdown was the alleged chanting of some anti-national slogans at JNU, and a meeting to mark the death anniversary of Afzal Guru. But the government's disproportionate response smacks of tyranny of the highest order.[3]

Mehta said, 'being anti-national is not a crime'.[4] It is true that in a free country like India, verbally attacking the authorities for their policies is not a crime. But the issue is whether the investors and founders consciously wanted to set up an anti-national university without proper balance. Mehta openly advocated for the vandalism that followed the passing of the CAA. He is quoted as saying, 'The direction is going to be set by mob, by brute power, by mobilisation while legal and philosophical work is necessary, don't count on them'.[5]

It is disturbing to see the vice chancellor of a leading university, formed with the lofty goals of upholding merit and hard work, encouraging hooliganism on campuses and streets rather than honest debates on campus. Ashoka's students are mimicking their peers at places like Harvard by adopting a Marxist anti-thesis against the Indian grand narrative.

Ashoka: An Incubator of Hinduphobia

A staunch critic of Prime Minister Narendra Modi, Mehta feels that populism is the only reason for the rise of the Bharatiya Janata Party. He spins a tale about the persecution complex of Hindus that according to him, leads them to create conspiracy theories against various minorities and their champions. This, he feels entitles him to dismiss their concerns. In an interview with *ThePrint* he said:

> There is much bravado about this moment – a new India rising out of the ashes of the last 70 years of wasted independence as the official narrative goes. But ... if you just scratch this ruling ideology, this combination of authoritarianism communalism, you notice how insecurities – it is an ideology largely in a sense founded on the anxiety and resentment. ... what it needs to sustain itself is a persecutory complex, the idea that somehow India's majority [Hindus] ... has constantly been persecuted through history and this is its moment to, ... claim its rightful historical agency. ... it is as much a constructed anxiety as it is a real one. ... it will always require an enemy to satiate itself right. It's Lutyens Delhi today, it's intellectuals the day after, it's Muslims today, it's Christians tomorrow, it's Ayodhya yesterday, and it's Krishna Janma bhoomi tomorrow. ... The philosophy of history that comes with this ideology is relatively simple: 'Let us not bother with the complexities of our history, this incredibly complex weave that made India what it is; history is relatively simple – the past is a conspiracy of a few elites – Islamic elites to begin with, secular elites later on and the future is going to be ... redeemed by a leader who is personification of the people.' ... It has a conspiratorial, as it were, politics at the base of its [BJP's] thinking about politics. Therefore, it will always need to find conspirators – minorities, liberal secularists, leftists, urban Naxals, now even Bollywood. And the targeting of them will not be driven by an ordinary calculus of politics, because when you legitimise yourself entirely by inventing enemies, truth ceases to matter, normal restraints of civilization decay, checks and balances don't matter.[6]

The fact is that history books in the Indian school curriculum have been heavily influenced by foreign Leftist historians. Unfortunately, any Indian attempt at reclaiming history gets condemned as a persecution complex. This attitude pervades Ashoka from the vice chancellor's office down to the students.

Ashoka's faculty includes well-known subversives like the professor of history, Dilip Simeon, an ex-Naxalite who 'directly participated in the first Naxalbari war against the Indian state'.[7] He is also the chairman and trustee of Aman Panchayat, a non-profit that receives funding from a number of NGOs and non-profits with a history of anti-India activity.[8] Some of these have also had Foreign Contribution (Regulation) Act, 2010 licences cancelled for violations.

Another example is the sociology and anthropology professor, Mitul Baruah who was accused in 2016 of sexual harassment and rape in student Raya Sarkar's #MeToo list of 'sexual harassers in academia'. Ashoka's investigation in this case dragged on for a year and a half, after which Baruah got away on a minor charge of 'professional misconduct' instead of sexual harassment, which would have made him unmarketable to fight for women and minorities. The Leftist newspaper *Greater Kashmir* reported the issue.[9]

In 2017, Baruah wrote a scathing article titled *Namami Brahmaputra* claiming that Hindu practices related to the river are an attempt to 'enrol it into the Hindutva imagination'. He says that 'the Brahmaputra is not considered "holy" by the local communities...'.[10] In another article he writes that although the Brahmaputra is worshipped, it is done only by some in the framework of Brahminical patriarchy and that too out of desperation:

> To the people of Majuli, the Brahmaputra is anything but sacred. There have been instances where some *sattradhikars* (the religious and administrative head of a *sattra*, a Vaishnavite monastery) have offered *bhog* to the Brahmaputra for the protection of the island from erosion. However, such rituals have been performed only in times of intense erosion activity on the island. Hence, these are desperate acts and not the norm ... such acts are always performed by the *sattradhikars* and not by the ordinary inhabitants of the island. ... these can be described ... as Brahmanic (sic) rituals that

perhaps help enhance the public reverence for the *sattradhikars*. They are not part of the local culture and tradition.[11]

Baruah was also among those who requested the president of India to consider a mercy plea against the execution of Yakub Memon, the terrorist convicted for the serial blasts in Mumbai in which 257 people were killed.[12]

Another example is of professor of contemporary history at Ashoka, Srinath Raghavan, who tweeted: 'The claim that ANYONE did satyagraha for the freedom of Bangladesh and were arrested is too ridiculous to require refutation'.[13] The twitterati rose to the occasion by quickly finding videos to falsify his claims of history. In 2021, Neelanjan Sircar, assistant professor of political science at Ashoka trolled the president of India on Twitter and made a Hinduphobic statement mocking Lord Ram. He later deleted the tweet after backlash.[14]

Besides their public utterances, the faculty teaches courses and recommends study materials that push the Hinduphobic agenda. For example, Aparna Vaidik, a history professor, came under scrutiny for her Great Books Foundation course that prescribed *A Gardener in the Wasteland: Jotiba Phule's Fight for Liberty* by Srividya Natarajan. The publisher, Navayana, known for its anti-Hindu publications, has admitted that the book is 'a scathing and witty attack on Brahmanism (sic) and the slavery of India's "lower" castes that it engendered'.[15]

This book depicts Adi Shankara as a 'devious brahmin' with a 'twisted intellect'. Brahmins, according to Natarajan, devised signs like the sacred thread and the highly revered Gayatri mantra from the *Rig Veda* to recognize one another and purified themselves by 'drinking urine of cows'. In response to public protests, Ashoka defended the faculty, saying: 'The university faculty are free to use a diverse range of materials to catalyze thinking'.[16] This would be fine provided the 'diverse range of materials' being mentioned were truly diverse and not entirely one-sided as they happen to be. There is no attempt by Ashoka to 'catalyze' the thinking of its students by explaining the contributions of Adi Shankara or the significance of the Gayatri mantra so they could debate the issue. Our issue is, once again, the lack of balance in the discourse.

Vaidik was awarded a large grant in 2018 from the Andrew W. Mellon Foundation as part of a project to research 'sexualities, gender, and the state in the postcolonial world' and uncover 'the persistence of gender inequalities in the Global South'.[17] In 2020, Vaidik received another grant of fifty thousand pounds from The British Academy in the UK. Ashoka and Flame universities were chosen for providing academic support. One of the goals is the creation of archives of 'experiential knowledge' from the point of view of groups that Vaidik decides to categorize as Subalterns. She calls this 'Public history'.[18] The aim is to incorporate this 'oppressor versus oppressed' history into academia and then introduce it into the school curriculum.

Meanwhile, the useful knowledge and experience of these rural peoples on plants, medicines, and other things of value have no place in such research because this would make them heroes rather than oppressed. Besides, it would expose the theft of such biological intellectual property by the Western pharma companies.

According to The British Academy:

> This research project has been co-developed and will be co-delivered by academic historians and community representatives of India's indigenous people, to bring marginalised epistemologies and knowledge into school and university pedagogy. The research team will do this by creating the first database of community public history initiatives and pedagogical resources in India. The project punctures conventional historical practice by relying on multilingual and multi-ethnic sources and centring community traditions, orality and experiential knowledge. In its conception, design and dissemination the project seeks to bring to the forefront community researchers from marginalised communities who make up the lowest proportion of Indians to engage with formal education to bring their voices to educational spaces. This will benefit local community development and re-valuation of their knowledge resources. It will also enable different audiences in the education sector to develop a new understanding of collective public history at the level.[19]

There seems to be hardly any oversight by anyone other than the foreign funding sources. Therefore, the university can be used as a platform for poor, vulnerable people to vent their grievances, and such narratives can then be used in international forums to foster mistrust and unrest between communities. The British university overseeing the project states:

> The project will raise awareness of history and memory amongst marginalised communities and encourage higher education institutions to integrate nonstandard community knowledge into the teaching and research programmes of Indian universities.[20]

Ashoka's website quotes Vaidik:

> A great deal of historical research is premised on institutionalised archives such as the one created by the states and corporate institutions. ... how do we decolonise the archives? How to build peoples' and communities' worldview into the archives? What are the traditional archive practices that one needs to do away with?
>
> Doing Public History fundamentally requires you to first shift the vision to community archives - the archives that a community creates instead of archives created for the communities. ... Janastu ... documents stories of pattachitra story-tellers as recorded by them on a push-button recorder. It also documents ... the Raika community where they have developed a mobile application for the shepherd to track their locations. This helps protect the commons and in the compiling of bio-cultural protocols by the community itself. The traditional archives are spaces of violence and erasure, created by the colonial administration, the state and people in power. They have written out genocide, massacres and land grabs. ... community knowledge archiving and record keeping is very important in re-imagining our histories.
>
> A great deal of history is really history of the state, rulers and big statesmen. They are seen as 'doers' in history ... Then came the subaltern historians who focused on the people on the margins of history - the working class, peasants, and women - as the agents of history.
>
> Public History ... seeks to engage the 'small voice of history' in the act of analysis and the manner of writing history itself. One has to be careful here because a conception of public history can feed the separation between 'real' history as done by historians for their peers and one they write for and with the public but both are complimentary.[21]

It is interesting how the British colonizers' hearts bleed for the colonized, such that they have commissioned people to rewrite the history of the colonized from their 'own point of view'. This is particularly intriguing because they refuse to restore the resources and artefacts that Britain looted from India, knowing all too well that these would help write the history of the period in an unbiased way.

Vaidik's implicit application of Critical Race Theory is clear in her analysis that Indian history and mythology are ridden with violence, and that *'upper-caste privilege plays a major role in people's inability to recognise this violence'*.[22] When asked what is the way out of the 'supremacist ideologies, such as Hindu nationalism', she explains the message in her book, *My Son's Inheritance: A Secret History of Lynching and Blood Justice in India*:

> The inheritance of our historical violence, ... comes to us in the form of a secret, a secret that is hidden in plain sight. It is visible and yet we don't see it. Only once the secret is unveiled the question of atonement or redemption will come up: How do we redeem ourselves? How do we atone? .... Atonement lies in the Indians first owning up to their history of violence. The choice is to either hide one's shame and generate even more violence or to own up to one's historical shame and break the silence around violence. For it is our silence borne out of privilege that perpetuates violence.[23]

In response to the question, 'Why do you think the upper caste and middle-class are not empathetic towards the minorities and oppressed in India?'[24] she says:

> One will have to unpack the myth of the 'Poor Brahmin'. The word Brahmin here is a metaphor for a savarna whose social capital is offset by insufficient economic capital and ... runs the risk of sinking below the line of survival. He encounters an uneven playing field by virtue of his birth which he is called on to level with hard work, honesty and his innate merit – all without inflicting violence ... His life was made worse in Independent India with provision of caste-based reservation and minority appeasement ... He had to work hard to acquire social respectability while others raced

ahead aided by caste-based reservation. ... the poorest of the Poor Brahmin never had to carry the nightsoil on his head, clean the sewages, clear the cattle carcasses or live on the fringes of the village. He was never prevented from drawing water from the village well ... His shadow never soiled another human being. This myth invisibilises Poor Brahmin's caste privilege and perpetuates the feelings of him being the historical victim. This myth as the collective unconscious of India's majority community makes them unsee oppression.[25]

Given this motivation driving her project of rewriting Indian history, one can expect that the marginalized communities will be fed divisive narratives against their own fellow citizens.

Our next example is Durba Chattaraj, a development economics fellow from Ashoka, who recently wrote on *Why India is Struggling to be Truly Open Defecation Free*, only to blame it on Hindu beliefs in ritual purity and the mother of all evils – the caste system. She cites Western research on how and why Hindus defecate:

Many scholars have analysed open defecation practices according to the Hindu caste system ... A study conducted by Dean Spears and Michael Geruso suggested that Hindus are far less likely to use toilets than Muslims in India. The difference in demand by Hindus and Muslims was seen across all levels of wealth. These findings were significant at the 5% level. Furthermore, Hindus were more likely to respond that defecating far away from home is considered pure.[26]

In 2021, Ashoka's Shahid Jameel, a virologist on the national COVID-19 panel wrote an op-ed in *The New York Times* criticizing the Modi government for the pandemic in India.[27] However, it has been pointed out elsewhere that his predictions were flawed and he wanted to undermine the credibility of India's indigenous vaccine.[28]

Another example of Ashoka's output is an article by journalist Maya Mirchandani, now head of media studies at Ashoka University, in which she condemned Ajit Doval, India's national security advisor, for waging war on civil society.[29]

We next examine the work of Ashwini Deshpande, professor of

economics and director of the Centre for Economic Data and Analysis at Ashoka. This example illustrates the problem with Ashoka wanting to be the Harvard of India. Deshpande says she has been working on the economics of discrimination in India with a focus on caste, gender, and affirmative action policies.[30] She is deeply concerned about the low participation rate of women in the workforce and attributes it to traditional gender roles and non-availability of suitable jobs.[31]

Our comment is that such experiments in the US of pushing women into the workplace have resulted in broken families, high rates of depression, suicides, divorces, rapes, and children being brought up by single parents. The West can hardly be considered a gold standard on the well-being of women. And therefore, the extent to which Western norms for women are adopted by India should be a matter of individual choice. It is important to take a nuanced approach given the cultural differences. Simply allowing the Americans to set the benchmarks, measure the results, and pronounce the verdict, is inappropriate. We consider this an issue that Indian society has to solve on its own terms. There is no law preventing women from working if they so desire. The percentage of poor women working for a living is evidence that women have the freedom to exercise this choice when they want.

Indian society has proven that it has the structure, intelligence, rhythm, and equilibrium that facilitates change without external intervention. Western cultures based on the imposition of order are prone to restricting choices and are less capable of adapting to situations. Indian culture is stronger in accommodating factors like the joint-family structure, care of the elderly, care for small children, following family traditions and culture, family business division of labor, division of responsibilities where one person is the breadwinner and the other is a homemaker, all of which are legitimate reasons why women may choose not to join the workforce. Indian culture is different, and India has the right to assert that uniqueness.

This kind of interference in the affairs of Indian women impinges on their ability to make choices based on their circumstances. It insults their intelligence and infringes on their right to choose a lifestyle. But it is also a matter of particular concern when foreign funded agencies, with no moral standing or accountability, try such experiments with the goal of controlling the discourse on India. Once their systems and standards are in place, they can press buttons from anywhere in the world, and monitor and manage the effects in the remotest of Indian villages. And they can quickly evaluate and pass judgment.

Ashwini Deshpande is an example of the foot soldiers that play an important role in making India vulnerable to external forces. Deshpande is a frequent contributor to *The Wire* writing about caste issues and supporting the recognition of caste as a category for discrimination under the law in the UK. She accuses the Indian diaspora of caste discrimination in Indian society as a form of racism.[32]

She was also invited by Harvard to the Harvard Shanghai Center in China to speak about India and meritocracy. But before getting into her anti-India contributions in Shanghai, we will give a little background on Ashoka's connection with Harvard on its China studies initiative.

Centre for China Studies

China has used its prominence on the world stage to increase its efforts to subvert and buy out Indian educational institutions, just as it is doing in the US. We do not wish to pass any sweeping judgment on the Indians who happen to be linked in some way because this could be entirely unintentional or a hangover from the past era of India-China friendship. We merely point out the risks that need to be evaluated in the present geopolitical context. Our concern is that Ashoka could be used by China to enter India to:

- Groom young China studies scholars in India;
- Set up China studies departments in universities across India; and
- Control the narrative of China studies in India

On the surface, Ashoka's Centre for China Studies' (ACCS) goals look well-meaning:

> The Centre will set the academic research focus and strategy for China studies, develop coursework and degree programs, and facilitate educational exchanges for faculty and students, and through the creation of a hub at Ashoka support the development of China Studies across prominent institutions in India.[33]

But because of the significant role it is intended to play with regard to a troublesome China, there should be more care to ensure its independence from foreign influences.

The Chinese could exploit existing institutional infrastructure to infiltrate India which can be explained by the role of Shivshankar Menon, India's former national security advisor, who chairs the ACCS.[34] In prior years, this would be normal, but recent geopolitical events concerning China call for a fresh review. Menon is a distinguished fellow in foreign policy at the Brookings Institution.[35] Brookings is influenced by China's CCP, and even Americans are concerned about its implications for US national security, as explained in Chapter 8. After he retired, Menon was made a Fisher Family Fellow at the Harvard Kennedy School, which influences government decisions and policy making.[36] He is also chairman of the advisory board at the Institute of Chinese Studies (ICS) in New Delhi, which is backed by the Indian Ministry of External Affairs. None of this suggests anything wrongful on the part of Menon or others. Furthermore, Pratap Bhanu Mehta, before his resignation from Ashoka as vice chancellor, was also a governing council member at ICS, a position he continues to hold.[37] It may not be too far fetched to conclude that the ICS has a degree of control over the scholarship coming out of Ashoka's Centre for Chinese Studies because it supports many of their scholars as visiting research associates on an an ongoing basis.[38]

The Harvard-Yenching Institute (HYI) relationship is yet another route of influence. The institute started out as a Christian missionary organization, founded in 1928 by the estate of Charles M. Hall. Hall, a businessman who founded American protestant missionary colleges in Asia.[39] From the late 1940s through the 1950s, the Chinese Communist government ended foreign control over Chinese educational institutions.[40] But because of Hall's Christian mission, at least three trustees of the HYI are still from the United Board for Christian Higher Education in Asia, a non-profit that claims to 'draw strength from our Christian identity and values and our collaboration with Asian colleges and universities'.[41] The United Board has funded eighty colleges in fifteen countries across Asia.[42]

Today, both India studies and China studies fellowships at HYI are 'facilitated' by leading Chinese universities which are under the control of the Chinese government. The HYI has two programs, a doctoral fellowship[43] and a postdoctoral fellowship[44] for Indian students and scholars. It directly recruits post-doctoral candidates from Ashoka, while the doctoral fellowship is a partnership between Harvard-Yenching Institute and the Institute of Chinese Studies in Delhi to 'encourage Chinese studies in India':[45]

> This program, facilitated by the participation of eight partner institutions in China, seeks to foster a cross-national network of scholars by bringing to the Harvard-Yenching Institute scholars of Indian Studies in China. They will be joined at HYI by selected candidates from HYI's Chinese Studies in India program (a joint doctoral fellowship program with the Institute for (sic) Chinese Studies in Delhi to encourage Chinese studies in India). The program's host institutions in China (Beijing Normal University, Central China Normal University, East China Normal University, Fudan University, Peking University, Sichuan University, and Yunnan University) will be invited to nominate a small number of outstanding doctoral students or younger faculty members in Indian studies to come to HYI as Visiting Fellows or Visiting Scholars. Selected candidates will join their Indian counterparts at the Harvard-Yenching Institute for a one-year stay.[46]

In order to expand the HYI program, Ashoka has roped in Shiv Nadar University in Noida, Christ University in Bengaluru (supported by the United Board of Christian Higher Education), IIM Shillong, Somaiya Vidyavihar University in Mumbai, Ahmedabad University, and Jadavpur University in Kolkata. Ashoka and HYI provide a generous two-year postdoctoral fellowship.[47] None of this is necessarily a problem and we merely wish to point out the extent of China's presence in India's higher education. Many of the links to China's authorities are indirect but need to be monitored closely.

Shanghai Meritocracy Workshop

As an example of the kind of scholarship emerging from the Ashoka-Harvard connection, Harvard conducted a workshop in Shanghai, China to discuss *Merit in China and India*. Many Indian scholars including

Ashwini Deshpande of Ashoka University, Ajantha Subramanian of Harvard, Ashutosh Varshney (ex-Harvard Kennedy fellow), Devesh Kapur and Madan Lal Sobti from University of Pennsylvania participated. The distinction between the Indian and Chinese experts was glaring. While the Chinese spoke proudly of the role meritocracy played in building the greatness and glory of China, the Indian participants tried to discredit meritocracy in India's context with a narrative of shame.

The China experts spoke about how the Chinese examination system based on meritocracy was renowned because it yielded great results that the rest of the world wanted to emulate. They presented papers on their history of meritocracy and described how the selection of bureaucrats by Chinese emperors was purely performance-based. One paper discussed the recent rise of Chinese universities in the global league measured on merit.[48] Another analyzed the 'key education policy and planning documents from the inception of the People's Republic of China up to the present time'. Yet another was on the history of meritocracy in China focusing on the Tang Dynasty.[49]

The Indian side was exactly the opposite. The Indian scholars went to Shanghai to tell the Chinese how unfair meritocracy is in the Indian context, citing caste-based oppression and how it is a systemic oppression of Hindu society. This echoes the work of Ajantha Subramanian analyzed in Chapter 4.

As a universal principle, Ashutosh Varshney supported merit, saying: 'Even if inclusionary principles are applied, those meritorious must be given their due weight.'[50] In academics, he wondered whether merit should mean 'academic performance, or an ability to perform and deliver regardless of academic achievement' and whether academic excellence needs to be supplemented with social intelligence. In the absence of a resolution of these dichotomies, he conceded that academic attainment was the only yardstick for measuring merit.

Varshney went on to explain that this general rule doesn't apply to India. He launched the subject of caste in India which he said was a hurdle in achieving true merit. In other words, in India's case, the meritorious don't deserve consideration because historically, caste-based division of labor forced people into professions that didn't reflect their aspirations or capabilities. He said: 'Merit essentially came to mean the reproduction of ascriptive social hierarchies in India, an idea a democracy could ill-afford.'

He then equated caste oppression with racism in America. The division of labor was 'tightly regulated' and enforced with violence: 'If violated, the social order, often legally buttressed, was enforced with violence, quite a bit like the Jim Crow American South after the US civil war.' [51]

He expressed concern with Indian democracy being able to 'handle the problem of the upper caste domination of education and public services'.[52] He remarked: 'Were only the upper castes meritorious?' [53]

Varshney differentiated between inclusion in India's public sector and merit in the private sector: 'Inclusionary projects basically mark the functioning of the public sector, whereas the idea of merit, in principle, has migrated to the private sector.'[54]

Ashwini Deshpande asserted that the private sector discriminates against certain castes:

> There is sufficient evidence to indicate that caste disparities in economic outcomes, ... in occupational attainment are neither mainly a hangover from the past, nor are they mainly a result of educational or skill gaps. Thus, members of SC-ST communities will face worse employment outcomes even if they were similarly qualified as the upper-castes, given discrimination in labour (job) markets.[55]

In line with the principles of Critical Race Theory, Deshpande said that difference in outcomes can only be attributed to an inherently biased system. To prove this, she claimed that 'teachers tended to give scripts marked low-caste and female, lower scores compared to those marked high-caste and male'.[56] She went on to suggest that under the pretext of checking applicants' 'family background', employers exercise caste-based discrimination.

> The fact that the two groups enter the labour market with substantial differences in "ability" or "merit" indicates "pre-market discrimination", which means that there are discriminatory factors at work in early childhood development. [57]

Deshpande believes that merit is not a 'neutral, objective characteristic, independent of the standard used to measure it, similar to height or weight or the number of teeth'.[58] She therefore questioned the notion that exam performance indicates merit by raising doubts about the very concept of exams.[59]

Discussing students who enter universities using the quotas reserved for lower castes, she said that their lower performance should be blamed on their psychological trauma for being unable to cope with 'micro-aggressions'. Her final conclusion was

> "family background", a catch-all phrase designed to capture the intertwined effect of class, caste, parental background and social networks, remains the most crucial indicator of individual merit, making the idea of equality of opportunity or establishment of a level-playing field – basic preconditions of meritocracy – very difficult to achieve.[60]

Both Varshney and Deshpande found merit to be a sham in the Indian context, and both proposed reservations in private-sector employment. We are not passing judgment on the merit of lower-caste students but merely presenting the arguments put forward by the cabal of caste-race-gender champions in academia.

We are in favor of an objective evaluation process that allows all students, irrespective of their background, to prove their mettle. We also believe that while affirmative action may be beneficial to remove imbalances for a finite number of years, its benefit deteriorates when continued indefinitely, because of the feeling of entitlement it sows in the youth that leads them to discount the virtues of toil and sweat. Moreover, extended protection to a section of the population actually disempowers it because many skills are lost in the process, and it is rendered incapable of becoming self-sufficient. In Chapter 6, we gave several examples of India's lower caste groups that have managed to climb up the socio-economic ladder with good leaders and internal efforts. None of these examples are featured at Ashoka's discussions on caste.

Harvard's Ajantha Subramanian presented a paper titled *Merit and Caste* in which she reiterated the thesis in her book we critiqued in Chapter 4. She said that merit 'has come to reference forms of caste distinction that have a much longer social life'. Her presentation centered on the argument that caste is reconstituted in technical science education and meritocracy produces inequality based on privilege.[61]

Finally, there was Devesh Kapur whose topic was *Selection Mechanisms and Meritocracy in a Hierarchical and Unequal Society: Indian Higher Education*. He said that meritocracy simply sounds great and fair, but in the Indian context, it amplifies inequalities because of the caste system. He did not propose any new ideas but simply regurgitated the same old concepts on privilege, inequality, and caste. He said the idea of meritocracy being fair is a myth because it doesn't produce equal outcomes. In fact, he felt that 'the high degree of tolerance that democracies have for inequality might, in some part, be due to the legitimizing myth of meritocracy'.[62]

Ashoka University could easily have balanced out the Indian panel by including pro-merit thinkers from IITs, IIMs, The Indus Entrepreneurs, and numerous other institutions that pride themselves on India's meritocracy.

The contrast between Indian and Chinese representations of meritocracy in their respective societies is glaring. The Chinese do not mention social issues like Tibet or the Uyghurs whereas the Indians are obsessed with attacking their country's social abuses. We are giving concrete examples to show how India is being attacked in places like Harvard in the US, in its own liberal arts universities, and in countries like China when Indians are invited to speak.

Trivedi Centre for Political Data

Collaborating with foreign entities, Ashoka's Trivedi Centre for Political Data (TCPD) produces sensitive databases on India, which could be of serious concern to India's national security. It is a joint project between political and computer scientists. Its executive board comprises Ashoka's founders, Ashish Dhawan and Ashok Trivedi, as well as India's former chief election commissioner, S.Y. Quraishi, political science professor, Gilles Verniers (from France), and practice in computer science professor, Sudheendra Hangal.

The Trivedi Centre's scientific board is responsible for project conception, academic direction, and implementation. It is dominated by foreign scholars (mostly French and American) and Quraishi. Christophe Jaffrelot of King's College, London, heads this effort. Francesca R. Jensenius, of the Norwegian Institute for International Affairs, Milan

Vaishnav, of the Carnegie Endowment for International Peace, Susan L. Ostermann, from University of Notre Dame, Tariq Thachil, from UPenn, and Mukulika Banerjee, from the London School of Economics are on the scientific board.

French institutes like Paris Institute of Political Studies (Sciences Po) and LIA SPINPER funded by the French Ministry of Foreign Affairs are primary partners driving the research at TCPD along with American universities like UPenn, University of Michigan, University of Notre Dame, and the thinktank, Carnegie Institute of Global Peace. The Trivedi Centre is also developing domestic partnerships in India with organizations like the Centre for Policy Research and *The Hindustan Times*. Its output is regularly published in Left-leaning publications.

The Trivedi Centre is employing big data/machine learning and AI technology to study the rise of the BJP. There is nothing intrinsically wrong with this but it is worth pointing out that the databases could potentially be useful in an effort to influence electoral outcomes in India, including potentially foreign driven influences.

It is collecting big data from the past as well, dating back to 1962, on people, outcomes and candidates that participated in the electoral system and governance. Under the 'Social Profiling of Legislators'[63] project, detailed statistics on religion, caste, gender, language, education, occupation, and other demographics are also being collected and verified. This helps them decode the Indian political landscape and thereby shape the desired narratives. The vast amount of disparate data is cleaned, curated, and made available to researchers, both Indian and foreign. According to the website, the institute

> ... aims at promoting data-driven research, policy work and journalism on India's political life by producing and disseminating in open access scientifically collected and treated political data. ... also ... improving the quality of existing public data by developing and providing access to web-based tools adapted to Indian data.[64]

The People and Institutions Behind the Trivedi Centre

We will briefly explore the backgrounds of some key members that run the Trivedi Centre to show the lens and approach that drive its database mining activities.

Christophe Jaffrelot

French native Christophe Jaffrelot,[65] chairman of the Trivedi Centre is also a non-resident fellow at the Carnegie Endowment for International Peace along with Milan Vaishnav, director and senior fellow at Carnegie Endowment's South Asia Program. Carnegie Endowment is alleged to have close ties to the CCP:

> The Carnegie Endowment for International Peace – formerly led by Joe Biden's Central Intelligence Agency Director Bill Burns – has continued its relationship with Chinese Communist Party influence groups despite Burns claiming otherwise during sworn testimony to the U.S. Senate.[66]

Besides his role as chairman of TCPD, Jaffrelot is a fellow at its current French partner CERI-Sciences Po/CNRS, Paris, in mining India's databases and as professor of Indian politics and sociology at King's India Institute, London. He has a well-known history of attacking the RSS and has authored numerous books on Hindu nationalism and caste-based mobilizations in India. He was a major participant in the Dismantling Global Hindutva Conference. He wrote: 'Jobless plebeians joined Bajrang Dal and other similar lumpen organisations and started to get a sense of identity by fighting for the cow'.[67] Some of his work is listed in the endnote.[68]

The *Indian Express* celebrates him by saying that he 'offers valuable insights on South Asian politics, particularly the methods and motivations of the Hindu right in India'.[69] Not surprisingly, he positions himself as a voice for Indian Muslims.

Milan Vaishnav, Carnegie's India expert has written a number of papers that reveal his political bias. (See list in endnote.[70])

Gilles Verniers

Frenchman Gilles Verniers is a student of Jaffrelot and assistant professor of political science at Ashoka's TCPD. Prior to Ashoka, Verniers recruited Indian students at all levels for Sciences Po's data mining work in India. He has also developed executive education programs for Indian civil servants, and worked for thinktanks, corporates, and media.[71]

S.Y. Quraishi

Quraishi, a former chief election commissioner of India, is a member of the executive and scientific board of the Trivedi Centre. He is also ambassador of democracy at the International Institute for Democracy and Electoral Assistance (IDEA),[72] an intergovernmental organization with a mission to 'support sustainable democracy worldwide'.[73] He provides the Trivedi Centre with credibility as well as connections for collecting big data.

When discussing his book, *The Population Myth: Islam, Family Planning and Politics in India,*[74] Quraishi expressed some of his controversial views openly, such as 'Muslims taking to family planning faster than Hindus'[75] and 'it is a myth that polygamy is rampant in India'.[76] As an apologist for Muslims, he says that polygamy among Muslims is far less than it is among Hindus, Jains, Buddhists, and tribals.[77]

On the Karnataka High Court ruling on the hijab, Quraishi said that it is not the judge who will decide about the hijab but the maulana.[78] On Kashmir, he said: '*The Kashmir Files* is dividing the masses just like the terrorists.'[79]

We do not in any way pass judgment on his political ideologies but point out that there is a specific slant among many of those in senior positions at this Centre.

Output from the Trivedi Centre for Political Data

As explained in Chapter 10, archive building and database mapping can be the first steps towards compromising India's ability to control the discourse. Many such databases are being prepared by the Trivedi Centre.

For example, the TCPD–IAS is a dataset on Indian Administrative Service officers from 1951 to 2020.[80] Similarly, TCPD has also created a dataset of all the chief ministers of Indian states and their electoral histories between 1962 and 2021.[81] This data has been systematized and verified. Yet another dataset relates to the sociological composition of governments in India, both at the center and the state levels. The purpose is to study the demography of Cabinet ministers in detail:

> There is a lot of emphasis on the study of Prime Ministers and Chief Ministers in India, perhaps owing to a tradition of the concentration of power within the executive. We know less

about Cabinets' composition. Who are India's ministers? Where do they come from? What is their political profile and sociological background? How do parties form their governments? How often do they reshuffle their cabinets? And what are the discernible trends across states and across time?[82]

The TCPD has also developed a similar database of governors and the judiciary. It boasts of the impressive 'Lokdhaba' project showcasing all Indian electoral outcomes at the national or state level from 1962 onwards with visualization for easy access.[83] As social media becomes a weapon in elections, Ashoka University is using machine learning to collect vast amounts of data on election campaigning using Facebook and Twitter. Facebook India is a partner of the TCPD:

> The objective ... is to analyze political campaigning on social media at the level of contesting candidates. [It] would be more granular ... by looking at individual candidates, and thus being able to provide insights at all levels, i. e., trends within and across constituencies, within and across parties etc. ... we employ a mixed-methods approach, using ML-assisted human annotations for creating the data needed for qualitative analysis, and machine learning models ... This is particularly a requirement for studying Facebook ads, because the content ... is predominantly visual, making it difficult to run automated ML methods to classify the content. We have also engaged with TTC Labs [Trust, Transparency, and Control Labs] at Facebook during their Ads Targeting Transparency Design Jam workshop, which focused on better transparency on how political ads are designed and run on Facebook.[84]

According to TCPD's 2021 report, it has released a Political Career Tracker tool 'that enables users to visualize the political career of every candidate who stood for elections ever since 1962'.[85] It carries out extensive analysis of state elections and related topics. It has published thirty-three articles in various media and embarked on a data partnership involving the University of Michigan.

This kind of data collection allows TCPD to glean insights on the real-time operations of each political party, enabling its algorithms to learn how campaigns are created and operated, the popularity level of individual candidates, the vulnerability of specific candidates to be compromised, and the modus operandi for influencing the judicial system. The Indian government has announced that the next census will be an e-census, which will also connect seamlessly with birth and death registrations and people being automatically included in the electoral roll when they turn eighteen. People will fill in details from their mobile phones. It is expected to be the foundation for the next twenty-five years of economic development.[86] Reading the TCPD data with such other datasets will also reveal information on places that can be repopulated to change the demographics, or places where certain sections of the electorate may be intimidated to change electoral outcomes. Building databases, studying the processes and outcomes, monitoring current electoral proceedings, and leveraging media relationships positions TCPD to cause changes in electoral outcomes.

Christophe Jaffrelot has bragged about using TCPD's data with the support of its French partner CNRS. He illustrates his use of the database to analyze the caste dynamics of the RSS in words that could be weaponized politically:

> Traditionally, the Sangh parivar has been supported by upper castes. RSS was primarily a Brahmin organisation and the Jana Sangh was known as a "*baniya*-Brahmin" party. BJP has retained this characteristic but has been able to attract low caste voters too. The fact that it has retained its upper caste legacy is evident from the social profile of the caste background of its ministers, MPs and MLAs – something very obvious from the CNRS-supported data base that Ashoka University and Sciences Po have built under the name of SPINPER. [87]

The French Connection: LIA SPINPER

The Social Profile of India's National and Provincial Elected Representatives or SPINPER project is created by a France-based institute called LIA SPINPER, dedicated to collecting data of the Indian polity.[88] Many French institutions are involved, including Sciences Po and its research units, CERI, CDSP, and Médialab. Facebook India is a partner of LIA SPINPER conferences.[89] All use Ashoka University's

Trivedi Centre to collect sensitive information on the Indian electoral landscape. Like Harvard, the Leftist French academics also seem troubled by the rise of the BJP. The LIA SPINPER's very raison d'être seems to be to undermine the current power structure in India:

> The trend towards more inclusiveness that had started in the late 1980s, with the election of low caste members in the assemblies, has been reversed across the country. The comeback of forward caste, urban "middle class" Hindu males at the expense of rural low caste, female and Muslim representatives has been amplified by the rise to power of the BJP, whose Hindu ethno-religious populism has helped the elite groups to regain power. ... This analysis relies on the biographical data of about 70,000 elected representatives. The data collection phase combining data scraping and web mining for the information available online and systematic fieldwork for the others and the phase of data processing have both associated Sciences Po-based research units ... and the Ashoka University-based Trivedi Center (sic) for Political Data. The phase of data analysis will result in several publications ...[90]

Indian data sources are in Indian languages or in print which make them inaccessible to the French.[91] This is why the comprehensive dataset profiling of India's elected representatives is being built with the help of Ashoka's Trivedi Centre with Jaffrelot and Verniers heading the effort to ensure French control. The plan is to link Ashoka's large databases to other datasets:

> The data collected will feed the dataset gathered by (TCPD) on Indian election results. The study of the social profile ... must be complemented by a detailed analysis of candidates and parties (sic) performance, ... with a broader analysis of electoral outcomes. Further, the coding of geospatial variables such as sub-regions, districts or the degree of urbanization of each constituency will help conduct the analysis at various levels of observation. The SPINPER dataset will thus be connected to other existing datasets, including the affidavit datasets assembled by the Association for Democratic Reforms (ADR). ADR has digitized the affidavits deposed by all contestants to Indian elections since

2004, providing data on occupation, assets and liabilities, as well as on the criminal profile of candidates to elections.[92]

Ashoka is responsible for the stature of both Jaffrelot and Verniers, now considered experts on Hindutva and Indian polity. In 2018, they conducted a workshop in UC Berkeley to train fellow academics on 'the limitations of democratic representations in India – the case of Muslims and women'.[93]

The LIA SPINPER itself is funded by France-Berkeley Fund,[94] a partnership between UC Berkeley and the French Ministry of Foreign Affairs. Though the French government and thinktanks get easy access to India's sensitive data, this has not set off alarm bells in India.

The LIA SPINPER holds annual conferences to discuss the data produced by the Trivedi Centre. The topics it is interested in are illustrated by some of the issues discussed during its 2018 conference shown in the diagram on the next page.

The anti-Hindu agenda comes through clearly from these subjects. For example, when TCPD conducted a workshop on land laws in India entitled *One Thousand Land Laws: Mapping the Maze of Land Regulation in India*,[95] it did not research the issue of government occupation of Hindu temples and the misappropriation of temple lands.

The Trivedi Centre also shares its work with Harvard's Mittal Institute. For example, Verniers presented TCPD data at a Harvard Mittal Institute event moderated by Ashutosh Varshney. The event was on the *2022 Legislative Assembly Elections*, held within a couple of weeks after the elections in India. The institute stressed the importance of monitoring India's elections:

> ... elections were held across 5 Indian states over seven phases in Uttar Pradesh, Punjab, Uttarakhand, Goa and Manipur from 10 February to 7 March 2022. The UP and Punjab polls coincided with the 70th anniversary of legislative assembly elections in both states. The outcome ... has the potential to shape India's political future as we approach the 2024 Lok Sabha elections. Join our dynamic panel as they discuss the crucial role these elections have played and what the results mean for the country's future.[96]

The diagram on page 544 shows the intricate relationships involving the Trivedi Centre at Ashoka.

Ashoka's Trivedi Centre Enabled: LIA SPINPER Conference on Indian Polity

MUSLIMS
- Assessing Muslims Under-Representation in Karnataka's State Assemblies
- Do Muslims Matter Electorally in BJP's Showcase State Gujarat?
- The Highs and Lows of Muslim Representation in Uttar Pradesh
- Odisha: Where Muslims Hardly Matter
- Analyzing the Case of Missing Muslims in Maharashtra Assembly
- The Fate of Indian Muslims
- Querying the Indian Parliament: What Can the Question Hour Tell Us About Muslim Representation in India?

BJP/RSS
- Can Modi and UP Achieve and Sustain Hegemony?
- Sangh and Sarkar: The RSS Power Centre Shifts from Nagpur to New Delhi
- Fables of Free Speech and Violence: India Towards a Politics of Mania and Modi
- Uttar Pradesh, One Year After the Rise to Power of BJP
- Gujarat: The Showcase of BJP Rule?
- Can BJP Win West Bengal?
- An Ascendant Party Machine: Understanding the BJP's Sweep in 2019
- To What Extent is Odisha Still a BJD Stronghold?

VOTING/ELECTORATE
- Counting Votes Without Party Agents: Political Competition and Partisan
- Uneven Expectations: The Geography of Citizenship Practice in Rural and Urban India
- Cultivating Clients: Reputation, Responsiveness, and Ethnic Indifference in India's Slums
- The Stabilization of the Indian Electorate? Volatility and Vote Swing
- Regional Facets of the Lok Sabha Elections
- The Tamil Resilience
- Return of the 'PAKSHA' in Gujarat
- West Bengal: Contested Nationalism, 'Bengali-ness' and Electoral Violence
- Profile of the New Lok Sabha
- The Fault Lines in Dalit Representation in Tamil Nadu

KASHMIR
- Who Governs Jammu And Kashmir? A Profile of The State Assembly, 1983-2014, and its Relevance in State Politics
- Kashmir Since 2014. Trends in the Civil Unrest and their Significance for Party Politics

DALIT/OBCs
- Conceptualizing, Measuring and Understanding Discrimination Against Dalits in Gujarat
- Who Represents the Scheduled Castes in Assemblies? The Paradox of Reservation and Castes in Rajasthan
- Ezhava Representation in Kerala: Questions and Conundrums
- Dominant Castes, From Bullock Capitalists to OBCs? The Impact of Class Differentiation in Rural India
- Identity Politics and Economic Policy
- Parachuters vs Climbers: Economic Consequences of Barriers to Political Entry in a Democracy
- Sub-Categorization of Backward Classes and Scheduled Castes in Telangana
- Dalit Representation in the Hindi Belt
- The Impact of Class Differentiation Among Dominant Castes in Rural India

GENDER
- Women's Representation and Resistance: Positive & Perverse Consequences of Indian Laws for Gender Equality
- Performing Representation: Prospects for Women's Substantive Representation in the 17th Lok Sabha
- Who Speaks for Women in the Lok Sabha
- Women in the 2019 Elections: What the Data Conceals
- The Profile of the Women Candidates in the 2019 General Elections
- A Methodological Note on Designing and Executing Surveys for Women Respondents in Rural Haryana
- Women Candidates, Women Voters, and Gender Politics in the 2019 Lok Sabha Elections

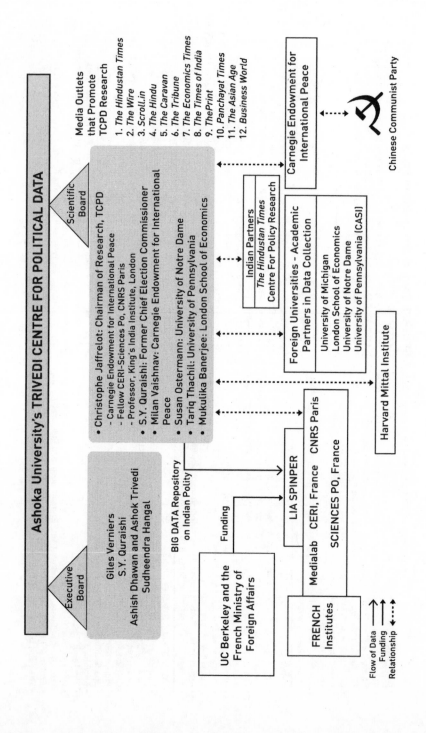

Ashoka University's TRIVEDI CENTRE FOR POLITICAL DATA

Executive Board

Giles Verniers
S.Y. Quraishi
Ashish Dhawan and Ashok Trivedi
Sudheendra Hangal

Scientific Board

- Christophe Jaffrelot: Chairman of Research, TCPD
  - Carnegie Endowment for International Peace
  - Fellow CERI-Sciences Po, CNRS Paris
  - Professor, King's India Institute, London
- S.Y. Quraishi: Former Chief Election Commissioner
- Milan Vaishnav: Carnegie Endowment for International Peace
- Susan Ostermann: University of Notre Dame
- Tariq Thachil: University of Pennsylvania
- Mukulika Banerjee: London School of Economics

Media Outlets that Promote TCPD Research

1. *The Hindustan Times*
2. *The Wire*
3. *Scroll.in*
4. *The Hindu*
5. *The Caravan*
6. *The Tribune*
7. *The Economics Times*
8. *The Times of India*
9. *ThePrint*
10. *Panchayat Times*
11. *The Asian Age*
12. *Business World*

Carnegie Endowment for International Peace

Chinese Communist Party

Indian Partners – *The Hindustan Times* | Centre For Policy Research

Foreign Universities – Academic Partners in Data Collection

University of Michigan
London School of Economics
University of Notre Dame
University of Pennsylvania (CASI)

Harvard Mittal Institute

BIG DATA Repository on Indian Polity

Funding

LIA SPINPER Medialab CERI, France CNRS Paris

SCIENCES PO, France

UC Berkeley and the French Ministry of Foreign Affairs

FRENCH Institutes

Flow of Data
Funding
Relationship

Between Kréa and Ashoka, big data on all significant areas of Indian life is being captured and stored in repositories outside India. High ranking ex-bureaucrats lead these efforts with funding from Indian billionaires and foreign NGOs, and under the direction and oversight from foreign academicians with well-known ideologies on India's internal political landscape. An entire cadre of professionals is being trained on Indian soil in the application of foreign social theories.

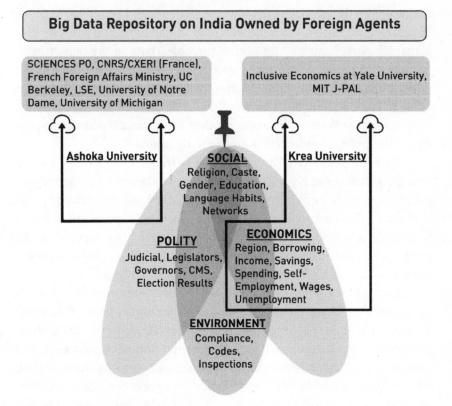

Centre for Studies in Gender and Sexuality

Gender bias, inequality, and related issues are significant areas to study, but we recommend these be done in the indigenous context. However, gender studies, as it exists in academics today, superimposes the Marxist idea of oppressors and oppressed upon gender and sex, and produce the anti-thesis to topple the established structures of society. This was explained in Chapter 1.

The Centre for Studies in Gender and Sexuality (CSGS) at Ashoka has an eclectic mix of faculty from diverse departments such as economics, biology, and English literature that have come together to propagate Woke ideas, and groom and recruit students for activism. To monopolize the discourse, they boycott many respected Indian scholars like Madhu Kishwar with decades of work on women's issues and Feminism in India. This preference for Western theories over Indian ones, and activists over actual scholars, leads us to question the objectivity of the department.

The US-based Wellesley Centers for Women is funding the development of the curriculum that is based on its framework, and this is being fed to CSGS students by Ashoka.[97] Ashoka is an effective pipeline for distributing Western ideas on gender, and a natural consequence of this is the political indoctrination of young minds.

One of Ashoka's founding members is Harshbeena Sahney Zaveri, managing director at NRB Bearings. Having studied as an anthropology graduate at Wellesley College, she played a key role in brokering this deal for CSGS. Her goal is to break the 'barriers of privilege',[98] which is amusing coming from one who owes a lot of her success to the privilege of inheriting her father's business. In 2016, Ashoka signed a Memorandum of Understanding with Wellesley College.[99]

There is a heavy use of Critical Race Theory imported from the US in the subjects being taught at Ashoka. For example, under *Governing Intimacies*, a five-year-long research project funded by the Andrew W. Mellon Foundation, various concepts like intimacy, sexuality, and queerness are framed in the context of caste and ethnicity. As expected, 'Hindu-Supremacist Politics' gets blamed for oppression. The categories of gender and sexuality are seen as having been 'racialized'. The law to ban triple *talaq* (the Islamic practice allowing a husband to declare divorce unilaterally simply by saying the word 'talaq' thrice) gets blamed as 'the BJP's and the Sangh's organised Islamophobia and anti-feminism'. The stated goal is to help in 'building political solidarities' among the victims of oppression.[100]

In the West, such 'Grievance'-based studies are being criticized as contrived academic fields, serving as Leftist propaganda machines.

Many of these 'studies' departments have been exposed by hoax papers. The high cost of these useless degrees is not only destroying the youth emotionally but also leaving them with no employable skills. Some countries are shutting down Gender Studies, and academics from the field call this pushback a Right-wing conspiracy for a heteronormative patriarchal society.[101]

American conservatives call such activism 'grooming', where young minds are tutored into activism that may include actually living 'trans' lives. They allege that these trends are due to organized top-down movements in education, Hollywood, and so on. They present data showing that many young people become confused about sexuality, or out of a desperate need for attention, fall prey to such grooming and undergo irreversible gender altering surgery which some later regret.[102]

In the West, there is healthy debate with both sides voicing concerns and presenting research data in support of their positions.[103] However, in India there is no debate at a serious level. Ashoka's connections with the sources of Critical Race Theories in America, combined with support from Indians, has turned this into one-sided activism. This is a far more sophisticated level of social engineering than even JNU.

These issues are being combined with other hot issues to increase the number of supporters. For instance, Ashoka's CSGS nurtures its Kashmiri research fellow Samreen Mushtaq, who writes about India's 'tyranny' in Kashmir and promotes secessionist propaganda. (See endnote for a list of papers that CSGS sponsored on the Kashmir issue.[104]) The Gender and Sexuality Centre combines these unrelated issues in a manner that is seen as trendy and cool by the youth.

The goal of Gender Studies departments in the US and their disciples in India is to introduce a certain kind of sex education in schools. This education is not for protecting children from abuse or pregnancy but rather to open them up to sexual encounters as early as possible in order to destroy their childhood innocence. As we saw in Chapter 1, childhood innocence is said to be a social construct created by White heterosexual males that brainwashed children into believing that sex between different genders is normal and preferred. This foisting is said to be a form of oppression. Therefore, it must be countered by introducing children to queerness at a very early age. The method results in making children rebellious and drawing a wedge between them and their parents, traditions, culture, and society at large. In other words, the manipulation of children away from their parents is part of the Marxist anti-thesis developed to fight the established order.[105]

Ashoka's CSGS is frantically importing the Western model for LGBTQ+ activism on its campus. As part of classroom instruction, it is systematically projecting the ideology through videos, study groups, and other methods. And in the spirit of Cancel Culture imported from the US, no opposing views or independent critical thinking is encouraged.

Under the self-proclaimed title of 'Centre of Excellence',[106] CSGS is also a nexus connecting leading centers bringing Wokeism to India to create new imagined minorities that perceive themselves as victims of the nation-state. Each new minority gets defined by a new set of grievances.

In a conference on Sex and Education organized by CSGS and its American partner Wellesley College, the goal was imported directly from the US: Views on sex should be included in the curriculum with the potential to drive a wedge between Indian children and their parents. This counter narrative will defeat the hegemonic narrative that has passed down from their identities and ancestral cultures. In turn, this will destroy the family structure and destabilize society, thus facilitating the creation of a new society. The conference participants comprised academics, activists, artists, and performers from the US and India. See endnote for the topics discussed.[107]

This seems to be Ashoka University's process of influencing Indian primary and secondary school children. The government's NCERT that is responsible for producing school textbooks, took an important step in this direction in 2021 by releasing a teacher training manual (later withdrawn) on gender diversity for schools. The manual included information on puberty blockers and blamed caste patriarchy as the cause of trans-phobia.[108] An external expert brought in by NCERT was Vikramaditya Sahai, a frequent speaker at CSGS, who makes no bones about the underlying agenda to destroy what he sees as the 'violent' concepts of gender, marriage, and monogamy. Here are some gems from Sahai's lectures at Ashoka:

> It's not simply the institution of marriage but I find institutions
> of monogamy and cultural ideas about [what] constitutes love as

oppressive institutions. These are institutions that uphold certain kinds of structures - no surprise patriarchy being one of them; and these are structures that do not allow for deep negotiation. I recognise gender to be deeply violent but it does not stop me from organising on grounds of gender; that is that which is violent that which is intrinsically violent can also become the condition of new possibilities of resistance of reimagining the world right.[109]

In some sense my critique of marriage is that I do not find anything worth salvaging in the institution of marriage. There is a history of marriage where it has been oppressive; it is oppressive both within and by leaving people outside but moreover I recognise that violence as such cannot be something I can give up in toto.[110]

Ashoka University's Bittu Kaveri Rajaraman was another advisor to NCERT. She is a Harvard educated trans-gender person, a professor of biology at Ashoka, and also on the CSGS faculty. Her discourses boil down to attacks on Brahminical patriarchy, male superiority, and anti-Hindu rhetoric with liberal doses of caste oppression thrown in.[111] She is also a popular speaker at JNU's Birsa Ambedkar Phule Students Association (BAPSA)[112] and Justice for Rohith, University of Hyderabad.[113]

To promote that gender is a social construct, despite being a professor of biology, she says that 'we should not biologize gender'.[114] She continues:

Organizers have asked me to address the question of gender fluidity as they put it. More fundamentally the overall question is gender itself because gender is a social construct that derives legitimacy from association with the biological category sex.[115]

Another 'victim' group nurtured by Ashoka's CSGS is the Bondage-Domination-Sado-Masochism (BDSM) community, which is also told it is 'struggling' under oppression from 'built-in caste and class structures'. This includes education on how kinky sex is practiced in India. Jaya Sharma, a member of the Kinky Collective, which conducts CSGS-sponsored lectures, has talked about the right to define pleasure and

change the paradigm that only what is pleasant is pleasurable.[116] She
has said that all desires including humiliation, and all fantasies including
rape are permissible as long as there is consent.[117] Anything deviant is
desirable because it challenges the existing ideas that have been propped
up by 'existing power structures and existing power hierarchies of
gender, caste class and religion and private property and all the rest
of it'.[118]

Centre for Social and Behaviour Change

The Bill & Melinda Gates Foundation has set up the Centre for Social
and Behaviour Change (CSBC) at Ashoka, and funds it along with
the Omidyar Network.[119] It has the clear goal of making 'impactful
behaviour change interventions' in 'low-income and marginalised
populations'.

> The vision of CSBC is to establish an institution, based out of India
> that is globally reputed for thought leadership and excellence in
> impactful behaviour change interventions for low-income and
> marginalised populations.[120]

The CSBC is bringing foreign influence into the Indian government
through several programs. This is a three-way partnership where the
government, through the NITI Aayog puts out a problem statement,
Ashoka produces the research to solve the problem and the Gates
Foundation funds Ashoka in line with its interests. The solution is then
adopted by the government. This kind of collaboration particularly
involves the governments of Uttar Pradesh and Bihar.

For example, the NITI Aayog worked with CSBC to address
behavioral barriers through communication and the 'framing' of public
health messages.

> To introduce a novel paradigm of behaviourally-informed
> policymaking in India, NITI Aayog partnered with the Bill and
> Melinda Gates Foundation (BMGF) and Centre for Social and
> Behaviour Change (CSBC) in 2019 for instituting India's first
> Behavioural Insights Unit (BIU).[121]

Dr Pavan Mamidi is director of CSBC and is charged with designing behavior altering experiments on the field with mobile labs and tents. Based on what is seen as 'problematic' behavior, the team offers solutions. Depending on the campaign or objective, the center builds suitable narratives through stories, folk music, and films. This format is more acceptable to the public and therefore, more effective in changing behavior. But research in brainwashing the masses can potentially be misused.

The CSBC suggests ways to change behavior using carrots and sticks as incentives[122] and espouses:

1. Policy changes through formal institutions;
2. Pricing to bring behavioral change in the markets; and
3. Changing social norms (informal institutions) that change behavior[123]

For example, during the COVID-19 crisis such experiments were conducted to change norms in society:

1. Bringing the norm of mask wearing;[124]
2. Breaking down ideas of 'fatalism' ('that pervades Indian' society); and
3. Dealing with what it considers dis/misinformation

One of the activities funded by the Bill & Melinda Gates Foundation is the reduction of vaccine hesitancy in India and promotion of the Gates' position on vaccines. By calling it 'fatalism', the Gates/Ashoka project is justifying changing the cultural attitudes of millions of unsuspecting Indians that believe in karma. This preying on innocent masses is unethical and could also undermine the civilizational ethos. And when people don't know what to believe, they become vulnerable to influence from Naxals, Marxists, and missionaries. We are not taking any position on the subject but simply drawing attention to the fact that this is the way people like Bill Gates could use Ashoka to change the behavior of the masses.

Through Ashoka, the Gates Foundation gains access to the World Bank aided Bihar Rural Livelihoods Project, locally known as Jeevika Trust.[125] The goal of this intervention is to increase vaccinations in Bihar by providing behavior changing solutions. Both the CSBC and the Gates Foundation also work closely with the Uttar Pradesh government.

In UP, we will work closely with the Government of Uttar Pradesh's Health Department, the Integrated Child Development Services (ICDS) department, the State Rural Livelihoods Mission (SRLM), the Information, Education, and Communication (IEC) department, and the UP Technical Support Unit (TSU).[126]

What many Indians are unaware of is that public trust in the Gates Foundation and its intentions are being questioned in the US.

Centre for Social Impact and Philanthropy

Chapter 22 discusses the Breaking India activities of Omidyar Network. Ashoka University's Centre for Social Impact and Philanthropy (CSIP) receives funds from Omidyar Network.[127] The CSIP aims to facilitate research for powerful Indian NGOs with foreign connections. Ashoka's infrastructure, faculty, and students play the role of consultants and lobbyists for policy changes with the government.

To appreciate the motives for funding CSIP, it is necessary to take a step back to 2015, when a Public Interest Litigation was filed in Delhi High Court by the NGO, Association for Democratic Reforms (ADR), seeking the creation of an independent body to implement the new FCRA rules.[128] This is a foreign interest litigation since ADR receives massive funding from Ford Foundation, Omidyar Network, Google, and Hivos (a Dutch NGO).[129] Ingrid Srinath, current head of CSIP was earlier CEO of Hivos in India, one of the parties that filed the PIL.[130] Clearly, the connections run deep. As early as 2014, watchdogs in India began to notice the work Hivos was doing:

> Hivos is a recipient of the Ford Foundation's generous grants. Stichting Hivos, the Netherlands, is also a donor who maintains a full-fledged country office in India, receiving $1.2 million (2014). Hivos (is) one of the co-financing agencies to the Government of the Netherlands, whose embassy funds Kejriwal and Sisodia's Kabir. Hivos co-funds ... CCD. It also supports, financially, one of the two Ford Foundation-funded NGOs of IIM Bangalore's Dean Trilochan Shastri, who also runs ADR. He has also been conferred Breton Woods Committee membership, thanks to the Ford Foundation's lobbying.[131]

Hivos is now partnered with Ashoka's CSIP on a project titled *Advocacy, Rights & Civil Society: The Opportunity for Indian Philanthropy* with funding from Omidyar and Azim Premji Philanthropic Initiatives. Its partners include Harvard Business School, the Gates Foundation, the ATE Chandra Foundation (Amit Chandra and Archana Chandra), Rohini Nilekani Philanthropies, and Oxfam.[132] It is investigating the devastating impact on foreign NGOs that violate India's FCRA laws. Its report proposed antidotes to the Indian government's clamp-down on foreign NGOs for non-compliance.[133]

The report examines the legal and regulatory frameworks of the government's 'heightened attention to inflows of funds and its impact on foreign NGOs which operate on the pretext of upholding social justice and human rights in India'. The report was based on grievances collected from NGOs selected by Ashoka. They are the usual suspects: Greenpeace, Hivos, People's Watch, Amnesty International, Oxfam, Ford Foundation, CRY, Open Society Foundations, MacArthur Foundation, Commonwealth Human Rights Initiative, Michael and Susan Dell Foundation along with the foundations of Ashish Dhawan, Azim Premji, and others. Some big NGOs have remained anonymous in the CSIP report. It says:

> ... opportunities have been identified for Indian philanthropists to play a larger enabling role in the non-profit sector, particularly by supporting certain kinds of rights and advocacy work that have a structural, longer-term impact.[134]

The research is based on anecdotal evidence and narratives by CSIP's own admission.[135] The CSIP started the process to undo the cancellation of twenty thousand FCRA licenses:

> CSIP along with research partners How India Lives and Lumen Consulting, spent many months studying government databases and speaking to a range of people to take a closer look at funding to non-profits in India. They've looked at how some of the changes made to the FCRA Act have affected our sector; and ... how philanthropy can step in to fill the gaps that have been created by around 20,000 FCRA licenses being cancelled.[136]

The report did not bother to investigate the violations by the NGOs. Instead, it focused on how to:

- Sue the Indian government including by creating a legal defense fund;
- Fund NGOs that lost their funding sources due to FCRA cancellations;
- Temporarily help those NGOs that have violated Indian law by providing stopgap measures in the form of 'bridge funding'; and
- Pressure Indian corporate houses to step up and fund 'social justice' and 'human rights' causes in India, thereby reducing the dependency on foreign funds.

The Ashoka CSIP project was concerned about a dip in FCRA funding from 2015-6 to 2016-7. Ingrid Srinath of Ashoka's CSIP, ex-Hivos executive, said:

> There are three broad things that Indian philanthropy can do to address nonprofits affected by the FCRA cancellations. One is to just support such organisations by creating a legal defence fund to challenge some of these rulings. The second is to extend support to organisations who have lost funding for no particular reason other than their funder being watch-listed. And thirdly, to look at creating some sort of bridge fund ... that will allow organisations who lose their FCRA to manage in the short run till they find alternatives.[137]

In India most of the rights and advocacy organizations are foreign funded while NGOs doing service on the ground are funded by CSR contributions and domestic philanthropy. Since 2009, philanthropy in India has exponentially increased from wealthy individuals, corporate CSR, and small donors. Indians and Indian companies still prefer to fund service and delivery NGOs rather than those fighting for social justice and human rights. The report provides information on how to change this balance and suggests ways to urge corporations and wealthy individuals to fund rights and advocacy.

While some Indian philanthropists have built universities, thinktanks and social organizations to do human rights and advocacy work, the bulk of such funding comes from foreign sources. The area of work includes governance, democracy, human rights, and so forth. For example, large portions of the budget of many reputed organizations such as Housing and Land Rights Network, Centre for Promotion of Social Concerns, Lawyers Collective, etc., are from foreign donors.[138]

The organizations behind some of the case studies presented by the report include the foreign funded organization Indian Social Action Forum whose license got canceled by the government when they organized protests against the Kudankulam nuclear power plant in Tamil Nadu.[139]

Ashoka's CSIP report coaches the foreign funding agencies on how to bypass trouble from the government. For instance, it has told its grantees 'to ensure that no project we fund has the word "rights" associated with it'.[140] *Another brilliant strategy it devised was to avoid non-profit organizations because they come under FCRA scrutiny and instead set up for-profit organizations that can do the same activism work using foreign funds without any FCRA constraints.*[141]

The CSIP also suggests that corporates can reduce the risk by collaborating with others rather than going solo. A good example is the Independent and Public-Spirited Media Foundation, which funds Left-wing media houses with some occasional crumbs thrown at neutral magazines like *Swarajya*.[142] This is explained in Chapter 20.

The CSIP report also suggests:

> Indian funders who are unable to take on more risk, could pledge to take over the low-risk grants from the portfolios of their peers who have a higher risk appetite. This would free up the latter's capital for more rights and advocacy work. ... foreign funders who are susceptible to actions under FCRA could take up low-risk grants from Indian funders and hand over the rights and advocacy work that Indian funders could support without the restrictions of FCRA.[143]

Ashoka University's Academic Partnerships

Harvard's early connections with Ashoka involved the co-opting of professors and the collaborations through the Harvard-Yenching

Institute. Over the last few years, Harvard has been preparing for more direct involvement with Ashoka.

For example, in 2015, Harvard offered Ashoka students a one-year online certification course in business for eighteen hundred dollars.[144] In 2017, Ashoka partnered with Harvard Business School to 'drive meaningful social change'[145] in the Indian non-profit sector. Harvard professors 'delivered classes to senior leadership, trustees and board members of non-profit organizations operating in South or Southeast Asia'.[146] Separately, Ashoka students partnered with Harvard US-India Initiative (HUII) in organizing conferences *in* India *about* India.[147]

A side-effect of partnerships with Harvard and other foreign universities is that they generate material that foreign scholars can use to create atrocity literature about India. The goal is to co-opt Indian students by feeding them biased versions of 'history', 'social sciences', and similar disciplines. These efforts are designed to help them develop a Western lens for viewing India.

For instance, in 2016, Ashoka University's conference on *Conservatism in India* generated the following kind of scholarship:

> Sharika Thiranagama, a scholar from Stanford University, presented her paper on 'The slow arc of emancipation? Communism and Dalit Lives in Kerala', and addressed the problems of inclusion when new identities break out through political transformations. ... she asked if transformations in caste practices is truly a sign of transformation, or whether policies that are enforced today are just a sign of accommodation, so these don't have to be addressed.[148]

Even a course on the history of cricket called *A Global History of Cricket* at Ashoka examines 'how racial, class and caste histories were intertwined with the game of cricket'.[149]

Of course, partnerships with a foreign university need not always be detrimental to a student's development. But as seen above, foreign partners are often interested in funding Woke 'scholarship', Grievance Studies or research on how to break India's culture, heritage and history, rather than build things of value.

Ashoka entered into partnerships with many Western institutions including with Yale University in 2015, expressing the hope that it would provide 'ways to further collaboration in research'.[150]

> 'During my discussions in India, again and again, Indian leaders told me that there is a vital need for liberal arts education in India,' Salovey said. 'I was impressed by the seriousness of purpose that Ashoka's founders and faculty have demonstrated.' Ashoka anthropology professor Durba Chattaraj said she hopes Yale and Ashoka will be able to enrich one another's anthropology and sociology departments through faculty and student exchanges, as well as research collaboration.[151]

Ashoka founders and funders are so enamored with the attention the university is receiving from Western universities that they haven't bothered to evaluate recent events like the closure of the Yale-National University of Singapore partnership. Singapore's bold stand against the partnership should have had these Indian do-gooders sit up and take notice.

On the contrary, after the passing of the NEP, Ashoka has gone on a partnership signing spree with UPenn, Carleton University, University of Michigan, Yale, UC Berkeley, King's College, London, and Sciences Po in France.[152] Harvard Business School now visits Ashoka to teach Indian students that merit itself is Brahminical patriarchy.

Western Academia's Intimidation of Ashoka University

In late 2021, Ashoka's vice chancellor, Pratap Bhanu Mehta resigned from his position. The events that followed illustrate how places like Harvard and Yale use Ashoka as a distribution channel for their 'research' and the nature and extent of their control on this distribution channel. Mehta's resignation letter stated that Ashoka found him to be a political liability. The Leftist masters in Western universities immediately got into action. Ashoka, after all, could only be allowed into the elite club if it toed their line. Sheldon Pollock of Columbia University lashed out immediately:

> Trustees must "provide a full, public, accounting of whatever policies or pressures brought about the circumstances that forced Pratap Bhanu Mehta's resignation ... My Respect for Ashoka

University Has Been Seriously Tested ... I gave the first of the
Ashoka 'Crossover' Series lecture unveiling the university to the
public later that year; I offered the commencement address at
the 2018 Ashoka convocation; I donated to its library my own
and my late wife's entire collections of books in 2019. And I have
known Professor Mehta for almost 30 years and have learned
from him for 30 years."[153]

Pollock noted that he was a consultant for Pramath Raj Sinha on the
founding of Ashoka University in 2013. He warned that if Ashoka did
not comply with his demands, there would be dire consequences: 'If
this is not done, and done soon,' he said, 'the stain on the university will
be indelible, and the support of its most fervent admirers permanently
lost.'[154]

Ex-Harvard fellow and Brown University professor, Ashutosh
Varshney (who in 2020 testified against India's CAA to the US
Commission on International Religious Freedom saying that it targets
Muslim immigrants) posted a threatening tweet:

If Ashoka founders think it was a company because they put so
much money in it, let us now talk business. Many in the leading
US universities were thinking of developing partnerships with
Ashoka and a lead founder came to me for a partnership with
Brown. Not possible anymore.[155]

Soon the who's who of Western academia wrote a letter with the usual
culprits as signatories. It was titled:

'"A Dangerous Attack on Academic Freedom" include Homi K
Bhabha of Harvard University, Erwin Chemerinsky of the Berkeley
School of Law, Rogers Smith of the University of Pennsylvania,
Milan Vaishnav of Carnegie Endowment for International Peace,
and Kate O'Regan of Oxford University.'[156]

Ashoka buckled under this pressure and apologized to its American
masters:

Ashoka University has admitted to "some lapses in institutional
processes which we will work to rectify in consultation with
all stakeholders", and also sung praises of the two professors

who have left. The members of the administration have also said that they "reaffirm our commitment to academic autonomy and freedom which have always been at the core of the Ashoka University ideals".[157]

The Western academicians' movements to champion dissent are a front to fuel sedition in India. They are known for ruining careers of scholars that merely have an alternate view from the one prescribed by them. Independently thinking scholars are often afraid to voice their opinions even if they are tenured, because of concerns around funding, student recruitment to their courses, and publication of their research.

Since Ashoka is not a research institution known for technological originality, it is entirely dependent as a foreign franchisee to build its brand. The withdrawal of foreign support would mean the loss of its propped-up image and prestige value. The Western academic cabal knows this only too well and mobilizes quickly to ensure that their position of power and privilege is not threatened. This is exactly what the British did in India with the zamindars and the rajas, allowing them to enjoy power, status, glory, and protection in exchange for subservience.

Ashoka was set up by Silicon Valley billionaires that are invested in the American ecosystem. They have convinced the Indian government that imported liberal arts is part of modernizing India. It is India's folly for naïvely buying into this idea. The Pratap Bhanu Mehta resignation corroborates this. The diagram that follows summarizes the vast ecosystem built by Ashoka University.

Ashoka University • Centers • Output • Who Controls it

Student Indoctrination at Ashoka

The university's strategy has turned it into a conduit for Harvard and other Western universities to create an ecosystem of knowledge supply and distribution. Ashoka organizes frequent propaganda talks by Marxists. Some of the prominent ones include Kavita Krishnan (on 'Hindu-supremacist' campaigns to criminalize triple talaq)[158] and musician T.M. Krishna (on ideas of equality, justice, and governance in his musical renditions). Thenmozhi Soundararajan of Equality Labs (discussed in Chapter 3) was invited to speak on *Engendering Caste, Sexualizing Race.*

Soundararajan blamed the violent 'Brahminical system' that is designed to exploit millions through sexual violence and gender control. She explained the unity of India's Dalit, Queer, Trans, and Feminist movements to fight Brahminical patriarchy, and draws parallels with American Black, Feminist, Queer, Trans, and related activism. She mapped White American heterosexual patriarchy with Brahmins and proclaims that caste dominance is built on rape, offering no evidence in support of her outlandish claim.[159]

The dangers of such an ideology-based education that Ashoka espouses is already becoming apparent. Two of Ashoka's graduates (Zainab Firdausi and Sparsh Agarwal[160]) founded Azaad India Collective (AIC) which was charged with undermining Indian interests by organizing anti-CAA protests.[161] This is aligned with an organization called Students Against Hindutva Ideology (SAHI) founded by the infamous Audrey Truschke of Rutgers University. It promotes the festival of Holi as being anti-Hindutva on US campuses. One of SAHI's causes as declared in its social media is 'Decolonize, Demilitarize, and Demand the Right to Self-determination in Kashmir'.[162]

When an Indian Army soldier was martyred in a stand-off with the Chinese in 2020, the social media chats of the privileged students of Ashoka University revealed their strong anti-national sentiments.[163] It is indeed amazing that the billionaires who fund Ashoka do not see these fruits of their investment as a disturbing outcome.

In 2016, a petition was drafted and signed by eighty-eight students, alumni, and faculty of Ashoka University calling for solidarity with scholars who were protesting the Indian state's atrocities in Kashmir, demanding a plebiscite in Kashmir, and calling Burhan Wani's (terrorist commander of Hizbul Mujahideen in Kashmir shot dead in a gun fight) death an 'extra-judicial killing'. When asked about this issue, Ashoka founder Vineet Gupta avoided taking responsibility and washed his hands off the matter, saying: 'With the Kashmir petition issue, university's objection was not with the petition or students signing it but with the misuse of the university name.'[164]

Ashoka is an echo chamber for Wokeism. YouTube has interesting testimonials of some students that throw light on the gravity of the situation. One student of economics said that the Ashoka ecosystem is diverse only in name because students of various identities don't necessarily mingle, the rich kids stick together, students from the northeast or foreign students all have their separate groups. The diversity of ideas is also absent. Additionally, the college has a prescribed narrative on issues and straying away from it is unwelcome.[165]

A physics student from a rural village said that Ashoka is teeming with rich kids that are on the Left but have no understanding of the ground realities. He said that Ashoka students will protest and demonstrate for the same things that JNU students protest against but with a difference. The JNU students are committed to their causes and end up in police arrests, whereas Ashoka students, because they come from affluent and well-connected families, will return home in a luxury bus after the protests. He also complained about the homogeneity of student ideas among Ashoka's privileged lot.[166]

A student of history said that the Ashoka culture is toxic, where students discriminate against other students based on their place of origin, with students from remote places in India feeling left out. The wealthy students deride how those from rural areas speak and look. The intense peer pressure makes vulnerable students unlearn their values and relearn new values just to fit in. Politically too, students with opposing ideas are treated as outcastes. The rich students are clueless about how to interact with people from lower socio-economic classes. Nor do they know what it takes to create something original.[167]

A survey was conducted by a student to find out how the non-Leftist students were represented. An article summarizing her findings stated:

> There's a general stereotyping of right sided people being homophobic and sexist with name-calling and being asked to 'fuck-off' even by close friends. One student said that 'campus does not let you have political discourse unless you think a certain way which in my opinion happens to be very elite-oriented'. This, she felt, makes Ashoka an elite echo-chamber of sorts. Another student said that many of his friends feel 'cornered' and don't feel comfortable expressing their views.[168]

It is interesting to note that students from the rural areas seem to be the ones questioning the lack of rationality and diversity of ideas at

Ashoka rather than the privileged urban metro kids.

As compared to our earlier work on Breaking India 1.0, NGOs now play a smaller role than universities that have not been scrutinized as much. Also, the universities have the protection of global brands like Harvard with Indian billionaires supporting them. The clamp-down on the abuses of FCRA as a route to fund dissent in India is made obsolete because the funding mechanisms we describe, do not fall under the purview of the FCRA laws.

Ashoka could have been India's answer to Western liberal arts. It could have been the go-to place for putting Indian civilization on the global stage. But both the elite businessmen that funded the institution, and the government that sought its advice, didn't care to do basic due diligence.

The end result is that an important Indian institution has become a shadow of Western academia, certainly not attracting talent back from the West as it was intended to do, but instead, helping foreign institutions expand their influence.

These are the consequences when Indians decide to imitate Harvard rather than re-building our own Nalanda.

20

Azim Premji's Media and Educational Impact

Overview

It is commendable that many billionaires are entering the field of education with their philanthropy, bringing their good intentions to educate India's poor and marginalized. Where successful governments have failed, the Indian elites have stepped up in large numbers to fill the void, expecting nothing in return. However, we raise an issue that is food for thought: What are these liberal arts universities producing and is it good for India? This issue is not about the conduct or motives of the philanthropists but about the performance of the scholars who enjoy their patronage.

Besides Ashoka University, the other prominent liberal arts universities in India include the Tata Institute of Social Sciences in Maharashtra, Azim Premji University in Karnataka, Shiv Nadar University in Uttar Pradesh, FLAME University in Maharashtra, and the O.P. Jindal Global University in Haryana. All of them lean on Western social sciences and humanities, ignoring India's own rich intellectual traditions in the same fields. Therefore, to a large extent our audit of their performance is driven by the very nature of Western liberal arts in which these institutions are grounded.

These private universities are intertwined with Harvard as the vishwa guru along with other Western universities. The exchange between them is twofold: The Indian affiliates supply data to their Western affiliates, and in the reverse direction they import Western theories and map them to the Indian context. Today, Critical Race Theory is explicitly or implicitly being applied to examine subjects like caste, minority religions, women, and so forth. The oppressor/oppressed and thesis/anti-thesis binaries from Marxism are foundational.

Essentially, the same theories, toolkits, and positions that we explained in Part 2 formulating in Harvard, are distributed by these universities, as their franchisees/agents, to the Indian government, thinktanks, corporate elites, entrepreneurial ecosystems, media, and the public at large.

This kind of an ecosystem was present in India even in colonial times. It has, however, recently become turbo charged because for the first time it is being funded and championed by Indian elites.

In this chapter we examine a mechanism in which Azim Premji plays a leading role to build a coalition of wealthy donors for funding media houses that propagate a certain genre of narratives. There is nothing wrong in doing this because it is one's freedom to espouse any ideology of one's choice and promote it openly.

We also discuss the role played by some of his people in developing India's National Education Policy 2020. Our critique is not specific to Premji's contributions to NEP 2020, but a much broader commentary on the Americanization of liberal arts in India. Under the NEP, American theories are being imported, adapted, and planted in schools, colleges, government, law, and just about every aspect of civic society.

Azim Premji University

Azim Premji University (APU) has a colloquium series in which students are exposed to selective outrage from voices like Harsh Mander talking about human rights, the activist Sudha Bharadwaj talking about labor unions,[1] musician T.M. Krishna on Brahminical patriarchy in the ecosystem of classical music,[2] and journalist Siddharth Varadarajan wondering 'What's gone wrong with the Indian media?'[3] The activist Teesta Setalvad is welcomed as an expert speaker to talk on history.[4] The billionaire, George Soros, too, has been a guest speaker at Azim Premji University.[5]

None of this violates any law or needs to be canceled. But students deserve a healthy balance with opposing views getting equal space, and this is what we find deficient.

The staple topics of research and discussion at APU are Hindutva, RSS, and Hindu nationalism. While focusing on such topics, they avoid researching or discussing issues like the activities of missionary-based NGOs, India's cultural and scientific contributions to the world, the digestion of Indian knowledge into Western frameworks, and so forth.

As an example of the stereotype scholar, Malini Bhattacharjee, a professor of political science talks about how a 'Hindu *rashtra*' or state, is being built by the RSS' notion of *seva* or service. She describes seva as 'creative and more covert forms of mobilisation that are seemingly benign and non-threatening. The strategy of seva is a classic illustration of this kind of political mobilisation'.[6] She worries that 'In the hands of the RSS leaders, it [seva] was consciously valorised as a distinct and "superior" category compared to the Western notions of charity and philanthropy'.[7] Her conclusion is that 'Seva thus becomes a process of identity performance'.[8]

As discussed in Chapter 1, a new trend in American universities is to blur the boundaries between scholarship and activism, and to replace rigor and objectivity with personal anecdotes that support the pet theories. Azim Premji University's faculty and its students, at times, push students into anti-national hooliganism. For example:

- When India's chief of defence staff, Bipin Rawat, died in a fatal helicopter crash, a graduate of the university's humanities department called him 'a war criminal'.[9]
- At least six members of the faculty have supported petitions by JNU students hampering efforts to clean up its campus politics and turn it into a place of serious learning.[10]
- At least four APU professors protested the arrest of a Delhi University professor for Naxalite (terrorism) activities.[11]
- Several faculty members attacked India's response to the terror attacks in Pulwama.[12]
- Many at APU protested the Citizenship (Amendment) Act, 2019 passed by the government.[13] They also protested the government's handling of the Delhi riots.[14]

Such activities by the faculty and students are well within their right to free speech and are not a reflection on the funding source. But we hope there would be a more open academic climate where opposing views get debated with mutual respect.

The Independent and Public-Spirited Media Foundation

Azim Premji has also started a separate non-profit entity known as Independent and Public-Spirited Media Foundation (IPSMF), which focuses specifically on funding media and journalism. Its donors include: Azim Premji Philanthropic Initiatives, Pirojsha Godrej Foundation, Cyrus Guzder, Rohini Nilekani Philanthropies, Kiran Mazumdar Shaw, Anu Aga Family, RDA Holdings, Lal Family Foundation, Sri Nataraja Trust, Manipal Education and Medical Group, Tejaskiran Pharmachem, Viditi Investment, Unimed Technologies, Quality Investment, and Piramal Enterprises.[15]

The foundation funds media outlets some of which are viciously anti-government leaning towards ultra-Left ideologies. These include *The Wire*, *The Caravan*, *MoJo Story* (of Barkha Dutt), *Economic and Political Weekly*, *Alt News*, and *Feminism in India*. They espouse controversial positions on issues like CAA, the farmer's protests, JNU protests, and support for the US-based Dismantling Hindutva conference.[16]

The IPSMF claims that its grants and fellowships are meant for 'independent and impactful digital-media entities, in encouraging digital-media ventures to focus on public-interest issues. In promising journalists to produce socially impactful content...'[17]

The Bill & Melinda Gates Foundation funded a *Global Media Philanthropy*[18] report that praised IPSMF for helping these new media start-ups in India's 'hostile climate' for journalism created by Hindu nationalism. It cited this report to expose what it considers harassment by Hindu extremists of journalists who were being frequently 'threatened, detained or arrested'.[19] We believe that it is for Indian courts to adjudicate on the rights of journalists versus what is in the best public interest.

Ashoka University's Centre for Social Impact and Philanthropy put out a report that hails this collaborative model. Since groups are harder to target than individuals, the report recommends this as one of the many strategies that non-profits should use to avoid the risk of violating the Foreign Contribution (Regulation) Act, 2010 and other Indian laws.[20]

The Azim Premji Foundation also funds some Christian missionary institutions based in India including the Rongmei Baptist Association

Nagaland; Rongmei Naga Baptist Association, Imphal,[21] which is also funded by the German missionary Brot für die Welt (Bread for the World),[22] an agency of the Protestant Churches in Germany;[23] and Christian Hospital, Bissamcuttack.[24] Again, there is nothing wrong with making one's own choices on what to fund, but by the same token, it is also fair for observers like us to point out the ideological tilt in such funding patterns.

Azim Premji Foundation's Role in the National Education Policy 2020

Azim Premji Foundation's current vice chancellor, Anurag Behar, was on the panel that drafted the National Education Policy 2020.[25] Behar, an ex-Wipro executive, supports the kind of Leftist/Marxist liberal arts education we have been criticizing. Behar praises the NEP for its liberal arts by saying it

> ...very explicitly expresses this strong commitment to liberal education, ... it is much talked about in the media; and the strong commitment in liberal education is not only at the level of undergraduate education but the notion of how grades 9, 10, 11, 12 are to be structured is also based on the essence of liberal education.[26]

He also praises that the NEP gives autonomy to these institutions from 'any kind of external interference'.[27] This autonomy prevents any government or other regulation from protecting our educational institutions. It thereby puts the nation's education at the risk of being taken over by governing boards selected by foreign masters and serving their interests. Foreign funding sources can end up driving the curriculum, course material, reading matter, research focus, and overall indoctrination of our youth aligned with their geopolitical interests.

In effect, the NEP throws open the Indian education field to foreign universities giving them access to a huge revenue-generating market.[28] This revenue could have been earned by educational institutions set up by and for Indians, with selective foreign educators invited to fill critical gaps.

The net effect is that nobody with a pro-India worldview can interfere, leaving the powerful Western institutions to run the show. Once again, India has turned into a mere consumer of Western education.

The NEP DISADVANTAGE – Outflow of Money, Data and Brains

The NEP Disadvantage: Outflow of Money, Data and Brains

A Gamechanger for Foreign Universities

- Easy Access to Indian Scholars for BI Work

- Ability to Freely Collect Donations from Indian Billionaires

- Education Business: Big Revenue Generator

- Access to, and Ownership of, Indian Big Data

- Distribution Channel for Scholarship

- Control of Narrative

India Stands to Lose

- Attack on STEM Institutions

- Flight of STEM Students – Brain Drain

- Indian Families Pay Hefty Fees for Useless Western Liberal Arts Education

- Students Turn to Activists, Sepoy Army

- Foreign Institutions Get Funding from Indians

- India Loses Taxes Revenues to Fund BI Programs of Foreign Agents

While it may seem that allowing Indian students to have access to 'world-class' education without having to travel overseas is a great idea, we must wake up to the fact that the curriculum and content are not under India's control. The research collaborations between Indian and global institutions simply have the façade of being a relationship between equals. But the statement below gives away the fact that as the junior partners in these collaborations, Indian institutions will basically adopt Western content and pedagogy just to appear 'global':

> World-class universities equipped with laboratories and research centres of international standards will be set up. Foreign partnerships will enable local institutes to design their curriculum in alignment with global teaching standards and offer a diverse

portfolio of subjects and specialisation to students.[29]

Besides, there is no clarification on who will conduct the research and in what areas; what resources will India have to contribute, who will store, control, and own the databases collected, and what will be its impact, especially in the context of Artificial Intelligence. In other words, what will be the short, intermediate, and long-term, outcomes of such projects?

The prior chapters discussed the biased research interests of Western academia. Also, in Chapter 4 we discussed the anti-meritocracy ideology being used to attack the IITs and other Indian STEM institutions. So, while foreign liberal arts and their ideologies brainwash our youth, the STEM graduates will continue to go abroad for better education and career opportunities. The strategy is already playing out, with MIT bringing J-PAL to India instead of bringing STEM collaborations. Clearly, India has failed to learn from China's strategy of focusing on STEM while banning Western liberal arts education from entering the country. This was explained in Chapter 8.

Foreign institutions are using the National Education Policy to set up non-profit institutions in India that solicit donations from Indians with tax benefits.[30] A good example is the Mumbai-based Harvard Global Research Support Centre India that enjoys this special tax status and carries out work for the US parent. Not only is Harvard colonizing Indians with its ideology and sucking out valuable and sensitive big data, but it is also doing this using Indian taxpayer money:

> Our local entity, Harvard Global Research Support Centre India,
> is registered as a section 8 nonprofit company, which enables us
> to support a broad range of activities and services across India
> on behalf of several Harvard Schools and centers.[31]

The Harvard T.H. Chan School of Public Health discussed in Chapter 13 has created a formal initiative called the HSPH–India Health Partnership to focus on database compiling in India as well as policy infiltrations at the highest levels. The Harvard Global Research Centre provides the Harvard Chan School with an important operational base to conduct research, teaching, and policy work throughout India. With staff in Mumbai, it serves as Harvard Chan School's physical presence facilitating the following activities: public health research; translation and communication of knowledge to promote evidence-based policies and programs; training the next generation of public health scholars and practitioners for leadership roles in advocacy and public service through field visits and placements; workshops; and various kinds of academic programming.[32]

Our main concern on NEP is this: *Though India has clamped down on foreign funding of NGOs that facilitate missionary work and Marxist/ Maoist inspired Breaking India activities, the NEP opens the door to all sorts of funding in the name of 'education' and 'research'.* And many enterprising Indians have joined this goldrush by becoming middlemen helping the foreign nexuses. The SANNAM S4 Group is a good example.[33]

The outflow of Indian big data and brains has accelerated with the NEP. It has opened the flood gates for the Breaking India forces to turn young students into sepoys that would destroy the Indian state. It's as if the Breaking India forces have scripted the National Education Policy themselves to facilitate their operations in the smoothest way possible. This is not the fault of Premji or any other Indian billionaire, but a critique of the government's policy.

21

Godrej and Queering

Overview

The industrialist family Godrej has set up an important organization that is leading India's Queer movement. India has its own respectful place for persons of all genders and sexuality, but Godrej is importing a Western model built on divisiveness, and inimical to Indian traditions. We hope this chapter sheds light on such potential pitfalls.

In the Vedic worldview, the one Supreme Being manifests as everything and everyone that exists. This is how we can celebrate all existence. Each distinct kind of experience enriches our collective experience of the world. The LGBTQ+ community has always been a contributing group to society by bringing its diversity. The LGBTQ+ individuals, and community as a whole, must be respected and given access to all resources for them to live meaningful lives.

Our concern is with the colonized manner in which the LGBTQ+ movement is being brought from the West to India, framed entirely in Western paradigms. Though our interest is to discuss the impact of this import into India, we will set the stage by giving the background of this movement in the US from where it is being spread worldwide.

Marxist Foundations

In Chapter 1, we explained the hallmarks of Marxism that have been the foundation of various American social movements including Wokeism and the LGBTQ+ movement. Some characteristics of Leftist social thought may be summarized as follows:

1. Society should be modelled in terms of the binary of oppressors and oppressed.

2. All kinds of marginalized identities must be discovered and taught that they have been victims of oppression for a long time.

3. The history of such oppression is old, and the structures of oppression remain buried beneath the surface. Until these structures are excavated and destroyed completely, the oppression will continue even if it is inactive and hidden.

4. The only way forward for society is by developing an anti-thesis to fight the prevailing thesis. The thesis is the discourse developed by the dominant groups and it is part and parcel of their oppression.

5. The fight between the anti-thesis and the incumbent thesis must be an all-out war leading to total destruction. There is no room for compromise or any win-win outcome.

6. For a massive revolution of this nature to succeed, the false discourse, called the hegemonic discourse, must be destroyed. It is the foundational narrative in all education, media, advertising, government policies, and indeed all organs of civic society. To fight this all-pervasive cancer, a counter-hegemonic discourse must be developed.

7. This requires suppressing free speech of the oppressors and only allowing the victim identities to articulate. All logic, rationality, and empirical evidence that the oppressors may put forth has to be blocked and outright rejected as part of the structure of oppression that is being dismantled.

8. Only the lived experiences of the oppressed communities should be heard in education, media, and policymaking. This amounts to Cancel Culture of the oppressors.

9. Since a given victim group is not likely to be strong enough to fight its own battle, all of them must unite and defeat the established order.

10. The single group of oppressors responsible for all these problems are Whites in the West and Brahmins in Indian society. These groups should be given no option other than to confess their oppression and apologize, and make amends by obeying what the social revolution demands.

11. One of the demands must be for equity, which is not tantamount

to equality. *Equality* means that everyone, regardless of race, caste, creed, challenges, and socio-economic background is treated the same, and given the same resources and opportunities to become successful. *Equity*, on the other hand, assumes that every individual has equal talent, skill, and other success factors in a given field; and any variance in outcomes is due to a rigged system built by White supremacy, patriarchy, casteism, transphobia, racism, and so on. The concept of merit is rigged. The focus should be to make the outcomes equal.

This doctrine, embedded in many successive generations of Marxist thought, is a sledgehammer approach to dismantle structures that were created far back in history by the dominant identities. Since race is not expandable to include new outside recruits, new minority groups and sub-groups are being created among the young, such as Blacks, Muslims, LGBTQ+, and women in the US.

Queer Movement in America

With the aid of billionaires and corporates, Wokeism for trans persons has penetrated the workplace, universities, elementary school curriculums, and everyday lexicon. A few years ago, the idea of various personal pronouns was unheard of. Today, it is an integral part of corporate email.

The Woke American youth are anxious, easily triggered, confused about their identity, gender, and sexuality. They want constant affirmation and social media is an echo chamber that provides emotional reinforcement. TikTok and other social media platforms for the youth are teeming with videos about entitled youth declaring their sexuality and their current place in the fluid gender spectrum. This is the current obsession. New categories of sexuality, gender, and personal pronouns emerge on a daily basis. The American youth are clearly going through a psychological crisis.

In the past decade, the number of Americans identifying as LGBTQ+ has skyrocketed suddenly and dramatically.[1] Also, by 2021 'gender' got decoupled from 'sexuality'. And the media has pushed the idea that the blame lies with White domination for making America heteronormative. The truth, according to latest theories is that gender, as we have known it for millennia, is actually a spectrum. It is non-binary and has *nothing* to do with sexuality. During the past decade, the number of sub-categories in the LBGTQ+ sexual group has increased and now includes: Lesbian, Gay, Bisexual, Queer, Asexual, Demisexual, Graysexual, Pansexual, Questioning, Queer, and Transsexual. Moreover, since gender itself is being considered a 'fluid, social construct', the categories of gender have also proliferated.[2]

In 2021, *Newsweek* published some shocking statistics: thirty percent of millennials and thirty-nine percent of Gen Z or Generation Z kids (aged eighteen to twenty-four) identified themselves as LBGTQ+.[3] This is three times the numbers for older persons, indicating this is a generational shift. Does this dramatic increase mean that more people are now comfortable identifying within these Queer categories? Or is this a socially constructed change caused by Wokeism?

Some people suggest that the obsession with gender identity and sexuality reflects the psychological state of attention-seeking youngsters that are taking refuge in such identities for security. This could be the result of American culture's latest crisis. For instance, *Newsweek's* pollster and sociologist, George Barna, attributes the trend to social and news coverage that makes it 'safe and cool' for young Americans to identify as LGBTQ+. He says that this is a lost generation searching for a meaning in life and the LGBTQ+ identity gives them a comfort group.[4] It also gives them a cause to channel their energies that put the blame for all their problems on some scapegoats like White heterosexual men.

National Public Radio reported that in an elite liberal arts college in the US, over half of the students identified as LGBTQ+.[5] The youth receive strong affirmation from mainstream media and even most US college applications ask students to talk about their sexual preferences and gender identities. There is also a sudden increase in persons undergoing brutal and multiple surgical procedures to alter their bodies to match their feelings.[6]

The Queer lifestyle in the US is being promoted as early as elementary school, thereby creating confusion in the minds of young children.[7] Due to their instability and loss of purpose, the youth are increasingly angry, narcissist, and are taught to accuse any counter viewpoint as a 'micro aggression'.

There is general understanding that discrimination and oppression based on gender identity and sexual preference is unacceptable. However, Wokeism is demanding the dismantling of the basic building blocks of society. It is changing the language, rejecting science, imposing its views on others, demanding reverse discrimination in its favor, and giving young people a sense of entitlement.

Trans rights have come at the cost of women's rights which took decades to achieve. Women's sports are being undermined by men transitioning to women and competing as trans-women. A transgender swimmer at UPenn has been on a winning spree in college championships, breaking many records. Teammates are uncomfortable changing in the locker room with the trans swimmer.[8] There are concerns of sexual assault when dedicated facilities like restrooms, spas, and even prisons are opened up to the opposite sex in the name of inclusivity. J.K. Rowling, author of the *Harry Potter* series, was trolled and 'cancelled' by trans-activists on Twitter when she said that the word 'women' should not be replaced by the term 'people who menstruate'.[9] She went on to say: 'If sex isn't real, the lived reality of women globally is erased.'[10] Gender fluidity would mean that there is no such thing as a 'woman' in the traditional sense.

We are not opposing any of these American social trends in which people freely make choices and propagate their preferences. However, we wish to discuss the manner in which this brand of Western social engineering has been adapted for India and penetrated liberal arts universities like Ashoka as well as initiatives like the Godrej India Culture Lab.

Trans-Queer and India

Indian civilization, unlike the Western, has historically had no issues with the idea of homosexuality and transgender peoples. There is an inherent acceptance in the Indian psyche that this is a private matter in which society should not meddle. And there is no injunction against them in Indian religious texts.

On the contrary, traditional Indian narratives have had representations of the male and female principles combined in the popular deity, Ardhanareeshwara. The iconography of this deity melds the female and male bodies, transcending the binary of gender and taking the seeker towards the realm of the limitless beyond all categories. There are also sacred stories of people changing their gender.[11] During pre-colonial times, up to the present, transgenders in India are specially invited to bless households during births, marriages, and other auspicious occasions.

But during Mughal and British rules, the Abrahamic views on sexuality were imposed, and the Queer community was marginalized and faced harassment. Even *The New York Times* has grudgingly acknowledged this fact, although it blamed only the British and remained silent on the role of Muslims:

> Hundreds of years ago, under traditional Hindu culture, hijras enjoyed a certain degree of respect. But Victorian England changed that. When the British colonized India in the mid-19th century, they brought a strict sense of judgment to sexual mores, criminalizing "carnal intercourse against the order of nature." That was the beginning, scholars say, of a mainstream discomfort in India with homosexuality, transgender people and hijras.[12]

However, Ashoka University's trans professor Bittu Kaveri Rajaraman blames Brahminical patriarchy for the stigma faced by the trans community. This is a blind copy of the way American Whites have been blamed, although Brahmins in India have not occupied the same social roles as Whites in the West. She writes:

> Traditional trans persons in Hijra and Kinner communities are already assigned forms of labour under Brahminical patriarchy which are stigmatised by mainstream society, and these forms of labour from badhai toli/mangti and dancing to sex work have all been shut down during the lockdown.[13]

In 2018, the trans community was finally freed of their illegal status introduced during colonial times. They are now slowly finding their lost place within Hindu society, even forming a trans-*akhara* (a type of spiritual group) to celebrate the Kumbh Mela:

> On Tuesday, her (trans woman Laxmi Narayan Tripathi's) religious movement, called the Kinnar Akhada, became the first transgender group to bathe at the confluence of the holy Ganges

and the Yamuna rivers on the first day of the ancient festival, traditionally reserved for reclusive Hindu priests, almost all of whom are men. "After centuries down the line, it was when the community finally got its due," Tripathi told Reuters, seated on a pedestal next to her Michael Kors bag, juggling calls on an iPhone. Many at the festival cheer Tripathi for reclaiming the lost place in Hinduism for India's "third gender", known as the hijras, worshipped as demi-gods for thousands of years, but ridiculed and sidelined during British colonial rule.[14]

In 2021, the Government of India awarded a Padma Shri to transgender artist Mata Manjamma Jogathi in recognition of her work in folk art. All of India cheered. The Ayushman Bharat Yojana or Healthy India Scheme now covers the cost of sex transition surgeries for transgenders. Various state governments are employing trans people. The government introduced a scheme to address health, education, welfare, skill upgradation, shelter and economic support for livelihood of transgender persons.[15] A new legislation was passed to protect their rights. Despite this progress, a lot more needs to be done for the community which continues to face stigma, harassment, sexual abuse, and poverty.

We must understand that the Western Queer/Trans movement is a revolt against the Abrahamic religions' bigotry on sexuality. If any old structures deserve to be dismantled, it is the structures of the Abrahamic religions. While it is true that India needs to work harder on the upliftment of the trans community, the Western Marxist approach is counter-productive.

As we saw in Chapter 1, Queer Theory has a larger scope of deconstructing and fighting all binaries and normative thinking, because it considers all normative thinking as rooted in power. We also compared this with Vedanta's central idea of knocking down binaries and recognizing duality as a myth. Queer Theory has borrowed these ideas and digested them in the same way as much of Postmodernism has borrowed from Indian thought. However, in Vedanta, the notion of the self is robustly held together by the integral unity. Unfortunately, Western Queer Theory misses this latter aspect because it is at the level of the ego and lacks an understanding of higher consciousness. *The real trans, according to Vedanta, is to transcend the ego.*

Western Querists have not thought through what one replaces the victim ego with. Hence, they end up with Nihilism. This is why their arbitrary and subjective lived experience has become the entire basis for truth. The oppressor's ego gets replaced by the victim's ego. The Indian path offers freedom on a grand scale, not only freedom from genders and sexuality but also from other kinds of ego-based identities. Woke activists, on the other hand, demand that to be in their movement one has to be an activist obsessed with bringing down others.

Godrej India Culture Lab

Apart from Ashoka University's Centre for Studies in Gender and Sexuality, which focuses on importing Western Queer Theory to fuel activism, the other dominant player in this space is the Godrej India Culture Lab. Both have very little to do with India's culture.

Nisaba 'Nisa' Godrej at the Godrej company is the sponsor of the Godrej India Culture Lab (GICL), an initiative created by the family to signal their progressive views on diversity by promoting the emerging and rapidly growing Queer/Trans movement in India.[16]

Most reasonable people in India are well aware that discrimination based on gender orientation or caste is totally unacceptable. Corporates are especially sensitive because hiring the best talent without discrimination helps business. Most Indians agree that transgenders need to be treated with respect and not be subject to harassment, just as seriously as one takes any sexual harassment against women.

Parmesh Shahani, a Yale University world fellow and a World Economic Forum young global leader, headed the Godrej India Culture Lab for over a decade, starting in 2011. A Queer activist himself, Shahani brought substantial programming related to LGBTQ+ issues and provided a platform for activists to voice grievances on caste, Feminism, gender and other forms of oppression. He is a successful DEI consultant to Indian business houses.

Shahani became a sought-after speaker for students everywhere including at Yale. Under him, Godrej also began funding fellowships to students to study contemporary issues in Indian society with a focus on identity politics.[17] Godrej India Culture Lab offers fellowships for students in the humanities and received the *India Today* award for

'Corporate Commitment to Art'.

An example of the kind of activist that Godrej promotes is Anish Gawande, brand ambassador for the Godrej India Culture Lab. A close ally of Shahani,[18] Gawande was a humanities student at Columbia University when he spent time on a fellowship at Godrej India Culture Lab and was moved by the experience. He is also a self-described anti-nationalist, founder of Pink List India, and the director of the Dara Shikoh Fellowship program, which is a partnership with the Harvard US-India Initiative.[19]

In his speech to promote Godrej India Culture Lab, Gawande closed by asking people to escalate the Kashmir secessionist movement. He said that GICL is a place to know more about activism by combining digital humanities with the Kashmir cause.[20] He also has a history of supporting rallies against the Citizenship (Amendment) Act, 2019. One of his articles against India was quoted at the US House Foreign Affairs Committee Hearing on South Asia Human Rights on Kashmir.[21] He has openly come out in support of persons responsible for inciting violence in Jawaharlal Nehru University[22] as well as in support of those who openly make claims of wanting to break India.[23] He has also spoken up against the Indian Army.[24]

Gawande shames LGBTQ+ activists who are patriotic Indians and refuse to align with his brand of Breaking India activism. A media report featured how GICL selectively de-platforms and cancels LGBTQ+ activists who do not support an anti-Hindu and anti-India narrative.[25] One such transgender activist is Gopi Shankar Madurai, who was de-platformed from a major event sponsored by Godrej. This, despite the fact that Godrej proudly claims to champion inclusivity and progressive policies.

As one can see, our critique is not about the rights of LGBTQ+ but about the way that community is being used politically to push unrelated agendas like Kashmir, CAA, and so on.

Human Resource Policies

Godrej's strategy is that LGBTQ+ activists should become aggressive once they infiltrate the corporate system. Parmesh Shahani brags about his success as an LGBTQ+ infiltrator inside the corporate world.[26]

Godrej has defined its human resource policies on LGBTQ+ issues and lobbies other companies to adopt them using corporate ESG ratings as a tool. By embedding aggressive demands for the LGBTQ+ community, their strategy is to pressure companies to follow the lead of Godrej.

Shahani has drafted *A Manifesto for Trans Inclusion in the Indian Workplace*[27] in which he lists demands that include a variety of costly plastic surgeries that company insurance should cover, in order to be considered inclusive for trans people. He also includes a tall order of feminizing and masculinizing surgical and non-surgical procedures.[28]

Shahani is clearly an activist when he says: 'It is important to remember that when an individual chooses to transition, the organisation also transitions along with them.' He accuses corporates of being transphobic if they don't accept his approach. The manifesto states that companies should 'avoid gendered language' (such as 'He/She'). He believes using gendered language shows an unconscious bias and corroborates the fact that the company is not a trans-friendly workplace.[29]

Shahani teaches Indian corporates the latest American practices including language, reorganizing of the workplace, and constant retraining of employees on trans issues. The manifesto also advocates a corporate standard that 'New employees should have a compulsory training module on gender identity'.[30] It wants that the 'dress code should be gender neutral', i.e., it should not be gendered (such as skirts for women, ties for men).[31]

While we agree that transgenders need restrooms that they are comfortable using, Shahani goes a step further by saying that women should be comfortable with transgenders (who usually have male genitalia) using women's restrooms. He writes:

> gender neutral washrooms are better as opposed to 'third gender'
> or 'transgender', because those would create an obvious divide.
> Trans employees that aren't 'out' yet might not want to use a
> 'third gender' restroom, whereas gender neutral washrooms are
> open to everyone.[32]

Also, he wants every company to consider special transportation options for transgender inclusivity and help them find secure housing.[33] On corporate recruitment, Shahani says that in order to be trans-friendly, companies 'should relax their criteria and evaluate skills such as communication and presentation if they truly want to further inclusion in the company'.[34]

Importing Intolerance from American Wokeism

During a talk at Yale, Shahani displayed his intolerance for anyone who disagreed with him. This is an imitation of American Wokeism's Cancel Culture against all dissent. A report on his talk says that he wants to

> leave no room for doubters. "When someone in the room stands up and says, 'let me play Devil's advocate for a moment,' say 'No.' If someone in the room can't be an angel of hope, of good sense, then no. Shut up the naysayers," Shahani said, smiling but serious. "We don't want you at this moment. We don't want you ever."[35]

While awareness, policies of equal opportunity, and non-harassment are noble pursuits, Shahani pushes his agenda aggressively in Godrej, and then uses the 'Godrej vantage point' to promote his activism to other corporations. His demands are steep and if an executive resists or wants to debate the proposals on LBGTQ+ within the corporation, he is simply bullied into silence. Shahani repeats the same points everywhere with increasing passion:

> There is always some person at a meeting who, when you suggest anything radical or innovative, and this person tends to be a man and in my experience to be an older man, this person will. ... the first thing that you should do when you encounter this person is put your hands up and say, 'NO', just 'NO!' Maybe you shouldn't play devil's advocate for a moment because you know the devil has many advocates...... that's my light answer...because there are so many good ideas that have been sacrificed this altar of this devil's advocate nonsense and this nonsense always comes from someone who is scared, someone who is older, who is scared, the world is changing around them, they don't know, so they want to maintain the status.[36]

As discussed in Chapter 1, this is the exact same strategy used by Critical Race Theory proponents in the US like Robin DiAngelo and Ibram

X. Kendi who say that any opponents must be dismissed, even if that means canceling the person or shouting them down. If we replace the term racism with transphobia in the writings of DiAngelo and Kendi, it is exactly the strategy that Shahani is adopting. Wokeism's toolkits teach that grievance groups should bully those who have doubts until they succumb.

Shahani refuses to entertain questions even from executives who inherently have a right and responsibility to debate the HR policy. We find his demands unreasonable: It is one thing to expect that the workplace gives everyone equal opportunities, and is harassment-free, but totally another to demand that the LBGTQ+ community be represented in huge numbers within the business. Shahani even wants to tie business leaders' compensation based on the queer and trans people they hire.[37]

Inadvertently, Godrej ends up supporting the Breaking India forces by providing a platform for political activists. For example, India Foundation for the Arts, an NGO that promotes Leftist artists, was on the Godrej India Culture Lab platform to talk about the importance of funding dissenting narratives through art.[38] Arundhati Ghosh of IFA openly said that they give grants for art that is political: 'We support a lot a work that is in unexplored areas that are looking at caste, gender, sexuality...'[39]

The India Foundation for the Arts has wealthy corporate donors and business leaders on its list of patrons and an annual budget of three to five crore rupees for grants and programming.[40] Many American and Indian corporates are also listed as donors.

In conclusion, we feel that Godrej has been a pioneer in introducing Indian businesses to LGBTQ+ sensitivites. But the manner in which their leading voices have implemented this vision has turned it into partisan politics on issues (like Kashmir, CAA, and so on) that are unrelated to the needs of the LGBTQ+ community. A better approach in our view would be one based on Indian traditional ideas respecting the LGBTQ+ individuals without meddling with divisive politics.

22

Omidyar Network:
Trojan Horse in India

Overview

Omidyar Network India (ONI), based out of Mumbai, is the Indian initiative by Pierre Morad Omidyar, the founder of eBay, a man with a net worth of around twenty billion dollars. He is a great example of a philanthropist wanting to change the fundamental workings of society and politics. A reasonable way to introduce him would be to think of him as a younger version of another billionaire, George Soros. Both are ultra-wealthy and self-made and want to use their wealth to bring about social change worldwide in accordance with their favorite model of how society ought to be.

Both are portrayed as humanitarians who are 'protecting democracies'. They want to help societies fight authoritarianism. Both are the proverbial 'good cops' operating on the global frontier where savages (i.e., those that disagree with their worldviews) and their cultures need to be civilized.

Between them, Omidyar is far more tech savvy and strategic in his approach to social engineering. His 'investments' are couched in carefully selected jargon, and one must dig deeper to tease out the socio-political disruptions hidden beneath the surface. A *Forbes* article depicts Omidyar as a champion protecting 'democracies under attack'.[1] When he invests in ventures that offer 'data protection and privacy rights', the long-term vision is to protect citizens from their own governments that might use the new technologies for surveillance and control. Ironically, many of his own ventures are specifically in the field of data collection, behavioral analysis, and different kinds of AI applications.

As a foreign entity, Omidyar is remarkable for having its own distribution channel in India, one that is deeply embedded in Indian affairs from the highest levels of government to businesses and all the way down to the level of individual citizens.

By using a web of technology partnerships with the Central and state governments and their various departments, the Omidyar Network India has positioned itself between the Indian people and their governments. Firstly, this allows it to collect valuable data on Indians and develop and study models of society and behavior for the purpose of future social engineering. Secondly, this positions it effectively as a parallel governance structure, ironically being built with the help of the Indian government itself. We will show various strategies used by Omidyar to facilitate the achievement of these ends.

By comparison, earlier civilizing missions from the West were less sophisticated, requiring more time, resources, and manpower. Omidyar's approach is far more efficient because the Indians themselves do the work, generate revenue and provide feedback for real-time monitoring. They are often young, inexperienced and bright, and are being carefully groomed into the kind of leaders that can fulfil his mission. Additionally, Omidyar has investments in organizations of strategic value that can yield datasets or provide the desired media coverage.

Background: The American Parent

Though our interest here is in Omidyar's Indian ventures implemented under Omidyar Network India, we will first explain his US-based activities to provide a global picture of how he operates.

At the outset we wish to clarify that we do not know of any unlawful activities he has performed. He has every right to spend his money to impact societies according to his ideology. In fact, many of the projects he funds in India help causes that are dear to us, and the entrepreneurs he supports are bright young men and women that deserve encouragement.

We will refer to an investigative report on Omidyar's US activities as a starting point to understand the big picture. Titled, *The Billionaire Takeover of Civil Society*, the Canadian author Roslyn Fuller characterizes Omidyar as part of an even bigger 'NGO-industrial complex, which includes an end-to-end web of political financing'.[2] She writes:

If one accepts what 'givers', like Omidyar et al, say, it becomes apparent that rather than participating in traditional acts of charity, like founding a hospital for the needy, they are attempting to engage in 'social engineering' – that is, using their resources to artificially change the structure of society to what they think it should be. If successful, this would amount to an extreme circumvention of democracy, utilizing money not just to win elections, but to substitute paid or subsidized content for actual support, and thereby flip an entire political culture on to a different track by amplifying some voices and drowning out others.[3]

The diagram opposite reveals that there is a dense network of funds, and these funds give money to other funds, which give to other funds, and so on. This obscures the transparency of where the funds originate and where they end up. This is ironic considering that a favorite word used to describe Omidyar's philanthropy is 'transparency' in governance worldwide.[4]

The funds shown in the top line of the diagram are all from organizations owned by Omidyar. The organizations at the bottom belong to other billionaires collaborating on similar causes. The purpose here is to show how these groups are part of a large ecosystem with interrelated agendas.

Let us zoom into one of the funding sources, Luminate, which is part of the Omidyar Group and chaired by Pierre Omidyar. One of the organizations that Luminate funds is New Media Ventures: Innovation Fund (NMV). According to an article by Luminate: 'New Media Ventures casts a wide net to defend democracy in the U.S.'.[5] It is described as a seed fund to support media and tech start-ups that 'disrupt politics and catalyze progressive change'. They are proud that their start-ups 'spark civic engagement', 'change culture' and 'build movements'. The goal is to invest in 'entrepreneurs and activists wrestling with the biggest challenges facing our democracy'.[6] All these are nice ideals to help save the world, but in reality, they are not neutral and are loaded with ideological biases from the social sciences.

For instance, we noted in an earlier chapter that NMV is the main funding source for Equality Labs, the champion of the movement to

THE OMIDYAR GROUP

Provide Funding

formally classify caste as racism in American industry, civic society, and college campuses. The flow of funds from Omidyar is as follows:

Omidyar ➔ Luminate ➔ New Media Ventures ➔ Equality Labs[7]

The following diagram zooms into a sample of the funding provided by Luminate in the US. This shows how vast the footprint of just one of Omidyar's funding mechanisms is.

Omidyar's activities are described with great precision – quite like an engineering project. There is the aura of a highly disciplined, formal process. Young technocrats are impressed by the jargon that makes them feel like proud members of a movement driven by 'facts', 'science', 'evidence-based decision-making', and various kinds of 'toolkits'. Omidyar also invests in an extensive network of 'research' institutes that compile information and develop position papers for advocacy. This so-called 'groundbreaking research' is part of the complex web that supports their ideology.

What Roslyn Fuller finds fake about Omidyar is that the youthful participants aren't so much being empowered as instrumentalized. After all, they are part of the portfolio of an investment fund that is using them to 'shift power'. Almost everyone involved is young and very inexperienced, but highly paid. They comprise an army of foot soldiers continuously on patrol, protecting the cause and expanding its reach. The system is incestuous. The inter-related organizations cite each other's work and partner among themselves. The same staff and leaders get recycled.

This complex web of start-ups, projects, and collaborations drives the hunger for oligarchic power. Glenn Greenwald, who co-founded *The Intercept* as a 'platform for voices too anti-establishment and radical for mainstream corporate outlets' talks about how 'it is simply unavoidable — inevitable — that the ideology, views and political agenda of a billionaire funder will end up contaminating and dominating any project for which they are the exclusive or primary funder'.

This is particularly true when the concerned billionaire-founder is on a mission to change the world according to his own ideology. In this case, it is not enough for him to uplift the underclasses, which is what he ostensibly tries to do and how he frames his activities. He must go a step further to control the discourse. Greenwald says:

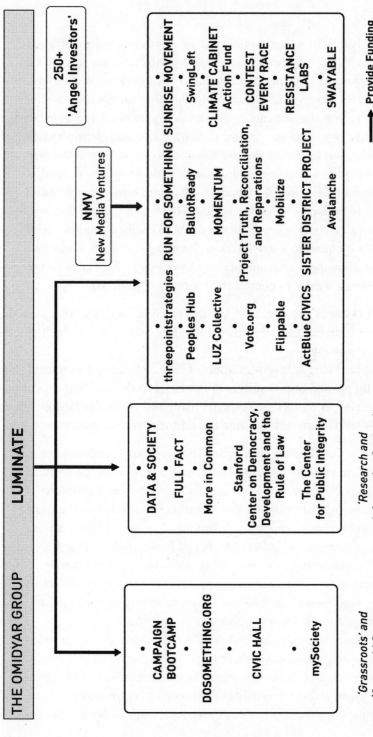

THE OMIDYAR GROUP

LUMINATE

250+ 'Angel Investors'

NMV New Media Ventures

'Grassroots' and 'Outreach' Groups
- CAMPAIGN BOOTCAMP
- DOSOMETHING.ORG
- CIVIC HALL
- mySociety

'Research and Information Centers'
- DATA & SOCIETY
- FULL FACT
- More in Common
- Stanford Center on Democracy, Development and the Rule of Law
- The Center for Public Integrity

- threepointstrategies
- RUN FOR SOMETHING
- SUNRISE MOVEMENT
- Peoples Hub
- BallotReady
- SwingLeft
- LUZ Collective
- MOMENTUM
- CLIMATE CABINET Action Fund
- Vote.org
- Project Truth, Reconciliation, and Reparations
- CONTEST EVERY RACE
- Flippable
- Mobilize
- RESISTANCE LABS
- ActBlue CIVICS
- SISTER DISTRICT PROJECT
- Avalanche
- SWAYABLE

→ Provide Funding

Omidyar is not some apolitical or neutral guardian of good internet governance; he is a highly politicized and ideological actor with very strong views on society's most debated questions. And that is why it is so dangerous that the campaign to control and police the internet — to launch pressure campaigns to further centralize the control over what can and cannot be said online, and to further restrict the range of views that is deemed permissible — is being funded almost entirely by a small handful of multi-billionaires like Omidyar. No matter how benevolent and well-intentioned they may be, the power and control they will *inevitably* wield, even if they try not to, will be limitless. And when it comes to a free internet, few things are more dangerous than allowing a tiny number of like-minded billionaires to use their vast wealth to control the contours of permissible speech.[8]

The end result is the commodification of civic society's norms for the benefit of billionaires and multimillionaires. They are the high priests on a holy mission.

Despite being the co-founder of *The Intercept*, Greenwald was eventually pushed out. Omidyar didn't need to do anything except pay hefty salaries to the senior editorial team and make his far-Left views well-known. Greenwald explains the editorial team's position:

> Despite Omidyar's genuine affirmation of editorial independence, they live in complete captivity to, and fear of, Omidyar's whims and preferences. ... editors and senior writers at The Intercept receive gigantic, well-above-the-market salaries. Because the site depends almost entirely on Omidyar's infinite wealth, it does not sell any subscriptions or ads and it therefore does not have any pressure to produce at all in order to generate revenue. ... enormous salaries, endless expense accounts, a complete lack of job requirements, and no need even to attract an audience...the money flows in from Omidyar no matter what.
>
> They work in an industry where jobs disappear with astonishing frequency, where layoffs are the norm, where the very existence of most organizations is precarious, and where the slightest dissent from liberal orthodoxies can render someone permanently unemployable. Those who work in outlets funded

by billionaires have essentially won a type of lottery, ... very few people are willing to risk losing a winning lottery ticket, especially if they know they have no alternatives in the event that their security blanket is taken away...

...The senior editorial management absolutely knows that their only real job is to foster a climate that will keep Omidyar happy, which means only hiring or publishing voices that will not offend him, ensuring that *The Intercept*'s political and journalistic posture is aligned with his ideological worldview and, most of all, prohibiting anyone or any journalism from remaining at The Intercept if it strays too far from Omidyar's political project.[9]

It is a none-too-subtle way of buying out people and relocating their loyalties while operating within legal boundaries.

While shouting about saving democracy, what these billionaires are actually doing is sidelining and diminishing the established structures and replacing them with their new model of how society ought to function. All this social engineering is a revolution for 'the greater good'.

Taxable Companies Replace Traditional Tax-exempt Non-Profits

As billionaires' ambitions to rule the world grow, they are choosing to establish for-profit companies as a new structure for 'philanthropy' instead of the traditional non-profit structure. Although non-profit structures are tax-exempt, the drawback is that their tax filings are public information. They want to keep their big ambitions of controlling the discourse and playing God confidential. Hence, the billionaires use a structure called 'impact investing' that is for-profit and pays tax, but the financial details are private. For example, Mark Zuckerberg of Meta Platforms is giving up tax exemption for his Chan Zuckerberg Initiative, as a recent *Forbes* article explained:

> 'By using an LLC instead of a traditional foundation, we receive no tax benefit from transferring our shares to the Chan Zuckerberg Initiative, but *we gain flexibility to execute our mission more effectively*,' Zuckerberg wrote. ... the LLC structure enables him and Priscilla Chan to invest in private (including for profit)

companies as well as engage in policy debates—also known as lobbying.[10]

The article also points to Pierre Omidyar, who prefers privacy and flexibility in how he 'invests' in impact investing. This is why he has so many front organizations that he funds with private money. The details are kept murky and obscured from public scrutiny. It states:

> A few other billionaires have pursued a similar strategy. Pierre Omidyar, the founder of eBay, is perhaps the best known for mixing investments in for-profit and donations to non-profit entities through his Omidyar Network.[11]

These billionaires have the financial strength to bypass FCRA regulations, and enter India as a for-profit business, to conduct their Breaking India activities. India needs to therefore take another look at foreign enterprises entering India on the pretext of doing business. It is going to be a challenge to separate the wheat from the chaff, but that is the need of the hour.

Omidyar Network India

In India, Omidyar's investments cover the entire spectrum of the political process. Here, the movement of money, influence, and big data is even more convoluted and murky than in the US and hides behind good public relations with officials, and lots of skillful rhetoric about helping the bottom layers of society. In effect, there is significant 'insider trading' among the various ventures and projects controlled by ONI.

Omidyar Network India presents itself in three ways: venture capitalist, social mobilization group, and mentor for young tech-savvy Indians.

It uses the term 'Next Half Billion' (NHB) to refer to the bottom half of India's population as its main target. Like the missionaries of the Joshua Project trying to spread the good news to the unreached, ONI targets those that have not been reached enough by technology to bring about social transformation. In the process, ONI builds databases that have financial and national security implications. There are four ways in which ONI wants to change Indian society:

1. Build <u>infrastructure</u> to implement tech solutions that will transform society and align it with ONI's ideology.

2. Invest in innovative <u>entrepreneurs and leaders</u>, especially the young using the latest technology, initiatives, and opportunities. Turn them into Omidyar's loyal army of youth leaders and help manage their careers.
3. Create a network of <u>tech start-ups</u> with equity enabling this social engineering to become financially self-sufficient.
4. Influence the <u>Indian government's policies</u> by funding various organizations, including its own start-ups, industry organizations, and established institutions.

This four-pronged approach is rapidly building ONI's footprint in India. It is very open about this multifaceted strategy and its websites and social media publicity are very informative.

The following diagram shows the four kinds of investments, while the circle in the centre shows the resulting leverage.

Surveillance and Disruption

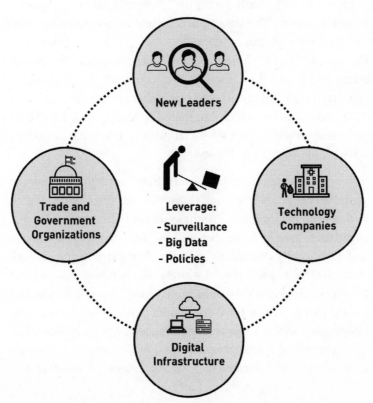

It can easily be surmised that Omidyar's global strategy is playing out in India as well. It is built around technology platforms that ostensibly serve the Indian people. The vision and specific goals are carefully couched in politically correct terms, such as 'inclusion', 'social mobility', 'helping the underclass', 'bringing rights to the masses', 'citizens' relationship to government', 'increasing transparency', and so on that draw attention away from the fact that their data is bleeding out.

Upon closer examination, one finds that this positions ONI to re-engineer the way Indians think, their aesthetics and values, the kind of products they like, the leaders they will be loyal to, etc.

The Reincarnation of the Joshua Project

Readers familiar with the Joshua Project will recall the outcry it created in India when our book, *Breaking India*, exposed this sinister project by the Church's global headquarters to develop an extensive database of every district in India with details on religious leaders, affiliations, and socio-demographics. The stated purpose was to micro-target individual communities for missionary work.[12]

The project profiles individual Indian communities for evangelical marketing and shares this data with Western intelligence agencies. This facilitates transnational agencies to remotely manage their interventions in Indian communities, which can include creating social turbulence in the guise of educating them on social justice. The book *Breaking India* summarized the project as follows:

> There are institutions which study India academically for the purpose of evangelism and have formal links with Indian evangelical institutions. All these factors ... create a strong population-base in India that will be financially, institutionally and emotionally dependent upon the West's right-wing. ... both state and non-state players—invest in building institutional infrastructural logistics in India, for effective control at social and political levels. A base for Western domination is being effectively constructed within India through evangelical organizations. The goal is to spread a fundamentalist kind of Christianity and create a population of believers with strong emotional bonding and

dependence on the West. The Christian right in the United States is particularly active and ambitious in this regard.[13]

We revealed that just one of several data gathering groups, Gospel for Asia, had deployed teams among one hundred communities of Joshua Project's list of the most 'unreached peoples' in terms of Christianity. Each team had at least thirty evangelists. Our report stated: 'This provides Christian multinationals with the type of market research one would expect from a commercial enterprise such as Coca Cola or IBM'.[14]

An investigative report stated that

> The plan was based on a military model with the intent to invade, occupy, control, or subjugate its population. It was based on solid intelligence emanating from the ground and well-researched information on various facets of selected people groups. The idea was to send out spying missions to source micro details on religion and culture. The social and economic divisions in the various Indian communities were closely examined.[15]

Such a multinational network empowers the US headquarters to direct local actions efficiently in India in coordination with India-based units:

> A letter written to an agency in the US is re-directed immediately to Bengaluru and the agency in Bengaluru ... tracks down the nearest evangelist and directs him to take upon the task of ministering the gospel to the newest seeker. ... the mission goal is: 'We need a church within cycling distance, then within walking distance and finally within hearing distance'.[16]

The Joshua Project has the leverage to trigger or manage local conflicts, which in turn can get reported internationally for sensationalism and further political interventions. Its mission is to identify and highlight the people groups with the greatest need and vulnerability, their hot buttons, as well as the optimum leaders and contacts through which to approach them.

The cited report also stated that the Joshua Project was mining the databases of the Indian government such as the official census and the People of India Project undertaken by the Anthropological

Society of India. Luis Bush, director of Global Consultation on World
Evangelization proudly claimed:

> Never before has this kind of information on India been so
> carefully surveyed, prepared, well published and distributed. ...
> We do not believe it is accidental. God is allowing us to 'spy out
> the land' that we might go in and claim both it and its inhabitants
> for Him.[17]

Below are the differences between the Joshua Project and what we
describe as Omidyar's project in India:

- Omidyar is developing databases and infrastructure for
  intervention on behalf of the Global Left and not the Church.
- While the Joshua Project was carried out manually, ONI
  collects much more precise data automatically and processes
  and distributes it, all in real time.
- The Joshua Project required massive funding on an ongoing
  basis whereas ONI profits by investing in equity of cutting-edge
  start-ups in India; the data generated is a by-product.
- The Joshua Project was open about its agenda whereas ONI hides
  behind the veneer of bringing technology and social justice to
  Indians especially in remote locations.
- The Joshua Project was contained in the evangelical world, while
  ONI has widespread acceptance as a respectable partner in the
  private sector, public sector, and academia.

Omidyar Grants Via Harvard's Mittal Institute

Early in 2012 the Mittal Institute provided a gateway into India for
Omidyar by providing scholars with grants to work on certain projects
in India. Omidyar funded the 'MOBILIZE! Digital Libraries' project in
India which uses technology (smart screens) for education, developed for
self-directed learning. The goal was to 'catalyze positive social change'.

> We operate at the intersection of education, technology and
> mobility, harnessing the best materials and practices to inspire
> students to new ways of thinking and generate greater interest
> in self-improved academic performance.[18]

Another project focussed on providing women internet access in Chennai

> The target for this intervention is middle income class working women, and will provide internet access, printing; coffee, regular educational seminars, and training events. Using the funds from the Omidyar Grant for Entrepreneurship in South Asia, iSpace will create a pilot cyber café in Chennai, and hope to grow this into numerous cyber café chains.[19]

After taking baby steps through the Mittal Institute a decade ago, Omidyar made major inroads entirely through its own organizations.

Omidyar Network India's Digital Infrastructure and Big Data

In this age of Artificial Intelligence, information on the actions, events, and behaviors of individuals and communities become a powerful database for analysis and prediction. The recent book, *Artificial Intelligence and the Future of Power*, gives examples of big data being used for political strategy, for understanding and manipulating social behavior, and for social re-engineering.[20]

Omidyar Network India's investments can be better understood in these terms as intelligence gathering mechanisms on a large scale and especially in sensitive communities. This data is amenable to powerful analysis and all kinds of social interventions, both constructive and disruptive. Building models on the workings of a society is a sophisticated activity requiring elaborate mechanisms of data collection and analysis. Omidyar's tech background makes him well-suited to dominate in developing and operating such infrastructure.

When seen in the light of the *big data game*, it becomes clear why ONI does what it does. Applications and services used by a large captive audience are rich in behavioral data. When engaging with India's vulnerable groups, there is a powerful impact that such data analysis brings for social engineering in the name of social justice. In all its ventures, ONI tries to position itself to control the flow of data.

At the heart of this strategy is eGovernments Foundation (eGov), in which Omidyar initially invested one million dollars back in 2014.[21]

Founded by technology stalwarts Nandan Nilekani and Srikanth Nadhamuni, eGov is intended to bring data-driven governance through an open-source technology backbone connecting the economy, society, and government. This software stack dubbed DIGIT[22] is its Open Digital Ecosystems (ODEs). It was built on the strategy of helping businesses and citizens interact with the government for approvals, taxation, service delivery, and grievance addressal. Therefore, the ability to do this seamlessly will, on the one hand, increase the government's operational efficiency, the effective use of its resources, facilitate the delivery of services, and improve its revenue collection. On the other hand, it will speed up processes for individuals and businesses.

This is good for Indians short-term, but in the long run it is ONI that assumes control of the technology on which the ecosystem operates, which positions it to capture all the valuable data being generated. This makes Omidyar the gatekeeper monitoring and directing the traffic of citizen-government interactions.

It is advantageous to facilitate the proliferation of this ecosystem that can be leveraged to develop insights and build models on how things work in India so it can be re-engineered later. Making it 'open source' helps to spread the system more universally. The more it is adopted, the more dependent the government, enterprises, and individuals will become, making it that much harder to switch. Therefore, eGov has partnerships with commercial enterprises and entrepreneurs to collaboratively create local solutions built on the platform and integrated with it. It also partners with civil society organizations to get them on to its platform, which helps it capture and analyze social phenomena.

Omidyar is already partnering with the Indian government, most of the states, and important government bodies like the Ministry of Housing and Urban Affairs and the National Institute of Urban Affairs. The goal here is to influence the framing of national standards and the development of policies and programs that can speed up the adoption of its DIGIT system by the government. One example is the adoption of its technology during the pandemic:

> ... the government announced that over 1 billion COVID vaccine certificates had been issued on the government's vaccination

portal COWIN using eGov's DIVOC software. DIVOC is a modular digital platform that enables countries to manage large-scale rollouts of last-mile vaccine administration programs. It has made carrying and storing a vaccine certificate convenient for millions by allowing for digitally signed and offline verifiable certificates using QR code technology.[23]

The ONI website proclaims:

> The much-overused phrase 'impact at scale' is the only way to describe what the organization has achieved over the past five years: eGov is now deploying the platform in 2,421 cities (653 live, 1858 in implementation) across 14 states, impacting over 160M Indian citizens... DIGIT has enabled over $2.5 billion in revenue collections.[24]

It proudly declares: 'This has been one of those investments that delivers on practically every dimension of our thesis and has done so at a staggering scale'.[25] In other words, the system is generating humongous amounts of data as well as influence that ONI is using to build its social models as the foundation for its interventions. Given the central role it is playing in India's governance at all levels, ONI has set the following specific goals for the future in line with its economic, social, and government themes.

- To continue driving public and private sector partnerships to 'co-own, improve, customize, deploy and service the platform across multiple cities'.
- To 'build and engage "offline architectures" or intermediaries (e.g., community-based organizations, local politicians etc.)' in the last mile to reach the most 'disenfranchised citizens'. This assumes even greater importance when one considers the claim that the system is 'holding governments accountable through enhanced transparency'.
- To expand the government's National Urban Governance Platform through the National Urban Digital Mission to leverage the cloud for the delivery of services, and in the process spur DIGIT's adoption across states and cities. The intention is to 'integrate various municipal services on a common platform so

that all states/cities may use customisable solutions to address their needs at speed and scale'. The nine reference service applications are property tax assessment/payment, building plan approval, municipal grievance redressal, trade license issuance and payment, no-objection certificate issuance, water and sewerage connection management, municipal accounting and finance, birth and death registration and user charges for public utilities like water, electricity, etc.[26]

Omidyar Network India's obsession with projects and organizations that influence data policy and data governance now make sense. Its focus is on building its own Open Digital Ecosystem. This digital ecosystem mimics a parallel governance and web of traffic of which ONI's designated leaders are the traffic cops and gatekeepers.

As founder of eBay, Omidyar is an expert in creating digital marketplaces that bring buyers and sellers together (on one platform) and very well knows the techniques of building databases from this activity. He is using this expertise in the following ventures, this time as the digital gatekeeper deep inside India's remotest communities.

- Bijak is a digital supply chain for farmers across twenty-eight plus states and one thousand plus regions of India, connecting buyers and sellers as their 'trusted digital marketplace'. Clearly, a rich real-time data source from rural farms.[27]
- IntrCity makes travel reservations by train or bus in one hundred plus cities, giving ONI a database on the movement of people, and trends in real-time.[28]
- CredR organizes the market for used motorcycles, and in the process tracks their movements through GPS and gathers behavioral data on the users.[29]
- Indifi provides digital credit for small businesses, giving it access to financial data and behavioral modelling, and giving it clout among small-scale entrepreneurs.[30]
- Sitara provides micro-loans to poor women with a footprint of more than sixty thousand as of now. This gives ONI data on families and their finances, and behavior modelling.[31]
- Doubtnut is a popular multi-lingual education platform for K-12 students. It answers over two million questions daily giving it

influence on the type of answers given.[32] It also gathers data on households with children, tracks their careers and transition to adulthood, and can put in hooks to understand their aspirations, and drive behavior.

- Vedantu offers another live online K-12 education platform. It has built databases of over forty million youth and teachers, with the ability to influence careers, recruit, and discover behavior hooks on a personal level.[33]
- Transerve is building geo-demographic databases useful for communities, rural areas, towns, and urban geographies with a footprint of over twenty-three million people.[34]

Omidyar Network India's Project Kaveri Investment has penetrated the prestigious Indian Institute of Science (IISc), Bengaluru, where it is positioned as a Centre of Excellence. Its mission is to 'unlock the massive untapped social and economic value of data'. While gaining access to valuable data and the talented pool of human resources, it also builds its brand value by association with this iconic institution.[35]

Omidyar Network India also has plans to work with the World Bank to get access to the census data in the guise of making this data more easily accessible.

Economic Influence and Leadership Building

Over the past several years, ONI has made 128 active investments,[36] amounting to a total of US$350 million.[37] It claims to have touched the lives of 550 million Indians. It has a total portfolio of 106 companies including at least 4 unicorns. All this is rapidly expanding.

Omidyar Network India's strategy is to win over young Indian entrepreneurs by funding exciting technology ventures, and to use these ventures to build infrastructure in rural India. We provide a few examples of ONI's investments. We must clarify that we are not opposing the organizations that receive these grants. In many cases, the work (*fes.org* for example) is extremely important. Our thesis is that they were chosen by ONI not from a purely financial perspective but with an overarching gameplan. It is this underlying motive that we intend to tease out.

The broad principles are well articulated and non-controversial when taken at face value:

- <u>Digital Society</u>: Using technology to foster inclusion, privacy, security, transparency, and good governance. Ambitious goal to impact the lives of the 'Next Half Billion' population that is 'most vulnerable'.
- <u>Education</u>: Influence textbooks and curricula and train teachers to 'reimagine what is taught' with 'empathy' towards students, i.e., influence the values and ideology.
- <u>Financial Inclusion</u>: Research and change the 'structural impediments to financial inclusion'. This brings ONI deep into India's Small and Medium Enterprises (SMEs) especially in sensitive rural areas.
- <u>Good Governance</u>: Play a role in the 'relationship between citizens and government'. ONI states: 'We enable citizens to be informed, have agency over the issues that matter most to them, and hold their political leaders to account'. Focus on digital technologies for citizens to disrupt politics and governance, independent media (meaning aligned with ONI), and defining and enforcing best practices for politicians and government.

In fact, ONI's websites and publicity are loaded with wonderful jargon. The Open Digital Ecosystems initiative is described as an engine comprising digital public infrastructure that supports 'Beneficial Technology'. It enables 'a community of actors to unlock transformative solutions for society, based on a robust governance framework'. Omidyar Network India states that India's digital systems are like silos, and it wants to be the engine for interoperability.

This is a fancy way of stating that it wants to be the gatekeeper and surveillance mechanism at the crossroads through which traffic flows between the various digital silos. Such an ambitious ecosystem development is quite complex and includes policies, practices, and behavior modification in governments, businesses, and citizens. Concerns related to ethics, privacy, access to data, vulnerability and national security risks abound.

Looking deeper, one clearly sees an agenda for a sort of parallel government, or at least a network of people, technologies, and databases aligned with ONI and under its control. In fact, ONI repeatedly states that its investments serve a dual purpose (which it calls its 'dual chequebook' approach): good financial investments on the one hand, and good social engineering interventions, on the other.

For example, let's look at the way its group company iMerit functions. iMerit states it is 'focussed on advancing key technologies such as machine learning algorithms and artificial intelligence' with application across the autonomous vehicle, medical AI, agricultural technology, geospatial and other robotics-based technology industries, in natural language processing, as well as for 'societal applications'.

iMerit's work begins with scouting out the territory: 'Two-thirds of the Indian workforce, however, is still employed within the agriculture and manufacturing sectors, and Information Technology (IT) employs only a fraction of the one-third of the population working in the services sector'.

Being engaged in AI operations, it needs huge volumes of cheap labor (it pays 3X to 10X the family income, which is subsistence level) for things like data labeling required for machine learning. For this it goes straight to 'underserved regions' in India, where people with no conventional degrees need 'greater opportunities to flourish'. It has picked up 5,500 people from these regions, 50% of whom are female.

iMerit works with Anudip Foundation, a skilling non-profit it founded to train people from these regions through its six centers in India and one in New Orleans. The output of the Indian centers feeds the New Orleans center. The various stages of the skilling program are on-job training, English enhancement program, contextual understanding, domain specialization, and leadership development to gradually move them up the value chain.

Radha Basu, founder of iMerit has talked about the social impact at the first Onward talk show. She says if you speak to these people, they say, 'our families consider our opinion very seriously, especially in family and village decisions'.

This clearly shows how the organization is adept at selecting people with low bargaining power and using the money to develop foot soldiers that are then leveraged to embed desired ideologies at the community and village level.

Clearly, iMerit does great work for the public. Our concern is over the foreign control because such interventions could pose a potential threat to the social unity of India's masses. Many of these grants and investments are direct interventions to study and influence the working of the Indian State. Some of them seek to plant their own policymakers or influence the existing ones. Omidyar Network India's LinkedIn[38] footprint makes it obvious that it is very keen to position the youth it funds as bold political leaders,[39] path-breaking, and aspirational. The grooming of a new generation of leaders and influencing the leadership ecosystem are significant moves.

Omidyar Backs the IDFC Institute and IDFC Foundation

We examine a couple of non-profit organizations: IDFC Foundation and IDFC Institute. These are wholly owned subsidiaries of India's Infrastructure Development Finance Company Limited (IDFC), which is a finance company and IDFC Bank's parent, established under the government's Department of Financial Services.

The IDFC Foundation was established in 2011 to focus on capacity building, policy advisory and sustainability initiatives. It oversees the Corporate Social Responsibility activities being pursued by IDFC Group.[40] It also funds the IDFC Institute and receives money from foreign NGOs like Ford Foundation, Rockefeller Foundation, Bill & Melinda Gates Foundation, and the Omidyar Network which are known to have anti-India agendas.[41] The IDFC Institute's website states:

> IDFC Institute has been set up as an independent, economic development-focused think/do tank to investigate the political, economic and spatial dimensions of India's ongoing transition from a low-income, state-led country to a prosperous market-based economy. We provide in-depth, actionable research and recommendations that are grounded in a contextual understanding of the political economy of execution.[42]

The diagram that follows shows the intricate web of relationships involving IDFC.

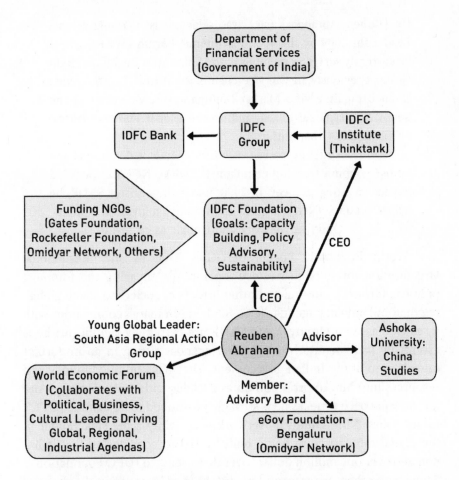

Given IDFC's role in infrastructure building and focus on rural development, Pierre Omidyar was likely interested in penetrating the organization. And IDFC Institute, headed by its founder-CEO Reuben Abraham, provided the opening. Abraham is a member of the advisory board of e-Gov Foundation in Bengaluru,[43] so it is perhaps not surprising that Omidyar's style of impact investing and his use of digital technology to gather data are reflected in the institute's activities.

It all became easier because Reuben Abraham is CEO of both IDFC Foundation and the thinktank IDFC Institute. Currently, he is also an adviser at Ashoka's Centre for China Studies, a Young Global Leader of the WEF and still holds positions there:

He [Ruben Abraham] (sic) was selected as a Young Global Leader for 2009 by the World Economic Forum (WEF), where he currently serves as member of the South Asia Regional Action Group. Previously, he was vice-chair of the WEF's Global Agenda Council on Emerging Market Multinationals, vice-chair of the South Asia regional board, and on the Global Futures Council on Cities and Urbanization.[44]

For a decade, he served as an independent director at the Soros Economic Development Fund (SEDF) in New York, a global impact investing pioneer. In 2008, under the aegis of SEDF, he helped set up SONG, one of the earliest impact investment funds, with Soros, Omidyar Network and Google as co-investors.[45]

The World Economic Forum describes itself as an 'International Organization for Public-Private Cooperation', 'engaging the foremost political, business, cultural and other leaders of society to shape global, regional and industry agendas'.[46] So Reuben Abraham's connections with it, as well as with Omidyar and SEDF are extremely significant; he is essentially *their* man, advancing their agendas sitting in an important organization of the Indian government. They have pumped money and resources into him to prop him up as a leader with their ideology. And it is now payback time, as he is strongly positioned to determine IDFC's future course. The Omidyar Network is certainly a big stakeholder in the digital infrastructure being built by IDFC, considering that it has donated over one million dollars over three years to IDFC Foundation.[47] Along with other overseas funders such as Ford Foundation, Rockefeller Foundation, and the Gates Foundation that have similar objectives, IDFC Foundation has received about three million dollars.[48]

The digital infrastructure being built by IDFC Institute is the basis for a social credit system that the WEF backs in its quest for a new world order called the 'Great Reset'. For Omidyar, this helps him guzzle more data and further expand influence. As one reporter commented about him:

> To [Omidyar] it's ... about ... integrating things together to give technocrats, business executives and government officials a God's-eye view of the world — to manage and control society more efficiently. — Yasha Levine, author of '*Surveillance Valley: The Military History of the Internet*'.[49]

Projects of the IDFC Institute

The institute has over twenty-five projects being run by teams that are highly skilled in AI, big data, econometric studies, and machine learning. It also runs a Data Governance Network which is a multidisciplinary community of professionals 'that can inform good governance practices and the trajectory of India's digital economy'.[50]

The institute has created many sophisticated digital tools that can help with decision-making based on satellite imagery, surveys, and big data from railways and other sources. Among the major projects at IDFC Institute are infrastructure projects such as mapping India's urbanization, Gross Domestic Product, internal migrations, urban mobility, regional divergences and infrastructure, and urban expansion.

The institute uses big data from satellite imaging to advise the government on economic policy issues, something that was traditionally achieved with number crunching. It monitors urbanization, and factors affecting it using AI-based analysis of satellite imagery and uses big data for policy analysis. For example, it studies internal migration 'using monthly data on unreserved railway passenger travel over five years as a proxy for migration in search of work. The data was collated for every pair of railway stations in India'.[51] Big data was also used to understand labor flows down to the district level. The Goods and Services Tax network data and central sales tax invoices were analyzed to get insights into inter-state trade.

The IDFC Institute is making maps of healthcare facilities all over India using interactive maps. With the justification that they are very useful during a crisis, massive amounts of data is being captured in them:

> Important healthcare data like locations of health facilities should be geotagged and publicly accessible. This encourages reuse of data for innovation, i.e., research, developing new services and tools, or improving evidence-based policies. ... it can be used to help decision makers and humanitarian agencies measure access to facilities, improve overall service delivery of the health sector and/or plan emergency response. As positive externalities of ongoing government programmes to improve road infrastructure, and the government's response to COVID-19, two new datasets

containing locations of Indian health facilities have now been added to the public sphere. These include:

Rural public health facilities surveyed under Pradhan Mantri Gram Sadak Yojana (PMGSY) Phase – III

Private facilities empanelled under Pradhan Mantri Jan Arogya Yojana (PM-JAY) (functioning as COVID-19 Vaccination Centres or CVCs)[52]

The IDFC institute uses the Brihanmumbai Municipal Corporation data on detailed indicators such as mortality, containment zones, bed capacity, vaccinations, etc. The IDFC states: 'As can be imagined, such data is extremely useful not only for formulating short-term policy measures but also for assisting longer term academic research'.[53]

> ... we've been able to gather all such PDFs from July 2020 until the present. We are in the process of converting all relevant indicators to a machine-readable output and will put them out as a public-facing database in due course. ... we will put out a brief analysis of them along with the related datasets. We've started by compiling and analysing all mortality data over time, as outlined below.[54]

The IDFC also collected data on COVID-19 vaccination rates, ICU bed availability during the pandemic, Case Fatality Rate, ICU bed occupancy rate, severe COVID-19 cases, doses administered for various demographic groups, and so forth. This is valuable data in the hands of a foreign funded private institute.

It also created a toolkit to change behavior for vaccine acceptance during the pandemic in India: 'We realised that there is a need for simple, empathetic and compelling communication to facilitate large-scale behaviour change to drive demand for vaccination'.[55]

The IDFC has access to NITI Aayog data of manufacturing firms and conducts surveys for it:

> The NITI Aayog-IDFC Institute Enterprise Survey covers approximately 3200 manufacturing firms, including manufacturing start-ups, in order to assess the business regulatory environment in states. The survey focuses on 9 areas of doing business viz. starting a business, land and construction related permits, environmental permits, labour regulations, infrastructure related

utilities like electricity, water and sewerage, taxes and customs, legal issues, access to finance, and exiting a business. Firms are asked whether they have completed compliance processes online, the time taken to complete processes, and the severity of obstacles they face in each of these areas. In addition, the survey also covers industry associations and experts to know their views regarding the business regulatory environment in states.[56]

The following table shows a sample of some of their projects.[57]

MAPPING INDIA'S URBANIZATION	Satellite imagery and machine learning techniques to analyze level and form of urbanization across India over the last four decades.
DEVELOPING INFRASTRUCTURE TO CREATE EMPLOYMENT	Study focuses on eighteen districts across states that show potential for growth. The project will involve conducting a firm-level survey of districts to understand infrastructural constraints enterprises face in operating, scaling, and hiring.
MAPPING INDIA'S GDP	New 3D web tool developed to assess the spatial distribution of India's GDP. This tool is based on 2006 GDP and population data (recent data will be added) and be used to understand variation in economic activity across the country at a higher resolution than administrative data, and at a granular level. Users can search for specific cities to view economic output at a one sq. km. cell level and population.
INDIA INFRASTRUCTURE REPORT	Government should focus on areas where market does not operate like providing mass public transit and public services, and facilitate effective functioning of land and housing markets. This will make housing affordable for low-income groups. IDFC Institute has developed a new web tool that illustrates the supply-side constraints that hinder access to affordable housing in India.

URBAN DEFINITIONS	Providing alternate definitions
COVID STUDIES: KARNATAKA	Seroprevalence studies conducted in random population-representative studies are essential for measuring the spread of COVID-19. To fill this critical evidence gap, researchers from IDFC Foundation undertook a study in Karnataka in collaboration with the Centre for Monitoring Indian Economy.
INDEX FOR LAND GOVERNANCE	The current government's interest in improving the existing land title system across all states presents a great opportunity to speed up implementation of the Digital India Land Records Modernisation Programme as a prerequisite to moving towards a system of conclusive titles. This is an opportunity to track states' performances in modernizing land records. IDFC Institute, in collaboration with World Bank, is involved in creating a state-level land governance index. Such an indicator will capture policymakers' attention at a high level, improve ability to regularly report on progress and possibly also allocate funds, support DILRMP management/implementation by allowing Department of Land Resources, GOI, to drill down to sub-registrar office/village level, and make it possible to assess the impact of modernization by correlating it with other sources of socio-economic data.

Omidyar is using IDFC as the front to build digital infrastructure in Karnataka. This is set up as a public-private partnership between IDFC, HDFC and the government of Karnataka called iDecK Infrastructure Development Corporation (Karnataka) Limited. iDeCK also 'assists governments in policy development, law making and in capacity building activities'. According to the IDFC Foundation website:

A joint venture between IDFC Foundation, Government of Karnataka (GoK) and Housing Development Finance Corporation Limited (HDFC), iDeCK is built on the stability of a dynamic government department and the impetus of pioneers in infrastructure strategy. Since the year 2000, iDeCK has been working closely with governments, its departments and agencies as well as private sector clients across the globe for development of infrastructure in transportation, tourism, urban development, social infrastructure, industrial infrastructure and renewable energy.[58]

Another project is in New Delhi, again an alliance between IDFC Foundation, and the Government of National Capital Territory of Delhi, called Delhi Integrated Multi-Modal Transit System Limited. The IDFC, backed by Omidyar, Gates, and Rockefeller are advising the government on policy in transportation:

A joint venture between IDFC Foundation and ... (GNCTD), DIMTS provides specialised end-to-end policy, technical and transaction advisory solutions in the transportation realm. It assists the Government and private clients in the development and improvement of public transport systems in several cities across India and in developing countries through a range of services like Transport planning, Intelligent Transport Systems, Infrastructure Engineering, Railways, Transport Technologies, Information technology, Transaction Advisory and operations. ... the involvement of these agencies has made a substantial difference to the way PPPs have been used to develop infrastructure in India.[59]

Omidyar-China Nexus

Omidyar's connection with the Chinese Communist Party and the fact that it seems to be working in 'cooperation' with the party is a direct national security risk to India. Whether this 'cooperation' means working for Chinese interests in India is the question. A 2017 report revealed that China was bragging about its control over President Joe Biden's national security team and names Omidyar among others:

A 2017 report effectively claims – on the CCP's behalf – that CNN host Fareed Zakaria, Twitter CEO Jack Dorsey, Facebook Oversight Board member Helle Thorning-Schmidt, NeverTrump philanthropist Pierre Omidyar and many others "co-operate" with the CCP and its goals.[60]

With this in mind, the CAC proclaims of promoting over 10,000 propaganda pieces to foreign audiences and, critically, brags of their work with Western think-tanks in achieving this goal: 'Through cooperation with think-tanks such as the Berggruen Institute in the United States, the Canadian Center for International Governance Innovation, and the Australian Lowy Institute for International Policy, we have attracted nearly 200 overseas think-tankers as special commentators on China Daily. In one year, it published more than 300 of their signed articles, enabling these influential people to influence more overseas audiences and tell China's stories well.'[61]

Omidyar is no stranger to investing in media companies in order to change the narrative in the US and is trying the same in India.[62] Omidyar has invested in a Bengaluru-based self-publishing platform called Pratilipi,[63] which also recently raised an investment from the China-based Qiming Venture Partners. Omidyar is reaching for the Next Half Billion through Pratilipi, which is India's largest digital platform for self-publishing. Pratilipi connects readers and writers in twelve Indian languages. Infused with foreign capital, the site already boasts a staggering scale of '2.5Cr+ readers, 27L+ stories, 2.7L+ writers, 12 languages'.[64] Once Pratilipi gains critical mass it will be easy for it to silence some voices while amplifying others. Since Pratilipi 'is the only online platform in India that caters to literature in regional languages', India appears to be handing over its contemporary literature to Omidyar and Chinese investors.

Social Impact

One of ONI's high impact projects brings the latest technology into areas already teeming with missionaries and separatist movements. The ReSolve Initiative project empowers some of those very NGOs we have been fighting over the previous decades that prey upon India's rural and marginalized populations. It targets the 110 million Indians that help run micro and small businesses and the migrant workers estimated to be between 80 and 130 million.

The opportunity ONI has seized upon is that the social and cultural needs of these small businesses and migrant workers 'have not been addressed systemically'. The vulnerability is identified as follows: 'How do gender biases against women and the girl child play out among migrant women and children? How many of them get adequate food, nutrition, and education?'[65]

This project brings entrepreneurs, thought leaders and policy makers together. So far ONI has funded sixty-seven rural projects in seventeen states of which twenty-one claim to have nationwide impact. At least 3.2 million people are directly involved; another 48 million Indians will get evangelized by ONI's social justice activities.[66]

Omidyar Network India is investing in Ashoka University's Centre for Social Impact and Philanthropy, which claims to be India's first academic center focused on enabling strategic and robust philanthropy for greater social impact. The ONI states: 'The Centre intends to achieve this by developing knowledge products that inform sector strategy and action, providing independent, non-partisan platforms that build sector vision, voice and norms'.[67] This is discussed in greater detail in Chapter 19.

In a previous chapter we explained the duplicity in the work of the Saudi funded Abdul Latif Jameel Poverty Action Lab (J-PAL) at MIT. Omidyar Network India funds and actively works with J-PAL. Assuming that Indians would not be aware of the scandalous activities of J-PAL, ONI claims that its mission is to 'reduce poverty by ensuring that policy is informed by scientific evidence. We do this through research, policy outreach, and training'.[68]

Janaagraha is another NGO funded by ONI claiming to 'transform the quality of life in India's cities and towns'. It claims to bring 'reforms to city governance' through its activism to educate the public on local political issues and advocacy. This project helps ONI infiltrate local, state and Central governments in four thousand-plus cities across India.[69] This is similar to the role Omidyar has played in US local politics to organize voters, promote specific policies, and pressure politicians.

The Foundation for Ecological Security (FES) facilitates rural citizens' legal rights to share, self-govern, and conserve common land. It represents landless communities at the grassroots level, in effect making it a high-tech upgrade for the traditional NGO bringing human rights to the lowest strata. With over nine million acres of Indian land in its databases already, it exerts influence over communities, gathers data on their social-political-religious hierarchies, and builds models of behavior.[70] Without doubt, FES is doing important work in very remote areas, but our concern is merely over foreign dependency, outflow of data, and inflow of ideological influences.

Jan Sahas is an NGO 'working for India's most marginalized communities' providing them 'counselling, legal aid, job skills, land and property rights, social support, social and behaviour change, awareness drives'. It claims it 'works with the local government, police and state apparatus to influence better policies'. This makes ONI an important grassroots activist bringing a form of shadow-governance to over five million people.[71]

Omidyar Network India along with MacArthur and Rockefeller Foundation run the Catalytic Capital Consortium (C3). Its social impact is among rural artisans in regions across Africa and India.[72]

Omidyar Network India's Diversity, Equity, and Inclusion work is to generate large-scale activism with legal support to bring about social justice for gender, caste, religion, and sexual orientation. It builds young leaders from a plethora of marginalized groups and provides bridges between them and ESG activities. It brings the Omidyar cultural framework into India's heartland.[73] It also funds Nudge Foundation's Centre for Social Innovation by building infrastructure to promote disruptive, differentiated thinking to solve critical social issues.[74]

The ONI has spent over a decade working with entrepreneurs focused on the segment, the last three of which were used for 'internal conversations, introspection, and sensitisation on DEI'.[75] Now, the DEI project is moving to the next level. In the inaugural issue of its bi-annual newsletter, *Vividh*, it laid out its insights and goals:

- It is time to move from general discourse to getting organizations to commit to specific goals.
- The intention is to embed DEI in the core business and organization strategy to accelerate success and impact.

- Foot soldiers are encouraged to 'face uncomfortable truths', 'have difficult conversations' and recognize their own 'unconscious biases' and most importantly, 'to be persistent, flexible and open-minded as many solutions can turn out to be ineffective or unexpectedly difficult to implement'.
- Data mining remains extremely important for gleaning continued insights and for creating desired solutions.
- Pushing for diversity in the funding by venture capitalists is now a target.

The Open Digital Ecosystem initiative provides non-tech layers of community and robust governance, also called 'phygital' (physical+digital). This is typically at the juncture where public digital infrastructure ends and the 'last mile' where the remotest people are, begins. This positions ONI as the digital gatekeeper for the most vulnerable and sensitive populations.[76]

Professional Assistance For Development Action (PRADAN) is making interventions in forest-based marginalized communities. These are the traditional vanavasis (inappropriately called 'tribals'). It is another sensitive region from which ONI seeks to recruit and groom foot soldiers for activism.[77]

The National Foundation for India gets grants from ONI to 'promote social justice'. Here ONI is open about using its network: 'Through our state partnerships and citizen engagement we have reached out to 26,000 Dalit and tribal families, more than 14,000 minorities, 30,000 women, 3,000 youth and 158 Members of Legislative Assemblies'. The implications for India are obvious.[78] Synergistic with this is ONI's Legal Tech Thesis: the country's digitization has opened up the opportunity for making reforms that 'extend beyond court-focused judicial reforms'. This tech-driven legal intervention gives ONI the potential to amplify its activism.[79]

Another initiative ONI is proud of is its 'award-winning program curriculum' for training social activists and mentoring young leaders of social justice. This role is strategically positioned as the power broker and middleman between grassroots activists and the government.

Omidyar Network India also has a strategic tie-up with GiveIndia, a crowd-funding platform that connects donors and non-profits. The former helps by bringing its brand value and credibility. To quote ONI, it is 'bridging the trust deficit among donors towards non-profits and helping trustworthy non-profits access retail donations at significantly lower costs'. In other words, it is the powerful matchmaker between donors and NGOs and explains the role as such:

> GiveIndia helps NGOs tap into the power of peer-to-peer fundraising through their employees, volunteers and donors. Individuals (employees, volunteers, donors, etc.) can create fundraising campaigns in favour of an NGO on GiveIndia's online crowd-funding platform.[80]

It goes on to explain how it ties up with CSR programs.

Omidyar Network India has developed a Rural E-Commerce Thesis which is to continually learn more about the Next Half Billion aspirations and how to enter their lives.[81]

Akin to its US parent, ONI is always looking for ways to influence media for political and sociological themes. For example, it has made equity investments in NewsLaundry[82] and Scroll.[83] Its grant to *Swarajya* raises eyebrows. One wonders if this is meant to be a public display of 'balance' or an entry point with long-term strategies to influence the editorial policy the way it did in the case of *The Independent*.

Policy Research and Influence on Government

Indians familiar with the East India Company know very well the risks and uncertainties of foreign interventions in political and government affairs. What starts as friendly cooperation can easily turn hostile when there is a conflict of ideological or commercial interests. In Omidyar's case, there is precedence of this in other countries. One example is the Omidyar funded movements that allegedly helped topple the previous Ukraine government.[84] It is reported that Omidyar was a major funder along with George Soros of an umbrella organization that helped create an uprising in Ukraine, according to the *Financial Times*. This led to the overthrow of Ukrainian president Viktor Yanukovych in 2014 because he chose closer ties with Russia than the European Union. The allegation is that American billionaires aligned with the CIA because removing countries out of Russia's orbit would create opportunities for American corporations.[85]

Below are some examples of Omidyar's direct, and indirect, penetration into Indian individuals and organizations involved in governance.

From the very beginning, Pierre Omidyar tapped some of India's best connected political leaders, giving him access to the who's who of India's power structure. One of them was C.V. Madhukar who has served as managing director of Omidyar Network. The Omidyar Network commends Madhukar for leading its strategic interventions in digital forms of identity and data privacy issues. He has been instrumental in shaping India's policies on foreign e-commerce entry into India, task forces on good governance and transparency, and other good-sounding affiliations. He has also worked with Azim Premji Foundation and World Bank, has a degree from Harvard Kennedy School, and has become a Young Global Leader at the World Economic Forum.

One of the reasons Omidyar tapped him as one of its main frontmen in India was that Madhukar was co-founder of the New Delhi-based Institute for Policy Research Studies (PRS).[86] To appreciate the importance of 'capturing' PRS, we refer to its website that describes its goals as 'to help legislators understand the nuances of various issues and use data and evidence to judge the implications of various policy alternatives'. Related to this is its goal 'of improving the transparency of legislatures', which means it sees itself as a watchdog ensuring that legislators have competence and integrity. The institute is also mentoring young Indians entering politics by pairing them with members of parliament for mentorship.

In summary: 'The Vision of PRS is to strengthen India's democracy by making legislatures more effective. The Mission of PRS is to make the legislative process better informed, more transparent and participatory'. It is noteworthy that among the other board members of PRS are Tarun Khanna (discussed earlier as head of Harvard Mittal Institute) and Pratap Bhanu Mehta (discussed as former head of Ashoka University).

For a foreign entity like Omidyar to hijack PRS at the highest level given the role that it plays in India is an impressive feat indeed. Omidyar Network has been successful at this kind of penetration into thinktanks largely because of the way it discusses its strategic initiatives to make the government feel like an 'ally'. This also helps to build personal relationships with bureaucrats and mentor them for long-term influence and to gain access to information.[87]

The digital intermediary eGov Foundation discussed above with its role in municipal operations, decision-making, and financial transparency, facilitates top-down policymaking at the Central government and bottom-up implementation at the local level. Its footprint already influences over 160 million people in India. This will become a great repository of policymaking debates, positions, and anticipation of policy changes.[88]

The Data Governance Network is another research initiative. It is described as

> a self-sustaining, multidisciplinary community of professionals that can inform good governance practices and the trajectory of India's digital economy. We aim to achieve this by bringing together institutional and individual experts, convening stakeholders across industry, government and academia, and fuelling an engine of implementable policy research.[89]

This gives ONI a front row seat inside government bodies making policies, staying one step ahead, as well as shaping the thinking through its research staff and reports, seminars and other activities. It is also useful to bring advance knowledge of policies for the benefit of its other start-ups.[90]

Yet another research involvement is in the Data Security Council of India, the industry body concerned with data protection. Omidyar Network India acknowledges that this gives it access to the 'central and state governments and their agencies, regulators, industry sectors, industry associations and think tanks for policy advocacy, thought leadership, capacity building and outreach activities'. Such collaborations give it access to policymakers, and advance information on India's data policy trajectory.[91]

It has a key relationship with the Centre for Internet and Society, a Bengaluru-based research organization working on 'interdisciplinary research on internet and digital technologies, such as privacy, freedom of expression, cybersecurity, digital identity, access to knowledge, Artificial Intelligence, digital labour, and accessibility, from policy and academic perspectives'. This gives ONI privileged access to the thinking of policymakers as well as a path to bring its own influences.[92]

Omidyar Network India points out a major opportunity to fill 'the many gaps in service delivery and localised government' across India. It states:

> From the largest metro areas to the smallest villages, the interests of citizens often do not translate into relevant public action due to opaque government processes, poor infrastructure around public services, and inadequate opportunities for citizen engagement. … Village Capital and Omidyar Network are looking to support startup ventures driving citizen engagement in government systems and in their communities. The program will support entrepreneurs with an award-winning program curriculum, 1:1 mentorship with sector leaders, and tailored engagements with strategic partners and investors.[93]

In effect, Omidyar is building a parallel civic-governance infrastructure that is digital and bypasses the brick-and-mortar infrastructure. It is openly justifying this on the grounds that the existing infrastructure is 'inadequate'.

India's Sovereignty at Risk

The dangers of allowing foreign ownership of India's critical infrastructure and foreign control over information flow on that infrastructure cannot be overstated. Especially when the foreign hand has a history of facilitating civil wars and regime changes. And specifically, when it explicitly states its intention of influencing every level of operation of the country, of advocating for the underclasses, and demanding accountability from the government. And when, by virtue of its control over the critical infrastructure, it can anticipate the government's response.

The process of driving a wedge between the government and the people of the country has already started. The foundation has been laid and the structure is being rapidly built up. The risk to India's sovereignty and democracy seems unprecedented.

Conclusion

The *Devatas* of Davos and the Digital Caste System

The introduction to the book began with four major stories that shape the discourse to undermine India. We explained how Wokeism is identifying many diverse kinds of victims of social oppression and organizing them into a unified movement, and how this movement is being used as a wrecking ball to dismantle the structures of society. We exposed a vast infrastructure in India and in the West that is carrying out this havoc, and we focused on the crucial role played by the Indian billionaires in this activity.

The core thesis of Wokeism is that all structures must be dismantled that are in any way linked to the oppression of any groups of people and that were erected by the oppressors. We support this in principle as a way to remedy the past and move forward to a better future for humanity. But we point out that:

- Entirely new structures of oppression are being erected using technologies like Artificial Intelligence and big data in which the oppressors are the new elites. Entirely new kind of oppressor/ oppressed categories will replace the identities of race, ethnicity, religion, gender and sexual orientation.
- Dismantling the old structures is helping pave the way for the new technology-driven structures of oppression to fill the vacuum of power. We are referring to a digital caste system.

Such a scenario ought to lead all well-wishers of humanity to investigate: What is the relationship between these two mega trends: Wokeism as a dismantling force, and the rise of the new techno-elites?

To understand the big picture, we must acknowledge that the world system as we know it, is coming apart at the seams with challenges like the COVID-19 pandemic, wars, climate change, and the technological revolution. Technology is galloping ahead faster than ever before, as a result of which the wealth asymmetry between the ultra-rich and the rest of humanity is deepening. The big tech companies have market valuations exceeding the GDPs of many sovereign nations.

Technology platforms controlled by the techno-elites enable them to direct the discourse by using big data and AI to predict and change behavior, and either silence or amplify specific voices. They are influential enough to sway elections using the large platforms they control. Their ownership of platforms and big data gives them control over the narratives; governments have been entering into alliances with them, be it to quell dissenting voices or censor what governments perceive as misinformation. One example of the narratives being controlled is big media groups coming together under the umbrella of the Trusted News Initiative (TNI). The TNI was started by the *BBC* and includes *The Hindu* media conglomerate in India. Tech companies and social media platforms are also part of TNI.[1] This group is the self-appointed gatekeeper of information.

Earlier chapters explained that Cancel Culture is being justified by Wokeism using the Marxist argument (put forth by Herbert Marcuse) that the oppressor must be silenced by a counter-hegemony. One oppression must be countered by another oppression. Could we not consider Cancel Culture and de-platforming as a Woke version of apartheid and untouchability?

The ability to use technology as a force multiplier has enabled the global oligarchs to influence governments and they are wasting no time in making political interventions. It is natural for this to translate into a widening gap in power.

This is not the first time there will be a large-scale destruction of civilizations. But this time, the weapons and soldiers are different. One would not have expected the billionaires to actively support this activity that is destroying the world order in which they are at the top. Unless, of course, they see it as an opportunity to build something grander in which their power will catapult even further.

One clue is the strange irony in the partnership between the Global Left's Wokeism and the global billionaires: The billionaires have outsourced the dismantling of the old order to the Left using them as useful idiots. This alliance will be a temporary one in which one side is using the other to do the dirty work. Once the job of dismantling is done, *the Woke Left will be rendered useless, and a new hierarchy will emerge*, with the billionaires at the helm.

Chapter 1 explained Marxism's main theory that every social system will generate its opposite force, called the anti-thesis. These two forces will fight to mutual destruction, and out of the rubble a new synthesis will emerge that will take us forward. But there is one big surprise and disappointment awaiting the Marxists this time!

It will shock Leftists to understand that this revolution will not lead to a dictatorship of the masses (as aspired by Marxism), but a dictatorship of the elites.

This new kind of dictatorship will be based on the latest technologies and will be far worse than the oppressive structures being toppled. The outcome will be a new hierarchical caste system and not an egalitarian society. Marxist methods are being used to produce an outcome that is exactly the opposite of what Marxism wants. Will the technology of blockchains turn into the new chains of slavery?

One can debate on who is using whom. Is Wokeism coming out ahead because the social media owned by the billionaires seems to help their cause? Or is the Left engaged in a self-defeating revolution because a new cabal of elites will emerge on top?

And who might be the new winners running the new world order? As in any transitory period of systemic breakdowns and chaos, there are multiple contenders competing to come out on top when the dust settles. Each camp wants to use the present turmoil as an opportunity to reposition itself. Some of the main contenders are:

- Global Left Based in the West – the focus of our attention here
- Global Christian Right
- China
- Pan-Islam

Therefore, the new world order and India's place in it may take a few different pathways. Each of these alternative scenarios that could emerge out of the ashes of this disruption deserve discussion. But that is a major topic for a future book.

In this brief conclusion, we will explore what we consider the lead contender. The diagram on the following page gives the big picture with India as the case study. It depicts the ultra-rich as the barbarians at the gate, using Wokeism as a useful tool for dismantling India. We will explain the scenario in which the global elites will run the new power structures with *the Indian billionaires as junior partners much like the zamindars served the East India Company.* The global elites have articulated their strategies openly and with clarity, and the events thus far indicate they have built up considerable momentum.

One of the big developments under way towards the new world order is the removal of the separation of business and government, leading to a concentration of power that is essentially a global oligarchy. This new paradigm has been termed stakeholder capitalism by its lead proponent, the World Economic Forum. Its main tenet is that corporates should take over many of the roles that governments play. This is being done in the guise of social justice and impact investing. Stakeholder capitalism will transform capitalists into oligarchs by merging business and politics.[2]

In varna terms, this merges the domains of Brahmin, Kshatriya, and Vaishya into a consolidated oligarch varna of sorts! This gives them more money and more power than they could achieve with the original form of capitalism called shareholder capitalism. This is why many of them want to dismantle the present system in which they are successful and replace it with this new system in which they plan to hold an unprecedented concentration of power.

The limited liability company, that was meant to pursue shareholder profit, is being repurposed as a vehicle for social interventions. The question arises, why do they not use the structure of independent non-profit philanthropies that are meant for charity? The answer is that public charities are open to public scrutiny under the laws. The limited liability private companies are not subject to the same accountability for their social impact the way public charities are.

For instance, India's FCRA laws monitor foreign funds coming to non-profit charities. But the FCRA laws do not apply to Foreign Direct Investment (FDI) because this comes as business investment and not as philanthropy. The use of business entities to indulge in social-political interventions is a ploy to maintain secrecy on the goals and activities. In Chapter 22 we saw how Omidyar has cleverly used venture capital

Barbarians at India's Gate

One Plausible Future Scenario: World Economic Forum Runs the Show

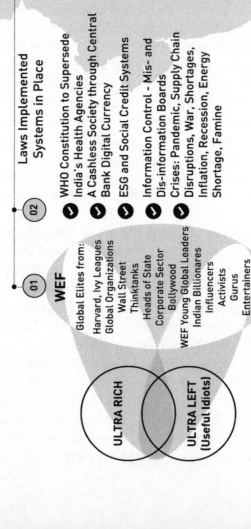

01

WEF

Global Elites from:

Harvard, Ivy Leagues
Global Organizations
Wall Street
Thinktanks
Heads of State
Corporate Sector
Bollywood
WEF Young Global Leaders
Indian Billionares
Influencers
Activists
Gurus
Entertainers
Celebrities

WOKEISM

ULTRA RICH

ULTRA LEFT
(Useful Idiots)

02

Laws Implemented /
Systems in Place

➤ WHO Constitution to Supersede India's Health Agencies
➤ A Cashless Society through Central Bank Digital Currency
➤ ESG and Social Credit Systems
➤ Information Control - Mis- and Dis-information Boards
➤ Crises: Pandemic, Supply Chain Disruptions, War, Shortages, Inflation, Recession, Energy Shortage, Famine

03

Intermediate: Long Term

Destruction of Family Life

Loss of Religious Life

Health: No Autonomy, Destructon of Ayurveda

Loss of Identity, Gender, Varna, Community, Culture, Language

Monitored for Social Credit: Own Nothing

Depopulation, Metaverse, Transhumanism

as a means to establish a vast infrastructure that impacts the social and political fabric of India. None of that passes through the FCRA regime.

The public is being deceived with the impression that the global elites have suddenly become big-hearted and selfless. The fact is that they are repositioning themselves for even greater concentration of wealth and power.

Besides the goal of bypassing government and social scrutiny, another obstacle the foreign nexuses want to remove are old structures of society that are deeply entrenched in every society worldwide. We explained that these must be dismantled to make room for any new order. This is where Wokeism is useful as a destructive force, and hence the support provided by many billionaires. Our argument is that far from removing the hierarchies of power and oppression, the new world order will implement its own kind of digital caste system.

Wokeism is channeling the anger of the masses against a target list of designated oppressors, and the victims of oppression are being promised lucrative employment, wealth redistribution, and even reparations. Some of the activists become successful as middlemen in the same way as some Africans were involved in slave trade selling out their fellow Africans, and the way Indians served as zamindars, babus, and sepoys to enable the British to maintain their empire. The vast majority of those mobilized as victims are mere pawns in a game they do not fully comprehend. The figure on the following page shows the destructive role of Wokeism.

The figure also shows the following two processes to build the new hierarchical structures:

- At the level of <u>companies</u>, there is a new system of rewarding good corporate citizenship based on the criteria of measuring Environmental, Societal, and Governance impact. This amounts to a *social credit system for companies* in accordance with the new rules being established by the strategists of this world order.
- At the <u>individual</u> level, each person's behavior will be monitored using digital identifications and surveillance, and constantly managed using a *social credit system for individuals*.

This combination of organizational and individual coercive methods will modulate the behavior of society, helping certain individuals and companies to compete and advance in the new game.

Oligarchy Caste System and The New World Order

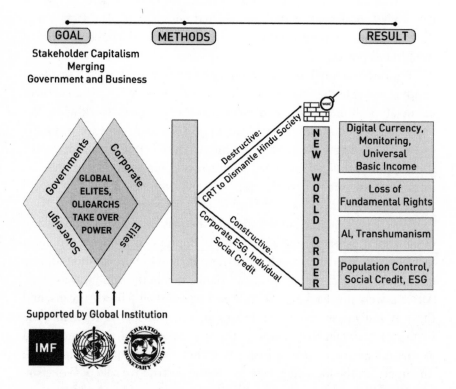

We will discuss who these global elites are and use their own words and activities to explain the revolution under way. In Part 2, we showed how Harvard University has been developing scholarship to function like a master puppeteer with a well-choreographed plan. This is driven not by the quest for truth but by the quest for power. We also saw that some Indian billionaires are hand in glove as Harvard's junior partners. A major motive behind this book is to expose the hypocrisy of this partnership.

Already, a group of global elites are using their massive assets to control central banks, several government bodies, and the corporate sector. They can control the public discourse and election outcomes through media houses they own. Even global institutions like the World Health Organization are influenced by oligarchs like Bill Gates. The following figure shows the extent of this concentration of power.

OLIGARCHS AMASS POWER

Global Elite Caste Controls

Control Through

Global Elite Caste Controls	Control Through
✔ FINANCIAL SECTOR	ESG
✔ MEDIA, NARRATIVE - MSM and SM	Media Ownership
✔ CENTRAL BANKS	Assets Under Management Worth Trillions
✔ GOVERNMENTS	Funding, Lobby, WEF Fellows
✔ GLOBAL INSTITUTIONS	Funding by Billionaires

Davos *Devatas*: Klaus Schwab and the World Economic Forum

Harvard University's influence and power stretch far beyond its ivory towers. We will show this by explaining the pivotal role being played by the WEF led by the technocrat Klaus Schwab, a product of the Harvard Kennedy School and a protégé of former US secretary of state, serving under Presidents Nixon and Ford, Henry Kissinger.[3] The WEF is in many ways a spinoff of Harvard that *operates outside all controls and is not accountable to anyone.* It is not monitored like other multilateral organizations such as the UN, IMF, WTO, World Bank, and WHO, nor a public charity scrutinized like Red Cross, Amnesty International, etc.

Klaus Schwab's power comes from the grand by-invitation-only annual party he throws called a global summit in Davos, Switzerland. It brings together the most powerful influencers from academics, corporations, governments, artists, royalty, celebrities, activists, and public figures of all kinds to join its carefully thought-out worldview. Through this networking clout, WEF has infiltrated most governments, businesses, and NGOS.

628 Snakes in the Ganga

Today, Schwab's World Economic Forum is a who's who of the richest, most powerful people all over the world. The members and partners of his group have a few commonalities:

- Most are very wealthy and/or hold powerful positions
- All share a vision for world domination, on their terms
- Everyone else is expendable in the search for 'sustainable development'
- Marxist revolution is their method of change, disguised as social justice
- A One World Order is their goal
- The goal justifies all means of execution

The important point is this: *Though the people are diverse, the discourse is not*. All the ideas fit within a Western Universalism framework of values. One does not find a Native American view on environmentalism, or an Islamic view on society, or a Confucian view on governance, or a Hindu view on ethics.

Schwab has been working on the WEF mission for a long time:

... Schwab studied at Harvard's John F. Kennedy School of Government (1966-67), where he earned a Master of Public Administration degree. ... he developed friendships with a number of luminaries, including the economist John Kenneth Galbraith, and the great godfather of *RealPolitik*, Henry Kissinger. Schwab's relationship with Kissinger, the trigger-happy Secretary of State in the Nixon and Ford administrations, was more than casual. Schwab described it as a "50-year-long mentorship" that continues paying dividends to this day.[4]

As the journalist Ernst Wolff explains, "the Harvard Business School had been in the process of planning a management forum of their own, and it is possible that Harvard ended up delegating the task of organizing it to him [i.e., Schwab]."[5]

Now that Klaus Schwab and the WEF have drafted up the blueprints for their highly coveted technocratic state, there remains one crucial key, and that is making sure leaders sympathetic to the message are in positions of power to see it through.[6]

Davos has been successfully turned into an echo chamber reinforcing a specific foundational worldview. There is a concerted effort to popularize phrases coined by WEF. Heads of states use WEF terminology like 'build back better' and 'private-public partnership', and corporate CEOs like that of BlackRock champion 'stakeholder capitalism'.

Klaus Schwab makes no secret about redefining life, as we know it, on a global scale. His ideas on global governance, use of social credit system to control the population and the environment, are explicit. He even has ideas on the use of technology for what is being called transhumanism.

One of his most audacious ideas is that 'you will own nothing and be happy'. In other words, your life will be a subscription model in which you will get a certain lifestyle delivered end to end depending on your level of participation. This could be seen as a new kind of digital slavery.

The primary agenda is to push for *stakeholder* capitalism replacing *shareholder* capitalism, a point made by tech entrepreneur, Vivek Ramaswamy as quoted in Chapter 1. Klaus Schwab has discussed his new world order in a book titled *COVID-19: The Great Reset*. He says that 'the pandemic has presented a rare opportunity to reset our world'. According to British journalist James Delingpole:

> *The Great Reset*, as every half-way informed person now knows, is part of the sinister plan by the World Economic Forum (and others) to turn the world into a gigantic slave state in we are the vassals ('You will own nothing and be happy') and the Davos elite rule over us like Pharaohs or Babylonian kings. But for some weird reason the puppet governments only obeying the orders of this elite just don't want to admit this in public.[7]

Many world leaders cultivated by WEF have publicly supported the principle of the Great Reset. At the launch event for The Great Reset project, during the WEF annual meeting in 2020, Prince Charles said in his opening remarks:

> We have a golden opportunity to seize something good from this crisis. Its unprecedented shockwaves may well make people more receptive to big visions of change.[8]

At a UN conference in 2020, Canadian prime minister, Justin Trudeau said:

> This pandemic has provided an opportunity for a reset. This is our chance to accelerate our pre-pandemic efforts, to re-imagine economic systems that actually address global challenges like extreme poverty, inequality and climate change.[9]

The main strategy is to use crises as opportunities to push the masses into behavior changes that would normally be unpopular, which would increase their dependency on the new technologies and the new hierarchical structures.

The Dismantling Process

To build a new system, ideas like Critical Race Theory and its popular version, Wokeism, are being used to destroy existing structures, systems, and institutions. In February of 2022, WEF put out a propaganda video titled, *This is what you need to know about critical race theory.*[10] The WEF's goal is to use Critical Race Theory to widen the schisms in society, and move the world towards stakeholder capitalism and The Great Reset.

The WEF is also pushing Wokeism's core belief of equity over equality. Equity will undermine hard work and merit and thereby create a mediocre society. This will make it easier for the privileged group of oligarchs to rule by reducing competition. Promising equity also appeases the masses by exploiting their sense of victimhood and making them believe that they are entitled to every kind of benefit as reparations for past injustices. Equity is a Marxist tool that's being used to make the masses a homogeneous group of serfs. We saw in earlier chapters that Wokeism also wants to break up family structures and social relationships – the oligarchs benefit because dismantling such structures makes society vulnerable and hence easier for them to manage.

We caught a glimpse of the wealth re-distribution during the pandemic when the big tech became even wealthier. Many changes were accepted by the public out of fear – such as digital IDs, use of private data, and so forth. Similarly, we could see a sudden worldwide rise in unemployment that will become an opportunity to implement Universal Basic Income (UBI), another mechanism to control the masses. This will be clothed as a genuine-sounding concern for humanity. The WEF website explains how it positions UBI:

> ... a new social contract needs to emerge from this crisis that rebalances deep inequalities that are prevalent across societies. ... The question should no longer be whether resources for effective social protection can be found – but how they can be found. UBI promises to be a useful element of such a framework.[11]

But the real reason for this sudden generosity is that the WEF fears massive social unrest in the absence of UBI. So, the purpose of UBI is to serve as a safety net that cushions the financial calamity people will have to face:

> The alternative to not having UBI is worse – the rising likelihood of social unrest, conflict, unmanageable mass migration and the proliferation of extremist groups that capitalize and ferment on social disappointment. ... we seriously need to consider implementing a well-designed UBI, so shocks may hit, but they won't destroy.[12]

Here is the smoking gun: The proposed *UBI will come with strings attached, and this is how more control and power will shift from the masses to the elites*. Schwab expects implicit obedience from the masses in exchange for receiving UBI:

> ... good arguments can be made for having very selective conditions [for Universal Basic Income] – ... some that relate to public goods, like vaccinating all children and ensuring they attend school. Such selective conditions would not undermine the main purpose of eliminating poverty and allow low-income people to take calculated risks, to try to lift themselves out of poverty.[13]

Gradually, the masses will become dependent on UBI for survival, making them obedient, while the global elites morph into oligarchs.

Once incomes are centrally controlled, it can be used to modulate behavior. Companies will play a role through stakeholder capitalism which is a way to evaluate companies on their social impact (i.e., ESG ratings) and not just on profit. The WEF has been promoting this as a way to re-organize the world and re-distribute wealth. Environment, Social Justice, and Governance are the pillars of stakeholder capitalism, and the ratings of companies will determine how businesses operate and who gets funded.

But the question is, who is deciding the criteria for rating under the ESG system? Answer: Big banks, big consulting and financial institutions, certain corporations, governments, and United Nations officials – all under the aegis of World Economic Forum's task forces. But this presents serious conflicts of interest because the global elites are designing the value system by which corporate social credit will be managed.

Despite the conflicts of interest, the ESG stakeholder capitalism system has become popular because central banks, governments, and wealthy investors have committed trillions of dollars to ESG funding. The Glasgow Financial Alliance for Net Zero (GFANZ), a group supported by the Joe Biden-US Democratic Party administration, claims to have 'more than 450 banks, insurers and other asset managers in dozens of countries' as members. Together, the members of GFANZ have pledged $130 trillion in assets.[14]

This makes WEF and its partners the new dictators. Anyone failing to comply will be subject to exclusionary policies – a form of Cancel Culture applied to institutions. So, every company is gearing up to comply.

> According to Schwab, the world must be rapidly transformed according to the designs of a technocratic elite, and "we" must adopt the ideas and policy preferences of 50 hand-picked "narrators" interviewed for the book, who he describes as "global thinkers and public intellectuals."[15]
>
> Klaus Schwab has an unbelievable God complex, and he frequently reminds the reader of his apparently unlimited technocratic faculties. He routinely reveals that he believes his group of colleagues have deity-like powers, and that once they unite their overall expertise, these technocrats, once in charge of all of us, can bring about unprecedented happiness and order.[16]

The system of ESG is being promoted as a way to eliminate poverty, eradicate inequality and improve access through control and technology.

Klaus Schwab is a comic book villain, and in *The Great Narrative,* he exposes the truly insane, extremist agenda of The World Economic Forum, which, through its Davos forum, acts as the go-to policy and ideas shop of the ruling class. It's important to read this book so that you are aware of the "great narratives" that will soon emerge from the global elites. Rarely do you find such genuine, overt evil in this world. Klaus and the World Economic Forum, through the attempted Trojan horse hijacking of our freedoms via the "climate emergency," fit the bill.[17]

The goal is to use Wokeism as the toolkit for dismantling the established structures and use inducements like UBI to get public support for stakeholder capitalism. The ESG ratings will control and monitor companies. The WEF saw an opportunity in the pandemic to mandate corporate ESG reporting and has partnered with major accounting firms like Deloitte, EY, KPMG, and PwC to promote, implement and eventually mandate its ESG framework.

Building a resilient business is increasingly dependent on preparing for the impact of non-financial factors, including those related to ... [ESG] issues. As we see with the current business impacts of COVID-19, companies are already dealing with financially material business factors that can develop suddenly. To succeed in the coming decade, investors and companies must equip themselves with forward-looking and proactive approaches to materiality.[18]

Vanguard Group, State Street, and BlackRock are the three largest institutional investors that own practically all major companies in all industries: pharmaceutical, consumer goods, agriculture, mining, automotive, energy, defense, and of course, big tech. *Bloomberg* published a report titled *BlackRock and Vanguard Are Less Than a Decade Away From Managing $20 Trillion – Two towers of power are dominating the future of investing.*[19]

Bloomberg goes as far as to say that BlackRock is the fourth branch of government[20] with strong ties to US and EU central banks.

Fink possesses a power that's more technocratic. BlackRock, the world's largest money manager, can do the things governments need right now.[21]

BlackRock's infusion of Wokeism in business is serious because BlackRock and a handful of inter-related oligarchs own practically all major companies. BlackRock is a WEF Partner[22] and has launched a Stake Holder Capitalism Center in a crusade to mandate ESG, universally leveraging its ten-trillion-dollar asset base.

> Although BlackRock cannot divest of companies in its index funds, Fink makes it clear that they will be 'increasingly disposed to vote against management and board directors when companies are not making sufficient progress on sustainability-related disclosures and the business practices and plans underlying them.'[23]

The World Economic Forum is also bringing ESG to the venture capital world, forcing companies to invest in only those start-ups that are ESG-compliant. Even more shocking is that it wants venture capitalists to use *organizations like Amnesty International to supply human rights reports.* It says that

> a report by Amnesty International highlighting the failure of VC firms over human rights due diligence demonstrate that venture capital has been a laggard when it comes to incorporating ... [ESG] considerations in investment processes.[24]

In this way the Woke becomes an ally because it gets empowered as the referees for rating capitalist enterprises. It is safe to assume that the rubric imposed on corporates via the ESG program, and the social credit system scorecard imposed on individuals, will all be based on Western social sciences ideas of what constitutes social justice, environmental compliance, and governance.

Interestingly, when BlackRock CEO Larry Fink came under criticism for embracing stakeholder capitalism,[25] the *Harvard Business Review* quickly jumped to his rescue through an article by someone whose social-impact consulting firm is funded by the Bill & Melinda Gates Foundation. It states:

> Rather than fault leaders like Fink for imposing a personal agenda on their businesses, we must censure those CEOs who fail to take social consequences into account and, as a result, harm their shareholders' returns.[26]

This concentration of power, combining money and politics, denies the diversity of views and values across cultures. For instance, India's culture may not be compatible with the stakeholder definitions of good values that WEF and its allies have formulated.

Digital Identifications as Control Mechanisms for Individuals

As we are seeing, the WEF has ambitious goals to control humanity on an unprecedented scale using draconian measures with the help of technology. Just as ESG is a way to control the behavior of corporations, individuals will be controlled through digital IDs and digital currency which will reward them on social credit earned with 'good behaviour' as prescribed by the elites. We witnessed this during the pandemic, where the poor were not given rations if they refused vaccinations. This is just the beginning!

The digital ID infrastructure is being pushed by WEF for the ostensible purpose of facilitating transactions. It has published several white papers promoting this, for instance, *How digital identity can improve lives in a post-COVID-19 world*[27] and *Digital identity can help advance inclusive financial services.*[28] It praises India for falling in line:

> India's Aadhaar system increases inclusion for over 1.2 billion Indians. World Bank Chief Economist Paul Romer calls it the most sophisticated digital ID system in the world. Given that one billion people globally are currently without access to a formal proof of identity, other governments should use such a system to streamline the delivery of services and payments, and massively increase financial inclusion.[29]

India is well poised for harnessing the surveillance system built into the Aadhaar card ID. Aadhaar is the world's biggest biometric ID information system with 1.1 billion people enrolled with data on retinal scans and fingerprints. It has received praise by Bill Gates.[30] Aadhaar serves as a government-issued ID accepted for government services, travel, banking etc. With the launch of the COVID-19 vaccines, patients providing Aadhaar were given a Unique Health ID[31] generated and maintained by the government. It is unclear, however, if it was with informed consent.[32] In October 2021, this program received a grant from the Bill & Melinda Gates Foundation.[33]

Similar to India's social credit system with biometric based digital ID, the Western world is working on rebranding vaccine passports and using them as digital IDs. The World Bank and the Bill & Melinda Gates Foundation have teamed with Nandan Nilekani, co-founder of Infosys and former chairman of Unique Identification Authority of India (UIDAI), to develop similar digital IDs in other countries.[34] It is interesting to note that Nilekani has been an important agenda contributor at WEF events for twenty years.[35] We are not against the use of technology for humankind's future, but we question the 'big brother' control of our lives through such technology.

The digital ID will become justified as a way to improve cyber security and authentication of transactions. However, the system can also be used insidiously to quell any form of dissent or expression of opinions. This was evident in the punitive actions taken by the Canadian government in tracking down and freezing bank accounts of citizens voicing support for the truckers' convoy.

In a report titled, *Advancing Digital Agency: The Power of Data Intermediaries*,[36] the WEF proposed the use of the digital ID to capture data on everyday transactions like credit, medical histories, social media, and online purchasing behaviors, and use the data for 'Judgements or decisions made based on authentication processes, profiles and histories (e.g. a bank decides the attractiveness of an individual for a loan)',[37] Or 'to book trips, to go through border control between countries or regions, vote and file taxes'.[38]

During a crisis situation, in order to survive, people readily comply with draconian measures without asking questions. Such opportunities are being exploited by WEF.

> The COVID 19 pandemic has led to a heightened focus on the power of medical data, specifically so-called vaccine passports. These passports by nature serve as a form of digital identity.[39]

The WEF applauds the use of vaccine passports to collect sensitive data and suggests this data can be re-used with or without consent.[40] It is clearly paving the way for a social credit system across the world using the invasive digital ID as the means. It suggests making 'use of a data intermediary, to overcome the limitations of notice and consent'.[41] It proposes that the data collected could be used in decision-making for things like loan eligibility.

Indian Businesses Becoming the Missionaries of a New Religion

The WEF has spawned yet another large initiative called Religious Freedom and Business Foundation (RFBF) headed by a former WEF official.[42] This organization deals with matters of faith and human rights in business and has set up a network of faith-based branches inside major multinational corporates. It has secured funding and endorsements from a large cabal of like-minded organizations.[43]

The RFBF is using businesses as fronts to bypass India's tightening restrictions on foreign proselytizing efforts. Working closely with the US Commission on International Religious Freedom (USCIRF), RFBF has already put out a 2021 report on religious freedom, giving India a score of 5.12 for government restrictions on religion on a scale of 0 to 10. India also scored a 5.74 on social hostilities involving religion on a scale of 0 to 7, from highest to lowest, while Pakistan scored 6.06 and China a mere 1.70. It is clear that the WEF and its affiliates are creating a problem where none exists.[44]

The RFBF is developing its own index to measure each business entity's commitment to religious freedom. The strategy is to make this index universally accepted as a rating system that could be used to supplement the ESG ratings.

> The Corporate Religious Equity, Diversity & Inclusion (REDI) Index is a benchmarking measure of a company's commitment to including religion as part of its overall diversity initiatives.[45]

Clearly, there is a lot of power in controlling such an index.

Grooming Future World Leaders

The World Economic Forum is promoting private-public partnerships in which corporations assume many functions of the government in the name of efficiency. To support the infiltration of governments, WEF is grooming business leaders and politicians worldwide. Schwab brags about this:

> ...what we are really proud of now, is the young generation like Prime Minister Trudeau, President of Argentina and so on, we penetrate the cabinets. So yesterday I was at a reception for Prime Minister Trudeau and I know that half of his cabinet or even more than half of his cabinet are from our, actually our Young Global Leaders of the WEF. [...] It's true in Argentina, it's true in France now, with the President [Macron] a Young Global Leader...[46]

The Young Global Leaders Program of WEF is designed to increase its influence by recruiting high potential individuals below the age of forty. The Harvard Kennedy School is involved as one of the donors.[47] The selection process is rigorous, and the leaders consider it an honor to be nominated to this elite club. The roster includes royalty, politicians, activists, business leaders, and journalists. The *Hill* recently reported:

> These young leaders are thrilled and also intimidated to be nominated and end up going along with ideas in order to not stand out. If everyone else is saying this is the thing that's right, we all agree on it even if they don't. People go along just to not be the lone contrarian. So groupthink is a minimum a consequence of being in this club. ... It's more likely the leadership is shaping this group to think a certain way, so that when they ultimately infiltrate cabinets they will likely tend to govern in a certain way. That makes sense because that is the stated goal of the World Economic Forum and its Great Reset. There is a stated agenda and of course their Global Young Leaders program is a grooming ground for getting leaders positions of power to usher in this agenda.[48]

Many world leaders, including a large number of Indians in important positions (such as Cabinet Minister Smriti Irani), are being groomed by WEF as part of this program. There is also an under-thirty program for grooming:

> In 2012, Schwab and the WEF founded yet another institution, the "Global Shapers Community," which brings together those

identified by them as having leadership potential from around the world who are under 30. Approximately 10,000 participants have passed through this program to date, and they regularly hold meetings in 400 cities. Wolff believes that it is yet another proving ground where future political leaders are being selected, vetted, and groomed before being positioned in the world's political apparatus.[49]

The chief ministers of Tamil Nadu, M.K. Stalin, and Andhra Pradesh, Y.S. Jagan Reddy are already working with the WEF. Even modern popular Hindu gurus such as Sri Sri Ravi Shankar and Sadguru Jaggi Vasudev are affiliated with the WEF. Many actors from the Indian film industry also are ambassadors of the WEF.

The former chairperson of PepsiCo, Indra Nooyi, is a trustee for the WEF Talent for Boards.[50] The WEF has also set up an office in Mumbai for what it calls the Fourth Industrial Revolution. The stated goal of the Centre for the Fourth Industrial Revolution India is to serve as a global hub for public-private partnerships in a broad spectrum of technologies and public services.[51]

The Indian government's NITI Aayog has a partnership with the Centre for the Fourth Industrial Revolution India and has developed a framework to promote data exchanges 'with open, scalable architectures and transparent and equitable governance models supported by sound incentivization principles'. Given the WEF's track record and motives, one wonders what these 'incentives' are, and how 'equitable' is being defined. The NITI Aayog is developing ideas jointly with WEF and advocating for public-private partnerships. The following statement echoes the framework of WEF:

> The Data Empowerment and Protection Architecture (DEPA) released by NITI Aayog in collaboration with iSPIRT is truly futuristic, providing data empowerment to the common citizen in the most comprehensive and transparent manner. A similar approach for developing data platforms through unique public-private partnership that moves data out of silos would help in data-driven decision-making for organizations and data-driven policy-making for the government. NITI Aayog has collaborated with (WEF) to prepare this paper on data exchange (DEx),

technical and commercial enablers for a flexible data governance framework. A data exchange allows data to be leveraged for broader sets of social outcomes and can play a pivotal role in unlocking the potential of a data economy. (It) ... is a critical step towards a data-driven economy and invites a dialogue on exploring government-led data exchanges for citizen services. ... sector-specific models and use cases need to be designed and developed. NITI Aayog and the World Economic Forum endeavour to ... focus on the approach for developing Logistics Data Exchange (LDEx), a framework for data exchange of public- and private-sector data in the logistics sector. We acknowledge the World Economic Forum team and NITI Aayog collaborators for their initiative and effort in preparing this white paper.[52]

To encourage the Indian government to continue complying with the WEF's policies, it has praised India for its digital reset:

This digital-first reset of a country of 1.3 billion people is not only technological advancement but, more importantly, it is the foundation of a new mechanism for the deliverance of goods of governance. ... This joint public-private push is making India a digital-first country, resetting the basic life experience and aspirations of more than a billion people.[53]

The Devatas of Davos

The Abrahamic faiths no longer need to impose their beliefs using missionaries or the sword to convert. The WEF's constellation of devatas of Davos can use industrialists and politicians as their puppets. Its commandments are based on Western Universalism with a Marxist toolkit to dismantle existing structures. Harvard University, the vishwa guru, has spent decades working on such scholarship. These knowledge systems will be used on an unprecedented scale with the aid of technology to undermine India and create the WEF's vision of the Great Reset.

We could also be headed towards a system of algorithmic justice in which Artificial Intelligence embeds the values of the global oligarchs. The World Economic Forum's devatas will punish the heretics who commit 'sins' as determined by the social credit system. Social credit will determine if one is eligible for services like healthcare, food, insurance, shelter, and travel/mobility. The digital IDs and personal data will prevent dissidents from availing of goods and services. Corporate ESG ratings will effectively shut down small businesses that are non-compliant.

The ratings will be based on the Woke definition of Diversity, Equity, and Inclusion. For instance, a Hindu could be penalized for carrying out Vedic rituals, lighting lamps, bursting firecrackers on the festival of Diwali, consuming dairy, performing Hindu prayers, and bathing in sacred rivers. The new ethics of the social credit system will become like a religion.

The irony of this new game is that it is being played in the name of saving humanity from a variety of problems. Sadly, many Indian elites are all in it as the new zamindars, sepoys, and shishyas. India has indeed been sold out by its very own elites!

Endnotes

Introduction

1   The evidence is complex because it entails multiple disciplines such as: archeology, linguistics, art history, textual evidence (mostly oral), etc. Many scholars have provided arguments against the Aryan Invasion Theory on linguistic and archaeological grounds. Some have even proposed that the homeland of the Indo-European language family is India, a theory known as Out of India Theory.

2   (Malhotra 2016, 20)

3   For her background: 'Deepthi Rao'. LinkedIn. Retrieved on April 30, 2022 (https://www.linkedin.com/in/deepthirao05)

4   For her background: 'Deepthi Rao'. LinkedIn. Retrieved on April 30, 2022 (https://www.linkedin.com/in/deepthirao05)

5   (Shafer 2016)

6   (Kumar 2020)

7   (Hindu Students Council 2021)

8   See: 'General Assembly Unanimously Adopts Texts on Combating Islamophobia, Protecting Rangelands, Tackling Difficulties for Widows, Bicycles as Public Transportation'. United Nations. Retrieved on April 30, 2022 (https://www.un.org/press/en/2022/ga12408.doc.htm)

1.   Dismantling the United States of America

1   The authors are indebted to the following two books for providing important insights that have helped in this chapter: 1) (Pluckrose and Lindsay 2020); 2) (Boghossian and Lindsay 2019).

2   Gramsci introduced the concept of cultural hegemony in the Marxist framework. It refers to the dominance of a diverse society by the ruling class who manipulate the culture of that society—the beliefs and explanations, perceptions, values, and mores—so that the worldview of the ruling class becomes the accepted cultural norm. Thus, the socio-economic and political status quo are misrepresented as being natural, inevitable, and beneficial to all classes, rather than being contrived for the exclusive benefit to the ruling class.

3   Gramsci proposed a *strategic distinction* between two kinds of war. The war of

<u>position</u> is an intellectual and cultural struggle to create a proletarian culture whose native value system counters the cultural hegemony of the bourgeoisie. Class distinctions are emphasized, changing the academic discourse and revolutionary organization. Then, in the <u>war of manoeuver</u>, popular and political support are mobilized for social revolution.

4   (Horkheimer, Critical Theory Selected Essays 1982, 244)

5   (Marcuse 1964, 8)

6   (Marcuse 1964)

7   (Butcher and Gonzalez 2020)

8   (Marcuse 1964, 256–57) and (Horkheimer and Adorno 2002, 106)

9   A big difference between the postmodernist deconstruction and Vedanta or Buddhism is that Vedanta and Buddhism also deconstruct binaries, the ego, the ideas we have of truth which are based on our own ego and our own language, etc. The difference being that Vedanta has a deeper absolute reality after one has transcended the relative reality. So, the relative reality of *Nama Rupa* is false, but that doesn't mean there is nothing else of a higher level, whereas in the case of Postmodernism, there is no higher reality, there is no ultimate, absolute reality, and once you deconstruct the reality as constructed by human power and social discourse, there is no other higher reality which would be of a universal kind. One ends up with identities, with their own separate realities, fighting each other and replacing one set of hegemony with another hegemony.

10   See: 'Critical Legal Theory'. Cornell Law School. Retrieved on April 30, 2022 (https://www.law.cornell.edu/wex/critical_legal_theory); (Kennedy and Klare 1984)

11   (Butcher and Gonzalez 2020)

12   (Delgado and Stefancic 2017, 3)

13   Richard Delgado and Jean Stefancic as cited in (Pluckrose and Lindsay 2020, 115)

14   (K. Crenshaw 1989)

15   (Collins 1990)

16   (Collins and Bilge 2016, 2)

17   (Beshara 2019)

18   (Malhotra, Open letter to Senator Cory Booker 2022a)

19   (NBC News@NBCNews 2021)

20   (Tamari 2009)

21   (Bowyer 2021)

22   (Abelove, Barale and Halperin 1993, 149) Gayle Rubin has taken an *extreme position on pedophilia*. She refers to pedophilia as one of these 'essentialized categories' and she adopts a position of moral relativism. She wants us to sympathize with pedophiles, writing: 'It is harder for most people to actually sympathize with boy-lovers. Like communists and homosexuals in the 1950s, boy-lovers are so stigmatized that it is difficult to find defenders for their civil liberties, let alone for their erotic orientation'. (Abelove, Barale and Halperin 1993, 147)

23   (Butler 1993, 2)

24   Dismantling Childhood Innocence: Julie C. Garlen explains: '...The construct of childhood innocence is a powerful social myth that structures children's social relations and culture and informs their rights and status in society. ... By examining the emotional investments and social tensions that have shaped concepts of childhood, which define who is entitled to innocence and what it means to "belong" with/in childhood, I reveal how *the doctrine of innocence has operated to maintain White supremacy*'. She considers childhood innocence as something unnatural and blames White supremacy. This innocence is built by parents through 'the magical childhood moments' they want the child to remember forever, such as 'bedtime songs and stories, lunch box love notes, kiss attacks, fort building, catching bugs and fireflies, bonfires, snowball fights, shoulder rides, gardening, cooking, organized adventures, and readily available art, music, and cultural experiences'. The parental goal is to implant memories of a happy childhood 'filled with music, laughter, exploration and sun'. Vacations, she says, are 'happiness anchors' that will later 'lighten the burdens of adulthood'. This parenting is fake, she maintains, because the goal is to 'Curate extraordinary adult memories for their children by creating a mythical period of wide-eyed wonder and magical moments'. Parents protect their children from natural things like sadness and stress by censoring topics such as sexuality, death, violence, and poverty. They want to regulate 'children's sexual agency' along with regulating race relations by producing a particular "childhood" that perpetuates White supremacy'. Garlen says that this amounts to the 'Conflation of innocence with conservative Christian values'. She feels that toys, games, video games and TV shows that depict violence are considered threats to innocence because they are a direct assault on Christian values. Gender fluidity is a threat to the parents' agenda to produce childhood innocence. The definition of innocence is incorrect as the need to protect children from adult knowledge of sexual desire, consumption, violence, and immorality. This presupposes that adult culture is corrupt and children need to be protected from it. Garlen challenges the adult-child binary. She explains the structural problem: 'The prioritization of childhood innocence reinforced the superiority of White elites who would serve as the models of the new Christian piety and emphasized the role of women as the primary nurturers of good Christian children. At a time when the morality of human enslavement could no longer be justified, the doctrine of childhood innocence also offered a sort of absolution by proxy for White Americans.' Her stated goal is to dismantle the traditional notions of innocence 'to advance conditions of social justice'. (All quotations from: (Garlen 2018)).

25   (Ramaswamy 2021, 216)
26   (Ramaswamy 2021, 231)
27   (Mitchell 2019)
28   (Mitchell 2019)
29   (Ramaswamy 2021, 258-59)
30   (Dougherty 2018)

31 An example of this was the encounter between a Yale professor, Nicholas Christakis, and students in a public courtyard in 2015. This video illustrates the dogmatic quality, and gang-like intimidation of free thinking: (Gravitahn 2017)

32 (Jay 1996, 69)

33 (Jolivette 2015, 5)

34 (Nanda 2001, 165)

35 (Riley 2008, 109)

36 See: 'Professor Argues Against "Truths and Knowledge"; Says Math=White Privilege'. *The New American*. Retrieved on April 30, 2022 (https://thenewamerican.com/professor-argues-against-truths-and-knowledge-says-math-white-privilege)

37 (Dougherty 2018)

38 Herbert Marcuse, 'Repressive Tolerance', in (Wolff, Moore, Jr. and Marcuse 1969, 110)

39 (Bell 1995, 893, 902) Also, quoted in (Butcher and Gonzalez 2020)

40 (DiAngelo, *White Fragility* 2011)

41 (Soave 2020). She used to charge fourteen thousand dollars per speech in 2020 and has now increased her fee to between thirty thousand to forty thousand dollars for speeches. According to media reports, she made '$728K a year' apart from the 7.5 percent in royalties from her best seller'. See: (Eberhart 2021)

42 (Sensoy and DiAngelo 2017, 20,23,24)

43 (Sensoy and DiAngelo 2017, 15)

44 (Sensoy and DiAngelo 2017, 84-85)

45 (DiAngelo 2011, 55-56). She gives a specific example of White fragility: 'A cogent example of White Fragility occurred recently during a workplace anti-racism training I co-facilitated with an inter-racial team. One of the white participants left the session and went back to her desk, upset at receiving (what appeared to the training team as) sensitive and diplomatic feedback on how some of her statements had impacted several people of color in the room. At break, several other white participants approached us (the trainers) and reported that they had talked to the woman at her desk, and she was very upset that her statements had been challenged. They wanted to alert us to the fact that she literally "might be having a heart-attack." Upon questioning from us, they clarified that they meant this literally. These co-workers were sincere in their fear that the young woman might actually physically die as a result of the feedback. Of course, when news of the woman's potentially fatal condition reached the rest of the participant group, all attention was immediately focused back onto her and away from the impact she had had on the people of color'. (DiAngelo 2011, 64-65)

46 (Applebaum 2010, 108)

47 (Applebaum 2010, 188-89)

48 (Bailey 2017, 880)

49 (Grey 2013)

50 (Perna 2018)

51 Ironically, the same logic is not applied when they attack the *Manusmriti*. To be

consistent, they must say that the *Manusmriti* cannot be assumed as a reliable source for understanding caste.

52 (Schofield 2021)
53 (Schofield 2021)
54 (Élysée 2020)
55 (Élysée 2020)
56 (wzgrl 2008, 00:02:08)
57 (Bonilla-Silva and Dietrich 2011)
58 "Our Constitution is color-blind, and neither knows nor tolerates classes among citizens. In respect of civil rights, all citizens are equal before the law" See: 'Plessy v. Ferguson, 163 U.S. 537 (1896)'. US Supreme Court. Retrieved on April 30, 2022 (https://supreme.justia.com/cases/federal/us/163/537). Also see: 'Parents Involved in Community Schools v. Seattle School Dist. No. 1 (6/28/07)'. US Supreme Court. Retrieved on April 30, 2022 (https://www.supremecourt.gov/opinions/06pdf/05-908.pdf)
59 (Apfelbaum, Norton and Sommers 2012)
60 See: 'Ibram X. Kendi defines what it means to be an antiracist'. Penguin. Retrieved on April 30, 2022 (https://www.penguin.co.uk/articles/2020/june/ibram-x-kendi-definition-of-antiracist.htm)
61 (VI-Control 2007)
62 (Bonilla-Silva and Dietrich 2011)
63 (Bonilla-Silva and Dietrich 2011)
64 (Coates 2015)
65 (Bonilla-Silva 2003)
66 (Dean 2013)
67 (Bonilla-Silva and Dietrich 2011)
68 (Bonilla-Silva and Dietrich 2011)
69 (Bonilla-Silva and Dietrich 2011)
70 (Crenshaw, et al. 2019, 128)
71 (Crenshaw, et al. 2019, 128)
72 (Ferlazzo, 2019)
73 'CRT questions the very foundations of liberalism, including equality theory, legal reasoning, Enlightenment rationalism, and neutral principles of constitutional law'. (Delgado and Stefancic 2017, 3)
74 (Ramaswamy 2021)
75 (Annenberg Public Policy Center 2021)
76 Address by Abraham Lincoln before the Young Men's Lyceum of Springfield, Illinois, as it appeared in the *Sangamo Journal*, February 3, 1838. Reprinted from (Basler 1953). See also (The Journal of the Abraham Lincoln Association 1984).
77 (Koop 2020)
78 See: 'About SHRM'. SHRM. Retrieved on April 30, 2022 (https://www.shrm.org/about-shrm/pages/default.aspx)
79 (DiAngelo, *White Fragility* 2018, xiv)

80   (Kendi 2019, 163)
81   (Ramaswamy 2021, 2)
82   (Ramaswamy 2021, 3)
83   (Ramaswamy 2021, 135)
84   (Ramaswamy 2021, 139)
85   (Ramaswamy 2021, 143)
86   (Ramaswamy 2021, 19)

2. The Americanization of Caste

1   (Malhotra and Neelakandan 2011, 11)
2   (Wilkerson 2020)
3   (Wilkerson 2020, 273)
4   (The New York Public Library 2020)
5   See: 'Isabel Wilkerson'. Isabel Wilkerson. Retrieved on February 15, 2022 (https://www.isabelwilkerson.com)
6   See: 'Caste and the Durban conference'. Ministry of External Affairs: Government of India. Retrieved on February 15, 2022 (https://www.mea.gov.in/articles-in-indian-media.htm?dtl/18479/Caste+and+the+Durban+conference)
7   (Wilkerson 2020, 176)
8   (Wilkerson 2020, 17)
9   (Wilkerson 2020, 24)
10   (Wilkerson 2020, 18)
11   (Wilkerson 2020, 19)
12   (Wilkerson 2020, 19)
13   (Wilkerson 2020, 26)
14   (Wilkerson 2020, 29)
15   (Wilkerson 2020, 25)
16   (Wilkerson 2020, 29)
17   (Wilkerson 2020, 74)
18   (Wilkerson 2020, 104)
19   (Wilkerson 2020, 268)
20   See: 'Africans in India: From Slaves to Generals and Rulers'. New York Public Library. Retrieved on February 15, 2022 (https://www.nypl.org/blog/2013/01/31/africans-india-slaves-generals-and-rulers). Also see: 'Indian Ocean and Middle Eastern Slave Trades'. Oxford Bibliographies. Retrieved on February 15, 2022 (https://www.oxfordbibliographies.com/view/document/obo-9780199846733/obo-9780199846733-0051.xml) and 'The story of East Africa's role in the transatlantic slave trade'. *The Conversation*. Retrieved on February 15, 2022 (https://theconversation.com/the-story-of-east-africas-role-in-the-transatlantic-slave-trade-43194)
21   (Levi 2002) When I first saw the PhD dissertation of Scott Levi being done at

University of Wisconsin-Madison, I did not notice any mention about slavery in India before the Muslims. The dissertation was about slavery during Islam in India, and it was based on archives of that period available in the former USSR. But then a warning was issued by academic scholars that his work would play into the hands of "Hindu activists" like me. The published version was adapted with a preamble saying that slavery pre-dates Islam in India because it is mentioned in the Vedic literature. However, that claim is incorrect because it is based on mistranslating the Vedic Sanskrit term "dasu" as "slave", which is an incorrect translation.

22   See: 'Caste Among Indian Muslims Is a Real Issue. So Why Deny Them Reservation?' *The Wire*. Retrieved on February 15, 2022 (https://thewire.in/caste/caste-among-indian-muslims-real-why-deny-reservation) and also 'Islam And Caste Inequality Among Indian Muslims'. Indian Dalit Muslims' Voice. Retrieved on February 15, 2022 (https://dalitmuslims.wordpress.com/2009/07/13/islam-and-caste-inequality-among-indian-muslims)

23   See: 'Debates on Muslim Caste in North India and Pakistan: from colonial ethnography to pasmanda mobilization'. *HAL Open Science*. Retrieved on February 15, 2022 (https://hal.archives-ouvertes.fr/hal-02697381) and also 'India's Muslim community under a churn: 85% backward Pasmandas up against 15% Ashrafs'. *The Print*. Retrieved on February 15, 2022 (https://theprint.in/opinion/indias-muslim-community-under-a-churn-85-backward-pasmandas-up-against-15-ashrafs/234599)

24   Spanish caste system: 'Spanish Caste System'. Nuestra Verdad Publicación. Retrieved on February 15, 2022 (https://www.nuestraverdad.com/post/spanish-caste-system); Latin American caste system: 'Figure 1 - uploaded by Hector Y Adames'. ResearchGate. Retrieved on February 15, 2022 (https://www.researchgate.net/figure/Latin-American-Social-Caste-Pyramid-LASCP_fig1_262107699); Pakistan's caste system: (Barth 1956); China's urban caste system: (Tang and Yang 2008); Japan's caste system: "Japan's hidden caste of untouchables." *BBC* News. Retrieved on February 15, 2022 (https://www.bbc.com/news/world-asia-34615972).

25   (Wilkerson 2020, 76)

26   See, for example, Cox's 1948 book that caste is not race. 'Caste, Class, and Race'. Global Social Theory. Retrieved on February 15, 2022 (https://globalsocialtheory.org/concepts/caste-class-and-race)

27   (Wilkerson 2020, 106)

3. Indian Americans Equated With White Racists

1   (Equality Labs 2018a)

2   (North Star Fund 2017)

3   See: 'Dr. T.S.S. Rajan MD'. *U.S. News*. Retrieved on April 30, 2022 (https://health.usnews.com/doctors/tss-rajan-1225010)

4   See: 'Thenmozhi Soundararajan'. Virginia Tech. Retrieved on April 30, 2022

(https://ccc.ipg.vt.edu/Programs/forum/Thenmozhi.html)

5   (Equality Labs 2018a)

6   (Equality Labs 2018b). See p.39 of the Full Report.

7   (Badrinathan, et al. 2021)

8   (Badrinathan, et al. 2021)

9   (Metcalf and Rolfe 2010)

10 (Equality Labs 2018b)

11 See: 'A Historic Congressional Hearing on Caste in the US'. *The Wire*. Retrieved on February 15, 2022 (https://thewire.in/caste/a-historic-congressional-hearing-on-caste-in-the-us)

12 (R. Rao 2021)

13 See: 'Who We Invest In'. New Media Ventures. Retrieved on February 15, 2022 (https://www.newmediaventures.org/investments). See also: 'Equality Labs has 1 Investor, New Media Ventures'. *Crunchbase*. Retrieved on February 15, 2022 (https://www.crunchbase.com/search/principal.investors/field/organizations/num_investors/equality-labs). And: https://mobile.twitter.com/by2kaafi/status/1247926029319987206. This tweet, which has been deleted, stated: 'New Media Ventures (NMV) is one Angel Investor in EqualityLabs. NMV has many investors of which one name is recognizable – Omidyar Network'.

14 (Equality Labs 2018b)

15 See: 'Thenmozhi Soundararajan'. Atlantic Fellows. Retrieved on April 30, 2022 (https://racialequity.atlanticfellows.org/fellow/thenmozhi-soundararajan); Also see: 'The Atlantic Institute'. *Rhodes Trust*. Retrieved on April 30, 2022 (https://www.rhodeshouse.ox.ac.uk/about/the-atlantic-institute)

16 See: 'Describing a system of oppression is not a slur'. *Scroll.in*. Retrieved on February 15, 2022 (https://scroll.in/article/902949/describing-a-system-of-oppression-is-not-a-slur-creator-of-smash-brahmanical-patriarchy-poster)

17 See: 'HAF Legal Team Writes to CDE to Investigate Assault Allegations'. HAF. Retrieved on February 15, 2022 (https://www.hinduamerican.org/press/haf-legal-team-writes-cde-investigate-assault-allegations)

18 See: 'Why We Must End Caste Oppression'. *Reappropriate*. Retrieved on February 15, 2022 (http://reappropriate.co/2018/05/why-we-must-end-caste-oppression/)

19 See: '2020.06.30 DFEH v. Cisco Systems, Et Al. Civil Complaint – FILED'. *Scribd*. Retrieved on February 15, 2022 (https://www.scribd.com/document/467774912/2020-06-30-DFEH-v-Cisco-Systems-Et-Al-Civil-Complaint-FILED)

20 (Rising Up With Sonali 2020). Timestamp: 8:01

21 (Rising Up With Sonali 2020). Timestamp: 9:05-9:41

22 See: 'Protecting Our People'. Cisco. Retrieved on February 15, 2022 (https://blogs.cisco.com/news/protecting-our-people). The case was dismissed in October 2020. But Cisco's defense included statements like the law doesn't say you can't discriminate based on caste!
See: 'California dept dismisses employee harassment case against Cisco'. *The Times*

of India. Retrieved on February 15, 2022 (https://timesofindia.indiatimes.com/business/india-business/california-dept-dismisses-employee-harassment-case-against-cisco/articleshow/78760768.cms)

23   (Mukherji 2021)

24   See: 'India's engineers have thrived in Silicon Valley. So has its caste system'. *The Washington Post*. Retrieved on February 15, 2022 (https://www.washingtonpost.com/technology/2020/10/27/indian-caste-bias-silicon-valley/)

25   BAPS stands for Bochasanwasi Akshar Purushottam Swaminarayan Sanstha.

26   See: 'Why Is Caste Inequality Still Legal in America?' *The New York Times*. Retrieved on February 15, 2022 (https://www.nytimes.com/2021/05/25/opinion/caste-discrimination-us-federal-protection.html)

27   See: 'American Colleges as beginning to recognize caste as a protected class'. *Quartz India*. Retrieved on February 15, 2022 (https://qz.com/india/2081765/us-universities-like-uc-davis-ban-indian-caste-system-on-campus/)

28   See: 'Companies Have Promised $35 Billion Toward Racial Equity. Where Is the Money Going?' *The Wall Street Journal*. Retrieved on February 15, 2022 (https://www.wsj.com/articles/companies-have-promised-billions-toward-racial-equity-where-is-the-money-going-11608570864)

29   See: 'The Unfinished Business of Office Diversity Training'. *The Wall Street Journal*. Retrieved on February 15, 2022 (https://www.wsj.com/articles/the-unfinished-business-of-office-diversity-training-11608512401)

30   See: 'Diversity Has Become a Booming Business. So Where Are the Results?' *Time*. Retrieved on February 15, 2022 (https://time.com/5696943/diversity-business)

31   See: 'EEO Data Collections'. The U.S. Equal Employment Opportunity Commission. Retrieved on February 15, 2022 (https://www.eeoc.gov/employers/eeo-data-collections)

32   See: 'Statement on the Interpretation of Caste Within the Brandeis Nondiscrimination Policy'. Brandeis University. Retrieved on February 15, 2022 (https://www.brandeis.edu/human-resources/policies/discrimination/caste-statement.html)

33   See: 'UC Davis quietly added caste to its antidiscrimination policy. Will it cause others to do the same?' *San Francisco Chronicle*. Retrieved on February 15, 2022 (https://www.sfchronicle.com/california/article/UC-Davis-quietly-added-caste-to-its-16626845.php). Also see: 'California University Board unanimously votes to recognise protection from caste discrimination'. *The Hindu*. Retrieved on February 15, 2022 (https://www.thehindu.com/news/international/california-varsity-board-unanimously-votes-to-recognise-protection-from-caste-discrimination/article38328354.ece)

34   For Colby College, see: 'Maine's Colby College bans discrimination based on caste'. *AP*. Retrieved on February 15, 2022 (https://apnews.com/article/asia-education-discrimination-maine-south-asia-a4934667f35e70733e4986474a5021b0)

35   (Tejeda and Chahal 2021)

36   (Tejeda and Chahal 2021)

37 (Tejeda and Chahal 2021)
38 (Tejeda and Chahal 2021)
39 (Tejeda and Chahal 2021)
40 (R. Rao 2021)
41 (County of Santa Clara 2020)
42 (County of Santa Clara 2020)
43 See: 'Minutes'. County of Santa Clara Human Rights Commission. Retrieved on February 15, 2022 (http://sccgov.iqm2.com/Citizens/FileOpen.aspx?Type=12&ID=8723&Inline=True)
44 (Diya TV 2021). Timestamp: 05:28:20. The speaker identified herself as Nikhila Lakshmana.
45 (Ambedkar King Study Circle USA 2021)
46 See: 'Subject: Caste Based Discrimination in the United States'. County of Santa Clara. Retrieved on February 15, 2022 (http://sccgov.iqm2.com/Citizens/FileOpen.aspx?Type=4&ID=213125)
47 (Borgonjon 2017)
48 (Equality Labs 2020)
49 See: 'A Muslim student levelled false allegations against 3 professors at Dartmouth College in the USA just because they are Hindus: Details'. *OpIndia*. Retrieved on February 15, 2022 (https://www.opindia.com/2021/10/muslim-student-made-false-allegations-against-hindu-professors-in-usa)
50 (End Forced Arbitration 2022). Timestamp: 30:43-32:11.
51 (King 2018)

4. Attacking Meritocracy at the Indian Institutes of Technology

1 See: 'South Asia Without Borders Seminar Series'. The Lakshmi Mittal and Family South Asia Institute at Harvard University. Retrieved on April 30, 2022 (https://mittalsouthasiainstitute.harvard.edu/event/south-asia-without-borders-seminar-series)
2 (Subramanian 2019, 23)
3 (Weber 1905)
4 See: 'Christianity's Meritocratic Dilemma: Reflections on Sandel's The Tyranny of Merit'. *Providence Magazine*. Retrieved on February 15, 2022 (https://providencemag.com/2021/11/christianitys-meritocratic-dilemma-reflections-michael-sandel-tyranny-of-merit/)
5 (Sandel 2020)
6 See: 'Michael Sandel: "The populist backlash has been a revolt against the tyranny of merit"'. *The Guardian*. Retrieved on February 15, 2022 (https://www.theguardian.com/books/2020/sep/06/michael-sandel-the-populist-backlash-has-been-a-revolt-against-the-tyranny-of-merit)

7   (Subramanian 2019, 27)

8   (Subramanian 2019, 28)

9   (Subramanian 2019, 31)

10   Unlike Britain, the mental and manual aspects of technical work are integrated in Germany, and students are expected to do intellectual, conceptual, abstract work along with physical tasks like carpentry and metal work. German engineering, in fact, prioritizes technique over theory. The engineer is first and foremost trained as a skilled technician.

11   (Subramanian 2019, 26)

12   (Malhotra, The Peer-Review Cartel 2022b)

13   This is a slightly edited version from the article: (Malhotra 2022b)

14   (Sambara 2021)

15   Larry Summers, president of Harvard, became controversial for saying that men and women had different kinds of aptitude. See: 'Why women are poor at science, by Harvard president'. *The Guardian.* Retrieved on February 15, 2022 (https://www.theguardian.com/science/2005/jan/18/educationsgendergap.genderissues)

16   (Sindwani 2020)

17   (Subramanian 2019, 260)

18   (Subramanian 2019, 268)

19   (Subramanian 2019, 293)

20   (Subramanian 2019, 299)

21   (Sambara 2021)

22   (Ambedkar King Study Circle USA 2020). Timestamps: 03:54 and 9:54.

23   (Sambara 2021)

24   (Ambedkar King Study Circle USA 2020). Timestamp: 20:28.

25   (Ambedkar International Center (AIC) 2021)

26   (Ambedkar International Center (AIC) 2021)

27   (Ambedkar International Center (AIC) 2021)

28   (Sambara 2021)

29   (Subramanian 2019, 304)

30   (Subramanian 2019, 305)

31   (Kodaikanal International School 2021). Timestamp: 00:00:43-00:00:51.

32   (Subramanian 2019, 314)

33   (Subramanian 2019, 303)

34   Subramanian shows her true colors when she starts supporting the Kashmir separatists, Maqbool Bhatt and Afzal Guru, who were charged for the 2001 terrorist attack on the Indian Parliament. It is interesting that her criticism is echoed in the reports by the US Commission on International Religious Freedom labeling India as a Country of Concern because it allegedly suppresses religious freedom. Positioning herself with the USCIRF, she accuses Modi of violent attacks on Muslims and Dalits, the arrest of civil and human rights activists, and the killing of journalists. She does not believe that such things ever happened under previous governments. She also criticizes the Modi government for celebrating Sanskrit and establishing

separate facilities for vegetarians and non-vegetarians, as though that is something contrary to lower caste interests.

35 (Subramanian 2019, 321)
36 (Sambara 2021)
37 (Sambara 2021)
38 (Higgins 2021)

5. The Rise of the Afro-Dalits

1 See: 'Suraj Yengde - Perspectives on Race and Caste in the U.S. and India Speaker Series on Global Racism'. Loyola University Chicago. Retrieved on February 15, 2022 (https://www.luc.edu/asianstudies/events)
2 See: 'As we debate Floyd and systemic prejudice, the power and need for such a moral force couldn't be more relevant today'. *The Indian Express*. Retrieved on February 15, 2022 (https://indianexpress.com/article/opinion/columns/george-floyd-us-india-dalit-advisasi-6479505)
3 (Leung 2021)
4 (*The Wire* 2021). Timestamp: 30:57.
5 See: 'Caste among the Indian Diaspora in Africa'. *Economic & Political Weekly*. Retrieved on February 15, 2022 (https://www.epw.in/journal/2015/37/notes/caste-among-indian-diaspora-africa.html)
6 (Yengde 2019)
7 (D'Souza 2020). Timestamp: 19:36-21:20.
8 (Hindu American Foundation 2019). Timestamp: 01:19:26.
9 (Hindu American Foundation 2019). Timestamp: 01:14:05.
10 (Hindu American Foundation 2019). Timestamp: 01:07:29.
11 (Yengde 2021)
12 (Samyak Chetna 2021). Timestamp: 24:19.
13 (Samyak Chetna 2021). Timestamp: 26:25.
14 (Samyak Chetna 2021)
15 (Samyak Chetna 2021). Timestamp: 07:08.
16 (Bangalore International Centre 2019). Timestamp: 01:07:29.
17 (JharGov TV 2021)
18 See: 'Adivasis were never Hindus, they never will be: Jharkhand CM'. *The Indian Express*. Retrieved on February 15, 2022 (https://indianexpress.com/article/india/adivasis-were-never-hindus-they-never-will-be-jharkhand-cm-7199096)
19 (Samyak Chetna 2021). Timestamp: 35:58
20 See: 'This ugly head dumpster—Shankaracharya is responsible for crimes such as this. The terrorists caste terrorism in India. Yet to come across proud bamans and Hindus who promote social harmony via inter caste marriages. The youngsters need to make a choice'. Twitter. Retrieved on February 15, 2022 (https://twitter.com/surajyengde/status/1368201526028697601)

21   (Samyak Chetna 2021). Timestamp: 36:22.

22   (Hindu American Foundation 2019). Timestamp: 01:20:23.

23   (Samyak Chetna 2021). Timestamp: 43:06.

24   (Samyak Chetna 2021). Timestamp: 43:48.

25   (Samyak Chetna 2021). Timestamp: 45:14.

26   (Samyak Chetna 2021). Timestamp: 37:13.

27   (Samyak Chetna 2021). Timestamp: 35:00.

28   (Samyak Chetna 2021). Timestamp: 40:51.

29   (*The Wire* 2021). Timestamp: 06:05.

30   (*The Wire* 2021). Timestamp: 03:50.

31   (*The Wire* 2021). Timestamp: 21:30.

32   (*The Wire* 2021). Timestamp: 25:50.

33   (*The Wire* 2021). Timestamp: 07:25.

34   (*The Wire* 2021). Timestamp: 13:55.

35   (Bangalore International Centre 2019). Timestamp: 09:18.

36   (*The Wire* 2021). Timestamp: 20:00.

37   (Bangalore International Centre 2019). Timestamp: 22:27.

38   (Bangalore International Centre 2019). Timestamp: 09:00.

39   (D'Souza 2020). Timestamp: 26:30.

40   (D'Souza 2020). Timestamp: 26:50.

41   (Asoka TV Channel 2017). Timestamp: 21:20.

42   (D'Souza 2020). Timestamp: 36:24.

43   (Bangalore International Centre 2019). Timestamp: 01:22:00.

44   (Bangalore International Centre 2019). Timestamp: 01:22:05.

45   (Bangalore International Centre 2019). Timestamp: 01:28:01.

46   (D'Souza 2020). Timestamp: 45:40.

47   (*The Wire* 2021). Timestamp: 09:40.

48   (*The Wire* 2021). Timestamp: 16:30.

49   (Rodrigues 2020)

50   (Bangalore International Centre 2019). Timestamp: 01:20:25.

51   (Bangalore International Centre 2019). Timestamp: 01:25:20.

52   (Asoka TV Channel 2017). Timestamp: 42:33.

53   (Bangalore International Centre 2019). Timestamp: 00:39:00.

54   See: 'Send 10,000 Dalit students every semester to foreign universities: Suraj
     Milind Yengde'. *The Economic Times*. August 14, 2016. Retrieved on February
     15, 2022 (https://economictimes.indiatimes.com/opinion/interviews/send-
     10000-dalit-students-every-semester-to-foreign-universities-suraj-milind-yengde/
     articleshow/53690113.cms)

55   See: 'Reservation is the most important state policy we have and we can't give
     up on that'. *The Kathmandu Post*. Retrieved on February 15, 2022 (https://
     kathmandupost.com/interviews/2019/07/09/reservation-is-the-most-important-
     state-policy-we-have-and-we-can-t-give-up-on-that)

56   (Hindu American Foundation 2019). Timestamp: 01:25:10.

57   See: 'RSS = Brahmin supremacy. AAP = Bania supremacy. Welcome to the Brahmin-Bania Raj'. Twitter. Retrieved on April 30, 2022 (https://twitter.com/surajyengde/status/1506530077412151300)

58   (Najar 2017)

59   (Rodrigues 2020)

60   See: 'The Brahmin, Bania, Kshatriya caste academics should invest in researching about their caste and subcastes. Stop anthropologizing Dalits like museum objects and pass disastrous judgments on their lives. Need greater scrutiny of Dalit studies done by non-Dalits'. Twitter. Retrieved on February 15, 2022 (https://twitter.com/surajyengde/status/1377266791513198598)

61   (D'Souza 2020). Timestamp: 08:42.

62   (D'Souza 2020). Timestamp: 10:39.

63   (Yengde 2020). Timestamp: 00:05:31.

64   (Yengde 2020). Timestamp: 00:49:35.

65   (Yengde 2020). Timestamp: 00:57:42.

66   (Yengde 2020). Timestamp: 00:49:20.

67   (Children Of Mahad 2020)

68   (Yengde 2020). Timestamp: 00:21:54.

69   (Yengde 2020). Timestamp: 00:11:46.

70   (Yengde 2020). Timestamp: 00:11:05.

71   (Yengde 2020). Timestamp: 00:16:03.

72   (Yengde 2020). Timestamp: 00:47:05.

73   (Yengde 2020). Timestamp: 00:19:00-00:20:30.

74   (Yengde 2020). Timestamp: 00:07:40.

75   (Yengde 2020). Timestamp: 00:14:40.

76   (Yengde 2020). Timestamp: 00:21:17.

77   (Children Of Mahad 2020)

78   (Yengde 2020). Timestamp: 00:55:48.

79   (Yengde 2020). Timestamp: 01:04:30.

80   (Yengde 2020). Timestamp: 00:17:11.

81   (Yengde 2020). Timestamp: 00:24:42.

82   (The Fletcher School 2021). Timestamp: 49:20.

83   See: 'Parents are the first casteist teachers. They are responsible for damaging their child's mind. When youngsters ask me how to get rid of caste I tell them to disown their casteist parents. If they can do it then we can talk about next steps'. Twitter. Retrieved on February 15, 2022 (https://twitter.com/surajyengde/status/1366737360646524930)

84   (D'Souza 2020). Timestamp: 35:00.

85   (Yengde 2020)

86   (Yengde 2020). Timestamp: 00:36:38.

87   (Yengde 2020). Timestamp: 00:06:50.

88   (Children Of Mahad 2020)

89   (Yengde 2020). Timestamp: 00:59:28.

90 (Yengde 2020). Timestamp: 00:38:40.
91 (Yengde 2020). Timestamp: 00:46:30.
92 (Hindu American Foundation 2019). Timestamp: 00:06:35.
93 (Yengde 2021)
94 (The Lakshmi Mittal and Family South Asia Institute at Harvard University 2018a)
95 (The Lakshmi Mittal and Family South Asia Institute at Harvard University 2018a)
96 (The Lakshmi Mittal and Family South Asia Institute at Harvard University 2018a)
97 (Yengde 2021)
98 (Yengde 2021)
99 (The Fletcher School 2021). Timestamp: 54:00-56:30.
100 (The Lakshmi Mittal and Family South Asia Institute at Harvard University 2018a)
101 (Yengde 2019)
102 (Yengde 2019)
103 (Yengde 2019)
104 (Yengde 2021)
105 (The Lakshmi Mittal and Family South Asia Institute at Harvard University 2018a)
106 (The Lakshmi Mittal and Family South Asia Institute at Harvard University 2018a)
107 (Leung 2021)
108 (The Fletcher School 2021). Timestamp: 38:57.
109 See: 'Chetna Association of Canada'. chetna.ca. Retrieved on February 15, 2022 (https://chetna.ca)
110 (Outlook Web Desk 2021)
111 (Outlook Web Desk 2021)

6. A Response: History of Indian Social Organization

1   (Ahuja 1993, 287)
2   (Ahuja 1993, 286)
3   (Ahuja 1993, 287)
4   (Ahuja 1993, 288)
5   (Ahuja 1993, 288)
6   (Ahuja 1993, 292)
7   Examples are Kavasa of *Rig Veda* and Mahidasa of *Aitreya Aranyaka*.
8   (Majumdar 2001, 546-47)
9   (Aiyangar 1934, 55)
10 (Law 1943, 350)
11 (Jaiswal 1998, 15)
12 (R. S. Sharma 1998, 58)
13 (Majumdar 2001, 548)
14 (U. Singh 2013, 168-69)
15 (Eraly 2007, 166)
16 (Eraly 2007, 166)

17 (Ambedkar, Who were the Shudras? 1979, 22)

18 Sharma, R.S. *Sudras in Ancient India,* p. 29, Motilal Banarsidass, New Delhi,1958 as cited in (A. Sharma 2000, 142)

19 See: 'The *Brihadaranyaka Upanishad* | Swami Krishnananda'. Retrieved on February 15, 2022 (https://www.swami-krishnananda.org/brdup/Brihadaranyaka_ Upanishad.pdf p. 39)

20 (A. Sharma 1996)

21 *Rg Veda* V 60.5. Translated by (Pandurangi 1999, 3)

22 (Radhakrishnan 1953)

23 (A. Sharma 2000, 136)

24 As quoted in: (A. Sharma 2000, 165)

25 (Gupta 2000, 190)

26 (Saha 2020)

27 (Saha 2020)

28 For many examples, see: (A. Sharma 2000, 132-80).

29 *Apasthambha dharmasutra* may have supported untouchability, but it is rarely read by practicing Hindus. It seems to be read mainly by those looking for ways to attack Hinduism. Most Hindus have never heard of it. And many other better known *dharmashastras* differed, 'Badari espoused the cause of the shudras and propounded the view that all (including shudras) were entitled to perform Vedic sacrifices.' See: '*History of Dharmashastra (Ancient and Medieval Religions and Civil Law in India). Volumes I-V'.* Bhandarkar Oriental Research Institute, Pune. Retrieved on February 15, 2022 (https://indianculture.gov.in/indian-culture-repository?search_ api_fulltext=History%20of%20Dharmasastra&f%5B0%5D=parent_library_ ic_repository%3AArchaeological%20Survey%20of%20India). And Ambedkar mentions that though the *Dharmashastras* says in one place that a Shudra is not entitled to upanayana, the text *Samskara Ganapti* explicitly declares Shudras to be eligible for it. He also shows that Jaimini, the author of *Purva Mimamsa,* said that Shudras could perform Vedic rites. Ambedkar cites *Bharadwaja Srauta Sutra* (v. 28) and *Katyayana Srauta Sutra* (1 & 5) to show the eligibility of shudras to perform Vedic rites. See: 'Shudras and the Counter Revolution' in (Ambedkar, Writings and Speeches. Vol. 3 1989a, 423)

30 (Olivelle 2005, 124)

31 (Olivelle 2005, 185)

32 (Olivelle 2000, 359)

33 (Chattopadhyaya 2014, 95)

34 (Olivelle 2000, 361)

35 (Ahmad 1988, 236)

36 (Olivelle 2000, 69)

37 (Olivelle 2005, 103)

38 (Kane 1941, 161)

39 (Kane 1941, 170)

40 (Kane 1941, 170)

41   (Kane 1941, 168)

42   (Kane 1941, 173-76). Similarly, the *Smrtyarthasara* states that no problem occurs upon physical contact on public roads leading to a market, in religious processions, in temples, during festivals, in sacrifices, at sacred places, in calamities or invasions of the country, on the banks of large sheets of water, in the presence of great persons, or when there is a fire or other calamity.

43   Also, *Apastambha Dharmasutra* says that Shudras may cook food for the masters of the higher castes. (Datta 1944, 27)

44   (R. N. Sharma 1977, 55)

45   *Rig Veda* (X.45.6). These included four from each varna and a fifth who was outside the varnas, i.e., a Dalit. Yaska in his Nirukta (VI.7) says this. See (Mookerji 1969, 52).

46   (R. S. Sharma 1958, 63)

47   (R. S. Sharma 1958, 68)

48   (McClish and Olivelle 2012, lxiv)

49   (Datta 1944, 30)

50   For instance, the *Baijavapa Grhya Sutra* says that seven samskaras are allowed to the Shudra from *garbhadhana* to *caula*. The view of lawgiver Apararka appears to be that the eight samskaras from garbhadhana to caula were meant for all the varnas, including the Shudras. According to the *Madanaratna, Rupanarayana* and the *bhashya* of Harihara as quoted in the *Nirnayasindhu*, the Shudras were entitled to perform six samskaras and the five daily mahayajnas. (Kane, History of Dharmashastra 1941, 198)

51   See: 'Lingayat SCs, OBCs may not welcome minority tag'. *The New Indian Express*. Retrieved on February 15, 2022 (https://www.newindianexpress.com/ states/karnataka/2018/mar/23/lingayat-scs-obcs-may-not-welcome-minority-tag-1791248.html)

52   For example: In the *Sigala Jataka*, Buddha denounces a man from a low varna for wanting the hand of a Kshatriya girl. In the *Simhakotthuka Jataka*, a monk of inferior birth wants to recite the religious texts monks born in higher varnas were reciting, but Buddha rebukes him saying that the monks born in superior varnas were like lions while he was like the offspring of a jackal. He is likened with the ass who wants to acquire the status of a lion by wearing the lion-skin. (Goyal 1987, 283)

     Also, in the *Kannakathalasutta* Buddha says, 'There are these four varnas – Kshatriyas, Brahmins, Vaishyas and Shudras, of these four varnas, two – the Kshatriyas and the Brahmins are given precedence in salutation, homage and obeisance'. (Datta 1944, 177)

53   (Goyal 1987, 285)

54   For example: Buddhist masters like Sariputra, Maudgalyayana, and Mahakashyap were all Brahmins. In the later Buddhist order, the intellectual stalwarts in philosophy, logic, ethics, poetry and drama were almost entirely from the Brahmin varna. Buddhist exemplars like Ashvaghosha, Nagarjuna, Aryadeva, Asanga, Vasubandhu,

Dignaga, Dharmakirti, and Dharmottara were born in Brahmin families, educated in Vedic lore, and reared in the orthodox Vedic tradition. They were intellectual giants that produced erudite works on dialectics and logic that established many of the core tenets of Buddhist philosophy. (Goyal 1987, 271-72)

55   (Goyal 1987, 392)

56   (Goyal 1987, 392)

57   (Goyal 1987, 419)

58   (Goyal 1987, 392)

59   (Goyal 1987, 397)

60   (Siddiqui 2014, 80)

61   (Siddiqui 2014, 80)

62   (Kapur 2010, 195)

63   (Biswas 2016)

64   (Biswas 2016)

65   (Biswas 2016)

66   (Biswas 2016)

67   (EWTN Global Catholic Network 2003)

68   See: 'Maneesha Panchakam". Chinmaya Mission. Retrieved on February 15, 2022 (https://www.v0.chinfo.org/images/userupload/Reflections/05_Manisha_Panchakam.pdf) and "manIShApanchakam". Sanskrit Documents. Retrieved on February 15, 2022 (https://sanskritdocuments.org/sites/snsastri/Manishapanchakam.pdf)

69   See: 'Sanskritisation' in (Srinivas 1971)

70   For example, one of the earliest Vedic texts, *Satapatha Brahmana,* refers to a Shudra king performing an important Vedic *yajna.* (Eggeling 1900, 397); Satapatha Brahmana (XIII.5.4.6), (Olivelle 2000, 131)

71   (Ambedkar, Who were the Shudras? 1979, 114)

72   (Roy 1923, 137)

73   (Ambedkar 1979, 119-22)

74   (R. S. Sharma 1958, 241)

75   See (Jayaswal 1934, 3) and (Jayaswal 1934, 45)

76   (Majumdar, *History of Ancient Bengal* 1971, 99)

77   See (Ray 2003, 98)

78   (A. Sharma 2015)

79   (R. S. Sharma 1958, 54)

80   (R. S. Sharma 1958, 48-49)

81   (R. S. Sharma 1958, 242)

82   (R. S. Sharma 1958, 53)

83   During Chhatrapati Shivaji's time, Mahar, Mang, and Ramoshi soldiers guarded the slopes and accesses to Maratha fortresses (Constable 2001, 447). The Ramoshis secured the hill forts while the Mahars and Mangs served in artillery and the garrisons. (Cadell 1938, 12) They were also intelligence agents, carrying out surveillance and misleading enemies. (Betham 1908, 141)

84   For example, Subedar Gopal Baba Valangkar (nineteenth Bombay Infantry), the Mahar leader in Dapoli in the late 1880s and a colleague of the social activist, Jyotirao Phule, called the Mahars 'polluted Kshatriyas'. (Constable 2001, 446-47)

85   See: 'Indian Army's Mahar regiment: Home to two army chiefs and a Param Vir Chakra'. *The Print*. Retrieved on February 15, 2022 (https://theprint.in/report/indian-armys-mahar-regiment-home-to-two-army-chiefs-and-a-param-vir-chakra/26313)

86   (K. Singh 1993, 6)

87   The Jatav community of Uttar Pradesh refuse to be referred to as Chamars. According to *Lomash Ramayana*, which is found in Nepal, the Jatavs trace their ancestry to a direct lineage from Lord Shiva. In *Jatav Jiwan* (1924) and *Yaduvansh ka Itihas* (1942), the Jatavs are mentioned as a Kshatriya jati. The Dabgar (often considered Chamars), is a Dalit community spread across Gujarat, Madhya Pradesh, and Rajasthan. Their oral tradition traces their origin to Rajputs who were downgraded because they worked with the skins of dead animals. The Meghwal Scheduled Caste community is divided into several exogamous communities like Chauhan, Parmar, Solanki etc. Many of these names are of Rajput origin. The Chamars of Madhopur (in Uttar Pradesh) also consider themselves degraded Kshatriyas (K. Singh 1993, 326, 387, 939, 304).

88   (Agarwal 1934, 69). Also (Longer 1981, 4)

89   (Constable 2001, 448-49)

90   Some chapters of the *Yajur Veda* are entirely devoted to enumeration of various industries that belonged to them. For example: *Yajur Veda* 30.15 mentions leather workers (Charmakar or present day Chamars), *Yajur Veda* 16.27 and 30.7 mention textile workers (Julahas), *Yajur Veda* 16.27 and 30.7 mention iron workers (Lohars or ironsmiths), *Yajur Veda* 16.27 and 30.6 mention Rathakar or the maker of chariots, *Yajur Veda* 16.46 and 30.6 mention the makers of bows and arrows, *Yajur Veda* 30.8 mentions the maker of nails and needles, *Yajur Veda* 30.12 mentions the sculptors or the maker of idols (Mahavir 2001, 116). Also, the *Atharva Veda* mentions that the craftsmen had very large residences and factories (See *Atharva Veda* 7.73.1. Also see (Mahavir 2001, 113).

91   (Mahavir 2001, 228)

92   (Mahavir 2001, 114)

93   For example, See *Rig Veda* 1.31.8, 1.31.9 and 8.46.3. Also See Pg. 112, *Vaidik Arthvyavastha*, Dr. Mahavir, Samaanantar Prakashan, New Delhi, 2001. Vedic mantras mention Shudra artisans who made iron weapons for the king in their factories and in return the king protected them, an indication of their cohesive and symbiotic relationship. (See *Rig Veda* 10.92.7 and *Rig Veda* 10.48.3.) The role of Shudras as engineers and architects continued in the later periods. During the Mauryan period, the area to the west of the royal palace was allotted to them for making woolen and cotton goods and armor (Sastri 1987, 79). A Shudra artisan community of the Andhra region that claimed to have originated from Vishvakarma (considered the divine architect in Hinduism) helped in the construction and

repair of temples, chariots, temple ornaments, religious vessels, and images. The Vijayanagar kings (fourteenth-seventeenth century) gave them certain temple honors and privileges, such as walking in front of chariots and offering puja standing on the chariots in their traditional dress. Also, in the Andhra region, the Kancharas or brass-workers were Shudras, and an inscription of 1645 CE says that the ruler waived all their taxes and tolls because of their importance. The Uppara Shudra community provided civil engineering to dig wells and construct houses. They were also involved in removing silt from rivers to make them viable for shipping. Another Shudra community were the Kammaras who manufactured tools, implements and wares of iron (Pandey 2015, Chapter 2).

94   For instance, in the Andhra region in the seventeenth-eighteenth century, several Brahmins and Kshatriyas worked under the Shudra chief of the village (Pandey 2015, Chapter 2).

95   (Kunhappa 1988, 2)

96   (Menon 2011, 133). Interestingly, in the *Mahabharata*, the twin Ashvins, physicians to the gods, are Shudras (R. S. Sharma 1958, 74).

97   (Datta 1944, 25)

98   The Indore copper-plate inscription (465-466 CE) of the Gupta emperor Skandagupta records an endowment that was made, and the interest was allocated to maintain the lamp in the temple of the Sun. The endowment was deposited with the guild of oilmen of Indrapura who invested it in their own business or lent it to others to gain interest. An inscription at Nashik from third century CE during the rule of King Isvarasena records the investment of an endowment with the guilds of potters, oil-millers, and others. An inscription from Junar (c. 1165 CE) records an investment with the guilds of bamboo-workers and braziers (Chakraborti 1960, 316-18). While some twelfth century records mention that Shudras traded in commodities prohibited for the Vaishyas, like salt, wine, curd, arms, poison, and so forth, the *Brihaspati Smriti* say that Shudras traded in all commodities. Also, *Kuvalayamala*, a Jain text from the eighth century CE, mentions Shudras being leaders of trade caravans. (S. Srivastava 2008, 51).

99   (S. Srivastava 2008, 53)

100 (Datta 1944, 27)

101 (Datta 1944, 148)

102 (Chakraborti 1960, 326)

103 For example, during the Maurya period such guilds were granted various concessions by the state. In the Andhra-Kushan period (c. 200-300 CE) and in the period of the Andhravrityas there were guilds of weavers, druggists, corn-dealers, oil manufacturers, etc. In the Gupta period (c. 320-500 CE) there were guilds of oilmen, silk weavers, and architects (Datta 1944, 147-48). An inscription of Emperor Vikramaditya II (c. 733-44 CE) in Karnataka shows that the state authorized the guild of brass-workers to collect taxes from the public (Chakraborti 1960, 318). The Siyadoni inscription (903 CE) of the Pratihara emperor, Mahendrapala I mentions guilds of potters, distillers of liquors, sugar-boilers, betel sellers, oil-makers, and

stone cutters. Such guilds facilitated the task of the government and rendered useful service in organising society and administering justice in internal affairs (Tripathi 1989, 345-46).

104 The existence of wealthy Shudras is mentioned in the *Krishna Yajur Veda* and *Sama Veda*. The *Alinachitta Jataka* mentions a prosperous guild of weavers near Benaras. The Buddhist *Jataka* stories tell us that blacksmiths intermarried with rich jewellers. See (Datta 1944, 29) and (Chakraborti 1960, 314, 319).

105 (Datta 1944, 151, 155)

106 For example, the Mathura inscriptions of the Kushana period (first century CE) record the names of many prosperous Shudra donors who were blacksmiths, barbers, washermen, and so on. They donated money for building temples, roads, and other public amenities. A blacksmith named Gova, son of Siha is also heard of in the inscription to have dedicated an image of Sarasvati. Similarly, a blacksmith Nada of Kalyana is recorded to have given money to build a road in the Kanheri inscription. One inscription belonging to the Kushana period (first century CE) mentions the term 'Rajanapita' which means chief of barber's guild. The Mathura inscription of the Kushana period records the name of a donor called 'Rayagini' which means the wife of a dyer or a washerman. The Jatakas also mention about the guilds of dyers or washermen (dhobi). The Taxila casket inscription of Emperor Kanishka (first-second century CE) mentions a religious gift by an architect. Many records of the period mention a craft-guild of the *navakarmikas* (architects) who built universities and temples, and also did repairs. The Mandasar inscription of (c. 437-38 CE) of Gupta emperors speaks of a guild that built 'a noble and unequalled temple of the bright-eyed sun with the stores of wealth acquired by the craft'. The artisans in the Gupta period were held in high esteem by the kings as shown by the Karitalai (c. 493-4 CE) and the Khoh (c. 497-512 CE) inscriptions. Inscriptions of Gurjara Pratihara (mid eighth to eleventh century) rulers of north India also show that persons following the same occupation normally formed themselves into organizations for regulating their business (Chakraborti 1960, 318-25).

107 They mention wealthy Shudra fishermen in India who hired many laborers to fish in the rivers. In another example, a Shudra is named as the owner of five hundred sheds for manufacturing earthenware, clearly a sign of flourishing entrepreneurs. Another Shudra woman is named as an affluent owner of a pottery business, and Jain monks frequently took shelter in such pottery shops and held them in high esteem. The Jain texts describe many prosperous towns with fine buildings, temples, gardens, roads, etc., where Shudra craftsmen resided and worked. They also point out that the leather industry was thriving and Shudra communities manufactured shoes, bags, musical instruments like drums, bellowing bags, sheaths, etc. (Jain 1980, 29, 56, 58)

108 (S. Srivastava 2008, 51)

109 (Basham 2004, 146)

110 (Basham 2004, 146). For instance, during the British period, the plan to set up a seminary in 1821 failed because the Shudra students refused to be seated with

the Shanars and Paraiahs whom they considered lower to them. This was to be a boarding school, and the different castes were expected to dine together. For the Shudra students, this was an emotionally charged situation. As a result, parents withdrew their children. (Tschurenev 2019, 304)

111 (K. Singh 1993, 11)

112 (K. Singh 1993, 11)

113 (K. Singh 1993, 29)

114 (K. Singh 1993, 6)

115 (Dharampal 1983, 21)

116 (Dharampal 1983, 29)

117 (Dharampal 1983, 29)

118 (Dharampal 1983, 29)

119 (Dharampal 1983, 35)

120 (Tschurenev 2019, 41)

121 (Keay 1918, 148)

122 (K. Singh 1993, 10)

123 (K. Singh 1993, 11)

124 (K. Singh 1993, 4)

125 (K. Singh 1993, 5)

126 (K. Singh 1993, 3)

127 (K. Singh 1993, 302)

128 (K. Singh 1993, 307)

129 (K. Singh 1993, 314)

130 (K. Singh 1993, 314)

131 (K. Singh 1993, 318)

132 (K. Singh 1993, 3)

133 (K. Singh 1993, 25)

134 (K. Singh 1993, 27)

135 (K. Singh 1993, 29)

136 (K. Singh 1993, 1070)

137 (K. Singh 1993, 1072)

138 (K. Singh 1993, 1072)

139 (Russell 1916, 380-81)

140 (K. Singh 1993, 105-12)

141 (Das 2003, 378-79)

142 (Ghurye 1959, 4)

143 (K. Singh 1994, 10)

144 (K. Singh 1994, 12)

145 (K. Singh 1994, 3)

146 (K. Singh 1994, 293)

147 (K. Singh 1994, 293)

148 (K. Singh 1994, 295, 324, 336). See also: (Von Furer Haimendorf and Von Furer Haimendorf 2022, 436, 439)

149 (K. Singh 1994, 118, 119, 127, 122)

150 (K. Singh 1994, 3, 773)

151 (K. Singh 1994, 774)

152 (K. Singh 1994, 776)

153 (K. Singh 1994, 776)

154 (Bag 1997, 106)

155 (K. Singh 1994, 842)

156 (A. Srivastava 1986, 18)

157 (A. Srivastava 1986, 18)

158 (A. Srivastava 1986, 20)

159 For example, the Gaddi Rajput Scheduled Tribe of Himachal Pradesh claim they migrated from Lahore during the medieval period to escape the onslaught by the Muslim rulers (K. Singh 1994, 272-74).

160 (K. Singh 1994, 436-38)

161 (K. Singh 1994, 436, 441-42)

162 For example, the great Veershaiva acharya and scholar, Sripati Panditacharya (thirteenth century CE) wrote a wonderful commentary on the *Vedanta Sutras* called *Srikara Bhashya*. The text begins with the following: 'I have composed this for the benefit of the Virasaivas. The Virasaivas who have the knowledge of the Vedas and Agamas and their inner spiritual meanings; who are fired with the desire to attain moksha; who are followers of the Vedic path; and who are strict in following the tenets of pure Saivism'. (C. H. Rao 1936, 24) Rupa Gosvami, a great Vaishnava scholar of the sixteenth century CE, also made the same point in his *Bhaktirasamrtasindhu*, a massive treatise on bhakti-rasa. He said that devotion to the Lord must be in accordance with the scriptures, shruti and smriti. (Haberman 2003, 41)

163 (B. Srivastava 1957, 87)

164 (Neelotpal 2013, 20-21)

165 (Chauhan 2014, 59-61)

166 (Gupt 1986, 48)

167 (Ghorpade 2011, 196)

168 (Upadhyaya 1954, 583)

169 (Auti 1970, 16)

170 (Kunhappa 1988, 34)

171 (Kunhappa 1988, viii)

172 (Kunhappa 1988, ix)

173 See: (Hardgrave Jr. 1969) and (Rudolph and Rudolph 1967)

174 See: 'Business Class Rises in Ashes of Caste System'. *The New York Times*. Retrieved on February 15, 2022 (https://www.nytimes.com/2010/09/11/world/asia/11caste.html)

175 (Charsley 1996)

176 (Charsley 1996)

177 The British Privy Council stated 'Clear proof of usage, outweighs the written text

of the Law'. In 1833, the British Parliament established the Privy Council in 1833 as the judicial body that heard appeals from various courts of the British colonies including India.

178 (Dharampal 2003, 12)

179 As quoted in: (Chakravorty 2019)

180 As quoted in: (Chakravorty 2019)

181 (Charsley 1996)

182 (Charsley 1996)

183 (Charsley 1996)

184 There are many instances showing that endogamy was not rigidly followed. Many of the great rishis mentioned in the *Puranas* and *Mahabharata* had mothers who were Shudras, such as Parashara Muni, known as the author of the *Vishnu Purana*, who was born of a *shvapaaka* (literally one who cooks the flesh of dogs) woman. (R. S. Sharma 1958, 63) The *Dharmashastras* discuss the instance when a Brahmin has a Shudra son and advocate that if the father is Brahmin, Kshatriya, or Vaishya, the son should inherit half the property. (R. S. Sharma 1958, 247) This shows that such cases were sufficiently common. During the Gupta period too, there are records mentioning marriages between people of different varnas. Buddhist texts also bear testimony to inter-marriages between persons of different varnas. For example, the *Matanga Jataka* mentions a merchant's daughter who became the wife of a *chandala*. (Datta 1944, 178)

185 As quoted in: (Chakravorty 2019)

186 As quoted in: (Chakravorty 2019)

187 (Charsley 1996)

188 (Charsley 1996)

189 (Charsley 1996)

190 (Charsley 1996)

191 (Charsley 1996)

192 (Charsley 1996)

193 (Charsley 1996)

194 (Charsley 1996)

195 (Charsley 1996)

196 (Charsley 1996)

197 (Charsley 1996)

198 (Charsley 1996)

199 (Charsley 1996)

200 (Ambedkar 1936)

201 (Ambedkar 1990)

202 See: Introduction of (Rathore and Verma 2011)

203 (Ambedkar 2015)

204 (Ambedkar 1936), Prologue

205 (Ambedkar 1936, 5)

206 (Ambedkar 1936, 5)

207 (Ambedkar 1936, 5)
208 (Ambedkar 1936, 24)
209 (Ambedkar 1936, 26)
210 (Ambedkar 1936, 3)
211 (Ambedkar 1936)
212 (Ambedkar 1936, 14)
213 (Ambedkar 1936, 20)
214 (Ambedkar 1936, 21)
215 (Ambedkar 1936, 23)
216 (Ambedkar 1936, 23)
217 (Ambedkar 1936, 24)
218 (Ambedkar 1990)
219 (Ambedkar 1990), Chapter X-I
220 (Ambedkar 1990), Chapter X-I
221 (Ambedkar 1990), Chapter X-I
222 (Ambedkar 1990), Chapter X-I
223 (Ambedkar 1990), Chapter X-I
224 (Ambedkar 1990), Chapter X-I
225 (Ambedkar 1990), Chapter X-I
226 (Ambedkar 1990), Chapter X-II
227 (Ambedkar 1990), Chapter XII-III
228 (Ambedkar 1990), Chapter XII-III
229 (Ambedkar 1990), Chapter XII-III
230 (Ambedkar 1990), Chapter XII-III
231 (Ambedkar 1990), Chapter XII-V
232 (Ambedkar 1990), Chapter X-II
233 (Ambedkar 1990), Chapter X-II
234 (Ambedkar 1990), Chapter X-II
235 (Ambedkar 1990), Chapter VII-III
236 (Ambedkar 1990), Chapter VII-III
237 (Ambedkar 1990), Chapter VII-III
238 (Rathore and Verma 2011, xxix-xxx)
239 (Rathore and Verma 2011, 50)
240 (Omvedt 2003, 262)
241 (Ambedkar 1989a, 23)
242 (Ambedkar 1989b, 416-17)
243 As mentioned in (Ramteke 1983, 127)
244 (Ambedkar 2015)
245 (Ambedkar 2015, 5)
246 (Ambedkar 2015, 7)
247 (Ambedkar 2015, 7)
248 (Ambedkar 2015, 8)
249 (Ambedkar 2015, 6)

250 (Ambedkar 2015, 6)

251 (Ambedkar 2015, 8)

252 (Ambedkar 2015, 8)

253 (Ambedkar 2015, 8)

254 (Ambedkar 2015, 8)

255 Many ideas in this section are borrowed from (Nadkarni 2003).

256 (Kane 1990, 531)

257 (Kane 1990, 66-67, 121)

258 (Ahuja 1993, 322)

259 (Ahuja 1993, 322)

260 (Ahuja 1993, 322)

261 (Ahuja 1993, 323)

262 (Ahuja 1993, 324)

263 (Ahuja 1993, 325)

264 (Ahuja 1993, 326) Harold Gould, in his study of *jajmani* system in Sherpur village in Faizabad district in Uttar Pradesh in 1954-5 found payments in the form of free residence site, free food for family, free clothing, free food for animals, free timber, free dung, rent free land, credit facilities, opportunity for supplementary employment, free use of tools, aid in litigation etc.

265 (Ahuja 1993, 324)

266 (Ambedkar 1936, 11)

7. Thirty Years of Encounters with Harvard University

1   See: 'Welcome to Infinity Foundation'. Infinity Foundation. Retrieved on April 30, 2022 (https://infinityfoundation.com)

2   See: 'U-Turn Theory by Rajiv Malhotra'. Spotify. Retrieved on April 30, 2022 (https://open.spotify.com/episode/50PZhCEtJihTO2B3IzA7fr) and 'The U-turn Theory: How Indian Ideas are Stolen by the West and Covered up'. YouTube. Retrieved on April 30, 2022 (https://www.youtube.com/watch?v=tR6QGe-a8gM)

3   (Wilson 2014, 82)

4   See: 'Tobacco Industry Records Held by the New York State Archives'. New York State Archives. Retrieved on April 30, 2022 (https://web.archive.org/web/20141212180722/http://www.archives.nysed.gov/a/research/res_topics_bus_tobacco.shtml). Original link last retrieved on January 30, 2013 is no longer active (http://www.archives.nysed.gov/a/research/res_topics_bus_tobacco.shtml)

5   (Benson, Alexander and Feldman 1975) See also: (Benson, Marzetta, et al. 1974)

6   (Wilson 2014, 80-82)

7   (Goleman 1971, 1-25)

8   (To The Best Of Our Knowledge 2014)

9   (To The Best Of Our Knowledge 2014)

10 (Goleman 1971, 1-25)

11 (Goleman 1971, 1-25)

12 (Goleman 1971, 1-25)

13 See: (Goleman 1972a) and (Goleman 1972b)

14 See: (Goleman 1972a) and (Goleman 1972b)

15 (Wilson 2014, 80-82)

16 (Goleman 1976)

17 (Wilson 2014, 80-82)

18 (To The Best Of Our Knowledge 2014)

19 (Parade 2020)

20 (Parade 2020)

21 (Purser 2017)

22 (Purser 2017)

23 (Purser 2017)

24 Quoted in (Verhoeven 2001)

25 (Kline 1963, 25)

26 This is still unpublished and will be part of the series on digestion of Indian knowledge.

27 (Thera 1999)

28 (Thera 1999)

29 Whitehead's tenure at Harvard (1924-37) was overlapped by the presence in the philosophy department of a number of professional philosophers such as William Earnest Hockings who were involved to some extent in Indic philosophy, having inherited the legacy of an earlier generation of Harvard philosophers such as William James, C.S. Peirce, George Santayana, whose philosophies were extensively influenced by Indic thought. During Whitehead's time at Harvard the Department of Sanskrit and Indian Studies flourished as did Buddhist Studies. As in the two previous decades, a fairly close relationship prevailed between Indic studies in general and Buddhist studies in particular and the philosophy department. Hockings is a prime example in this respect. In an essay on his personal recollection of Whitehead, *Whitehead as I knew Him* (Hocking 1963), Hocking fondly recalls Whitehead's tenure at Harvard and how he was a member of the Josiah Royce philosophy club, the members of which had included William James and those others at Harvard with interest in Indic thought. In another essay in the same volume ("Whitehead's Novel Intuition", pp.18-26), Charles Hartshorne, a student of Whitehead destined to become a prominent philosopher and theologian takes note of the resemblance of Whitehead's Process Philosophy to Buddhism, drawing particular attention to Whitehead's concept of *Prehension* (pp.2-26). As we have argued above, Whitehead's theory of prehension was likely developed on the basis of the Buddhist Abhidharma concept of *Prapti* (refer) to table above (third item from bottom). Hartshorne himself embraced both Process Philosophy (of which he became the foremost theorist post-Whitehead and Buddhism) and called the philosophy of becoming or Process Philosophy 'the Buddhisto-Whiteheadian doctrine', thus indirectly confirming the Buddhist antecedence of Whitehead's Process Philosophy.

30 God in either Primordial Nature or Consequent Nature is a curious superimposition on a self-organizing universe in radical flux. For many Buddhists as well as other scientists, the curious blend of science and theology, especially evolutionary theory imposed on an incompatible Christian theological framework is highly problematic. For a trenchant critique of the attempts of Christian theologians to impose evolution on an incompatible Christian theological framework, see (Dharmasiri 1988)

31 (Harvard Square Library 2017)

32 (Gordon 2007)

33 (Oldmeadow 2004, 27)

34 (Thoreau 1932)

35 (Thoreau 1932)

36 (Thoreau 1932)

37 (Institute Of Noetic Sciences (IONS) 2010)

38 (Hodder 2001)

39 (R. Higgins 2017)

40 T.S. Eliot's *After Strange Gods* as cited in (Kearns 1987, 13)

41 (Kearns 1987, 13)

42 The following book is devoted to this inner conflict Eliot faced: (Kearns 1987)

43 See, for example, his extensive article at: (Asani 2007)

44 See: (Infinity Foundation 2002a)

45 (Infinity Foundation 2002b)

46 (Nussbaum 2009, 214-215, 246-261)

8. China's Trojan Horse in America

1   (Yemma and Golden 1998) and (Online Burma/Myanmar Library 1998)

2   (Yemma and Golden 1998) and (Online Burma/Myanmar Library 1998)

3   (Diamond and Schell 2018)

4   (Wong 2020)

5   (Wong 2020)

6   (Rodman and Zhu 2015)

7   (Hava 2020a)

8   (Horwitz 2017)

9   (Redden 2017)

10 See: 'Change in personnel in Beijing department dealing with Dalai Lama's Envoys'. *World Tibet Network News*. Jan 30, 2004. Retrieved on April 30, 2022 (https://web.archive.org/web/20040408192139/http://www.tibet.ca/en/wtnarchive/2004/1/30_2.html) Alternate source: (Smith 2009, 232)

11 See: 'A Discussion on Tibetan Issue With American Experts on China'. *China News and Report*. September 17 2002. Retrieved on April 30, 2022 (https://web.archive.org/web/20040225014441/http://www.china.org.cn/baodao/english/newsandreport/2002sep/17-1.htm)

12 (Kynge 2021)
13 (Kynge 2021)
14 (Kynge 2021)
15 (Hoagland 2012)
16 (Office of Foreign Assets Control 2022)
17 (United States Department of the Treasury 2022)
18 (Winters 2020a)
19 (Winters 2020a)
20 (Schneider 2020)
21 It entered into a contract to open a Chinese government-funded Confucius Institute on its campus, with the goal of promoting Chinese culture and language. And in 2012, under Stanford President John Hennessy, the Stanford Center at Peking University was also opened for Stanford students in China. In 2014, Stanford received $58.1 million in China-based gifts and contracts for 'Advancement in U.S.-China Relations'. See: (Schneider 2020)
22 (FCCED 2020)
23 (Neuman and Turner 2020)
24 (Neuman and Turner 2020)
25 (Neuman and Turner 2020)
26 (Neuman and Turner 2020)
27 (Tan 2021) In China, the dream of an American education loses some of its gleam
28 (Ramaswamy 2021, 161)
29 (Ramaswamy 2021, 165)
30 (Ramaswamy 2021, 168)
31 (Ramaswamy 2021, 178)
32 (Ramaswamy 2021, 175). See: (Craymer 2020)
33 (Ramaswamy 2021, 194)
34 (Harvard Kennedy School 2015c)
35 (Xie 2018)
36 (Squawk Box @SquawkCNBC 2021)
37 (Squawk Box @SquawkCNBC 2021)
38 (Harvard Kennedy School 2016a)
39 (P. Schweizer 2021)
40 See: (Fish, What China experts have to do to get on Beijing's visa 'whitelist' 2019)
41 (Patrick 2021)
42 Examples: John Cena's apology (Boom 2021); (The Late Show with Stephen Colbert 2021); Gap apology for map of China: (Sanchez 2018); US companies that have apologized to China. (Nextshark - Editorial Staff 2019)
43 See: 'China theft of technology is biggest law enforcement threat to US, FBI says'. *The Guardian*. Retrieved on April 30, 2022 (https://www.theguardian.com/world/2020/feb/06/china-technology-theft-fbi-biggest-threat) and 'The Middle Kingdom Meets Higher Education'. FDD. Retrieved on April 30, 2022 (https://www.fdd.org/analysis/2021/12/09/the-middle-kingdom-meets-higher-education/)

44 See: '1 in 5 corporations say China has stolen their IP within the last year: CNBC CFO survey'. CNBC. Retrieved on April 30, 2022 (https://www.cnbc.com/2019/02/28/1-in-5-companies-say-china-stole-their-ip-within-the-last-year-cnbc.html)

45 (Harvard Kennedy School 2016b)

46 (Harvard Kennedy School 2016b)

47 (Harvard Kennedy School 2015b)

48 (Harvard Kennedy School 2021a)

49 (Harvard Kennedy School 2021a)

50 (Harvard Kennedy School 2015c)

51 (Harvard Kennedy School 2015c)

52 (Diamond and Schell 2018)

53 (Winters 2020b)

54 (Winters 2021b)

55 (Diamond and Schell 2018, 45-46)

56 (Winters 2021b)

57 (Winters 2021b)

58 (Winters 2021b)

59 (Winters 2020b)

60 (Winters 2020b)

61 (Winters 2020b)

62 (Diamond and Schell 2018, 46)

63 (Cunningham, Saich and Turiel 2020)

64 (Winters 2020a)

65 (Kakutani 2020a)

66 (Kakutani 2020a)

67 (Kakutani 2020a)

68 (Kakutani 2020a)

69 (Winters 2020a)

70 (Winters, 2020a)

71 (Winters, 2020a)

72 (Harvard University 2012a). Timestamp: 00:15-01:50.

73 (Winters 2021a)

74 (Winters 2021a)

75 (Winters 2021a)

76 (Winters 2021a)

77 (Winters 2021a)

78 (Burns and Manuel 2020)

79 (Burns 2020). Timestamp: 08:20.

80 (*The Hindu* 2021)

81 (Burns 2020). Timestamp: 23:37.

82 (Burns 2020). Timestamp: 25:08.

83 See: 'Future HBS case studies on failure: 1. Covid19. 2. Demonetisation. 3. GST

implementation'. Twitter. Retrieved on April 30, 2022 (https://twitter.com/ RahulGandhi/status/1279963844027183105)

84   (Luce 2021)
85   (Winters 2020d)
86   (Winters 2020d)
87   (Beyrer 2021)
88   (Harvard T.H. Chan School of Public Health 2019a)
89   (Donovan and Nilsen 2021)
90   (Walker 2021)
91   (Walker 2021)
92   (Winters and Kassam 2021)
93   (Christenson 2021)
94   (Christenson 2021)
95   (Christenson 2021)
96   (Harvard T.H. Chan School of Public Health 2021b)
97   (Harvard T.H. Chan School of Public Health 2021b)
98   (C. Ross 2021a)
99   (C. Ross 2021a)
100 (C. Ross 2021b)
101 (C. Ross 2021b)
102 (C. Ross 2021b)
103 (Fish, Huawei's surprising ties to the Brookings Institution 2018)
104 (Fish, Huawei's surprising ties to the Brookings Institution 2018)
105 (*The Daily Wire* 2022)
106 (*The Daily Wire* 2022). Timestamp: 0:00.
107 (*The Daily Wire* 2022). Timestamp: 0:32.
108 (*The Daily Wire* 2022). Timestamp: 1:19.
109 See: 'Tag Archives: China'. Law and Society Alliance. Retrieved on April 30, 2022 (https://lawandsocietyalliance.in/tag/china). To download the pdf see: 'Mapping Chinese Foorprints and Influence Operations in India'. Law and Society Alliance. Retrieved on April 30, 2022 (https://defence.capital/wp-content/uploads/2021/09/ MAPPING-CHINESE-FOOTPRINTS-AND-INFLUENCE-OPERATIONS-IN-INDIA2.pdf)

9. The Importance of Investigating Harvard University

1   (Tocqueville 2004)
2   Winston Churchill, Speech at Harvard University, September 6, 1943.
3   (Binkley 2022)
4   (Hanson 2022)
5   (*The Harvard Gazette* 2008)
6   (*The Harvard Gazette* 2008)

7   (Mission Kaali 2020)
8   (*The Times of India* 2010)
9   (*Financial Express* 2018)
10 (*Financial Express* 2018)
11 (*Financial Express* 2018)
12 (Vikaspedia 2019)
13 (Harvard Global 2017a)
14 (Boyd 2021)

10. Databases, Taxonomies, and Archives

1   (Malhotra 2021)
2   (Anderson 1983)
3   (Anderson 1983, 168)
4   (Anderson 1983, 177-78)
5   (Anderson 1983, 188)
6   Another related frame of reference on India has been the colonial theory of foreign Aryans dominating the native Dravidians. As discussed in Chapter 3, this has been further developed at Harvard into a three-tier model: The Munda language speakers are considered the original natives of India (now championed as 'tribals' or 'Adivasis' or Dalits). Above them are the Dravidians who came from the Middle East to build the Indus Valley Civilization, and they oppressed the Mundas. At the top are the Aryans who came from Central Asia and oppressed both the layers above.
7   (Malhotra and Babaji 2020)
8   (Symonds 1986)
9   (Harvard University 2012b) Also see: 'Mapping the Kumbh Mela'. Mapping the Kumbh Mela. Retrieved on April 30, 2022 (https://mappingthemela.wordpress.com)
10 (Mittal Institute 2013). Timestamp: 01:17:33; (Nitnaware 2015)
11 (Ganesh N 2015a)
12 (Ganesh N 2015b)
13 (Harvard University 2014a)
14 (Barnett, Khanna and Onnela 2016)
15 (The Lakshmi Mittal and Family South Asia Institute at Harvard University 2016, 24)
16 (The Lakshmi Mittal and Family South Asia Institute at Harvard University 2016, 8)
17 (Harvard University 2015a)
18 (The Lakshmi Mittal and Family South Asia Institute at Harvard University 2016, 9)
19 (The Lakshmi Mittal and Family South Asia Institute at Harvard University 2016, 17)

20   (The Lakshmi Mittal and Family South Asia Institute at Harvard University 2016, 17)

21   (Mittal Institute 2016)

22   (Harvard University 2020a)

23   (Harvard University 2020b)

24   (Harvard University 2020c)

25   (Harvard University 2019a)

26   (Harvard University 2017a)

27   (The Lakshmi Mittal and Family South Asia Institute at Harvard University 2021, 38)

28   (The Lakshmi Mittal and Family South Asia Institute at Harvard University 2019, 67)

29   (The Lakshmi Mittal and Family South Asia Institute at Harvard University 2019, 67-68)

30   (The Lakshmi Mittal and Family South Asia Institute at Harvard University 2017, 24)

31   (The Lakshmi Mittal and Family South Asia Institute at Harvard University 2017, 24)

32   See: 'Project Prakash'. Project Prakash. Retrieved on April 30, 2022 (https://www.projectprakash.org)

33   (The Lakshmi Mittal and Family South Asia Institute at Harvard University 2020, 27)

34   (The Lakshmi Mittal and Family South Asia Institute at Harvard University 2018b, 74)

35   (Harvard University 2021a)

36   (Harvard University 2021a)

37   (The Lakshmi Mittal and Family South Asia Institute at Harvard University 2020, 37); (Linda Hall Library 2022)

38   See for examples: (Harvard University 2018a); (Harvard University 2019k); (Harvard University 2020g);

39   (The Lakshmi Mittal and Family South Asia Institute at Harvard University 2021, 65)

40   (The Lakshmi Mittal and Family South Asia Institute at Harvard University 2019, 15-16)

41   (The Lakshmi Mittal and Family South Asia Institute at Harvard University 2020, 28)

42   (The Lakshmi Mittal and Family South Asia Institute at Harvard University 2021, 28)

43   (Harvard University 2013a)

44   (The Lakshmi Mittal and Family South Asia Institute at Harvard University 2014, 22)

45   (The Lakshmi Mittal and Family South Asia Institute at Harvard University 2019, 43)

46 (The Lakshmi Mittal and Family South Asia Institute at Harvard University 2020, 39)

11. Anand Mahindra and Postmodernism

1   (Mukherjee 2010)
2   (Merrigan 2010)
3   (Merrigan 2010)
4   (Mukherjee 2010)
5   (Mukherjee 2010)
6   See: (Eakin 2001)
7   See: 'Infosys Prize | Jury'. Infosys Science Foundation. Retrieved on April 30, 2022 (https://www.infosys-science-foundation.com/prize/jury/jury-2017.asp)
8   (Golikeri and John 2011)
9   (Golikeri and John 2011)
10 (Rayman and Spitzer 2010)
11 (Grossman 1999)
12 Cited in (Grossman 1999)
13 (Eakin 2001)
14 (Eakin 2001)
15 See: 'Customer Review | David Schweizer'. Amazon. Retrieved on April 30, 2022 (https://www.amazon.com/gp/customer-reviews/R1Q3POGMK3H1F6)
16 (Young 1990, 186)
17 See: (Davies 2012). There are other versions of this story that Foucault said ten percent rather than twenty-five percent, but the implication is still the same.
18 (Mohanty 2005)
19 (Bhabha 1994)
20 Jacques Lacan, 'The Line and Light', *Of the Gaze*, cited in (Bhabha 1994, 121)
21 (Harvard University 2017b)
22 (Rosario 2017)
23 (Rosario 2017)
24 (Pratap 2017)
25 (Pratap 2017)
26 (R. Liu 2019)
27 (Srinivasan 2020)
28 All references and quotes in this section are from: (Mahindra Humanities Center 2020)
29 (Harvard University 2017c)
30 See: 'Prasenjit Duara'. Institute of Chinese Studies. Retrieved on April 30, 2022 (https://www.icsin.org/faculty/prasenjit-duara)
31 (Law and Society Alliance 2021, 15). Incidentally, this institute is supported by: Indian Council of Social Science Research; the Ministry of External Affairs of India;

Gargi and Vidya Prakash Dutt Memorial; TATA Trusts; Jamnalal Bajaj Foundation; Pirojsha Godrej Foundation.

32   (Mahindra Humanities Center 2020). Timestamp: 01:01:15.
33   (Johnson 2016)

12. Lakshmi Mittal and Social Justice

1   (*The Harvard Gazette* 2017)
2   (Gulf News 2017)
3   (Harvard University 2018d)
4   (The Lakshmi Mittal and Family South Asia Institute at Harvard University 2020, 55)
5   (Harvard University 2019b)
6   (Harvard University 2019b)
7   (Soshi and Walsh 2021)
8   (Harvard University 2019c)
9   (Harvard University 2021b)
10   (Harvard University 2016a)
11   (Harvard University 2019d)
12   (Harvard University 2019e)
13   See: 'SAI Event Type: Lecture'. The Lakshmi Mittal and Family South Asia Institute. Retrieved on April 30, 2022 (https://mittalsouthasiainstitute.harvard.edu/events/ types/lecture/page/2/)
14   (Harvard University 2015b)
15   (The Lakshmi Mittal and Family South Asia Institute at Harvard University 2020, 51)
16   (Harvard University 2019f)
17   (Harvard University 2013c)
18   (The Lakshmi Mittal and Family South Asia Institute at Harvard University 2021, 47)
19   (A. Datta 2014)
20   (The Lakshmi Mittal and Family South Asia Institute at Harvard University 2020, 54)
21   (Harvard University 2019g)
22   (Harvard University 2020d)
23   (The Lakshmi Mittal and Family South Asia Institute at Harvard University 2014, 13)
24   (The Lakshmi Mittal and Family South Asia Institute at Harvard University 2012)
25   (The Lakshmi Mittal and Family South Asia Institute at Harvard University 2012)
26   (The Lakshmi Mittal and Family South Asia Institute at Harvard University 2014, 13)

27 (The Lakshmi Mittal and Family South Asia Institute at Harvard University 2015, 15)
28 (Harvard University 2013d)
29 (Harvard University 2020e)
30 (The Lakshmi Mittal and Family South Asia Institute at Harvard University 2020, 52)
31 (Harvard University 2018e)
32 (Harvard University 2019h)
33 (Harvard University 2014b)
34 (The Lakshmi Mittal and Family South Asia Institute at Harvard University 2014, 31)
35 (The Lakshmi Mittal and Family South Asia Institute at Harvard University 2014, 45)
36 (Harvard University 2014c)
37 (Harvard University 2016b)
38 (Harvard University 2017d)
39 (Harvard University 2021c)
40 (Harvard University 2016c)
41 (The Lakshmi Mittal and Family South Asia Institute at Harvard University 2015, 49)
42 (The Lakshmi Mittal and Family South Asia Institute at Harvard University 2014, 49)
43 (DeBenedictis 2016)
44 (Hartocollis 2022)
45 (Harvard University 2014d)
46 (Harvard University 2013a)
47 (Harvard University 2014d)
48 See: 'Livelihood Creation Project'. The Lakshmi Mittal and Family South Asia Institute at Harvard University. Retrieved on April 30, 2022 (https://mittalsouthasiainstitute.harvard.edu/about-livelihood-creation-project)
49 (Harvard University 2018f)
50 (Harvard University 2018g)
51 (Harvard University 2018h)
52 (Harvard University 2018i)
53 (Harvard University 2019i)
54 (Harvard University 2014e)
55 (Harvard University 2013b)
56 (The Lakshmi Mittal and Family South Asia Institute at Harvard University 2016, 15)
57 (The Lakshmi Mittal and Family South Asia Institute at Harvard University 2020, 16-17)
58 (The Lakshmi Mittal and Family South Asia Institute at Harvard University 2019, 49)

59   (Pelaez 2019)

60   (The Lakshmi Mittal and Family South Asia Institute at Harvard University 2017, 32)

61   (The Lakshmi Mittal and Family South Asia Institute at Harvard University 2018b, 74, 77)

62   (The Lakshmi Mittal and Family South Asia Institute at Harvard University 2014, 33)

63   (The Lakshmi Mittal and Family South Asia Institute at Harvard University 2016, 21)

64   (The Lakshmi Mittal and Family South Asia Institute at Harvard University 2020, 55)

65   (The Lakshmi Mittal and Family South Asia Institute at Harvard University 2020, 55)

66   (The Lakshmi Mittal and Family South Asia Institute at Harvard University 2020, 55)

67   (The Lakshmi Mittal and Family South Asia Institute at Harvard University 2020, 55)

68   (Harvard University 2015c)

69   (Harvard University 2019j)

70   (The Lakshmi Mittal and Family South Asia Institute at Harvard University 2019, 68)

71   (The Lakshmi Mittal and Family South Asia Institute at Harvard University 2020, 29)

72   (The Lakshmi Mittal and Family South Asia Institute at Harvard University 2017, 16)

73   (The Lakshmi Mittal and Family South Asia Institute at Harvard University 2017, 29)

74   (The Lakshmi Mittal and Family South Asia Institute at Harvard University 2020, 17)

75   (Harvard University 2021d)

76   (The Lakshmi Mittal and Family South Asia Institute at Harvard University 2017, 29)

77   (Harvard University 2021e)

78   (The Lakshmi Mittal and Family South Asia Institute at Harvard University 2017, 25)

79   (The Lakshmi Mittal and Family South Asia Institute at Harvard University 2017, 25)

80   For example, the cookstoves being invented and their data being sent all the way to Berkeley for evaluation is something an IIT related startup in India could easily have done. See: (The Lakshmi Mittal and Family South Asia Institute at Harvard University 2019, 71)

81   (The Lakshmi Mittal and Family South Asia Institute at Harvard University 2017, 20)

82 For example, what value does Harvard's Kennedy School bring to the study of India's coal industry, other than perhaps arming the US in pressuring India during the climate change negotiations? See: (Harvard University 2018b)

83 (Harvard University 2020f)

84 (Harvard University 2021f)

85 Mittal Institute's advisory board members include many influential Indians: 1) K.P. Balaraj, Bengaluru, India; he is co-founder and managing director of WestBridge Capital. 2) Kushagra Bajaj is chairman of the Bajaj Group, chairman and managing director of Bajaj Hindusthan Limited, and chairman of Bajaj Corp Limited. 3) Kuntala Das (New York) and Bharat Das. 4) Meera Gandhi is CEO and founder of The Giving Back Foundation, which she created in 2010 as a catalyst to aid women and children, to create a new generation of leaders and thinkers. 5) Vikram Gandhi is founder of Asha Impact, an impact investing and advocacy platform and VSG Capital Advisors, senior advisor to The Canadian Pension Plan and Greenhill and Company. 6) Mala Gaonkar Haarmann is partner and managing director at a six billion dollars private investment partnership fund that comprises three equity hedge funds. She oversees the fund's media, technology, and telecommunications investment portfolio, 7) Dr. Dipti Mathur has built a highly regarded collection of modern and contemporary South Asian art. She has served on the Collections Committee of the Asia Society Museum, New York, on the Contemporary Art Advisory Panel of the Asian Art Museum, San Francisco, and on the Board of Trustees of the Seattle Art Museum. 8) Sanjeev Mehra, New York, is managing director and partner of Goldman Sachs, where he leads the Business Practices Committee and Operating Committee for its Principal Investment Area, and serves on its Investment Committee. 9) Victor Menezes (PA; New York) is senior advisor with New Silk Route Partners LLC, an international private equity firm. He was formerly senior vice chairman of Citigroup Inc., and after a thirty-two-year global career in the company, retired in January 2005. He chairs the American India Foundation, is a vice chairman of Catholic Charities. 10) Gaurav and Parul Swarup (Kolkata) – head Paharpur Cooling Towers Limited in Kolkata. Paharpur is a well-diversified business house with interests in industrial process cooling equipment, flexible packaging, saw milling & forestry, realty and investments. 11) Rajiv and Anupa Sahney (Mumbai). Rajiv is a founding and managing partner at New Vernon Capital, LLC, a private equity firm that managed $2.1B in assets as of September 2008. Prior to founding New Vernon Capital, he was founder and CEO of Medusind, a healthcare services outsourcing company. 12) Sribala Subramanian and Arvind Raghunathan. Arvind is CEO and CIO of Roc Capital Management. 13) Dalip and Chandrika Pathak. Dalip is senior advisor to Warburg Pincus. He joined Warburg Pincus in 1994 and has previously been both head of India and head of Europe for the firm. 14) Mukesh (AB '93) and Chandni Prasad (New York). Mukesh is an MD from The Johns Hopkins Medical College and completed training in otolaryngology and head and neck surgery at Columbia University. 15) Tom Varkey (New York) has participated in the management of the Stonehill portfolios since joining the

firm in 2001 and has been a partner since 2004. See: (Harvard University 2022a)

86 (The Lakshmi Mittal and Family South Asia Institute at Harvard University 2021, 56)

87 (The Lakshmi Mittal and Family South Asia Institute at Harvard University 2019, 27)

88 (Chughtai 2015, 203)

89 (The Lakshmi Mittal and Family South Asia Institute at Harvard University 2018b, 22)

13. The Piramals: Harvard University's Gateway to India

1   (Capstone Report 2020b)

2   (Clarida 2014)

3   (Hava 2020b)

4   (Kakutani 2020b)

5   See: '@jimmylaiapple | This account doesn't exist'. Twitter. Retrieved on April 30, 2022 (https://twitter.com/jimmylaiapple)

6   See: (Ramzy 2017) and: (Davidson 2020)

7   (Asia Sentinel 2017)

8   For example, see: (Capstone Report 2020a)

9   (Kakutani 2020b)

10 (Hava 2020b)

11 (Lam and Chung 2018)

12 (Nietzel 2022)

13 (Hava 2020b)

14 (Hava 2020b)

15 See: 'ISB Governing Board'. Indian School of Business (ISB). Retrieved on April 30, 2022 (https://www.isb.edu/en/about-isb/leadership/governing-board.html)

16 (ToHim89 Live 2019)

17 See: 'What is Public Health?' CDC Foundation. Retrieved on April 30, 2022 (https://www.cdcfoundation.org/what-public-health)

18 (Harvard T.H. Chan School of Public Health 2021a)

19 See: 'Harvard Center for Population and Development Studies'. Harvard T.H. Chan School of Public Health. Retrieved on April 30, 2022 (https://www.hsph.harvard.edu/population-development/tag/caste/)

20 (Blanding 2021)

21 (Blanding 2021)

22 (Harvard University 2018c)

23 (Hancock 1987)

24 (The New York Public Library 2013)

25 (Witzenrath 2015) Another book that gives details is: (Levi 2002)

26 (Feldscher 2014)

27 (Feldscher 2014)

28 (Business France 2021)

29 (Feldscher 2014)

30 (Feldscher 2014)

31 (Feldscher 2014)

32 (Saathi Re 2017)

33 (Harvard T.H. Chan School of Public Health 2016)

34 (Harvard T.H. Chan School of Public Health 2017)

35 (Harvard T.H. Chan School of Public Health 2016)

36 (Harvard T.H. Chan School of Public Health 2019b)

37 See: 'Artificial Intelligence and Tuberculosis'. Harvard T.H. Chan School of Public Health. Retrieved on April 30, 2022 (https://www.hsph.harvard.edu/india-center/research/artificial-intelligence-and-tuberculosis/)

38 (Liu and Zhang 2016)

39 (Harvard T.H. Chan School of Public Health 2019a)

14. Harvard University's Control of the Media Ecosystem in India

1 (Peters 2010)

2 (Peters 2010)

3 (MacArthur Foundation 2022)

4 (Nieman Foundation for Journalism at Harvard 2010)

5 (K. Jain, International Reporting Must Distinguish Hindu Nationalism from Hinduism 2019)

6 (MacArthur Foundation 2022)

7 (Poynter 2017)

8 (Poynter 2017)

9 (Poynter 2017)

10 (Poynter 2017)

11 (Pulitzer Center 2016). Timestamp: 00:00:00-00:01:42

12 See: 'The Pulitzer Center on Crisis Reporting extends its greatest appreciation to our supporters and donors'. Pulitzer Center. Retrieved on April 30, 2022 (https://pulitzercenter.org/about/donors)

13 (InfluenceWatch 2020)

14 (Sanghamitra 2018)

15 (Sanghamitra 2018)

16 (OpIndia 2021c)

17 (Safikul Hasan 2018). Timestamp: 47:51. Accessed and downloaded on April 1, 2022. Link no longer active.

18 (PARI - People's Archive of Rural India 2021a)

19 (PARI - People's Archive of Rural India 2021a)

20   (PARI - People's Archive of Rural India 2021a)

21   (PARI - People's Archive of Rural India 2021b)

22   See: 'Acknowledgments'. People's Archive of Rural India. Retrieved on May 15, 2022 (https://ruralindiaonline.org/en/pages/acknowledgements/)

23   (Thakur 2021)

24   (OpIndia 2021a)

25   (Ross and Dobson 2022)

26   (Safikul Hasan 2018). Timestamp: 46:56. Accessed and downloaded on April 1, 2022. Link no longer active.

27   (PARI Education - People's Archive of Rural India 2020a)

28   (PARI Education - People's Archive of Rural India 2020a)

29   (PARI Education - People's Archive of Rural India 2020b)

30   (PARI Education Team 2021)

31   (PARI Education Team 2021)

32   (PARI Education 2020)

33   (Behl 2021)

34   (Karthikeyan 2014)

35   (Karthikeyan 2014). Also see: 'Faces'. PARI - People's Archive of Rural India. Retrieved on April 30, 2022 (https://ruralindiaonline.org/en/categories/faces/)

36   (Karthikeyan 2014)

37   See: 'Leadership in The Digital Century'. GBH. Retrieved on April, 30 2022 (https://www.wgbh.org/foundation)

38   (Martin, Ray and Pillay, Caste Discrimination in the USA: A Public Radio and Online Series 2019)

39   (Martin, Ray and Pillay, Caste Discrimination in the USA: A Public Radio and Online Series 2019)

40   (Martin, Ray and Pillay, Caste Discrimination in the USA: A Public Radio and Online Series 2019)

41   (Martin, Ray, et al., 'Caste in America' Receives 2020 Gabriel Award 2020)

42   See: 'Article'. Pulitzer Center. Retrieved on April 30, 2022 (https://pulitzercenter.org/article)

43   (NiemanReports 2014)

44   See: 'Fellowships in Journalism'. Editors Guild of India. Retrieved on April 30, 2022 (https://editorsguild.in/awards-fellowships/)

45   (NiemanLab 2021)

46   (Nieman Foundation for Journalism at Harvard 2021a)

47   (Nieman Foundation for Journalism at Harvard 2021a)

48   (Nieman Foundation for Journalism at Harvard 2021b)

49   (Nieman Foundation for Journalism at Harvard 2020)

50   (Krishnan 2021)

51   (Krishnan 2021)

52   (Nieman Foundation for Journalism at Harvard 2017)

53   (Gipson, et al. 2021)

54 (Sikora 2021)
55 (Gipson, et al. 2021)
56 (Sikora 2021)
57 (Sikora 2021). The original link in YouTube is: (Berkley Center 2021). Timestamp: 00:08:12.
58 (Malhotra 2016)

15. Harvard Kennedy School: Geopolitics

1 See: 'Learn. Lead. Serve'. Harvard Kennedy School. Retrieved on April 30, 2022 (https://www.hks.harvard.edu/more/about)
2 (Harvard University 2021g)
3 (Harvard Kennedy School 2017a)
4 (IAMC Official Channel 2020). Timestamp: 00:07:00-00:07:15
5 (The Harbus 2020)
6 (Maqbool and Naik 2017)
7 (IAMC Official Channel 2020)
8 (OpIndia 2021b)
9 (OpIndia 2020b)
10 See: 'Rashad Hussain, 2003'. Paul & Daisy Soros Fellowship for New Americans. Retrieved on April 30, 2022 (https://www.pdsoros.org/meet-the-fellows/rashad-hussain)
11 (Arenas 2010)
12 (J. Weber 2021)
13 See: 'Religious freedom includes the ability to choose one's religious attire. The Indian state of Karnataka should not determine permissibility of religious clothing. Hijab bans in schools violate religious freedom and stigmatize and marginalize women and girls.' Twitter. Retrieved on April 30, 2022 (https://twitter.com/IRF_Ambassador/status/1492153532350402564)
14 (The Harvard Gazette 2021)
15 (Haniffa 2020)
16 (Haniffa 2020)
17 (Crawford 2021)
18 (The Hindustan Times 2004)
19 (USCIRF 2004)
20 (Harvard Law School 2018)
21 (The American Bazaar 2018)
22 (USCIRF 2020)
23 (MOJO STORY 2020)
24 (Varshney 2021a)
25 (Varshney 2020b)
26 (D'Amore-McKim School of Business 2019). Timestamp: 29:20.

27   (Varshney, Ayyangar and Swaminathan 2021)

28   (Levi 2002)

29   (Varshney 2020b)

30   See: 'Shorenstein Center on Media, Politics and Public Policy'. Shorenstein Center. Retrieved on April 30, 2022 (https://shorensteincenter.org/about-us/)

31   (Jolly 2016)

32   (Jolly 2016)

33   (*The National Pulse* 2021)

34   (*The National Pulse* 2021)

35   (*The National Pulse* 2021)

36   (*The National Pulse* 2021)

37   (*The National Pulse* 2021)

38   (*The National Pulse* 2021)

39   (Gockowski 2017)

40   (Gockowski 2017)

41   See: 'The HKS Misinformation Review'. Shorenstein Center. Retrieved on April 30, 2022 (https://shorensteincenter.org/programs/misinformation/)

42   (Carney 2022)

43   (Garimella and Eckles 2020)

44   (Abhishek 2021)

45   (Abhishek 2021)

46   (Abhishek 2021)

47   (Kazemi, et al. 2022)

48   (Kuo and Marwick 2021)

49   (Kuo and Marwick 2021)

50   (Kuo and Marwick 2021)

51   (Reis, et al. 2020)

52   (Marcus 2021)

53   (Marcus 2021)

54   (Carney 2022)

55   (Carney 2022)

56   (HKS Misinformation Review Editorial Staff 2021)

57   (HKS Misinformation Review Editorial Staff 2021)

58   (HKS Misinformation Review Editorial Staff 2021)

59   (Carney 2022)

60   (Desai 2015)

61   (Parkin 2019)

62   (Agrawal 2017)

63   (Walt 2019)

64   (Dizikes 2020)

65   (Varshney 2021)

66   (Varshney 2021)

67   (The Heritage Foundation 2018)

68 See: 'Board & Leadership'. Freedom House. Retrieved on April 30, 2022 (https://freedomhouse.org/about-us/board-leadership)

69 (Harvard Kennedy School 2016c)

70 (Chuang, Williams and Wong 2019)

71 (Williams and Wong 2020)

72 (Williams 2020)

73 (Harsha 2019)

74 (Sarma 2020)

75 (Timalsina and Michel 2021)

76 (K. Visweswaran, M. E. Witzel, et al. 2009)

77 (Chandra and Michael 2020)

78 (Chandra and Michael 2020)

79 (Harvard Kennedy School - Women and Public Policy Program 2014)

80 (Field, Jayachandran and Pande 2010)

81 (Field, Jayachandran and Pande 2010)

82 (Field, Jayachandran and Pande 2010)

83 (Field, Jayachandran and Pande 2010)

84 (Harvard Center for Population and Development Studies 2021)

85 (Vyas, Gupta and Khalid 2021)

86 (Jayachandran and Pande 2015)

87 (Jayachandran and Pande 2015)

88 (Beaman, Pande and Cirone, Politics as a Male Domain and Empowerment in India 2012)

89 See: 'Sushma Raman - Social Change Strategist | Author | Coalition Builder'. LinkedIn. Retrieved on April 30, 2022 (https://www.linkedin.com/in/sushmaraman/details/experience)

90 (*The Hindustan Times* 2017)

91 (OpIndia 2020a)

92 (Chenoweth, Smith and Shetty 2020)

93 (Harvard Kennedy School 2018). Timestamp: 00:03:37.

94 (Shetty and Sahgal 2019)

95 (Shetty and Sahgal 2019)

96 (Shetty and Sahgal 2019)

97 (Shetty and Sahgal 2019)

98 (Shetty and Sahgal 2019)

99 (Rajgarhia 2020)

100 (Rajgarhia 2020)

101 (Rajgarhia 2020)

102 (Rajgarhia 2020)

103 (*Harvard Law Review* 2021)

104 (Chenoweth, Smith and Shetty 2020)

105 (Sabhikhi 2019)

106 The report states: 'This paper examines the hypothesis that the persistence of low

spatial and marital mobility in rural India, despite increased growth rates and rising inequality in recent years, is due to the existence of sub-caste networks that provide mutual insurance to their members. Unique panel data providing information on caste loans and sub-caste identification are used to show that households that out-marry or migrate lose the services of these networks, which dampens mobility when alternative sources of insurance or finance of comparable quality are unavailable. At the aggregate level, the networks appear to have coped successfully with the rising inequality within sub-castes that accompanied the Green Revolution. Indeed, this increase in inequality lowered overall mobility, which was low to begin with, even further. The results suggest that caste networks will continue to smooth consumption in rural India for the foreseeable future, as they have for centuries.' See: (Munshi and Rosenzweig 2005).

107 The report states: 'Sustained high economic growth since the early 1990s has brought significant change to the lives of Indian women, and yet female labor force participation has stagnated at under 30%, and recent labor surveys even suggest some decline since 2005. Using a nationally representative household survey, we lay out five descriptive facts about female labor force participation in India that help identify constraints to higher participation. First, there is significant demand for jobs by women currently not in the labor force. Second, willing female non-workers have difficulty matching to jobs. Third, obtaining vocational training is correlated with a higher likelihood of working among women. Fourth, women are more likely to be working in sectors where the gender wage gap and unexplained wage gap, commonly attributed to discrimination, is higher. Finally, female-friendly policies, including quotas, are correlated with higher female participation in some key sectors. Combining these facts with a review of the literature, we map out important areas for future investigation and highlight how policies such as employment quotas and government initiatives focused on skilling and manufacturing should be better investigated and leveraged to increase women's economic activity.' (Fletcher, Pande and Moore 2017)

108 The report says: 'Female labor force participation varies significantly even among countries with similar levels of economic development. Recent studies have shown that gender norms can help explain these differences in women's work, but the channels through which norms impact women's employment decisions are not well understood. We present novel data on spouses' preferences and perceptions of community attitudes about female labor in rural India and document associations with female work. We find that the perceived social cost of women's work falls on men and that husbands' opposition to female labor is associated with their wives' lower take-up of employment.' (Bernhardt, et al. 2018)

109 The report states: 'We exploit random assignment of gender quotas across Indian village councils to investigate whether having a female chief councillor affects public opinion towards female leaders. Villagers who have never been required to have a female leader prefer male leaders and perceive hypothetical female leaders as less effective than their male counterparts, when stated performance is identical.

Exposure to a female leader does not alter villagers' taste preference for male leaders. However, it weakens stereotypes about gender roles in the public and domestic spheres and eliminates the negative bias in how female leaders' effectiveness is perceived among male villagers. Female villagers exhibit less prior bias but are also less likely to know about or participate in local politics; as a result, their attitudes are largely unaffected. Consistent with our experimental findings, villagers rate their women leaders as less effective when exposed to them for the first, but not second, time. These changes in attitude are electorally meaningful: after 10 years of the quota policy, women are more likely to stand for and win free seats in villages that have been continuously required to have a female chief councillor.' (Beaman, Chattopadhyay, et al. 2008)
110 (Barboni, et al. 2018)
111 (Harvard Kennedy School 2021b)
112 (Anand 2020)
113 (Khare, et al. 2021)
114 (K. Jain, *Cow Vigilantes and the Rise of Hindu Nationalism* 2019)
115 (Mehta 2016)
116 (Mehta 2016)
117 (*The Times of India* 2006)
118 (Harvard Kennedy School 2019a)
119 (The Training Division, Department of Personnel and Training, Government of India 2018)
120 (The Training Division, Department of Personnel and Training, Government of India 2018)
121 (Jaschik 2021)
122 (Harvard Kennedy School 2019b)
123 (Harvard Kennedy School 2019c)
124 See: 'Mukul Saxena | Founding Professor at Kautilya School of Public'. LinkedIn. Retrieved on April 30, 2022 (https://www.linkedin.com/in/mukul-saxena)
125 (BW Education 2020)
126 (Rai 2018)
127 (Moshik Temkin @moshik_temkin 2020)
128 (Temkin 2020)
129 (Mint 2021)
130 See: 'Thanks @AkbaruddinIndia & all the @KautilyaSPP team for your hospitality. Both @DavidWhiteDelhi & I were most impressed by the students & excellent facilities with @Kennedy_School inspired decor – we hope explore how tangible collaborations with GB institutions might evolve'. Twitter. Retrieved on April 30, 2022 (https://twitter.com/Andrew007Uk/status/1466337552386781189)
131 (Burnley 2017)
132 (Harvard University 2020h)
133 (Harvard T.H. Chan School of Public Health 2018)

16. Harvard Business School

1   (Iyer, Khanna and Varshney 2011)
2   (A. Gupta 2015)
3   (A. Gupta 2015)
4   See: 'Events - Advancing Racial Equity | Managing Diversity Speaker Series'. Harvard Business School. Retrieved on April 30, 2022 (https://www.hbs.edu/racialequity/news-commentary/Pages/events.aspx)
5   (Banerjee, Iyer and Somanathan 2006)
6   (Banerjee, Iyer and Somanathan 2006)
7   (Harvard Business School 2021)
8   (Jones 2017)
9   (Bhalotra, et al. 2013)
10 (Philanthropy News Digest 2016)
11 (Bhattacharya 2012)
12 (Dallmeyer 2021)
13 (Jack, Harvard's 'teaching power' puts business school in the lead for influence 2021)
14 (Jack, Harvard's 'teaching power' puts business school in the lead for influence 2021)
15 (Jack, Why Harvard's case studies are under fire 2018)
16 (The Lakshmi Mittal and Family South Asia Institute at Harvard University 2014, 47)
17 (Harvard University 2014f)
18 (Shaw 2022)
19 (CEIBS 2016)
20 (*The Economist* 2020)
21 (Byrne 2021)
22 (Byrne 2021)
23 (Byrne 2021)

18. The Nexus of Saudis, Americans, and Indian Billionaires

1   (IAMC Official Channel 2022). Timestamp: 0:00-1:20
2   (The Intercept 2022). Timestamp: 42:10-42:50
3   (Barnes, Rosenberg and Harris 2018)
4   (Wolters and Dumas 2018)
5   (Schwartz 2018)
6   The *New York Times* reported: 'One Saudi student in the United States whom I asked to interview said he would participate only if I shielded his identity. "Thanks for reaching out, please DO NOT use my name, affiliation or any descriptive

information in any published work," he wrote me in an email. When we met, he said that in contrast to what he considered some forward economic reforms by the government, "freedom of expression has been going in the other direction. You can't risk even moderate criticisms. And if you're an explicit critic, I feel like you could end up in prison."' (Sokolove 2019)

7   (Hsu, Yaffe-Bellany and Tracy 2020)
8   (Sokolove 2019)
9   (Sokolove 2019)
10   (Sokolove 2019)
11   (Sokolove 2019)
12   (Binkley 2018)
13   (Macropolis 2015)
14   (MIT News Office 2014)
15   (Sokolove 2019)
16   Its website states: 'Our work is generously supported by visionary foundations, governments, and individuals. Major donors include Arnold Ventures, Co-Impact, Community Jameel, Echidna Giving, The Bill and Melinda Gates Foundation, Google.org, The William and Flora Hewlett Foundation, King Philanthropies, The John D. and Catherine T. MacArthur Foundation, The Douglas B. Marshall Jr. Family Foundation, Omidyar Network, The Alfred P. Sloan Foundation, the Australian Department of Foreign Affairs and Trade, and the UK Department for International Development.' (J-PAL 2010)
17   (OpIndia Staff 2020)
18   (J-PAL South Asia 2021)
19   See: (xSDG 2021b) and (Belongg 2019)
20   (Belongg Circle 2022)
21   (Belongg Mental Health Collective 2021)
22   (House Of Belongg 2021). Timestamp: 15:52
23   (Patnaik and Jha 2020)
24   (Patnaik and Jha 2020)
25   (Thorat, et al. 2015)
26   (xSDG 2021c)
27   See: 'India Exclusion Report 2019–2020'. Centre For Equity Studies. Retrieved on May 15, 2022 (http://centreforequitystudies.org/wp-content/uploads/2021/01/India-Exclusion-Report-2019-20-e-copy.pdf)
28   (Centre for Equity Studies 2021)
29   See: 'US based Indian Muslims Relief & Charity a UK based Minority Rights Grop pumped money to Harsh Mander's CES during peak anti #CAA_NRC_Protests period, which frowns common Indians n motive of the donors n action of NGO on ground speaks lots seeing its role in #DelhiRiots (Cont)'. Twitter. Retrieved on May 15, 2022 (https://twitter.com/legallro/status/1308969510968479751)
30   (Subramanian 2020)
31   (The Peace Research Institute Oslo (PRIO) 2021). Also see: (Satyaagrah 2022)

32 (OpIndia Staff 2021)
33 (Soros 2020)
34 (The Sikh Coalition 2021)
35 (The Sikh Coalition 2021)
36 (J-PAL 2020a)
37 (Jeanne Lafortune's Homepage 2022)˙ See also: (J-PAL 2020b)
38 (J-PAL 2020c)
39 (J-PAL 2020d)
40 (J-PAL 2020e)
41 (J-PAL 2021)
42 (J-PAL 2014a)
43 (J-PAL 2020f)
44 (Mohan and Rego 2020)
45 (J-PAL 2014b)
46 (Kundu 2020)
47 (Kundu 2020)
48 (Aiyar 2019)
49 (Arthan 2021)
50 (*Al Jazeera* 2021)
51 (Silas 2019)
52 (Bharathi, et al. 2020)
53 (Vaidyanathan 2019)
54 (National Association of Science Writers 2021)
55 (Datta 2021)
56 (Raman 2022)
57 See: 'This is really irritating. There is more than ENOUGH documentation that all IITs, and IIT Madras too, is a hotbed of casteist discrimination. In fact, IITs survive on casteism; IITs *produce* caste to continue the myth of merit.'. Twitter. Retrieved on May 15, 2022 (https://twitter.com/queersprings/status/1485216011666157572)
58 See: 'Any analysis of Ayurveda without understanding how it is inexorably linked to caste and casteism is, for the most part, bullshit. Promoting Ayurveda = promoting caste'. Twitter. Retrieved on May 15, 2022 (https://twitter.com/queersprings/status/1502551645569564672)
59 (Yale Macmillan Center 2022)
60 (Yale Macmillan Center 2022)
61 (Yale Economic Growth Center 2020a)
62 (Yale Economic Growth Center 2022a)
63 (Yale Economic Growth Center 2021a)
64 (Yale Economic Growth Center 2021b)
65 (Yale Economic Growth Center 2022b)
66 (Field, Pande, et al. 2021c)

19. Ashoka University: Harvard University's Junior Partner

1   (Meet the Founders 2017) (8:53 – 9:29)
2   (Nanda 2021)
3   (Mehta 2016)
4   (Mehta 2016)
5   (Swarajya Staff 2021)
6   (*ThePrint* 2020). Timestamp: 06:37-09:30
7   (Balakrishna 2020)
8   (National Foundation For India 2019). (Aman Public Charitable Trust 2018)
     The donors were Oxfam, Habitat for Humanity, the Ford Foundation, National
     Foundation of India (which itself receives funding from Oxfam, the Ford foundation,
     Gates Foundation, the Rockefeller Foundation and the Azim Premji Foundation.)
9   (Krishnam 2021)
     The publication reported: 'These so-called liberal spaces are not at all different
     from other spaces or institutions that we may consider as patriarchal. Ashoka did
     everything in its capacity to protect the perpetrator. One may think a university
     in Bihar or Uttar Pradesh may act in this manner, not some place like Ashoka
     which had the famed public intellectual Pratap Bhanu Mehta as the VC during
     my complaint'. This is an excerpt from the previously unpublished interview of
     the survivor in Ashoka University Sexual Harassment case.
10   (Baruah 2017a)
11   (Baruah 2017b)
12   (*The Hindu* 2016)
13   (A. Singh 2021a)
14   (OpIndia Staff 2021a)
15   (Navayana 2012)
16   (Apoorvanand 2018)
17   (Ashoka University 2019a)
18   (Ashoka University 2020a)
19   (The British Academy 2020a)
20   (Keele University 2020)
21   (Ashoka University 2020a)
22   (Chandra 2020)
23   (*Asia Now* 2020)
24   (S. Gupta 2020)
25   (S. Gupta 2020)
26   (A. Sharma 2021a)
27   (Jameel 2021)
28   (Koshy 2021)
29   (Venu and Mirchandani 2021b)
30   (Ashoka University 2019b)
     She is working on a 'big project which is about looking at why women's participation

in the labour force in India is so persistently low. What are the issues around that and that's been a big policy question right now. And so there we find that the fact that women have to do domestic chores I don't mean things like cooking cleaning etc. but even things like maintenance, household maintenance, washing clothes etc., with every additional domestic chore, when you account for all other factors, women's participation in economic activity goes down. That's one thing that we find and the other thing that we find is that while education of women has been rising, availability of suitable jobs is not. What I'm hoping is that this evidence based research contributes to the formulation of meaningful policy to tackle these persistent problems that we see'.

31 (Ashoka University 2019b)
32 (Deshpande 2018a)
33 (Ashoka University 2022a)
34 (Ashoka University 2022a)
35 (Brookings 2015)
36 (Harvard Kennedy School 2017c)
37 (Institute of Chinese Studies 2020)
38 (Institute of Chinese Studies 2021)
39 (Harvard-Yenching Institute 2020a)
40 (Rosenbaum 2012)
41 (United Board 2019)
42 See: "Our Network". United Board. Retrieved on May 15, 2022 (https:// unitedboard.org/about-us/our-network/). In India, it supports CHRIST University in Bangalore, C.S.I. Ewart Women's Christian College Fatima College, Holy Cross College, Trichy, Lady Doak College, Madras Christian College, Maris Stella College, Nesamony Memorial Christian College, Union Christian College, Kerala, Union Christian College, Shillong and the Women's Christian College in Chennai to name a few.
43 (Harvard-Yenching Institute 2020b)
44 (Chinese Studies Association of Australia 2021)
45 (Harvard-Yenching Institute 2020c)
46 (Harvard-Yenching Institute 2020c)
47 (Chinese Studies Association of Australia 2021)
48 (Harvard University 2018j)
49 (Yeung 2018)
50 (Varshney 2018)
51 (Varshney 2018)
52 (Varshney 2018)
53 (Varshney 2018)
54 (Varshney 2018)
55 (Deshpande, Meritocracy and Affirmative Action in India 2018)
56 (Deshpande, Meritocracy and Affirmative Action in India 2018)
57 (Deshpande, Meritocracy and Affirmative Action in India 2018)

58   (Deshpande, Meritocracy and Affirmative Action in India 2018)
59   (Deshpande, Meritocracy and Affirmative Action in India 2018)
60   (Deshpande, Meritocracy and Affirmative Action in India 2018)
61   (Harvard University 2018j, 9). 'First is the role of technical education in caste formation. Rather than a space of universal knowledge where caste is no longer relevant, what we are seeing is the reconstitution of caste within and through the technical sciences. What this suggests is that caste is both resilient within and foundational to the makeup of the most modern, apparently identity-free institutions. Second is how we understand the relationship between meritocracy and democracy. By bracketing out historically accumulated advantages and disadvantages, the notion of meritocracy, like that of a color-blind society, has come to service the reproduction of inequality. Of course, the ideal meaning of meritocracy as a system which corrects for historical privilege has not vanished. However, the divergence between its ideal meaning and its social life should call into question the easy assumption that meritocracy is indeed a leveller of opportunity'.
62   (The Lakshmi Mittal and Family South Asia Institute 2019a); (Harvard University 2018j, 15).
63   (Trivedi Centre for Political Data 2018)
64   (Trivedi Centre for Political Data 2020c)
65   (Sciences Po 2017)
66   (Winters and Kassam, EXC: Joe Biden's CIA Director Told Congress He Terminated a Relationship With a Chinese Communist Influence Group – New Evidence Suggests This Was a Lie 2022)
67   (Mahaprashasta 2020)
68   (Jaffrelot and Laliwala, The segregated city 2018). 'The segregated city - Ghettoisation and Disturbed Areas Act are dividing urban spaces in Gujarat, pushing Muslims to the edge'; (Jaffrelot and Laliwala 2018b) 'Inside Ahmedabad's Juhapura: What It's Like for Muslims to Live in a Ghetto - If ghettoes promote orthodoxy, sectarianism and self-help, the rise of Hindutva has also prompted efforts to reach out to wider civil society'; (Jaffrelot 2021) 'Narendra Modi and Hindu Nationalism – The police is even acting directly against the minorities and the Delhi riots of 2020 showed that the police could be on their side in the street in their rioting activities'.
69   (The Indian Express 2015)
70   (Carnegie Endowment for International Peace 2016) His papers are: Nationalism, not Hindutva Will Be the Big Theme for 2019; BJP is insecure about the youth vote; NRC Could Be the 21st Century Ram Janmabhoomi; The Dismal Functioning Of Democracy In Indian States; Has India's 'Flailing State' Been Turned Upside Down?; Introduction to E-symposium: Urbanisation, Gender, & Social Change in North India; Urbanisation, Gender, And Social Change: Do Working Women Enjoy More Agency?
71   See: 'Gilles Verniers'. LinkedIn. Retrieved on May 15, 2022 (https://www.linkedin.com/in/gillesverniers/?originalSubdomain=in)
72   See: 'Dr. S.Y. Quraishi'. LinkedIn. Retrieved on May 15, 2022 (https://www.linkedin.com/in/dr-s-y-quraishi-bab17365/)

73 (The International Institute for Democracy and Electoral Assistance 1998)

74 (Dhawan 2021)

75 (Jeelani 2021)

76 (OpIndia Staff 2022)

77 (*The Hindustan Times* 2022). Timestamp: 2:00

78 (OpIndia Staff 2022)

79 (OpIndia Staff 2022)

80 (Trivedi Centre for Political Data 2021a)

81 (Trivedi Centre for Political Data 2021b)

82 (Trivedi Centre for Political Data 2020b)

83 (Trivedi Centre for Political Data 2022)

84 (Trivedi Centre for Political Data 2021c)

85 (Trivedi Centre for Political Data 2021d)

86 (Zee Media Bureau 2022); See also: 'E-Census will shape development of next 25 years, every birth and death will be registered: Amit Shah'. *Times Now*. Retrieved on April 30, 2022 (https://www.timesnownews.com/india/e-census-will-shape-development-of-next-25-years-every-birth-and-death-will-be-registered-amit-shah-article-91444323)

87 (CNRS 1997) and (Mahaprashasta 2020)

88 (LIA SPINPER 2019a)

89 (LIA SPINPER 2019b)

90 (LIA SPINPER 2019a)

91 (LIA SPINPER 2019c)

92 (LIA SPINPER 2019d)

93 (LIA SPINPER 2019e)

94 (LIA SPINPER 2019f)

95 (Trivedi Centre for Political Data 2021e)

96 (Harvard University 2022b)

97 (Wellesley College 2016a). 'The signed memorandum of understanding represents a five-year agreement. The main components of the proposed academic program include: the joint development of innovative course content; research between faculty members and students in the areas of mutual interest; faculty exchange; and the possibility of wintersession programs, student exchange and study abroad programs. Further, as part of the agreement, the Wellesley Centers for Women has proposed to collaborate with Ashoka to support the development of the Center for Research on Gender and Sexuality, and the Albright Institute has proposed the sharing of their curricular and pedagogical global affairs model. A small cohort of Ashoka students was on campus to observe the 2016 Albright Institute winter session'.

98 (Pocket News Alert 2016)

99 (Wellesley College 2016a)

100 (Ashoka University 2020b)

101 Brazil, Romania, and Russia are examples where Gender Studies are under attack

from the governments. See: (Redden 2018b))

102 (Duffy 2021). 'Students are being asked to pretend they're trans or non-binary during mock discussions about initiating sex. This is from a federally funded sex education program.' The sudden rise in gender dysphoria in teens is blamed on trans activism and some even call it 'social engineering' by the Marxists of academia in the US. Snapchat, the social media platform for trans activism is also blamed for actively promoting the trans agenda and gender transitioning has emerged into a multibillion-dollar industry.

103 (Jones 2021); See: 'The number of kids who identify as LGBT, especially trans and bisexual, has absolutely skyrocketed. If you think this is a natural or organic development, you're deluded. The media, Hollywood, and the school system actively recruit children into the LGBT ranks'. Twitter. Retrieved on May 15, 2022 (https://twitter.com/MattWalshBlog/status/1364639405605027840)

104 Kashmir papers sponsored by CSGS: *On Kashmiri Women's Songs of Resistance, LSE Engenderings*; *Why does Kashmir's internet matter, when Kashmiri lives don't? Middle East Eye*; *On Kashmiri Women's Resistance, Asia Dialogue Post,* University of Nottingham; *The Myth of Empowerment: Gender, Conflict, and 'Development' in Kashmir, in Minorities and Populism – Critical Perspectives from South Asia and Europe* (edited by Volker Kaul and Ananya Vajpeyi), Springer; *On solidarity: reading love, loss, and longing in Kashmir, Identities Journal*; *In Kashmir, Resistance is Mainstream, Himal* SouthAsian; *Kashmir: Coronavirus is a new tool for India to oppress us, Middle East Eye*; *India takes another leaf from Israel's playbook by denying funerals in Kashmir, MiddleEast Eye*; *Kashmir and the politics of solidarity,* Identities Journal Blog; *India's settler colonialism in Kashmir is not starting now, eliminating the natives is a process long underway,* The Polis Project; *Home as the Frontier,* in *Can You Hear Kashmiri Women Speak?* Edited by Nitasha Kaul and Ather Zia, Women Unlimited; *In Kashmir, like Palestine, tourism glosses over reality of occupation, Middle East Eye.*

105 (New Discourses 2021)

106 (Ashoka University 2019)

107 (Wellesley Centers for Women 2020). The topics were: *Can sex be 'educated' in a culture of fear victimhood & trauma?*; *Intersections between gender and sexuality,* discussed educational policy and theory; *The relationship between sex and education in history, art, literature, law, and culture; Sex & Education – in the Indian context; Relationship between sex, education, history, and culture; Laws regulating 'desire' in educational institutions and public spaces; Sex, Education, and the Classroom.*

108 (K. Bhattacharjee 2021)

109 (Ashoka University 2016b). Timestamp: 31:48

110 (Ashoka University 2016b). Timestamp: 34:23

111 (Tariq 2020)

112 (BAPSA (Birsa Ambedkar Phule Students Association), JNU 2016)

113 (Justice For Rohith, University of Hyderabad 2016)

114 (Cogito 137 2020). Timestamp: 1:40

115 (Cogito 137 2020). Timestamp: 0:23

116 (Ashoka University 2017b). Timestamp: 9:17

117 (Ashoka University 2017b). Timestamp: 13:24

118 (Ashoka University 2017b). Timestamp: 08:53

119 (Omidyar Network India 2020b)

120 (Omidyar Network India 2020b)

121 (Ashoka University 2021a)

122 (Omidyar Network India 2020b)

123 (Rethinking Economics JNU 2021). Timestamp: 14:45

124 (PIB Delhi 2020)

125 (Ashoka University 2022b)

126 (Ashoka University 2021b)

127 (Omidyar Network India 2021a)

128 (*The Indian Express* 2015)

129 (Association for Democratic Reforms 2016)

130 See: 'Ingrid Srinath'. LinkedIn. Retrieved on May 15, 2022 (https://www.linkedin. com/in/ingrid-srinath-355552)

131 (Hindu Janajagruti Samiti 2014)

132 (Ashoka University 2018)

133 (Centre for Social Impact and Philanthropy 2019)

134 (Centre for Social Impact and Philanthropy 2019, 5)

135 (Centre for Social Impact and Philanthropy 2019)

136 (Philip 2018)

137 (Philip 2018)

138 (Centre for Social Impact and Philanthropy 2019, 10)

139 (Centre for Social Impact and Philanthropy 2019, 17)

140 (Centre for Social Impact and Philanthropy 2019, 24)

141 (Centre for Social Impact and Philanthropy 2019, 25)

142 (Independent and Public-Spirited Media Foundation 2019a)

143 (Centre for Social Impact and Philanthropy 2019, 40)

144 (Bhattacharya 2015)

145 (Ashoka University 2018a)

146 (Ashoka University 2018a)

147 (Ashoka University 2017a)

148 (Ashoka University 2016a)

149 (Ashoka University 2021)

150 (Shimer 2015)

151 (Shimer 2015)

152 (Wellesley College 2016a)

153 (*The Wire* Staff 2021a)

154 (*The Wire* Staff 2021a)

155 See: 'If Ashoka founders think it was a company because they put so much money in it, let us now talk business| Many in the leading US universities were thinking

of developing partnerships with Ashoka and a lead founder came to me for a partnership with Brown| Not possible any more|'. Twitter. Retrieved on May 15, 2022 (https://twitter.com/profvarshney/status/1372747919242235904)

156 (Pullanoor 2021)

157 (*The Wire* Staff 2021b)

158 (CSGS@Ashoka 2019)

159 (CSGS@Ashoka 2020). Timestamp: 00:03:45-00:07:45

160 (Stop Hindu Hate Advocacy Network 2020)

161 (K. Bhattacharjee 2020)

162 See: 'Students Against Hindutva Ideology'. Instagram. Retrieved on May 15, 2022 (https://www.instagram.com/studentsagainsthindutva).

163 (Dubey 2020)

164 (K. Sharma 2017)

165 (Blatantly Honest 2021b)

166 (Blatantly Honest 2021a)

167 (Blatantly Honest 2022)

168 (Goswami 2020)

20. Azim Premji's Media and Educational Impact

1   (Azim Premji University 2016)

2   (Azim Premji Foundation 2020); (Azim Premji University 2020)

3   (Varadarajan 2014)

4   (Azim Premji University 2014)

5   (Azim Premji University 2012)

6   (M. Bhattacharjee 2021)

7   (M. Bhattacharjee 2021)

8   (M. Bhattacharjee 2021)

9   (A. Singh 2021b)

10   (*The Wire* Staff 2018)

11   (*The Wire* Staff 2019)

12   (*The Hindu* 2019)

13   (Countercurrents 2020)

14   (Shireen 2021)

15   (Independent and Public-Spirited Media Foundation 2019c)

16   Since 2016 they have made grants of up to rupees seventy-nine crores. The following is the list of grantees: *Kashmir Observer*, *The Wire*, *ThePrint* (of Shekhar Gupta), *The Caravan*, *Mojo Story* (of Barkha Dutt), *Economic & Political Weekly*, *Janjwar*, *The Bastion*, *Down to Earth*, *Feminism In India*, *The Citizen*, *Alt News*, *India Spend*, *Max Maharashtra*, *India Development Review*, *Live History India*, *Saptahik Sadhana*, *The News Minute*, *Swarajya*, *Think Pragati*, *Supreme Court Observer*, *Article 14*, *The Ken*, *The Better India*, *Azhimukham*, *Live Law*, *Dool*

News, YouTurn, Asiaville, The India Forum, Suno India, CGNet Swara, Imphal Free Press, East Mojo, Sikkim Chronicle, Khabar Lahariya, and *Gaon Connection.* See: (IPSMF News 2021). According to IPSMF's website, as of January 2022, the following publications are still in their active grantee portfolio: *Article 14, The Citizen, Mojo Story, Supreme Court Observer, The India Forum, Imphal Free Press, Kashmir Observer, Feminism In India, Asiaville, Janjwar, Live History India, India Development Review, The Bastion, Suno India, Sikkim Chronicle, Saptahik Sadhana, Max Maharashtra, East Mojo, Alt News, Khabar Lahariya, The Caravan, Down to Earth, ThePrint, Swarajya, Think Pragati, The News Minute* and *Economic & Political Weekly.*

17   (Independent and Public-Spirited Media Foundation 2019b)
18   (Armour-Jones, Clark and Schwartz-Henderson 2019)
19   (Armour-Jones, Clark and Schwartz-Henderson 2019, 39)
20   (Centre for Social Impact and Philanthropy 2019, 30)
21   (Azim Premji Foundation 2021a); (Azim Premji Foundation 2021b)
22   (Brot für die Welt 2020)
23   (RNBA Manipur 2020)
24   (Azim Premji Foundation 2021)
25   (Arkitect India 2021)
26   (Arkitect India 2021). Timestamp: 09:40
27   (Arkitect India 2021). Timestamp: 11:36
28   (Rozario 2020)
29   (Basha 2020)
30   (K. Sharma 2021)
31   (Harvard Global 2017b)
32   (Harvard Global 2017a)
33   (Sannam S4 Group 2008)

21. Godrej and Queering

1   A 2011 study by the UCLA Williams Institute estimated the size of the LGBTQ+ population in the US and four other countries. The study found 3.5% identified as LGBTQ+ and 0.3% identified as transgender and 8.2% of Americans reported that they engaged in same-sex sexual behaviour. See: (Gates 2011). In 2020, that number increased: 4.5 % of the US population was found to be LGBTQ+ by the same research group. See: (Conron and Goldberg 2020)

2   Some of the main categories as of today are: **Agender:** does not identify with any gender; **Bigender:** identifies as two genders, either simultaneously or at different times; **Cis-gender, cisgender:** identifies as the same gender as the biological sex assigned at birth; **Genderfluid:** has a shifting or changing gender identity or identifies differently at different times; **Genderqueer:** has gender identity different from the societal norms of their assigned biological sex; **Neutrois:** neutral gender;

Trans, transgender, trans-man, trans-woman: identifies with a different gender than the sex assigned at birth. Sometimes trans people identify as either MTF (male to female) or FTM (female to male). A trans man is a person who was assigned female at birth and identifies as male. A trans woman is a person who was assigned male at birth and identifies as female. See: (Evan 2015)

3   (Bond 2021)

4   (Bond 2021)

5   (Harmon 2020)

6   (Shrier 2020)

7   (New Discourses 2022). Timestamp: 02:15:20 – 02:16:00

8   (Reilly 2022)

9   (Cost 2021)

10   (Cost 2021)

11   For instance, Vishnu assuming the form of Mohini. This is an annual festival trans-gender people can celebrate.

12   (Gettleman and Lyons 2018b)

13   (Bittu 2021)

14   (*Reuters* 2019)

15   (ANI 2021b)

16   (Godrej India Culture Lab 2019a)

17   (Godrej India Culture Lab 2019b)

18   (N. J. Sharma 2020c)

19   (N. J. Sharma 2020c)

20   (IndiaCultureLab 2019). Timestamp: 02:00

21   (N. J. Sharma 2020c)

22   (N. J. Sharma 2020c)

23   (N. J. Sharma 2020c)

24   (N. J. Sharma 2020c)

25   (N. J. Sharma 2020c)

26   (IndiaCultureLab 2020a). Timestamp: 19:22

27   (Nambiar and Shahani 2018)

28   For instance, feminizing includes the following surgical procedures: Scalp Hair Reconstruction (including both crown and hairline reconstruction); Scalp Advancement/Hairline lowering; Forehead contouring/Brow burnishing; Brow Lift; Blepharoplasty; Rhytidoplasty; Rhinoplasty; Cheek enhancement/reduction; Upper lip reduction/enhancement; Genioplasty, feminizing; Jaw Contouring; Liposuction of neck; Tracheal Shave; Breast Augmentation/Augmentation Mammoplasty; Suction-assisted lipectomy/body contouring; Penectomy; Orchiectomy; Vaginoplasty; Clitoroplasty; Vulvoplasty; Labiaplasty. Masculinizing includes surgeries for the following: Forehead Lengthening; Forehead Augmentation; Cheek Augmentation; Nasal Augmentation; Genioplasty, masculinizing; Thyroid Cartilage Enhancement; Mastectomy; Suction-assisted lipectomy/body contouring; Hysterectomy/Oophorectomy; Reconstruction of the

fixed part of the urethra; Metoidioplasty; Phalloplasty; Vaginectomy Scrotoplasty; Implantation of erectile or testicular prostheses. (Nambiar and Shahani 2018)

29   (Nambiar and Shahani 2018, 37)
30   (Nambiar and Shahani 2018, 41)
31   (Nambiar and Shahani 2018, 39)
32   (Nambiar and Shahani 2018, 42)
33   (Nambiar and Shahani 2018, 51)
34   (Nambiar and Shahani 2018, 51)
35   (Yale School of Management 2014)
36   (IndiaCultureLab 2020a). Timestamp: 24:08
37   (IndiaCultureLab 2020a). Timestamp: 22:33
38   (India Foundation for the Arts 2014); See: 'Storytelling Special | June 14, 15, 27 & 28, 2013 | Mumbai'. India Foundation for the Arts. Retrieved on April 30, 2022 (http://indiaifa.org/events/storytelling-special-june-14-15-27-28-2013-mumbai. html)
39   (IndiaCultureLab 2020b). Timestamp: 07:50
40   (India Foundation for the Arts 2021)

22. Omidyar Network, Trojan Horse in India

1   See: (A. Field 2019)
2   See: (Fuller 2021). We are indebted to Fuller's investigative work that enabled us to dig deeper.
3   See: (Fuller 2021)
4   Fuller's investigation reveals the following: 'Omidyar, whose Omidyar Network funds AELP, also funds the Democracy Fund which is now part of Omidyar Group (1). The Democracy Fund, in turn, together with the Knight Foundation, Quadrivium, the McArthur Foundation and Luminate (also funded by Omidyar) fund Democracy Works (2). Omidyar also funds Democracy Fund Voice, which in turn contributes to Defending Democracy Together (3). Then there is Healthy Democracy which is funded by the Democracy Fund, Silicon Valley Community Foundation (which also receives money from Democracy Fund) (4) and the Ford Family Foundation. The Omidyar Network also co-funds New Public by Civic Signals, along with the Knight Foundation, One Project, the National Conference on Citizenship and the University of Texas at Austin, Centre for Media Engagement. Of course, the University of Texas at Austin, Centre for Media Engagement is also funded by the Omidyar Network, the Democracy Fund (funded by Omidyar), the Knight Foundation, Robert McCormick Foundation, and Google. To name just a few others, the Ada Lovelace Institute also receives funding from Luminate, the Wellcome Trust and Nuffield Foundation, while TicTec, a MySociety event about 'civic tech', is funded by Facebook, Luminate and Google, among others'.

5   (Luminate 2019)

6   See: 'NMV'. New Media Ventures. Retrieved on May 15, 2022 (https://www. newmediaventures.org)

7   There is also a direct flow to Equality Labs. Equity Initiative Omidyar's website states: 'Equality Labs is a critical conduit for information, services, and rapid response for South Asian and broader racial justice communities. With a grant from the Omidyar Network, we will increase direct services to our base and update our mutual aid resource kit, grow our COVID-19 public health guide and *create more culturally sensitive materials*; and bring on a new digital security contractor'. See: (Omidyar Network India 2021j)

8   (Greenwald 2021)

9   (Greenwald 2021)

10   (Dolan 2015)

11   (Dolan 2015)

12   (Malhotra and Neelakandan 2011)

13   (Malhotra and Neelakandan 2011, 336-37)

14   (Malhotra and Neelakandan 2011, 363-64)

15   (Shashikumar 2004)

16   (Shashikumar 2004)

17   (Shashikumar 2004)

18   See: 'Summer 2012, Pilot Project'. Harvard University. Retrieved on April 30, 2022 (https://mittalsouthasiainstitute.harvard.edu/wp-content/uploads/2012/08/ Final-Report-MOBILIZE-Digital-Libraries-2012-Pilot3.pdf)

19   (Harvard University 2019)

20   (Malhotra 2021)

21   (Mishra 2014)

22   Digital Infrastructure for Governance, Impact and Transformation. See: 'DIGIT by eGov Foundation'. digit.org. Retrieved on May 15, 2022 (https://www.digit.org/)

23   (Musthafa, Kumar and Sharalaya 2022a)

24   (Musthafa, Kumar and Sharalaya 2022a)

25   (Musthafa, Kumar and Sharalaya 2022a)

26   (Musthafa, Kumar and Sharalaya 2022a); (ANI 2021a)

27   (Omidyar Network India 2021b)

28   See: 'How IntrCity Mobility Changed with Intrcity Smart Buses'. Omidyar Network India. Retrieved on May 15, 2022 (https://www.omidyarnetwork.in/theboldones/ intrcity)

29   (Omidyar Network India 2021f)

30   See: 'Helping Small business grow via Easy Loans'. Omidyar Network India. Retrieved on May 15, 2022 (https://www.omidyarnetwork.in/theboldones/indifi)

31   (Omidyar Network India 2021i)

32   (Omidyar Network India 2021c)

33   (Omidyar Network India 2022c)

34   See: 'Transforming India using Data Driven Technology – Transverse'. Omidyar

Network India. Retrieved on May 15, 2022 (https://www.omidyarnetwork.in/theboldones/transerve)

35   (Omidyar Network India 2021g)

36   (Omidyar Network India 2019a) See Homepage for latest investment Tracker

37   The investments are in the categories of Equity, Grants, Support for Projects and Research

38   See: 'Omidyar Network India'. LinkedIn. Retrieved on May 15, 2022 (https://in.linkedin.com/company/omidyar-network-india)

39   See: 'The Bold Ones'. LinkedIn. Retrieved on May 15, 2022 (https://www.linkedin.com/posts/omidyar-network-india_the-bold-ones-activity-6868452932489121792-v6AO)

40   (IDFC Foundation 2016a)

41   (IDFC Institute 2015)

42   (IDFC Institute 2015)

43   (IDFC Institute 2017a)

44   (IDFC Institute 2017b)

45   (IDFC Institute 2017b)

46   (World Economic Forum 2016)

47   (IDFC Foundation 2016a)

48   (IDFC Foundation 2016a)

49   (Rubinstein and Blumenthal 2019)

50   (Data Governance Network 2020)

51   (Rajadhyaksha 2017)

52   (Parasa 2021a)

53   (Imad, et al. 2021b)

54   (Imad, et al. 2021b)

55   (Rajan, et al. 2021c)

56   (Tandel, et al. 2017a)

57   Data in the table is copied from (IDFC Institute 2017c)

58   (IDFC Foundation 2016b)

59   (IDFC Foundation 2016b)

60   (Winters and Kassam 2021b)

61   (Winters and Kassam 2021b)

62   (Ganguly 2019)

63   (Pratilipi 2014)

64   (Pratilipi 2014)

65   (Omidyar Network India 2022a)

66   (Omidyar Network India 2020a)

67   (Omidyar Network India 2021a)

68   (J-PAL 2003)

69   (Omidyar Network India 2019b)

70   (Omidyar Network India 2021e)

71   (Omidyar Network India 2021h)

72 See: 'Catalytic Capital Consortium Announces Awards to 14 Research Projects'. LinkedIn. Retrieved on May 15, 2022 (https://www.linkedin.com/posts/omidyar-network_catalytic-capital-consortium-announces-awards-activity-6856272421377458177-8iLe) and (New Venture Fund 2021)

73 See: '#NextHalfBillion: Diversity, Equity and Inclusion'. LinkedIn. Retrieved on May 15, 2022 (https://www.linkedin.com/posts/omidyar-network-india_nexthalfbillion-diversity-equity-activity-6853955345090441216-JV0e) and (Kudva 2021)

74 See: 'This duo incubates early-stage non-profits. Their goal: Bring 1 crore Indians out of poverty by 2025'. LinkedIn. Retrieved on May 15, 2022 (https://www.linkedin.com/posts/omidyar-network-india_forbes-india-this-duo-incubates-early-stage-activity-6863754490013614081-atzY) and (Shekhar 2021)

75 (Omidyar Network India 2022b)

76 See: 'Widening India's Digital Highways: The Next Frontiers for Open Digital Ecosystems (ODEs)'. LinkedIn. Retrieved on May 15, 2022 (https://www.linkedin.com/posts/omidyar-network-india_odes-opendigitalecosystems-digitalindia-activity-6859007168834760704-Xpd1). And also: "The Next Frontiers for ODEs'. LinkedIn. Retrieved on May 15, 2022 (https://www.linkedin.com/posts/omidyar-network-india_the-next-frontiers-for-odes-activity-6859736951080140800-0ULs).

77 (Professional Assistance for Development Action 2021); See: 'Leveraging Technology to Secure Tribal Land Rights: Why We Invested in Pradan'. LinkedIn. Retrieved on May 15, 2022 (https://www.linkedin.com/posts/omidyar-network-india_leveraging-technology-to-secure-tribal-land-activity-6851831041959710720-PEdZ/); See: 'Professional Assistance For Development Action (PRADAN): Overview'. LinkedIn. Retrieved on May 15, 2022 (https://www.linkedin.com/company/professional-assistance-for-development-action).

78 (NFI 2019)

79 (Kumar, Musthafa and Kamra 2021a)

80 (Omidyar Network India 2020c)

81 (Tandan, Nautiyal and Kudva 2019)

82 (Omidyar Network India 2019c)

83 See: 'Scroll.in'. Omidyar Network India. Retrieved on May 15, 2022 (https://www.omidyarnetwork.in/investees/scroll)

84 (Rieder 2014)

85 As reported in: (Valentine 2017, 130-131). Also see: (Cohen 2014)

86 See: 'PRS Legislative Research'. PRS. Retrieved on May 15, 2022 (https://prsindia.org) and (Omidyar Network 2020)

87 See: 'Entrepreneurship-In-Government_ Part I with Dr K.P. Krishnan and Varad Pande'. LinkedIn. Retrieved on May 15, 2022 (https://www.linkedin.com/posts/omidyar-network-india_entrepreneurship-in-government-part-i-with-activity-6838355897102807040-L1ts)

88 (Omidyar Network India 2021d)

89 (Data Governance Network 2020)

90 (Data Governance Network 2013)
91 (Omidyar Network India 2020d)
92 (The Centre for Internet and Society 2008); and See: 'The Centre for Internet and Society'. LinkedIn. Retrieved on May 15, 2022 (https://in.linkedin.com/company/centre-for-internet-and-society)
93 Village Capital: (Omidyar Network India 2020e)

Conclusion

1 (*BBC* News 2020)
2 (Schwab and Vanham 2021); (Bakker and Elkington 2020)
3 (Harvard Kennedy School 2017b)
4 (kenlej 2022)
5 (kenlej 2022)
6 (kenlej 2022)
7 (Delingpole 2021)
8 (Young and Addison 2020); (Taylor 2020)
9 (Wherry 2020); (Global News 2020). Timestamp: 2:05.
10 See: 'This is what you need to know about critical race theory. Learn more about racial equality: http://ow.ly/PUbR50HPGga'. Twitter. Retrieved on May 15, 2022 (https://twitter.com/wef/status/1491094355444219906)
11 (Wignaraja and Horvath 2020)
12 (Wignaraja and Horvath 2020)
13 (Wignaraja and Horvath 2020)
14 (Stein 2021)
15 (Schachtel 2022)
16 (Schachtel 2022)
17 (Schachtel 2022)
18 (World Economic Forum 2020b)
19 (Evans, et al. 2017)
20 (Massa and Melby 2020)
21 (Massa and Melby 2020)
22 (World Economic Forum 2022a); See: 'BlackRock'. World Economic Forum. Retrieved on May 15, 2022 (https://www.weforum.org/organizations/blackrock-inc)
23 (Kramer 2020)
24 (Sheth 2022)
25 (Barrabi 2022)
26 (Kramer 2019)
27 (Dawson and Duda 2021)
28 (Joshi 2021)
29 (Joshi 2021)
30 (Dhillon 2018)

31   (Rao 2021)

32   (Nevradakis 2022)

33   (Nevradakis 2022)

34   (Nevradakis 2022)

35   (Infosys 2020). Timestamp: 01:05

36   (World Economic Forum 2022b, 22)

37   (World Economic Forum 2022b, 22)

38   (World Economic Forum 2022b, 22)

39   (World Economic Forum 2022b, 24)

40   (World Economic Forum 2022b, 24)

41   (World Economic Forum 2022b, 29)

42   See: 'Brian J. Grim | Faith & Business Build a Better World'. LinkedIn. Retrieved on May 15, 2022 (https://www.linkedin.com/in/briangrim)

43   For instance, the Templeton Foundation with its strong experience in funding Christian initiatives is a sponsor of the RFBF's Asian expansion engagement. See: (Religious Freedom & Business Foundation 2019)

44   For instance, one of the participants in their focus group said: 'The World Trade Centers are very active in India. They have a very strong business community. They now have almost 40 World Trade Centers throughout India. I know many people on the board and have been active the past couple decades. This issue [religious freedom] never came up there...But through the roundtables, I connected. I then realized how intense this issue was. I was not aware of it. In the business community, it was going past me.' (Religious Freedom & Business Foundation 2021, 7)

45   See: 'Corporate Religious Equity, Diversity & Inclusion (REDI) Index'. REDI. Retrieved on May 15, 2022 (https://religiousfreedomandbusiness.org/redi)

46   (Da Alternative 2022)

47   (The Forum of Young Global Leaders 2020)

48   (*The Hill* 2022). Timestamp: 05:38-06:23

49   (Lord 2021)

50   (Dellacherie 2017)

51   (World Economic Forum 2020a)

52   (Jeedigunta, et al. 2021, 4)

53   (Sharma and Sengupta 2020)

Acknowledgments

A book of this magnitude and scope can only be developed with the help of a competent team. The authors wish to acknowledge the assistance given by several individuals working in a variety of specific capacities. T.N. Sudarshan has helped in the huge research that was required to put together a book of this magnitude. Sejuti Banerjea edited each chapter in parallel as we were writing, as well as the entire manuscript at the end, to help improve the flow, consistency, and clarity. Anurag Sharma and Divya Sharma improved the diagrams significantly. Anurag also provided extensive research support for Chapter 6. Subhodeep Mukhopadhyay built the bibliography very systematically in the standard format. Divya Reddy has helped with the transcription of audio files and videos that were used in the compilation of the text of this book. Gerald Surya led the effort to verify the quotations and find alternative urls where the original urls were dead. Aditya Pai downloaded all the references and organized them into an archive for future research, besides helping verify the quotations. Sanjana Roy Choudhury, our highly experienced editor, painstakingly went through the manuscript multiple times to ensure that the use of language and special terms are correct and consistent. Biswajit Malakar has been responsible for the book's website as well as all the video production related to the book's launch and marketing. Aditi Banerjee reviewed several chapters and provided helpful comments and feedback. Deepthi Rao reviewed the sections pertaining to the LGBTQ+ topics, and her extensive feedback is quoted in the Introduction. Rajeev Rao provided much of the early leads on Equality Labs. Prateek Uniyal helped transcribe some of the dictations by the authors. Manogna Sastry coordinated and oversaw the successful publication of the book.

Bibliography

Abelove, Henry, Michele Aina Barale, and David M Halperin. 1993. *The Lesbian and Gay Studies Reader*. New York: Routledge.

Abhishek, Aman. 2021. "Overlooking the political economy in the research on propaganda." *Harvard Kennedy School, Misinformation Review*. 1 April. Accessed March 31, 2022. https://misinforeview.hks.harvard.edu/wp-content/uploads/2021/03/abhishek-_political_economy_research_propaganda_20210401.pdf.

Agarwal, C.B. 1934. *The Harijans in Rebellion*. Bombay: Taraporewala and Sons.

Agrawal, Riju. 2017. *A Rare Opportunity for India's Congress Party*. 10 October. Accessed March 31, 2022. https://ksr.hkspublications.org/2017/10/10/a-rare-opportunity-for-india-and-the-congress-party/ .

Ahmad, Qeyamuddin. 1988. *India by Al-Biruni*. 2nd. New Delhi: National Book Trust.

Ahuja, Ram. 1993. *Indian Social System*. Jaipur: Rawat Publishers.

Aiyangar, K.V. Rangaswami. 1934. *Aspects of Ancient Indian Economic Thought*. Benares Hindu University: Benares.

Aiyar, Swaminathan S. Anklesaria. 2019. *View: Experimental economics not perfect but has potential*. 20 October. Accessed May 15, 2022. https://economictimes.indiatimes.com/news/economy/policy/view-experimental-economics-not-perfect-but-has-potential/articleshow/71670694.cms.

Al Jazeera. 2021. *Rihanna creates flutter in India with tweet on farmer protests*. 3 February. Accessed May 15, 2022. https://www.aljazeera.com/news/2021/2/3/rihanna-creates-flutter-in-india-with-tweet-on-farmer-protests.

Aman Public Charitable Trust. 2018. *DONORS & PARTNERS*. Accessed May 15, 2022. http://amanpanchayat.org/about/donors-partners/.

Ambedkar International Center (AIC). 2021. *Cisco Caste Discrimination: AIC Press Release*. 2 March. Accessed February 15, 2022. https://ambedkarinternationalcenter.org/2021/03/cisco-caste-discrimination-aic-press-release/.

Ambedkar King Study Circle USA. 2020. *Practice of Caste in USA - HOW CASTE TRAVELS? by Dr.Ajantha Subramanian, Harvard University, USA*. 25 July. Accessed February 15, 2022. https://www.youtube.com/watch?v=gVweqgyGvKM.

——. 2021. *Santa Clara County HRC on Caste Discrimination*. 30 April. Accessed April 30, 2022. https://akscusa.org/santa-clara-county-hrc-on-caste-discrimination/.

Ambedkar, Bhimrao Ramji. 2015. *'Buddha or Karl Marx?* CreateSpace Independent Publishing Platform. https://www.baiae.org/index.php/ja/downloads-baiae.html?download=12:buddha-or-karl-marx-pdf.

——. 1936. *Annihilation of Caste with a reply to Mahatma Gandhi*. Lahore: Self-Published.

http://www.ambedkar.org/ambcd/02.Annihilation%20of%20Caste.htm.

——. 1990. *Pakistan: The Partition of India*. Mumbai: Education Department, Govt. of Maharashtra. https://mea.gov.in/Images/attach/amb/Volume_08.pdf.

——. 1979. *Who were the Shudras?* New Delhi: Ministry of External Affairs, Government of India. Accessed February 15, 2022. https://www.mea.gov.in/Images/attach/amb/Volume_07.pdf.

——. 1989a. *Writings and Speeches. Vol. 3*. Bombay: Government of Maharashtra.

——. 1989b. *Writings and Speeches. Vol. 5*. Bombay: Government of Maharashtra.

Ames, Mark. 2014b. *Just as we predicted, India's new leader is about to make Pierre Omidyar a lot richer*. 5 June. Accessed April 30, 2022. https://pandodaily.com/2014/06/04/just-as-we-predicted-indias-new-leader-is-about-to-make-pierre-omidyar-a-lot-richer/.

——. 2014a. *Pierre Omidyar's man in India is named to Modi's cabinet*. 9 November. Accessed April 30, 2022. https://pandodaily.com/2014/11/09/pierre-omidyars-man-in-india-is-named-to-modis-cabinet.

Anand, Abhishek. 2020. "Gendered impact of Covid-19 lockdown on employment: The case of India." *Center for International Development at Harvard University*. 24 March. Accessed March 31, 2022. https://www.hks.harvard.edu/sites/default/files/centers/cid/files/publications/CID_Wiener_Inequality%20Award%20Research/Policy%20Briefs/Abhishek%20Anand%20(1-A).pdf.

Anderson, Benedict. 1983. *Imagined Communities: Reflections on the Origin and Spread of Nationalism* . London: Verso.

ANI. 2021a. *DIGIT now the National Platform for Urban Governance, transforming urban landscape*. 30 October. Accessed May 15, 2022. https://www.aninews.in/news/business/business/digit-now-the-national-platform-for-urban-governance-transforming-urban-landscape20211030124256/.

——. 2021b. *MHA asks states, UTs to protect, rehabilitate transgenders*. 23 January. Accessed May 15, 2022. https://www.livemint.com/politics/policy/mha-asks-states-uts-to-protect-rehabilitate-transgenders-11611378131197.html.

Annenberg Public Policy Center. 2021. "Annenberg Public Policy Center 2021 Civics Knowledge Survey." September. Accessed April 30, 2022. https://cdn.annenbergpublicpolicycenter.org/wp-content/uploads/2021/10/APPC_2021_Civics_SCOTUS_Appendix.pdf.

Apfelbaum, Evan P., Michael I. Norton, and Samuel R. Sommers. 2012. *Racial Color Blindness: Emergence, Practice, and Implications*. June. Accessed April 30, 2022. https://www.hbs.edu/faculty/Pages/item.aspx?num=41856.

Apoorvanand. 2018. *Ashoka University did what famed Delhi University could not – stand by its teachers*. 19 December. Accessed May 15, 2022. https://theprint.in/opinion/ashoka-university-did-what-famed-delhi-university-could-not-stand-by-its-teachers/165093/ .

Applebaum, Barbara. 2010. *Being White, Being Good: White Complicity, White Moral Responsibility, and Social Justice Pedagogy*. New York: Lexington Books.

Arenas, J. C. 2010. *Pro-jihadist Rashad Hussain : Obama appointee's connection to Soros*. 18 February. Accessed March 31, 2022. https://www.americanthinker.com/

blog/2010/02/projihadist_rashad_hussain_oba.html.

Arkitect India. 2021. *NEP-What is New Education Policy 2020- Prof. Anurag Behar, VC, AzimPremji University.* 2 February. Accessed May 15, 2022. https://www.youtube.com/watch?v=2CWOCnkknlw .

Armour-Jones, Sarah, Jessica Clark, and Laura Schwartz-Henderson. 2019. "Global Media Philanthropy." *Media Impact Funders.* March. Accessed April 30, 2022. https://mediaimpactfunders.org/wp-content/uploads/2019/03/Gates-Report-Final-3-25-19-2.pdf.

Arthan. 2021. *Nobel Laureate Dr. Esther Duflo joins Krea University's Governing Council.* 28 December. Accessed May 15, 2022. https://blog.arthancareers.com/nobel-laureate-dr-esther-duflo-joins-krea-universitys-governing-council/.

Asani, Ali S. 2007. *Reflections on Pluralism and Islam.* 30 April. Accessed March 31, 2022. http://worldmuslimcongress.blogspot.com/2007/04/pluralism-and-islam-asani.html.

Ashoka University. 2019. *About us.* Accessed May 15, 2022. http://csgs.ashoka.edu.in/about-us/.

——. 2022a. *Ashoka Centre for China Studies (ACCS).* Accessed May 15, 2022. https://www.ashoka.edu.in/centres_list/centre-for-china-studies/.

——. 2020a. *Ashoka History Faculty Aparna Vaidik awarded £50,000 (about Rs.50 lacs) grant for research by The British Academy, UK.* 29 December. Accessed May 15, 2022. https://www.ashoka.edu.in/ashoka-history-faculty-aparna-vaidik-awarded-50000-about-rs-50-lacs-grant-for-research-by-the-british-academy-uk/ .

——. 2016a. *Ashoka University hosts a conference on 'Conservatism in India'.* 14 December. Accessed May 15, 2022. https://www.ashoka.edu.in/ashoka-university-hosts-a-conference-on-conservatism-in-india/ .

——. 2018a. *Ashoka University in Partnership with Harvard Business School Hosted the First Batch of the Executive Programme on Strategic Nonprofit Management in India.* 3 August. Accessed May 15, 2022. https://www.ashoka.edu.in/ashoka-university-in-partnership-with-harvard-business-school-hosted-the-first-batch-of-the-executive-programme-on-strategic-nonprofit-management-in-india/.

——. 2017a. *Ashoka University students partner with Harvard US India Initiative.* 4 January. Accessed May 15, 2022. https://www.ashoka.edu.in/ashoka-university-students-partner-with-harvard-us-india-initiative/ .

——. 2019a. *Ashoka University welcomes Professor Sourav Pal.* 21 May. Accessed May 15, 2022. https://www.ashoka.edu.in/ashoka-university-welcomes-professor-sourav-pal/.

——. 2021a. *Behavioural Insights Unit of India, NITI Aayog.* Accessed May 15, 2022. https://csbc.org.in/niti-biu.php.

——. 2022b. *Centre for Social and Behaviour Change (CSBC).* 4 January. Accessed May 15, 2022. https://www.compendium.ashoka.edu.in/post/centre-for-social-and-behaviour-change-csbc-1.

——. 2019b. *Faculty@Ashoka: Prof. Ashwini Deshpande.* 25 March . Accessed May 15, 2022. https://www.youtube.com/watch?v=txohUgHF49o.

——. 2020b. *Governing Intimacies.* Accessed May 15, 2022. http://csgs.ashoka.edu.in/governing-intimacies-a-research-meeting/.

——. 2021. *History and International Relations Programme.* Accessed May 15, 2022. https://www.ashoka.edu.in/courses/history-and-international-relations-b-a-hons/.

——. 2017b. *Jaya Sharma on BDSM.* 18 January. Accessed May 15, 2022. https://www.youtube.com/watch?v=mPKybSZyOvI.

——. 2018. *Our Partners.* Accessed May 15, 2022. https://csip.ashoka.edu.in/partnerships/.

——. 2021b. *State Behavioural Insights Units.* Accessed May 15, 2022. https://csbc.org.in/state-biu.php.

——. 2016b. *Vikram Aditya Sahai - Full Interview with CSGS.* 10 May. Accessed May 15, 2022. https://www.youtube.com/watch?v=kyJ4FdLR4jU .

Asia Now. 2020. *My Son's Inheritance: India's Invisible Violence.* 27 August. Accessed May 15, 2022. https://www.asianstudies.org/my-sons-inheritance-indias-invisible-violence/.

Asia Sentinel. 2017. *Forbes Magazine Dumps an Article on an Influential HK Tycoon.* 20 July. Accessed April 30, 2022. https://www.asiasentinel.com/p/forbes-magazine-dumps-article-ronnie-chan.

Asoka TV Channel. 2017. *Dr. Suraj Yengde, Harvard University, USA: On Higher Education in India and Overseas.* 16 September. Accessed February 15, 2022. https://www.youtube.com/watch?v=IEIMtnG7jTY.

Association for Democratic Reforms. 2016. *FCRA Declarations.* Accessed May 15, 2022. https://adrindia.org/content/fcra-declarations.

Auti, V. M. 1970. *Varkari Sampradaya Ke Kaviyon Ki Hindi Rachnaon Ka Anushilan.* Pune: Pune University.

Azim Premji Foundation. 2021. *Christian Hospital Bissamcuttack, Rayagada, Odisha.* Accessed May 15, 2022. https://azimpremjifoundation.org/content/christian-hospital-bissamcuttack-rayagada-odisha.

——. 2020. *Colloquium Series: We are the Music Makers.* 9 October. Accessed May 15, 2022. https://azimpremjifoundation.org/content/colloquium-series-we-are-music-makers .

——. 2021a. *Rongmei Naga Baptist Association (RNBA), Imphal.* 10 April. Accessed May 15, 2022. https://azimpremjifoundation.org/content/rongmei-naga-baptist-association-rnba-imphal.

——. 2021b. *Rongmein Baptist Association Nagaland, Nagaland.* 10 April. Accessed May 15, 2022. https://azimpremjifoundation.org/content/rongmein-baptist-association-nagaland-nagaland.

Azim Premji University. 2012. *'A conversation with George Soros,' at the Azim Premji University.* 12 January. Accessed May 15, 2022. https://www.youtube.com/watch?v=epjGg_dO3oQ.

——. 2016. *'Fighting in the Courts and on the Streets... ' by Sudha Bharadwaj.* 23 September. Accessed May 15, 2022. https://www.youtube.com/watch?v=g4v_lWyYZzo.

———. 2014. *Towards A Modern Indigenous Historical Framework*. 12 February. Accessed May 15, 2022. https://www.youtube.com/watch?v=82Fmf6s231o.

———. 2020. *We are the Music Makers by T M Krishna*. 27 October. Accessed April 30, 2022. https://www.youtube.com/watch?v=eIatArSxTNc.

Badrinathan, Sumitra, Devesh Kapur, Jonathan Kay, and Milan Vashnav. 2021. *Social Realities of Indian Americans: Results From the 2020 Indian American Attitudes Survey*. 9 June. Accessed 2022 15, February. https://carnegieendowment.org/2021/06/09/social-realities-of-indian-americans-results-from-2020-indian-american-attitudes-survey-pub-84667.

Bag, A.K. 1997. *History of Technology in India*. Vol. I. New Delhi: Indian National Science Academy.

Bailey, Alison. 2017. "Tracking Privilege-Preserving Epistemic Pushback in Feminist and Critical Race Philosophy Classes." *Hypatia: A Journal of Feminist Philosophy* 32 (4): 876-892. doi:https://doi.org/10.1111/hypa.12354.

Bakker, Peter, and John Elkington. 2020. *To build back better, we must reinvent capitalism. Here's how*. 13 July. Accessed May 15, 2022. https://www.weforum.org/agenda/2020/07/to-build-back-better-we-must-reinvent-capitalism-heres-how/.

Balakrishna, Sandeep. 2020. *Untangling the Oxfam Labyrinth: What Unites George Soros, Harsh Mander and Ashoka University?* Accessed May 15, 2022. https://www.dharmadispatch.in/commentary/untangling-the-oxfam-labyrinth-what-unites-george-soros-harsh-mander-and-ashoka-university .

Banerjee, Abhijit, Lakshmi Iyer, and Rohini Somanathan. 2006. "Public Action for Public Goods." *Harvard Business School*. September. Accessed March 31, 2022. https://www.hbs.edu/ris/Publication%20Files/07-061.pdf.

Bangalore International Centre. 2019. *Caste matters: Suraj Yengde's book on caste in the 21st century*. 21 August. Accessed February 15, 2022. https://www.youtube.com/watch?v=k6PMii3sdNg.

BAPSA (Birsa Ambedkar Phule Students Association), JNU. 2016. *Karthik Bittu Kondaiah speech on 'Society without Civility'- Part 2*. 21 November. Accessed May 15, 2022. https://www.youtube.com/watch?v=J4mZtpL705A.

Barboni, Giorgia, Erica Field, Rohini Pande, Natalia Rigol, and Simone Schaner. 2018. "A Tough Call: Understanding Barriers to and Impacts of Women's Mobile Phone Adoption in India." *Harvard Kennedy School, Evidence for Policy Design* . October. Accessed March 31, 2022. https://epod.cid.harvard.edu/sites/default/files/2018-10/A_Tough_Call.pdf.

Barnes, Julian E., Matthew Rosenberg, and Gardiner Harris. 2018. *U.S. Spy Agencies Are Increasingly Convinced of Saudi Prince's Ties to Journalist's Disappearance*. 17 October. Accessed May 15, 2022. https://www.nytimes.com/2018/10/17/world/middleeast/pompeo-khashoggi-murder.html.

Barnett, Ian, Tarun Khanna, and Jukka-Pekka Onnela. 2016. "Social and Spatial Clustering of People at Humanity's Largest Gathering." *PLOS ONE*. 3 June. Accessed March 31, 2022. https://journals.plos.org/plosone/article?id=10.1371/journal.pone.0156794.

Barrabi, Thomas. 2022. *BlackRock CEO says stakeholder capitalism isn't 'woke,' just good business.* 18 January. Accessed May 15, 2022. https://nypost.com/2022/01/18/larry-fink-says-stakeholder-capitalism-isnt-woke-just-good-business/.

Barth, Fredrik. 1956. "Ecologic Relationships of Ethnic Groups in Swat, North Pakistan." *American Anthropologist* 58 (6): 1079-1089. https://www.jstor.org/stable/666295.

Baruah, Mitul. 2017b. *"NAMAMI BRAHMAPUTRA" IS A DISSERVICE TO THE PEOPLE OF THE BRAHMAPUTRA VALLEY.* 4 April. Accessed May 15, 2022. https://raiot.in/namami-brahmaputra-is-a-disservice-to-the-people-of-the-brahmaputra-valley/.

——. 2017a. *"Namami Brahmaputra": Worshipping a river, ignoring its materialities.* 27 April. Accessed May 15, 2022. https://entitleblogdotorg3.wordpress.com/2017/04/27/namami-brahmaputra-worshipping-a-river-ignoring-its-materialities/.

Basha, Sadiq. 2020. *NEP opens doors to foreign universities and fulfils many dreams.* 16 September. Accessed May 15, 2022. https://bloncampus.thehindubusinessline.com/b-learn/nep-opens-doors-to-foreign-universities-and-fulfils-many-dreams/article32622859.ece.

Basham, A.L. 2004. *The Wonder That Was India.* 3rd. London: Picador.

Basler, Roy P. 1953. *The Collected Works of Abraham Lincoln.* New Brunswick, NJ: Rutgers University Press.

BBC News. 2020. *Media and tech firms join forces to tackle harmful Covid vaccine myths.* 10 December. Accessed May 15, 2022. https://www.bbc.com/news/entertainment-arts-55257814.

Beaman, Lori, Raghabendra Chattopadhyay, Esther Duflo, Rohini Pande, and Petia Topalova. 2008. "Powerful Women: Does Exposure Reduce Bias?" *Digital Access to Scholarship at Harvard.* July. Accessed March 31, 2022. https://dash.harvard.edu/bitstream/handle/1/37366185/175.pdf?sequence=1&isAllowed=y.

Beaman, Lori, Rohini Pande, and Alexandra Cirone. 2012. "Politics as a Male Domain and Empowerment in India." *Women and Public Policy Program, Harvard Kennedy School.* Accessed March 31, 2022. https://wappp.hks.harvard.edu/files/wappp/files/14._politics_as_a_male_domain_and_empowerment_in_india__0.pdf.

Behl, Riya. 2021. *Rights and democracy.* 6 October. Accessed March 31, 2022. https://pari.education/learning-resource/rights-and-democracy/.

Bell, Derrick A. 1995. "Who's Afraid of Critical Race Theory?" *University of Illinois Law Review* (4).

Belongg. 2019. *About.* 4 November. Accessed May 15, 2022. https://belongg.net/about/.

Belongg Circle. 2022. *7 experts you can invite to understand religion-based discrimination in terms of access to development.* Accessed May 15, 2022. https://belonggcircle.com/collections/0f06d411-05d1-45ff-84f9-6dd471f2d6a9.

Belongg Mental Health Collective. 2021. *Belongg Student Ambassador Program 2021.* 22 March . Accessed May 15, 2022. https://belonggmentalhealth.com/initiatives/belongg-student-ambassador-program/.

Berkley Center. 2021. *Understanding Religion and Populism.* 12 March. Accessed April 30, 2022. https://www.youtube.com/watch?v=DPUF-Pjtjgk.

Bernhardt, Arielle, Erica Field, Rohini Pande, Natalia Rigol, and Simone Schaner. 2018.

"Male Social Status and Women's Work." *Harvard Business School*. May. Accessed March 31, 2022. https://www.hbs.edu/ris/Publication%20Files/pandp.20181086_5907afa6-2831-43f0-a7bb-d2fd848e3e14.pdf.

Beshara, Robert. 2019. *Decolonial Psychoanalysis: Towards a Critical Islamophobia*. London: Routledge.

Betham, R.M. 1908. *Marathas and Dekhani Musalmans*. Calcutta: Superintendent of Government Printing.

Beyrer, Jack. 2021. *Ivy League Colleges Partner With Chinese Health Institutions Tied to Military*. 10 March. Accessed March 31, 2022. https://freebeacon.com/national-security/ivy-league-colleges-partner-with-chinese-health-institutions-tied-to-military/.

Bhabha, Homi K. 1994. *The Location of Culture*. London, New York: Routledge.

Bhalotra, Sonia, Guilhem Cassan, Irma Clots Figueras, and Lakshmi Iyer. 2013. "Religion, Politician Identity and Development Outcomes: Evidence from India." *Harvard Business School*. 21 June. Accessed March 31, 2022. https://www.hbs.edu/ris/Publication%20Files/13-102_ef340026-34b1-4b90-af4f-dc022a137e9a.pdf.

Bharathi, Naveen, Deepak Malghan, Sumit Mishra, and Andaleeb Rahman. 2020. "Fractal Urbanism: City Size and Residential Segregation in India." *Dyson School of Applied Economics and Management Cornell University*. June. Accessed May 15, 2022. https://dyson.cornell.edu/wp-content/uploads/sites/5/2020/07/WP_2020_06-VD.pdf.

Bhattacharjee, K. 2021. *NCERT goes Woke, claims separate toilets for boys and girls is a problem, suggests puberty blockers, blames 'caste patriarchy' for stigma*. 1 November. Accessed May 15, 2022. https://www.opindia.com/2021/11/ncert-training-manual-teachers-gender-identity-transgender-woke-puberty-blockers/ .

———. 2020. *The 'protests' that burnt the nation: How American citizen Siddharth Varadarajan's The Wire collaborated with anti-CAA 'protesters'*. 13 June. Accessed May 15, 2022. https://www.opindia.com/2020/06/azaad-india-collective-siddharth-varadarajan-the-wire-anti-caa-protests/ .

Bhattacharjee, Malini. 2021. *Building a 'Hindu Rashtra' through 'Seva'*. 14 January. Accessed May 15, 2022. https://www.epw.in/engage/article/building-hindu-rashtra-through-seva.

Bhattacharya, Saumya. 2015. *Harvard Business School's digital platform HBX enters into first tie-up in India with Ashoka University*. 20 October. Accessed May 15, 2022. https://economictimes.indiatimes.com/industry/services/education/harvard-business-schools-digital-platform-hbx-enters-into-first-tie-up-in-india-with-ashoka-university/articleshow/49460004.cms .

———. 2012. *Xander Group founder Siddharth Yog gifts $11 million to Harvard Business School*. 28 January. Accessed April 30, 2022. https://economictimes.indiatimes.com/news/company/corporate-trends/xander-group-founder-siddharth-yog-gifts-11-million-to-harvard-business-school/articleshow/11655935.cms.

Binkley, Collin. 2022. *'A real yearning to right the wrongs of our past': The fight to end legacy admissions at Ivy League schools*. 13 February. Accessed April 30, 2022. https://www.boston.com/news/politics/2022/02/13/ending-legacy-admissions-harvard-yale-brown/.

——. 2018. *MIT report recommends against cutting ties with Saudi Arabia.* 7 December. Accessed May 15, 2022. https://apnews.com/article/edee57a4171f406694f57eb16f26dd0e.

Biswas, Soutik. 2016. *Why are many Indian Muslims seen as untouchable?* 10 May. Accessed February 15, 2022. https://www.bbc.com/news/world-asia-india-36220329.

Bittu, Karthik. 2021. *Pride month in Times of COVID-19 Pandemic.* 20 July. Accessed May 15, 2022. https://gaurilankeshnews.com/pride-month-in-times-of-covid-19-pandemic-community/?fbclid=IwAR1lNLJmLy7GH5b2U3q3JVbhzAH_LDh2FnaSZzfcD0JvmL3e6PgNI8TkThY.

Blanding, Michael . 2021. *Making the case for reparations.* 14 December. Accessed March 31, 2022. https://www.hsph.harvard.edu/news/features/making-the-case-for-reparations/.

Blatantly Honest. 2021a. *'At Ashoka University, the academics is rigorous,' a mathematics major talks about his journey.* 31 December. Accessed May 15, 2022. https://www.youtube.com/watch?v=zJMmOt4WO7Q.

——. 2022. *Despite a cutting-edge pedagogy, most of the Ashoka students are still stuck in the CBSE mindset.* 6 January. Accessed May 15, 2022. https://www.youtube.com/watch?v=8A6qOUMKtQ8 .

——. 2021b. *'It's not easy to survive at Ashoka University at all,' a student recalls of his time there.* 29 December. Accessed May 15, 2022. https://www.youtube.com/watch?v=QjqJCTW7Wb4.

Boghossian, Peter, and James A. Lindsay. 2019. *How to Have Impossible Conversations: A Very Practical Guide.* Da Capo Lifelong Books.

Bond, Paul. 2021. *Nearly 40 Percent of U.S. Gen Zs, 30 Percent of Young Christians Identify as LGBTQ, Poll Shows.* 20 October. Accessed May 15, 2022. https://www.newsweek.com/nearly-40-percent-us-gen-zs-30-percent-christians-identify-lgbtq-poll-shows-1641085.

Bonilla-Silva, Eduardo. 2003. *Racism without Racists: Color-Blind Racism and the Persistence of Racial Inequality in America.* Lanham: Rowman & Littlefield Publishers.

Bonilla-Silva, Eduardo, and David Dietrich. 2011. "The Sweet Enchantment of Color-Blind Racism in Obamerica." *The Annals of the American Academy of Political and Social Science* (Sage Publications, Inc.) 190-206. http://www.jstor.org/stable/29779402.

Boom, Daniel Van. 2021. *John Cena's China apology: What you need to know.* 26 May. Accessed April 30, 2022. https://www.cnet.com/news/john-cenas-apology-to-china-everything-you-need-to-know/.

Borgonjon, David. 2017. *Artist Interview: Thenmozhi Soundararajan.* 20 April. Accessed February 15, 2022. https://www.eyebeam.org/five-questions-around-technology-and-stories-for-social-change/.

Bowyer, Jerry. 2021. *An unexpected message from Silicon Valley .* 19 October. Accessed April 30, 2022. https://wng.org/opinions/an-unexpected-message-from-silicon-valley-1634728806 .

Boyd, Jordan. 2021. *Communist China Adds Video Promoting Critical Race Theory To Propaganda Lineup.* 18 August. Accessed April 30, 2022. https://thefederalist.

com/2021/08/18/communist-china-adds-video-promoting-critical-race-theory-to-propaganda-lineup/.

Brookings. 2015. *Ambassador Shivshankar Menon joins Brookings as Distinguished Fellow in Foreign Policy.* 16 June. Accessed May 15, 2022. https://www.brookings.edu/research/ambassador-shivshankar-menon-joins-brookings-as-distinguished-fellow-in-foreign-policy/.

Brot für die Welt. 2020. *About us : Brot für die Welt (Bread for the World).* Accessed May 15, 2022. https://www.brot-fuer-die-welt.de/en/bread-for-the-world/about-us/.

Burnley, Malcolm. 2017. *How the Harvard Kennedy School Abandoned America.* 22 January. Accessed March 31, 2022. https://www.bostonmagazine.com/news/2017/01/22/harvard-kennedy-school-america/2/.

Burns, Nicholas. 2020. *India's Transforming Horizon: A Conversation with Rahul Gandhi.* 8 October. Accessed March 31, 2022. https://www.belfercenter.org/publication/indias-transforming-horizon-conversation-rahul-gandhi.

Burns, Nicholas, and Anja Manuel. 2020. *On India, the U.S. Must Think Bigger.* 16 October. Accessed March 31, 2022. https://www.belfercenter.org/publication/india-us-must-think-bigger.

Business France. 2021. *Swati Piramal.* 12 October. Accessed March 31, 2022. https://events-export.businessfrance.fr/ambition-india/swati-piramal/.

Butcher, Jonathan, and Mike Gonzalez. 2020. *Critical Race Theory, the New Intolerance, and Its Grip on America.* 7 December. Accessed April 30, 2022. https://www.heritage.org/civil-rights/report/critical-race-theory-the-new-intolerance-and-its-grip-america.

Butler, Judith. 1993. *Bodies that Matter: On the Discursive Limits of "Sex".* London: Routledge.

BW Education. 2020. *Harvard, Stanford & IIM Alumni Together Establishes The Kautilya School Of Public Policy In Hyderabad.* 11 November. Accessed March 31, 2022. http://bweducation.businessworld.in/article/Harvard-Stanford-IIM-Alumni-Together-Establishes-The-Kautilya-School-Of-Public-Policy-In-Hyderabad/11-11-2020-341653/.

Byrne, John A. 2021. *CEIBS's New MBA Director On Getting An MBA In China.* 1 December. Accessed March 31, 2022. https://poetsandquants.com/2021/12/01/ceibs-new-mba-director-on-getting-an-mba-in-china/?pq-category=b-schools.

Cadell, Patrick. 1938. *A History of the Bombay Army.* London: Longmans.

Capstone Report. 2020a. *Billionaire linked to Chinese Communist Party has given extensively to Americans including to Evangelical Christians.* 16 December. Accessed April 30, 2022. https://capstonereport.com/2020/12/16/billionaire-linked-to-chinese-communist-party-has-given-extensively-to-americans-including-to-evangelical-christians/35257/.

——. 2020b. *China uses money to seduce, divide geopolitical rivals.* 21 October. Accessed April 30, 2022. https://capstonereport.com/2020/10/21/china-uses-money-to-seduce-divide-geopolitical-rivals/35077/.

Carnegie Endowment for International Peace. 2016. *Milan Vaishnav.* Accessed May 15,

2022. https://carnegieendowment.org/experts/714.

Carney, Leo. 2022. *Harvard Kennedy School Misinformation Review Retracts Hit Piece Against ADOS*. 7 January. Accessed March 31, 2022. https://www.mississippifreepress. org/19539/harvard-kennedy-school-misinformation-review-retracts-hit-piece-against-ados/.

CEIBS. 2016. *CEIBS Establishment*. Accessed March 31, 2022. https://www.ceibs.edu/ ceibs-establishment.

Centre for Equity Studies. 2021. "Centre for Equity Studies: Balance Sheet as at 31st March 2019." *Centre for Equity Studies*. February. Accessed May 15, 2022. http:// centreforequitystudies.org/wp-content/uploads/2021/02/Balance-Sheet-F.Y-18-19. pdf.

Centre for Social Impact and Philanthropy. 2019. "Advocacy, Rights & Civil Society: The Opportunity for Indian Philanthropy." *SDG Philanthropy Platform*. January. Accessed May 15, 2022. https://www.sdgphilanthropy.org/system/files/2019-01/ Advocacy%2C%20Rights%20%26%20Civil%20Society%3A%20The%20 Opportunity%20for%20Indian%20Philanthropy.pdf.

Chakraborti, Haripada. 1960. *Trade and Commerce of Ancient India*. Calcutta: Academic Publishers.

Chakravorty, Sanjoy. 2019. *Viewpoint: How the British reshaped India's caste system*. 19 June. Accessed February 15, 2022. https://www.bbc.com/news/world-asia-india-48619734.

Chandra, Abhimanyu. 2020. *Privilege keeps many from seeing the violence in India: Historian Aparna Vaidik*. 4 October. Accessed May 15, 2022. https://caravanmagazine. in/interview/privelege-keeps-many-from-seeing-the-violence-in-india-historian-aparna-vaidik .

Chandra, Rohit Walton, and Michael. 2020. *Big potential, big risks? Indian capitalism, economic reform and populism in the BJP era*. 19 May. Accessed March 31, 2022. https://www.tandfonline.com/doi/full/10.1080/14736489.2020.1744997.

Charsley, Simon. 1996. "'Untouchable': What is in a Name?" *The Journal of the Royal Anthropological Institute* (Royal Anthropological Institute of Great Britain and Ireland) 2 (1): 1-23.

Chattopadhyaya, Brajdulal. 2014. *Essays in Ancient Indian Economic History*. 2nd. Delhi: Indian History Congress and Primus Books.

Chauhan, G.S. 2014. *Bani of Bhagats Part 2*. Amritsar: All India Pingalwara Charitable Society.

Chenoweth, Erica, Matthew Smith, and Salil Shetty. 2020. "Reimagining Social Movements and Civil Resistance during the Global Pandemic." *Harvard Kennedy School, Carr Center for Human Rights Policy*. 17 April. Accessed March 31, 2022. https://carrcenter.hks.harvard.edu/files/cchr/files/200416_covid_discussion_paper. pdf.

Children Of Mahad. 2020. *Caste Oppression thrives on Oppression of Women- Suraj Yengde*. 22 July. Accessed February 15, 2022. https://www.youtube.com/watch?v=LGf-MjCH5eg.

Chinese Studies Association of Australia. 2021. *China Studies Postdoctoral Fellowship.* 13 August. Accessed May 15, 2022. https://www.csaa.org.au/2021/08/china-studies-postdoctoral-fellowship/.

Christenson, Josh. 2021. *WHO Director Who Covered for China to Be Harvard Commencement Speaker.* 28 January. Accessed March 31, 2022. https://freebeacon.com/coronavirus/who-director-who-covered-for-china-to-be-harvard-commencement-speaker/.

Chuang, Callia A., Luke A. Williams, and Matteo N. Wong. 2019. *Hundreds of Harvard Affiliates Sign Letter Protesting India's Citizenship Amendment Act.* 20 December. Accessed March 31, 2022. https://www.thecrimson.com/article/2019/12/20/indian-citizenship-act-letter/.

Chughtai, Mariam. 2015. "What Produces a History Textbook?" *Digital Access to Scholarship at Harvard.* Accessed March 31, 2022. https://dash.harvard.edu/bitstream/handle/1/16461056/CHUGHTAI-DISSERTATION-2015.pdf?sequence=1&isAllowed=y.

Clarida, Matthew Q. 2014. *School of Public Health Renamed with $350 Million Gift, Largest in Harvard History.* 8 September. Accessed March 31, 2022. https://www.thecrimson.com/article/2014/9/8/chan-gift-public-health/.

CNRS. 1997. *CNRS.* Accessed May 15, 2022. https://www.cnrs.fr.

Coates, Ta-Nehisi. 2015. *Color-Blind Policy, Color-Conscious Morality.* 13 May. Accessed April 30, 2022. https://www.theatlantic.com/politics/archive/2015/05/color-blind-policy-color-conscious-morality/393227/.

Cogito 137. 2020. *Dr Bittu explains the science of gender fluidity.* 24 October. Accessed May 15, 2022. https://www.youtube.com/watch?v=h1TsrL7QgoI.

Cohen, Rick. 2014. *The Role of Pierre Omidyar and Big Charity in the Ukraine.* 4 March. Accessed April 30, 2022. https://nonprofitquarterly.org/the-role-of-pierre-omidyar-and-big-charity-in-the-ukraine/.

Collins, Patricia Hill. 1990. *Black Feminist Thought: Knowledge, Consciousness, and the Politics of Empowerment.* New York and London: Routledge.

Collins, Patricia Hill, and Sirma Bilge. 2016. *Intersectionality.* Malden, MA: Polity Press.

Conron, Kerith J., and Shoshana K. Goldberg. 2020. "Adult LGBT Population in the United States." *Williams Institute School of Law.* July. Accessed May 15, 2022. https://williamsinstitute.law.ucla.edu/wp-content/uploads/LGBT-Adult-US-Pop-Jul-2020.pdf.

Constable, Philip. 2001. "The Marginalization of a Dalit Martial Race in Late Nineteenth- and Early Twentieth-Century Western India." *The Journal of Asian Studies* 60 (2): 439-478. doi:https://doi.org/10.2307/2659700.

Cornell Law School. n.d. *Critical Legal Theory.* Accessed April 30, 2022. https://www.law.cornell.edu/wex/critical_legal_theory.

Cost, Ben. 2021. *J.K. Rowling slams trans activists for sharing address on social media.* 22 November. Accessed May 15, 2022. https://nypost.com/2021/11/22/j-k-rowling-slams-trans-activists-for-sharing-address-on-twitter/.

Countercurrents. 2020. *Over 350 Acadamics Issue Statement on the anti-Muslim pogrom* *in Delhi.* 2 March. Accessed May 15, 2022. https://countercurrents.org/2020/03/over-350-acadamics-issue-statement-on-the-anti-muslim-pogrom-in-delhi/.*

County of Santa Clara. 2020. *Receive report from Equity Labs relating to caste discrimination in Silicon Valley, and approve recommendations, if any.* 12 November. Accessed February 15, 2022. http://sccgov.iqm2.com/Citizens/Detail_LegiFile.aspx ?ID=103782&highlightTerms=Caste.*

Crawford, Abijah. 2021. *Religious Freedom in India Is In Trouble.* 2 August. Accessed March 31, 2022. https://providencemag.com/2021/08/religious-freedom-india-trouble/.

Craymer, Lucy. 2020. *China's National-Security Law Reaches Into Harvard, Princeton Classrooms.* 19 August. Accessed April 30, 2022. https://www.wsj.com/articles/chinas-national-security-law-reaches-into-harvard-princeton-classrooms-11597829402?page=1.

Crenshaw, Kimberle. 1989. *Demarginalizing the Intersection of Race and Sex: A Black Feminist Critique of Antidiscrimination Doctrine, Feminist Theory and Antiracist Politics.* Accessed April 30, 2022. chicagounbound.uchicago.edu/uclf/vol1989/iss1/8.

Crenshaw, Kimberlé Williams, Luke Charles Harris, Daniel Martinez HoSang, and George Lipsitz. 2019. *Seeing Race Again.* Oakland, California: University of California Press.

CSGS@Ashoka. 2019. *Governing Intimacies | Keynote Address | Kavita Krishnan.* 11 December. Accessed May 15, 2022. https://www.youtube.com/watch?v=8mFepS-OuPg.

——. 2020. *Theory & Practice | Engendering Caste, Sexualizing Race.* 12 November. Accessed May 15, 2022. https://www.youtube.com/watch?v=YcIX4Ph5tMw.

Cunningham, Edward, Tony Saich, and Jessie Turiel. 2020. *Understanding CCP Resilience: Surveying Chinese Public Opinion Through Time.* July. Accessed March 31, 2022. https://ash.harvard.edu/publications/understanding-ccp-resilience-surveying-chinese-public-opinion-through-time.

Da Alternative. 2022. *Klaus Schwab 2017 Young Global Leaders.* 3 February. Accessed May 15, 2022. https://www.youtube.com/watch?v=PbVD4tB4cVQ.

Dallmeyer, McKenna. 2021. *Harvard Business School Club of NY cancels speaker from... cancel culture talk: report.* 26 February. Accessed March 31, 2022. https://www.campusreform.org/article?id=16920.

D'Amore-McKim School of Business. 2019. *Democracy in India: Achievements and Deficits | Ashutosh Varshney | India Lecture Series.* 26 October. Accessed March 31, 2022. https://www.youtube.com/watch?v=uZyEnOMEjxA.

Das, Veena. 2003. *The Oxford Companion to Sociology and Social Anthropology.* New Delhi: Oxford University Press.

Data Governance Network. 2020. *About | Data Governance Network.* Accessed May 15, 2022. https://datagovernance.org/about.

——. 2013. *Data Governance Network.* Accessed May 15, 2022. https://datagovernance.org/.

Datta, Aveek. 2014. *PSUs could be engaged in CSR more productively: Tarun Khanna.*

6 February. Accessed March 31, 2022. https://www.livemint.com/Companies/NVQioMXAzDgPYweaoS22lM/PSUs-could-be-engaged-in-CSR-more-productively-Tarun-Khanna.html.

Datta, Bhupendranath. 1944. *Studies in Indian Social Polity.* Calcutta: Purabi Publishers.

Datta, Sayantan. 2021. *Intersectionality and privilege in Indian science practice.* 28 April. Accessed May 15, 2022. https://thelifeofscience.com/2021/04/28/intersectionality-and-privilege-in-indian-science-practice/.

Davidson, Helen. 2020. *Pro-democracy leader Joshua Wong arrested in Hong Kong.* 24 September. Accessed March 31, 2022. https://www.theguardian.com/world/2020/sep/24/pro-democracy-leader-joshua-wong-arrested-in-hong-kong.

Davies, Jim. 2012. *Academic obfuscations: the psychological attraction of postmodern nonsense - Document - Gale Academic OneFile.* Summer. Accessed March 31, 2022. https://go.gale.com/ps/i.do?id=GALE%7CA313159923&sid=googleScholar&v=2.1&it=r&linkaccess=abs&issn=10639330&p=AONE&sw=w&userGroupName=anon%7Ef3ce69b3.

Dawson, Julie, and Cristian Duda. 2021. *How digital identity can improve lives in a post-COVID-19 world.* 14 January. Accessed May 15, 2022. https://www.weforum.org/agenda/2021/01/davos-agenda-digital-identity-frameworks/.

Dean, Paul. 2013. *Obama and Color-Blindness.* 16 December. Accessed April 30, 2022. https://www.thesociologicalcinema.com/videos/obama-and-color-blindness.

DeBenedictis, Julia E. 2016. *Tackling Gender Inequality at HBS: A Case Study.* 4 May. Accessed April 30, 2022. https://www.thecrimson.com/article/2016/5/4/tacking-gender-inequality-at-hbs/.

Defence.Capital. 2021. *Law and Society Alliance study report exposes Communist China's overt, covert influence operations in India.* 4 September. Accessed March 31, 2022. https://defence.capital/2021/09/04/law-and-society-alliance-study-report-exposes-communist-chinas-overt-covert-influence-operations-in-india.

Delgado, Richard, and Jean Stefancic. 2017. *Critical Race Theory: An Introduction.* New York and London: New York University Press.

Delingpole, James. 2021. *Delingpole: Watch Brave Dutch MP Skewer Klaus 'Anal' Schwab's Great Reset.* 23 July. Accessed May 15, 2022. https://www.breitbart.com/europe/2021/07/23/delingpole-watch-brave-dutch-mp-skewer-klaus-anal-schwabs-great-reset/.

Dellacherie, Olivier. 2017. *World Economic Forum announces Børge Brende to new role of President alongside Klaus Schwab as Executive Chairman.* 15 September. Accessed May 15, 2022. https://talent4boards.com/world-economic-forum-announces-borge-brende-new-role-president-alongside-klaus-schwab-executive-chairman/.

Desai, Ronak D. 2015. *Prime Minister Modi's First Year In Office: A Report Card.* 26 May. Accessed March 31, 2022. https://www.belfercenter.org/publication/prime-minister-modis-first-year-office-report-card.

Deshpande, Ashwini. 2018a. *Caste in the UK: Denial of Discrimination Is Not the Solution.* 5 August. Accessed May 15, 2022. https://thewire.in/caste/caste-discrimination-uk-denial-equality .

——. 2018. "Meritocracy and Affirmative Action in India." *Harvard China Fund.* 8 May. Accessed May 15, 2022. https://hcf.fas.harvard.edu/wp-content/uploads/2018/05/Deshpande_Shanghai.pdf.

Dharampal. 2003. *Rediscovering India: Collection of Essays and Speeches, 1956-1998.* Mussoorie: Society for Integrated Development of Himalayas.

——. 1983. *The Beautiful Tree: Indigenous Indian Education in the Eighteenth Century.* Mapusa: Goa.

Dharmasiri, Gunapala. 1988. *A Buddhist Critique of the Christian Concept of God.* Antioch, CA: Golden Leaves Publishing.

Dhawan, Himanshi. 2021. *'Islam is the pioneer of the concept of family planning ... and it is a myth that polygamy is rampant in India'.* 25 February. Accessed May 15, 2022. https://timesofindia.indiatimes.com/blogs/the-interviews-blog/islam-is-the-pioneer-of-the-concept-of-family-planning-and-it-is-a-myth-that-polygamy-is-rampant-in-india/.

Dhillon, Dilsher. 2018. *Bill Gates backs India's scheme to make a database of every citizen by scanning people's fingerprints and eyeballs.* 4 May. Accessed May 15, 2022. https://www.insider.com/bill-gates-denies-biometric-id-breaches-human-rights-2018-5.

Diamond, Larry, and Orville Schell. 2018. *China's Influence & American Interests: Promoting Constructive Vigilance.* Stanford, CA: Hoover Instituition Press. Accessed March 31, 2022. https://www.hoover.org/sites/default/files/research/docs/00_diamond-schell_fullreport_2ndprinting_web-compressed.pdf.

DiAngelo, Robin . 2018. *White Fragility.* Boston: Beacon Press.

DiAngelo, Robin. 2011. "White Fragility." *International Journal of Critical Pedagogy* 3 (3): 54-70.

Diya TV. 2021. *EXCLUSIVE: Santa Clara County Human Rights Commission debates caste | Diya TV.* 30 April. https://www.youtube.com/watch?v=9b6KJptrArU.

Dizikes, Peter. 2020. *Democracy in distress?* 30 October. Accessed March 31, 2022. https://news.mit.edu/2020/democracy-distress-starr-1030.

Dolan, Kerry A. 2015. *Mark Zuckerberg Explains Why The Chan Zuckerberg Initiative Isn't A Charitable Foundation.* 4 December. Accessed May 15, 2022. https://www.forbes.com/sites/kerryadolan/2015/12/04/mark-zuckerberg-explains-why-the-chan-zuckerberg-initiative-isnt-a-charitable-foundation/?sh=19fc033370c5.

Donovan, Joan, and Jennifer Nilsen. 2021. *Cloaked Science: The Yan Reports.* 3 January. Accessed March 31, 2022. https://mediamanipulation.org/case-studies/cloaked-science-yan-reports.

Dougherty, Michael Brendan. 2018. *The Church of Grievance.* 14 May. Accessed April 30, 2022. https://www.nationalreview.com/magazine/2018/05/14/victim-mentality-identity-politics-dominate-modern-left/.

D'Souza, Faye. 2020. *Pass The Mic - Suraj Yengde On Why Caste Matters | Faye D'Souza.* 6 October. Accessed February 15, 2022. https://www.youtube.com/watch?v=nhBAV1XbDL8.

Dubey, Ashutosh J. 2020. *This incident happened at Ashoka University in Delhi | Ashoka University Exposed.* 25 September. Accessed May 15, 2022. https://www.naradasbuzz.com/this-incident-happened-at-ashoka-university-in-delhi-ashoka-university-exposed.

Duffy, Evita. 2021. *Snapchat Is A Transgender Propaganda And Grooming Machine.* 27 February. Accessed May 15, 2022. https://thefederalist.com/2021/02/27/snapchat-is-a-transgender-propaganda-and-grooming-machine/.

Eakin, Emily. 2001. *Harvard's Prize Catch, a Delphic Postcolonialist.* 17 November. Accessed March 31, 2022. https://www.nytimes.com/2001/11/17/arts/harvard-s-prize-catch-a-delphic-postcolonialist.html.

Eberhart, Christopher. 2021. *Anti-racist author DOUBLES speaking fees as America goes woke: 'White fragility' writer Robin DiAngelo charges an average of $14,000 per speech and makes '$728K a year.* 2 July. Accessed April 30, 2022. https://www.dailymail.co.uk/news/article-9749517/An-anti-racist-author-Robin-DiAngelo-makes-728K-year-speaking-engagements.html.

Eggeling, Julius. 1900. *The Satapatha Brahman Part V.* Oxford: Clarendon Press.

Élysée. 2020. *Fight against separatism – the Republic in action: speech by Emmanuel Macron, President of the Republic, on the fight against separatism.* 2 October. Accessed April 30, 2022. https://www.elysee.fr/emmanuel-macron/2020/10/02/fight-against-separatism-the-republic-in-action-speech-by-emmanuel-macron-president-of-the-republic-on-the-fight-against-separatism.en .

End Forced Arbitration. 2022. *A Conversation on Caste Discrimination with Thenmozhi Soundararajan.* 19 April. Accessed April 30, 2022. https://www.youtube.com/watch?v=rXyzbWAuPWQ.

Equality Labs. 2018b. *Caste in the United States - Reviews.* Accessed April 30, 2022. https://www.equalitylabs.org/castesurvey/#reviews.

——. 2018a. *Mission.* Accessed February 15, 2022. https://www.equalitylabs.org/mission.

——. 2020. *Why Do We Say No to Holi? A Guide To Challenge Casteism.* Accessed April 30, 2022. https://www.kractivist.org/why-do-we-say-no-to-holi-a-guide-to-challenge-casteism/.

Eraly, Abraham. 2007. *The Mughal World.* New Delhi: Penguin Books.

ET Bureau. 2020. *Assam NRC data: Wipro says IT services contract not renewed after October 2019.* 13 February. Accessed May 15, 2022. https://economictimes.indiatimes.com/tech/ites/assam-nrc-data-wipro-says-it-services-contract-not-renewed-after-october-2019/articleshow/74100062.cms.

Evan. 2015. *L, G, B, T, Q, Q, I, A... What do all the letters mean?* 8 July. Accessed May 15, 2022. http://queergrace.com/letters/.

Evans, Rachel, Sabrina Willmer, Nick Baker, and Brandon Kochkodin. 2017. *BlackRock and Vanguard Are Less Than a Decade Away From Managing $20 Trillion.* 4 December. Accessed May 15, 2022. https://www.bloomberg.com/news/features/2017-12-04/blackrock-and-vanguard-s-20-trillion-future-is-closer-than-you-think.

EWTN Global Catholic Network. 2003. *Bishops' Conference India - 6.* Accessed April 30, 2022. https://www.ewtn.com/catholicism/library/bishops-conference-india--6-8243.

FCCED. 2020. *US DoE probes millions of dollars in foreign donations to Harvard, Yale.* 17 March. Accessed March 31, 2022. https://fcced.com/doj-probes-foreign-donations-harvard-yale-173201632/.

Feldscher, Karen. 2014. *Gift from Alumna Swati Piramal and family inspires new HSPH-India collaborations.* Accessed March 31, 2022. https://www.hsph.harvard.edu/magazine/magazine_article/gift-from-alumna-swati-piramal-and-family-inspires-new-hsph-india-collaborations/.

Ferlazzo, Larry. 2019. *When People Say They Don't See Race, 'I Ask Them If They Don't See Me.* 17 September. Accessed April 30, 2022. https://www.edweek.org/teaching-learning/opinion-when-people-say-they-dont-see-race-i-ask-them-if-they-dont-see-me/2019/09.

Field, Anne. 2019. *Omidyar Network's Luminate Spinoff Seeks To Protect Democracies Under Attack.* 31 January. Accessed May 15, 2022. https://www.forbes.com/sites/annefield/2019/01/31/omidyar-networks-luminate-spinoff-seeks-to-protect-democracies-under-attack/?sh=580d917164dc .

Field, Erica, Rohini Pande, Natalia Rigol, Simone Schaner, and Charity Troyer Moore. 2021c. *On Her Own Account: How Strengthening Women's Financial Control Impacts Labor Supply and Gender Norms.* July. Accessed May 15, 2022. https://egc.yale.edu/her-account.

Field, Erica, Seema Jayachandran, and Rohini Pande. 2010. "Do Traditional Institutions Constrain Female Entrepreneurship? A Field Experiment on Business Training in India ." *Women and Public Policy Program, Harvard Kennedy School.* May. Accessed March 31, 2022. https://wappp.hks.harvard.edu/files/wappp/files/entrepreneur.pdf.

Financial Express. 2018. *$50 million gift from Tata Trusts to Harvard Business School under scrutiny.* 26 May. Accessed March 31, 2022. https://www.financialexpress.com/industry/50-million-gift-from-tata-trusts-to-harvard-business-school-under-scrutiny/1181574/.

Fish, Isaac Stone. 2018. *Huawei's surprising ties to the Brookings Institution.* 7 December. Accessed April 30, 2022. https://www.washingtonpost.com/opinions/2018/12/08/chinese-companys-surprising-ties-brookings-institution/.

——. 2019. *What China experts have to do to get on Beijing's visa 'whitelist'.* 5 September. Accessed April 30, 2022. https://www.washingtonpost.com/opinions/2019/09/05/what-china-experts-have-do-get-beijings-visa-whitelist/.

Fletcher, Erin K., Rohini Pande, and Charity Troyer Moore. 2017. "Women and Work in India: Descriptive Evidence and a Review of Potential Policies." *Harvard Kennedy School.* 30 December. Accessed March 31, 2022. https://research.hks.harvard.edu/publications/getFile.aspx?Id=1624.

Fuller, Roslyn. 2021. *The billionaire takeover of civil society.* 29 January. Accessed May 15, 2022. https://www.spiked-online.com/2021/01/29/the-billionaire-takeover-of-civil-society/.

Ganesh N. 2015b. *Kumbh Mela hit by condom controversy amid claims 5.40 lakh have been ordered 'to meet demand' during holy festival.* 8 July. Accessed March 31, 2022. http://www.dailymail.co.uk/indiahome/indianews/article-3154032/AIDS-prevention-activists-deny-condom-supply-surge-linked-Kumbh-Mela.html.

——. 2015a. *Reports of surge in condom supply annoys Kumbh Mela planners.* 9 July.

Accessed March 31, 2022. http://indiatoday.intoday.in/story/condom-supply-surge-vexes-kumbh-planners-mela/1/450131.html.

Ganguly, Shreya. 2019. *China-Based Qiming Venture Partners Lead $15 Mn Funding Round In Pratilipi*. 6 June. Accessed May 15, 2022. https://inc42.com/buzz/china-based-qiming-venture-partners-invests-in-pratilipi/.

Garimella, Kiran, and Dean Eckles. 2020. *Images and misinformation in political groups: Evidence from WhatsApp in India*. 7 July. Accessed March 31, 2022. https://misinforeview.hks.harvard.edu/article/images-and-misinformation-in-political-groups-evidence-from-whatsapp-in-india/ .

Garlen, Julie C. 2018. "Interrogating innocence: "Childhood" as exclusionary social practice." 22 November. Accessed April 30, 2022. https://journals.sagepub.com/doi/pdf/10.1177/0907568218811484.

Gates, Gary J. 2011. *How many people are lesbian, gay, bisexual, and transgender?* April. Accessed May 15, 2022. https://williamsinstitute.law.ucla.edu/publications/how-many-people-lgbt/.

Gettleman, Jeffrey, and Eve Lyons. 2018b. *The Peculiar Position of India's Third Gender*. 17 February. Accessed May 15, 2022. https://www.nytimes.com/2018/02/17/style/india-third-gender-hijras-transgender.html.

Ghorpade, Arjun. 2011. *Chokhamela*. Aurangabad: Baba Saheb Ambedkar Marathwada University.

Ghurye, G.S. 1959. *The Scheduled Tribes*. 2nd. Bombay: Popular Book Depot.

Gipson, Abigail, John Fea, Kalpana Jain, and Ann Peters. 2021. *Religion, Populism, and the Media*. 15 March. Accessed March 31, 2022. https://pulitzercenter.org/blog/religion-populism-and-media.

Global News. 2020. *Coronavirus: Trudeau tells UN conference that pandemic provided "opportunity for a reset"*. 30 September. Accessed April 30, 2022. https://www.youtube.com/watch?v=n2fp0Jeyjvw.

Gockowski, Anthony. 2017. *Harvard pushes list calling conservative websites 'fake news'*. 10 March. Accessed March 31, 2022. https://www.campusreform.org/?ID=8895.

Godrej India Culture Lab. 2019a. *India Culture Lab: LGBTQ*. Accessed May 15, 2022. https://indiaculturelab.org/lgbtq.

——. 2019b. *The India Culture Lab National Fellowship*. Accessed May 15, 2022. https://indiaculturelab.org/nationalfellowship.

Goleman, Daniel. 1976. "Meditation and Consciousness: An Asian Approach to Mental Health." *American Journal of Psychotherapy* 30 (1): 41–54.

——. 1971. "Meditation as meta-therapy: Hypotheses toward a proposed fifth state of consciousness." *Association for Transpersonal Psychology*. Accessed March 31, 2022. https://www.atpweb.org/jtparchive/trps-03-71-01-001.pdf.

——. 1972a. "The Buddha on meditation and states of consciousness, Part 1: The teachings." *Association for Transpersonal Psychology*. Accessed March 31, 2022.

——. 1972b. "The Buddha on meditation and states of consciousness, Part II: A typology of meditation techniques." *Association for Transpersonal Psychology*. Accessed March 31, 2022. https://www.atpweb.org/jtparchive/trps-04-72-02-151.pdf.

Golikeri, Priyanka, and Satish John. 2011. *If you don't have humanities, the sciences, tech, finance won't have a strong framework of values*. 31 January. Accessed April 30, 2022. https://www.dnaindia.com/business/interview-if-you-don-t-have-humanities-the-sciences-tech-finance-won-t-have-a-strong-framework-of-values-1501124.

Gordon, Robert C. 2007. *Emerson and the Light of India*. New Delhi: National Book Trust.

Goswami, Devika. 2020. *Is Ashoka a Safe Space for Political Discourse?* 1 February. Accessed May 15, 2022. http://edictarchive.the-edict.in/index.php/2020/02/01/why-ashoka-needs-to-be-more-inclusive-of-its-political-right/.

Goyal, S.R. 1987. *A History of Indian Buddhism*. Meerut: Kusumanjali Prakashan.

Gravitahn. 2017. *Public Shaming MOB demand groveling apology from Yale Professor*. 6 March. Accessed April 30, 2022. https://www.youtube.com/watch?v=iAr6LYC-xpE.

Greenwald, Glenn. 2021. *Pierre Omidyar's Financing of the Facebook "Whistleblower" Campaign Reveals a Great Deal*. 25 October. Accessed May 15, 2022. https://greenwald.substack.com/p/pierre-omidyars-financing-of-the.

Grey, Sandra J. 2013. "Activist Academics: What Future?" *Policy Futures in Education* 11 (6): 700-711. doi:https://doi.org/10.2304/pfie.2013.11.6.701.

Grossman, Ron. 1999. *IN THIS WRITING CONTEST, IT'S GOOD TO BE BAD*. 28 January. Accessed April 30, 2022. https://www.chicagotribune.com/news/ct-xpm-1999-01-28-9901280242-story.html.

Gulf News. 2017. *Lakshmi Mittal donates $25m to Harvard University*. 17 October. Accessed March 31, 2022. https://gulfnews.com/world/asia/india/lakshmi-mittal-donates-25m-to-harvard-university-1.2107905.

Gupt, Harihara Prasad. 1986. *Vaishnava Kabir*. Allahabad: Bhasha Sahitya Samsthan.

Gupta, Arvind. 2015. *Book Review : Prof R Vaidyanathan, Caste as Social Capital, Westland Books, 2019, Chennai, PP. 131*. 15 April. Accessed March 31, 2022. https://www.vifindia.org/bookreview/2019/april/15/caste-as-social-capital.

Gupta, Dipankar. 2000. *Interrogating Caste - Understanding Hierarchy and Difference in Indian Society*. New Delhi: Sage.

Gupta, Surbhi. 2020. *'The book is an outcome of my disquiet... my book of mourning'*. 11 November. Accessed May 15, 2022. https://indianexpress.com/article/books-and-literature/aparna-vaidik-interview-7047876/.

Haberman, David L. 2003. *The Bhaktirasamrtasindhu of Rupa Gosvamin*. New Delhi: Indira Gandhi National Centre for the Arts.

Hancock, Ian F. 1987. *Pariah Syndrome: An Account of Gypsy Slavery and Persecution*. Ann Arbor, MI: Karoma Publishers.

Haniffa, Aziz. 2020. *India's controversial citizenship laws are 'troubling,' says Hindu American commissioner*. 11 March. Accessed March 31, 2022. https://www.indiaabroad.com/india/india-s-controversial-citizenship-laws-are-troubling-says-hindu-american-commissioner/article_865fadb8-63fa-11ea-99dd-27ca3a74507c.html.

Hanson, Melanie. 2022. *Student Loan Debt Statistics*. 1 March. Accessed March 31, 2022. https://educationdata.org/student-loan-debt-statistics.

Hardgrave Jr., Robert L. 1969. *The Nadars of Tamilnad: The Political Culture of a Community in Change*. Berkeley and Los Angeles: University of California Press.

Harmon, Grace. 2020. *More than half of the student body at Evergreen identifies as LGBTQ or questioning.* 18 February. Accessed May 15, 2022. https://www.knkx.org/youth-education/2020-02-18/more-than-half-of-the-student-body-at-evergreen-identifies-as-lgbtq-or-questioning.

Harsha, Dan. 2019. *India's pluralistic political system at stake in national elections.* 13 May. Accessed March 31, 2022. https://www.hks.harvard.edu/faculty-research/policy-topics/politics/indias-pluralistic-political-system-stake-national.

Hartocollis, Anemona. 2022. *A Lawsuit Accuses Harvard of Ignoring Sexual Harassment by a Professor.* 8 February. Accessed April 30, 2022. https://www.nytimes.com/2022/02/08/us/harvard-sexual-harassment-lawsuit.html.

Harvard Business School. 2021. *Can Historic Social Injustices be Addressed Through Reparations?* 2 March. Accessed March 31, 2022. https://hbswk.hbs.edu/item/cold-call-can-historic-social-injustices-be-addressed-through-reparations.

Harvard Center for Population and Development Studies. 2021. *Gender norms in rural north India may play role in slow adoption of cleaner, government-endorsed fuel sources for cooking.* 27 October. Accessed March 31, 2022. https://www.hsph.harvard.edu/population-development/2021/10/27/gender-norms-in-rural-north-india-may-play-role-in-slow-adoption-of-cleaner-government-endorsed-fuel-sources-for-cooking/.

Harvard Global. 2017a. *Public Health Center in India.* Accessed May 15, 2022. https://www.harvardglobal.org/our-projects/public-health-center-india.

——. 2017b. *Where we Operate : India.* Accessed May 15, 2022. https://www.harvardglobal.org/where-we-operate/india.

Harvard Kennedy School - Women and Public Policy Program. 2014. *About WAPP.* Accessed March 31, 2022. https://wappp.hks.harvard.edu/about-wappp.

Harvard Kennedy School. 2021a. *Bay Area Development and Innovation Research Project.* Accessed March 31, 2022. https://ash.harvard.edu/bay-area-development-and-innovation-research-project.

——. 2016b. *China Philanthropy.* Accessed March 31, 2022. https://ash.harvard.edu/china-philanthropy-project.

——. 2015a. *China Programs.* Accessed March 31, 2022. https://ash.harvard.edu/china-programs.

——. 2021b. *CID/Malcolm Wiener Center Joint Awards on Inequality Research.* Accessed March 31, 2022. https://www.hks.harvard.edu/centers/cid/about-cid/news-announcements/joint-award-inequality-research.

——. 2015b. *Conferences.* Accessed March 31, 2022. https://ash.harvard.edu/china-conferences.

——. 2016a. *Dalio Scholarship.* Accessed March 31, 2022. https://ash.harvard.edu/dalio-fellowship.

——. 2017a. *Guide to Center & Program Fellows.* Accessed March 31, 2022. https://www.hks.harvard.edu/research-insights/library-knowledge-services/research-services-policies/research-policies/guide-hks.

——. 2019b. *Harvard Kennedy School Admissions Blog.* 16 December. Accessed March 31, 2022. https://hksadmissionblog.tumblr.com/post/189701921903/

fellowshipscholarship-series-public-service.

——. 2019a. *Harvard Kennedy School establishes new fund to support training and development for civil servants in Croatia.* 17 January. Accessed March 31, 2022. https://www.hks.harvard.edu/announcements/harvard-kennedy-school-new-fund-support-training-civil-servants.

——. 2016c. *PM Narendra Modi's Notes Ban Neither Intelligent Nor Humane: Amartya Sen To NDTV.* 30 November. Accessed March 31, 2022. https://www.hks.harvard.edu/centers/mrcbg/programs/growthpolicy/pm-narendra-modis-notes-ban-neither-intelligent-nor-humane.

——. 2018. *Salil Shetty.* 15 October. Accessed March 31, 2022. https://carrcenter.hks.harvard.edu/people/salil-shetty.

——. 2017b. *Schwab's Wiener Lecture points to challenges and opportunities of new industrial revolution.* 2 October. Accessed May 15, 2022. https://www.hks.harvard.edu/more/alumni/alumni-stories/collaboration-fractured-world-klaus-schwab-mcmpa-speaks-harvard-kennedy.

——. 2017c. *Shivshankar Menon.* 6 January. Accessed May 15, 2022. https://www.belfercenter.org/person/shivshankar-menon-0.

——. 2019c. "Student Financial Services Financing Your Education." *Harvard Kennedy School, Student Financial Services.* July. Accessed March 31, 2022. https://www.hks.harvard.edu/sites/default/files/student%20financial%20services/files/282548%20HKS%20Finance%20Education_WEB.pdf.

——. 2015c. *Teaching.* Accessed March 31, 2022. https://ash.harvard.edu/china-programs-executive-education.

Harvard Law Review. 2021. *From Domicile to Dominion: India's Settler Colonial Agenda in Kashmir.* 10 May. Accessed March 31, 2022. https://harvardlawreview.org/2021/05/from-domicile-to-dominion-indias-settler-colonial-agenda-in-kashmir/.

Harvard Law School. 2018. "Celebrating 65 years of Alumnae, September 14-16, 2018, Speaker Biographies." *Harvard Law School.* Accessed March 31, 2022. https://hls.harvard.edu/content/uploads/2018/08/Speaker-Bios-8.31.pdf.

Harvard Square Library. 2017. *The Living Legacy of Ralph Waldo Emerson.* Accessed March 31, 2022. https://www.harvardsquarelibrary.org/collection/living-legacy-ralph-waldo-emerson/.

Harvard T.H. Chan School of Public Health. 2021a. *'A Catalyst for Humanity' A Conversation with Isabel Wilkerson.* 1 February. Accessed March 31, 2022. https://theforum.sph.harvard.edu/events/catalyst-for-humanity/.

——. 2018. *Acknowledgment of Native Land and Peoples.* 24 May. Accessed March 31, 2022. https://www.hsph.harvard.edu/social-and-behavioral-sciences/2018/05/24/acknowledgment-of-native-land-and-peoples/.

——. 2019b. *India Research Center - Evidence-Based Public Policy and Practice.* 16 January. Accessed March 31, 2022. https://www.hsph.harvard.edu/india-center/research/initiative-on-evidence-based-public-policy-and-practice/.

——. 2017. *India Research Center - Improving Health in India.* 15 December. Accessed March 31, 2022. https://www.hsph.harvard.edu/india-center/improving-health-in-india/.

——. 2019a. *India Research Center - Our Donors.* Accessed March 31, 2022. https://www.hsph.harvard.edu/india-center/press-releases/.

——. 2016. *India Research Center.* Accessed March 31, 2022. https://www.hsph.harvard.edu/india-center/.

——. 2021b. *India's COVID-19 Crisis: Variants, Vaccines and Surges.* 13 May. Accessed March 31, 2022. https://theforum.sph.harvard.edu/events/indias-covid-19-crisis/.

Harvard University. 2017b. *"The Social Texture of an Artist" – reflections on the 2017 SAI Mahindra Lecture.* 13 April. Accessed March 31, 2022. https://mittalsouthasiainstitute.harvard.edu/2017/04/the-social-texture-of-an-artist-reflections-on-the-2017-sai-mahindra-lecture/.

——. 2015b. *"The Water, Forest, and Land Belong to Us": Collective action and property in an Indian forest.* 14 January. Accessed March 31, 2022. https://mittalsouthasiainstitute.harvard.edu/event/south-asia-without-border-seminar-2/.

——. 2013a. *2013 Prasad Fellowship Luncheon.* 1 October. Accessed March 31, 2022. https://mittalsouthasiainstitute.harvard.edu/2013/10/2013-prasad-fellowship-luncheon/.

——. 2014d. *2014 Prasad Fellowships.* 16 May. Accessed March 31, 2022. https://mittalsouthasiainstitute.harvard.edu/2014/05/2014-prasad-fellowships/.

——. 2019e. *A Harvard Team Brings an Educational Outreach Program to Life in Manipur, India.* 20 February. Accessed March 31, 2022. https://mittalsouthasiainstitute.harvard.edu/2019/02/harvard-educational-outreach-manipur-india/.

——. 2018j. "Abstracts for Feb Meritocracy Workshop." *Harvard University.* May. Accessed April 30, 2022. https://hcf.fas.harvard.edu/wp-content/uploads/2018/05/Abstracts-for-Feb-Meritocracy-Workshop.pdf.

——. 2020h. *Acknowledgement of Land and People.* Accessed March 31, 2022. https://hunap.harvard.edu/land-acknowledgement.

——. 2022a. *Advisory Council.* Accessed March 31, 2022. https://mittalsouthasiainstitute.harvard.edu/mittalinstitute-advisory-council/.

——. 2012a. *Anthony Saich on US-Chinese relations ‖ American Conversation Essentials.* 12 June. Accessed March 31, 2022. https://www.youtube.com/watch?v=GaqIXrpVZBU.

——. 2022b. *Assembly Elections and After.* Accessed May 15, 2022. https://mittalsouthasiainstitute.harvard.edu/event/assembly-elections-and-after/.

——. 2020e. *Breaking the Mould: Girl Power and Beyond in Contemporary India.* 2 January. Accessed March 31, 2022. https://mittalsouthasiainstitute.harvard.edu/event/breaking-the-mould-girl-power-and-beyond-in-contemporary-india/.

——. 2021a. *Buddhist Nuns and Biodiversity: Winter Student Grant Report.* 13 May. Accessed March 31, 2022. https://mittalsouthasiainstitute.harvard.edu/2021/05/buddhist-nuns-and-biodiversity-winter-student-grant-report/.

——. 2020d. *Caste in Tech Town Hall.* 14 August. Accessed March 31, 2022. https://mittalsouthasiainstitute.harvard.edu/event/caste-in-tech-town-hall/.

——. 2020c. *Cities and Settlements: Impacts of Partition on Urbanization in the Subcontinent.* 28 July. Accessed March 31, 2022. https://mittalsouthasiainstitute.harvard.edu/partition-cities-and-settlements/.

——. 2020b. *Crowdsourcing Memories.* 4 August. Accessed March 31, 2022. https://mittalsouthasiainstitute.harvard.edu/partition-crowdsourcing-memories/.

——. 2016a. *Development and Politics in Indian Democracy.* 1 December. Accessed March 31, 2022. https://mittalsouthasiainstitute.harvard.edu/event/armed-politics-violence-order-and-the-state-in-southern-asia/.

——. 2018i. *Fall Class: Contemporary Developing Countries: Entrepreneurial Solutions to Intractable Social and Economic Problems (SW47).* 14 August. Accessed March 31, 2022. https://mittalsouthasiainstitute.harvard.edu/2018/08/fall-class-contemporary-developing-countries-entrepreneurial-solutions-to-intractable-social-and-economic-problems-sw47/.

——. 2017d. *Film Screening and Q+A with Deepa Mehta: Anatomy of Violence.* 1 February. Accessed March 31, 2022. https://mittalsouthasiainstitute.harvard.edu/event/film-screening-and-qa-with-deepa-mehta-anatomy-of-violence/.

——. 2013b. *Financial Inclusion: Its Challenges and Prospects.* 5 December. Accessed March 31, 2022. https://mittalsouthasiainstitute.harvard.edu/event/social-enterprise-seminar-2/.

——. 2021g. "Financial Report Fiscal Year 2021." *Harvard University.* October. Accessed March 31, 2022. https://finance.harvard.edu/files/fad/files/fy21_harvard_financial_report.pdf.

——. 2019f. *Fractal Urbanization: Spatial Segregation in Liberalizing India.* 12 November. Accessed March 31, 2022. https://mittalsouthasiainstitute.harvard.edu/event/fractal-urbanization-spatial-segregation-in-liberalizing-india/.

——. 2018h. *Free Online edX Course: "Entrepreneurship in Emerging Economies".* 27 February. Accessed March 31, 2022. https://mittalsouthasiainstitute.harvard.edu/2018/02/entrepreneurship-emerging-economies/.

——. 2016b. *Gender Challenges.* 14 September. Accessed March 31, 2022. https://mittalsouthasiainstitute.harvard.edu/event/gender-challenges/.

——. 2018e. *Gender, Violence and Vulnerabilities of Adolescents in India.* 17 September. Accessed March 31, 2022. https://mittalsouthasiainstitute.harvard.edu/event/gender-violence-and-vulnerabilities-of-adolescents-in-india/.

——. 2019j. *Harnessing Science to Serve Humanity: Vision of Tata Institute for Genetics and Society.* 25 February. Accessed March 31, 2022. https://mittalsouthasiainstitute.harvard.edu/event/harnessing-science-serve-humanity/.

——. 2014f. *Harvard faculty share corporate social responsibility lessons with leaders in Mumbai.* 12 February. Accessed March 31, 2022. https://mittalsouthasiainstitute.harvard.edu/2014/02/harvard-faculty-share-corporate-social-responsibility-lessons-with-leaders-in-mumbai/.

——. 2013d. *Harvard Gender Violence Project : Gender Justice and Criminal Law Reform Conference.* 10 June. Accessed March 31, 2022. https://mittalsouthasiainstitute.harvard.edu/gender-violence-project_delhi-event/.

——. 2018d. *Harvard's New "Embassy" in India.* 22 March. Accessed March 31, 2022. https://mittalsouthasiainstitute.harvard.edu/2018/03/harvards-new-embassy-in-india/.

——. 2015c. *Health and Human Rights in Burma.* 16 January. Accessed March 31, 2022. https://mittalsouthasiainstitute.harvard.edu/event/burma-panel/.

——. 2019g. *How Does Caste Impact America?* 27 March. Accessed March 31, 2022. https://mittalsouthasiainstitute.harvard.edu/2019/03/caste-impact-america/.

——. 2018a. *India International Center: Annexe Building: Lecture Room- I.* Accessed March 31, 2022. https://mittalsouthasiainstitute.harvard.edu/events/venue/india-international-center-annexe-building-lecture-room-i.

——. 2018b. *India Seminar Series: The Past, Present and Potential Future of Coal in India.* 1 August. Accessed April 30, 2022. https://mittalsouthasiainstitute.harvard.edu/2018/08/the-past-present-and-future-of-coal-in-india/.

——. 2014e. *Informal Workers, Enterprises, and Cities: Addressing Informality in South Asia.* 3 March. Accessed March 31, 2022. https://mittalsouthasiainstitute.harvard.edu/sai-symposium-2014-informal-economy/.

——. 2021b. *Joint Seminar on South Asian Politics Archives.* Accessed March 31, 2022. https://mittalsouthasiainstitute.harvard.edu/events/topic/joint-seminar-on-south-asian-politics/.

——. 2015a. *Kumbh Mela book launch in Delhi.* 20 August. Accessed March 31, 2022. http://southasiainstitute.harvard.edu/kumbh-mela/post/kumbh-mela-book-launch-in-delhi/7.

——. 2021f. *Kushagra Nayan Bajaj's New Gift to LMSAI Remarkably Expands Opportunities for South Asian Scholars.* 13 October. Accessed March 31, 2022. https://mittalsouthasiainstitute.harvard.edu/2021/10/bajaj-fellowship/.

——. 2020a. *Looking Back, Informing the Future: the 1947 Partition of British India.* 4 August. Accessed April 30, 2022. https://mittalsouthasiainstitute.harvard.edu/partition-home/.

——. 2012b. *Mapping India's Kumbh Mela.* 21 September. Accessed April 30, 2022. http://southasiainstitute.harvard.edu/kumbh-mela/.

——. 2019i. *Meritocracy: Perspectives from China Past and Present.* 10 December. Accessed March 31, 2022. https://mittalsouthasiainstitute.harvard.edu/event/meritocracy-perspectives-from-china-past-and-present/.

——. 2013c. *Na Hindu, Na Musalman: The Dilemma of a Bengali Artisan Caste.* 3 September. Accessed March 31, 2022. https://mittalsouthasiainstitute.harvard.edu/event/na-hindu-na-musalman-the-dilemma-of-a-bengali-artisan-caste/.

——. 2019. *Omidyar Grant for Innovative Solutions.* Accessed May 15, 2022. https://mittalsouthasiainstitute.harvard.edu/omidyar-grant-for-innovative-solutions/.

——. 2019k. *Primary Health Care Reforms in India: Field Lessons from Early Implementation.* Accessed March 31, 2022. https://mittalsouthasiainstitute.harvard.edu/event/primary-health-care-reforms-in-india-field-lessons-from-early-implementation/.

——. 2019h. *Property, Power, and Women: Positive and Perverse Consequences of Indian Reforms for Gender Equality.* 25 October. Accessed March 31, 2022. https://mittalsouthasiainstitute.harvard.edu/event/womens-representation-and-resistance-rachel-brule/.

——. 2014a. *Religion and Culture: Mapping India's Kumbh Mela.* 10 March. Accessed April 30, 2022. https://web.archive.org/web/20140310060958/http://southasiainstitute. harvard.edu/kumbh-mela/page/religion-and-culture/.

——. 2016c. *SAI hosts women's empowerment workshop.* 3 February. Accessed March 31, 2022. https://mittalsouthasiainstitute.harvard.edu/2016/02/womens-empowerment-educational-social-and-economic-solutions/.

——. 2014b. *SAI Research Affiliates, 2014-2015.* 12 October. Accessed March 31, 2022. https://mittalsouthasiainstitute.harvard.edu/2014/10/sai-research-affiliates-2014-2015/.

——. 2017a. *SAI to host weekly seminar series on Partition of British India.* 13 February. Accessed March 31, 2022. https://mittalsouthasiainstitute.harvard.edu/2017/02/sai-to-host-weekly-seminar-series-on-partition/.

——. 2019b. *Salil Shetty: Decoding the Kashmir Crisis.* 12 September. Accessed March 31, 2022. https://mittalsouthasiainstitute.harvard.edu/2019/09/salil-shetty-decoding-kashmir-crisis/.

——. 2017c. *Spiritual Ecologies: Sustainability and Transcendence in Contemporary Asia.* 16 November. Accessed March 31, 2022. https://mahindrahumanities.fas.harvard. edu/event/spiritual-ecologies-sustainability-and-transcendence-contemporary-asia.

——. 2019d. *The Fears Have Gone Away: Exploring the Roots of Insurgent Citizenship in India's Bhil Heartland.* 22 August. Accessed March 31, 2022. https:// mittalsouthasiainstitute.harvard.edu/event/exploring-roots-insurgent-citizenship-bhil-heartland/.

——. 2018f. *The Mittal Institute and Tata Trusts Begin Social Enterprise Partnership in India.* 13 February. Accessed March 31, 2022. https://mittalsouthasiainstitute.harvard. edu/2018/02/sai-tata-trusts-begin-social-enterprise-partnership-india/.

——. 2021d. *The Mittal Institute's Winter 2020 Student Grant Recipients.* 7 January. Accessed March 31, 2022. https://mittalsouthasiainstitute.harvard.edu/2021/01/the-mittal-institutes-winter-2020-student-grant-recipients/.

——. 2018c. *The Roma Program.* 21 February. Accessed March 31, 2022. https://fxb. harvard.edu/the-roma-program/.

——. 2018g. *Trust and Creativity: Fostering Entrepreneurship in Developing Countries.* 15 March. Accessed March 31, 2022. https://mittalsouthasiainstitute.harvard.edu/event/ trust-and-creativity-fostering-entrepreneurship-in-developing-countries/.

——. 2021e. *VAF Spotlight: Bunu Dhungana on Gender Norms in Art and Artistic Expression.* 1 December. Accessed March 31, 2022. https://mittalsouthasiainstitute. harvard.edu/2021/12/bunu/.

——. 2020f. *Vijay Shekhar Sharma Provides New Fund for the Mittal Institute.* 7 December. Accessed March 31, 2022. https://mittalsouthasiainstitute.harvard.edu/2020/12/ vijay-shekhar-sharma-provides-new-fund/.

——. 2021c. *Visiting Artist Fellow Pragati Jain Reflects on Being a Practicing Artist and Woman in India Today.* 17 November. Accessed March 31, 2022. https:// mittalsouthasiainstitute.harvard.edu/2021/11/pragati-jain/.

——. 2019a. *Visiting Artist Fellows Exhibition Reception: Partition Perspectives.* 22

February. Accessed March 31, 2022. https://mittalsouthasiainstitute.harvard.edu/event/visiting-artist-fellows-exhibition-2019/.

———. 2019c. *Voting for Strongmen: Nationalist and Populist Leadership in Brazil and India.* 9 September. Accessed March 31, 2022. https://mittalsouthasiainstitute.harvard.edu/event/voting-for-strongmen/.

———. 2020g. *Webinar: The Response to COVID-19 in South Asia.* Accessed March 31, 2022. https://mittalsouthasiainstitute.harvard.edu/event/webinar-is-the-response-to-covid-19-in-south-asia-adequate-and-proportionate.

———. 2014c. *Women in Politics: The Case of India.* 15 May. Accessed March 31, 2022. https://mittalsouthasiainstitute.harvard.edu/2014/05/women-in-politics-the-case-of-india/.

Harvard-Yenching Institute. 2020b. *Chinese Studies in India.* Accessed May 15, 2022. https://www.harvard-yenching.org/programs/chinese-studies-in-india/.

———. 2020a. *History of The Harvard-Yenching Institute.* Accessed May 15, 2022. https://www.harvard-yenching.org/history-of-the-harvard-yenching-institute/.

———. 2020c. *Indian Studies in China.* Accessed May 15, 2022. https://www.harvard-yenching.org/programs/south-asian-studies-in-china-program/.

Hava, Guillermo S. 2020a. *In China, Harvard More Than Turns a Blind Eye.* 12 February. Accessed April 30, 2022. https://www.thecrimson.com/article/2020/2/12/hava-harvard-china-ties/.

———. 2020b. *The Other Chan: Donation Sanitization at the School of Public Health.* 19 October. Accessed April 30, 2022. https://www.thecrimson.com/column/for-sale/article/2020/10/19/hava-the-other-chan/.

Higgins, Michael. 2021. *Minority professor denied grants because he hires on merit: 'People are afraid to think'.* 24 November. Accessed February 15, 2022. https://nationalpost.com/news/canada/minority-professor-denied-grants-because-he-hires-on-merit-people-are-afraid-to-think.

Higgins, Richard. 2017. *The Harvard in Thoreau.* 29 June. Accessed April 30, 2022. https://news.harvard.edu/gazette/story/2017/06/near-the-bicentennial-of-thoreaus-birth-a-look-at-his-harvard-years/ .

Hindu American Foundation. 2019. *WGBH News "Caste in America" panel discussion, part 1.* 2 April. Accessed February 15, 2022. https://www.youtube.com/watch?v=NEjfA47QcG0.

Hindu Janajagruti Samiti. 2014. *Ford Foundation's link with Congress, NAC, AAP.* 3 May. Accessed May 15, 2022. https://www.hindujagruti.org/news/19538.html .

Hindu Students Council. 2021. *Hinduphobia at Harvard University.* 2 February. Accessed April 30, 2022. https://www.hindustudentscouncil.org/open-letter-to-harvard-signatories/.

HKS Misinformation Review Editorial Staff. 2021. *Retraction note to: Disinformation creep: ADOS and the strategic weaponization of breaking news.* 20 December. Accessed March 31, 2022. doi:https://doi.org/10.37016/mr-2020-86.

Hoagland, Kate. 2012. *Ash Center: Two Senior Chinese Officials Perform Key Research at the Ash Center.* 3 February. Accessed March 31, 2022. https://ash.harvard.edu/news/

ash-center-two-senior-chinese-officials-perform-key-research-ash-center.

Hocking, William Ernest. 1963. "Whitehead as I knew Him." In *Alfred North Whitehead: Essays on His Philosophy*, by George L. Kline, 7-17. New Jersey.

Hodder, Alan D. 2001. *Thoreau's Ecstatic Witness*. New Haven, Connecticut: Yale University Press.

Horkheimer, Max. 1982. *Critical Theory Selected Essays*. New York: Continuum Publishing Corporation.

Horkheimer, Max, and Theodor W. Adorno. 2002. *Dialectic of Enlightenment: Philosophical Fragments*. Stanford, CA: Stanford University Press.

Horwitz, Josh. 2017. *A visit by the Dalai Lama is dividing a US campus where 14% of students are from China.* 15 June. Accessed March 31, 2022. https://qz.com/1004386/ the-uproar-over-the-dalais-lamas-ucsd-visit-has-unveiled-chinas-meddling-influence-over-foreign-campuses/.

House Of Belongg. 2021. *Belongg Inclusive Schools Festival: What is an Inclusive School?* 21 July. Accessed May 15, 2022. https://www.youtube.com/watch?v=UGgIFnDoSSs.

Hsu, Tiffany, David Yaffe-Bellany, and Marc Tracy. 2020. *Jeffrey Epstein Gave $850,000 to M.I.T., and Administrators Knew.* 10 January. Accessed May 15, 2022. https://www. nytimes.com/2020/01/10/business/mit-jeffrey-epstein-joi-ito.html.

IAMC Official Channel. 2022. *Pathology of Islamophobia Taking Most Lethal Form in India under Narendra Modi: Prof. Noam Chomsky.* 10 February. Accessed May 15, 2022. https://www.youtube.com/watch?v=hRrPBvWQmq4.

——. 2020. *Raqib Hameed Naik Briefing on Kashmir Before the United States Congress on Dec 12, 2019.* 5 March. Accessed March 31, 2022. https://www.youtube.com/ watch?v=ZZZOrzU6pAs.

IDFC Foundation. 2016a. *IDFC Foundation: Grants.* Accessed May 15, 2022. http:// idfcfoundation.com/#grants.

——. 2016b. *Joint ventures.* Accessed May 15, 2022. http://idfcfoundation.com/.

IDFC Institute. 2015. *About Us - IDFC Institute.* Accessed May 15, 2022. https://www. idfcinstitute.org/about/.

——. 2017c. *Projects.* Accessed May 15, 2022. https://www.idfcinstitute.org/projects/.

——. 2017b. *Reuben Abraham - IDFC Institute.* Accessed May 15, 2022. https://www. idfcinstitute.org/about/people/team/reuben-abraham/.

——. 2017a. *Reuben Abraham - IDFC Institute.* Accessed May 15, 2022. https://www. idfcinstitute.org/about/people/executive-council/reuben-abraham/.

Imad, Sofia, Harsh Vardhan Pachisia, Sridhar Ganapathy, Rajeswari Parasa, and Manvi Mehta. 2021b. *Covid-19 Mortality Data for Mumbai.* 26 May. Accessed May 15, 2022. https://www.idfcinstitute.org/blog/2021/may/covid-19-mortality-data-for-mumbai/.

Independent and Public-Spirited Media Foundation. 2019a. *Grantee Portfolio – IPSMF.* Accessed May 15, 2022. https://ipsmf.org/grantee-portfolio/.

——. 2019c. *Introduction to Donors.* Accessed May 15, 2022. https://ipsmf.org/donors/.

——. 2019b. *The Mandate.* Accessed May 15, 2022. https://ipsmf.org/about-us/the-mandate/.

India Foundation for the Arts. 2014. *About IFA*. Accessed May 15, 2022. https://indiaifa. org/about-us/about-ifa.html.

———. 2021. "India Foundation for the Arts : Annual Report 2020-2021." *India Foundation for the Arts*. Accessed May 15, 2022. https://indiaifa.org/website/about_ifa/ifa_ar/ AnnualReport2020-2021.pdf.

IndiaCultureLab. 2019. *Fellowships at Godrej India Culture Lab- Join us now!* 26 November. Accessed May 15, 2022. https://www.youtube.com/watch?v=rEo2WUIe7xI.

———. 2020a. *Nisaba Godrej and Parmesh Shahani on the imperative for companies to be inclusive.* 8 July. Accessed May 15, 2022. https://www.youtube.com/ watch?v=qFV7OiPcRzg.

———. 2020b. *The Money Question | Strategies and models for funding the arts in India.* 13 July. Accessed May 15, 2022. https://www.youtube.com/watch?v=Oeb3Dv5RiZo.

Indian Express. 2015. *Party funding: Delhi HC asks govt about system in place to enforce FCRA.* 25 November. Accessed May 15, 2022. https://indianexpress.com/article/ india/india-news-india/party-funding-delhi-hc-asks-govt-about-system-in-place-to-enforce-fcra/.

Infinity Foundation. 2002b. *Sangamani: A Conference for India Studies.* 7 December. Accessed March 31, 2022. https://www.infinityfoundation.com/mandala/s_pr/s_pr_ sangamani_frameset.htm.

———. 2002a. *The Infinity Foundation Visiting Professor at Harvard University.* Accessed March 31, 2022. https://infinityfoundation.com/harvard/.

InfluenceWatch. 2020. *Pulitzer Center on Crisis Reporting.* Accessed March 31, 2022. https://www.influencewatch.org/non-profit/pulitzer-center-on-crisis-reporting/.

Infosys. 2020. *Nandan Nilekani at WEF 2020.* 22 January. Accessed May 15, 2022. https:// www.youtube.com/watch?v=njqLhi0Ukfc.

Institute of Chinese Studies. 2021. *Barnali Chanda.* Accessed May 15, 2022. https:// www.icsin.org/faculty/barnali-chanda.

———. 2020. *Pratap Bhanu Mehta.* Accessed May 15, 2022. https://www.icsin.org/faculty/ pratap-bhanu-mehta.

Institute Of Noetic Sciences (IONS). 2010. *The Physical and Psychological Effect of Meditation.* 9 November. Accessed March 31, 2022. https://www.psychologyofjoy. com/the-physical-and-psychological-effect-of-meditation/.

IPSMF News. 2021. "Grantees Build Strong Presence Through Videos." *IPSMF News.* May. Accessed May 15, 2022. https://ipsmf.org/wp-content/uploads/2021/05/ IPSMF-Quarterly-Newsletter-April202134121.pdf.

Iyer, Lakshmi, Tarun Khanna, and Ashutosh Varshney. 2011. "Caste and Entrepreneurship in India." *Harvard Business School.* 18 October. Accessed March 31, 2022. http://www. hbs.edu/research/pdf/12-028.pdf.

Jack, Andrew. 2021. *Harvard's 'teaching power' puts business school in the lead for influence.* 31 May. Accessed March 31, 2022. https://www.ft.com/content/beb77be1-f735-45e9-82cb-ec834eb39565.

———. 2018. *Why Harvard's case studies are under fire.* 29 October. Accessed March 31, 2022. https://www.ft.com/content/0b1aeb22-d765-11e8-a854-33d6f82e62f8.

Jaffrelot, Christophe. 2021. *Narendra Modi and Hindu Nationalism.* 13 July. Accessed May 15, 2022. https://carnegieendowment.org/publications/84978.

Jaffrelot, Christophe, and Sharik Laliwala. 2018b. *Inside Ahmedabad's Juhapura: What It's Like for Muslims to Live in a Ghetto.* 12 September. Accessed May 15, 2022. https://thewire.in/communalism/juhapura-ahmedabad-ghetto-muslims.

——. 2018. *The segregated city.* 26 May. Accessed May 15, 2022. https://indianexpress.com/article/opinion/columns/muslims-in-india-hindus-jains-gujarat-love-jihad-5191304/.

Jain, Dinendra Chandra. 1980. *Economic Life in Ancient India as Depicted in Jain Canonical Literature.* Vaishali, Bihar: Research Institute of Prakrit, Jainology & Ahimsa.

Jain, Kalpana. 2019. *Cow Vigilantes and the Rise of Hindu Nationalism.* 3 May. Accessed March 31, 2022. https://ksr.hkspublications.org/2019/05/03/cow-vigilantes-and-the-rise-of-hindu-nationalism/.

——. 2019. *International Reporting Must Distinguish Hindu Nationalism from Hinduism.* 3 December. Accessed March 31, 2022. https://niemanreports.org/articles/international-reporting-must-distinguish-hindu-nationalism-from-hinduism/.

Jaiswal, Suvira. 1998. *Caste: Origin, Function and Dimension of Change.* New Delhi: Manohar Publishers.

Jameel, Shahid. 2021. *How India Can Survivethe Virus.* 13 May. Accessed May 15, 2022. https://www.nytimes.com/2021/05/13/opinion/india-coronavirus-vaccination.html Majumdar, R .C. 1971. History.

Jaschik, Scott. 2021. *Buying Progress in Rankings?* 27 April. Accessed March 31, 2022. https://www.insidehighered.com/admissions/article/2021/04/27/study-charges-qs-conflicts-interest-international-rankings.

Jay, Martin. 1996. *The Dialectical Imagination.* Berkeley, Los Angeles and London: University of California Press.

Jayachandran, Seema, and Rohini Pande. 2015. *Why Are Indian Children So Short? |CID Faculty Working Paper No. 292.* April. Accessed March 31, 2022. https://www.hks.harvard.edu/sites/default/files/centers/cid/files/publications/faculty-working-papers/Indian_Children_Short_Pande_293.pdf.

Jayaswal, K.P. 1934. *An Imperial History of India in a Sanskrit Text.* Lahore: Motilal Banarsidass.

Jeanne Lafortune's Homepage. 2022. *Jeanne Lafortune: Curriculum Vitae.* Accessed May 15, 2022. https://sites.google.com/site/jeannelafortune/curriculum-vitae.

Jeedigunta, Satyanarayana, Nadia Hewett, Purushottam Kaushik, and Arushi Goel. 2021. "Towards a Data Economy: An enabling framework." *World Economic Forum.* Accessed May 15, 2022. https://www3.weforum.org/docs/WEF_Towards_a_Data_Economy_2021.pdf.

Jeelani, Gulam. 2021. *Muslims taking to family planning faster than Hindus; Polygamy a myth: Former CEC SY Quraishi.* 20 March. Accessed May 15, 2022. https://www.moneycontrol.com/news/politics/muslims-taking-to-family-planning-faster-than-hindus-polygamy-a-myth-former-cec-sy-quraishi-6669901.html/amp.

JharGov TV. 2021. *INDIA CONFERENCE AT HARVARD - 20-02-2021.* 20 February.

Accessed February 15, 2022. https://www.youtube.com/watch?v=MJ4yqgc_gkM.

Johnson, Ion. 2016. *On the Role of Chinese Religion in Environmental Protection* . 17 October. Accessed March 31, 2022. https://www.nytimes.com/2016/10/18/world/asia/china-religion-prasenjit-duara.html.

Jolivette, Andrew J. 2015. *Research Justice: Methodologies for Social Change.* Bristol, UK: Polity Press.

Jolly, Joanna. 2016. *Rape Culture in India: The Role of the English-Language Press.* 20 July. Accessed April 30, 2022. https://shorensteincenter.org/rape-culture-india-english-language-press/.

Jones, Geoffrey. 2017. "International Business and Emerging Markets: A Long-Run Perspective." *Harvard Business School.* 29 September. Accessed March 31, 2022. https://www.hbs.edu/ris/Publication%20Files/18-020_0da6ca17-091e-4491-8ec1-974156463cb7.pdf.

Jones, Jeffrey M. 2021. *LGBT Identification Rises to 5.6% in Latest U.S. Estimate.* 24 February. Accessed May 15, 2022. https://news.gallup.com/poll/329708/lgbt-identification-rises-latest-estimate.aspx.

Joshi, Mohit. 2021. *Digital identity can help advance inclusive financial services.* 30 April. Accessed May 15, 2022. https://www.weforum.org/agenda/2021/04/digital-id-is-the-catalyst-of-our-digital-future/.

J-PAL. 2010. *About Us - The Abdul Latif Jameel Poverty Action Lab (J-PAL).* Accessed May 15, 2022. https://www.povertyactionlab.org/about-j-pal.

——. 2020d. *Ankit Agarwal.* Accessed May 15, 2022. https://www.povertyactionlab.org/person/agarwal.

——. 2014b. *Business Training for Women in Ahmedabad, India.* Accessed May 15, 2022. https://www.povertyactionlab.org/evaluation/business-training-women-ahmedabad-india.

——. 2014a. *Discrimination in Grading in India.* Accessed May 15, 2022. https://www.povertyactionlab.org/evaluation/discrimination-grading-india.

——. 2020e. *H.Y. Gowramma.* Accessed May 15, 2022. https://www.povertyactionlab.org/person/gowramma.

——. 2020b. *Jeanne Lafortune.* Accessed May 15, 2022. https://www.povertyactionlab.org/person/lafortune.

——. 2020a. *Marianne Bertrand.* Accessed May 15, 2022. https://www.povertyactionlab.org/person/Bertrand .

——. 2020c. *Priyal Patil.* Accessed May 15, 2022. https://www.povertyactionlab.org/person/patil.

——. 2020f. *Reducing Farmers' Risk through Flood-Tolerant Rice in India.* Accessed May 15, 2022. https://www.povertyactionlab.org/evaluation/reducing-farmers-risk-through-flood-tolerant-rice-india.

——. 2021. *Reducing Prejudice Through Cross-Caste Cricket Teams in India.* Accessed May 15, 2022. https://www.povertyactionlab.org/evaluation/reducing-prejudice-through-cross-caste-cricket-teams-india.

J-PAL South Asia. 2021. *xSDG UnConference: Making global development inclusive.*

August. Accessed May 15, 2022. https://www.povertyactionlab.org/event/xsdg-unconference-making-global-development-inclusive.

J-PAL. 2003. *The Abdul Latif Jameel Poverty Action Lab (J-PAL).* Accessed May 15, 2022. https://www.povertyactionlab.org/.

Justice For Rohith University of Hyderabad. 2016. *MAHA DHARNA – Speech by Karthik Bittu Kondaiah – Justice For Rohith.* 30 August. Accessed May 15, 2022. https://www.youtube.com/watch?v=b9U_-Jz1Hes.

Kakutani, Yuichiro. 2020b. *Ex-China Official a Top Donor to D.C. Think Tank.* 13 July. Accessed April 30, 2022. https://freebeacon.com/national-security/ex-china-official-a-top-donor-to-d-c-think-tank/.

——. 2020a. *Harvard Taps Former CCP Official to Conduct Polling in China.* 31 July. Accessed March 31, 2022. https://freebeacon.com/coronavirus/harvard-hires-ex-regime-official-to-poll-china/.

Kane, Pandurang Vaman. 1941. *History of Dharmashastra.* Vol. II. Poona: Bhandarkar Oriental Research Institute.

——. 1990. *History of Dharmashastras: Ancient and Medieval Religions and Civil Law in India Vol II. Part 1.* Pune: Bhandarkar Oriental Research Institute.

Kapur, Kamlesh. 2010. *Portraits of a Nation: History of Ancient India.* New Delhi: Sterling Publishers.

Karthikeyan, Aparna. 2014. *Everyday lives, Everyday people.* 13 December. Accessed March 31, 2022. https://www.thehindu.com/features/magazine/everyday-lives-everyday-people/article10945235.ece.

Kazemi, Ashkan, Kiran Garimella, Gautam Kishore Shahi, Devin Gaffney, and Scott A Hale. 2022. "Research note: Tiplines to uncover misinformation on ." *Harvard Kennedy School, Misinformation Review.* 31 January. Accessed March 31, 2022. https://misinforeview.hks.harvard.edu/wpcontent/uploads/2022/01/kazemi_tiplines_whatsapp_20220131.pdf.

Kearns, Cleo McNelly. 1987. *T. S. Eliot and Indic Traditions.* Cambridge [Cambridgeshire]; New York: Cambridge University Press.

Keay, F.E. 1918. *Ancient Indian Education.* London: Oxford University Press.

Keele University. 2020. *Keele Researcher Awarded Funding to Promote Inclusive Education in India.* 15 December. Accessed May 15, 2022. https://www.keele.ac.uk/about/news/2020/december/funding-inclusive/education-india.php .

Kendi, Ibram X. 2019. *How to Be an Anti-Racist.* New York: One World.

kenlej. 2022. *World Economic Forum.* 4 March. Accessed May 15, 2022. https://www.dinardaily.net/t103534-world-economic-forum.*

Kennedy, Duncan, and Karl E. Klare. 1984. "A Bibliography of Critical Legal Studies." *Yale Law Journal* 94 (461).

Khare, Pallavi, Agastya Dev, Bhavya Jha, Diya Agarwal, and Nivya Raghu. 2021. "Measuring Effectiveness of Chatbot to Change Gender Attitudes in Underserved Adolescent Children in India." *Center for International Development at Harvard University.* Accessed March 31, 2022. https://www.hks.harvard.edu/sites/default/files/centers/cid/files/publications/CID_Wiener_Inequality%20Award%20

Research/Pallavi%20Khare%20(1-A).pdf.

King, Ruth. 2018. *Mindful of Race: Transforming Racism from the Inside Out.* Boulder, Colorado: Sounds True.

Kline, George L. 1963. *Alfred North Whitehead: Essays on His Philosophy.* New Jersey: Englewood Cliffs.

Kodaikanal International School. 2021. *Quad Talks I Politics of Meritocracy with Prof. Ajantha Subramanian '86.* 17 March. Accessed February 15, 2022. https://www.youtube.com/watch?v=xNDM6aYx7uM.

Koop, Chacour. 2020. *Smithsonian museum apologizes for saying hard work, rational thought is 'white culture'.* 17 July. Accessed April 30, 2022. https://www.miamiherald.com/news/nation-world/national/article244309587.html.

Koshy, Jacob. 2021. *Coronavirus | A vaccine is a vaccine... regulators never approve a backup, says virologist Shahid Jameel.* 9 January. Accessed May 15, 2022. https://www.thehindu.com/sci-tech/health/a-vaccine-is-a-vaccineregulators-never-approve-a-backup-says-virologist-shahid-jameel/article33537424.ece.

Kramer, Mark R. 2020. *Larry Fink Isn't Going to Read Your Sustainability Report.* 20 January. Accessed May 15, 2022. https://hbr.org/2020/01/larry-fink-isnt-going-to-read-your-sustainability-report.

——. 2019. *The Backlash to Larry Fink's Letter Shows How Far Business Has to Go on Social Responsibility.* 31 January. Accessed May 15, 2022. https://hbr.org/2019/01/the-backlash-to-larry-finks-letter-shows-how-far-business-has-to-go-on-social-responsibility.

Krishnam, Ujjawal. 2021. *The Patriarchal Burden of Indian Liberalism.* 2 October. Accessed May 15, 2022. https://www.greaterkashmir.com/op-ed-2/the-patriarchal-burden-of-indian-liberalism.

Krishnan, Vidya. 2021. *In India, the Last Few Bastions Of The Free Press Stand Guard Against Rising Authoritarianism.* 20 September. Accessed March 31, 2022. https://niemanreports.org/articles/in-india-the-last-few-bastions-of-the-free-press-stand-guard-against-rising-authoritarianism/.

Kudva, Roopa. 2021. *Diversity, Equity and Inclusion: Our promise to our team and our partners.* Accessed May 15, 2022. https://www.omidyarnetwork.in/diversity-equity-inclusion.

Kumar, Avantas. 2020. *Hinduphobia in the Academy.* 15 December. Accessed April 30, 2022. https://indiacurrents.com/hinduphobia-in-the-academy/.

Kumar, Shilpa, Tariq Musthafa, and Aastha Kamra. 2021a. *Our LegalTech Thesis: Building contractual trust in India.* 16 December. Accessed May 15, 2022. https://www.omidyarnetwork.in/insights/our-legaltech-thesis.

Kundu, Prerna. 2020. *Can information lead to better voting decisions? Evidence from information campaigns in India.* 30 March. Accessed May 15, 2022. https://www.povertyactionlab.org/blog/3-30-20/can-information-lead-better-voting-decisions-evidence-information-campaigns-india.

Kunhappa, Murkot. 1988. *Sree Narayana Guru.* New Delhi: National Book Trust.

Kuo, Rachel, and Alice Marwick. 2021. *Critical disinformation studies: History, power, and politics.* 12 August. Accessed March 31, 2022. doi:https://doi.org/10.37016/mr-2020-76.

Kynge, James. 2021. *Xinjiang officials overseeing detention camps studied at Harvard.* 19 October. Accessed March 31, 2022. https://www.ft.com/content/39404813-472c-455d-98d6-60aa865033d0.

Lam, Jeffie, and Kimmy Chung. 2018. *University of Texas at Austin rejects funding from Hong Kong-based foundation, citing its links to Communist Party.* 15 January. Accessed March 31, 2022. https://www.scmp.com/news/hong-kong/education/article/2128338/university-texas-austin-rejects-funding-hong-kong-based.

Law and Society Alliance. 2021. "Mapping Chinese Footprints and Influence Operations in India." *Defence.Capital.* August. Accessed May 15, 2022. https://defence.capital/wp-content/uploads/2021/09/MAPPING-CHINESE-FOOTPRINTS-AND-INFLUENCE-OPERATIONS-IN-INDIA2.pdf.

Law, Bimal Churn. 1943. *Tribes in Ancient India.* 1st. Poona: Bhandarkar Oriental Research Institute.

Leung, Russel. 2021. *Harvard researcher and NU profs. discuss Black and Dalit community solidarity.* 6 May. Accessed February 15, 2022. https://dailynorthwestern.com/2021/05/07/campus/harvard-researcher-and-nu-profs-discuss-black-and-dalit-community-solidarity/.

Levi, Scott C. 2002. "Hindus beyond the Hindu Kush: Indians in the Central Asian slave trade." *Journal of the Royal Asiatic Society* 12 (3): 277-288.

LIA SPINPER. 2019a. *About : SPINPER.* Accessed May 15, 2022. http://liaspinper.com/.

——. 2019c. *About the Project.* Accessed May 15, 2022. http://liaspinper.com/about-the-project/.

——. 2019e. *Berkeley, October 2018.* Accessed May 15, 2022. http://liaspinper.com/berkeley-october-2018/.

——. 2019d. *Data.* Accessed May 15, 2022. http://liaspinper.com/data/.

——. 2019b. *Paris, 24-25th June – LIASPINPER.* Accessed May 15, 2022. http://liaspinper.com/paris-24-25th-june/.

——. 2019f. *Sonipat, 21 December 2018.* Accessed May 15, 2022. http://liaspinper.com/sonipat-21-december-2018/.

Linda Hall Library. 2022. *Iris Yellum (Travel Fellow, 2020-21).* Accessed April 30, 2022. https://www.lindahall.org/fellow-iris-yellum/.

Liu, Rebecca. 2019. *Homi K Bhabha: Why we need a new, emotive language of human rights.* 5 November. Accessed April 30, 2022. https://www.prospectmagazine.co.uk/arts-and-books/homi-k-bhabha-interview-degradation-populism-immigration-postcolonialism-ica.

Liu, Siqi, and Hellary Y. Zhang. 2016. *School of Public Health Opens Research Center In Mumbai.* 16 January. Accessed March 31, 2022. https://www.thecrimson.com/article/2016/1/16/public-health-center-mumbai/.

Lok Dhaba. 2022. *2022 Assembly Elections at a glance.* Accessed May 15, 2022. https://lokdhaba.ashoka.edu.in/dash.

Longer, Victor. 1981. *Forefront Forever: The History of the Mahar Regiment.* Saugar: Mahar Regiment Centre.

Lord, Michael. 2021. *Exposed: Klaus Schwab's School For Covid Dictators, Plan for 'Great Reset' (Videos).* 10 November. Accessed May 15, 2022. https://rairfoundation.com/exposed-klaus-schwabs-school-for-covid-dictators-plan-for-great-reset-videos/.

Luce, Dan De. 2021. *U.S. universities retain ties to Chinese universities that support Beijing's military buildup, new report says.* 10 December. Accessed April 30, 2022. https://www.nbcnews.com/politics/national-security/us-universities-retain-ties-chinese-schools-support-chinas-military-bu-rcna8249.

Luminate. 2019. *New Media Ventures casts a wide net to defend democracy in the U.S.* 8 May. Accessed May 15, 2022. https://luminategroup.com/posts/blog/new-media-ventures-casts-a-wide-net-to-defend-democracy-in-the-us .

MacArthur Foundation. 2022. *Pulitzer Center on Crisis Reporting.* Accessed March 31, 2022. https://www.macfound.org/grantee/pulitzer-center-on-crisis-reporting-41986/.

Macropolis. 2015. *Mohammed Abdul Latif Jameel.* 5 May. Accessed May 15, 2022. https://marcopolis.net/mohammed-abdul-latif-jameel.htm.

Mahaprashasta, Ajoy Ashirwad. 2020. *Not Hindu Nationalism, But Society That Has Changed': Christophe Jaffrelot.* 25 January. Accessed May 15, 2022. https://thewire.in/religion/christophe-jaffrelot-rss-narendra-modi.

Mahavir. 2001. *Vaidik Arthvyavastha.* New Delhi: Samaanantar Prakashan.

Mahindra Humanities Center. 2020. *Indian Sex Life: Durba Mitra in conversation with Lisa Lowe and Sharon Marcus.* 17 March. Accessed April 30, 2022. https://www.youtube.com/watch?v=PQ7-_pOSpAA.

Majumdar, R.C. 1971. *History of Ancient Bengal.* Calcutta: G. Bharadwaj & Company.

——. 2001. *The Age of Imperial Unity - History and Culture of Indian People.* 7th. Vol. 2. Bharatiya Vidya Bhavan.

Malhotra, Rajiv. 2021. *Artificial Intelligence and the Future of Power: 5 Battlegrounds.* New Delhi: Rupa Publications India.

——. 2022a. *Open letter to Senator Cory Booker.* 1 January. Accessed April 30, 2022. https://www.linkedin.com/posts/rajivmalhotra2007_open-letter-to-senator-cory-booker-11-activity-6883190755465154560-yXhe/.

——. 2016. *The Battle For Sanskrit.* Noida: HarperCollins Publishers India.

——. 2022b. *The Peer-Review Cartel.* 3 February. Accessed April 30, 2022. https://www.outlookindia.com/website/story/the-peer-review-cartel/222822.

Malhotra, Rajiv, and Aravindan Neelakandan. 2011. *Breaking India: Western Interventions in Dravidian and Dalit Faultlines.* New Delhi: Amaryllis.

Malhotra, Rajiv, and Satyanarayana Dasa Babaji. 2020. *Sanskrit Non-Translatables: The Importance of Sanskritizing English.* New Delhi: Amaryllis.

Maqbool, Majid, and Raqib Hameed Naik. 2017. *India's far-right turns hostile toward Rohingya refugees.* 28 June. Accessed March 31, 2022. https://www.trtworld.com/magazine/india-s-far-right-turns-hostile-toward-rohingya-refugees-8327 .

Marcus, Adam. 2021. *Harvard journal retracts paper on Black advocacy in elections.*

22 December. Accessed March 31, 2022. https://retractionwatch.com/2021/12/22/harvard-journal-retracts-paper-on-black-advocacy-in-elections/.

Marcuse, Herbert. 1964. *One-Dimensional Man: Studies in the Ideology of Advanced Industrial Society* . Boston: Beacon Press.

Martin, Phillip, Tinku Ray, and Kavita Pillay. 2019. *Caste Discrimination in the USA: A Public Radio and Online Series.* 25 February. Accessed March 31, 2022. https://pulitzercenter.org/projects/caste-discrimination-usa-public-radio-and-online-series.

Martin, Phillip, Tinku Ray, Kavita Pillay, and Kayla Edwards. 2020. *Caste in America' Receives 2020 Gabriel Award.* 27 May. Accessed March 31, 2022. https://pulitzercenter.org/blog/caste-america-receives-2020-gabriel-award.

Massa, Annie, and Caleb Melby. 2020. *In Fink We Trust: BlackRock Is Now 'Fourth Branch of Government'.* 21 May. Accessed May 15, 2022. https://www.bloomberg.com/news/articles/2020-05-21/how-larry-fink-s-blackrock-is-helping-the-fed-with-bond-buying.

McClish, Mark, and Patrick Olivelle. 2012. *The Arthasastra: Selections from the Classic Indian Work on Statecraft.* Indianapolis: Hackett Publishing Company Inc.

Meet the Founders. 2017. *Sanjeev Bikhchandani and Ashish Dhawan | Meet the Founders, Ashoka University.* 29 November. Accessed May 15, 2022. https://www.youtube.com/watch?v=eE0eLYrbJWo.

Mehta, Malika Noor. 2016. *How Weddings Condemn India's Poorest to Bonded Labor.* 8 August. Accessed March 31, 2022. https://ksr.hkspublications.org/2016/08/08/how-weddings-condemn-indias-poorest-to-bonded-labor/.

Mehta, Pratap Bhanu. 2016. *An act of tyranny: 'Modi govt threatened democracy; that is the most anti-national of all acts'.* 16 February. Accessed May 15, 2022. https://indianexpress.com/article/opinion/columns/jnu-sedition-case-kanhaiya-kumar-arrest-afzal-guru-event/ .

Menon, A. Sreedhara. 2011. *Kerala History and Its Makers.* New Delhi: DC Books.

Merrigan, Tara W. 2010. *International Giving Increases, Especially from India's Tata.* 28 October. Accessed March 31, 2022. https://www.thecrimson.com/article/2010/10/28/business-school-harvard-donations/.

Metcalf, Hilary, and Heather Rolfe. 2010. "Caste discrimination and harassment in Great Britain." *National Institute of Economic and Social Research.* December. https://www.niesr.ac.uk/wp-content/uploads/2021/10/caste-discrimination.pdf.

Mint. 2021. *Mentoring the leaders of tomorrow.* 2 July. Accessed March 31, 2022. https://www.livemint.com/brand-stories/mentoring-the-leaders-of-tomorrow-11625201641694.html.

Mishra, Pankaj. 2014. *Nandan Nilekani reboots eGovernments Foundation.* 20 November. Accessed May 15, 2022. https://economictimes.indiatimes.com/industry/services/education/nandan-nilekani-reboots-egovernments-foundation/articleshow/45199769.cms.

Mission Kaali. 2020. *HOW RONEN SEN MISUSED HIS POSITION TO GRANT VISAS FOR CHRISTIAN MISSIONARIES IN INDIA.* 9 April. Accessed March 31, 2022. https://missionkaali.org/how-ronen-sen-misused-his-position-to-grant-visas-for-christian-missionaries-in-india/.

MIT News Office. 2014. *MIT alumnus Mohammed Abdul Latif Jameel gives major gift to solve urgent challenges in world food and water security.* 6 May. Accessed May 15, 2022. https://news.mit.edu/2014/mohammed-abdul-latif-jameel-gives-major-gift-to-solve-food-water-issues-0506.

Mitchell, Joshua. 2019. *Dead Conservative Memes Can't Defeat the Identity Politics Clerisy.* 6 June. Accessed April 30, 2022. https://americanmind.org/salvo/dead-conservative-memes-cant-defeat-the-identity-politics-clerisy/ .

Mittal Institute. 2013. *Harvard without Borders: Mapping the Kumbh Mela.* 1 May. Accessed March 31, 2022. https://www.youtube.com/watch?v=8T1boAZX-8M2.

——. 2016. *The 1947 Partition of British India: The Demographic and Humanitarian Consequences.* 13 May. Accessed March 31, 2022. https://www.youtube.com/watch?v=fTAddznUy-w.

Mohan, Moulshri, and Anna Rego. 2020. *Measuring social attitudes and norms in impact evaluations: Examples from India.* 13 March. Accessed May 15, 2022. https://www.povertyactionlab.org/blog/3-13-20/measuring-social-attitudes-and-norms-impact-evaluations-examples-india.

Mohanty, Sachidananda. 2005. *Towards a global cultural citizenship.* 3 July. Accessed March 31, 2022. https://web.archive.org/web/20050706092138/http://www.hindu.com/lr/2005/07/03/stories/2005070300020100.htm.

MOJO STORY. 2020. *Testimony on CAA and Religious freedom in India at United States Commission Hearing.* 8 March. Accessed March 31, 2022. https://www.youtube.com/watch?v=pmDbrooDvck.

Mookerji, Radha Kumud. 1969. *Ancient Indian Education.* 4th. New Delhi: Motilal Banarsidass.

Moshik Temkin @moshik_temkin. 2020. *Thanks for the reminder. This has nothing to do with Biden's xenophobic ad, which did not mention it. The state of the Uighurs - like the state of the Palestinians, or of Muslims in India - is something that does not interest the Democratic Party leadership in the slightest.* 20 April. Accessed March 31, 2022. https://twitter.com/moshik_temkin/status/1252036147066347522.

Mukherjee, Shubham. 2010. *Mahindra gifts alma mater Harvard $10 m.* 4 October. Accessed April 30, 2022. https://timesofindia.indiatimes.com/business/india-business/Mahindra-gifts-alma-mater-Harvard-10-m/articleshow/6680909.cms.

Mukherji, Anahita. 2021. *California's Legal Ground in Battling Caste Discrimination Takes Centre Stage in Historic Cisco Case.* 10 March. Accessed February 15, 2022. https://thewire.in/caste/cisco-case-caste-discrimination-silicon-valley-ambedkar-organisations.

Munshi, Kaivan, and Mark R. Rosenzweig. 2005. "Why is Mobility in India so Low? Social Insurance, Inequality, and Growth." *Center for International Development at Harvard University.* July. Accessed March 31, 2022. https://www.hks.harvard.edu/sites/default/files/centers/cid/files/publications/faculty-working-papers/121.pdf.

Musthafa, Tariq, Shilpa Kumar, and Nandan Sharalaya. 2022a. *Building Digital Rails for Urban India – Why We Invested in eGovernments Foundation.* 2 February. Accessed May

15, 2022. https://www.omidyarnetwork.in/blog/why-we-invested-in-egovernments-foundation.

Nadkarni, M. V. 2003. "Is Caste System Intrinsic to Hinduism? Demolishing a Myth." *Economic and Political Weekly* (Economic and Political Weekly) 38 (45): 4783-4793. Accessed February 15, 2022.

Najar, Nida. 2017. *India Picks Ram Nath Kovind, of Caste Once Called 'Untouchables,' as President.* 20 July. Accessed April 30, 2022. https://www.nytimes.com/2017/07/20/world/asia/india-dalit-president-ram-nath-kovind.html .

Nambiar, Nayanika, and Parmesh Shahani. 2018. "A Manifesto for Trans Inclusion in the Indian Workplace." *Godrej India Culture Lab.* December. Accessed May 15, 2022. https://indiaculturelab.org/assets/Uploads/Godrej-India-Culture-Lab-Trans-Inclusion-Manifesto-Paper3.pdf.

Nanda, Meera. 2001. "We are all hybrids now: The dangerous epistemology of post-colonial populism." *The Journal of Peasant Studies* 28 (2): 162-186. doi:https://doi.org/10.1080/03066150108438770.

Nanda, Prashant K. 2021. *Ashoka University to raise Rs. 1.5K crore for expansion.* 8 September. Accessed May 15, 2022. https://www.livemint.com/education/news/ashoka-university-to-raise-1-5k-crore-for-expansion-11631121634731.html .

National Association of Science Writers. 2021. *NASW Diversity Reporting Grant recipients for 2021 announced.* 2 December. Accessed May 15, 2022. https://www.nasw.org/article/nasw-diversity-reporting-grant-recipients-2021-announced.

National Foundation For India. 2019. *Who we are | National Foundation For India.* 20 July. Accessed May 15, 2022. https://www.nfi.org.in/who-we-are/#link-115.

Navayana. 2012. *A Gardener in the Wasteland.* 10 October. Accessed May 15, 2022. https://navayana.org/books/2012/10/10/a-gardener-in-the-wasteland-2/?v=7516fd43adaa .

NBC News@NBCNews. 2021. *The University of Maryland is facing backlash after an administrative graphic separated students into two categories — "students of color, minus Asians" and "white or Asian students.".* 20 November. Accessed April 30, 2022. https://twitter.com/NBCNews/status/1461844255027175425.

Neelotpal, S. 2013. *Meera Padavali.* Delhi: Prabhat Prakashan.

Neuman, Scott, and Cory Turner. 2020. *Harvard, Yale Accused Of Failing To Report Hundreds Of Millions In Foreign Donations.* 13 February. Accessed April 30, 2022. https://www.npr.org/2020/02/13/805548681/harvard-yale-targets-of-education-department-probe-into-foreign-donations.

Nevradakis, Michael. 2022. *Bill Gates, Indian Government Targeted in Lawsuit Alleging AstraZeneca Vaccine Killed 23-Year-Old.* 20 January. Accessed May 15, 2022. https://childrenshealthdefense.org/defender/bill-gates-indian-government-lawsuit-astrazeneca-vaccine-killed-shri-hitesh-kadve/.

New Discourses. 2021. *Groomer Schools 2: Queer Futurity and the Sexual Abuse of Your Children.* 25 November. Accessed May 15, 2022. https://www.youtube.com/watch?v=-OQL1Jja3p4.

——. 2022. *Paulo Freire's Politics of Education and a New Hope.* 18 January. Accessed May 15, 2022. https://www.youtube.com/watch?v=v2aGMCpgpjU.

New Venture Fund. 2021. *Catalytic Capital Consortium Announces Awards to 14 Research Projects.* 13 October. Accessed May 15, 2022. https://newventurefund.org/for-grant-seekers/c3grantmaking/catalytic-capital-consortium-announces-awards/.

Nextshark - Editorial Staff. 2019. *At Least 25 Global Brands Have Apologized to China Since 2017.* 14 October. Accessed April 30, 2022. https://nextshark.com/global-brands-apologize-to-china/.

NFI. 2019. *Impact.* 20 July. Accessed April 30, 2022. https://www.nfi.org.in/impact.

Nieman Foundation for Journalism at Harvard. 2021a. *India's Caravan Magazine wins the Louis M. Lyons Award for Conscience and Integrity in Journalism.* 8 February. Accessed March 31, 2022. https://nieman.harvard.edu/news/2021/02/indias-caravan-magazine-wins-louis-lyons-award-for-conscience-integrity-journalism/.

——. 2017. *Nieman Foundation announces 2017 Knight Visiting Nieman Fellows.* 7 February. Accessed May 15, 2022. https://nieman.harvard.edu/news/2017/02/nieman-foundation-announces-2017-knight-visiting-nieman-fellows/.

——. 2021b. *Nieman Foundation for Journalism - Class of 2022.* 25 May. Accessed March 31, 2022. https://nieman.harvard.edu/alumni/class-of-2022/.

——. 2020. *Nieman Foundation for Journalism at Harvard announces fellows in the class of 2020-2021.* 22 July. Accessed March 31, 2022. https://nieman.harvard.edu/news/2020/07/nieman-foundation-for-journalism-announces-2021-fellows/.

——. 2010. *Nieman Foundation, Pulitzer Center join forces to strengthen global health reporting.* 7 September. Accessed March 31, 2022. https://nieman.harvard.edu/news/2010/09/nieman-foundation-pulitzer-center-join-forces-to-strengthen-global-health-reporting/.

NiemanLab. 2021. *India's Caravan Magazine wins the Louis M. Lyons Award for Conscience and Integrity in Journalism.* 10 February. Accessed March 31, 2022. https://www.niemanlab.org/reading/indias-caravan-magazine-wins-the-louis-m-lyons-award-for-conscience-and-integrity-in-journalism/.

NiemanReports. 2014. *About Nieman Reports.* 8 January. Accessed March 31, 2022. https://niemanreports.org/about-nieman-reports/.

Nietzel, Michael T. 2022. *MIT Receives $100 Million Gift To Form New Multidisciplinary Design Center.* 17 March. Accessed April 30, 2022. https://www.forbes.com/sites/michaeltnietzel/2022/03/17/mit-receives-100-million-gift-to-form-new-multidisciplinary-design-center/?sh=5a9ed7193526.

Nitnaware, Himanshu. 2015. *Condom shortage: Jitters in Nashik ahead of Kumbh | India News - Times of India.* 4 July. Accessed March 31, 2022. http://timesofindia.indiatimes.com/india/Condom-shortage-Jitters-in-Nashik-ahead-of-Kumbh/articleshow/47932804.cms.

North Star Fund. 2017. *North Star Fund Rapid Response Grants 2016-17.* 8 November. Accessed February 15, 2022. https://northstarfund.org/2017/11/north-star-fund-rapid-response-grants-2016-17/.

Nussbaum, Martha C. 2009. *The Clash Within: Democracy, Religious Violence, and India's Future.* Harvard: Harvard University Press.

Observer Research Foundation. 2020. *Jayant Sinha: Chairperson, Standing Committee on*

Finance and Member of Parliament, India. 1 April. Accessed April 30, 2022. https://www.orfonline.org/about/jayant-sinha/.

Office of Foreign Assets Control. 2022. *Sanctions List Search.* Accessed March 31, 2022. https://sanctionssearch.ofac.treas.gov/Details.aspx?id=34119.

Oldmeadow, Harry. 2004. *Journeys East: 20th Century Western Encounters with Eastern Religious Traditions.* Bloomington, Indiana: World Wisdom.

Olivelle, Patrick. 2000. *Dharmasutras.* New Delhi: Motilal Banarsidass.

——. 2005. *Manu's Code of Law.* New York: Oxford University Press.

Omidyar Network. 2020. *CV Madhukar: Managing Director, Beneficial Technology.* Accessed April 30, 2022. https://omidyar-network.jjzizzr3-liquidwebsites.com/omidyar-team/cv-madhukar/.

Omidyar Network India. 2021b. *Bijak | Increasing farmers' income across 28+ states and 1000+ regions of India.* Accessed May 15, 2022. https://www.omidyarnetwork.in/theboldones/bijak.

——. 2020b. *Centre for Social and Behaviour Change (CSBC).* Accessed May 15, 2022. https://www.omidyarnetwork.in/investees/centre-for-social-and-behaviour-change.

——. 2021a. *Centre for Social Impact and Philanthropy (CSIP).* Accessed May 15, 2022. https://www.omidyarnetwork.in/centre-for-social-impact-philanthropy-ashoka-university.

——. 2021f. *CredR | Offering independence and ease of travel through the medium of used motorcycles.* Accessed May 15, 2022. https://www.omidyarnetwork.in/theboldones/credr.

——. 2020d. *Data Security Council of India.* Accessed May 15, 2022. https://www.omidyarnetwork.in/data-security-council-of-india.

——. 2021c. *Doubtnut | India's most used education platform.* Accessed May 15, 2022. https://www.omidyarnetwork.in/theboldones/doubtnut.

——. 2021d. *EGOV | Technology solutions for better urban governance.* 16 November. Accessed May 15, 2022. https://www.omidyarnetwork.in/theboldones/egov.

——. 2021e. *FES | Giving local villagers property rights across 9 million acres.* Accessed May 15, 2022. https://www.omidyarnetwork.in/theboldones/fes.

——. 2020c. *GiveIndia.* Accessed May 15, 2022. https://www.omidyarnetwork.in/giveindia.

——. 2021g. *Indian Institute of Science.* Accessed May 15, 2022. https://www.omidyarnetwork.in/indian-institute-of-science.

——. 2019a. *Investments that drive empowerment and social impact at scale.* Accessed May 15, 2022. https://www.omidyarnetwork.in/.

——. 2021h. *Jan Sahas | Working for India's most marginalized communities.* 16 November. Accessed May 15, 2022. https://www.omidyarnetwork.in/theboldones/jan-sahas.

——. 2019b. *Janaagraha Centre for Citizenship & Democracy.* Accessed May 15, 2022. https://www.omidyarnetwork.in/investees/janaagraha.

——. 2019c. *NewsLaundry.* Accessed May 15, 2022. https://www.omidyarnetwork.in/investees/newslaundry.

——. 2022a. *Omidyar Network India's Post - The Indian Express Thinc Migration series.*

20 January. Accessed May 15, 2022. https://www.linkedin.com/posts/omidyar-network-india_migration-migrationinindia-migrants-activity-6889827276704366592-v6n1.

——. 2020a. *Omidyar Network India's ReSolve Initiative: Next phase of response to Covid-19 focuses on migration and MSMEs.* 22 July. Accessed May 15, 2022. https://www.omidyarnetwork.in/blog/omidyar-network-indias-resolve-initiative-next-phase-of-response-to-covid-19-focusses-on-migration-and-msme .

——. 2021i. *Sitara | Affordable housing loans to low-income women borrowers.* 17 November. Accessed May 15, 2022. https://www.omidyarnetwork.in/theboldones/sitara.

——. 2021j. *The Community Infrastructure Fund for Mutual Aid.* Accessed May 15, 2022. https://omidyar.com/the-community-infrastructure-fund-for-mutual-aid/.

——. 2022c. *Vedantu | India's first LIVE online interactive K-12 education platform.* Accessed May 15, 2022. https://www.omidyarnetwork.in/theboldones/vedantu.

——. 2020e. *Village Capital.* Accessed May 15, 2022. https://www.omidyarnetwork.in/investees/village-capital-c.

——. 2022b. *Vividh: A bi-annual newsletter on Diversity, Equity & Inclusion (DEI).* 27 January. Accessed May 15, 2022. https://www.omidyarnetwork.in/blog/vividh-bi-annual-newsletter-on-diversity-equity-inclusion-dei.

Omvedt, Gail. 2003. *Buddhism in India: Challenging Brahmanism and Caste.* New Delhi: Sage Publications.

Online Burma/Myanmar Library. 1998. *Harvard: The Cost of Excellence.* 1 June. Accessed April 30, 2022. https://www.burmalibrary.org/reg.burma/archives/199806/msg00033.html.

OpIndia. 2020a. *Did Amnesty International India have to shut due to Delhi Riots report?* 29 September. Accessed March 31, 2022. https://www.opindia.com/2020/09/fact-check-amnesty-international-shut-operations-india-report-delhi-riots/.

——. 2021a. *ED probe reveals Chinese funding to Newsclick, Elgar Parishad case accused Gautam Navlakha also one of the beneficiaries: Details.* 18 July. Accessed March 31, 2022. https://www.opindia.com/2021/07/ed-newsclick-china-funding-gautam-navlakha-prabir-purkayastha/.

——. 2020b. *Hussain Haidry rues inaction by 'progressive non-Muslims' for not protesting against the construction of Ram Mandir in Ayodhya.* 4 August. Accessed March 31, 2022. https://www.opindia.com/2020/08/hussain-haidry-progressive-non-muslims-construction-of-ram-mandir-in-ayodhya/.

OpIndia Staff. 2022. *'Maulana will decide about hijab and not Judge': What ex-Chief Election Commissioner Dr SY Quraishi said on love jihad, hijab, and Kashmiri Pandits.* 26 March. Accessed May 15, 2022. https://www.opindia.com/2022/03/former-chief-election-commissioner-sy-quraishi-love-jihad-hijab-yogi-adityanath-kashmiri-pandits/.

——. 2021a. *Ashoka University Assistant Professor mocks Lord Ram while trying to troll President of India over false accusations.* 25 January. Accessed May 15, 2022. https://www.opindia.com/2021/01/neelanjan-sircar-ashoka-university-mocks-lord-ram-president-kovind-netaji-portrait/.

———. 2021. *How George Soros is fueling a dangerous anti-India narrative through media and 'civil society'.* 18 July. Accessed May 15, 2022. https://www.opindia.com/2021/07/how-george-soros-fund-open-society-foundation-anti-india-narrative-media-ngos/.

———. 2020. *Unmasking Care India: A Board member with accusations of involvement in fraud, soliciting funds in the name of GoI and funding evangelical organisations.* 29 June. Accessed May 15, 2022. https://www.opindia.com/2020/06/care-india-evangelical-organisations-fcra-neera-saggi-mani-shankar-aiyer-daughter/.

OpIndia. 2021b. *The Wire journalist Arfa Khanum Sherwani compares Nazi Germany with India in 2020, netizens explain the difference.* 17 January. Accessed March 31, 2022. https://www.opindia.com/2020/01/arfa-khanum-sherwani-nazi-germany-india-2020-compare/.

———. 2021c. *When 'activist' Teesta Setalvad was accused financial fraud and embezzling money meant for Godhra riot victims.* 30 May. Accessed March 31, 2022. https://www.opindia.com/2021/05/teesta-setalvad-was-accused-of-fraud-in-the-name-of-gujarat-riot-victims/.*

Outlook Web Desk. 2021. *Harvard's Biggest Dalit Voice Unhappy After Its New Caste Sensitive Policy, Here's Why.* 4 December. Accessed February 15, 2022. https://www.outlookindia.com/website/story/harvards-biggest-dalit-voice-unhappy-after-new-caste-sensitive-policy-heres-why-suraj-yengde-instagram/403707.

Pandey, Alpana. 2015. *Medieval Andhra: A Socio-Historical Perspective.* Partridge India.

Pandurangi, K.T. 1999. *Indian Thought on Human Values.* 2nd. Bangalore: Bharatiya Vidya Bhavan.

Parade. 2020. *Meet Mr. Mindfulness: How Jon Kabat-Zinn Brought Mindfulness to the Masses.* 22 April. Accessed April 30, 2022. https://parade.com/717983/parade/meet-mr-mindfulness-how-jon-kabat-zinn-brought-mindfulness-to-the-masses/amp/.

Parasa, Rajeswari. 2021a. *Status Quo of Spatial Datasets of Health Facilities in India.* 29 April. Accessed May 15, 2022. https://www.idfcinstitute.org/blog/2021/april/status-quo-of-spatial-datasets-of-health-facilities-in-india/.

PARI - People's Archive of Rural India. 2021b. *In 2014-15, only about 0.24% of front page news came out of rural India. We want to change that.* Accessed March 31, 2022. https://ruralindiaonline.org/en/pages/donate/.

———. 2021a. *Rural India: a living journal, a breathing archive.* Accessed March 31, 2022. https://ruralindiaonline.org/en/pages/about/.

PARI Education - People's Archive of Rural India. 2020a. *A one-stop resource for students and teachers.* 22 June. Accessed March 31, 2022. https://pari.education/p-sainath/.

———. 2020b. *Participating organisations.* Accessed March 31, 2022. https://pari.education/participating-institutions/.

PARI Education Team. 2021. *PARI Education years 1, 2 & 3.* 27 August. Accessed March 31, 2022. https://pari.education/articles/pari-education-years-1-2-3/.

PARI Education. 2020. *What is a PARI Education.* 17 June. Accessed April 30, 2022. https://pari.education/what-is-a-pari-education/.

Parkin, Siodhbhra. 2019. *How China Regulates Foreign Non-Governmental Organizations.*

27 August. Accessed March 31, 2022. https://www.chinafile.com/ngo/latest/how-china-regulates-foreign-non-governmental-organizations.

Pathak, Priya. 2019a. *NRC protests: Wipro celebrates company's role in NRC project in Assam, first deletes page then restores it.* 23 December. Accessed May 15, 2022. https://www.indiatoday.in/technology/news/story/wipro-celebrates-its-role-in-nrc-project-in-assam-first-deletes-page-then-restores-it-1630865-2019-12-23 .

Patnaik, Sasmita, and Shaily Jha. 2020. *Caste, Class and Gender in Determining Access to Energy.* June. Accessed May 15, 2022. https://www.ceew.in/publications/caste-class-and-gender-determining-access-energy.

Patrick, Jim. 2021. *Infiltrating America: China paid DC-based radio station millions to air Chinese propaganda.* 24 December. Accessed April 30, 2022. https://www.lawenforcementtoday.com/infiltrating-america-china-paid-dc-based-radio-station-millions-to-air-chinese-propaganda/.

Pelaez, Eduardo. 2019. *(Slum)scapes of adaptation Weak Grounds, Risk Ecologies, Community Initiatives.* Accessed March 31, 2022. https://www.gsd.harvard.edu/project/slumscapes-of-adaptation-weak-grounds-risk-ecologies-community-initiatives/.

Perna, Laura W. 2018. *Taking it to the Streets: The role of scholarship in advocacy and advocacy in scholarship.* Baltimore: Johns Hopkins University Press.

Peters, Ann. 2010. *Nieman Foundation and Pulitzer Center join forces to strengthen global health reporting.* 7 September. Accessed March 31, 2022. https://pulitzercenter.org/blog/nieman-foundation-and-pulitzer-center-join-forces-strengthen-global-health-reporting.

Philanthropy News Digest. 2016. *Harvard, Tata Companies Announce $8.4 Million Research Partnership.* 30 August. Accessed April 30, 2022. https://philanthropynewsdigest.org/news/harvard-tata-companies-announce-8.4-million-research-partnership.

Philip, Sneha. 2018. *IDR Shorts | Philanthropy's role in rights-based advocacy.* 19 December. Accessed May 15, 2022. https://idronline.org/idr-shorts-philanthropys-role-in-rights-based-advocacy/ .

PIB Delhi. 2020. *NITI Aayog Launches Behaviour Change Campaign, 'Navigating the New Normal',and Website (Essential focus on mask-wearing by all).* 15 June. Accessed May 15, 2022. https://pib.gov.in/PressReleasePage.aspx?PRID=1634328 .

Pluckrose, Helen, and James A. Lindsay. 2020. *Cynical Theories: How Activist Scholarship Made Everything about Race, Gender, and Identity—and Why This Harms Everybody.* Durham: Pitchstone Publishing.

Pocket News Alert. 2016. *Ashoka University, Wellesley College partnership commences with student exchange programme.* 1 April. Accessed May 15, 2022. https://www.pocketnewsalert.com/2016/04/Ashoka-University-Wellesley-College-partnership-commences-with-student-exchange-programme.html.

Porayouw, William. 2022. *Yale looks to India and South Asia as global research expands.* 17 February. Accessed May 15, 2022. https://yaledailynews.com/blog/2022/02/17/yale-looks-to-india-and-south-asia-as-global-research-expands/.

Poynter. 2017. *Meet the tiny nonprofit behind the world's most ambitious journalism.*

21 March. Accessed March 31, 2022. https://www.poynter.org/reporting-editing/2017/the-tiny-nonprofit-behind-the-worlds-most-ambitious-journalism/.

Pratap, Rashmi. 2017. *'Now we have a tit-for-tat democracy'.* 8 September. Accessed March 31, 2022. https://www.thehindubusinessline.com/blink/know/now-we-have-a-titfortat-democracy/article9850190.ece.

Pratilipi. 2014. *About | Pratilipi.* Accessed May 15, 2022. https://www.pratilipi.com/about.

Professional Assistance for Development Action. 2021. *PRADAN - Professional Assistance for Development Action.* 10 February. Accessed May 15, 2022. https://www.pradan.net/.

Pulitzer Center. 2016. *Meet the Journalist: George Black.* 18 July. Accessed March 31, 2022. https://www.youtube.com/watch?v=GVnaiBdIjdE.

Pullanoor, Harish. 2021. *Dangerous Attack: Yale, MIT, Harvard Academics On Pratap Bhanu Mehta's Ashoka Exit.* 20 March. Accessed May 15, 2022. https://www.ndtv.com/india-news/yale-mit-harvard-academics-on-pratap-bhanu-mehtas-ashoka-university-exit-2394968.

Purser, Ron. 2017. *The Branding of Mindfulness.* 16 December. Accessed March 31, 2022. https://www.huffpost.com/entry/the-branding-of-mindfulness_b_5a35a283e4b02bd1c8c60750.

Radhakrishnan, S. 1953. *The Principal Upanishads.* New Delhi: Harper Collins.

Rai, Siddhartha. 2018. *Rahul Gandhi retains Harvard professor Steve Jarding's services to trump Modi in 2019 polls.* 1 September. Accessed March 31, 2022. https://www.mynation.com/news/rahul-gandhi-congress-bjp-steve-jarding-narendra-modi-bjp-samajwadi-party-pedtx6.

Rajadhyaksha, Niranjan. 2017. *Big Data enters Indian policy.* 16 August. Accessed May 15, 2022. https://www.livemint.com/Opinion/qSvFZxqhXBgWTmw0AARdeP/Big-Data-enters-Indian-policy.html.

Rajan, Kalyani, Shilpa Rao, Sofia Imad, and Anushka Bhansali. 2021c. *Covid-19 Vaccine Acceptance Communication Campaign.* 27 September. Accessed May 15, 2022. https://www.idfcinstitute.org/projects/state-capacity/covid-vaccine-acceptance/.

Rajgarhia, Sanjana. 2020. "Media Manipulation in the Indian Context: An Analysis of Kashmir-Related Discourse on Twitter." *Harvard Kennedy School, Mossavar - Rahmani Center for Business and Government.* June. Accessed March 31, 2022. https://www.hks.harvard.edu/sites/default/files/centers/mrcbg/files/Final_AWP_147.pdf.

Raman, A. Ragu. 2022. *'Reaching out to rural talent, homegrown technology to be priority of IIT Madras'.* 21 January. Accessed May 15, 2022. https://timesofindia.indiatimes.com/city/chennai/reaching-out-to-rural-talent-homegrown-technology-to-be-priority-of-iit-madras/articleshow/89034539.cms.

Ramaswamy, Vivek. 2021. *Woke, Inc.: Inside Corporate America's Social Justice Scam.* New York: Hachette Book Group.

Ramteke, D.L. 1983. *Revival of Buddhism in Modern India.* New Delhi: Deep and Deep.

Ramzy, Austin. 2017. *Asia Society Blames Staff for Barring Hong Kong Activist's Speech.* 7 July. Accessed March 31, 2022. https://www.nytimes.com/2017/07/07/world/asia/

hong-kong-joshua-wong-censorship.html.

Rao, C. Hayavadana. 1936. *The Srikara Bhashya: Being the Virasaiva commentary on the Vedanta Sutras by Sripati.* Bangalore: Bangalore Press.

Rao, Raj. 2021. *Exclusive: Santa Clara County Human Rights Commission to hold hearing on caste.* 29 April. Accessed February 15, 2022. https://diyatvusa.com/2021/04/29/exclusive-santa-clara-county-human-rights-commission-to-hold-hearing-on-caste/.

Rao, Sunitha R. 2021. *Govt to generate unique health IDs for people giving Aadhaar for vaccination.* 11 January. Accessed May 15, 2022. https://timesofindia.indiatimes.com/india/govt-to-generate-unique-health-ids-for-people-giving-aadhaar-for-vaccination/articleshow/80205336.cms.

Rathore, Akash Singh, and Ajay Verma. 2011. *B.R. Ambedkar: The Buddha and his Dhamma – A Critical Edition.* New Delhi: Oxford University Press.

Ray, Rajat Kanta. 2003. *The Felt Community.* New Delhi: Oxford University Press.

Rayman, Noah S., and Elyssa A. L. Spitzer. 2010. *Sanskrit Dept. To Change Name, in Pursuit of Interdisciplinary Work.* 27 May. Accessed March 31, 2022. https://www.thecrimson.com/article/2010/5/27/department-witzel-sanskrit-current/.

Redden, Elizabeth. 2018. *Global Attack on Gender Studies.* 5 December. Accessed May 15, 2022. https://www.insidehighered.com/news/2018/12/05/gender-studies-scholars-say-field-coming-under-attack-many-countries-around-globe.

———. 2017. *Is China Punishing a U.S. University for Hosting the Dalai Lama?* 20 September. Accessed March 31, 2022. https://www.insidehighered.com/news/2017/09/20/china-punishing-american-university-hosting-dalai-lama.

Reilly, Patrick. 2022. *Teammates say they are uncomfortable changing in locker room with trans UPenn swimmer Lia Thomas.* 27 January. Accessed May 15, 2022. https://nypost.com/2022/01/27/teammates-are-uneasy-changing-in-locker-room-with-trans-upenn-swimmer-lia-thomas/.

Reis, Julio C. S., Philipe Melo, Kiran Garimella, and Fabrício Benevenuto. 2020. "Can WhatsApp benefit from debunked fact-checked stories to reduce misinformation?" *Harvard Kennedy School, Misinformation Review.* 20 August. Accessed March 31, 2022. https://misinforeview.hks.harvard.edu/wp-content/uploads/2020/08/WhatsApp_India_Brazil_Copyedited.pdf.

Religious Freedom & Business Foundation. 2021. "New Directions: Global Opportunities for Expanding and Coordinating Religious Freedom Initiatives." *Religious Freedom & Business Foundation.* July. Accessed May 15, 2022. https://religiousfreedomandbusiness.org/wp-content/uploads/2021/07/IRF-Global-Survey-2021-FINAL.pdf.

———. 2019. *Templeton Religion Trust grant helps expand RFBF Asia engagement.* 3 October. Accessed May 15, 2022. https://religiousfreedomandbusiness.org/2/post/2019/10/templeton-religion-trust-grant-helps-expand-rfbf-asia-engagement.html.

Rethinking Economics JNU. 2021. *Interactive Session on Behavioral Research with Dr. Pavan Mamidi.* 3 August. Accessed May 15, 2022. https://www.youtube.com/watch?v=fNq5aGbBH2s .

Reuters. 2019. *From pariah to demigod: Transgender Laxmi becomes a star at Kumbh*

Mela with her Kinnar Akhara. 20 January. Accessed May 15, 2022. https://www. indiatoday.in/india/story/transgender-laxmi-narayan-tripathi-kumbh-mela-kinnar-akhara-1435168-2019-01-20.

Rieder, Rem. 2014. *Rieder: Pierre Omidyar's Ukrainian connection.* 2 March. Accessed May 15, 2022. https://www.usatoday.com/story/money/columnist/rieder/2014/03/02/ flap-over-omidyar-support-for-ukrainian-group/5948821/.

Riley, Donna. 2008. *Engineering and Social Justice.* San Rafael, California: Morgan & Claypool Publishers.

Rising Up With Sonali. 2020. *How India's Caste Discrimination Made it to the USA.* 21 July. Accessed February 15, 2022. https://vimeo.com/440440045.

RNBA Manipur. 2020. *Donors - RNBA Manipur.* Accessed May 15, 2022. https://rnba. in/about-rnba/donors/.

Rodman, Melissa C., and Yehong Zhu. 2015. *Calls for Divestment: A Retrospective.* 27 May. Accessed April 30, 2022. https://www.thecrimson.com/article/2015/5/27/ divest-retrospective-reunion-1990/.

Rodrigues, Shaunna. 2020. *Dalit is the New Political and Epistemic Horizon: An Interview with Suraj Yengde.* 23 November. Accessed February 15, 2022. https://www. borderlines-cssaame.org/posts/2020/11/23/dalit-is-the-new-political-and-epistemic-horizon-an-interview-with-suraj-yengde.

Rosario, Kennith. 2017. *'A populist nationalism is now alive'.* 16 September. Accessed March 31, 2022. https://www.thehindu.com/opinion/interview/a-populist-nationalism-is-now-alive/article19697534.ece.

Rosenbaum, Arthur Lewis. 2012. *New Perspectives on Yenching University 1916-1952: A Liberal Education for a New China.* Leiden, the Netherlands: Brill Academic Publishers.

Ross, Alexander Reid, and Courtney Dobson. 2022. *The Big Business of Uyghur Genocide Denial.* 18 January. Accessed March 31, 2022. https://newlinesmag.com/reportage/ the-big-business-of-uyghur-genocide-denial/.

Ross, Chuck. 2021b. *Brookings Institution Boosts China Initiatives Linked to Board Member.* 1 November. Accessed March 31, 2022. https://freebeacon.com/national-security/brookings-institution-boosts-china-initiatives-linked-to-board-member/.

———. 2021a. *Top California Democrat and Think-Tank Titans Slated to Attend Chinese Communist Diplomacy Event.* 13 May. Accessed March 31, 2022. https://freebeacon. com/national-security/top-california-democrat-and-think-tank-titans-slated-to-attend-chinese-communist-diplomacy-event/.

Roy, Pratap Chandra. 1923. *The Mahabharata of Krishna Dwaipayana Vyasa Volume VIII.* Calcutta: Oriental Publishing Co.

Rozario, Anthony S. 2020. *NEP: US Welcomes Decision to Allow Foreign Universities in India.* 4 August. Accessed May 15, 2022. https://www.thequint.com/news/education/ nep-us-welcomes-decision-to-allow-foreign-universities-in-india.

Rubinstein, Alexander, and Max Blumenthal. 2019. *PIERRE OMIDYAR_ Sultan of Surveillance Valley and Funding Agent for CIA Regime Changes Worldwide.* 11 March. Accessed May 15, 2022. https://themillenniumreport.com/2019/03/pierre-omidyar-sultan-of-surveillance-valley-and-funding-agent-for-cia-regime-changes-worldwide/.

Rudolph, Lloyd I., and Susane Hoeber Rudolph. 1967. *Modernity of Tradition: Political Development in India.* Chicago: University of Chicago Press.

Russell, R.V. 1916. *The Tribes And Castes Of The Central Provinces Of India.* Vol. IV. London: Macmillan.

Saathi Re. 2017. *Harvard Global Research Support Centre India.* Accessed March 31, 2022. https://www.saathire.com/TTQ/harvard-global-research-support-centre-india/.

Sabhikhi, Inayat. 2019. *In Solidarity: Harvard Students Join Indian Demonstrations Against New Citizenship Bill.* 20 December. Accessed March 31, 2022. https://citizen.hkspublications.org/2019/12/20/in-solidarity-harvard-students-join-indian-demonstrations-against-new-citizenship-bill/.

Safikul Hasan. 2018. *Palagummi Sainath Amazing Talk On Rural India.* 25 October. Accessed March 31, 2022. https://www.youtube.com/watch?v=aSlKpLhfVg.

Saha, Sharmistha. 2020. *Rereading History: On Ambedkar's "The Untouchables: Who Were They and Why They Became Untouchables".* 17 October. Accessed February 15, 2022. https://www.allaboutambedkaronline.com/post/an-outline-of-the-untouchables-who-were-they-and-why-they-became-untouchables.

Sambara, Sraavya. 2021. *Caste and Colonialism Beyond the Subcontinent: An Interview with Ajantha Subramanian.* 1 September. Accessed February 15, 2022. https://harvardpolitics.com/caste-and-colonialism-beyond-the-subcontinent-an-interview-with-ajantha-subramanian/.

Samyak Chetna. 2021. *Special Discussion on Ambedkarism Struggle And Budhdhism by Ajahn Sujan With Dr. Suraj Yengde.* 25 June. https://www.youtube.com/watch?v=Zj1_t7slNzU.*

Sanchez, Luis. 2018. *Gap apologizes to China for selling T-shirt with map omitting Taiwan.* 16 May. Accessed April 30, 2022. https://thehill.com/blogs/blog-briefing-room/387984-gap-apologizes-to-china-for-selling-t-shirt-with-map-that-omitted.

Sandel, Michael J. 2020. *The Tyranny of Merit: What's Become of the Common Good?* Farrar, Straus and Giroux.

Sanghamitra. 2018. *Sordid tale of Congress' sanction and hateful anti-Hindu brainwashing of children by Teesta Setalvad.* 29 May. Accessed March 31, 2022. https://www.opindia.com/2018/05/sordid-tale-of-congress-sanction-and-hateful-anti-hindu-brainwashing-of-children-by-teesta-setalvad/.

Sannam S4 Group. 2008. *Sannam S4 Group.* Accessed May 15, 2022. https://sannams4.com/.

Sarma, Ajay. 2020. *Protecting Cows and Persecuting People.* 4 February. Accessed March 31, 2022. https://harvardpolitics.com/protecting-cows/.

Sastri, K. A. Nilakanta. 1987. *A Comprehensive History of India Volume 2.* New Delhi: People's Publishing House.

Satyaagrah. 2022. *George Soros's Open Society Foundation-funded Institute Peace Research Institute Oslo (PRIO) names Open Society functionary Harsh Mander in unofficial shortlist for Nobel prize.* 4 February. Accessed May 15, 2022. https://satyaagrah.com/global/global-news/1231-george-soros%E2%80%99s-open-society-foundation-funded-institute-peace-research-institute-oslo-prio-names-open-society-functionary-harsh-mander-in-unofficial-shortlist-for-nobel-prize .

Schachtel, Jordan. 2022. *The Great Reset, part two: the World Economic Forum's Great Narrative Project*. February. Accessed May 15, 2022. https://dossier.substack.com/p/the-great-reset-part-two-the-world.

Schneider, Christian. 2020. *Stanford accepts $58 million in Chinese cash while pushing global human rights*. 2 July. Accessed March 31, 2022. https://www.thecollegefix.com/stanford-accepts-58-million-in-chinese-cash-while-pushing-global-human-rights/.

Schofield, Hugh. 2021. *France resists US challenge to its values*. 13 December. Accessed April 30, 2022. https://www.bbc.com/news/world-europe-59584125 .

Schwab, Klaus, and Peter Vanham. 2021. *What is stakeholder capitalism?* 22 January. Accessed May 15, 2022. https://www.weforum.org/agenda/2021/01/klaus-schwab-on-what-is-stakeholder-capitalism-history-relevance/.

Schwartz, Natalie. 2018. *MIT report finds no 'compelling case' to cut Saudi ties*. 10 December. Accessed May 15, 2022. https://www.highereddive.com/news/mit-report-finds-no-compelling-case-to-cut-saudi-ties/543938/.

Schweizer, Peter. 2021. *China's US Enablers*. 19 December. Accessed March 31, 2022. https://www.gatestoneinstitute.org/18035/china-us-enablers.

Sciences Po. 2017. *Christophe Jaffrelot*. Accessed May 15, 2022. https://www.sciencespo.fr/ceri/en/cerispire-user/7143/586.

Sensoy, Özlem, and Robin DiAngelo. 2017. *Is Everyone Really Equal?* New York: Teachers College Press.

Shafer, Leah. 2016. *Dismantling Islamophobia*. 23 November. Accessed April 30, 2022. https://www.gse.harvard.edu/news/uk/16/11/dismantling-islamophobia.

Sharma, Ananya. 2021a. *Here's Why India Is Struggling to Be Truly Open Defecation Free*. 28 October. Accessed May 15, 2022. https://thewire.in/government/heres-why-india-is-struggling-to-be-truly-open-defecation-free.

Sharma, Ankita, and Hindol Sengupta. 2020. *COVID-19 has accelerated India's digital reset*. 5 August. Accessed May 15, 2022. https://www.weforum.org/agenda/2020/08/covid-19-has-accelerated-india-s-digital-reset/.

Sharma, Arvind. 2000. *Classical Hindu Thought*. Oxford University Press: New Delhi.

——. 1996. *Hinduism for our Times*. New Delhi: Oxford University Press.

Sharma, Arvind. 2015. "Review of The Pariah Problem: Caste, Religion, and the Social in Modern India by Rupa Viswanath." *International Journal of Dharma Studies* 3 (8): 1-2. doi:https://doi.org/10.1186/s40613-015-0018-0.

Sharma, Kritika. 2017. *Ashoka University says problem with misuse of University name, not Kashmir petition*. 27 March. Accessed May 15, 2022. https://www.dnaindia.com/india/report-ashoka-university-says-problem-with-misuse-of-university-name-not-kashmir-petition-2369645.

——. 2021. *Indian universities are being taught how to generate funds like Harvard & Cambridge*. 21 August. Accessed May 15, 2022. https://theprint.in/india/education/indian-universities-are-being-taught-how-to-generate-funds-like-harvard-cambridge/719113/.

Sharma, Nupur J. 2020c. *Godrej, a deeply problematic association with anti-Hindu, anti-India elements and the silencing of a Dharmic LGBTQIA+ activist.* 19 February. Accessed May 15, 2022. https://www.opindia.com/2020/02/lgbtqia-event-rise-pride-circle-godrej-de-platform-gopi-shankar-madurai-pressure-anti-india-elements/.

Sharma, Ram Sharan. 1998. *Perspectives in Social and Economic History of India.* New Delhi: Munshiram Manoharlal Publishers.

——. 1958. *Sudras in Ancient India.* New Delhi: Motilal Banarsidass.

Sharma, Ravindra Nath. 1977. *Culture and Civilization as Revealed in the Srauta Sutras.* Delhi: Nag Publishers.

Shashikumar, V. K. 2004. "Bush's Conversion Agenda for India: Preparing for the harvest ..." *Tehelka.* February. Accessed May 15, 2022. https://baixardoc.com/preview/bush39s-conversion-agenda-for-india-preparing-for-the-harvest-tehelka-5cf8268d22593.

Shaw, Jonathan. 2022. *Climate-Solutions Investments Near 1 Percent of Endowment Assets.* 3 February. Accessed March 31, 2022. https://www.harvardmagazine.com/2022/02/endowment-climate-solution-investment.

Shekhar, Divya J. 2021. *This duo incubates early-stage non-profits. Their goal: Bring 1 crore Indians out of poverty by 2025.* 29 October. Accessed May 15, 2022. https://www.forbesindia.com/article/innovation-nation-2021/this-duo-incubates-earlystage-nonprofits-their-goal-bring-1-crore-indians-out-of-poverty-by-2025/71259/1.

Sheth, Shrinal. 2022. *ESG is coming to venture capital. Here's how startup founders can stay ahead of the curve.* 5 January. Accessed May 15, 2022. https://www.weforum.org/agenda/2022/01/esg-is-coming-to-venture-capital-here-s-how-early-stage-startup-founders-can-stay-ahead-of-the-curve/.

Shetty, Salil, and Tara Sahgal. 2019. "India's Soft Power: Challenges and Opportunities." *Rajiv Gandhi Institute for Contemporary Studies.* December. Accessed March 31, 2022. https://www.rgics.org/wp-content/uploads/RGICS-Paper-Indias-Soft-Power-Challenges-Opportunities.pdf.

Shimer, David. 2015. *Yale and Ashoka engage further.* 26 October. Accessed May 15, 2022. https://yaledailynews.com/blog/2015/10/26/yale-and-ashoka-engage-further/.

Shireen, Rabia. 2021. *Delhi Riots: Azim Premji University students protest the incarceration of UAPA accused Gulfisha Fatima.* 15 October. Accessed May 15, 2022. https://thehindustangazette.com/national/new-delhi/delhi-riots-azim-premji-university-students-protest-the-incarceration-of-uapa-accused-gulfisha-fatima-5792 .

Shrier, Abigail. 2020. *How 'peer contagion' may play into the rise of teen girls transitioning.* 27 June. Accessed May 15, 2022. https://nypost.com/2020/06/27/how-peer-contagion-plays-into-the-rise-of-teens-transitioning/.

Siddiqui, Iqtidar Husain. 2014. *Delhi Sultanate: Urbanization and Social Change.* 2nd. New Delhi: Viva Books.

Sikora, Krysia. 2021. *Religion and Populism Are Critical Challenges for Media Worldwide, Scholar John Fea and Journalist Kalpana Jain Say.* 10 March. Accessed March 31, 2022. https://berkleycenter.georgetown.edu/features/religion-and-populism-are-critical-challenges-for-media-worldwide-scholar-john-fea-and-journalist-kalpana-jain-say.

Silas, Karen. 2019. *Who is Rihanna's boyfriend Hassan Jameel?* 13 September. Accessed May 15, 2022. https://www.hola.com/us/celebrities/gallery/2019091328003/who-is-rihanna-boyfriend-hassan-jameel/1/.

Sindwani, Prerna. 2020. *India tops the world in producing female graduates in STEM but ranks 19th in employing them.* 28 February. Accessed April 30, 2022. https://www.businessinsider.in/careers/news/india-tops-the-world-in-producing-female-graduates-in-stem-but-ranks-19th-in-employing-them/articleshow/74117413.cms.

Singh, Abhinav. 2021a. *"Can we see a photograph of this Satyagraha?" Liberals suffer a glorious meltdown after PM Modi talks about participating in Bangladesh liberation struggle.* 27 March. Accessed May 15, 2022. https://tfipost.com/2021/03/can-we-see-a-photograph-of-this-satyagraha-liberals-suffer-a-glorious-meltdown-after-pm-modi-talks-about-participating-in-bangladesh-liberation-struggle/.

——. 2021b. *A massive hunt for people who mocked CDS Gen Bipin Rawat's death has begun across states.* 10 December. Accessed May 15, 2022. https://tfipost.com/2021/12/a-massive-hunt-for-people-who-mocked-cds-gen-bipin-rawats-death-has-begun-across-states/ .

Singh, K.S. 1993. *The Scheduled Castes.* New Delhi: Anthropological Survey of India and Oxford University Press.

——. 1994. *The Scheduled Tribes.* New Delhi: Anthropological Survey of India and Oxford University Press.

Singh, Upinder. 2013. *Rethinking Early Medieval India.* New Delhi: Oxford University Press.

Smith, Warren W. 2009. *China's Tibet: Autonomy or Assimilation?* Lanham, Maryland: Rowman & Littlefield Publishers.

Soave, Robby. 2020. *UConn Will Pay White Fragility Author Robin DiAngelo $20,000 To Train School Administrators.* 14 August. Accessed April 30, 2022. https://reason.com/2020/08/14/uconn-will-pay-white-fragility-author-robin-diangelo-20000-to-train-school-administrators/.

Sokolove, Michael. 2019. *Why Is There So Much Saudi Money in American Universities?* 3 July. Accessed May 15, 2022. https://www.nytimes.com/2019/07/03/magazine/saudi-arabia-american-universities.html.

Soros, George. 2020. *Frightening setback in India, democratically elected Modi creating Hindu state: George Soros.* 24 January. Accessed May 15, 2022. https://theprint.in/world/frightening-setback-in-india-democratically-elected-modi-creating-hindu-state-george-soros/353960/.

Soshi, Mayesha R, and Lucas J. Walsh. 2021. *UC Endorses Calls on Harvard to Condemn Alleged Human Rights Violations During Protests in India.* 8 March. Accessed March 31, 2022. https://www.thecrimson.com/article/2021/3/8/uc-condemns-indian-protest-crackdown/.

Squawk Box @SquawkCNBC. 2021. *"What they have is an autocratic system and one of the leaders described it that the U.S. is a country of individuals and individualism...in China it is an extension of the family," says @RayDalio. "As a top down country what they are doing is–they behave like a strict parent.".* 30 November. Accessed March 31,

2022. https://twitter.com/SquawkCNBC/status/1465660719756681218.

Srinivas, M N. 1971. *Social Change in Modern India.* New Delhi: Orient Longman.

Srinivasan, Ragini Tharoor. 2020. *The Nation We Knew: After Homi Bhabha's "DissemiNation".* 19 May. Accessed March 31, 2022. https://post45.org/2020/05/the-nation-we-knew-after-homi-bhabhas-dissemination/.

Srivastava, A.R.N. 1986. *Tribal Freedom Fighters of India.* New Delhi: Publications Division of Ministry of Information and Broadcasting, Government of India.

Srivastava, Badrinarayan. 1957. *Ramanand Sampradaya Tatha Hindi Sahitya Par Unka Prabhaav.* Prayag: Hindi Parishad, Prayag Vishvidyalaya.

Srivastava, Surabhi. 2008. *Socio-economic History of the Gurjara Pratihara Times.* Lucknow: New Royal Book Company.

Stein, Jeff. 2021. *Financial firms announce $130 trillion in commitments for climate transition, but practical questions loom.* 3 November. Accessed May 15, 2022. https://www.washingtonpost.com/us-policy/2021/11/03/climate-glasgow-bloomberg-carney/.

Stop Hindu Hate Advocacy Network. 2020. *The Wire.* 14 July. Accessed May 15, 2022. https://stophinduhate.org/hindu-haters-2/media/the-wire/.

Subramanian, Ajantha. 2019. *The Caste of Merit.* Cambridge, MA: Harvard University Press.

Subramanian, Balaji. 2020. *Centre for Equity Studies, NGO run by Harsh Mander received crores from Christians and Islamic donors.* 25 September. Accessed May 15, 2022. https://thecommunemag.com/centre-for-equity-studies-ngo-run-by-harsh-mander-received-crores-from-christians-and-islamic-donors/.

Swarajya Staff. 2021. *Did Pratap Bhanu Mehta Do The Right Thing?* 18 March. Accessed May 15, 2022. https://swarajyamag.com/ideas/did-pratap-bhanu-mehta-do-the-right-thing.

Symonds, Richard. 1986. *Oxford and Empire: The Last Lost Cause?* New York: St. Martin's Press.

Tamari, Tal. 2009. "The Development of Caste Systems in West Africa." *The Journal of African History* (Cambridge University Press) 32 (2): 221-250. doi:10.1017/S0021853700025718.

Tan, Rebecca. 2021. *In China, the dream of an American education loses some of its gleam.* 13 August. Accessed March 31, 2022. https://www.washingtonpost.com/world/asia_pacific/chinese-students-america-university/2021/08/13/6f38368a-ef47-11eb-81b2-9b7061a582d8_story.html.

Tandan, Madhav, Siddharth Nautiyal, and Roopa Kudva. 2019a. *E-Commerce 2.0:Designed for India's Next Half Billion.* 29 November. Accessed May 15, 2022. https://www.omidyarnetwork.in/insights/e-commerce-2-0.

——. 2019. "E-Commerce 2.0:Designed for India's Next Half Billion." *Omidyar Network India.* 29 November. Accessed May 15, 2022. https://uploads-ssl.webflow.com/61b9a0d531bc5e31aa66a38d/6245a663e0c6e3ae2edb2c8a_E-commerce-2.0-26_09.pdf.

Tandel, Vaidehi, Shamika Ravi, Vivek Dehejia, and Kadambari Shah. 2017a. *NITI Aayog – IDFC Institute Enterprise Survey.* 1 September. Accessed May 15, 2022. https://www.

idfcinstitute.org/projects/state-capacity/nitiaayog-idfcinstitute_enterprise-survey/.

Tang, Wenfang, and Qing Yang. 2008. "The Chinese Urban Caste System in Transition." *The China Quarterly* (Cambridge University Press) (196): 759-779. http://www.jstor. org/stable/20192266.

Tariq, Varisha. 2020. *In Conversation With Professor Bittu: A Neuroscientist And A Queer Activist.* 6 March. Accessed May 15, 2022. https://feminisminindia.com/2020/03/06/ professor-bittu-a-neuroscientist-and-an-anti-caste-queer-activist/.

Taylor, Chloe. 2020. *Coronavirus crisis presents a 'golden opportunity' to reboot the economy, Prince Charles says.* 3 June. Accessed April 30, 2022. https://www.cnbc. com/2020/06/03/prince-charles-covid-19-a-golden-opportunity-to-reboot-the-economy.html.

Tejeda, Amanda, and Manmit Singh Chahal. 2021. "Resolution #21-01: RESOLUTION CALLING FOR CAL POLY AND THE CALIFORNIA STATE UNIVERSITY (CSU) TO INCLUDE CASTE IN ANTI-DISCRIMINATORY POLICY." *CalPoly.* 4 March. Accessed February 15, 2022. https://www.asi.calpoly.edu/wp-content/ uploads/2021/03/21-01-Resolution-Call-for-CP-and-CSU-to-Include-Caste-in-the-Anti-Discriminatory-Policy_BODappr.pdf.

Temkin, Moshik. 2020. *Bernie Offered Us the Future. Why Did He Fail—and What Did We Forfeit?* 14 April. Accessed March 31, 2022. https://www.belfercenter.org/ publication/bernie-offered-us-future-why-did-he-fail-and-what-did-we-forfeit.

Thakur, Pradeep. 2021. *ED probes media portal's funding from businessman 'linked' to China regime.* 18 July. Accessed March 31, 2022. http://timesofindia. indiatimes.com/articleshow/84514212.cms?utm_source=contentofinterest&utm_ medium=text&utm_campaign=cppst.

The American Bazaar. 2018. *Indian American Preeta Bansal honored at APAICS gala.* 16 May. Accessed March 31, 2022. https://www.americanbazaaronline.com/2018/05/16/ indian-american-preeta-bansal-honored-at-apaics-gala/.

The British Academy. 2020. *The Ownership of Public History in India (TOPHI).* Accessed May 15, 2022. https://www.thebritishacademy.ac.uk/projects/humanities-social-sciences-tackling-global-challenges-ownership-public-history-india/.

The Centre for Internet and Society. 2008. *The Centre for Internet and Society.* Accessed May 15, 2022. https://cis-india.org/.

The Daily Wire. 2022. *China: The Enemy Within. Episode 3. Education.* 18 February. Accessed April 30, 2022. https://www.dailywire.com/episode/3-education.

The Economist. 2020. *Chinese management schools are thriving.* 15 February. Accessed March 31, 2022. https://www.economist.com/business/2020/02/13/chinese-management-schools-are-thriving.

The Fletcher School. 2021. *Shattering Brahminical Supremacy and White Supremacy.* 5 March. Accessed February 15, 2022. https://www.youtube.com/ watch?v=3KQf9E8fKMM.

The Forum of Young Global Leaders. 2020. *Supporters.* Accessed May 15, 2022. https:// www.younggloballeaders.org/supporters.

The Harbus. 2020. *Harvard India Conference 2020 Discusses "India: Foresight".* 7 March.

Accessed March 31, 2022. https://harbus.org/2020/harvard-india-conference-2020-discusses-india-foresight/.

The Harvard Gazette. 2021. *Bhargava is Class of 1996's pick for chief marshal.* 10 March. Accessed March 31, 2022. https://news.harvard.edu/gazette/story/2021/03/harvard-alumni-association-announces-chief-marshal-for-2021/.

——. 2008. *Government of India gives $4.5M to support grad students.* 18 December. Accessed March 31, 2022. https://news.harvard.edu/gazette/story/2008/12/government-of-india-gives-4-5m-to-support-grad-students/.

——. 2017. *Strengthening Harvard's ties to South Asia: Mittal family gift expands opportunities for South Asia engagement.* 11 October. Accessed March 31, 2022. https://news.harvard.edu/gazette/story/2017/10/mittal-family-gift-expands-opportunities-for-south-asia-engagement/.

The Heritage Foundation. 2018. *Freedom House Turns Partisan.* 16 February. Accessed March 31, 2022. https://www.heritage.org/global-politics/commentary/freedom-house-turns-partisan.

The Hill. 2022. *Kim Iversen: GREAT RESET Has INFILTRATED Cabinets Around The World With Young Leaders Like Trudeau.* 23 February. Accessed May 15, 2022. https://www.youtube.com/watch?v=-p1_8-jLQkI.

The Hindu. 2019. *Appeal for Reason from over 600 concerned citizens on Indo-Pak tension.* 1 March. Accessed May 15, 2022. https://www.thehindu.com/news/national/appeal-for-reason-from-over-600-concerned-citizens-on-indo-pak-tension/article26410066.ece.

——. 2016. *Eminent persons request President to consider Yakub Memon's mercy plea.* 2 April. Accessed May 15, 2022. https://www.thehindu.com/news/national/Eminent-persons-request-President-to-consider-Yakubs-mercy-plea/article60329906.ece.

——. 2021. *Rahul Gandhi questions U.S.' silence on happenings in India.* 3 April. Accessed April 30, 2022. https://www.thehindu.com/news/national/rahul-gandhi-questions-us-silence-on-happenings-in-india/article34226862.ece.

The Hindustan Times. 2017. *Ford Foundation officer connived with Teesta Setalvad's company for fund grant: CBI.* 4 February. Accessed March 31, 2022. https://www.hindustantimes.com/india-news/ford-foundation-officer-sushma-raman-connived-with-teesta-setalvad-s-company-sabrang-for-fund-grant-cbi/story-Msc2TQzKPNmXKigysB7X9J.html.

——. 2022. *Former CEC S.Y. Quraishi explains how religious polarisation is paying dividends in Indian elections.* 18 January. Accessed May 15, 2022. https://www.youtube.com/watch?v=yuIjUsNhfRM.

——. 2004. *Preeta Bansal.* 8 January. Accessed March 31, 2022. https://www.hindustantimes.com/india/preeta-bansal/story-m6puAx3G4JGAVWTSueHi1I.html.

The Indian Express. 2015. *Christophe Jaffrelot.* 29 April. Accessed May 15, 2022. https://indianexpress.com/profile/columnist/christophe-jaffrelot/.

The Intercept. 2022. *Noam Chomsky and Jeremy Scahill on the Russia-Ukraine War, the Media, Propaganda, and Accountability.* 15 April. Accessed May 15, 2022. https://www.youtube.com/watch?v=8Jr0PCU4m7M.

The International Institute for Democracy and Electoral Assistance. 1998. *About us.* Accessed May 15, 2022. https://www.idea.int/.

The Journal of the Abraham Lincoln Association. 1984. *The Perpetuation of Our Political Institutions (Address by Abraham Lincoln before the Young Men's Lyceum of Springfield, January 27, 1838).* Accessed April 30, 2022. https://quod.lib.umich.edu/j/jala/2629860.0006.103/--perpetuation-of-our-political-institutionsaddress?rgn=main;view=fulltext.

The Lakshmi Mittal and Family South Asia Institute at Harvard University. 2018a. *Q + A with Suraj Yengde: Caste, Apartheid and a Fourth World Think Tank.* 1 August. Accessed February 15, 2022. https://mittalsouthasiainstitute.harvard.edu/2018/08/q-a-with-suraj-yengde-caste-apartheid-and-a-fourth-world-think-tank/.

——. 2012. "SAI Faculty Grant Profile: The Champions Project." *The Lakshmi Mittal and Family South Asia Institute at Harvard University.* Accessed March 31, 2022. https://mittalsouthasiainstitute.harvard.edu/wp-content/uploads/2012/10/Jacuqeline-Bhabha-Champions-Project-Report.pdf.

——. 2018b. "The Mittal Institute Year in Review 2017-2018." *issuu.* 25 April. Accessed March 31, 2022. https://issuu.com/sainit/docs/the_mittal_institute_year_in_review_74f9ee41f07a9c.

——. 2019. "The Mittal Institute Year in Review 2018-2019." *issuu.* 28 May. Accessed March 31, 2022. https://issuu.com/sainit/docs/yir_mittalinstitute_5.7.

——. 2020. "The Mittal Institute Year in Review 2019-2020." *issuu.* 19 May. Accessed April 30, 2022. https://issuu.com/sainit/docs/mittal_institute_2019-20_year_in_review.

——. 2021. "The Mittal Institute Year in Review 2020-21." *issuu.* 24 June. Accessed March 31, 2022. https://issuu.com/sainit/docs/mittal_institute_yir_2020-21.

——. 2014. "Year in Review 2013-2014." *issuu.* 6 May. Accessed March 31, 2022. https://issuu.com/sainit/docs/sai_year_in_review_final__1_.

——. 2015. "Year in Review 2014-2015." *issuu.* 22 April. Accessed March 31, 2022. https://issuu.com/sainit/docs/sai_year_in_review_1415.

——. 2016. "Year in Review 2015-2016." *issuu.* 13 May. Accessed March 31, 2022. https://issuu.com/sainit/docs/year_in_review_2015_2016.

——. 2017. "Year In Review 2016-2017." *issuu.* 23 June. Accessed March 31, 2022. https://issuu.com/sainit/docs/yir_2016-17/1.

The Lakshmi Mittal and Family South Asia Institute. 2019a. *Talent and Meritocracy in China and India.* 16 April. Accessed May 15, 2022. https://mittalsouthasiainstitute.harvard.edu/talent-and-meritocracy-in-india-and-china-february-2018-workshop/.

The Late Show with Stephen Colbert. 2021. *Here's John Cena's Full Apology To China.* 27 May. Accessed April 30, 2022. https://www.youtube.com/watch?v=XI2IkPNteO4.

The National Pulse. 2021. *China-Backed Harvard Center Fellow Luke O'Brien Engages in Targeted Harassment Against The National Pulse.* 27 July. Accessed March 31, 2022. https://thenationalpulse.com/2021/07/27/china-backed-harvard-center-fellow-luke-obrien-engages-in-targeted-harassment-against-the-national-pulse/.

The New York Public Library. 2013. *Africans In India: From Slaves to Generals and Rulers.* Accessed March 31, 2022. https://www.nypl.org/events/exhibitions/africans-india-slaves-generals-and-rulers.

——. 2020. *Caste in America: Isabel Wilkerson with John Dickerson | LIVE from NYPL.* 6 August. Accessed February 15, 2022. https://www.youtube.com/watch?v=FxpouTYfJKY.

The Peace Research Institute Oslo (PRIO). 2021. *Nobel Peace Prize 2022: PRIO Director's Shortlist.* Accessed May 15, 2022. https://www.prio.org/nobelshortlist.

The Sikh Coalition. 2021. *Farmers' Protest Work.* 28 June. Accessed May 15, 2022. https://www.sikhcoalition.org/our-work/empowering-the-community/farmers-protest-work/.

The Times of India. 2010. *Harvard gets biggest international donation in 102 yrs, from Tata Group.* 15 October. Accessed March 31, 2022. https://timesofindia.indiatimes.com/business/india-business/Harvard-gets-biggest-international-donation-in-102-yrs-from-Tata-Group/articleshow/6752185.cms.

——. 2006. *Harvard to train desi IAS officers.* 15 April. Accessed March 31, 2022. http://timesofindia.indiatimes.com/articleshow/1491724.cms.

The Training Division, Department of Personnel and Training, Government of India. 2018. "F.No.12037/41/2018-FTC." *Centralized Circular Information System, Department of Personnel and Training.* 9 November. Accessed March 31, 2022. http://documents.doptcirculars.nic.in/D2/D02trn/DFFT%20Circular%202019-207z2n1.pdf .

——. 2018. "F.No.12038/01/2018-FTC." *Centralized Circular Information System, Department of Personnel and Training.* 9 November. Accessed March 31, 2022. http://documents.doptcirculars.nic.in/D2/D02trn/Partial%20Funding%20Circular%20091118dLTpe.pdf.

The Wire. 2021. *Answering the Upper Caste: Suraj Yengde Lays to Rest Questions the Privileged Often Ask About Caste.* 11 June. Accessed February 15, 2022. https://www.youtube.com/watch?v=nhBAV1XbDL8.

The Wire Staff. 2021b. *Ashoka University Acknowledges 'Some Lapses' but Pratap Bhanu Mehta Insists on Moving On.* 21 March. Accessed May 15, 2022. https://thewire.in/education/ashoka-university-pratap-bhanu-mehta-lapses-protests.

——. 2018. *In Solidarity Against JNU Administration's 'Witch-Hunt Against Dissenting Voices'.* 29 March. Accessed May 15, 2022. https://thewire.in/education/in-solidarity-against-jnu-administrations-witch-hunt-against-dissenting-voices.

——. 2019. *'Knowledge Deemed Crime Against the State': Students, Professors Stand With Hany Babu.* 15 September. Accessed May 15, 2022. https://thewire.in/rights/hany-babu-solidarity-statements-delhi-university.

——. 2021a. *Sheldon Pollock: 'My Respect for Ashoka University Has Been Seriously Tested'.* 19 March. Accessed May 15, 2022. https://thewire.in/education/sheldon-pollock-my-respect-for-ashoka-university-has-been-seriously-tested.

ThePrint. 2020. *India is passing through an era of darkness where Constitution is a facade, says Pratap Bhanu Mehta.* 19 October. Accessed May 15, 2022. https://www.youtube.com/watch?v=6F3YKnduUDI.

Thera, Nyanaponika. 1999. *Analysis of Consciousness.* Accessed March 31, 2022. http://www.buddhanet.net/abhidh05.htm.

Thorat, Sukhadeo, Anuradha Banerjee, Vinod K Mishra, and Firdaus Rizvi. 2015. "Urban Rental Housing Market: Caste and Religion Matters in Access." *JSTOR*. 27 June. Accessed May 15, 2022. https://www.jstor.org/stable/24482557?seq=1.

Thoreau, Henry David. 1932. *The Transmigration of the Seven Brahmans.* Accessed March 31, 2022. https://www.sacred-texts.com/hin/tsb/tsb03.htm.

Timalsina, Tarun Nehme, and Michel. 2021. *IPL During COVID: The Nexus Between Cricket and Politics in India.* 7 May. Accessed March 31, 2022. https://harvardpolitics.com/ipl-during-covid/.

TNM Staff. 2020. *'Vengeful state repression deeply concerning': Azim Premji Uni profs on CAA-NRC.* 16 January. Accessed May 15, 2022. https://www.thenewsminute.com/article/vengeful-state-repression-deeply-concerning-azim-premji-uni-profs-caa-nrc-116239 .

To The Best Of Our Knowledge. 2014. *Transcript for Emotional Intelligence - Daniel Goleman.* 28 February. Accessed April 30, 2022. http://archive.ttbook.org/book/transcript/emotional-intelligence-daniel-goleman.

Tocqueville, Alexis De. 2004. *Alexis de Tocqueville: Democracy in America.* New York: Library of America.

ToHim89 Live. 2019. *Message 1 Young Working Saints Conference SPS Church in Belmopan-- Ronnie Chan.* 14 October. Accessed March 31, 2022. https://www.youtube.com/watch?v=HYAEzmLRWwY.

Tripathi, Rama Shankar. 1989. *History of Kanauj.* New Delhi: Motilal Banarsidass.

Trivedi Centre for Political Data. 2020c. *About : Trivedi Centre for Political Data.* Accessed May 15, 2022. https://tcpd.ashoka.edu.in/about-the-centre/.

——. 2021a. *Bureaucrats of India.* 1 December. Accessed May 15, 2022. https://tcpd.ashoka.edu.in/bureaucrats-of-india/.

——. 2021b. *Chief Ministers of India.* 30 June. Accessed May 15, 2022. https://tcpd.ashoka.edu.in/chief-ministers-of-india/.

——. 2020b. *Indian Council of Ministers.* 10 August. Accessed May 15, 2022. https://tcpd.ashoka.edu.in/indian-council-of-ministers/.

——. 2021e. *One Thousand Land Laws: Mapping the Maze of Land Regulation in India.* Accessed May 15, 2022. https://tcpd.ashoka.edu.in/event/one-thousand-land-laws-mapping-the-maze-of-land-regulation-in-india/.

——. 2022. *Political Career Tracker.* Accessed May 15, 2022. https://lokdhaba.ashoka.edu.in/pct/.

——. 2021c. *Social Media and Elections.* 11 November. Accessed May 15, 2022. https://tcpd.ashoka.edu.in/social-media-and-elections/.

——. 2018. *Social Profiling of Legislators.* 10 August. Accessed May 15, 2022. https://tcpd.ashoka.edu.in/social-profiling-of-legislators/.

——. 2021d. "TCPD Annual Report: 2020-21." *Trivedi Centre for Political Data.* August. Accessed May 15, 2022. https://tcpd.ashoka.edu.in/wp-content/uploads/2021/08/TCPD-Annual-Report-2020-2021.pdf.

Tschurenev, Jana. 2019. *Empire, Civil Society, and the Beginnings of Colonial Education in India.* New Delhi: Cambridge University Press.

U.S. Ambassador-at-Large Rashad Hussain@IRF_Ambassador. 2022. *Religious freedom includes the ability to choose one's religious attire. The Indian state of Karnataka should not determine permissibility of religious clothing. Hijab bans in schools violate religious freedom and stigmatize and marginalize women and girls.* 11 February. Accessed April 30, 2022. https://twitter.com/IRF_Ambassador/status/1492153532350402564.

United Board. 2019. *Mission and Identity - United Board.* Accessed May 15, 2022. https://unitedboard.org/about-us/about-united-board/mission-vision/.

United States Department of the Treasury. 2022. *Specially Designated Nationals And Blocked Persons List (SDN) Human Readable Lists.* Accessed April 30, 2022. https://home.treasury.gov/policy-issues/financial-sanctions/specially-designated-nationals-and-blocked-persons-list-sdn-human-readable-lists\.

Upadhyaya, Baldev. 1954. *Bhagavat Sampradaya.* Varanasi: Kashi Nagari Pracharini Sabha.

USCIRF. 2004. *Testimony by Preeta D. Bansal, Chair.* 6 October. Accessed March 31, 2022. https://www.uscirf.gov/resources/testimony-preeta-d-bansal-chair-0.

———. 2020. *USCIRF - Citizenship Laws and Religious Freedom.* 5 March. Accessed March 31, 2022. https://www.youtube.com/watch?v=IcGgWJG5qxA.

Vaidyanathan, R. 2019. *Caste as Social Capital.* Chennai: Westland Publications Private Limited.

Valentine, Douglas. 2017. *The CIA as Organized Crime: How Illegal Operations Corrupt America and the World.* Atlanta, Georgia: Clarity Press.

Varadarajan, Siddharth. 2014. *Siddharth Varadarajan : What's gone wrong with the Indian media?* 14 August. Accessed May 15, 2022. https://azimpremjifoundation.org/author/siddharth-varadarajan .

Varshney, Ashutosh. 2018. "Democracy and Meritocracy." *Harvard China Fund.* 8 May. Accessed May 15, 2022. https://hcf.fas.harvard.edu/wp-content/uploads/2018/05/Varshney-Abstract-Shanghai.pdf.

———. 2020b. *Hindu nationalism, White supremacism threaten to morally impoverish the two democracies.* 6 July. Accessed April 30, 2022. https://indianexpress.com/article/opinion/columns/the-same-shrinking-6491627/.

———. 2021. *India's democratic exceptionalism is now withering away. The impact is also external.* 23 February. Accessed March 31, 2022. https://indianexpress.com/article/opinion/columns/elected-government-death-of-democracy-india-7200030/.

———. 2021a. *Jim Crow Hindutva.* 20 October. Accessed March 31, 2022. https://indianexpress.com/article/opinion/columns/jim-crow-hindutva-7577159/.

Varshney, Ashutosh, Srikrishna Ayyangar, and Siddharth Swaminathan. 2021. "Populism and Hindu Nationalism in India." *Springer.* 3 July. Accessed March 31, 2022. https://link.springer.com/content/pdf/10.1007/s12116-021-09335-8.pdf.

Venu, M. K., and Maya Mirchandani. 2021b. *Locating Pegasus in Doval's Civil Society as New Frontier of War.* 29 November. Accessed May 15, 2022. https://thewire.in/government/locating-pegasus-in-dovals-civil-society-as-new-frontier-of-war.

Verhoeven, Martin J. 2001. "Buddhism and Science: Probing the Boundaries Of Faith and Reason." *Religion East and West* (1): 77-97.

VI-Control. 2007. *Quotes from Barack Obama speech in Selma Alabama.* 5 March. Accessed April 30, 2022. https://vi-control.net/community/threads/quotes-from-barack-obama-speech-in-selma-alabama.6237/.

Vikaspedia. 2019. *Atal Innovation Mission.* Accessed March 31, 2022. https://vikaspedia. in/education/policies-and-schemes/atal-innovation-mission.

Visweswaran, Kamala, Michael E.J. Witzel, Nandini Manjrekar, Dipta Bhog, and Uma Chakravarti. 2009. "The Hindutva View of History: Rewriting Textbooks in India and the United States." *Georgetown Journal of International Affairs* 10 (1): 101-112.

Von Furer Haimendorf, Christoph, and Elizabeth Von Furer Haimendorf. 2022. *The Gonds of Andhra Pradesh.* New York: Routledge.

Vyas, Sangita, Aashish Gupta, and Nazar Khalid. 2021. *Gender and LPG use after government intervention in rural north India.* 6 September. Accessed March 31, 2022. https://www.sciencedirect.com/science/article/abs/pii/ S0305750X21002977?via%3Dihub.

Walker, Jonathan. 2021. *CCP-Linked Harvard Center Could Be Covering Up COVID-19 Origin - Vision Times.* 24 February. Accessed March 31, 2022. https://www.visiontimes. com/2021/02/24/ccp-linked-harvard-center-could-be-covering-up-covid-19-origin. html.

Walt, Stephen. 2019. *The World Didn't Change Much in 2019. That's Bad News for 2020.* 31 December. Accessed April 30, 2022. https://foreignpolicy.com/2019/12/31/united-states-world-changes-2019/.

Weber, Jeremy. 2021. *Biden Names First Muslim Religious Freedom Ambassador.* 30 July. Accessed March 31, 2022. https://www.christianitytoday.com/news/2021/july/ rashad-hussain-irf-ambassador-religious-freedom-uscirf-khan.html.

Weber, Max. 1905. *The Protestant Ethic and the Spirit of Capitalism.* Pantianos Classics.

Wellesley Centers for Women. 2020. *Sex/Ed: International Conference Brought Together Perspectives from U.S., India, and Beyond.* Accessed May 15, 2022. https://www. wcwonline.org/News-Events/sex-ed-international-conference-india.

Wellesley College. 2016a. *Wellesley Partners With Ashoka University, India's First Private Ivy League-Caliber Institution.* 27 January. Accessed May 15, 2022. https://www. wellesley.edu/news/2016/january/node/82096.

Wherry, Aaron. 2020. *The 'Great Reset' reads like a globalist plot with some plot holes.* 27 November. Accessed April 30, 2022. https://www.cbc.ca/news/politics/great-reset-trudeau-poilievre-otoole-pandemic-covid-1.5817973.

Wignaraja, Kanni, and Balazs Horvath. 2020. *Universal basic income is the answer to the inequalities exposed by COVID-19.* 17 April. Accessed May 15, 2022. https://www. weforum.org/agenda/2020/04/covid-19-universal-basic-income-social-inequality/.

Wilkerson, Isabel. 2020. *Caste: The Origins of Our Discontent.* New York: Random House.

Williams, Luke A. 2020. *Forty Protest Indian Consul General at Harvard India Conference.* 18 February. Accessed March 31, 2022. https://www.thecrimson.com/ article/2020/2/18/harvard-india-conference-protest/.

Williams, Luke A., and Matteo N. Wong. 2020. *Harvard Affiliates Stage 24-Hour Protest Against India's Citizenship Amendment Act.* 27 January. Accessed March 31, 2022.

https://www.thecrimson.com/article/2020/1/27/indian-citizenship-act-protest/.

Wilson, Jeff. 2014. *Mindful America: The Mutual Transformation of Buddhist Meditation and American Culture.* Oxford and New York: Oxford University Press.

Winters, Natalie. 2021a. *"We Need China" – Biden's China Ambassador Worked at a CCP-Linked Consulting Firm, And A Harvard Group Advising China's Military.* 17 April. Accessed April 30, 2022. https://thenationalpulse.com/2021/04/17/bidens-china-ambassador-former-ccp-consultant/.

——. 2021b. *COMPROMISED: Harvard Subjects Students To Trips, Research Papers Authored By Chinese Communist Party Propaganda Front.* 21 May. Accessed March 31, 2022. https://thenationalpulse.com/2021/05/21/harvard-kennedy-school-takes-ccp-trips/.

——. 2020d. *EXC: Harvard China Conference Collaborates With TikTok Parent Company & Chinese Military Proxies.* 16 August. Accessed March 31, 2022. https://thenationalpulse.com/2020/08/16/harvard-ccp-forum/.

——. 2020a. *EXCLUSIVE: Harvard Center Hypes Chinese Communist Party Popularity While Receiving MILLIONS From Chinese Govt and CCP-Linked Companies.* 23 July. Accessed March 31, 2022. https://thenationalpulse.com/2020/07/23/harvard-chinese-funding/.

——. 2020b. *STUNNING: All Major Western Media Outlets Take 'Private Dinners', 'Sponsored Trips' from Chinese Communist Propaganda Front.* 29 December. Accessed March 31, 2022. https://thenationalpulse.com/2020/12/29/media-private-ccp-dinners-trips/.

Winters, Natalie, and Raheem J. Kassam. 2021. *EXC: Harvard Center Attacking COVID Lab Theory Has Extensive Financial and Personnel Links With The Chinese Communist Party.* 13 February. Accessed March 31, 2022. https://thenationalpulse.com/2021/02/13/harvard-shorenstein-center-ccp-ties/.

——. 2022. *EXC: Joe Biden's CIA Director Told Congress He Terminated a Relationship With a Chinese Communist Influence Group – New Evidence Suggests This Was a Lie.* 30 March. Accessed May 15, 2022. https://thenationalpulse.com/2022/03/30/cia-directors-think-tank-continues-cusef-relationship/.

Winters, Natalie, and Raheem Kassam. 2021b. *REVEALED: China's State Propaganda Group Boasts Control Over Western Think Tanks, 'Election Integrity' Groups, And Even Joe Biden's National Security Team.* 1 April. Accessed April 30, 2022. https://thenationalpulse.com/2021/04/01/exc-china-state-propaganda-boasts-control-over-think-tanks/.

Witzenrath, Christoph. 2015. *Eurasian Slavery, Ransom and Abolition in World History, 1200-1860.* Surrey, England: Ashgate Publishinf Ltd.

Wolff, Robert Paul, Barrington Moore, Jr., and Herbert Marcuse. 1969. *A Critique of Pure Tolerance.* Boston: Beacon Press.

Wolters, Lukas, and Nicolas Dumas. 2018. *President Reif, cut MIT's ties to Saudi Arabia now!* 25 October. Accessed May 15, 2022. https://thetech.com/2018/10/25/reif-cut-ties-saudi-arabia.

Wong, Matteo N. 2020. *The End of the Harvard Century.* 23 April. Accessed March

31, 2022. https://www.thecrimson.com/article/2020/4/23/harvard-china-scrutiny/.

World Economic Forum. 2022b. "Advancing Digital Agency: The Power of Data Intermediaries." *World Economic Forum*. February. Accessed May 15, 2022. https://www3.weforum.org/docs/WEF_Advancing_towards_Digital_Agency_2022.pdf.

——. 2022a. *BlackRock's Larry Fink on the launch of a Center for Stakeholder Capitalism.* 18 January. Accessed May 15, 2022. https://www.weforum.org/partners/live-updates/davos-agenda-2022#blackrocks-larry-fink-calls-on-ceos-to-step-up.

——. 2020a. "Centre for the Fourth Industrial Revolution Network." *World Economic Forum*. Accessed May 15, 2022. https://weforum.ent.box.com/v/C4IR-India.

——. 2016. *Our Mission | World Economic Forum.* Accessed May 15, 2022. https://www.weforum.org/about/world-economic-forum.

——. 2020b. *World Economic Forum Releases Framework to Help Business Identify ESG Factors for Long-Term Resilience.* 19 March. Accessed May 15, 2022. https://www.weforum.org/press/2020/03/world-economic-forum-releases-framework-to-help-business-identify-esg-factors-for-long-term-resilience.

wzgrl. 2008. *Obama's Response to Wright: Time for a Post-Racial America.* 15 March. Accessed April 30, 2022. https://www.youtube.com/watch?v=9_6aLDQTleU.

Xie, Stella Yifan. 2018. *Bridgewater Wins License to Sell Investment Products in China.* 4 July. Accessed March 31, 2022. https://www.wsj.com/articles/bridgewater-wins-license-to-sell-investment-products-in-china-1530707031.

xSDG. 2021b. *About Us.* 1 March. Accessed May 15, 2022. https://xsdg.dev/about-us/#rakesh-basant.

——. 2021c. *xSDG by Belongg: A Knowledge Platform For SDGs and Intersectionality.* 6 April. Accessed May 15, 2022. https://xsdg.dev/xsdg-by-belongg-a-knowledge-platform-for-sdgs-and-intersectionality/.

Yale Economic Growth Center. 2020a. *EGC-CMF Survey in Tamil Nadu, India.* Accessed May 15, 2022. https://egc.yale.edu/data/egc-cmf-survey-tamil-nadu-india.

——. 2022b. *Reducing Industrial Air Pollution: Data Systems and Policy Innovations.* Accessed May 15, 2022. https://egc.yale.edu/ie/projects/reducing-industrial-air-pollution.

——. 2021a. *Studies on Early Childhood Development.* Accessed May 15, 2022. https://egc.yale.edu/data/studies-early-childhood-development.

——. 2021b. *Tamil Nadu Social Network Mapping Survey.* Accessed May 15, 2022. https://egc.yale.edu/data/tamil-nadu-social-network-mapping-survey.

——. 2022a. *TNSMS Users Reference.* Accessed May 15, 2022. https://egc.yale.edu/tnsms-users-reference.

Yale Macmillan Center. 2022. *Post-Doctoral Research Fellow (2) - Inclusion Economics India Centre at IFMR/Krea University.* Accessed May 15, 2022. https://southasia.macmillan.yale.edu/post-doctoral-research-fellow-2-inclusion-economics-india-centre-ifmrkrea-university.

Yale School of Management. 2014. *The Only People for Godrej Are the Mad Ones.* 11 December. Accessed May 15, 2022. https://som.yale.edu/blog/the-only-people-for-godrej-are-the-mad-ones .

Yemma, John, and Daniel Golden. 1998. *The Sun Never Sets on Harvard's Empire.* https:// web.archive.org/web/20091015101243/http://www.harvard60.org/china.html.

Yengde, Suraj. 2020. *Brahminical Patriarchy — UPenn | Suraj Yengde.* 28 February. https://www.youtube.com/watch?v=SApNw5FuLSM.

——. 2021. *Castes of Mind.* 24 March. Accessed February 15, 2022. https://thebaffler. com/latest/castes-of-mind.

——. 2019. *The Fourth World of the untouchables.* 3 January. Accessed February 15, 2022. https://www.aljazeera.com/opinions/2019/1/3/the-fourth-world-of-the-untouchables.

Yeung, Bernard. 2018. "Notes on Meritocracy: Insights from Tang's Civil Servant Exam and Poetry." *Harvard China Fund.* 1 May. Accessed May 15, 2022. https://hcf.fas. harvard.edu/wp-content/uploads/2018/05/Yeung-Bernie-For-May-2018-b.pdf.

Young, Robert. 1990. *White Mythologies: Writing History and the West.* London, New York: Routledge.

Young, Sarah, and Stephen Addison. 2020. *UK's Prince Charles says coronavirus reset is a new chance for sustainability.* 3 June. Accessed April 30, 2022. https://www.reuters. com/article/us-health-coronavirus-britain-royals-idUSKBN23A2AC.

Zee Media Bureau. 2022. *Next census to be e-census, announces Amit Shah, says 'it will be '100 per cent perfect'.* 10 May. Accessed May 15, 2022. https://zeenews.india.com/ india/next-census-to-be-e-census-announces-amit-shah-says-it-will-be-100-per-cent-perfect-2461986.html.

*Note: Any errors in links, articles, tweets, etc. are presented as they appear in the original.

Index